Who's Who

IN CONTEMPORARY
WOMEN'S WRITING

Who's Who
IN CONTEMPORARY
WOMEN'S WRITING

Edited by Jane Eldridge Miller

London and New York

First published 2001
by Routledge
11 New Fetter Lane, London EC4P 4EE

Simultaneously published in the USA and Canada
by Routledge
29 West 35th Street, New York, NY 10001

Second edition first published 2002

Routledge is an imprint of the Taylor & Francis Group

© 2001, 2002 Jane Eldridge Miller

Typeset in Sabon by RefineCatch Limited, Bungay, Suffolk
Printed and bound in Great Britain by
TJ International Ltd, Padstow, Cornwall

British Library Cataloguing in Publication Data
A catalogue record for this book is available from the British Library

Library of Congress Cataloging in Publication Data
A catalog record for this book has been requested

ISBN 0–415–15981–4

Contents

Contributing editors

African: Marie Umeh, John Jay College, CUNY; Gay Wilentz, East Carolina University

Arab: Joseph T. Zeidan, Ohio State University

Australian and New Zealander: Mary-Robyn Adams, Roseville College

Caribbean: Sonita Sarker, Macalester College

Chinese: Jingyuan Zhang, Georgetown University

French and Francophone: Joëlle Vitiello, Macalester College

German, Austrian, and Swiss: Anke Gleber, University of California, Irvine

Italian: Grazia Menechella, University of Wisconsin–Madison

Japanese: Tomoko Kuribayashi, University of Wisconsin–Stevens Point

Latin American: María Inés Lagos, Washington University

Scandinavian: Monika Žagar, University of Minnesota, Twin Cities

Slavic: Helena Goscilo, University of Pittsburgh

South Asian and South Asian Diaspora: Josna Rege, Dartmouth College

Advisers

Arab: Issa J. Boullata, McGill University

Australian and New Zealander: David Callahan, Universidade de Aveiro, Portugal

Brazilian: Cristina Ferreira-Pinto, University of Texas at Austin; Susan Canty Quinlan, University of Georgia

Canadian: Allan Hepburn, McGill University

Caribbean: Magali Roy-Féquière, Knox College

Chinese: Sung-sheng Yvonne Chang, University of Texas at Austin; Xiaomei Chen, Ohio State University; Amy D. Dooling, Connecticut College; Edward Gunn, Cornell University; David Der-wei Wang, Columbia University; Lingzhen Wang, Brown University; Michelle Yeh, University of California, Davis

Dutch and Flemish: Agnes Andeweg, University for Humanist Studies in Utrecht; Maaike Meijer, University of Maastricht

Greek: Helen D. Kolias, Cornell University

Iranian: Kamran Talattof, University of Arizona

Israeli: Nancy E. Berg, Washington University in St Louis; Yael S. Feldman, New York University

Italian: Robin Pickering-Iazzi, University of Wisconsin–Milwaukee

Japanese: Mizuho Terasawa, Waseda University

Korean: Kyeong-Hee Choi, University of Chicago; Yung-Hee Kim, University of Hawaii at Manoa; Carolyn So, Claremont McKenna College

Latin American: Sharon Magnarelli, Quinnipiac College

Portuguese: Ana Paula Ferreira, University of California, Irvine

Romanian: Ioana Both, 'Babes-Bolyai' University in Cluj-Napoca

South Asian: Meenakshi Mukherjee, University of Hyderabad

Southeast Asian: Pamela Allen, University of Tasmania; Vicky Bowman; Marjorie Evasco, De La Salle University, Manila; Minfong Ho; Nor Faridah Abdul Manaf, International Islamic University, Malaysia; Connie J. Maraan, De La Salle University, Manila; Nitaya Masavisut; Dinah T. Roma, De La Salle University, Manila

Spanish: Geraldine Cleary Nichols, University of Florida; Randolph D. Pope, Washington University in St Louis

Turkish: Sibel Erol, New York University

Contributors

MBr	Marvie Brooks, John Jay College of Criminal Justice, CUNY
JLB	Joan L. Brown, University of Delaware
UB	Urvashi Butalia, Kali for Women, New Delhi
DCa	David Callahan, Universidade de Aveiro, Portugal
SGC	Susan Gasster Carrière, Aquinas College
TFC	Tania Franco Carvalhal, Federal University of Rio Grande do Sul, Brazil
JC	Jöelle Cauville, St Mary's University, Halifax, Nova Scotia
S-sYC	Sung-sheng Yvonne Chang, University of Texas at Austin
F-SC	Fabienne-Sophie Chauderlot, Wayne State University
SC	Shunxin Chen, Lingnan College, Hong Kong
XC	Xiaomei Chen, Ohio State University
VC	Vitaly Chernetsky, Columbia University
FC	Frédérique Chevillot, University of Denver
K-HC	Kyeong-Hee Choi, University of Chicago
LC	Loretta Collins, University of Iowa
DCo	David Connolly, University of Athens
IC	Isabelle Constant, Boise State University
ALC	Anne L. Critchfield, University of Portland
GC	Gordana Crnković, University of Washington
PC-D	Pilar Cuder-Dominguez, University of Huelva, Spain
IAD'A	Irène Assiba D'Almeida, University of Arizona
VD	Vasudha Dalmia, University of California, Berkeley
SDD	Shamita Das Dasgupta, Rutgers University
GdB	Gabriella de Beer, City College of New York
ED	Elizabeth DeLoughrey, University of Maryland
JD	Jill Didur, Concordia University, Montreal
ADD	Amy D. Dooling, Connecticut College
APD	Aliki P. Dragona, University of California, Davis
CD	Chandana Dutta, editor, Katha, New Delhi
GE-C	Gun Edberg-Caldwell, University of Minnesota, Twin Cities
SE	Sibel Erol, New York University
ME	Marjorie Evasco, De La Salle University, Manila
VLSdBF	Vânia L.S. de Barros Falcão, Federal University of Rio Grande do Sul, Brazil
HF	Helen Fehervary, Ohio State University
YSF	Yael S. Feldman, New York University
APF	Ana Paula Ferreira, University of California, Irvine
CF-P	Cristina Ferreira-Pinto, University of Texas at Austin
FG	Francesca Galante, University of Wisconsin – Madison
CJG	Carmen J. Galarce, Otterbein College
MAG	Mary Anne Garnett, University of Arkansas, Little Rock
MGi	Monika Giacoppe, Pennsylvania State University
DGi	David Gilbey, Charles Sturt University
MGl	Miriyam Glazer, University of Judaism
AG	Anke Gleber, University of California, Irvine
HG	Helena Goscilo, University of Pittsburgh
CG	Christine Goulding, California State University, Chico
JGra	Jolisa Gracewood, Cornell University
JGre	Jill Greaves, James Cook University of North Queensland, Cairns

DGr	Dawn Green, University of Wisconsin–Madison
LPG	Lyubomira Parpulova Gribble, Ohio State University
KG	Kaaren Grimstad, University of Minnesota, Twin Cities
JBG	Jan Berkowitz Gross, Grinnell College
JH	Julie Hagedorn, New York University
CHa	Cynthia Hahn, Lake Forest College
DH	Doris Hambuch, University of Alberta
MHa	Margaret Harp, University of Nevada, Las Vegas
IEH	Ida Eve Heckenbach, Louisiana State University
DBH	Deirdre Bucher Heistad, University of Illinois, Urbana-Champaign
YH	Yolande Helm, Ohio University
MHe	Margaret Henderson, Monash University
MAH	Margaret A. Henderson, University of Queensland
AH	Allan Hepburn, McGill University
MHo	Minfong Ho, writer and member of PEN, USA
CHo	Chandra Holm, City University, Zürich
GH-W	Gail Holst-Warhaft, Cornell University
TH	Torild Homstad, St Olaf College
NBH	Naana Banyiwa Horne, Indiana University, Kokomo
MHH	Marte Hvam Hult, University of Minnesota, Twin Cities
NH	Neelam Hussain, Simorgh Women's Resource and Publication Centre, Pakistan
SIr	Susan Ireland, Grinnell College
SIy	Sujata Iyengar, University of Georgia
LJ	Lyn Jacobs, The Flinders University of South Australia
KJJ	Keala J. Jewell, Dartmouth College
KEJ	Karen E. Jones, East Carolina University
JK	Jayasree Kalathil, Central Institute of English and Foreign Languages, Hyderabad
KKa	Keiko Kanai, Asia University, Japan
KHK	Ketu H. Katrak, University of California, Irvine
LK	Lisa Kerrigan, freelance reviewer and writer, Melbourne
SK	Saleem Kidwai, Delhi University, emeritus
Y-HK	Yung-Hee Kim, University of Hawaii at Manoa
HDK	Helen D. Kolias, Cornell University
KKo	Kimberly Kono, University of California, Berkeley
RK	Rita Kothari, St Xavier's College
PK	Priya Kumar, McGill University
TK	Tomoko Kuribayashi, University of Wisconsin–Stevens Point
CLa	Christine Lac, Carleton College
MIL	María Inés Lagos, Washington University in St Louis
CSL	C. S. Lakshmi, SPARROW, Mumbai
CL-W	Carol Lazzaro-Weis, Southern University
MHL	Maria Helena Lima, State University of New York, Geneseo
ELi	Elaine Lindsay, University of Sydney
ELo	Elizabeth Locey, Emporia State University
JML	Jeffrey M. Loree, University of California, Los Angeles
DCGL	Dagmar C. G. Lorenz, University of Illinois, Chicago
SL	Stefania Lucamante, Georgetown University
CLu	Chris Lupke, Bowdoin College

BMab	Barbara Mabee, Oakland University
SMag	Sharon Magnarelli, Quinnipiac College
CPM	Christiane P. Makward, Pennsylvania State University
NFAM	Nor Faridah Abdul Manaf, International Islamic University, Malaysia
BMan	Bakirathi Mani, Stanford University
CJM	Connie J. Maraan, De La Salle University, Manila
PM	Paola Marchionni, University of London; Commonwealth Institute, London
KMM	K. Melissa Marcus, Northern Arizona University
EM	Elaine Martin, University of Alabama
NM	Nitaya Masavisut, literary scholar and president emeritus of PEN International, Thai Center
MAMM-M	Monita A. M. Mascitti-Meuter, Monash University
SMat	Suchitra Mathur, University of Wisconsin–Whitewater
RMa	Rinita Mazumdar, University of New Mexico, Albuquerque
LMcM	Lyn McCredden, Deakin University, Burwood
EMcM	Elizabeth McMahon, University of Tasmania
KMcN	Kathleen McNerney, West Virginia University
MMc	Maaike Meijer, University of Maastricht, the Netherlands
GMe	Grazia Menechella, University of Wisconsin–Madison
RMen	Ritu Menon, Kali for Women, New Delhi
DM	D. Mesher, San José State University
E-MM	Eva-Maria Metcalf, University of Mississippi
RMey	Ronald Meyer, Columbia University
YM	Yvonne Miels, Flinders University of South Australia
EBM-A	Eileen B. Mikals-Adachi, University of Notre Dame
JEM	Jane Eldridge Miller, writer and editor
F-yM	Feng-ying Ming, Whittier College
GMi	Giuliana Minghelli, Harvard University
PM-K	Peter Morris-Keitel, Bucknell University
JM	Jane Moss, Colby College
LM	Laura Moss, Queen's University, Canada
MMu	Magda Mueller, California State University, Chico
TN	Tahira Naqvi, Westchester Community College
EN	Ellen Nerenberg, Wesleyan University
JMN-A	Juliana Makuchi Nfah-Abbenyi, University of Southern Mississippi
NTT	Nguyen Thi Thanh, School for International Training
GCN	Geraldine Cleary Nichols, University of Florida
JN	Jonathan Noble, Ohio State University
MRO-W	María Rosa Olivera-Willliams, University of Notre Dame
JNO	José N. Ornelas, University of Massachusetts, Amherst
FO	Francesca Orsini, University of Cambridge
JLP	Janis L. Pallister, Bowling Green State University
AP-Z	Agnès Peysson-Zeiss, Baylor University
PP-W	Pary Pezechkian-Weinberg, Augsburg College
RP-I	Robin Pickering-Iazzi, University of Wisconsin–Milwaukee
MGP	Magdalena García Pinto, University of Missouri, Columbia
RDP	R. D. Pope, Washington University in St Louis
TJP	Tracy J. Prince, University of Nebraska
PJP	Patrice J. Proulx, University of Nebraska at Omaha

GP	Gus Puleo, State University of New York, Buffalo
SCQ	Susan Canty Quinlan, University of Georgia
SRah	Samina Rahman, Women's Action Forum, Pakistan
SRao	Sujata Rao, Sri Venkateswara College, New Delhi
LR	Lily Rattok, Tel Aviv University
TMR-P	Thelma M. Ravell-Pinto, Olympus College, Rotterdam
SDR	Sharon D. Raynor, East Carolina University
AMR	Annabelle M. Rea, Occidental College
MR	Michael Reder, Connecticut College
JR	Josna Rege, Dartmouth College
MBR	Myrna Bell Rochester, independent scholar
SVR	Sara Viola Rodrigues, Federal University of Rio Grande do Sul, Brazil
DTR	Dinah T. Roma, De La Salle University, Manila
LRR	Leah R. Rosenberg, Cornell University
NR	Natania Rosenfeld, Knox College
MR-F	Magali Roy-Féquière, Knox College
PR	Patricia Rubio, Skidmore College
GR	Gill Rye, Roehampton Institute, London
MSa	Maxine Sample, State University of West Georgia
JSa	Jose Santos, Russell Sage College
JHS	Judith Holland Sarnecki, Lawrence University
LMS	Lucy M. Schwartz, Buffalo State College
FS	Frankie Shackelford, Augsburg College
DMS	Dina M. Siddiqi, New School for Social Research, New York
PS	Pat Sieber, Ohio State University
NS	Neluka Silva, University of Colombo, Sri Lanka
AS	Atamjit Singh, San José State University
TSi	Tuulikki Sinks, University of Minnesota, Twin Cities
HS	Heather Smyth, University of Alberta
CS	Carolyn So, Claremont McKenna College
ES	Elena Sokol, The College of Wooster
SS	Sasson Somekh, Tel Aviv University
JSp	Jennifer Sparrow, Wayne State University
TSp	Thomas Spear, Lehman College and CUNY Graduate Center
RS	Ruth Starke, Flinders University of South Australia
MSt	Mark Stein, University of Frankfurt/Main
NSS	Nancy Saporta Sternbach, Smith College
JES	Jocelyn E. Stitt, University of Michigan
DS	Dana Strand, Carleton College
PT	Proma Tagore, McGill University
KTa	Kamran Talattof, University of Arizona
MLT	Mary Lawrence Test, independent scholar
KT-C	Kathleen Thompson-Casado, University of Toledo
HT	Helen Thomson, Monash University
KTo	Kris Torgeson, Columbia University
TT	Thúy Tranviet, Cornell University
MU	Marie Umeh, John Jay College of Criminal Justice, CUNY
CV	César Valverde, The College of Wooster
KVD	Karen Van Dyck, Columbia University
GAHVS	Gonda A. H. Van Steen, University of Arizona, Tucson

DVT	Desiree Van Til, independent scholar
JV	Jöelle Vitiello, Macalester College
MV	Martin Votruba, University of Pittsburgh
JW	Jing Wang, Ohio State University
LW	Lingzhen Wang, Brown University
KMW	K. Marianne Wargelin, independent scholar
AWa	Ann Waters, independent scholar
PW	Patrick West, Edith Cowan University
RW	Rebecca West, University of Chicago
GW	Gay Wilentz, East Carolina University
NW-T	Nana Wilson-Tagoe, University of London
AWi	Adi Wimmer, University of Klagenfurt, Austria
LY	Lingyan Yang, University of Massachusetts, Amherst
JY	Jack Yeager, University of New Hampshire
MY	Michelle Yeh, University of California, Davis
MŽ	Monika Žagar, University of Minnesota, Twin Cities
JTZ	Joseph T. Zeidan, Ohio State University
JZ	Jingyuan Zhang, Georgetown University
RJZ	Robert J. Zydenbos, independent scholar

Introduction

This is a biographical and bibliographical guide to contemporary women writers from around the world. It deals primarily with fiction writers, poets, and playwrights, but some writers of literary nonfiction, such as biographers, memoirists, and literary critics, have also been included. This work is unique in its combination of international coverage and contemporary focus. Though many other reference works on women's writing are available, none is devoted exclusively to contemporary women writers, and most of these works, due to either a broad historical scope or a national or ethnic emphasis, do not adequately represent writers from around the world whose careers began in the 1960s or later. The aim of this book is to provide, for students and general readers who are interested in contemporary writing, an international and comprehensive introductory guide to women writers of the last four decades of the twentieth century.

The international nature of this volume is perhaps its most significant feature. Although there has been a great deal of talk in recent years about multiculturalism and globalisation, most readers in English-speaking countries continue to read in national or cultural isolation. Most publishers, reviewers, and bookstores in these countries give readers barely a hint of the amazing wealth and variety of writing produced by women in other parts of the world. Many of the writers included here, perhaps the majority of them, are unknown to American and British readers. This volume offers readers an opportunity to discover hundreds of 'new' writers and gives those writers an opportunity to be known outside their own countries, to acquire new readers, and perhaps even to receive new translations. The Internet has made global communication instantaneous and effortless, and it is inevitable that awareness of and interest in global literature will grow, particularly as that literature becomes increasingly available for purchase on-line. One of the intentions of this book is to promote that growth and to help readers sort out who is who, and what it is they've written.

As is surely always the case with reference works such as this, the selection process has been the most difficult aspect of putting this book together. In order for this guide to be accessible and affordable, the number of entries had to be strictly limited, and as a result, many painful choices and omissions had to be made. An explanation of the procedures and principles of selection follows. For thirteen major literatures, contributing editors were chosen, and they, in consultation with advisers, selected the authors they wished to include. In other areas, I worked with advisers and contributors to determine which authors would be represented. Originally, 'contemporary' was defined as those writers whose careers began in 1960 or after. But it quickly became evident that this criterion had to be made more flexible, for a variety of reasons. First of all, there are many important and influential writers who began their writing lives in the 1950s, but who continued publishing and writing throughout the subsequent decades of the century. In most cases, these writers were included. But the time frame of the book was adjusted for other reasons as well. In China, for example, though many important women writers were published in the 1950s, political and social circumstances resulted in very few women writers being published in the 1960s and 1970s. Thus, for Chinese writers, the definition of contemporary was expanded to include the 1950s. A question also arose about how much weight to give older, yet extremely influential, writers. In Chinese, Korean, Italian, and other literatures, there are several important women writers whose careers began in the first half of the century but who, for various reasons, did not become influential or prominent until the latter half, and thus are often considered contemporary writers in their countries. Some, but not all, of these writers were also included. But just as I had to be careful not to go too far back into the twentieth century, I also had to limit the number of very new writers to be included. For the most part, writers who are just starting out and who currently have only one or two books to their credit have not been included, but will be considered for any future edition.

These criteria were applied with the greatest strictness to American, British, and Canadian writers because I wanted the volume to be truly international and not dominated by those who write in English. Since many reference works are already available on American, British, and Canadian writers, only those who fit precisely within the contemporary time frame have been included. In addition, although I have encouraged the inclusion of writers of non-canonical genres such as romance fiction and children's writing, representation of American, British, and Canadian practitioners of these genres has been limited, due to both space constraints and the availability of many specialized reference works on these genres in English. In all cases, my objective has been to create a balanced and international representation which does not slight important writers who are lesser-known because they do not write in English.

That writers have at least one book available in English translation was the other key principle of selection. The rationale for this was that since this volume is intended for an English-speaking audience, readers who become interested in a particular writer should be able to find something of her work to read. But as with the book's time frame, I soon realized that a more flexible policy was necessary in order to prevent the exclusion of many important writers. I have been surprised and dismayed to discover how many women writers remain largely or even wholly untranslated; this is most noticeable among but not limited to those who write in the Slavic languages and in Portuguese, Italian, and Chinese. To accommodate this fact, writers who have at least some work published in English-language anthologies were considered for inclusion. Also included are a handful of writers who have never been translated into English but who were too significant to leave out. Nevertheless, the necessary emphasis on writers whose work is available in translation resulted in many difficult decisions. In India, for example, there are twenty-two official languages, some of which have rich literatures dating back as far as the second century. Yet the contemporary literature in these languages is just beginning to be translated. Although the contributing editor for South Asia tried to represent the best-known writers from as many of the major languages as possible, many talented writers had to be left out in favor of Indian writers who write in English. It is my strong hope that this guide will increase awareness of how little of the work of these writers has been translated and will inspire publishers and translators to produce new translations of women's writing from around the world.

I have envisioned many different uses for this book, but I see it primarily as a guide for reading. It offers the reader an opportunity to move beyond bestseller lists or college reading lists, and by shifting into a global perspective, truly to read the world. It is important to note that this is an introductory guide and not a critical work. The entries are brief and factual, most averaging about 200 words, and the biographical narratives and literary descriptions they contain are necessarily summary. The aim has been to include as many writers as possible while providing readers with the essential information they need to start reading and exploring. This book is intended as a beginning. The entries provide some background information, but those who wish to learn about the historical, political, and social contexts of the author's life and works must look to the books listed in the bibliography and elsewhere.

An alphabetical organization was decided upon as the most logical and useful, but it is also appealing in that it increases the chances of stumbling onto new writers by reading beyond the specific entry sought or by simply browsing. As I gathered the entries together for the first time, I was thrilled by the unusual juxtapositions created by the book's alphabetical order and by the rich variety of the writers' lives and works. But it also seemed quite useful to be able to survey and categorize these writers by nationality, so they are identified that way at the beginning of the entry and grouped that way in an appendix. The writers' wishes, when known, have been followed in this matter. But national identity is increasingly a complicated concept, as national boundaries disappear or shift, or as nations are redefined, or as people move back and forth between countries and cultures and languages. A significant percentage of the writers represented here cannot accurately be identified by a single nationality, and instead are identified by their own hyphenated nationality which reflects the circumstances of their family background and their lives; in many cases, these writers are listed under several different nations in the appendix.

Finally, I would like to comment on the book's exclusive focus on women writers. This guide makes no claims about women's writing as a separate category or a distinct tradition. In addition, there was no requirement that the writers included define themselves as feminists or write on feminist or women-oriented themes and subjects. The decision to include only women was born out of frustration with the fact that women have consistently been given less coverage than men in reference works that include both women and men. It became clear to me that the only way to compensate for this past neglect and to provide adequate representation of important contemporary women writers from around the world was to give them a volume of their own. That said, I would like to acknowledge the fact that women's writing has been and continues to be vital to feminism and the expansion of women's rights. For many of the writers included in this volume, their identity as a woman is central to their writing; their commitment to writing about women's experiences is inseparable from their commitment to writing itself. For some, such as the Afghan writers included here, to identify oneself as a woman writer is in itself a radical and dangerous act. The entries on these writers, incomplete due to both censorship and the writers' concerns for their personal safety, provide an eloquent testimony to the position of women in Afghanistan today. But though I recognize how vitally important both parts of the identification 'woman writer' are to many of the authors included here, the most compelling link between the vastly disparate women in this collection is, for me, that of their common desire to create, communicate, enlighten, enchant, challenge, and inspire through their writing.

I would like to thank the following people for their advice and assistance: Leslie A. Adelson, Anna Allott, Carolyn Bliss, Rodica Botoman, Matei Calinescu, Joyce Carlson-Leavitt, Jerry Clinton, Louise Rodriguez Connal, Niedja Carvalho Fedrigo, Eva Geulen, Edward Gunn, Tineke Hellwig, Anne Golomb Hoffman, Christina Illias-Zarifopol, Amy Kaminsky, Susan F. Kepner, Ross King, Anna Klobucka, Miri Kubovy, Ann Lee, A. Walton Litz, John McGlynn, Margo Milleret, Luiza Franco Moreira, Harriet Murav, Suzanne Nash, Magda Al-Nowaihi, Carol Poore, Patrick Rumble, Darlene Sadlier, Ellen W. Sapega, Victor Schifferli, Peggy Sharpe, Elaine Showalter, Susan Rubin Suleiman, Katie Trumpener, Anne Ulmer, Jacqueline Vansant, Roxana Verona, and Rudi Wester. I am also grateful to the staff of the reference room at Firestone Library, Princeton University, for their help, and to Marilyn Yates, for her meticulous work on the typescript. I owe personal thanks to my family, especially Mac and Emma, and my friends, for their patience and support. My deepest gratitude is reserved for all the contributing editors, contributors, and advisers, whose knowledge, enthusiasm, generosity, and hard work made this book possible. I know that, like myself, all the contributing editors, at one time or another during the years we worked on this project, despaired that they had taken on far more than they had anticipated. But all of us were sustained by our commitment to and love of the work of the writers represented here.

Editor's note: The entries are organized alphabetically. An appendix groups authors together by nationality. Authors are listed by their best-known name; other names follow in parentheses. Works which were not written in English but are available in English translation are referred to by the translated title only. If a work has not been translated, the original title is given, followed by a literal translation in parentheses. Cross-references are marked by an asterisk before the author's name.

A

Abouzeid, Leila (b. 1950), Moroccan novelist, journalist. Abouzeid was born in El Ksiba, Morocco, into a middle-class family; her father was active in the resistance against the French. She was educated at a Moroccan school where Arabic and French were taught. She studied journalism at Mohammad V University in Rabat and the London School of Journalism. In addition to contributing to local periodicals, she has produced a daily radio program and worked as an anchorwoman for Moroccan television. Her first book *Bid' Sanābil Khudr* ('Few Green Wheat Stalks,' 1978), which she wrote during her stay in England, is a collection of articles, travel impressions and short stories. *Year of the Elephant* (1983), the first Arabic novel by a Moroccan woman to be translated into English, tells the story of the last years of fighting against the French in Morocco through the eyes of Zahra, a young woman who has taken part in the national struggle. Zahra's husband, who secures a high position in the new regime, decides to marry another woman. The devastated Zahra is forced to go back to her hometown to start anew on her own. *Rujū' ilā al-Tufūla* ('Return to Childhood,' 1993), an autobiography that Abouzeid had originally written in English and later translated into Arabic, is characterized by its frankness.

JTZ

Abū Khālid, Fawziyya (b. 1955), Saudi Arabian poet, essayist. Born in Riyadh, Saudi Arabia, to a traditional Bedouin family, Abū Khālid earned her BA in sociology from the American University of Beirut in 1978 and an MA in the same field from Lewis and Clark College in Portland, Oregon. She held a teaching position at the Women's College of King Saud University in Riyadh. She began contributing poetry to local journals at an early age. Her first collection *Ila Matā Yakhtatifānaki Laylalt al-'Urs* ('How Long Will They Keep Raping You on Your Wedding Night,' 1973) was published in Beirut and banned in Saudi Arabia. In 1985 she published her second collection, *Qirā'a fī al-Sirr li-Tārīkh al-ṣamt al-'Arabī* ('Secret Reading in the History of Arab Silence'), again in Beirut. In both collections, Abū Kāhlid wrote primarily about political themes with a revolutionary tone. She was deeply moved by the Arab defeat in the 1967 war: 'It was the blade over which I walked barefoot from childhood into womanhood.' Her use of the Arabic language is strikingly bold and she often refers to intimate parts of the female body. She was fiercely attacked by conservative groups, which caused her to lose her teaching job in Riyadh. Abū Khālid has also written stories for children.

JTZ

Accad, Evelyne (b. 1943), Lebanese-Swiss-US novelist. Born in Beirut of a Lebanese father and Swiss mother, Accad studied at Beirut University College before obtaining a PhD in Comparative Literature at Indiana University–Bloomington in 1973. She received the Prix Delta Kappa Gamma International Educator's Award for *Veil of Shame: The Role of Women in the Contemporary Fiction of North Africa and the Arab World* (1978). Since 1974, she has taught African, Caribbean, and Middle Eastern literatures and women's studies at the University of Illinois (Urbana). A Fulbright Scholar, she returned to Beirut to teach, and researched women's issues across Africa. Her first novel *The Excised* (1982) recounts her youth in Beirut followed by the story of an encounter with African traditions such as excision. Her third novel *Wounding Words: A Woman's Journal in Tunisia* (1993) documents the Tunisian women's movement in 1985. *Coquelicot du Massacre* ('Flower of Massacre,' 1988) depicts women's reactions to civil war in Beirut. Her book of essays about the link between representations of women and war, *Sexuality and War: Literary Masks of the Middle East*, received the Prix France-Liban in 1990. Accad's life and writing in French express her belief in the 'personal' as 'political'.

CHa

Acholonu, Catherine (*b.* 1950), Nigerian poet, dramatist, essayist, fiction writer. Born in Orlu in Imo State, Nigeria, to the family of Chief Lazarus Olumba, Acholonu was the first African woman to obtain a master's degree (1977) and a doctorate (1982) from the University of Dusseldorf, Germany. Married with four children, she is recognized as one of Nigeria's most gifted female poets. She has thirteen published works comprising poetry, plays, essays, and children's books to her credit and a forthcoming novel, *Oyidiya: The Story of an African Woman*. She founded Afa Publications, becoming one of Africa's few woman publishers. Her outstanding books include the play *Trial of the Beautiful Ones* (1982), a poetry collection

The Spring's Last Drop (1982), and the nonfiction works *The Igbo Roots of Olaudah Equiano* (1989) and *The Earth Unchained: A Quantum Leap in Consciousness* (1989). In *Motherism: The Afrocentric Alternative to Feminism* (1995), she redefines feminism from an African perspective. The former Fulbright Scholar and winner of multiple literary awards has also written collections of children's poetry in English and Igbo. Her poems and short stories have been published in many anthologies.

MU

Acker, Kathy (1948–1997), US novelist. Acker, who originally published under the daunting pen name 'Black Tarantula' and whose work has been variously categorized as postmodern, punk, or avant-garde, was born and grew up in New York City, received her BA from Brandeis University in 1968, and continued her studies at University of California, San Diego. She worked in a variety of professions, including secretary, stripper, and performer in live sex shows. Her influences were numerous and diverse: the Black Mountain poets, conceptual art, French surrealism, Sade, Freud, Gertrude Stein, William Burroughs, the Language poets. Her radically experimental novels, which include *The Childlike Life of the Black Tarantula by the Black Tarantula* (1973), *I Dreamt I was a Nymphomaniac* (1974), *Blood and Guts in High School* (1984), and *Empire of the Senseless* (1988), subvert traditional notions of narrative structure, character development, and authorial distance. Her intensely visceral prose, replete with depictions of violence, incest, rape, and suicide, has been criticized for being pornographic; her technique of openly 'plagiarizing' from other texts has also been attacked. In *Don Quixote* (1986), *Great Expectations* (1988), and *Pussy, King of the Pirates* (1996), a novel based loosely on Stevenson's *Treasure Island*, she rewrote 'male' stories from a feminist viewpoint. In her last work, *Eurydice in* *the Underworld* (1997), she turned her attention to Greek myth. Acker died of cancer in 1997.

DVT

Adams, Alice (1926–1999), US novelist, short story writer. A graduate of Radcliffe College in 1946, Adams captures and then challenges the educated, successful woman in her fiction. Born in Fredericksburg, Virginia and having lived most of her adult life in San Francisco, she taught at the University of California, Davis, the University of California, Berkeley, and Stanford University. Her novels include *Careless Love* (1966), *Families and Survivors* (1975), *Listening to Billie* (1978), *Rich Rewards* (1980), *Second Chances* (1988), *Caroline's Daughters* (1991), *Almost Perfect* (1993), and *Southern Exposure* (1995). Praised for the elegance and clarity of her prose, she often depicts women on a quest for independence and significance in their lives while trying to foster meaningful relationships. *Superior Women* (1984) depicts the intertwining lives of five Radcliffe women from their acceptance into the college through their middle age. Adams also published several collections of short stories including *Beautiful Girl* (1979), *To See You Again* (1982), and *After You've Gone* (1989). She was a frequent contributor to the *New Yorker*, and wrote articles for the *Paris Review* and the *Atlantic Monthly*, among others. She died in San Francisco in 1999.

DVT

Adams, Glenda (*b*. 1939), Australian novelist. After graduating with a BA from the University of Sydney, Adams studied in Indonesia and taught Indonesian at the University of Sydney before going to New York in 1964. In 1990 she returned to Australia and became Senior Lecturer in Writing at the University of Technology, Sydney. Adams's intricately structured novels are feminist, without subscribing to any particular orthodoxy. Her female characters struggle toward an understanding of their own identities from within a nexus of patriarchy and oppression. *Games of the Strong* (1982), in particular, with its Orwellian 'Big Brother' overtones and enigmatic authority figures, explores the role of contemporary women. Another recurring theme is that of the peripatetic wanderer, searching for identity between two worlds. In *Dancing on Coral* (1987; Miles Franklin Award and NSW Premier's Award), Lark Watter is stuck between Australia and the US, while in *Longleg* (1990; *Age* Fiction Book of the Year and National Book Council Banjo Award for fiction) William Badger is torn between Sydney and Europe. Adams has also published two short story collections. Her latest novel *The Tempest of Clemenza* (1996) is set in the US and Australia.

LK

Adcock, Fleur (*b*. 1934), New Zealand-born poet, translator. Born near Auckland, but along with her sister *Marilyn Duckworth, attended schools in England during World War II. Adcock returned to New Zealand during her teens and attended Wellington Girls' College. Subsequently she briefly married twice, completed her BA and MA in Classics at Victoria University, lectured at the University of Otago, and served as a librarian. In 1963 she moved to London, and eventually became a full-time writer. Her first collection of poetry *The Eye of the Hurricane* (1964) was followed by numerous other volumes including *The Inner Harbour* (1979), *The Incident Book* (1986), and *Looking Back* (1997); *Selected Poems* (1983) won the New Zealand National Book Award for Poetry. While generally lyric, her poetry sometimes employs traditional forms and sometimes is free verse. Her perspective often seems detached and has a mythic element, but frequently her poetry is pointed and ironic. Usually her poems are short and comment upon human relationships and experiences. She has also translated medieval Latin and Romanian poetry and has edited significant poetry collections. She has held fellowships in England and Australia and was awarded an Order of the British Empire.

M-RA

Adisa, Opal Palmer (*b*. 1954), Jamaican novelist, poet. Born in Kingston, Adisa earned an MA in creative writing and a PhD in Ethnic Studies. Her sensibilities were shaped by Jamaican sugar estates and rural communities, the setting for *Bake-Face and Other Guava Stories* (1986). Her first novel *It Begins with Tears* (1977) is an exhilarating exploration of primal human drives and conflicts in a Jamaican village not yet contaminated by colonization. Her harassed, sensual women are of a piece with Jamaica's sun and vibrant colors. Her best work, which includes the piquant, earthy poetry of *Tamarind and Mango Women* (1992), dramatizes in effervescent language the heroic lives of impoverished women with a strong sense of self-affirmation, and is a candid but loving evocation of Jamaican life. She has written stories for children and plays for Black Repertory Theater, and her poems and essays have appeared in several journals and anthologies in the US, Canada, and London. She has taught Caribbean and African literature at San Francisco State University and is presently Chair of Ethnic/Cultural Diversity Program at California College of Arts and Crafts.

HB

Adnan, Etel (*b*. 1925), Lebanese-US poet, novelist, essayist. Born in Beirut, Adnan is a writer and a painter. Educated in Lebanon, France (Lyon, 1949; the Sorbonne, 1950), and the US (University of California–Berkeley, 1955–7; Harvard, 1957–8), she taught at Al-Ahliya High School (Beirut 1947–9) then at Dominican College as professor of philosophy (1958–72). Written in French and in English, the majority of her work is poetic: ten volumes have been published since 1971 and others are unedited at this time. She contributed to Lebanese French-language newspapers (1972–5). Her work includes essays: *Journey to Mount Tamalpais* (1986), *Paris, When It's Naked* (1993), and *Of Cities and Women: Letters to Fawwaz* (1993). She has written articles and short stories as well as scripted films and television commentaries. Her novel *Sitt Marie Rose* (1978) is widely translated and received the Prix France–Pays Arabes. Her best-known work, it is inspired by actual events in the Lebanese civil war. It explores the development of violence and its impact on Lebanese society in general and on women in particular. Her poetry also reflects concern with issues related to peace and the preservation of the earth.

IEH

Ağaoğlu, Adalet (*b*. 1929), Turkish novelist, short story writer. Born near Ankara, Ağaoğlu received a BA in French literature. Through the 1950s and 1960s she worked for the cultural programs division of Ankara radio while she also wrote plays. She quit her job in 1970 to devote all her time to writing. Of her eight novels published to date, *Ölmeye Yatmak* ('Lying Down to Die,' 1973), *Bir Düğün Gecesi* ('The Night of a Wedding,' 1979) and *Hayır* ('No,' 1987) constitute a trilogy that depicts the social history of modern Turkey from 1938 to the late 1980s. *Curfew* (1984) covers several hours of one night as seven people come to realizations about their lives. Her latest novel *Romantik: Bir Viyana Yazı* ('Romantic: A Vienna Summer,' 1993) depicts a novelist looking for a character that s/he finds with the help of an ideal reader. Her stories are published in three volumes, and her essays are collected in three volumes. Her works have received many literary prizes such as the Saik Faik Story Award for the collection of stories *Sessizliğin İlk Sesi* ('The First Sound of Silence,' 1978), whose title story is available in English. She was honored with the presidential medal for literature in 1995, and most recently with an honorary doctorate by Ohio State University in 1998. She is married.

SE

Agosín, Marjorie (*b.* 1955), Chilean-US poet, essayist, critic. Daughter of Jewish immigrants, Agosín was born in Bethesda, Maryland, but grew up in Chile. She was educated in the US, receiving her PhD at Indiana University, Bloomington. Her book *A Cross and a Star: Memoirs of a Jewish Girl in Chile* (1994) chronicles her mother's experiences as a Jewish girl growing up as an outsider in a predominantly Catholic country, and in a region populated by German immigrants. As a journalist, Agosín has strongly denounced human rights violations throughout Latin America. In her stories and poetry, she explores the pain caused by torture and repression, and the brutality of the violence that occurred in Chile during the Pinochet regime (1973–90). In *Zones of Pain* (1988) and *Circles of Madness: Mothers of the Plaza de Mayo* (1992), she makes an 'alliance with the language of sorrow' through the use of aesthetic and metaphoric images, writing a poetic text based on the pictures and tapestries of the mothers of the 'disappeared.' In her collections of critical articles, Agosín argues that Latin American women are creating a new politics of resistance based on humility and motherhood. She teaches at Wellesley College.

CJG

Aguilar, Ma. Luisa B. (*b.* 1962), Philippine poet, essayist. Born in Baguio City, she earned an AB in humanities in 1980 from UP Baguio, an MA in English literature in 1988 from Ateneo de Manila University, and a PhD in English and creative writing in 1995 from the University of Illinois at Chicago, where she was a Fulbright Fellow and studied with the poets Ralph J. Mills, Jr. and Michael Anania. Winner of many literary awards, she is also in the Palanca Hall of Fame for having won five first prizes in poetry and essays. As part of a

community of Filipino women writers writing in English, she actively searches for the continuities of her culture, country, and identity in poetry. She locates the source of her poetry in an inspiring blend of native lore and personal history. But being woven into the dreams of a foreign tongue has given Aguilar the resolve to venture into the rich layers of multi-ethnic/cultural life which inevitably renders her poetry and teaching tensile and singular. Her collections of poetry include *Cartography/A Collection of Poetry on Baguio* (1992; Philippine National Book Award), *Encanto* (1994), *In the Garden of the Three Islands* (1995), and *Blood Sacrifice* (1997).

DTR

Aguilar, Mila (*b.* 1949), Philippine poet. When martial law was declared in 1972, Aguilar, who took the pen name 'Clarita Roja,' was among the progressive student writers rounded up and detained by the military. The rebellion case filed by the Marcos government against her had to be dropped since the military could not find evidence to support their allegations. She then worked with the extension service of St Joseph's College in Quezon City, and was active in fighting for the families of the disappeared victims of military executions or 'salvaging' during the dictatorship. She was again arrested for subversion in 1984. When the Aquino administration was installed by the people power revolution in 1986, she was finally released from detention. In 1984 her first poetry collection *A Comrade is as Precious as a Rice Seedling* was published with an introduction by * Audre Lorde. In the same year the poems she wrote in prison were collected in *Why Cage Pigeons*. Clarita Roja's poems are also found in *Pintig* (1985), an anthology of prose and poetry by political prisoners. The nationalist fervor in her poetry confronts forms of oppression based on political color, socio-economic class, and gender. *Journey: An Autobiography in Verse (1964–1995)* (1996) clarifies the complexities of the paths traversed by this activist-poet. Aguilar finished her bachelor's and master's degrees at the University of the Philippines. She is married to Magtanggol Roque; they have a son.

ME

Aidoo, Ama Ata (*b.* 1942), Ghanaian writer, activist. Aidoo was born in the central region of Ghana to Nana Yaw Fama, chief of the town Abeadzi Kyiakor, and Maame Abasema. After graduating with a BA from the University of Ghana, Legon in 1964, she made her debut with the play *The Dilemma of a Ghost* (1965), becoming the first published African woman dramatist, and one of the first to address the issues of slavery and Africans in the diaspora. *Dilemma* explores the complexities informing the return of New World Africans to the motherland, while her next play *Anowa* (1970) reveals her fascination with Ghanaian lore, African history, and women's lives – recurrent themes in all her works. She has published two collections of short stories – *No Sweetness Here* (1970) and *The Girl Who Can* (1997); two novels – *Our Sister Killjoy* (1977) and *Changes* (1991); two collections of poetry – *Someone Talking to Sometime* (1985) and *An Angry Letter in January* (1992); and children's books, essays, and interviews on the politics of identity and writing. Following a series of academic appointments, Aidoo became Secretary of Education in 1983. The founder of She-Kings in 1996, a consultancy on writing and books in Africa, she lives in Ghana and writes full-time, doing readings and speaking engagements combined with periodic teaching all over the world.

NBH

Aini, Leah (*b.* 1962), Israeli poet, fiction writer. Primarily a poet but also a prolific writer of novellas, short stories and children's fiction, Aini was born in a poor neighborhood in south Tel Aviv. Her Salonika-born father was a Holocaust survivor and her mother was born in Soviet Kurdestan. As a child, Aini was a voracious reader despite the dearth of books in the house. After her army service, she took a variety of jobs while studying literature. She published her first poetry at the age of 24. She is the winner of numerous Israeli prizes for literature. Clearly autobiographical, Aini's literary world is one of memory in which two central elements intersect: the community of her childhood and the Holocaust. She recreates her childhood milieu in precise detail: junk-filled yards, crowded shops, derelict old houses and lively relationships among the neighborhood's inhabitants. These include Holocaust survivors unable to free themselves from the past, whose experiences impinge upon the emotional and even physical lives of their descendants. Her stories are redolent of blight and disability, madness and perverted eroticism juxtaposed with fantasies of sweetness and warmth. These preoccupations converge in *Gibborei Kayitz* ('The Sea Horse Race,' 1991), a collection of stories and a novella. Her novel *Mishehi Tzerikha Lehiyot Kan* ('Someone Must Be Here,' 1995) has been translated into German.

GAb

Akello, Grace (*b. c.* 1940s), Ugandan poet, essayist, folklorist. Born in Uganda, Akello attended Makerere University where she studied English and history. Her book *Iteso Thought Patterns in Tales* (1975) reflects Teso worldviews and philosophy. Before traveling to England in 1981, she worked as an editor for magazines in Kenya and Tanzania, where one of her controversial poems, 'My Dear Brother,' appeared in *VIVA* in 1977. In 1979, she published a collection of her poetry titled *My Barren Song*. This woman-centered text, containing fifty-eight poems, champions women's rights and argues for equality between men and women in her sociocultural environment. *Self Twice-Removed: Ugandan Woman* (1982) gives a short history of Uganda –

pre- and post-colonialism – highlighting women's subordinate position in the society. One of Akello's essays, 'Problems Women Face,' was included in *Women and Health in Kenya* (1995). A mother of four sons, she lives with her second husband in Kenya.

MU

Åkesson, Sonja (1926–1977), Swedish poet. Born in Buttle on Gotland, an island east of Sweden, Åkesson left for Stockholm in 1951. An autodidact, she tried a wide range of occupations. Her working-class background and perspective are obvious in her oeuvre, which consists of about twenty books, some written in collaboration with her husband, the poet and artist Jarl Hammarberg. Her importance for the new wave of feminism is indisputable. She died of cancer in 1977. Her breakthrough came with the collection *Husfrid* ('Domestic Peace,' 1963). Here the well-known poem 'Marriage Question' appeared, written in 'pidgin Swedish,' where marriage is compared to a master-slave relationship. In 'Autobiography' – a line-by-line reply to the Beat poet Lawrence Ferlinghetti's 'Autobiography' – Åkesson describes her life while questioning gender, class, and artistry. She became the poet of everyday life, belonging to a new school of poetry called 'the new simplicity' Åkesson eschews linguistic rules in *Jag bor i Sverige* ('I Live in Sweden,' 1966), writes haiku poems in *Sagan om Siv* ('The Saga of Siv,' 1974), and uses collage in *Pris* ('Price,' 1968); her innovative techniques became a hallmark of her elaborate poems and prose. English translations of her poems can be found in several anthologies.

GE-C

Akhmadulina, Bella (Izabella) Akhatovna (*b.* 1937), Russian poet, prose writer. Born into a middle-class family in Moscow, Akhmadulina always prized her closeness to her unconventional maternal grandmother and her literary links with the poets Akhmatova and Tsvetaeva. After her poetic debut in 1955, she graduated from the Gorky Literary Institute in 1960, brought out her first collection, *Struna* ('The String') in 1962, and started translating Georgian poetry. Her major volumes of verse include *Oznob* ('Chill,' 1968), *Stikhi* ('Verses,' 1975), *Svecha* ('Candle,' 1977), *Sny o Gruzii* ('Dreams of Georgia,' 1977), *Taina* ('Secret,' 1983), *Stikhotvoreniia* ('Poems,' 1988), and *Izbrannoe* ('Selected Works,' 1988). *Griada kamnei* ('Row of Stones,' 1995) contains her best poems from 1957 to 1992. Themes of poetic creativity, alienation, moral values, and friendship dominate her verses, which often capture a transcendent moment concretely imaged in nature, animals, individuals, and locations. Symbols, fantasy, developed narrative, lexical diversity, syntactic inversions, complex rhymes and near-rhymes, evocative instrumentation, and, with the years, an increasing meditativeness and metric experimentation, mark her poetic style. Palpable in atmosphere and elegant in form, her poems earned her the State Prize for Literature in 1989. Formerly married to the poet Evgeny Evtushenko and the prose writer Turi Nagibin, Akhmadulina travels abroad extensively with her current husband, the artist Boris Messerer. She has become a 'revered member' of the generation born during Stalin's repressions, an identity that emerges clearly in her recent essay-memoirs titled *A Moment of Being* (1997). English translations include *Fever and Other New Poems* (1969), *The Garden* (1990), and poems in the anthology *Contemporary Russian Poetry* (1993).

HG

Albu, Florenţa (*b.* 1934), Romanian poet. Better known in her youth as a reporter for the main Romanian Communist Youth journal, Albu is an interesting and prolific poet who has changed her style several times, starting with a 'literature of political activism' (typical for the Romanian 1950s), then slowly turning to traditionalism, classical expression, and even autochtonism (in her later, nostalgic poems, evoking her native village, its archaic traditions and the edenic nature surrounding it). Her most important volumes are *Cîmpia soarelui* ('The Field of the Sun,' 1962), *Intrare în anotimp* ('Entering the Season,' 1964), *Petrecere cu iarbă* ('Party with Grass,' 1973), *65 de poeme* ('65 Poems,' 1978), and *Kilometrul Unu* ('Kilometer One,' 1988). Her representativeness lies within her continuous 'style-seeking': the changing aesthetic canons (and political context) in her country, after World War II, made the paths of creativity difficult for many writers of her generation.

IB

Alegría, Claribel (*b.* 1924), Salvadoran novelist, poet. Born in Nicaragua, Alegría moved to El Salvador at the age of 1. She graduated from George Washington University and married the late US-born Darwin Flakoll. They had three children. Her life is itself a testimony to the very issues about which she writes. Having witnessed the 'Massacre' of 30,000 Salvadoran peasants as a child, she incorporates this traumatic event into much of her fiction, poetry, and testimony. She collaborated on many projects with Flakoll, who also translated many of her collections of poetry and prose. Known as an indefatigable worker for human rights, her work responds to these concerns. Her early volumes of poetry and her novel *Ashes of Izalco* (1966) did not attract the attention she was to receive for *Sobrevivo* ('I Survive'), which was awarded the coveted Casa de las Américas poetry award in 1978. In *Flowers from the Volcano* (1982), *They Won't Take Me Alive* (1983), *Family Album* (1984), *Luisa in Realityland* (1987) and *Woman of the River* (1988), Alegría successfully intersects women's political realities in Central American settings. She has lived in Nicaragua since 1980.

NSS

Aleksievich, Svetlana (*b. c.* 1948), Belorus-

sian prose writer. Born in Minsk to a Belarus father and Ukrainian mother, Aleksievich graduated from Minsk University as a journalist in 1972. She worked for a local paper before turning to her life's major work: accounts of tragic events. Real-life catastrophe is her dominant concern, which she recreates with painful vividness in her signature genre of literary documentary. Combining materials gleaned from interviews with her own commentary and devices characteristic of fiction, she has assembled devastatingly powerful portraits of women's experience in World War II (*War's Unwomanly Face*, 1985), Russia's war with Afghanistan (*Zinky Boys: Soviet Voices from a Forgotten War*, 1991), suicide in Russia (*Bewitched by Death*, 1994), and, most recently, the nuclear disaster at Chernobyl (*Chernobyl Prayer: Chronicle of the Future*, 1997). Though awarded a prize by the Swedish PEN Club and officially commended by Western Europeans for her health-imperiling research in Chernobyl, at home Aleksievich was hounded by authorities who feared her revelations about Soviets' failure to control nuclear power. She amply documents the hideous, unendurable effects of radiation for current and future generations in Belarus. Alongside physical and psychological torments, Aleksievich's *Chernobyl Prayer* records incidents of love and superhuman generosity, courage, and self-sacrifice – which presages her next envisioned project, a quasi-documentary about love.

HG

Alexander, Meena (*b.* 1951), Indian-US poet, novelist. Born to a Christian family in Allahabad, India, Alexander spent much of her childhood in the state of Kerala, before the family moved to the Sudan in 1969. She studied at the University of Khartoum and the University of Nottingham, England, where she wrote a doctoral dissertation on the British Romantic poets. During this time, she also established herself as a poet, publishing several long poems later collected into *House of a Thousand Doors* (1988). In 1975, Alexander returned to teach English literature in India, an experience that inspired her first novel *Nampally Road* (1991). In her memoir *Fault Lines* (1993), Alexander traced the life-journey between continents that finally led her to the US in 1979. Merging poetry and autobiographical prose, she examined the space occupied by those who live between multiple cultures, a theme she resumed in *The Shock of Arrival: Reflections on Postcolonial Experience* (1996). She has increasingly turned her gaze on her home in New York, exploring both the trauma and rebirth that is part of an immigrant's experience in *River and Bridge* (1996) and the novel *Manhattan Music* (1997). She currently teaches at Hunter College and the Graduate Center, City University of New York.

MAg

Alfon, Estrella D. (1917–1983), Philippine fiction writer, playwright. The daughter of a grocer on Espleta Street in Cebu (a district which was to become the setting for a number of her stories), Alfon moved to Manila after high school to enroll at the University of the Philippines. There, she pursued studies in medicine and law, but was forced to abandon these due to a lung ailment. She obtained an Associate in Arts certificate instead, and became a member of the university writers' club, spending her time with a clique later acknowledged to be the first generation of Philippine writers in English. She is perhaps best remembered for her much anthologized story 'Magnificence,' which dramatizes a mother's valiant attempt to rescue her young daughter from sexual abuse. In 1955, the Catholic Women's League filed an obscenity suit against her and the publisher of *This Week Sunday Magazine* because her story 'Fairy Tale for the City' was deemed 'pornographic,' although the central conflict revolves around a young man who allows his parish priest to absolve him of his sins. *Magnificence and*

Other Stories was published in 1960; a retrospective, *The Stories of Estrella D. Alfon*, appeared in 1994.

CJM

Alkali, Zaynab (*b.* 1952), Nigerian novelist, short story writer, essayist. The first woman novelist from northern Nigeria, Alkali originates from Garkida, Adamawa, a village in Bornu State. Born a Muslim, she was raised in a Christian village in Gongola State, Nigeria. She received her BA in English in 1973, her MA in African literature in 1980, and her PhD in African literature in English in 1995 from Bayero University in Kano. After holding both administrative and teaching positions in Nigeria for over twenty-five years, she is currently an associate professor of African literature and creative writing and the editor of *Ganga: A Journal of Language and Literature* at the University of Maiduguri, Bornu. Her first novel *The Stillborn* (1984) received the Association of Nigerian Authors' prose prize in 1985 for the Best Novel. The novel presents a combination of themes that concern the condition of women, especially Muslim women in contemporary Nigeria, such as polygamy, child-brides, the generation gap, urbanization versus traditionalism, and women's roles and social change. Alkali believes that African women as subjects are too often ignored and not adequately represented. Her other works include her second novel *The Virtuous Woman* (1987), a coming of age story about three girls, and a collection of short stories titled *The Cobwebs and Other Stories* (1997). She has received several prestigious awards for her writing. She is married to Mohammed Nur Alkali; they have five children.

SDR, MU

Allen, Paula Gunn (*b.* 1939), US poet, essayist, novelist. As a woman of mixed heritage – her mother is Laguna Pueblo, Sioux, and Scottish, her father is Lebanese – Allen often expresses in her writing the struggle to combine a variety of cultural backgrounds into one coherent identity. A registered member of the Laguna Pueblo tribe, Allen was born and raised in New Mexico. She received a BA, an MFA in creative writing, and a PhD from the University of New Mexico, and is currently a professor of English at University of California, Los Angeles. Her poetry, fiction, and essays explore Native American traditions and cultures from an explicitly feminist and lesbian perspective. Her collections of poetry include *The Blind Lion* (1974), *Coyote's Daylight Trip* (1978), *Shadow Country* (1982), *Star Child* (1981) and *Skins and Bones* (1988). The protagonist of her novel *The Woman Who Owned the Shadows* (1983) is a lesbian of mixed racial heritage who seeks to understand herself by making a spiritual connection to the past. *The Sacred Hoop: Recovering the Feminine in American Indian Traditions* (1986) is an important collection of Allen's critical essays. She has also edited several anthologies of Native American literature.

DVT

Allende, Isabel (*b.* 1942), Chilean novelist, journalist. Allende was born in Lima, Peru, where her father was a Chilean diplomat. After graduating from high school in Santiago, she worked for a UN agency for six years, before becoming a successful journalist and editor at *Paula* magazine. She left Chile after the military coup of 1973, in which her uncle, President Salvador Allende, was overthrown. In Venezuela, while working as a school administrator, she began the novel that would make her internationally famous, *The House of the Spirits* (1982). She weaves the story of the Trueba family with the events that led to the Chilean coup. Her spellbinding narration, imaginative characters, and attention to women's experiences manage to move the reader seamlessly from the private to the social and political. More a reporter than an advocate, she makes use of her journalistic training in her novels. Her second novel *Of Love and Shadows* (1984) evokes the repression of life under the Pinochet dictatorship, while in *The Infinite Plan* (1991) she focuses on her new country of residence since 1988, the US. *Paula* (1994), the autobiographical narration of the death of her daughter in a Madrid hospital, has a superb mix of humor, pathos, and insight that makes it memorable and spellbinding. *Daughter of Fortune* (1999) is an historical novel set in nineteenth-century Chile. She has received numerous awards and honors.

RDP

Allfrey, Phyllis Shand (1908–1986), Dominican novelist, poet, journalist. Born to a white Creole family in Dominica, the second of four sisters, Phyllis Byam Shand married an Englishman, Robert Edward Allfrey, in 1930, had two children and adopted three Dominican children. While in London from 1936 to 1953, she wrote nearly forty short stories, and published two books of poetry titled *In Circles* (1940) and *Palm and Oak* (1950). Her most acclaimed work, *The Orchid House* (1953), examines the brown elite's ascendancy in Dominica and the rise of the predominantly black trade union movement. All her writing expresses her commitment to peace and the establishment of a racially tolerant and equitable society, as did her work for the British Labour Party and the Fabian Society. In 1953, she returned to Dominica, cofounding the Dominica Labour Party (DLP) in 1955, being elected Member of Parliament to the West Indian Federation, and serving as Federal Minister of Labour and Social Affairs (1958–62). Ousted from the DLP in 1962, she used the two newspapers she edited with her husband, *The Dominica Herald* (1962–5) and *The Star* (1965–82), as forum for her political views. She also wrote three unpublished novels, including the unfinished *In the Cabinet*, which relates her experience as Federal Minister.

LRR

Allison, Dorothy (b. 1949), US novelist, poet, short story writer. Born in Greenville, South Carolina, Allison first made a name for herself within the lesbian community with a collection of poetry, *The Women Who Hate Me* (1983), and a collection of short stories, *Trash* (1988). She found a much larger audience with her first novel, the critically acclaimed *Bastard Out of Carolina* (1992), which was a National Book Award finalist. Based in part on Allison's life and told from the perspective of a young girl named Bone, this coming-of-age novel tells a harrowing story of poverty, violence, incest, and survival while powerfully evoking the milieu of the rural south. Allison's outspoken sexual and political views are presented in *Skin: Talking about Sex, Class, and Literature* (1993), a collection of essays, and in her autobiographical memoir *Two or Three Things I Know for Sure* (1996), which was originally written for performance. Allison's second novel, *Cavedweller*, was published in 1999.

DVT

Almog, Ruth (b. 1936), Israeli novelist, journalist. Unique among Israeli women writers in her openly autobiographical (and psychoanalytical) fiction, Almog has foregrounded the 'female condition' throughout her work, from the stories in *Hasdei Halaylah Shel Marguerite* ('Marguerita's Nightly Charities,' 1969) through *Shorshei 'Avir* ('Roots of Air,' 1987), the ambitious novel that won the prestigious Brenner prize and catapulted her to public recognition. In this novel she for the first time let her heroine cut the umbilical cord that bound her earlier protagonists to father figures and (unresponsive) lovers, bringing them to the brink of insanity and disease: *Be'eretz Gzerah* ('The Exile,' 1970), *'Aharei To Bishvat* ('After To Bishvat,' 1980), *'Et Hazar Vehá oyev* ('The Stranger and the Foe: A Report on A [Writer's] Block,' 1980) and *Nashim* ('Women,' 1986). Steeped in philosophy and psychology (which she studied at Tel

Aviv University), Almog's unique blend of Israeli color and European culture is at the heart of *Death in the Rain* (1982), a Rashomon-style novel in which she first crossed over the gender boundaries of her earlier fiction. This process continues in *Tikkun 'Omanuti* ('Invisible Mending,' 1993), where her delicately wrought stories mend the wounded lives of children, new immigrants and other outsiders. A mother of two, she is also a prolific writer of children's literature, for which she has won three prestigious awards.

YSF

Alther, Lisa (b. 1944), US novelist. A native of Tennessee, Alther attended Wellesley College, receiving her BA in 1966. Her best-selling first novel *Kinflicks* (1976) was praised for its humor and its honesty, and the tough, lively voice of its heroine Ginny was compared to that of Holden Caulfield and Huck Finn. The novel is a *Bildungsroman* of the 1960s: Ginny, a Southern belle, is transformed by the women's liberation movement, the civil rights movement, the Vietnam War, and the sexual revolution. In this and her other novels, Alther's characters are on a continual quest for self-discovery that leads them to experiment with various identities and lifestyles. Her second novel *Original Sins* (1981), also a coming-of-age novel, follows the development of five different protagonists as they grow up in the South. *Other Women* (1984) explores the various kinds of relationships that women form – professional, romantic, or friendly, while *Five Minutes in Heaven* (1995) depicts how the friendship between two women develops into a lesbian relationship. *Bedrock* (1990) is set in Vermont, where Alther now lives.

DVT

Alunan, Merlie M. (b. 1943), Philippine poet. Alunan received her BA in education from the University of the Visayas in Cebu City. In 1967, she joined the Silliman University Graduate School under the tutelage of Edilberto and * Edith Tiempo. Though Alunan majored in creative writing, she never wrote during her student days. Being a teacher proved a more practical career and enabled her to help her family. But fifteen years after graduate school, teaching, and mothering, what she had earlier thought of as merely acts of living became a source of poetic vision. Her first volume of poetry *Hearthstone Sacred Tree* (1993) deals with loyalties invented and sustained in human relationships. Her second collection *Amina Among Angels* (1997) is, by her own declaration, a 'book of grieving.' One of its subjects is the Ornoc flash flood in 1991 which killed several members of her family. The author continues to live and teach at the University of the Philippines, Tacloban College (Visayas), where she is also actively involved in creative writing workshops.

DTR

Alvarez, Julia (*b*. 1950), Dominican-US novelist, poet. Born in the Dominican Republic, Alvarez came to the US in 1960. She earned a BA in English from Middlebury College in 1971, and an MA in Creative Writing from Syracuse University in 1975. She has held several academic appointments and is currently a professor at Middlebury College. She lives in Vermont with her second husband. The poems collected in *Homecoming* (1984) challenge the homemaking ideals of her Dominican background. Her second collection *The Other Side/El Otro Lado* (1995) succeeds in articulating her Latina self, bilingual and bicultural. In her first novel *How the García Girls Lost their Accents* (1991), she gives a polyphonic account of the immigrant experiences of a Dominican family. Attesting to her growing political awareness, *In the Time of the Butterflies* (1994) tells of the true struggle of the Mirabal sisters against the dictatorship of Trujillo in the Dominican Republic of the 1950s. The four García sisters and their parents return in *Yo!* (1997), in which Alvarez moves freely among settings (in the US and

the Dominican Republic), characters (above all, the García's extended family), and topics, in interrelated stories of a decidedly autobiographical cast. *Something to Declare* (1998) is a collection of essays.

PC-D

Alves, Miriam (*b*. 1952), Brazilian poet, short story writer. Alves works as a social worker in the city of São Paulo where she was born and raised. She has been associated with 'Quilombhoje,' a group of black writers who edit *Cadernos negros* ('Black Notebooks'), since 1983. She edited the bilingual volume *Enfim . . . Nós / Finally Us* (1995), a collection of texts by contemporary Brazilian black women. Her work has been published in numerous anthologies, including *Cadernos negros*. Her poems have been collected in two volumes of poetry: *Momentos de busca* ('Moments of Searching,' 1983) and *Estrelas no dedo* ('Stars in the Finger,' 1985). In her fiction, as well as in essays, she often analyzes what it means to be black and female in Brazil. Though her texts discuss her experience as an Afro-Brazilian, ethnicity and historical rage do not constitute the core themes in her fiction. Through the recreation of a unique poetic language, she describes her quest as a black woman for a social and personal position in Brazilian society.

MJB

Amadiume, Ifi (*b*. 1947), Nigerian poet, ethnographer, essayist. Born in Kaduna, a Muslim town in northern Nigeria, to Igbo parents, Amadiume had her early education in Nigeria before moving to Britain in 1971. There, as well as being an academic and poet, she was active in local politics and was editor of *Pan-African Liberation Platform*, an educational and human rights journal. In 1993, she moved to the US with her two children; she is currently chair of the African and African-American Studies program at Dartmouth College. She earned a BA (Honors) in 1978 and PhD in 1983 in social anthropology from the School of Oriental and African Studies, University of London. She has done field-work in Africa and has written two ethnographic monographs and a theoretical book of essays: *African Matriarchal Foundations: The Igbo Case* (1987), *Male Daughters, Female Husbands: Gender and Sex in an African Society* (1987; *Choice Magazine* award), and *Reinventing Africa: Matriarchy, Religion and Culture* (1997). Her work has made a tremendous contribution to new ways of thinking about sex and gender, the question of power, and women's place in history and culture. Her poetry also deals with women's experiences and concerns as mediated through her complex geographics. She has published two award-winning books of poetry – *Passion Waves* (1985) and *Ecstasy* (1995). A third collection, *Returning* (forthcoming), deals with her diasporic experiences and political activism.

MU

Ambai (C.S. Lakshmi) (*b.* 1944), Indian writer, researcher. Ambai (the pen name of C. S. Lakshmi) was born in Coimbatore, Tamilnadu and brought up in Mumbai and Bangalore. A novel written for children won a prize in 1961 and set her on a writing career. Although she wrote and published an early novel *Andhi Malai* ('Twilight') in 1966, her serious writing began in 1967 with *Siragugal Muriyam* ('Wings Get Broken'), a long short story, published in her first collection of the same title (1976). This and a second collection, *Veetin Moolayil Oru Samayalarai* ('A Kitchen in the Corner of the House,' 1988), have established her as a major short story writer. She experiments with form, genre, and narrative technique and her fiction is characterized by her eye for detail and sense of irony, which ranges from playful to biting. Her feminism permeates but does not restrict the subject matter of her work, which investigates the ways gender is constructed in society, explores communication between human

beings, and celebrates ordinary women's courage and resourcefulness. *A Purple Sea: Short Stories by Ambai* (1992) is a selection of her fiction in English translation. She has also written a book on women writers, *Face Behind the Mask: Women in Tamil Literature* (1984). Ambai lives in Mumbai and is involved in the task of establishing a women's archive.

JR

Amin, Khalidah Adibah (*b.* 1936), Malaysian columnist, essayist, radio/television/film scriptwriter. Amin is one of Malaysia's most versatile writers; she writes in both English and the national language, Bahasa Melayu. While most of her works are written in Malay, she is best known as the affable columnist/essayist 'Sri Delima,' author of the successful column called 'As I Was Passing,' which ran in a widely circulated English daily for more than five years in the 1970s. Two volumes also titled *As I Was Passing*, containing 212 witty pieces of social, cultural, and political commentaries on Malaysia and the world outside it, were published in 1976 and 1978. Amin's writing in English has been largely ignored by local literary critics and compilers of Malaysian writings in English, but she has been a great influence to young Malaysian Anglophone women writers of the 1980s and 1990s such as Bernice Chauly, *Dina Zaman, Sheena Gurbakhash Singh, and Ann Lee. Amin was born in Johor Bahru. She was accepted as a medical student at the University of Malaya in Singapore but later quit to study arts. She started writing professionally at 13, when she began to adapt English novels and stories, writing them in Malay. By 14, she was known as a bold critic who dared to criticize aristocrats for being arrogant and proud of their 'royal' blood. Amin is recipient of many honorary awards including the Asian Journalist Award of the Year (1979), the Southeast Asia (S.E.A.) Write Award (1983) and the Esso-Gapena Award (1991).

NFAM

Amīr, Daisy al- (*b.* 1935), Iraqi short story writer. Born in Alexandria, Egypt to an Iraqi father and a Lebanese mother (both graduates of the American University in Beirut), al-Amīr attended Baghdad University and the Institute for Fine Arts. In 1959, she traveled to London to pursue her studies, but a year later she came to Beirut, where she stayed for more than a quarter of a century working as the director of the Iraqi Cultural Center. In 1985 she returned to Iraq and lived there until she was invited to visit the US in 1989. In 1991 she returned to Beirut, where she eventually settled. In 1964 she published her first collection of short stories *Al-Balad al-Ba'īd Alladhī Tuḥibb* ('The Distant Land She Loves'), which set the tone for her future writings; the main character is always a woman, often suffering from alienation, anxiety and a sense of loss, but determined to stand up for herself. In *Fī Dawwāmat al-Ḥubb wa-al-Karāhiya* ('The Vortex of Love and Hate,' 1978), she focuses on the Lebanese civil war. The dilemma of the heroine of al-Amīr's sixth collection *The Waiting List* (1988) is the agonizing passage of time, as well as the re-examination of intellectual and cultural values. Her most recent collection *'Amali-yyat Tajmīl li-al-Zaman* ('Plastic Surgery for Time,' 1997) is permeated with the taste of death.

JTZ

AmirShahi, Mahshid (*b.* 1940), Iranian novelist. Born into a wealthy family in the city of Qazvin, AmirShahi attended high school and college in England. She received her MA from Oxford and returned to Iran to begin a writing career mostly in children's literature and translations. She married and divorced before going into self-exile after the 1979 Islamic Revolution in Iran. She was a Rockefeller Fellow in Middle Eastern studies for 1990–1 at the University of Michigan. Besides translations, her publications include the novels *Kusheh-ye Bonbast* ('The Blind Alley,' 1960), *Sar-e Bibi Khanom* ('Bibi Khanom's

Starling,' 1968), *Badaz Ruz-e Akher* ('After the Last Day,' 1969), and *Be-Sigheh-ye Avval Shakhas-e Mofrad* ('In the First Person Singular,' 1971). Most of these works deal with the lives of upper-class and somewhat intellectual characters who reflect the social and psychological dilemmas of the individual in a transitional society. Her *Dar Hazar* ('At Home,' 1987) relates her experience and understanding of (and disapproval of) the revolutionary events of 1978–9. *Dar safar* ('On Travel,' 1995) deals with her experiences in exile. Her only work currently available in English is *Tales of a Persian Teenage Girl* (1995).

KTa

Amrouche, Fadhma Aïth Mansour (1882?–1967), Algerian memoirist. Born an illegitimate child in a small Berber village in Algeria, she and her mother became outcasts. To protect her, her mother decided to have her educated by the White Sisters. She converted to Catholicism and later was married to a Catholic Algerian man, with whom she had six children. She convinced her husband to leave the village where they had no chance of prospering. He joined the railway company and the family moved to Tunis, where they remained most of their lives. Her only book, *Story of My Life* (1968), is the first narrative written by a Maghrebian woman. As such, it is an important testimony about the life of women in North Africa at the turn of the century and after. In addition to having been displaced all her life, she lost three sons in the space of a few years and another one in later years. Her greatest accomplishment perhaps remains all the Berber songs, tales and proverbs she communicated to her son Jean and only daughter Taos – who eventually became a singer and a novelist – precious material they both translated and published.

JSa

Anagnostaki, Loula, Greek dramatist. Born and raised in Salonica, Anagnostaki earned a law degree from the local university. Influenced by absurdist theater, the innovative trilogy of her first one-act plays (1965) raised existential issues that struck home with the Greek post-war generation. Games of dehumanizing victimization dominate *The City* (as well as subsequent works) and a pervasive pessimism runs through *Overnight Stop* and *The Parade*. Her first full-length play *He Synanastrophe* ('Keeping Company,' 1967) is again set in a militarist and demoralizing urban milieu, in which characters collide rather than communicate. *Antonio e to menyma* ('Antonio or the Message,' 1972) dissolves conventional structure and instead presents disconnected images of terror. *He Nike* ('The Victory,' 1978) paints the agony of entrapment within the Greek family, itself a metaphor for the oppressive sociopolitical system. Psychological reality is again at the center of *He Kaseta* ('The Cassette,' 1983), which exposes the dangers of advancing Westernization. *Ho Ecos tou Hoplou* ('The Sound of the Gun,' 1986) and *Diamantia kai Blues* ('Diamonds and Blues,' 1990) both focus on idealism lost to bourgeois selfishness. *To Taxidi Makria* ('The Journey Far Away,' 1995) makes the stage and the real life of a group of exiles interact.

GAHVS

Anchan (Anchalee Vivatanachai) (*b.* 1952), Thai short story writer, poet. Anchan was born in Thonburi, the city across the river from Bangkok. Her mother's experience as a nurse in a mental hospital and her father's obsession with astronomy and the world of fantasy left a profound impression on her as a child which, later in her life, had a great impact on her as a writer. She graduated from Chulalongkorn University with a BA in Thai language and literature. Subsequently she went to live with her parents in New York, where she met her husband, a graphic designer. Although she studied gemology at the Gemological Institute of America and worked at a well-known jewelry company

in New York, her consuming passion has always been writing. Her first published short story, 'Mother Dear,' was named the best short story of the year by the Thai PEN Center in 1985. Her collection of short stories *Anyamanee Haeng Cheewit* ('Jewels of Life'), which won the Southeast Asia (S.E.A.) Write Award in 1990, has been highly praised for its daring themes and innovative techniques. Her collection of short poems *Lai Sue* ('The Letters'), was shortlisted for the S.E.A. Write Award in 1995, and has been lauded by many literary scholars for its unconventional content and innovative form.

NM

Anderson, Barbara (*b.* 1926), New Zealand novelist, short story writer. Anderson received a BA in science from the University of Otago in 1946 and a BA in arts from Victoria University in 1983. Married in 1951 and having two sons, she has worked as a science teacher and a laboratory technician. The stories in *I Think We Should Go into the Jungle* (1989) and her first novel *Girls High* (1990) introduce Anderson's later interests in raw human emotions, wit, and shifting perspectives. The protagonist of *Portrait of the Artist's Wife* (1992; Goodman Fielder Wattie Book Award) is a painter, Sarah, who deals with motherhood (bearing her first child when she is 17 and another when she is 36) and an unfaithful marriage to a difficult man who becomes a famous writer. Her personal struggles are set within the context of social concerns in New Zealand and the world. *All the Nice Girls* (1993) concerns Royal New Zealand naval wife Sophie who has an affair with a Commodore while her First Lieutenant husband is away. Most recently she has published the novels *Proud Garments* (1996) and *The House Guest* (1997), and a collection, *The Peacocks and Other Stories* (1997).

M-RA

Anderson, Jessica (*b.* 1916), Australian novelist. Born in Queensland, Australia,

Anderson attended Brisbane Technical Art School, and has lived in Sydney most of her adult life. She has been married twice and has one daughter. Her early writing includes radio drama and literary adaptations, and magazine stories. Since *An Ordinary Lunacy* (1963), she has published seven more novels and a collection of short stories. Anderson has received numerous awards for her fiction including the prestigious Miles Franklin Award for her most acclaimed work *Tirra Lirra by the River* (1978), and again for *The Impersonators* (1980); and the *Age* Book of the Year Award for the short stories, *Stories from the Warm Zone* (1987). Much of Anderson's fiction provides an ironic view of Australian society, often through the eyes of the returned expatriate. Her fiction also investigates the operation of memories or hauntings on the construction of the present. Her more recent novels *Taking Shelter* (1989) and *One of the Wattle Birds* (1994) simultaneously acknowledge and undercut attempts to fashion patterns of meaning across time and experience.

EMcM

Anderson-Dargatz, Gail (*b.* 1963), Canadian novelist, short story writer. Born in Kamloops, British Columbia, Anderson-Dargatz worked for several years as a reporter, photographer, and cartoonist for a small town newspaper. She earned a BA in creative writing at the University of Victoria. She is married to Floyd Dargatz, a dairy herdsman and farmer. Her first book *The Miss Hereford Stories*, a collection of short stories, was published in 1994. She established an international reputation with her best-selling first novel *The Cure for Death by Lightning* (1996). The coming-of-age story of Beth, a girl in rural British Columbia in the 1940s, it is a narrative of suspense and the supernatural, told with psychological insight and magic realism. Beth learns from both a local Native American elder and her mother, whose scrapbook, filled with newspaper clippings and recipes (which are reprinted in the novel), provides the link that renews their relationship. Anderson-Dugatz's second novel *A Recipe for Bees* (1998) recounts the history of the marriage of an elderly couple who live on Vancouver Island. In particular, it examines, with sensitivity and insight, the wife's frustrations, compromises, and pleasures.

JEM

Andiievs'ka (Andiyewska), Emma (*b.* 1931), Ukrainian poet, prose writer. Born in Staline (now Donets'k), Andiievs'ka moved with her family to Kiev. In 1943 she was taken to Germany as an Ostarbeiter. After the war, she stayed there, and settled in Munich, where she has been living since, except for brief sojourns in Paris and New York during the 1950s. The leading woman poet of the Ukrainian diaspora, Andiievs'ka has been associated with the so-called New York group of Ukrainian poets, who in the late 1950s and early 1960s sought to bring Ukrainian literature in line with contemporaneous developments in Western writing. Hermeticism, unusual syntax, and surrealistic imagery mark her poetry. Her prose, simpler in tone and style, conveys a fairy-tale ambience and explores the riches of the Ukrainian language, but has received less acclaim then her poetry. Her first verse collection, titled *Poeziia* ('Poetry'), came out in 1951, followed by a volume of short stories *Podorozh* ('A Journey,' 1955). Her second book of poems *Narodzhennia idola* ('The Birth of an Idol,' 1958) established her literary reputation. The poetry collections *Ryba i rozmir* ('Fish and Dimension,' 1961), *Kuty opostin'* ('Corners behind the Wall,' 1962) and two volumes of prose sketches, *Tyhry* ('Tigers,' 1962) and *Dzhalapita* (1962) followed. Moving away from the New York group, she produced seven more collections of poetry, including *Kavarnia* ('Coffeehouse,' 1983) and *Vigilii* (1987), and three novels, including *Roman pro liuds'ke pryznachennia* ('Novel about Human Destiny,' 1982). In recent years, she has contributed more poetry to

Ukrainian literary journals, while turning to painting as a form of self-expression.

VC

Angel, Albalucía (b. 1939), Colombian novelist, playwright. Angel grew up in a coffee plantation family which had founded the town of Pereira, Colombia. She studied art history with *Marta Traba at the Universidad de los Andes in Bogotá and in 1963, moved to Europe to continue her studies. She published her first book *Los girasoles en invierno* ('Sunflowers in Winter'), in Colombia in 1970. Her family did not support her aspiration to become a writer, and were opposed to her lesbian lifestyle. In 1972, Carlos Barral published her second novel *Dos veces Alicia* ('Twice Alice') in Seix Barral, the publishing house of major Latin American writers. In 1975, she published the best known of her novels, *Estaba la pájara pinta sentada en el verde limón* ('The petite colored bird perched in a green lemon tree,' 1975), which became an instant best-seller and was recipient of the prize for the best Colombian novel of the year. Her increasingly problematic relationship with her native Colombia reached its zenith with the publication of her novel *Misiá señora* ('Madam Lady,' 1982), which was not well received. In 1984 she published a collection of texts titled *Las andariegas* ('The Wayfarers') that establishes a dialogue with *Monique Wittig's *Les Guérrillères*.

MGP

Angelou, Maya (b. 1928), US poet, autobiographer. Angelou, born Marguerite Johnson, has become one of the most famous voices of the modern African-American experience. She was born in St Louis and attended public schools in Arkansas and California. She has written five volumes of autobiography, of which the first, *I Know Why the Caged Bird Sings* (1970), which records her traumatic and violent childhood, is best known. The other volumes are *Gather Together in My Name* (1974), *Singing and Swinging and Gettin' Merry Like Christmas* (1976), *The Heart of a Woman* (1981), and *All God's Children Need Travelling Shoes* (1986). In the last volume, she recounts her extended visit in Ghana, which was instumental in shaping her identity as an American. She has published several volumes of poetry including *Just Give Me a Cool Drink of Water 'fore I Die* (1971), *And Still I Rise* (1978), and *Shaker, Why Don't You Sing?* (1983). In 1993, she read her poem, 'On the Pulse of Morning,' at President Bill Clinton's inauguration. She has also written plays, and television and film scripts, as well as performed as an actress, singer, and dancer. The recipient of numerous awards, she published *Even the Stars Look Lonesome*, her collected poems, in 1998.

DVT

Anghelaki-Rooke, Katerina (b. 1939), Greek poet. Born in Athens, Anghelaki-Rooke is one of Greece's best-known contemporary poets. She studied foreign languages and literature at the Universities of Nice, Athens and Geneva. Her first poems were published in the journal *Nea Epohi* ('New Age') in 1956. Since then she has published twelve volumes of poetry and her poems have been translated into more than ten languages. Her collections of poetry include *Magdalini to Megalo Thilastiko* ('Magdalene the Vast Mammal,' 1974), *The Body is the Victory and the Defeat of Dreams* (1975), *O Thriamvos tis Statheris Apoleias* ('The Triumph of Constant Loss,' 1978), *Beings and Things on Their Own* (1982), *I Ministires* ('The Suitors,' 1984), *Epilogos Aeras* ('Wind Epilogue,' 1990), *Ssfris Gydi* ('Empty Nature,' 1993), *Oraia Erimos, I Sarka* ('A Beautiful Desert, the Flesh,' 1995), and *From Purple into Night* (1998). Unlike many of her contemporaries in Greece, she does not address political and national issues in her work, but concentrates on the themes of love, sexuality, and loss. She has also translated many works of literature from French, Russian, and English into Greek. She is the current President of the Council of European Poets. Anghelaki-Rooke is married to British librarian Rodney Rooke and divides her time between Athens and the island of Aegina.

GH-W

Appachana, Anjana, Indian novelist, short story writer. Appachana was born in India and educated at Scindia Kanya Vidyalaya, Delhi University, Jawaharlal Nehru University, and Pennsylvania State University. She moved to the US in 1984 and lives in Tempe, Arizona with her husband and daughter. Her first book, *Incantations and Other Stories* (1992), was published in Britain, the US, and India and was translated into German. Her stories have been published in several journals, magazines, and anthologies. 'Sharmaji' was included in the collection *Mirrorwork: 50 Years of Indian Writing* (1997), edited by Salman Rushdie and Elizabeth West. Appachana is known for the sharply defined female perspectives in her stories. She consistently and convincingly portrays the strains on women in contemporary India, showing how the forces of modernization and nationalism affect women's daily lives. Her first novel *Listening Now* (1998) explores female sexuality and mother–child relationships across three generations in a narrative that is not chronological, but elliptical. Appachana is the recipient of an O. Henry Festival Prize and a National Endowment for the Arts Creative Writing fellowship.

KA

Ariyoshi Sawako (1931–1984), Japanese novelist, dramatist. Born in rural Wakayama, Ariyoshi grew up in Tokyo and lived in Java for three years due to her father's job. Baptized a Catholic in 1947, she only uses Christian themes occasionally in works like *The Village of Eguchi* (1971). Graduating from Tokyo Christian Women's Junior College as an English major in 1952, she worked for a publishing company while assisting a theatrical troupe. Her 1962 marriage to Akira Jin, Art Friend Association Director, ended in divorce in 1964; they have one daughter. Focusing on women, Ariyoshi's works deal with two main subjects: Japanese traditions and contemporary social issues. The award-winning novel *Kabuki Dancer* (1969) and two novels depicting family values, *The Doctor's Wife* (1978) and *The River Ki* (1980), demonstrate respect for tradition. Two best-sellers, *The Twilight Years* (1972) and *Fukugo osen* ('Compound Pollution,' 1975), deal with matters of social concern: care of the elderly and environmental pollution. *Hishoku* ('Because of Color,' 1964) is based on material gathered during one of her many trips abroad. She adapted several of her works for the stage and screen. Constantly plagued by poor health, she died in her sleep aged 53.

EBM-A

Árnadóttir, Nína Björk (*b.* 1941), Icelandic poet, playwright, novelist. Nína Björk was born in northwestern Iceland, where she lived until her family moved to Reykjavik. She developed an interest in theater, graduated in 1965 from the Reykjavik Theater Company's Actors Training School, and from 1973 to 1975 studied drama and drama theory at the University of Copenhagen. Currently she and her family live in Reykjavik. Her first collection of poetry *Ung Ijóð* ('Young Poems'), was published in 1965. Since then, she has published seven volumes of poetry, several plays for stage and radio, and two works of fiction. She is also well-known as a performer on radio and television as well as on the stage. For her literary production, she was honored in 1983 with the Icelandic Radio Literary Award, and in 1989 she became the official 'City Poet' for the city of Reykjavik. In English, Nína Björk's poems are included in several anthologies of Icelandic writers, chiefly *Icelandic Writing Today* and *The Postwar Poetry of Iceland*. Characteristic of her work is a concern for lonely, often marginalized, individuals struggling to find their role in life and to experience meaningful relationships. As in the novel *Móðir Kona Meyja* ('Mother Wife Maiden,' 1987), the search for self-fulfillment is fraught with both intense joy and excruciating pain.

KG

Arnothy, Christine (*b*. 1930), French auto-biographer, novelist, short story writer. Born in Hungary, Arnothy immigrated to France shortly after World War II, where she began a writing career. Her first work, the critically acclaimed *I am Fifteen and I Don't Want to Die* (1956), vividly depicts her experiences in hiding with her family during the German siege of Budapest. Other autobiographical works include *It is Not so Easy to Live* (1958), which recounts her time in a refugee camp and her sub-sequent move to France, and the richly tex-tured *Jeux de mémoire* ('Memory Games,' 1981), in which she reflects on significant events from her childhood. She has also written many popular novels, including the thrillers *Le Bonheur d'une manière ou d'une autre* ('Happiness Somehow or Other,' 1978) and *Vent africain* ('African Wind,' 1989). Her exploration of the fan-tastic is reflected in her prize winning col-lection of short stories *Le Cavalier mongol* ('The Mongolian Cavalier,' 1976).

PJP

Ashapurna Devi (1909 – 1995), Indian novelist, short story writer. Ashapurna was born into a conservative Bengali Brahmin family. Although there was en-couragement for learning in her family, she received no formal education. She began her writing career at 13 by publish-ing short stories and poetry in a children's magazine. After marriage, her husband helped her continue her self-education. She published her first story for adults in 1936 and remained vigorously productive until her death. Ahsapurna once remarked that as a homemaker in a joint (extended) family, she worked all day and wrote only when everyone was asleep at night. She has

written over 150 novels and numerous short stories. Her stories usually center on women's oppression and their struggles for dignity and autonomy. While her stor-ies reflect Bengali women's day-to-day ex-periences within the family, they transcend reality by their subtle artistry. Her most noteworthy work is a trilogy of novels that tells the story of three generations of women in a family: *Pratham Pratisruti* ('The First Promise,' 1964), *Subarnalata* (1966), and *Bakul Katha* ('Bakul's Tale,' 1973). These novels are unparalleled in Bengali literature for their feminist theme. *Pratham Pratisruti* won Ashapurna the Rabindra Puraskar award in 1965 and the prestigious Jnanpith award in 1976. Eng-lish translations of her stories are included in *Noon in Calcutta* (1992) and *Women Writing in India* (1993).

SDD

'Āshūr, Raḍwā (*b*. 1946), Egyptian novelist, literary critic. Born in Cairo, Egypt, to a middle-class family, 'Āshūr earned both her BA and MA degrees in English litera-ture from Cairo University and her PhD, focusing on Afro American literature, from University of Massachusetts in 1975. Her scholarly works have focused on the African novel, William Blake, Kahlil Gi-bran and the Palestinian writer, Ghassān Kanafānī. Her stay in the US between 1973 and 1975 provided the material for her book *Al-Riḥla* ('The Journey,' 1983). In her first novel *Ḥajar Dāfi'* ('Warm Stone,' 1985) she is chiefly concerned with depict-ing Egypt of the 1970s rather than creating credible characters. In *Khadīja wa-Sawsan* (1989), which took her three years to com-plete, she changes course to focus on two characters, Mother Khadīja and Daughter Sawsan; the story is told from the per-spective of each of them. In 1995, she won first prize in the Arab Women's Book Fair held in Cairo for *Gharnāṭa* ('Granada,' 1994–5), an historical trilogy of life in Andalusia, Spain, after the 1492 expulsion of Muslims. 'Āshūr is currently a pro-fessor of English at 'Ayn Shams in Cairo.

Her works have been translated into English, French, and German. She and her husband, Palestinian poet Murīd Barghūthī, have one son.

JTZ

Assunção, Leilah (Maria de Lourdes Torres de Almeida Prado Teixeira) (*b.* 1944), Brazilian dramatist, novelist. Born in São Paulo, Assunção has been interested in literature since she was a child: she wrote the novel *Sorriso na Alvorada* ('Smile at Dawn') when she was 11. Her singular performance as a dramatist is due largely to her special intuition and understanding of women's condition as well as her wide range of interests and activities. Interested in sports and the fine arts since adolescence, she studied philosophy, drama, and literary criticism at São Paulo University; she has also worked as a model, fashion designer, and actress. She is sensitive to the problems faced by people in the middle class yet at the same time her plays denounce the pressures of the established social and political system. She is particularly interested in exploring the oppressions suffered by women. Her plays include *Vejo um Vulto na Janela, me Acudam que Sou Donzela* ('I See a Shadow at the Window, Help me, I'm a Maiden,' 1963–4), *Fala Baixo, senão Eu Grito* ('Keep your Voice Down, or I'll Shout,' 1969; Molière Theatre Prize), *SobreviviDos* ('Survivors,' 1978), and *Lua Nua* ('Naked Noon,' 1986). *Roda côr de roda* ('Pink's Turn,' 1975) was banned for two years under Brazil's censorship laws. Assunção won the São Paulo drama critics' award for best Brazilian playwright of 1969.

SVR

Astley, Thea (*b.* 1925), Australian novelist. Astley was born in Brisbane and obtained a BA from the University of Queensland. She married Jack Gregson in 1948 and moved to Sydney; they have one son. Astley worked as a schoolteacher for many years; from 1968 to 1979, she was senior tutor in English at Macquarie University. Her first novel *Girl with a Monkey* (1958) is her most autobiographical, although her love of the Queensland littoral informs most of her thirteen novels, her volume of novellas (*Vanishing Points*, 1992), and her collection of short stories (*Hunting the Wild Pineapple*, 1979). Academic recognition of Astley's work was undeservedly slow, although eventually she won many awards including the Patrick White Award for lifetime achievement in literature (1989). She has been most often depicted as a satirist, but after *It's Raining in Mango* (1987), critics recognized the compassion that informed her criticisms of racist, sexist, exploitative and self-absorbed attitudes and began reading her more positively. Astley has described her books as 'a plea for charity . . . to be accorded to those not ruthless enough or grand enough to be gigantic tragic figures, but which, in their own way, record the same *via crucis.*'

ELi

Atkinson, Kate (*b.* 1952), British novelist, short story writer. Born in York, educated at Dundee University, earning an MA in 1974, Atkinson worked as a chambermaid and an English department tutor before beginning her career as a fiction writer. Her dazzlingly inventive first novel *Behind the Scenes at the Museum* (1995) won the prestigious Whitbread Prize. Full of rich characterizations and wry humor, the novel follows the life of the extraordinary and omniscient Ruby Lennox from her conception, an event which she recalls, through adulthood. Ruby's narration of her life as part of a dysfunctional Yorkshire family is interspersed with 'footnotes' which move the reader back and forth in time through four generations of family history. Atkinson's next novel *Human Croquet* (1997) also centers upon family history as the adolescent narrator moves through space and time in search of the truth about her long-lost mother. Atkinson's short fiction is included in two anthologies, *Pleasure Vessels* (1997) and *Snap Shots* (1999). Her third novel *Emotionally Weird* (2000), set on an island off the coast of Scotland, explores the nature of language and meaning through the stories that a mother and daughter tell one another. Atkinson lives in Edinburgh with her two daughters.

DVT

'Attar, Samar al- (*b.* 1945), Syrian novelist, translator. Born in Damascus, Syria into a middle-class family, 'Attar earned her BA in Arabic literature and her MA in English literature, both from Damascus University. She obtained another MA in English from Dalhousie University in Canada. In 1973 she received her PhD in comparative literature from the State University of New York at Binghamton. She has taught Arabic and English in Canada, the US, Algeria, and Germany. Today, she is a professor of Arabic Studies at the University of Sydney, Australia. Her publications include scholarly studies and textbooks for teaching Arabic, in addition to some translations of Arabic poetry. Her first novel *Lina: A Portrait of Damascene Girl* (1982) portrays the emotional and intellectual growth of Lina, the daughter of a middle-class Damascene family. The backdrop for the story is the turbulent period of the 1950s and 1960s in Syria. Her second novel *The House on Arnus Square* (1988) contains some autobiographical elements. She is married to a German scholar and has one daughter.

JTZ

Atwood, Margaret (*b.* 1939), Canadian novelist, poet. Daughter of an entomologist, Atwood, born in Ottawa, spent her childhood in bush country in northern Ontario and Quebec. She took a BA at the University of Toronto and did graduate studies at Harvard. Mythic structures of consciousness based on gender, nationalism, and urban–rural differences – define the parameters of her writings. Malevolent wilderness appears in her critical works *Survival* (1972) and *Strange Things* (1995), the story collection *Wilderness Tips* (1991), and the poems in *The Journals of Susanna Moodie* (1970). Wilderness, sometimes narrowed to ravines in Toronto, also appears in *The Edible Woman* (1969), *Surfacing* (1972), and *Cat's Eye* (1988). A strong polemical voice in the feminist debates of the 1970s, Atwood writes about misunderstandings between men and women in volumes of poetry such as *Power Politics* (1971) and *You Are Happy* (1974), as well as in novels such as *Lady Oracle* (1976), *Life Before Man* (1979), and *Bodily Harm* (1981). A chapbook, *Double Persephone* (1961), and her first published book, *The Circle Game* (1966), inaugurate a career-long fascination with myths that overlay human actions. Both *Bluebeard's Egg* (1983) and *The Robber Bride* (1993) allude to fairy tales. *The Handmaid's Tale* (1985) concerns a dystopic future, whereas *Alias Grace* (1996) mines nineteenth-century history. Atwood's works have been translated into over thirty languages and have won numerous prizes.

AH

Aude (Claudette Carbonneau-Tissot) (*b.* 1947), Canadian novelist, short story writer. A native of Montreal, Aude has published two novels, four short story collections and two children's books. She obtained an MA in French literature in 1974 and a PhD in creative writing from Laval University in 1985. She has taught writing primarily at a CEGEP (prep school) in Quebec. In 1983, she adopted the pseudonym Aude. While a student, her summer work in a hospital psychiatric ward made her attentive to forms of mental distress; her narratives demonstrate the workings of the unconscious mind, as in *La chaise au fond de l'oeil* ('The Chair in the Bottom of the Eye,' 1979). She broaches feminist themes such as breaking isolation barriers and self-definition in *Banc de brume, ou les aventures de la petite fille que l'on croyait partie avec l'eau du bain* ('Bank of Fog, or the Adventures of the Little Girl Believed Thrown Out With the Bathwater,' 1987). Her surreal and postmodern tone is also found in *Cet imperceptible mouvement* ('This Imperceptible Movement,' 1997; winner, Prix du Gouverneur Général). Several of her short stories have appeared in translation in anthologies and journals ('The Hot House,' 'Compulsion,' 'Cracks').

CHa

Aung San Suu Kyi (*b.* 1945), Burmese writer, politician. The daughter of Aung San, founder of independent Burma, who was assassinated in 1947, Aung San Suu Kyi was educated in Delhi and at Oxford before working for the UN in New York and in Bhutan. In 1988, she was living with her husband, Tibetologist Michael Aris, and her two sons in Oxford, when she was called back to Burma to care for her sick mother. Her return coincided with anti-government demonstrations and she emerged as the leader of the main opposition party, the National League for Democracy, which won a landslide victory in 1990 elections. She was not herself elected, as she was placed under house arrest in July 1989. Since her release in July 1995, she has stayed in Burma where she and her party have faced mounting repression. Her husband died in 1999. Prior to 1988, she was author of several monographs on India and Burma and her father, which are collected together with other writings and speeches in *Freedom from Fear* (1991), edited by Aris. The title essay was delivered in absentia in 1991 when she received the European Parliament's Sakharov Prize for Freedom of Thought. She has received many other awards including the Nobel Peace Prize (1991). The prize money has been invested into a trust fund for health and education in Burma, and she has had to support herself through writing columns for a Japanese newspaper, fifty-two of which are collected in *Letters from Burma* (1997).

VBo

Avril, Nicole (*b.* 1939), French novelist. Born in Rambouillet, Avril received her education in Lyon, earning her BA and CAPES degree in letters. An actress and model, she also taught literature in Paris and the north of France. She made her literary debut in 1972 with two novels, *L'été de la Saint-Valentin* ('The Saint Valentine Summer') and *Les gens de Misar* ('The People from Misar'). The latter received the Prix des Quatre Jurys. In 1975 she wrote a television screenplay from which she produced a novel, *Les remparts d'Adrien* ('Adrian's Ramparts'). Her themes often emphasize the coming of age of a young girl or woman. Her many novels include *Le jardin des absents* ('The Absents' Garden,' 1977), *Monsieur de Lyon* (1979), *La disgrâce* ('The Disgrace,' 1981), and *Jeanne* (1984). *Une personne déplacée* ('A Displaced Person,' 1996) tells the story of a young woman from Eastern Europe discovering freedom in Paris during the tumultuous 1968 student uprisings. *Dans les jardins de mon père* ('In My Father's Garden,' 1989) is her autobiographical memoir. Her most recent book is *Roman d'un inconnu* ('Novel of an Unknown Man,' 1998).

MHa

'Azzām, Samīra (1927–1967), Palestinian short story writer, journalist, translator. The daughter of a Christian Orthodox father, 'Azzām was born in Acre, Palestine. She received her primary education in her hometown and Haifa, but was forced to take a teaching position before completing her studies. She then pursued her studies by correspondence. At an early age, she contributed to local periodicals under a pseudonym. During the 1948 war, she fled with her family from Palestine to Lebanon and from there she traveled to Iraq, where she worked in radio broadcasting and journalism. In 1959, she returned to Beirut to edit two magazines, and worked as a teacher and translator. A great portion of her time and writing was devoted to the Palestinian question. Her first collection of short stories *Ashyāʾ Ṣāghīra* ('Small Things,' 1954) explores the world of the socially disadvantaged, especially women, but without blaming the patriarchal system for their plight. Later, she tackled the Palestinian problem in some of her stories, as in *Al-Sāʿa wa-al-Insān* ('The Clock and the Man,' 1963). She tried her hand at writing a novel, but was so shocked after the Arab defeat in 1967 that she destroyed the manuscript. Her fifth collection *Al-ʿĪd min al-Nāfidha* ('The Holiday from the Window,' 1971) was published posthumously, as was *Aṣdāʾ* ('Echoes,' 1997) which contains short stories that ʿAzzām wrote between 1945 and 1960 but had never before been published.

JTZ

B

Bâ, Mariama (1929–1981), Senegalese novelist, essayist. Bâ accomplished much in her short life, as a pioneering scholar, educator, writer, feminist activist, and divorced mother of nine. She was born in Dakar, Senegal. A traditional Moslem family background counterbalanced her education in French schools through Teachers' College. She taught for twelve years, and became a regional school inspector. Her father and her husband held high government positions, inspiring her work in women's associations and her conviction that writing could be a weapon of change. Her feminist epistolary novel *So Long a Letter* (1979), winner of the prestigious Noma Prize, has become a classic for the complexity of its ideas and the beauty of its style. In her presentation of love and marriage, she examined traditional, Islamic, and European values, rejecting 'imported vices,' praising 'ancient virtues,' but criticizing excess in all systems. This ode to friendship shows the value of female solidarity over Western individualism. Her posthumous novel *Scarlet Song* (1981), although less successful artistically, explored important issues surrounding biracial and bicultural marriage, and polygamy, in a postcolonial context.

AMR

Bachmann, Ingeborg (1926–1973), Austrian novelist, short story writer, poet. After studying in Graz, Innsbruck, and Vienna, Bachmann earned her PhD in philosophy from the University of Vienna. She gained public recognition in 1953 with *Borrowed Time*, an anthology of poems for which she won her first literary award from Gruppe 47. Many other literary awards would follow. Her experiences as a teenager in Nazi-occupied Austria, described in her memoir *Jugend in einer österreichischen Stadt* ('Youth in an Austrian City,' 1961), inform much of her work. Her masterful use of language and metaphor to evoke images of the devastation and atrocity of war, and her vision of a possible utopian world, made her poetry known throughout Europe. In her later years, she increasingly turned from poetry to prose. Feminist themes are evident in her short stories in *The Thirtieth Year* (1961) and *Three Paths to the Lake* (1972), and particularly in her novel *Malina* (1971). Here she portrayed women as unhappy victims of a male-dominated society. Her posthumously published, unfinished novels *The Book of Franza* and *Requiem for Fanny Goldman* (published together in English translation in 1999) also exhibit Bachmann's feminist and antifascist attitudes. She died at the age of 47 after suffering burns in a fire in her apartment in Rome.

CG

Badr, Liana (*b.* 1951), Palestinian novelist, short story writer, journalist. Born in

Jerusalem, Badr has lived in the Palestinian diaspora since her childhood. Her family was forced to flee its home many times, and Badr has lived in Syria, Egypt, and Jericho in Palestine, among other places. Due to the financial hardships that resulted, she lived for three years in an orphanage in Jerusalem. It was during this period that she began to develop her literary interests and skills. In 1969, she started attending the Jordanian University in Amman. She married Yāsir ʿAbd Rabbih, a prominent Palestinian activist. She graduated from the Lebanese University of Bei rut with a degree in psychology in 1973. Her novel *A Compass for the Sunflower* (1979) reflects many of the events of her childhood and the dislocation and instability inherent in the Palestinian national identity, using the memory of the protagonist as means of revealing the story. The Palestinian experience in diaspora is the focus of the three novellas in *A Balcony over the Fakihani* (1983). She has also written stories for children. The siege and massacre that took place at Tal-al-Zaʾtar, a Palestinian refugee camp in Lebanon, in the mid 1970s, serve as a backdrop for Badr's novel *The Eye of the Mirror* (1991). Today, she lives in the West Bank with her husband, who is the spokesman for the Palestinian Authority, and two sons.

JTZ

Bai Fengxi (*b.* 1934), Chinese playwright. Born in Wenʾan, Hebei Province, Bai Fengxi attended North China People's Revolutionary University in 1949 and became an actress in the China Youth Theater in 1954. She is married to Yan Zhongying, director and actor, and they have one daughter. Writing exclusively about women's issues, Bai is best known for *The Women Trilogy*, which depicts the concerns of intellectual women during the transition from Maoist China (1949–76) to post-Mao (1976–present) China. The first play in the trilogy *First Bathed in Moonlight* (1981), remarkable for the ab-

sence of men on stage, represents a miniature cultural history of PRC women through the life experiences of three generations of mothers and daughters who struggle between their official roles as leaders of women's liberation and their private identities as women in search of love, happiness, and freedom. The second play in the trilogy, *An Old Friend Returning in a Stormy Night* (1983), probes more deeply into women's multiple protests against a sexist society that glorifies fathers who make it impossible for women to stay at home and impossible for them to leave. The third play in the trilogy, *Where Is Longing in Autumn?* (1986), presents a group of courageous women whose daring and unconventional decisions in marriage and career shocked contemporary Chinese audiences.

XC

Bainbridge, Beryl (*b.* 1934), English novelist, short story writer. Raised in Liverpool, Bainbridge pursued an acting career for many years before turning to fiction writing. *Harriet Said*, her first novel, completed in 1958 but not published until 1972, chronicles the macabre activities of two young girls, including murder, voyeurism, and premature sexuality. Like most of Bainbridge's other novels, it is marked by a dark comedic tone which mingles the bizarre with the banal. As in *The Bottle Factory Outing* (1974; Guardian Prize) and *Injury Time* (1977; Whitbread Prize), violence and death make appearances in odd and unexpected ways. Other novels include *The Dressmaker* (1973), which portrays the despondency of a working-class household in Liverpool during World War II, *Sweet William* (1975), *Winter Garden* (1980), and *An Awfully Big Adventure* (1989), which is based on Bainbridge's experiences in the theater in the 1940s. She has written several historical novels, including *The Birthday Boys* (1991), about Scott's expedition to the South Pole; *Every Man for Himself* (1996), about the *Titanic*; and *Master Georgie*, set during the Crimean War. *Forever England* (1999) is a nonfiction work in which Bainbridge scrutinizes national myths.

DVT

Bakr, Salwā (*b*. 1949), Egyptian novelist, short story writer. Bakr was born in Cairo, Egypt; her father died before she was born. She earned her BA in business studies (1972) from ʿAyn Shams University and another degree in literary criticism (1976) from the High Institute for Dramatic Arts in Cairo. As a student, she was politically active – although she quit politics out of frustration and switched to writing as a means for change. Before leaving Egypt to work for a Palestinian magazine in Cyprus, she worked as a rationing inspector for the Ministry of Provisions in Cairo (1974–80). In 1986, she returned to Cairo, where she lives with her artist husband and their two children. In her writings, she questions the values of Egyptian society, especially with regard to women. In her novel *The Golden Chariot* (1991), Bakr deals with women's oppression. She believes that Arabic is a male-oriented language and that 'women should create a language for themselves.' She does not believe in the war between the sexes, but rather sees both women and men as victims of traditional society. Her short stories began to appear in the press during the 1970s. Her first collection of short stories, *Zīnāt fī Janāzat al-Raʾīs* ('Zīnāt in the President's Funeral'), was published in 1986. Bakr's first collection to be translated into English, *The Wiles of Men and Other Stories*, appeared in 1992.

JTZ

Baʿlabakkī, Laylā (*b*. 1936), Lebanese novelist, short story writer, journalist. Born in Beirut, Lebanon to a conservative Shiʿite Muslim family which had emigrated from southern Lebanon, Baʿlabakkī struggled to get an education in the face of family opposition. She claimed that her mother's illiteracy sparked her anger, and she began writing at the age of 14. She attended the Jesuit University of Beirut, but interrupted her studies to work as secretary in the Lebanese parliament. In 1960, she traveled to Paris on a one-year scholarship from the French government. She has traveled to a number of Arab countries, and presently resides in London with her Christian husband and three children. Her first novel *Anā Aḥyā* ('I Am Alive,' 1958) tells the story of a young woman who attempts to pursue personal freedom and self-fulfillment in a hostile, conservative society. It is groundbreaking in that it is the first Arab women's novel to use first-person narration to stress the identity of the protagonist. *Safīnat Ḥanān ilā al-Qamar* ('Spaceship of Tenderness to the Moon,' 1964) is a collection of short stories that is even more militant in advocating the total freedom of women from socially imposed codes of ethics. It raised a storm of controversy, and Baʿlabakkī was brought to trial after interrogation by the Beirut vice squad, but was later vindicated.

JTZ

Balle, Solvej (*b*. 1962), Danish prose writer. One of Denmark's most outstanding prose writers of the new generation, Balle studied comparative literature and philosophy at the University of Copenhagen. Her engagement with philosophical issues is obvious in her writing. In 1987–9 she attended the Writer's School. Her 1984 debut was a futuristic novel *Lyrefugl* ('The Lyre Bird'), which depicts Freia, a lone survivor of a plane crash on a Pacific island, who is forced to reconstruct not only her world but also her world-view. Balle has traveled extensively in Europe, Australia, the US and Canada. Her 1990 text *&* stands stylistically between short prose texts and prose poems. Her breakthrough came with *According to the Law: Four Stories about Humankind* (1993), a highly complex investigation of eternal human questions set in a contemporary scientific setting and against philosophical contemplation. Four protagonists – a biochemist, a lawyer, a mathematician, and an artist – search and find answers to their scientific or existential pursuits. Inspired by and alluding to European writing tradition, this prose gem by Balle, simultaneously classical and modernist, with its insistent focus on our most universal questions, has won her international acclaim.

MŽ

Bantaş, Ioana (Elena Mustaţă) (1937–1987), Romanian poet. Wife of Cezar Baltag, an important Romanian poet, Bantaş had her time of glory as a writer in the mid-1960s. Her poems were translated, at that time, into English and included in several anthologies. When the 'strong and loud voices' of the celebrated poets of communism were the most easily heard, she wrote lyrics of discreet feelings, about the miracle of life, as in *Memorie de iulie* ('Memory of July,' 1966), but also about the fear of death and void, as in *Poarta spre vid* ('The Gate to the Void,' 1969) and *Scrisori către Orfeu* ('Letters to Orpheus,' 1972). Literary allusions are there to compensate for a certain loss of energy, as in *Vertebra lui Yorick* ('Yorick's Vertebra,' 1970) and for a difficulty in defining a personal poetic style, a fact partly due to her husband's writings. In their shadow, Bantaş always appeared as an eternal, fragile, hesitant teenager.

IB

Banuş, Maria (1914–1999), Romanian poet, translator. A witness to this century's major events, Banuş started publishing poetry and translations from European poets (such as Rilke and Rimbaud) when she was a student in philosophy and letters at the University of Bucharest, from which she graduated in 1934. Her first volume of poems *Ţara fetelor* ('The Country of the Girls,' 1937) was hailed by critics as an important expression of 'feminist tendencies' in Romanian literature of that time. She was active in an anti-fascist underground network during World War II, which is evoked in her diary *Sub camuflaj*

('Under Cover,' 1978). Her poetry in the immediate postwar period, such as *Ţie-ţivorbesc, Americă* ('To You, America, I Speak,' 1955), is part of the official communist propaganda literature. A dramatic change took place in her writings around 1965, implying not only a reconsideration of her political options, but also of her aesthetic ones. The volumes that followed – *Portretul din Fayum* ('The Portrait of Fayum,' 1970), *Oricine şi ceva* ('Anybody and Something,' 1972), *Carusel* ('Carousel,' 1989) – speak of an intimate universe, of time going by, of childhood and old age, defending a strong, eternal feminine energy, opposed to femininity as a beautiful literary cliché. In reviewing her prolific career, this capacity to redefine her style and themes of poetic reflection, thus saving her literature from becoming pure political propaganda, must be saluted in Banuş as her most important achievement.

IB

Barakāt, Hudā (*b.* 1952), Lebanese novelist, journalist. Born in Beirut, Lebanon, Barakāt earned her license in French literature from the Lebanese University in 1974 and taught for one year. In 1975 she went to Paris to pursue her higher education, but decided to return to Beirut where she worked in teaching and journalism throughout the Lebanese civil war. Her first work *Zā'irāt* ('Visitors'), a collection of short stories that failed to attract attention, was published in 1985. In 1990, she published *The Stone of Laughter*, a novel that won the prestigious Al-Nāqid literary prize, for which she received wide literary acclaim. In this novel, which took her five years to write, Barakāt examines the life and transformation of an androgynous young man who lives in the war-torn city of Beirut and gradually progresses from his feminine character to a more masculine one. The protagonist of her second novel *Ahl al-Hawā* ('The Love People,' 1994) is again a man. She lives in Paris with her husband and children, and works as a journalist.

JTZ

Baranskaia, Natalia Vladimirovna (*b.* 1908), Russian prose writer. Born into a doctor's family in St Petersburg, Baranskaia spent her childhood abroad because of her parents' revolutionary activity. Returning to Russia with her mother during World War I, she majored in philology at Moscow State University, and graduated in 1930 with secondary specializations in history and ethnography. Her employment at literary museums entailed research and supervision of exhibits. Upon retirement, already a long-widowed grandmother, she turned to fiction. Her literary reputation rests on her novella *A Week Like Any Other* (1969), which chronicles the daily vicissitudes of a working urban wife and mother. Interpreted as a feminist tract, it reflects Baranskaia's signature focus on a female protagonist, a sensitive grasp on human psychology, and use of mild irony. *Den' pominoveniia* ('Memorial Day,' 1989), her sole novel, pays homage to her husband, who perished in World War II, and to the women who 'remained true' to their spouses' memory. Her semi-fictional study of Natalia Goncharova, 'Tsvet temnogo medu' ('The Color of Dark Honey,' 1981), attempts to vindicate Pushkin's wife, generally held indirectly responsible for the poet's premature death. Baranskaia subscribes to an essentialist concept of women as inherently maternal, self-sacrificing, stoic, and attuned to nature. Her prose in its unremarkable transparency sometimes borders on journalese.

HG

Barfoot, Joan (*b.* 1946), Canadian novelist. Born and raised in Owen Sound, Ontario, Barfoot graduated with a degree in English from the University of Western Ontario in 1969. She has worked as a reporter for the *London Free Press* in Ontario. She published her award-winning first novel *Abra* in 1978. In this story of a woman who leaves her family behind to live in solitude in northern Ontario, Barfoot establishes her concern with the domestic lives of women and interest in the extremes to which women will go to make new lives for themselves. In *Dancing in the Dark* (1982), the perfect housewife is driven to insanity by her husband's infidelity. *Plain Jane* (1992) is the story of a librarian who finds solace in her fantasies and in a pen-pal relationship with a convicted murderer. *Charlotte and Claudia Keep in Touch* (1994) traces the fifty-year friendship of two women and their changing views on love, sex, and aging. In 1992, Barfoot was honored with the Marian Engel Award for a women writer in mid-career. Other novels include *Duet for Three* (1985), *Family News* (1989), *Some Things about Flying* (1997), and *Getting Over Edgar* (1999).

JEM

Barker, Pat (*b.* 1943), English novelist. Born in the industrial town of Thornaby-on-Tees in northern England, Barker received a BSc from the London School of Economics in 1965. Upon graduation, she worked as a teacher in London for five years before taking a writing course taught by *Angela Carter. Carter encouraged Barker to use her working-class background as material for her fiction; Barker responded with *Union Street* (1982), which recounts the difficult lives of several women living in a factory town in northern England. *Blow Your House Down* (1984), a novel about a group of prostitutes living in fear of a Jack the Ripper-like serial killer, followed. *The Century's Daughter* (1986) is told from the point of view of an older woman looking back on life. Barker shifted her focus with her critically acclaimed trilogy of novels about World War I: *Regeneration* (1991), *The Eye in the Door* (1993; Guardian Prize), and *The Ghost Road* (1995; Booker Prize). The novels mingle fictional characters with historical figures and deal with questions of patriotism, masculinity, and postwar trauma. Other novels include *The Man Who Wasn't There* (1989), about a fatherless adolescent boy; and *Another*

World (1999), about three generations of a Newcastle family.

DVT

Barlas, Fevziye Rahgozar (*b.* 1955), Afghan poet, journalist, short story writer. Born in Balkh, Afghanistan, Barlas is the daughter of the well-known Afghan journalist, poet, and novelist, M. Shafee Rahgozar. After completing high school in Kabul, she married Rai Barlas and moved to Turkey. She received her degree in English and modern Turkish literature from Istanbul University in 1977. She worked in Kabul as a writer and journalist in the Ministry of Information and Culture and for Kabul State Radio and Television, while publishing her literary works and translations from English and Turkish literature in various Afghan magazines and newspapers. With the arrival of the communist regime in Kabul in 1979, she was fired from all her positions and her writings were banned. Accused of being a propagandist of imperialism and capitalism and threatened with arrest, she fled the country and returned to Istanbul, where she earned an MA in classical Turkish literature. She worked as a radio journalist in Munich, frequently writing about the political, economic, and social affairs of Afghanistan and Tajikistan. In 1996, she moved to Seattle to earn an MA in Persian language and literature at the University of Washington. Barlas's short stories regularly appear in Persian publications in the US and Europe. *Deyar-e Shegeftiha* ('Wonderland'), a collection of her poetry, was published in 1999, and *Wondering Eyes*, a collection of her short stories, is forthcoming.

FRB

Baroche, Christiane (*b.* 1935), French novelist, short story writer, poet. A biologist at the Institut Curie, Paris-born Baroche was awarded the Prix Drakkar for her first collection of short stories *Les feux du large* ('Lights of the Open Sea,' 1975). She also won the Bourse Goncourt de la

Nouvelle (1978) and the Grand Prix de la Nouvelle SGDL (1994). Her short stories portray moments of life with realism and humor. Her first major novel *L'hiver de beauté* ('Winter of Beauty,' 1987) is a powerful meditation on beauty and ugliness, resurrecting the character Mme de Merteuil from Choderlos de Laclos's *Dangerous Liaisons* (1782), to explore one of her recurrent themes – life in the aftermath of loss or disaster. Much of her writing has an oral quality, as in both *La rage au bois dormant* ('Sleeping Fury,' 1995) and *Petit traité des mauvaises manières* ('Short Treatise on Bad Manners,' 1998), in which women recount their life stories through memories of people and events of the past. Translations of her short stories can be found in the journal *Interstice* 2 (1997) and her poetry in *Elles: A Bilingual Anthology of Modern Poetry by Women* (1996).

GR

Barreno, Maria Isabel (*b.* 1939), Portuguese fiction writer, essayist. Born in Lisbon, Barreno studied history and philosophy at the University of Lisbon. In the 1960s and 1970s she became one of the best-known advocates for women's rights in Portugal through key nonfictional works such as *A Condição da Mulher Portuguesa* ('Portuguese Women's Condition,' 1968), *A Morte da Mãe* ('The Death of the Mother,' 1972), and *A Imagem da Mulher na Imprensa* ('The Image of Women in the Press,' 1976). However, she is best known internationally as one of the 'Three Marias' who co-wrote the famous *New Portuguese Letters* (1972), together with *Maria Velho da Costa and *Maria Teresa Horta. Barreno has since become one of Portugal's major writers of the late twentieth century, with works of historical fiction such as *A Crónica do Tempo* ('The Chronicle of Time,' 1990), on the Portuguese twentieth century, and *O Senhor das Ilhas* ('The Lord of the Islands,' 1994), on colonial Cape Verde. She has also developed a semi-fantastic literary genre (unique for Portugal) in *O Mundo Sobre o Outro Desbotado* ('The World Unleashed Upon the Other,' 1986) and in *O Chão Salgado* ('The Salted Ground,' 1992). In *Os Sensos Incomuns* ('The Uncommon Senses,' 1993) she explores issues of identity, difference, ethics, and solidarity among human beings, in a purportedly 'post-feminist' era.

FA

Basheva, Miryana Ivanova (*b.* 1947), Bulgarian poet. Born in Sofia, the daughter of the reform-minded Bulgarian foreign minister of the 1970s who perished under mysterious circumstances, Basheva graduated from the University of Sofia in 1972 with a BA in English. She worked for Bulgarian Television, the Film Company 'Boyana,' and the publishing company and magazine *Fakel*. Her first poems were published in 1972. Despite their frequently iconoclastic themes, imagery, and style, her works are usually published in leading literary periodicals. Her books *Tezhuk kharakter* ('Difficult Personality,' 1976) and *Malka zimna muzika* ('A Small Winter Music,' 1979) present a highly sophisticated female lyric persona, whose vulnerability is inextricably intertwined with irreverence, wit, and sarcasm. In *Sto godini sueta* ('A Hundred Years of Folly,' 1992) the brashness of her earlier works is somewhat tempered by the extended temporal perspective. During the 1970s, disillusioned young urban dwellers found Basheva's poetry particularly congenial. Many of her poems were set to music and performed by various pop singers. English translations of Basheva's works may be found in the anthologies *Poets of Bulgaria* (1985), *The Devil's Dozen* (1990), *Clay and Star* (1992), *The Many-Voiced Wave* (1993), and *An Anthology of Contemporary Poetry* (1994).

LPG

Bat Shahar, Hannah (*b.* 1944), Israeli fiction writer. Hannah Bat Shahar is the literary pseudonym of an author who is unable to reveal her true identity since she is a member of an ultra-Orthodox group in Israel. Jerusalem-born, she began publishing fiction in the mid-1980s after studying Hebrew literature, literary history and creative writing. She has published four collections of stories and novellas that deal predominantly with the inner world of women who are bound by the strict rules and customs of religious communities, as in her short story collection, *Calling the Bats* (1990). Her writing deals with forbidden and disappointed love. Her women are caught between their own romantic and erotic needs and the organized and controlled world of their husbands, who are unable and unwilling to understand their wives' frustrations. In lyrical and evocative prose, she allows the reader a glimpse into the lives of women who dare not give expression to their desperate desire for intimacy and passion. They therefore create an alternative life in the mind which is often erotic and redolent of tenderness and love. These fantasies often concern men who, for various reasons, are unsuitable or unattainable (*Look, the Fishing Boats*, 1997).

GAb

Bawden, Nina (*b.* 1925), British novelist, children's writer. In her youth, during World War II, Bawden was evacuated from her birthplace of London and sent to Wales, where she lived with various mining families. Her award-winning children's book *Carrie's War* (1973) is based on this experience, as is her adult novel *Anna Apparent* (1972). She earned a BA and an MA from Somerville College, Oxford, in 1946 and 1951 respectively. Bawden, who has explored a variety of genres including the *Bildungsroman*, the murder mystery, and the Gothic romance, has written over twenty novels for adults and as many for children. To both audiences, she offers her ironic, shrewd, and often comic observations of the family lives of the middle class, paying attention to intergenerational relationships and feminist themes. Among her novels are *Glass Slippers Always Pinch* (1960), *In Honour Bound* (1961), *A Woman of My Age* (1967), *Afternoon of a Good Woman* (1976), *The Ice House* (1983), *Circles of Deceit* (1987), and *Family Money* (1991). Her juvenile works, several of which have been made into television programs, include such books as *Squib* (1971) and *The Peppermint Pig* (1975). *In My Own Time: Almost an Autobiography* was published in 1994.

DVT

Beattie, Ann (*b*. 1947), US short story writer, novelist. Beattie has been characterized as one of the defining voices of her generation. Born in Washington, D.C., she completed her undergraduate studies in 1969 at American University, and received an MA from the University of Connecticut in 1970. Her writing focuses on the generation that came of age in the 1960s, expressing, through the lives of her characters, its sense of despair and alienation, its loss of direction and purpose. Those characters, usually well-educated and middle-class, suffer from a poignant angst as they seek to understand themselves in the contemporary world. The minimalist style with which she depicts their aimlessness and passivity, exacerbated by popular culture and casual drug use, and the absence of clear moral assessments, can be seen as satirical or symptomatic. Her short story collections include *Distortions* (1976), *Secrets and Surprises* (1979), *The Burning House* (1982), *Where You'll Find Me, and Other Stories* (1986), and *What Was Mine* (1991). Her novels include *Chilly Scenes of Winter* (1976), *Falling in Place* (1980), *Love Always* (1985), *Picturing Will* (1989), and *Another You* (1995) – all written in her characteristically plain, unadorned prose. Beattie, who has taught writing at Harvard and the University of Virginia, was awarded a Guggenheim Fellowship in 1978.

DVT

Beck, Beatrix (*b*. 1914), French-Belgian novelist, poet. Born in Switzerland, the daughter of Belgian poet Christian Beck (1879–1916), Beck was raised in France by her widowed Irish mother. She studied law in Grenoble, but was denied French citizenship until she gained literary success. Her husband died young, and to support her infant daughter (now novelist-artist Bernadette Szapiro), Beck took a series of menial jobs. She was also André Gide's last secretary. A sense of alienation pervades the five volumes of Beck's semi-autobiographical Barny cycle – *Barny* (1948) to *Le Muet* ('The Mute,' 1963). *The Passionate Heart* (1952; Prix Goncourt) relates an unsettling encounter between the young leftist Barny and a sincere populist priest during the Occupation. It gained acclaim in a 1961 film adaptation by J.-P. Melville. Barny finally finds strength and sanity when she herself begins to write. In the late 1970s, after a ten-year hiatus teaching in North American universities, Beck radically altered her style, experimenting with language, the unconscious, and the fantastic, as in *L'Enfant chat* ('The Cat Child,' 1984) and *Plus loin mais où* ('Further but Where,' 1997). Her work totals over thirty titles.

MBR, MLT

Bedford, Jean (*b*. 1946), Australian novelist, short story writer. Born in Cambridge, England, Bedford came to Australia in 1947 and was raised in rural Victoria. She graduated in Arts at Monash University and University of Papua New Guinea. She taught classes in creative writing and English as a second language, and worked as a journalist and publisher's editor. In 1982, Bedford moved to the US to accept the Stanford Writing Fellowship. Many of her short stories have appeared in publications such as *National Review*, *National Times* (where she was literary and arts editor) and *Meanjin*. Bedford received the NSW Premier's grant for her fiction (1983) and a Bicentennial writing fellowship (1986). Her first selection of short stories *Country Girl Again* (1979) was followed by *Sister*

Kate (1982) and *Love Child* (1986). Bedford co-authored *Colouring In* (1986), a novella of witty love stories, with Rosemary Creswell. Bedford has written numerous novels, including *Now You See Me* (1997), part of the private eye Anna Southwood series, and *Worse than Death* (1998). Bedford and her second husband Peter Corris live in Morton Bay with her three daughters and one step-daughter.

RMB

Beer, Patricia (1924–1999), British poet, non-fiction writer. Born in Exmouth, Devon, Beer was raised in a family that belonged to the strict Plymouth Brethren sect. She attended the University of Exeter, the University of London (BA), and St Hugh's College, Oxford, where she earned a B.Litt. In 1964, she married John Damien Parsons, an architect. She taught at the University of Padua, the British Institute in Rome, and the University of London, but later returned to Devon to write full-time. Her first book of poetry, *Loss of the Magyar*, was published in 1959. Her rural childhood and her religious background were important influences on her poetry, which is straightforward and elegantly economical, filled with close observations of the natural world and daily life, marked by a dry humor, and shadowed throughout by a preoccupation with death. Other volumes of poetry include *The Survivors* (1963), *The Estuary* (1971), the highly praised *Driving West* (1975), *The Lie of the Land* (1983), *Collected Poems* (1988), *Friends of Heraclitus* (1993), and *Autumn* (1997). She also wrote two novels, a memoir of her childhood, *Mrs. Beer's House* (1968), and *Reader, I Married Him* (1974), a study of female characters in nineteenth-century novels.

JEM

Bejerano, Maya (*b.* 1949), Israeli poet. Daughter of musicians, Bejerano was born in Kibbutz Ailon, grew up in Jaffa, served in the Israeli army, and took a BA in literature and philosophy at Bar-Ilan University.

She lives in Tel Aviv, and has one daughter. Her first books, *Bat Yaana* ('Ostrich,' 1978) and *Ha-Chom Ve-Ha-Kor* ('The Heat and the Cold,' 1981), are linguistic breakthroughs, revolutionary in the way they overcome the linear limits of language and in their use of scientific and technological elements. *Ibud Netunim 52 Shishah Maamarim u Maamar al Mosad Meen Makamah* ('Data Processing 52 Six Essays and an Essay about the Social Security Institution, sort of macama,' 1983) is a philosophical collection of poems which describe the consciousness observing the world and defining itself. *Shirat Ha-Tsiporim* ('Songs of the Birds,' 1985) is a collection of epic poems offering a panoramic and encyclopedic view of the universe and the human condition. *Retsef Ha-Shirim* ('Selected Poems, 1972–1986,' 1987) has been followed by several other collections. In *Anase La-Gaat Be-Tabur Bitny* ('Trying to Touch my Belly Button,' 1997) Bejerano returns to her biographical self in early childhood, writing in a comparatively more conservative style than previous works. Her latest work is a CD-ROM titled *Optical Poems: Thirteen Poems of Maya Bejerano Produced to Interactive Media Works* (1999). She has been honored with the Prime Minister Award (1986, 1995–6).

IA

Béji, Hélé (*b.* 1948), Tunisian essayist, novelist. Born in Tunisia, currently residing in Paris, Béji's first critical work, *Le désenchantement national: Essai sur la décolonisation* ('National Disenchantment: Essay on Decolonization,' 1982), discusses Tunisia's postcolonial system. She sees her country's problems in terms of internal forces of oppression causing a stifling of voices, intellectual and political. Her poetic narrative *Itinéraire de Paris à Tunis, Satire* ('Itinerary: Paris to Tunis,' 1992) is a meandering of thoughts on various topics, such as the reading experience. Her detailed, Proustian style is reflected in her novel *L'oeil du jour* ('The

Eye of Day,' 1993), which takes place within the memory of the narrator as she juxtaposes two generations, one the traditional, mystical world of her grandparents, the other characterized by modern, Westernized modes of thought. In reconciling the two, she undertakes a search for the self. In her poetic essay *L'art contre la culture, Nûba* ('Art versus Culture, Nûba,' 1994) she explores the dynamics of art in its context. Her latest essays *La fièvre identitaire* ('Identity Fever,' 1997) and *L'imposture culturelle* ('Cultural Deception,' 1997) address the main themes of her work. She is currently the most influential woman writer in Tunisia.

CHa

Belli, Gioconda (*b.* 1948), Nicaraguan poet, novelist. Belli was born in Managua, Nicaragua, but was educated in the United States and Europe. She married and worked in advertising in Managua. Before she became active in the Sandinista Liberation Front, which led to her divorce and exile, she had begun publishing poetry in several Latin American publications. Her first book of poems *Sobre la grama* ('On the Grass,' 1974) exalts womanhood and is viewed as a harbinger of the revolution. She worked in Mexico and Costa Rica on behalf of the Sandinista movement and raised funds in Europe. In 1979, after Anastasio Somoza was deposed, she returned to Nicaragua to work in the Ministry of Planning. Her second collection of poetry *Línea de fuego* ('Line of Fire,' 1978), which won the prestigious Casa de las Américas Prize, deals with the new roles of revolutionary women and sexual desire. Another book of poetry, *From Eve's Rib*, was published in 1987. Her novels *The Inhabited Woman* (1988) and *Sofía de os presagios* ('Sophie and the Omens,' 1990) explore the lives of contemporary women in political struggles in Nicaragua. Since the mid-1990s, she has lived in Los Angeles.

CJG

Bennett, Louise (*b.* 1919), Jamaican poet, folklorist. Born in Kingston, Bennett popularized 'patwah' (patois) and folk traditions in the arts. A British Council Scholarship supported her studies at the Royal Academy of Dramatic Art. In Jamaica, she taught drama for the Social Welfare Commission and the University of West Indies Extra Mural Department. Along with her husband Eric Coverley, she also contributed significantly to the Little Theatre Movement and the annual Pantomime, playing leading roles and adapting folk material for many productions. Her folklore research is collected in several audio anthologies and publications such as *Anancy Stories and Poems in Dialect* (1944), *Jamaica Folk Songs* (1954), *Children's Jamaican Songs and Games* (1957), *Laugh with Louise* (1961), *Anancy and Miss Lou* (1979), and *Anancy Stories* (undated audio). Her ballads, published in *Dialect Verses* (1942), *Jamaica Labrish* (1966), and *Selected Poems* (1982), deploy the verbal witticisms of Caribbean city streets and rural yards to provide trenchant commentary on daily life, national politics, the legacies of colonialism, immigration, war, and gender relations. She has earned an honorary Doctorate in Literature from the University of the West Indies, a Musgrave Silver Medal, and the Norman Manley Award for Excellence.

LC

Ben Yehuda, Netiva (*b.* 1928), Israeli author, editor. Until 1981 Ben Yehuda was known in Israel as the living emblem of the legendary Palmach, the elite units that spearheaded the struggle for Israel's independence in 1947–8. Her fearlessness as a young fighter, a specialist in topography, reconnaissance, and demolition, constituted a major part of the myth of that generation. A few years past independence, after studying at home and abroad (art, language, and philosophy), she became a freelance editor, openly 'fighting' against the elevated, highly stylized standards 'required' then by Hebrew *belles* *lettres*. This resulted in her first publication, the hilariously irreverent *World Dictionary of Hebrew Slang* (1972; co-authored). She waited over thirty years, however, to tell her personal story. The publication of *1948 – Bein hasfirot* ('1948 – Between Calendars') in 1981 took Israeli readers by surprise. It was followed by two sequels, *Miba'ad la'avotot* ('Through the Binding Ropes,' 1985) and *Keshepartza hamedinah* ('When the State Broke Out,' 1991). Her amazing story, 'spoken' in colloquial Hebrew and full of both humor and pathos, gives a personal, 'unorthodox' accounting of the national narrative. It exposes the gap between the Palmach's promise for 'sexual equality' and the reality in its ranks, thereby shedding light on the reasons behind the author's thirty-year-long silence.

YSF

Berberova, Nina Nikolaevna (1901–1993), Russian prose writer, poet, autobiographer, critic, translator. Born in St Petersburg into a middle-class family, Berberova left Russia in 1922, and spent a quarter-century (1925–50) in Paris with her lover, the émigré poet Vladimir Khodasevich. Upon emigrating to the US in 1950, she taught Russian literature at Yale University (1953–63) and Princeton University (1963–71). A woman of formidable discipline and wide-ranging talents, she first captured the attention of Anglophones with her fascinating autobiography, *The Italics Are Mine* (1969), which recounts the Parisian life of Russian expatriates. Until then, Slavic specialists knew her chiefly as an enthusiastic reviewer of Nabokov in learned journals, the editor of a collection of Khodasevich's verses (1960), and biographer of Tchaikovsky (1937), Borodin (1938), and the symbolist poet Alexander Blok (1948). The many stories, novellas, and poems Berberova wrote in Paris came into their own only in the 1980s with the translated collections *The Revolt* (1989), *Three Novels* (1990), and *The Tattered Cloak and Other*

Novels (1991). Her masterpiece 'The Accompanist' became a successful film by the same title. An understated realist, Berberova, in her fiction as in her poetry, largely treats the tribulations, compromises, and discoveries of everyday émigré life. With dispassionate irony and a discerning eye for eloquent detail, she reveals the loneliness, desperation, and pragmatic aspirations of her sometimes repellent, often pathetic, and invariably limited protagonists. Seemingly amorous relations especially are exposed as self-seeking and end in disillusionment, suicide ('Astashev in Paris') or murder ('The Waiter and the Slut').

HG

Berková, Alexandra (*b.* 1949), Czech novelist, essayist. Born in Trencin, Slovakia, the daughter of an orchestra conductor and a journalist who wrote fiction for women's magazines, Berková studied Czech literature and applied arts at Charles University in Prague, graduating in 1973. She earned a graduate degree in 1980. From her marriage to the painter Vladimir Novak, she has two children. After serving as an editor at publishing houses (1973–81), she wrote scenarios for Czechoslovak Television (1983–91). Following the 1989 revolution, she helped organize the Writers' Council and the feminist group New Humanity, which (unsuccessfully) promoted a candidate for Parliament, ran assertiveness-training groups for women, and made contact with women's groups abroad. She has taught creative writing in high school since 1995. Her first published prose, *Knížka s červeným obalem* ('Book with a Red Cover,' 1986), is a loose cycle of stories which, in a linguistically playful style, depicts a woman's fate from birth to death, emphasizing absurd aspects of reality. Her novel *Magorie* ('Land of Fools,' 1991) conveys a highly variegated metaphor for the degenerate society of pre-1989 Czechoslovakia. In fragmentary style, her latest novel, *The Sorrows of a Devoted Scoundrel*

(1993), achieves a more universal contemplation of human fate through the travels of a picaresque protagonist after his rejection by a supreme being.

ES

Berman, Sabina (*b.* 1955), Mexican playwright. Born in Mexico City, Berman studied at the Universidad Iberoamericana and earned a degree in clinical psychology and Mexican literature. Her first play, *Mariposa* ('Butterfly'), was staged in 1974. She has won numerous prizes. Several of her plays have appeared with more than one name. Her most recent work, *Krisis* (1996), stages the political intrigues and rivalries that led to Mexico's current economic crisis. Her box-office success, *Entre Villa y una mujer desnuda* ('Between Villa and a Naked Woman,' 1993) highlights gender roles and their relation to historical narratives. Several of her plays center on historical themes, such as *Aguila o sol* ('Eagle or Sun,' 1985), which reexamines the Conquest; and *Herejía* ('Heresy,' 1984) (also called *Anatema* ['Anathema'], *Los Carvajales* ['The Carvajals'], and *En el nombre de Dios* ['In the Name of God']), which dramatizes the predicament of a Jewish family in sixteenth-century Mexico. *Yankee* (also known as *Bill*) (1980), *El jardín de las delicias* ('The Garden of Delights,' 1978) (also called *El suplicio del placer* ['The Torture of Pleasure']), and *Muerte súbita* ('Sudden Death,' 1988) foreground searches for identity and autonomy within interpersonal relationships.

SMag

Bersianik, Louky (*b.* 1930), French-Canadian novelist, poet. Born Lucile Durand in Montreal, Bersianik earned a doctorate at the Université de Montreal, and did graduate work in France at the Sorbonne and at the Centre d'Etudes de Radio et Television. She has written several scripts for radio, television, and film. She began by writing children's books, but with her best-selling science fiction novel *The Euguelion* (1976), she became known as one of Canada's foremost feminist writers. The novel powerfully explores feminist themes while satirically rethinking the Bible; the title character is a female version of Christ who searches Earth for her male counterpart. Bersianik's feminist fiction, intelligent, humorous, and disruptive, focuses on relations between men and women and the subversion of male myths and theories. The novel *Picnic on the Acropolis* (1979) is a scathing parody of Plato's *Symposium*. She has also published *La Page de Garde* ('The Flyleaf,' 1978), *Au beau milieu de moi* ('At the Very Heart of Me,' 1983), and *Axes et eau* ('Axis and Water,' 1984), collections of poetry and prose-poems on feminist themes, and the novel *Permafrost* (1997).

DVT

Bessa-Luís, Agustina (*b.* 1922), Portuguese novelist. The most prolific woman writer of contemporary Portugal, Bessa-Luís has published close to one hundred titles since her debut, in 1948, with *Mundo Fechado* ('Closed World'). Besides fiction, she has written fictionalized biographies; literary, artistic, cultural and philosophical commentary; and drama. Born to a rural landowning family of northern Portugal, she became familiar when young with a vast array of Western literary masterpieces that reportedly were decisive in shaping her creative sensibility. Among these, she is fond of mentioning the '*One Thousand and One Nights*,' the Old and New Testaments, and, particularly, the Spanish picaresque novel. Her fascination with cinema has led her to write works readily adapted to the screen by Portuguese filmmaker Manoel de Oliveira (e.g. *The Convent*). Her *A Sibila* ('The Sybil,' 1954) is credited as marking a decisive turn in contemporary Portuguese letters, owing to its detour away from neo-realist commitment and toward a more universal, archetypal rendering of how irrational psychic forces and traditional systems of beliefs shape gender identities and power relations.

Bessa-Luís' style is characteristically metaphoric and aphoristic; her female figures often embody strength, willfulness and cunning.

APF

Bethel, Marion (*b*. 1953), Bahamian poet. Born in Nassau, Bethel studied law at Cambridge and has a private law practice in Nassau. She has been a teacher and consultant on educational and cultural issues, and as the national chair of CAFRA (Bahamas) for three years, worked on women's reproductive rights and violence against women. In her bilingual poetry collection *Guanahaní, mi amor/Guanahaní, my love* (1994), winner of the Casa de las Américas Prize, the Bahamian landscape and indigenous mythology provide inspiration for strength and resistance. She addresses the country's colonial legacy, using birth imagery, musical rhythms, and images of powerful women to write of self-definition, the writing process, and loss, in sensual language. She has published several essays and a short story, and co-authored a play and musical. Her work has appeared in *From the Shallow Seas* (1993), *Sisters of Caliban* (1996), and *Moving Beyond Boundaries* (1995), and in the journals *WomanSpeak*, *Massachusetts Review*, *The Caribbean Writer*, and *Callaloo*. Bethel won the James Michener Fellowship in 1991, the Bahamas National Poetry Award in 1996, and a 1997–8 creative arts fellowship at the Bunting Institute, Radcliffe College.

HS

Beyala, Calixthe (*b*. 1961), Cameroonian novelist. Born in Douala, Beyala was separated from her mother at age 5 and raised by female relatives in a ghetto. She attended Francophone schools and left for France at the age of 17 where she later earned a BA in literature. She is divorced and lives in Paris with her two children. Set in Africa, *The Sun Hath Looked Upon Me* (1987) relates the effects of poverty and social degradation on a teenage girl who is

abandoned by her mother and raised by her aunt in an urban slum. Similarly, child abuse and women's oppression are dominant issues in *Your Name Shall Be Tanga* (1988) and *Seul le diable le savait* ('Only the Devil Knew That,' 1990). In *Loukoum* (1992) and *Maman a un amant* ('Mother Has a Lover,' 1993), the Traoré family saga launches a series of novels that explore the discrimination and adjustments that post-colonial migrant Africans, especially women and children, have to confront in the French metropolis. Beyala won the Prix Tropiques for *Assèze l'Africaine* ('Assèze, the African Woman,' 1994) and the Grand Prix de l'Académie française for *Les honneurs perdus* ('Lost Honors,' 1996).

JMN-A

Bhandari, Mannu (*b*. 1931), Indian fiction writer, playwright, scriptwriter. Until the age of 16 Bhandari lived in Ajmer, then moved to Calcutta where she lived until 1964 and lectured in Hindi. From 1964 to 1991 she taught at the University of Delhi and from 1992 to 1994 was the director of the Premchand Srijanpith (Premchand School of Creative Writing). She is noted for her presentation of an authentic picture of society, especially the family unit, with a rare compassion and depth of emotion. Her five collections of short stories, two novels, and two plays are marked by a signal simplicity. She has also published a collection of stories and a novel for children. *Bunty* (1971) has been her most popular novel and concentrates on the psychology of a child caught in the harsh winds of marital and domestic strife. Her novel *The Great Feast* (1979) is a moving representation of the rampant corruption in contemporary politics. *Bina Diwaron ka Ghar* ('The House without Walls,' 1966), translated into several languages, is a play about the clash of the sexes, where the husband bears an inferiority complex in the face of the superior ability of his wife. Her work has been widely translated; two works, including *Bunty*, have been made into full-length films. She has scripted many popular television serials, including Premchand's *Nirmala*.

BA

Bihbahani, Simin (*b.* 1927), Iranian poet. Bihbahani was born in Tehran. She has been married twice, and has three children. In terms of poetic dynamics, innovative style, and mastery of poetic expression, she is on a par with one of Iran's most acclaimed poets, Furugh Farrukhzad (1935–67). Bihbahani is a prolific poet whose pre-revolutionary works alone exceed five volumes. In her works, social themes and the struggle to promote the leftist cause echo the pre-revolutionary discourse. Gender issues and feminist themes and ideas have also emerged in her recent works. She versifies the lives of women who must endure untold daily burdens such as bargaining for food in crowded markets and waiting in long lines for rationed foods, as well as the larger responsibilities of giving birth and raising children. In her most recent work, Bihbahani challenges masculine power by portraying an autonomous woman who freely transgresses traditional boundaries. Her works include *Guzinah-i Ash'ar* ('Selected Poems,' 1988), *An Mard Mard-i Hamraham* ('That Man, My Fellow Man,' 1990), and *Simin Chilchiragh* ('Chandelier,' 1991).

KTa

Bille, Stéphanie Corinna (1912–1979), Swiss short story writer, dramatist, poet, novelist. Considered one of the most important Franco-Swiss women writers, Bille was the daughter of a peasant girl taken as second wife by painter Edmond Bille. Her golden Valais childhood is evoked in fictional and autobiographical texts. A compulsive writer since age 15, without much formal education but a fertile, inspiring background, she eventually married poet Maurice Chappaz, who indefatigably promoted her work. They had three children. Her link to her mother's peasant heritage was exceptionally positive. Ex-

ploring sexual desire and denouncing religious, patriarchal repressive traditions were her most powerful motivations. In over thirty volumes of creative writing, she favored short forms from five to eighty lines, exploiting her dreams and fantasies in the wake of surrealist freedom. She was awarded the prestigious Prix Goncourt for her short stories in *The Savage Woman* in 1975. The title novella was made into a film in 1991. Other books include *Deux Passions* ('Two Passions,' 1979) and *Le bal double* ('The Double Ball,' 1980). Bille stands out as an elegant, transparent writer and a compassionate observer of early twentieth-century rural Catholic life.

CPM

Billetdoux, Raphaële (*b.* 1951), French novelist. Born in Neuilly, with a playwright as her father, Billetdoux wrote her first novel shortly after completing high school. *Jeune fille en silence* ('Young Girl in Silence,' 1971) is an autobiographical novel in which she explores the sexuality of adolescent girls. Her second novel *L'Ouverture des bras de l'homme* ('The Opening of the Man's Arms,' 1973) received two literary prizes. *Prends garde à la douceur des choses* ('Pay Attention to the Tenderness of Things,' 1976) is perhaps her best-known novel, in which she renders again the desires, sexual feelings, and rebellious moods of a bourgeois adolescent girl and her two sisters. *La lettre d'excuse* ('The Letter of Apology,' 1980) is a wrenching portrayal of the place of married women in privileged families. *Night Without Day* (1985) received the prestigious Prix Renaudot for its daring portrayal of sexuality, desire, and violence. Her most recent book is *Mélanie dans un vent terrible* ('Melanie in a Terrible Wind,' 1994). She also directed a film about a familiar topic, *La femme-enfant* ('The Child Woman,' 1980).

JV

Bilotserkivets', Natalka (*b.* 1954), Ukrainian poet. Born in the village of Kuianivka near Sumy, Bilotserkivets' was 'discovered' at the age of 13, and published her first collection of poetry, *Balada pro neskorenykh* ('Ballad of the Undefeated,' 1976), while at college. Now working as an editor, she lives in Kiev with her husband, the critic Mykola Riabchuk, and their two children. Her intimate, emotionally charged lyrics offer extraordinarily powerful portrayals of the dilemmas of an individual's survival under totalitarianism and the personal tragedy of the 'lost' generation of the 'stagnation years' preceding the liberalization of the late 1980s. Precisely in the 1980s, however, her poetry acquired a new existential poignancy, as demonstrated by her collections *Pidzemnyi vohon'* ('Subterranean Fire,' 1984) and *Lystopad* ('Falling Leaves,' 1989). Bilotserkivets' has also published a number of critical essays on contemporary Ukrainian writing. English translations of her poetry have appeared in several anthologies, most notably *From Three Worlds: New Writing from Ukraine* (1996).

VC

Binchy, Maeve (*b.* 1940), Irish novelist, short story writer. Born in Dublin and educated at University College, Dublin, Binchy worked as a teacher before she started writing short stories and plays such as *End of Term* (1976) and *The Half Promised Land* (1979). Her early short fiction, collected in *The Central Line: Stories of a Big City Life* (1978), *Victoria Line* (1980), and *Dublin Four* (1983), depicts the challenges, temptations, and monotony of urban life. She turned to the novel with *Light a Penny Candle* (1982), a tale of friendship set during World War II, which, like *Echoes* (1985) and *Firefly Summer* (1987), takes place in rural Ireland. Popular and prolific, she is known for her believable characterizations, her understanding of human behavior, her evocation of place (usually Ireland), and her compelling storytelling ability. Her best-seller *A Circle of Friends* (1991) sensitively chronicles the relationships of three ambitious young women in 1950s Dublin; it was made into a major film in 1995. Binchy has also written two books of interconnected short stories – *The Copper Beech* (1992) and *Lilac Bus* (1991) – as well as other short story collections and novels, including *The Evening Class* (1997), in which lives are changed when a schoolteacher organizes a class in Italian, and *Tara Road* (1999), in which two women trade houses and lives.

DVT

Bing Xin (1900–1999), Chinese poet, fiction writer, essayist. Born Xie Wanying, Bing Xin grew up in a naval family in Fujian and Shandong provinces. After studying classical Chinese at home, she entered the Bridgman Academy for Girls, a Beijing missionary school, in 1914, and then obtained a BA from Peking Union College for Women (later Yenching University) in 1923. She received an MA in literature from Wellesley College in 1926 and then returned to China to teach literature in several universities, including the National Minorities Institute. She married Wu Wenzao, a sociologist, in 1929; they had three children. Bing Xin remained in China after the Communist revolution of 1949 and served in numerous government-sponsored cultural posts. Her first short story, 'Two Families,' appeared in a popular Beijing daily in late 1919, and she subsequently published numerous stories on being a woman during China's transition from traditional to modern. Bing Xin also achieved renown at a young age for her poetry, particularly her short poems on natural and sentimental themes. Her collections *Fanxing* ('Myriad Stars,' 1923) and *Spring Water* (1923), inspired by the work of the Indian poet Tagore, sparked a fad for short, free verse poetry. Her series of short essays, 'Ji xiao duzhe' ('Letters to young readers'), also published in the 1920s, established her as one of China's most beloved children's writers. Until the end of her life, she continued to write and publish widely read essays.

KTo

Bint al-Shāṭiʾ (1913–1998), Egyptian prose writer, short story writer, literary critic. Born ʿĀʾisha ʿAbd al-Raḥmān in Damietta, Egypt, she wrote under the pseudonym of 'Bint al-Shāṭiʾ', so as not to upset her conservative father, who was an instructor at the Damietta Religious Institute. In spite of her own illiteracy, Bint al-Shāṭiʾ's mother encouraged her daughter's education and overcame her husband's objection to her continued schooling. As a result, Bint al-Shāṭiʾ received her first degree from Cairo University in the Arabic language in 1939. This was followed by an MA and a doctorate in Arabic from the same university in 1941 and 1950 respectively. She married her professor and mentor, Amīn al Khuli, who was polygamous. A religious individual, she believed that women have played an integral role in Muslim society throughout history. She therefore wrote many biographies of early Muslim women, including the Prophet's mother and wives. Her literary career really began with the publication of Al-Rīf al-Miṣrī ('The Egyptian Countryside,' 1936) and Qadiyyat al Fallāḥ ('The Problem of the Peasant,' 1938), two nonfiction works which criticized social conditions in rural Egypt. In her novel Sayyad al-ʿIzba ('Master of the Estate,' 1942) she dramatized the plight of a powerless peasant woman subject to the vicissitudes of patriarchal society. In 1967, she published her autobiography ʿAlā al-Jisr ('On the Bridge').

JTZ

Birdsell, Sandra (b. 1942), Canadian novelist. Born in Hamiota, Manitoba, Birdsell left school at 15, married early, and had two children. She divorced in 1984. She began writing stories in the mid-1970s, and published her first book Night Travellers, a collection of stories, in 1982. Ladies in the House (1984) is a collection of linked stories which draws on her small-town background and the tales she heard as a girl. Like her stories, her novels The Missing Child (1989) and The Chrome Suite (1992) are dark depictions of the lives of women and the oppressions they endure. The latter is realistic in structure, but The Missing Child, which concerns the rape and murder of young girls, is a complex and experimental narrative. The Two-headed Calf (1997) is a collection of stories. Birdsell has won numerous literary awards and prizes.

JEM

Blais, Marie-Claire (b. 1939), French-Canadian novelist, poet. Born in Quebec City, Blais left convent school when she was 15 years old to work as a secretary. She studied French literature and philosophy at Université Laval, Quebec. Her first novel Mad Shadows (1959), published when Blais was only 20, was a popular and critical success. She has gone on to become one of Quebec's most prolific and important writers. Her experimental fiction is powerful, lyrical, and dark; she deals compassionately with themes of sexuality, perversion, and evil. Using stream-of-consciousness and fairy-tale surrealism, her work often has a dream-like (or nightmare-like) quality. Although she has published several volumes of poetry, including Veiled Countries (1984) and Existence (1964), she is best known for her fiction. She established an international reputation with A Season in the Life of Emmanuel (1965; Prix France-Quebec), which depicts the hardships of a farming family in rural Quebec. The Manuscripts of Pauline Archange (1968, 1969) and Dürer's Angel (1970) are semi-autobiographical novels about a girl growing up in Quebec. Her numerous other novels include Tête Blanche (1960), The Day is Dark (1963), The Fugitive (1966), David Sterne (1973), The Wolf (1974), Nights in the Underground (1978), and Deaf to the City (1980).

DVT

Blandiana, Ana (Otilia-Valeria Coman) (b. 1942), Romanian poet. The most successful and widely translated Romanian writer of her generation, Blandiana offers a perfect example of a talented woman writer's career in postwar Romania: she graduated from the 'Babes-Bolyai' University of Cluj (in 1967), worked as an editor of two literary journals, and later as a librarian at the Institute of Fine Arts in Bucharest. She became a freelance writer in the 1980s. Having explicitly disagreed with the communist dictatorship, her works were denied publication and she took 'refuge' in a small village near Bucharest (transformed in her lyrics into a mythical village, part of an allegoric, cosmic biography). After the fall of communism, she embarked on a political career (and eventually became the president of the Romanian Civic Alliance and of the Romanian PEN Club) to the point of giving up her literary writing. Her numerous books of poetry, including *Călciiul vulnerabil* ('The Vulnerable Heel,' 1966), *Octombrie, Noiembrie, Decembrie* ('October, November, December,' 1972), *Somnul din somn* ('The Sleep Within the Sleep,' 1977), and *Ochiul de greier* ('The Cricket's Eye,' 1981), brought her several national and international prizes and worldwide fame. Her writing's main features are a strong taste for parables, a lyricism emanating from reflection, a violent, feminine sensuality, matched with a peculiar note of elegiac intimacy. Apart from poetry, she also written essays, fiction, and several books for children.

IB

Blazková, Jaroslava (*b.* 1933), Slovak novelist, editor. Born in Valasské Meziríci, Moravia, in her youth Blazková moved repeatedly between Slovakia and the Czech lands. While working at Slovak Radio and later in the culture section of the newspaper *Smena*, she graduated from Comenius University, Bratislava. Fired from the paper for political reasons, thanks to the thaw of 1956 she started publishing short stories in various periodicals. Her first novel *Nylon Moon* (1960), though censored in its first two editions, achieved instant success and was translated into

several languages. Its contemporary language, absence of positive communist heroines, elements of sensuality (after the prudery of socialist realism), and symbolic reference in the title to the fashionable fiber slowly reaching Czechoslovakia from the West, all heralded the country's political relaxation of the 1960s. While her short story 'Poviedka plná snehu' ('A Tale Full of Snow,' 1964) triggered controversy about her supposed immorality, her fiction for children enjoyed considerable success, including the UNESCO-prize-winning novel *Fireworks for Granddad* (1963), and the short stories collected in the volume *Little Lamb and Big Shots* (1964), which refracts the everyday world through a child's eyes. After the Soviet invasion of Czechoslovakia, Blazková settled in Canada, where she worked for the Canadian Broadcasting Corporation and later for 68 Publishers until her retirement. The collapse of communism brought her works back to Slovakia.

MV

Bloem, Marion (*b.* 1952), Dutch novelist, filmmaker. The child of Dutch/Indonesian parents who repatriated from Indonesia after the War of Independence in the late 1940s, Bloem's work is dominated by her experience of being a second-generation Dutch-Indonesian girl and woman. She became widely known with the novel *Green gewoon Indisch meisje* ('Not an Ordinary Indonesian Girl,' 1983), which describes the feelings and self-images of a girl torn between two worlds – that of the white Dutch and the colored Dutch-Indonesians – in neither of which does she feel at home. Bloem depicts this state of mind as verging on the schizophrenic and her fragmentary, non-linear and associative style of writing is very functional in this respect. This first novel generated a revival of Dutch postcolonial literature dealing with the East Indies. She often writes about conflicts between the experiences of different generations, as in *Slipi's Dogs* (1992), an account of a journey to present-day Indonesia in which the dream of the old Dutch Indies, her parents' lost paradise, is reconciled with the new Indonesia. *The Cockatoo's Lie* (1993) is a novel in which a successful author attempts to write an autobiography but instead composes a letter to her 90-year-old grandmother, setting down the stories of four generations of women. Bloem, a clinical psychologist, has also written children's books and made several documentary films.

AAn, MMe

Blume, Judy (*b.* 1938), US children's writer, novelist. Born in Elizabeth, New Jersey, Blume attended New York University, where she received a BA in 1960. She has been married three times and has three children. A prolific and immensely popular author of fiction for young adults, Blume has won numerous awards for her often controversial work. Her first book *The One in the Middle is the Green Kangaroo* was published in 1969. She made her mark with her third book, *Are You There, God? It's Me, Margaret* (1970). Narrated by 12 year old Margaret, the novel confronts the trials of puberty, in particular, menstruation, with an engaging frankness. Blume's insistence on treating with openness previously taboo sexual topics such as masturbation and loss of virginity was criticized by some, but her young readers responded with enthusiasm. Her novels, usually narrated in the first person in a realistic, accessible, and humorous style, are free from overt moralizing and accurately capture the everyday life of adolescents. *Starring Sally J. Freedman as Herself* (1977), featuring a young writer, is autobiographical. *Tiger Eyes* (1981), the story of a girl's recovery after the murder of her father, was praised for its sensitivity. Blume has also written novels for adults, including *Summer Sisters* (1998).

JEM

Bobis, Merlinda (*b.* 1959), Philippine-Australian poet, dramatist, fiction writer.

The cartographies of desire and war are among the main themes in Bobis's poetry, prose fiction, and performance texts. She grew up in the Philippines, in a city at the foot of an active volcano which inspired *Cantata of the Warrior Woman Daragang Magayon* (bilingual editions, 1993, 1997), an epic poem that interrogates war and rigid definitions of female sexuality, and which she herself performs as theater. Her other poetry books, *Rituals* (1990), *Flight Is Song On Four Winds* (bilingual edition, 1990) and *Summer Was A Fast Train Without Terminals* (1998), constantly move between sensual celebration and lyrical protest. That also best describes *Rita's Lullaby* (1998; Prix Italia) which is a poetic drama about child prostitution and militarization. Now living in Australia, Bobis also writes about migration and the problem of difference – its joyful affirmation, on one hand, and on the other, the danger of making it precious. This tension, along with variant themes on love and death, is explored in her collection of short stories *White Turtle* (1999) in a style that is alternately mythic, wistful, and quirky.

MBo

Bødker, Cecil (*b.* 1927), Danish novelist, poet, playwright. Born in Fredericia, Denmark, Bødker served a four-year apprenticeship as a silversmith after completing high school. She worked for four years as a silversmith for Georg Jensen in Copenhagen and for Markstroem's in Uppsala, Sweden. Her first collection of poetry *Luseblomster* (1955) was awarded the Edith Rodes grant in 1956, which encouraged Bødker to concentrate on writing full time. Her novels and short stories for adults are popular in Denmark but have not been translated into English. Internationally, she is best known for her children's fiction. *Silas and the Black Mare* (1967) earned her the prestigious prize of the Danish Academy. *Silas* was followed by *Silas and Ben-Godik* (1969) and *Silas and the Runaway Coach* (1972). This trilogy of picaresque adventure tales about

Silas makes effective use of suspense and, together with her young adult novel *The Leopard* (1970), gained her international recognition. *The Leopard* was written after a stay in an Ethiopian village and intended for use in East African secondary schools. Her novels are praised for their vivid characterizations and their stylistic beauty. In 1976, Bødker was given the highest honor in children's literature, the Hans-Christian Andersen Medal.

E-MM

Boland, Eavan (*b.* 1944), Irish poet, critic. Born in Dublin, Boland earned a BA (first-class honors) in English from Trinity College, Dublin in 1967. She married Ken Casey in 1969; they have two daughters. She is currently a lecturer at the School of Irish Studies in Dublin. Her first book of poetry *23 Poems* was published in 1962. Central to her poetry is her consciousness of her identity as an Irish woman poet and all the conflicts and contradictions inherent in that role. She strives to define her place within the history, myths, and literary traditions of Ireland, but is also concerned, particularly in her quietly detailed reflections on domesticity and motherhood, with her own particular experiences as a woman. Her volumes of poetry include *New Territory* (1967), *In Her Own Image* (1980), *Night Feed* (1982), *The Journey* (1983), *Selected Poems* (1989), *Outside History* (1990), *In a Time of Violence* (1994), *Collected Poems* (1995; published in the US as *An Origin Like Water* [1996]), and *The Lost Land* (1999). Her pamphlet *A Kind of Scar: The Woman Poet in a National Tradition* (1989) is an important examination of the radical changes that occur when women move from being objects of art to creators of it. *Object Lessons: The Life of a Woman and Poet in Our Time* (1995) is a collection of autobiographical essays.

JEM

Bonner, Elena (*b.* 1923), Russian memoirist. Known primarily as the physician Andrei Sakharov's wife, Bonner is a talented, gutsy woman in her own right. Born in Turkmenstan to a prominent Communist father and a puritanically ideological mother, she volunteered for the army in 1941, and as a nurse at the front received wounds that permanently affected her vision. After graduation in 1953 from the First Leningrad Medical Institute, she practiced as a district doctor and a foreign-aid health worker in Iraq. Despite joining the Communist Party in 1965, she engaged in political dissent in the late 1960s. Sakharov, whom she married in 1972, became her second husband and her partner in dissident activities. Both spent the years 1980–6 in exile in Gorky. Bonner's memoirs of this period, translated as *Alone Together* (1986), provide a sobering account of their isolated existence in this provincial town. A considerably richer, more complex work is her childhood memoir, *Mothers and Daughters* (1991), written after Sakharov's death in 1989. Bonner's account of a privileged life in Stalinist Russia, her troubled relationship with her Party-committed mother, and her loving closeness with her art-loving grandmother, constitutes a paradigm of sorts for multigenerational female autobiography.

HG

Boonlua (M. L. Boonlua Kunchon Thepyasuwan) (1911–1984), Thai novelist. Born in Bangkok, M. L. Boonlua was the youngest child of a high-ranking government official. She received a BA from Chulalongkorn University, Bangkok, in 1936, and an MA in education from the University of Minnesota in 1950. Although by profession Boonlua was a teacher and an educator, her novels and numerous short stories received high esteem from literary scholars. Recurring themes include the necessity of education and economic parity for women, the need for new paradigms for male–female relationships, and the struggle of Thais at mid-century to preserve traditional values while pursuing contemporary objectives. Her most controversial novel, *Suratnarii* ('Land of Women') is a utopian fable about a kingdom in which gender roles are reversed. None of her novels has been translated in full. The most accessible sources of her translated fiction are *Modern Thai Literature: An Ethnographic Interpretation* (1987) by Herbert P. Phillips and *A Civilized Woman: A Cultural Biography of M. L. Boonlua Thepyasuwan* – a PhD dissertation by Susan F. Kepner (University of California, Berkeley, 1998).

NM

Botan (Supa Sirisingha) (*b*. 1947), Thai novelist, short story writer, children's writer. Born in Thonburi, the twin city of Bangkok, Botan is the youngest daughter of a Chinese immigrant. Although her father saw no need for a girl to receive higher education, Botan managed to win many scholarships which enabled her to realize her dream. With BA and MA degrees from Chulalongkorn University, she began her career as a teacher before joining the editorial staff of two leading magazines. Married to Viriya Sirisingha, a well-known publisher, she now has a career as a freelance writer. Her highly acclaimed novel *Letters from Thailand*, which depicts the life of ethnic Thais and the conflict between Chinese–Thai culture, won the SEATO Literary Award in 1969 and has been translated into ten languages. As a writer, Botan is concerned with the plight of women in the male-dominated Thai society. The female protagonists in her novels, particularly in *Waewvan* ('Waewvan') and *Phu Ying Khon Nan Chue Boonrod* ('That Woman's Name is Boonrod,' 1980), clearly reflect her concerns. They are ambitious, driven, and single-minded in their fight for women's rights and independence. Many of her novels have been made into television series and films and acclaimed for their crisp dialogue and social overtones.

NM

Botelho, Fernanda (*b*. 1926), Portuguese novelist. One of the first prominent women novelists in contemporary Portugal, Botelho was born in Oporto and studied classics at the universities of Coimbra and Lisbon. She started out as a poet with *As Coordenadas Líricas* ('Lyrical Coordinates,' 1951) and regularly contributed to the experimental magazines of the 1950s, which introduced a highly intellectualized anti-realist aesthetics in Portuguese letters. Following in this mode, she became known primarily for her novels published between 1957 and 1971. *Xerazade e os Outros* ('Scheherazade and the Others,' 1964) and *Lourenço É Nome de Jogral* ('Lourenço is a Minstrel's Name,' 1971) are good examples of her characteristic recourse to intricate geometric structuring of plot and character design, the latter tending to assume symbolic stature owing to intertextual evocation. This makes for densely woven, anti-representational, and overtly ironic depictions of gender relations, especially with regard to women living in an authoritarian patriarchal regime. After a long period of silence, her prize-winning novel *Esta Noite Sonhei com Bruegel* ('Tonight I Dream of Brueghel,' 1987) was followed by the publication of three more novels to date. *As Contadoras de Histórias* ('The Women Storytellers,' 1998) was awarded the Portuguese Writers Association Prize, a recognition of her lifetime achievement.

APF

Boučková, Tereza (*b*. 1957), Czech prose writer. Born in Prague, the last of writer Pavel Kohout's three children with Anna Cornová, Boučková was raised by her mother. After high school, rejected by the Drama Academy for political reasons, she studied English for a year. She passed the state exam, signed *Charter 77* in 1978, and held several menial jobs. In 1985 she married Jiří Bouček and moved to her grandparents' cottage outside Prague. In addition to her biological son, she has two adopted Romany boys. Since 1988, she has devoted her free time to writing, in 1991 publishing the prose piece *Indian Run*, of which three more parts appeared in the following year. Boučková first draws on childhood experiences to link an individual world to larger social and political events, then raises issues of biological and adoptive parenthood, all in montage-like style. A similar approach characterizes her next short work *Quail* (1993), a portrayal of a woman's emotionally complex, ultimately unsuccessful search for a relationship with a man. Her latest (untraditional) novella, *Když milujete muže* ('When You Love a Man,' 1995), through a lyrical first-person narrative, depicts a woman's determined love.

ES

Boullosa, Carmen (*b*. 1954), Mexican novelist, poet. Boullosa, born in Mexico City, studied at the Universidad Iberoamericana and the Universidad Nacional Autónoma de México. She is married to Alejandro Aura and has two children. Her fiction illustrates her concern with the family, a nostalgia for earlier times, and a preoccupation with Mexico's environment and political system. Her earliest publications were poetry – *El hilo olvida* ('The Thread Forgets,' 1978) and *La memoria vacía* ('Empty Memory,' 1978). Her first novel *Mejor desaparece* ('Get Lost,' 1987) is fragmentary and creates an image of a disintegrating family. *Antes* ('Before,' 1989) is a narration of a young girl's passage from childhood to adolescence in a world where reality and fantasy struggle for control. Two novels set in colonial times are *They're Cows, We're Pigs* (1991), about pirates on the island of Tortuga where women are proscribed, and *Duerme* ('Sleep,' 1994), concerning the adventures of a young Frenchwoman who dresses as a man. *Llanto. Novelas imposibles* ('Weeping. Impossible Novels,' 1992) and *The Miracle-Worker* (1993) recreate history in contemporary times. The first describes the reappearance of Moctezuma in Mexico City, and the latter depicts Mexico's

political situation prior to the 1994 presidential elections.

GdB

Bouraoui, Nina (*b*. 1967), French novelist. Born in Rennes, France, of an Algerian father and French mother, Bouraoui grew up in Algeria, Switzerland, and the United Arab Emirates, where she attended French schools. In Paris, she studied law and philosophy at the university, but terminated her studies to write full time. She won the Prix du Livre Inter in 1991 for her first novel *Forbidden Vision*. Because of the strength of her memories about Algeria, she wanted her first novel to be about that country. She writes about how difficult it is to be an Algerian woman and acknowledges the extreme sexual tensions felt by both men and women because of the segregation of the sexes and their respective roles, still dictated to a great degree by tradition. She portrays Algerian society as 'boiling,' 'dangerous,' and 'exciting.' For Bouraoui, style and the craft of writing are as important as the content of her novels. Her care in evoking particular colors, sensations, odors, moods, and feelings is evident in the energetic play of language, striking images, and deliberate exaggeration in her texts. *Poing mort* ('Dead Fist') was published in 1992 and *Le bal des murènes* ('The Muraenas's Ball') in 1996.

KMM

Bowering, Marilyn (*b*. 1949), Canadian poet, novelist. Born in Winnipeg, Manitoba, Bowering was educated at the University of Victoria, British Columbia, the University of British Columbia, and the University of New Brunswick. She married Michael S. Elcock in 1982; they have one daughter. Her first book of poetry *The Liberation of Newfoundland* was published in 1973. Her early poems, as in her first volume and in *One Who Became Lost* (1976), are preoccupied with the natural world, most often as a projection of personal concerns. The later volumes have a wider range and greater variety. She is in-

creasingly interested in poetic monologues, as in *Anyone Can See I Love You*
(1987), a cycle of poems as told by Marilyn Monroe about her life, and in narrative, as in *Calling All the World* (1989),
which follows the adventures of Laika, the
Soviet canine astronaut, and his trainer.
Bowering's interest in narrative has led
her to fiction; her novels include *The Visitors All Returned* (1979), *To All Appearance a Lady* (1989), and *Visible Worlds*
(1997). Her other volumes of poems include *Sleeping with Lambs* (1980), *Giving
Back Diamonds* (1982), *Love As It Is*
(1993), *Autobiography* (1996), and
*Human Bodies: New and Collected
Poems* (1999).

JEM

Boylan, Clare (*b.* 1948), Irish novelist,
short story writer. Born and raised in Dublin, Boylan worked as a journalist for
many years before turning to fiction. Her
first novel *Holy Pictures* (1983), set in Dublin in the 1920s, is the coming-of-age story
of two girls. Its richly visual, lively, and
humorous style, its detailed evocation of a
time period, and its realistic depictions of
the joys and traumas of female adolescence are characteristic of Boylan's subsequent fiction. In *Room for a Single Lady*
(1997), a young girl and her sisters in Dublin in the 1950s are given an education in
life when their parents begin to take in
boarders. Both these novels depict the gulf
between the adolescent and the adult
world, and the inevitable loss of innocence
that accompanies crossing that gulf. Another of her favorite themes – the human
capacity for self-delusion – is at the center of *Last Resorts* (1984), in which a
middle-aged woman expects romance but
finds disappointment instead during a
vacation in Greece. *Black Baby* (1989)
concerns an unlikely relationship between
an elderly Irish woman and a younger
vivacious black woman she takes in. Boylan's short stories are collected in *A Nail
on the Head* (1983), *Concerning Virgins*
(1990), and *That Bad Woman* (1995). The

novel *Beloved Stranger* was published in
1999.

JEM

Brabcová, Zuzana (*b.* 1959), Czech novelist. Prague-born Brabcová is the daughter
of literary historians Jiří Brabec and Zina
Trochová. From a dissident family, after
high school graduation in 1978 she worked
first at the University Library and from
1980 to 1988 as a cleaning woman. Married, with a daughter, in 1995 she became
an editor at the publishing house *český
spisovatel* (Czech Writer), in charge of a
series featuring young prose writers. After
her debut in *samizdat*, she published her
first novel *Daleko od stromu* ('Far from the
Tree,' 1987) abroad. A dense, stream-of-
consciousness text, with abundant intertextual references, it is narrated from the
point of view of a young woman coming
of age in post-1968 Czechoslovakia, making a strong generational statement. Brabcová's second novel, *Zloděina* ('Thievery,'
1995) is an even more metaphorically
complex blend of dream and fantasy with
historical reality, juxtaposing the lives of
two apparently unrelated protagonists
whose separate searches for meaning
uncannily intersect in the end.

ES

Bradley, Marion Zimmer (1930–1999), US
novelist. Born in Albany, New York, Bradley received a BA from Hardin-Simmons
University in Texas in 1964 and did graduate work at the University of California,
Berkeley. She was married twice and had
three children. A prolific and influential
writer of science fiction and fantasy, she
first achieved notice with *The Planet
Savers* (1962), the first in her best-selling
Darkover series. Set on the planet Darkover, a colony of Earth, the series is innovative in its featuring of gay, lesbian, and
Amazonian characters. She also wrote
many fantasy and romance novels, many
of which are distinguished by their gay
and feminist themes. Bradley is best
known for *The Mists of Avalon* (1982), a

feminist retelling of Arthurian legend from the perspective of the women in the story. Similarly, *The Firebrand* (1987) focuses on Kassandra and other women in its reworking of the story of the fall of Troy.

JEM

Brainard, Cecilia Manguerra (*b. c.* 1948), Philippine fiction writer, essayist. Born and raised in Cebu, Brainard says she first started writing at the age of 9, after her father died, by keeping a diary in which she would update him on her life. A graduate of Maryknoll College in Quezon City, she pursued graduate studies in film at UCLA. She married lawyer and former Peace Corps volunteer Lauren Brainard; they have three sons. Brainard is the author of two short fiction collections – *Woman with Horns and Other Stories* (1988), a series of tales set in fictional Ubec; and *Acapulco at Sunset and Other Stories* (1995), which deals mostly with the lives of Filipinos, in the Philippines or elsewhere. Her novel *Song of Yvonne* (1991), which relates the experience of a young girl separated from members of her family during the Japanese occupation, was published in the US in 1994 as *When the Rainbow Goddess Wept*. She has also published a collection of essays, *Philippine Woman in America* (1991), and edited the following anthologies: *Seven Stories from Seven Sisters* (1992), *Fiction by Filipinos in America* (1993), *The Beginning and Other Asian Folktales* (1995), and *Contemporary Fiction by Filipinos in America* (1997). She teaches creative writing at UCLA Extension.

CJM

Brand, Dionne (*b.* 1953), Trinidadian-Canadian poet, essayist. Born in Guayguayare, Trinidad, Brand has lived in Toronto, Canada, since 1970. She earned a BA in English and philosophy in 1975, and an MA in the philosophy of education in 1989, from the University of Toronto. Her political involvement in the black and feminist communities is reflected in her documentary film work, and in her non-fictional studies of black working women and racism in Canada. Her poetry ranges from dealing with the 'tunnels called history' through explorations of love to cataloging immigrant experiences in Canada. *'Fore Day Morning* (1978), her first collection of poetry, was followed by six others, including *Chronicles of the Hostile Sun* (1984), a powerful series written in response to the American invasion of Grenada. Similarly, *No Language is Neutral* (1990) explores the 'blood-stained blind of race and sex.' That much of Brand's writing stems from her position as a cultural and social critic is particularly evident in her collection of essays *Bread Out of Stone* (1994). Her most recent collection of poetry, *Land to Light On* (1997), won the Governor's Award in Canada. Brand has written two novels: the critically acclaimed *In Another Place Not Here* (1996) and *At the Full and Change of the Moon* (1999).

LM

Brantenberg, Gerd (*b.* 1941), Norwegian novelist. Born in Oslo, Brantenberg grew up in Fredrikstad, a small city in southeastern Norway. She studied at the University of Oslo, then taught secondary school until 1982 when she became a fulltime writer. *What Comes Naturally* (1973), a humorous coming-out story confronting society's homophobia, was her first published book. *Egalia's Daughters* (1977) is an international best-seller. In this satirical novel, she creates new feminist terminology emphasizing the underlying phallocentricity of language. *Sangen om St Croix* ('The Song of St Croix,' 1979) and *Ved fergestedet* ('At the Ferry Landing,' 1985) are the first two volumes in a trilogy about life in Norway following World War II. In the third volume, *The Four Winds* (1989), the protagonist is first an *au pair* in Edinburgh, then studies at the University of Oslo, where she gradually comes to terms with her lesbianism.

Brantenberg is an active, radical feminist, and her eleven books, as well as her plays, short stories and essays, reflect the individual's search for identity as an individual and within society. *Augusta og Bjørnstjerne* ('Augusta and Bjørnstjerne,' 1977), a novel about Brantenberg's great grandmother's secret engagement to Bjørnstjerne Bjørnson, Norway's future national poet, shows how women's lives were restricted in nineteenth-century Norway.

Breeze, Jean 'Binta' (*b.* 1956), Jamaican poet, film writer. The daughter of a midwife and a Public Health inspector, Breeze grew up in Hanover, Jamaica. After her first marriage ended in 1978, she enrolled in the Jamaica School of Drama. She became a Rastafarian, retreating to the Clarendon hills for three years, where she had the second of her three children. She began performing in 1983 and has since toured extensively, as a poet and storyteller, in the Caribbean, Europe, North America, Southeast Asia, and Africa. In addition to her three published poetry collections, she has made several recordings, including *Tracks* (1991) and *Riding On De Riddym* (1996). Her film *Hallelujah Anyhow* aired on BBC, and her work was featured in the film *Moods and Moments*. *Riddym Ravings and Other Poems* (1988) includes the well-known title poem about a 'mad' woman, a tribute to Maroon Nanny, the Jamaican national hero, and 'baby madda,' a poem declaring the strength of a woman abandoned by the father of her child. *Spring Cleaning* (1992) evokes the voices of Caribbean mothers, sisters, and daughters. *On the Edge of an Island* (1997) includes humorous stories in the Jamaican vernacular.

LC

Brodber, Erna (*b.* 1940), Jamaican novelist. Born in Woodside, Jamaica, Brodber came to fiction through her work as a sociologist. Trained at University College

of the West Indies (now UWI), she attained her BA in sociology in 1963 and her MA in 1968. Because of her long affiliation with the Institute for Social and Economic Research, she approaches her own fiction as part of her sociological method. As a declared 'activist,' she deconstructs colonial myths and reconstructs a syncretic Jamaican identity in her works. Her first novel *Jane and Louisa Will Soon Come Home* (1980) examines the importance of traditional Jamaican life and its role in a communal healing process. The phrase 'the half has never been told' echoes in *Myal* (1988), which tells the other half of a Jamaican story through the story of Ella O'Grady, and emphasizes that the interpretation of stories must be done with an 'awareness' of their blindnesses in order for the healing, or myal, to begin. Similarly, Brodber's most recent novel *Louisiana* (1997) explores the connection between the living and the dead, and the healing that arises from such a connection.

LM

Brøgger, Suzanne (*b.* 1944), Danish novelist, essayist. One of Denmark's most creative and controversial writers, Brøgger was born in Copenhagen, spent part of her childhood in Southeast Asia, attended the University of Copenhagen, and worked as a journalist. It is difficult to assign genre classifications to her work, as part of her objective as a writer is to break down conventional categories in literature as well as in society as a whole. Her first book *Deliver Us from Love* (1973), a combination of several forms including essays and stories, is a polemic against marriage and monogamy. Her best-known works include the autobiographical *Crème Fraiche* (1978) and *A Fighting Pig's Too Tough to Eat* (1979), the first describing a life of erotic discovery and cosmopolitan life, the second a series of musings from the quiet rural village where she lives. In its English translation, the latter includes a selection of later essays. She has also written an epic prose poem *Tone* (1981), with a series of anecdotes about a strong woman who is not afraid to break the norms of society, and reinterpreted the Old Norse poem *Voluspá* (1994). She has written several plays and children's books. The winner of many prestigious awards, she writes predominantly in an autobiographical vein in the first person, which has occasioned confusion between the writer's persona and the actual person Brøgger.

MHH

Brooke-Rose, Christine (*b.* 1923), British novelist, critic. Born in Geneva, raised in Brussels, bilingual in French and English, married to a Polish author, and of Swiss, American, and British origins, Brooke-Rose, not surprisingly, is an adventurer in language. She worked as an intelligence officer in the British Women's Auxiliary Air Force during World War II before earning her BA from Somerville College, Oxford, in 1949 and an MA and a PhD from University College London. She taught English language and literature at the University of Paris VIII in the 1970s and 1980s. She began writing novels in 1956 when her husband Jerzy Peterkiewicz fell ill, publishing her first novel *The Languages of Love* in 1957. After writing several conventional novels in the 1950s and early 1960s, she began to publish experimental fiction with her novel *Out* (1964), a post-nuclear dystopia set in Africa. Her formally innovative novels have been compared to the *nouveau roman* of *Nathalie Sarraute and Alain Robbe-Grillet. A structuralist whose critical work includes *The Grammar of Metaphor* (1958) and *A ZBC of Ezra Pound* (1971), Brooke-Rose became increasingly concerned with language and influenced by scientific terminology in works like *Such* (1966; James Tait Black Memorial Prize), *Between* (1968), and *Thru* (1975). In *Amalgamemnon* (1984), *Xorander* (1986), *Verbivore* (1990), and *Textermination* (1996), she experiments with the genres of science fiction and fantasy. In *Subscript* (1999), she takes

as her subject the history of human evolution. *Remake* (1996) is Brooke-Rose's unique version of an autobiography.

DVT

Brookner, Anita (*b.* 1928), English novelist. Born in London to Polish Jewish parents, Brookner attended King's College London before obtaining her PhD in art history from the Courtauld Institute of Art. A historian of late-eighteenth- and early-nineteenth-century French art, she was the first woman to be named the Slade Professor of Fine Arts at Cambridge University. Beginning with *Watteau* in 1968, she has written several scholarly works of art history. In 1981 she published her first novel, aptly titled *A Start in Life*, which concerns the search for romantic and social fulfillment of Dr. Ruth Weiss, a scholar of Balzac – a writer who, along with Flaubert, strongly influenced Brookner's own work. In the novels *Providence* (1982) and *Look at Me* (1983), she continues her focus on intelligent, affluent women who are dissatisfied with the relationships in their lives. She won the Booker Prize for *Hotel du Lac* (1984), the story of a British romance novelist staying at an upscale hotel in Switzerland. Centered upon moral dilemmas, quietly witty and beautifully written, Brookner's novels include *Family and Friends* (1985), *The Misalliance* (1986), *A Friend from England* (1987), *Brief Lives* (1990), *Fraud* (1993), *A Private View* (1994), *Altered States* (1997), and *Undue Influence* (1999).

DVT

Brossard, Nicole (*b.* 1943), Canadian poet, essayist. Born and deeply rooted in Montreal, Brossard pursued a higher degree in arts and became an activist, an editor (*Nouvelle Barre du Jour* among other journals) and a frequent conference keynote speaker. She has a daughter. She has received several national or Quebecois awards and grants, and participated in a ground-breaking feminist play, *La nef des* *sorcières* ('The Witch Nave') in 1976. She is considered a leading feminist intellectual and a unique French-writing lesbian poet. Her works, often translated into English, explore the transmutation of life into writing and the affirmation of the female body's difference. An occasionally hermetic writer, she uses French psychoanalytical and feminist theory and North American philosophy on cultural identity. She co-directed the film *Some American Feminists* (1977). *The Aerial Letter* (1985), *Le centre blanc* ('The White Center,' 1978), and the complex narrative *Mauve Désert* ('Mauve Desert,' 1987) which was made into a CD-ROM in 1997, are among her best-known books.

CPM

Brown, Rita Mae (*b*. 1944), US novelist, poet. Born in Hanover, Pennsylvania, Brown spent part of her childhood in Florida and identifies herself as a Southern writer. She received a BA from New York University in 1968 and a PhD from the Institute for Policy Studies in Washington, D.C. She is best known for her first novel *Rubyfruit Jungle* (1973), a lively and humorous coming-of-age story about a young woman from Florida who moves to New York and discovers her lesbian sexuality and the women's rights movement. Brown is interested in revising male-dominated history, as in *High Hearts* (1986), about the Civil War, and *Six of One* (1978), in which a young woman tells her own version of her family's history during the twentieth century. With *Wish You Were Here* (1990), Brown turned to detective fiction, 'co-authored' with her cat, Sneaky Pie Brown. Other works in the series include *Rest in Pieces* (1992) and *Murder She Meowed* (1997). Her novels, which include *Southern Discomfort* (1982), *Sudden Death* (1983) and *Riding Shotgun* (1996), are written in a straightforward and humorous style, and characteristically feature lesbian characters and lesbian and feminist themes.

JEM

Brückner, Christine (*b*. 1921), German novelist, fiction writer. Born in Waldeck (Hessen), daughter of a pastor, Brückner was shaped by the parsonage, village life, and National Socialism. Her first novel *Ehe die Spuren verwehen* ('Before the Traces Disappear') won the 1954 Bertelsmann prize. Early novels such as *Die Zeit danach* ('The Time Afterwards,' 1961) and *Das glückliche Buch der a.p.* ('The Happy Book of a.p.,' 1970), have middle-class, female protagonists and treat women's emancipation issues. She gained fame with her Poenichen Trilogy, which narrates the wartime and postwar exploits of a young noblewoman from Pomerania: *Gillyflower Kid* (1975; television series 1978), *Flight of Cranes* (1977), and *Die Quints* ('The Quints,' 1985). Dismissed by some as a popular writer, Brückner has demonstrated increased literary ambition in her later works. *Desdemona – if you had only spoken!* (1983) presents fictive speeches by famous women (Sappho, Laura, terrorist Gudrun Ensslin), and *Früher oder Später* ('Sooner or Later,' 1994) investigates the East/West problem in Germany. Married since 1967 to author Otto Heinrich Kühner, with whom she has occasionally collaborated, her autobiographical writings include *Überlebensgeschichten* ('Survival Stories,' 1971) and *Woher und Wohin* ('Coming From, Heading Toward,' 1995). Vice President of the German PEN from 1980 to 1984 and recipient of the Goethe award of Hessen in 1982, Brückner has lived most of her adult life in Kassel.

EM

Burnier, Andreas (Catharina Irma Dessaur) (*b*. 1931), Dutch novelist, essayist. After a happy childhood in The Hague, Burnier survived the chaos and horror of World War II in hiding, separated from her parents. The novel *Het Jongensuur* ('The Boy's Hour,' 1969) is a beautiful literary account of the embattled existence of a young girl who aspires to be a boy, always on the move from one unsafe address to the next. The chronology is reversed: the novel moves back in time, beginning when the war is over, and ending when it has just begun. Burnier started her writing career 'as a man,' only to later reveal that she is a lesbian. She has written a series of novels in which feminist rebellion is combined with philosophy, mysticism and the longing for a masculine or transgendered existence. She is a prolific essayist and has worked as a professor of criminology at the University of Nijmegen. She has also written extensively on abortion, opposing what she sees as practices and feminist standpoints that are too easy. She has always created her own literary and intellectual space: 'I am a group of one' is a characteristic statement in which she aptly describes herself. After a long spiritual search, she has rediscovered the Jewish religion and tradition. Only one short story is available in English translation ('Next year in Jerusalem') and some of her poems can be found in the anthology *The Defiant Muse* (1998).

AAn, MMe

Butala, Sharon (*b.* 1940), Canadian short story writer, essayist. Born in Nipawin, Saskatchewan, Butala was educated at the University of Saskatchewan, where she earned a BA in art and English. After later earning her BEd, she taught children with learning disabilities for several years. Her first novel *Country of the Heart* was published in 1984. Her fiction is realistic and centered on rural life. It is concerned with the natural world and its rhythms of seasons and weather, as well as with the struggles and dreams of ordinary, middle-aged people, usually women, and their families. Three of her novels form a loosely connected trilogy. *The Gates of the Sun* (1986) traces the life and spiritual growth of man from childhood to death against a background of the history of Saskatchewan. *Luna* (1988) contrasts women's indoor lives of home and family with the outdoor life of men. *The Fourth Archangel* (1992) is a portrait of a small Canadian town and an elegy for a

disappearing way of rural life. Butala is also known for her short stories, which are collected in *Queen of the Headaches* (1985) and *Fever* (1990). *Upstream: 'Le Pays d'en Haut'* (1991) is an autobiographical novel about her father's French-Canadian heritage. The immensely popular *The Perfection of the Morning: An Apprenticeship in Nature* (1994) is a spiritual autobiography.

JEM

Butler, Octavia E. (*b.* 1947), US novelist, short story writer. Born in Pasadena, California, Butler was raised in a strict Baptist sect and educated at Pasadena College and California State University. She is a prolific and popular writer of science fiction, a field where few African-American writers like herself have ventured. Her novels are vividly imaginative and are notable for their engagement with issues of race and gender. Her first novel *Patternmaster* (1976) inaugurated the five-novel Patternist series, which includes *Mind of My Mind* (1977) and *Survivor* (1978). Her second series is the Xenogenesis trilogy. *Kindred* (1979), like several of Butler's other works, features a black female protagonist; she travels back in time to the antebellum South and must fight to survive slavery. *Parable of the Sower* (1993) and its sequel, *Parable of the Talents* (1998), deal with telepathy and environmental issues. Butler has also published two collections of short stories. She was awarded a prestigious MacArthur Fellowship in 1996.

JEM

Byatt, A(ntonia) S(usan) (*b.* 1936), English novelist, critic. Born in Sheffield, England, Byatt, sister to novelist *Margaret Drabble, graduated with first class honors from Newnham College, Cambridge, and continued her education at Bryn Mawr College and Somerville College, Oxford. She has taught at University College, London, and has written critical works on Wordsworth, Coleridge, and *Iris Murdoch, one of her influences. Her scholarly work informs her fiction, which is erudite, richly allusive, and self-conscious about literary critical issues. Her first novel *Shadow of a Sun* (1964) is a *Bildungsroman* of an adolescent girl with literary aspirations whose father is a novelist. *The Game* (1967) is about the complicated relationship of two sisters. Her novels *The Virgin in the Garden* (1979), *Still Life* (1985), and *Babel Tower* (1996) are three volumes of a projected tetralogy which follows Frederica Potter and her family and friends through several decades. The first volume takes place in the early 1950s and introduces the intelligent and passionate Frederica; the second volume concerns her years at Cambridge; and the third takes place in London in the 1960s, as Frederica leaves an abusive marriage and struggles to support herself and her son. Byatt's Booker Prize-winning novel *Possession: A Romance* (1990) combines the genres of academic novel, detective fiction, and historical fiction, as two literary scholars fall in love while researching a love affair between two nineteenth-century poets. Byatt has also published *Angels and Insects: Two Novellas* (1992) and a series of interlocking tales in *The Matisse Stories* (1994).

DVT

C

Cabrera, Lydia (1899–1991), Cuban short story writer. Born in Havana, Cabrera is best known for her research of Afro-Cuban culture. In the late 1920s, she went to Paris to pursue her studies in painting, where she was exposed to Surrealism, which would later shape her innovative writing style. Her first, and most widely read, collection of short stories (initially published in French in 1936) is *Cuentos negros de Cuba* ('Negro Stories of Cuba,' 1940). Other collections are *Ayapá, cuentos de jicotea* ('Ayapá, Wasp Stories,' 1971) and *Cuentos para adultos, niños y retrasados mentales* ('Stories for Adults, Children and the Mentally Retarded,' 1983). Years of dedication to anthropological, ethnological, and literary studies about Cuba and its African heritage earned her several honorary degrees from various US universities, including the University of Miami. Cabrera died in Miami where she spent her last years of exile, after her departure from Cuba in 1960.

MAMM-M

Campbell, Hazel (*b.* 1940), Jamaican short story writer. Campbell was educated during the 1940s and 1950s, a time of rising nationalism throughout the colonial world. She earned her BA from the University of the West Indies with diplomas in mass communications and management studies. In spite of the prevalence of foreign textbooks, patriotism, political activism, and the urge to 'think Jamaican,' as Campbell puts it, were part of the general consciousness. This is reflected in her short stories which explore the complex realities of contemporary Caribbean life: issues of black identity, relationships between men and women, and the enduring legacy of slavery in contemporary Jamaican society, among others. 'The Carrion Eaters,' her first published work, appeared in the Jamaican *Sunday Gleaner* in 1970. Campbell's short stories have been published in four volumes: *The Rag Doll and Other Stories* (1978), *Woman's Tongue* (1985), *Singerman* (1991), and *'Tillie Bummie' and Other Stories: Life in Jamaica, Country and Town* (1993), as well as in several anthologies. In 1997, she received the Vic Reid Award for Children's Literature from the Book Development Council of Jamaica. She now lives in Jamaica, where she works as a media consultant and teaches the writing of children's literature.

JSp

Campos, Julieta (*b.* 1932), Cuban-Mexican novelist, critic. Born in Havana, Campos earned a doctoral degree in literature in Cuba, and later studied at the Sorbonne. In Paris she married Enrique González Pedrero, a Mexican who in 1982 was elected governor of the State of Tabasco; they have one son. A resident of Mexico since 1955, Campos taught at the

Universidad Nacional Autónoma de México. As a literary critic she published *La imagen en el espejo* ('The Image on the Mirror,' 1965), and *La función de la novela* ('The Novel's Role,' 1973). In her 1982 study *La herencia obstinada. Análisis de cuentos nahuas* ('Persistent Heritage. Analysis of Nahuatl Tales') she moves away from an exclusive European centered criticism. Her first narratives, *Muerte por agua* ('Death by Drowning,' 1965) and *Celina or the Cats* (1968), explore family relationships and the inner world of characters secluded in interior spaces. In 1974 Campos was honored with the Xavier Villaurrutia Prize for *She has Reddish Hair and Her Name is Sabina*, a novel that focuses on the writing process and the relationship between gender and writing. In 1978 she published *The Fear of Losing Eurydice*. Campos was president of the PEN Club of Mexico in 1978, and authored a play, *Jardín de invierno* ('Winter Garden,' 1988).

MIL

Can Xue (*b.* 1953), Chinese fiction writer. Born Deng Xiaohua, Can Xue grew up in Changsha, Hunan Province. When she was 4 years old, her father, then working as the chief editor of the *New Hunan Daily*, was labeled an 'ultrarightist' and was sent to a rural area for reform through labor. The family of nine lived in a tiny hut of about ten square meters and often struggled on the verge of starvation. In 1979 her father was rehabilitated and restored to a post in the provincial Political Advisory Bureau, and the condition of the family improved. Can Xue and her husband then started a family business, a tailoring shop which was later run solely by her husband. She published her first story 'Yellow Mud Street' in 1985. Her works have won critical acclaim for their modernist surrealism and use of absurdity as a form of cultural criticism. Entering Can Xue's fictional world is like entering a strange world, where dream and reality merge. Fear, paranoia, absurdist humor,

sexual menace, grotesquery, and mystery run rampant. Her works have been compared with those of Western modernists such as Kafka and Bruno Schulz. Can Xue's works have been translated into many different languages, including two story anthologies in English: *Dialogues in Paradise* (1989) and *Yellow Mud Street* (1991).

JZ

Capriolo, Paola (*b.* 1962), Italian novelist, short story writer, translator. Born and residing in Milan, Capriolo has translated Mann and Goethe into Italian. Her narrative style is distinctive: symbolic use of mirrors; search for the self, beauty, art; suggestive and sophisticated writing; magic realism; fascination with music. Her first book *La grande Eulalia* ('The Great Eulalia,' 1988) is a collection of four short stories about the world of art in everyday life in a magical and mysterious atmosphere. Two of these stories have appeared in English: 'The Woman of Stone' in *Conjunctions* and 'Letters to Luisa' in the *Review of Contemporary Fiction*. Acclaimed by critics, this book was awarded the Premio Giuseppe Berto. Her second book *The Helmsman* (1989) was also well-received and was awarded the Premio Rapallo. In *Il doppio regno* ('The Double Reign,' 1991), the labyrinthine hotel symbolizes a prison in which the protagonist is challenged to decipher objects and people around her. *Floria Tosca* (1992) is a rewriting of Giacomo Puccini's *Tosca* with the focus shifted to Baron Scarpia, a police chief obsessed with Floria Tosca. *Con i miei mille occhi* ('With My Thousand Eyes,' 1997) is the sequel to the story of Echo and Narcissus, where Echo falls in love with a painter obsessed with mirrors. In 1991, in Munich, she was awarded the Bertelsmann Buchclubs' Fördepreis.

GMe

Cardinal, Marie (*b.* 1929), French novelist. Born to a French colonial family in Algeria, Cardinal studied philosophy at the

University of Algiers and at the Sorbonne. She taught high school and worked as a journalist following her marriage to producer Jean-Pierre Ronfard and before publishing her first novel *Ecoutez la mer* ('Listen to the Sea,' 1962). *The Words to Say It* (1975), a popular and critical success, followed by *In Other Words* (1977) with *Annie Leclerc, illustrates a recurrent theme in Cardinal's texts – the fundamental physical and psychological alienation of women in society, especially mothers, as in *Devotion and Disorder* (1987). Cardinal's narrative project, in part, has been to question women's peripheral status in myth and history. She undertakes a revisionist mythmaking strategy in *Le Passé empiété* ('The Backstitch,' 1983), in which she reinvents the story of Clytemnestra, and in *La Médée d'Euripide* ('Euripides' Medea,' 1986). In the autobiographical *Au Pays de mes racines* ('In My Native Land,' 1980), she candidly explores the implications of exile and colonialism in her own life, as she returns to Algeria after an absence of more than two decades. Most of her texts bear witness to Cardinal's continuing passion for Algeria and her desire to recover her origins through writing. She currently resides mostly in Montreal.

PJP

Cârneci, Magda (*b.* 1955), Romanian poet, art critic. Until 1990, Cârneci used to sign her poems with the pen name of Magdalena Chica, and was well-known as one of the most important young authors of the 1980s. She published three books of poetry: *Hipermateria* ('The Hypermatter,' 1980), *Oliniște asurzitoare* ('A Deafening Silence,' 1984), *Haosmos* ('Chaosmos,' 1992). Poetry meant to her a space of freedom and refuge – through the magic of words – for the fragile, solitary girl she has chosen as an alter-ego. In 1990, she 'recovered' her real name – Magda Cârneci – but she seems to have also moved her emphasis to art and art criticism (she has an MA and a PhD in history and theory of

art), publishing studies and organizing exhibitions and artistic experiments. She is among the founders of the Group for Social Dialogue, a postcommunist discussion group of intellectuals with a central role in civic and political life.

IB

Carson, Anne (*b.* 1950), Canadian poet, essayist. Born in Toronto, Ontario, Carson was educated at the University of Toronto, where she earned a BA (1974), an MA (1976), and a PhD (1980). She is a professor of classics at McGill University in Montreal. In her writing, the boundaries between genres are fluid; she uses prose or verse for her poetry and her essays. Her densely allusive work demonstrates a wide range of influences, which include the Greek texts that are the subject of her scholarly work, Emily Dickinson, and Gertrude Stein. Her poetry is dramatic and funny and daring, emotionally accessible but intellectually rich and formally inventive. *Glass, Irony and God* (1995) explores family relationships, romantic love, and the love of God, and features 'The Glass Essay,' a long poem sequence which powerfully juxtaposes autobiographical fragments with events from the life of Emily Brontë. The critically acclaimed *Autobiography of Red* (1998) is a novel in verse that updates the myth of Geryon and Herakles, placing it in modern times and figuring the monster Geryon as a gay teenaged boy. The ancient and the modern are also combined in *Men in the Off Hours* (2000), a collection of verse and prose poems that includes works on a variety of historical and mythical figures, including Antigone, Antonin Artaud, Lazarus, Freud, and Catherine Deneuve. *Eros the Bittersweet* (1986) is an essay on Sappho and erotic desire. *Short Talks* (1992) is a collection of prose poems which were also later included in *Plainwater: Essays and Poetry* (1995). In 1996, Carson won the Lannan Literary Award.

JEM

Carter, Angela (1940–1992), English novelist, short story writer, essayist. Born in Eastbourne, England, Carter moved to Yorkshire during the war years and grew up in London. She studied medieval literature at Bristol University, earning a BA in 1965; it was there that she developed her interests in French literature and fairy tales. She taught creative writing in England, the US, and Australia. She wrote over a dozen novels and short story collections as well as the essay collections *Nothing Sacred* (1982) and *Expletives Deleted* (1992), screenplays, and a 'cultural history,' *The Sadeian Woman* (1979). She characteristically used eroticism, violence, fantasy, Gothic elements, and the macabre to explore themes of sexuality and gender identity, as in *The Passion of New Eve* (1977), in which a man, surgically made female, experiences rape. Her first novel, *Shadow Dance* (1966), is about a disturbing and destructive young man who is a master at scavenging and seducing. *The Magic Toyshop* (1967) uses magic realism to explore Freudian theories of sexual development. Carter's startling, imaginative, and vivid prose was influenced by surrealism as well as by fairy tales, some of which she rewrote from a feminist perspective in *The Bloody Chamber and Other Stories* (1979). Other novels include *The Infernal Desire Machines of Doctor Hoffman* (1972), a science fiction fantasy about a mad scientist; the award-winning *Nights at the Circus* (1984); and *Wise Children* (1991).

DVT

Carvalho, Maria Judite (1921–1998), Portuguese short story writer. Although considered the most accomplished woman writer of the modern short story in Portugal, with several of her works translated into French and Spanish, Carvalho's literary career went by as discreetly as the everyday, lonely, and uneventful lives of her fictional characters. Born in Lisbon, she studied humanities at the university, going on to live with her husband, anti-Fascist writer Urbano Tavares Rodrigues, in France and Belgium between 1947 and 1955. Her first collection of short stories *Tanta Gente, Mariana* ('So Many People, Mariana,' 1955) set the tone of her subsequent work. This includes eleven volumes of short stories; the novel *Os Armários Vazios* ('The Empty Closets,' 1966); and two volumes of literary chronicles originally published in Lisbon newspapers. She is a master of concision and dramatic tension in the portrayal of the interior gloom of middle-class and lower-middle-class characters, enclosed in traditional gender myths and in the social-economic structures of oppression left unaltered by the democratic revolution of 1974. It was not until the publication of *Seta Despedida* ('Dismissed Arrow,' 1995) that she was finally recognized with a literary prize by the Portuguese critical establishment.

APF

Cassian, Nina (*b.* 1924), Romanian poet, composer. Daughter of a Romanian poet, Cassian studied fine arts and became involved with avant-garde circles in Bucharest before World War II; her first volume *La scara 1/1* ('On a Scale of 1 to 1,' 1947) is influenced by their style. After the war, she became one of the most active supporters of communist propaganda, writing a poetry of political inspiration but little aesthetic value. Like *Banuş, she went through a crisis around 1957, changing her style and aesthetic options, and reasserting her rebellious nature. Her work allegorizes everyday experience and concerns anxiety and destructive force, as in *Dialogul vîntului cu marea* ('The Wind's Dialogue with the Sea,' 1957), *Sîngele* ('The Blood,' 1966), *Recviem (*1971), *Life Sentence* (1990) and *Cearta cu haosul* ('The Fight with Chaos,' 1993). A playfulness is evident in *Loto-Poeme* ('Loto-Poems,' 1972), *Jocuri de vacanţă* ('Holiday Games,' 1983), and in her books for children. The main theme of her latest volumes, such as *Call Yourself Alive?* (1988) is love in its widest sense: love of life, of mankind, of one's native country and language. Since 1985, she has been living in the US; she teaches creative writing at New York University. Her successes as a composer of vocal lieds and symphonic poems are also to be noted.

IB

Castel-Bloom, Orly (*b.* 1960), Israeli short story writer, novelist. Born in Tel Aviv to an Egyptian Jewish family, Castel-Bloom studied film at Tel Aviv University. In addition to three collections of short stories and three novels, she has also written several plays. The hostile urban environment described in her stories is inhabited with marginal characters who suffer from alienation, a sense of meaninglessness, and, often, a bad case of nerves. She combines the banal with the fantastic in a hyper-realistic style. Her stories are celebrated for their irrational logic, capriciousness, and uncompromising irreverence. *Dolly City* (1992), a story of the maternal instinct taken to horrifying extremes, firmly established its author as the quintessential voice of the decade and her city. Recognized as an original and witty writer from her first collections – *Lo Rahok Mi-Merkaz Ha-'Ir* ('Not Far from the City Center,' 1987) and *Sevivah 'Oyenet* ('Hostile Surroundings,' 1989) – she continues to delight, surprise, and influence with her picaraesque-type adventure tales – *Hekhan Ani Nimtset* ('Where Am I,' 1990) and *HaMinah Liza* ('The Mina Lisa,' 1995) – and her hilarious *Sipurim Bilti-Retsoniyim* ('Involuntary Stories,' 1993). Her writing has won Castel-Bloom the Tel Aviv (1990), the Prime Minister's (1992), and the Nathan Alterman (1996) prizes for literature.

NEB

Castellanos, Rosario (1925–1974), Mexican poet, novelist. Born in Mexico City, Castellanos grew up in Chiapas, a region known for the conflicts between the native population and white property owners.

Her landowning family moved to Mexico City in 1941. She attended the Universidad Autónoma de México, earning a degree in philosophy in 1950. She married Ricardo Guerra, a philosophy professor, in 1957. They had one son, and were later divorced. Her autobiographical first novel *The Nine Guardians* (1957), which was awarded the 1957 Mexican Critic's Award for best novel, and the Chiapas Prize in 1958, tells the story of a white girl who grows up in Chiapas during the period of land reforms in post-revolutionary Mexico. Her second novel *The Book of Lamentations* (1962) focuses on a Tzotzil Indian woman. Her collected poems, *The Selected Poems of Rosario Castellanos* (1972), deal with her experiences as a woman in a male-dominated society. Other publications include several books of stories, essays on women, newspaper articles, and a play. She died in Tel Aviv in 1974 while serving as Ambassador to Israel. Posthumous publications are *Cartas a Ricardo* ('Letters to Ricardo,' 1994) and *Rito de iniciación* ('Rite of Passage,' 1997).

MIL

Castillo, Ana (*b.* 1953), US poet, fiction writer, essayist. Born in Chicago, Castillo attended Northeastern Illinois University (BA, 1975), the University of Chicago (MA, 1979), and the University of Bremen (PhD, 1991). She has taught at many universities and colleges, including San Francisco State University and Mount Holyoke College. Her identity as a Chicana woman is central to her work, which is consistently concerned with feminism and multiculturalism, and the oppressions of sexism and racism. Her volumes of poetry include the chapbook *Otro Canto* (1977), *Women Are Not Roses* (1984), and *My Father Was a Toltec* (1988), which emphasizes bilingualism by juxtaposing poems in English and Spanish without translation. Castillo is best known for *The Mixquiahuala Letters* (1986; American Book Award), a fragmentary epistolary novel in which she offers alternative narratives through suggested rearrangements of the letters. In *Sapagonia: An Anti-Romance in 3/8 Meter* (1990), she uses magic realism to imagine a mestizo utopia. Her other novels include *So Far from God* (1993) and *Peel My Love Like an Onion* (1999). *Loverboys* (1996) is a collection of short stories. In *Massacre of the Dreamers: Essays on Xicanisma* (1994), she posits a new Chicana feminism ('xicanisma') as she considers Mexican myths, history, and racial politics in the US.

JEM

Cato, Nancy (1917–2000), Australian novelist. Born in Adelaide, South Australia, Cato studied literature at Adelaide University, then worked as a journalist from 1935 to 1941. She married Eldred de Bracton Norman in 1941 (died 1971) and had children. She became the art critic for the Adelaide *News and Mail* (1957–8) and worked as a freelance writer. Her prominence as a writer occurred with the publication of her trilogy of historical novels *All the Rivers Run* (1958), *Time, Flow Softly* (1959), and *But Still the Stream* (1962). The trilogy was reissued in 1978 as a single volume in Australia, England, and the US, and was adapted for television in 1983. Cato also published numerous other novels, works of nonfiction, two volumes of poetry, a collection of short fiction, and a children's book. She was assistant editor of *Poetry* (1947–8), and also edited two collections: the *Jindyworobak Anthology* (1950) and *Southern Festival* (1960). In both her fiction and nonfiction Cato's writing commonly investigates the relationship among place, history and identity and between human communities and the natural environment. She was made a Member of the Order of Australia in 1984 for services to literature.

EMcM

Cavarero, Adriana (*b*. 1947), Italian philosopher. Philosopher and professor of political philosophy at the University of Verona, author of several books on Greek philosophers and one on John Locke's political philosophy, Cavarero has become one of the principal exponents of Italian feminist theoretical thought. In 1983, she founded, with Luisa Muraro and others, a group called Diotima, a community of women united by a love of philosophy and the goal of investigating the possibility of philosophy conceived and elaborated exclusively by women and from women's point of view. In *In Spite of Plato: A Feminist Rewriting of Ancient Philosophy* (1990), Cavarero rereads the Western tradition of philosophical thought through several female figures such as Penelope, Demeter and Diotima, to show how the myths and stories concerning these women have functioned to suppress originary female difference and hence the possibility for women's knowledge of themselves and participation in the body politic. In *Corpo in figure: Filosofia e politica della corporeità* ('The Body in Figures: Philosophy and the Politics of Corporeality,' 1995) she extends her critique of the expulsion of the female body from political thought through an analysis beginning with Sophocle's *Antigone*. In her most recent work, *Tu che mi guardi, tu che mi racconti: Filosofia della narrazione* ('You Who Look At Me, You Who Write About Me: The Philosophy of Narration,' 1997), Cavarero draws upon the work of Hannah Arendt to propose a way for women to emphasize their unique sexed nature.

CL-W

Césaire, Ina (*b*. 1942), French-Martinican dramatist. Daughter of the famous negritude poet Aimé Césaire, Ina studied and taught ethnography in France before retiring to Martinique. Her sister Michèle is also an academic and a playwright. While she is a social recluse, Césaire is committed to preserving Martinique's cultural heritage and Creole language. She has directed several ethnographic films, has compiled numerous oral testimonies and folk stories, and has served as an administrator in archival research and oral tradition preservation in Martinique. Her plays have been staged in Paris as well as in New York by the Ubu Repertory Theatre. Some have been translated into English, such as *Island Memories* (1985) and *Fire's Daughters* (1992), which are primarily constructions of oral traditions and of Martinique's history from the perspective of the little people. Her works include a humorous narrative mosaic of authentic stories, *Zonzon tête carrée* ('Square-Headed Zonzon,' 1994) and several collections of 'daytime' and 'nighttime' tales. She has also adapted works by *Simone Schwarz-Bart, *Marie Chauvet, and Jacques Roumain among others.

CPM

César, Ana Cristina (1952–1983), Brazilian poet, essayist. One of the most talented Brazilian poets of the modern generation, César was born in Rio de Janeiro. She earned a degree in literature and an MA in the theory and practice of literary translation from University of Essex in 1980. Her literary legacy is her poetry: *Cenas de Abril* ('April Scenes,' 1980), *Luvas de Pelica* ('Kid Leather Gloves,' 1980), and *A teus pés* ('At Your Feet,' 1982). The essays collected in *Literatura não é documento* ('Literature is not a Document,' 1980) are part of her MA thesis. By investigating documentary films made about writers and literary works in Brazil from 1939 to 1978, she attempted to define the concept of literature implicit in each of these films. Posthumously published edited works include *Inéditos e Dispersos* ('Unpublished and Dispersed,' 1985), a collection of poems and prose; *Escritos da Inglaterra* ('Writing from England,' 1988), essays about translation and literature; and *Escritos no Rio* ('Writing in Rio,' 1993). *Portsmouth Notebook* (1993) includes poems translated by César. The presence of many foreign language fragments and allusions in her poetic writing is probably due to her work as a translator and to her familiarity

with different rewritings of the same literary work.

TFC

Cesereanu, Ruxandra (*b.* 1963), Romanian poet. Daughter of a poet and wife of a specialist in comparative literature, Cesereanu has a BA in philology; she taught Romanian in several secondary schools during the communist period. Soon after 1989, she became an editor of the cultural magazine *Steaua* ('the Star') and a part-time senior lecturer in the Department of Theatre of the 'Babes-Bolyai' University in Cluj-Napoca (from which she had graduated in 1985). She earned a PhD in Letters in 1997. Since 1982 she has been publishing essays, poetry, prose and translations. Although her first book was a fantastic novel, *Călătorie prin oglinzi* ('Voyage through Looking Glasses,' 1989), she is better known as a poet. Her volumes of verse – *Grădina deliciilor* ('Garden of Delights,' 1993), *Zona vie* ('Live Zone,' 1993), *Cădere deasupra orasului* ('Fall over the City,' 1994) – won several prizes and were translated into German, Hungarian and English (*The Schizoid Ocean*, 1997). Femininity – an identity balanced between Death, Fear, and Madness – is the main theme of her writings. Bestiariums and apocalyptic images are there to evoke the loneliness of a woman 'who'll never be a grandmother or a sister or a mother/ ... just a daughter and a lover.'

IB

Chalfi, Rahel (Rachel) (*b. c.* 1940s), Israeli poet. Born in Tel Aviv, daughter of poets and niece to the Israeli poet Avraham Chalfi, Chalfi served in the Israeli army and worked as a military reporter. She took her MA degree in English literature at the Hebrew University in Jerusalem, worked as a documentary editor at Israeli public radio and as a director in public television. In the early 1970s she studied at the American Film Institute and later taught film at Tel Aviv University. In addition to being a poet, she is a documentary film maker and award-winning dramatist. In her expressive first book *Shirim Tat Yamiim Ve-Aherim* ('Under Water and Other Poems,' 1975) there are two important themes: illusion as an insupportable part of life and the desire to cross the boundaries of existence through multifaceted nature. In the books *Nefilah Hofshit* ('Free Fall,' 1979), *Zikit o Ekron i Ha-Vadaut* ('Chameleon or the Principle of Uncertainty,' 1986) and *Homer* ('Matter,' 1990) the logical element becomes stronger. She strives to define the world and its elements while dealing with the physical, changeable nature of the self and the complexity of being in a world both apocalyptic and ordinary. In her latest book *Ahavat Ha-Derakon* ('Love of the Dragon', 1995) she confronts the impact of time and the fragile existence of man.

IA

Chamnongsri Rutnin (Khunying Chamnongsri Hanchanlash) (*b.* 1939), Thai poet, biographer, translator. Born into a prominent banking family, Chamnongsri spent her teenage years at school in England. Prior to 1999, she was best known for her poetry and prose tales, some of which have been translated into several languages. In 1999, her first biographical work, *As a Boat in Mid-Ocean*, was published. It became a best-seller and won critical acclaim for its sensitive and poignant exploration into the origin and migration of her mother's family from China, the family's 130 years of struggles and assimilation into the fabric of Thai society, and its rise in Thailand's elite business circle. Her English language anthology of reflective poems *On the White Empty Page* has been described as a marriage of the two cultures, while her Thai language collection *Fon Tok Yang Tong, Fa Rong Yang Thueng* ('Touched by Rain, Reached by Thunder'), is an introspective journey during a three-month meditation retreat in a Buddhist forest monastery. One of her plays *Where Dusk Ends*, which deals with the deep-seated male double-standard in

marriage relationships, won the John A. Eakin Award in 1987. The play *Kaewta's Horizon* deals with a mother-daughter relationship during the mentally retarded daughter's sexual awakening. Chamnongsri's English translations of Thai literature have been widely praised for their artistic rendering and sensitivity to the original works.

NM

Chandernagor, Françoise (*b.* 1945), French novelist, biographer. Born in La Creuse, France, daughter of André Chandernagor, a government official and congressman, Françoise graduated from the Ecole Nationale d'Administration in 1969. She was nominated to the Conseil d'Etat (State Council) in 1978, where she occupied a high position, and is currently member of the literary Académie Goncourt. After an important political career, she published her first novel *The King's Way* (1981), inspired by the life of Madame de Maintenon, Louis XIV's mistress; it was made into a film in 1995. Having taken a sabbatical from her public service position, she started writing a romantic trilogy in a historical context: *Leçons de ténèbres* ('Lessons of Darkness'). In *La sans pareille* ('The Unequalled Woman,' 1988), *L'archange de Vienne* ('Vienna's Archangel,' 1989), and *L'enfant aux loups* ('The Wolf Child, 1990), she depicts the mores of political figures, particularly Christine Valbray's, 'la sans pareille,' a Machiavellian character. With *La première épouse* ('The First Wife,' 1998), she abandons the historical genre to write a confessional novel about the degree of servitude that a woman can reach to keep her husband from leaving her.

AP-Z

Chang, Eileen (*see* Zhang Ailing)

Chauvet, Marie (Marie Vieux) (1919–1972), Haitian novelist. Chauvet was born in Port-au-Prince. Her father was a well-known political figure and her mother was from the Virgin Islands. She studied at the Ecole Normale d'Institutrices to teach in elementary school. She married and divorced twice and died in exile in New York, where she had been teaching at Columbia University. Her first publication was a play, *La légende des fleurs* ('The Legend of Flowers,' 1947), which expressed her desire for solidarity. *Fille d'Haïti* ('Daughter of Haiti,' 1954) and *Dance on a Volcano* (1957) were her first two novels, anchored in the culture and injustices of her island. *Fonds-des-Nègres* (1960) is a peasant novel about poverty, deforestation, and the role of voodoo in politics. *Amour, Colère, Folie* ('Love, Anger, Madness,' 1968), which precipitated Chauvet's exile, is a courageous indictment of the cruelty of the Duvalier dictatorship and the corruption rampant in upper-class Haitian society, as well as an avant-gardist take on female sexuality. The book was quickly withdrawn from circulation. *Rapaces* ('Predators,' 1986) was published in Haiti posthumously the year of the Duvaliers' departure. A painful portrayal of oppression, it also presents the writer as an agent of change.

JV

Chavez, Denise (*b*. 1948), US novelist, playwright. Born in Las Cruces, New Mexico, Chavez earned an MA in creative writing from the University of New Mexico. The author of many plays, she is well-known for her performance art, especially her one-woman play *Women in the State of Grace*. Her work is informed by feminism, her Mexican heritage, the American Southwest, and her desire to give voice to the poor and the marginalized. Her first novel *The Last of the Menu Girls* (1986), comprised of seven related stories, tells of the coming of age of Rocio Esquibel, who, in trying to decide what kind of woman she will be, decides to write the stories of the women in her community. *Face of an Angel* (1994; American Book Award) is a comic novel about a waitress in New Mexico who writes 'The Book of Service,'

ostensibly a handbook for waitresses, but really a series of reflections on what waiting and serving means to women. A highly unconventional narrative, it is interspersed with anecdotes, monologues, and polemics. Chavez has edited an anthology of Latina dramatists *Shattering the Myth: Plays by Hispanic Women* (1992).

JEM

Chawaf, Chantal (*b*. 1943), French writer. Born in Boulogne during a bomb raid that left both her parents dead, Chawaf was adopted by an upper-class couple. She studied at the Ecole du Louvre and lived briefly in the Middle East. She has two children. Her first novel *Mother Love Mother Earth* (1974) relates the difficult birth of a girl and the symbiotic relationship between mother and daughter. The language used in this narrative attempts to translate the body into words, an attempt she sees as liberating for men and women alike. *Redemption* (1989) presents a reflection on language and its symbolic function. Other themes that recur in her texts are motherhood in *Cercoeur* (1975) and *Chair chaude* ('Warm Flesh,' 1976); childhood in *Blé de semences* ('Sowing Wheat,' 1976) and *Fées de toujours* ('Forever Fairies,' 1988); death in *Crépusculaires* ('Dusks,' 1982) and *Rougeâtre* ('Reddish,' 1978). She wrote a theoretical series of texts in *Le corps et le verbe: la langue en sens inverse* ('Body and Verb: Language in Reverse,' 1992). Her last autofiction *Le manteau noir* ('Black Coat,' 1998) goes back to the search for her lost origins, linking death and birth once more.

JV

Chedid, Andrée (*b*. 1920), French novelist, poet. Born Andrée Saab in Cairo in an Egyptian family of Lebanese ancestry, Chedid received her education mostly in French schools in Cairo and Paris. She studied journalism at the American University in Cairo. She married Louis Chedid, a medical scientist. After three years in Lebanon, they moved to Paris in

1946. They have two children. She wrote her first of over fifteen collections of poetry, *On the Trails of My Fancy*, in English in 1943. Carefully constructed, her poems present a polysemic reflection on the role of the poet, archetypes, poetic form, sound, space, rhythm, and meaning. Her first novel *From Sleep Unbound* (1952), which takes place in the Middle East, tells of the harsh life of a young woman married without her consent, and of the solidarity among women that transcends all religious, age, and class differences. *The Sixth Day* (1960), about the relationship of a young boy and his grandmother, has been made into a movie (1986). Her fiction often returns to Egypt or to Lebanon, as in *Return to Beirut* (1985). *Les saisons de passage* ('Passing Seasons,' 1996) is a nonlinear autobiography revolving around her mother's death. Chedid has been awarded many prestigious literary prizes worldwide.

JV

Chen Jingrong (1917–1995), Chinese poet, essayist, translator. A native of Sichuan Province, Chen audited courses at the Peking and Qinghua Universities in Beijing in 1935–6 but for the most part studied literature on her own. In the 1940s she published two volumes of poetry, a collection of essays, and translations of Hans Christian Andersen and Victor Hugo, among others. In 1948 she went to Shanghai where she worked as an editor for the journal *Xin shi* ('New Poetry'). After the founding of the People's Republic of China in 1949, she worked primarily as an editor for various literary journals and as a translator. Her translations of Baudelaire and Rilke, in particular, exerted a significant influence on aspiring young writers during the Cultural Revolution (1966–76), some of whom were to become major poets in their own right when China opened its door to the free world in the late 1970s and early 1980s. Chen's poetry of the 1940s, along with that of eight fellow poets, was rediscovered and given the

recognition that it deserves. Collectively, the nine poets are referred to as 'the School of Nine Leaves'; they have inspired a new generation of poets in the 1980s and beyond. Chen's early poetry is introspective, meditative, and symbolist, while her later work from the 1970s onward bespeaks unswerving faith in beauty, nature, and life. English translations of her poetry appear in several anthologies.

MY

Ch'en Jo-hsi (*see* Chen Ruoxi)

Chen Lucy (*see* Chen Ruoxi)

Chen Ran (*b.* 1962), Chinese fiction writer. Chen Ran was born in Beijing. After her graduation from a college in Beijing in 1986, she first remained at her alma mater as a teacher, and then worked as a newspaper reporter and later as a publishing house editor. She now resides in Beijing, working as a professional writer. Chen began publishing stories during her college years; her early stories were about college life and the restless urban youth. Her first collection of stories, *Zhi pan'er* ('Paper,' 1989), however, was a departure from her college themes: the stories are mystic and indeterminate, centering on the characters' internal conflicts. In addition to her novella *Siren shenghuo* ('Private Life,' 1996), she has published several story collections, including *Zuichun li de yangguang* ('The Sunbeam from the Lips,' 1992), *Yu wangshi gaobei* ('Saying Goodbye to Things Past,' 1994), and *Du yu ren* ('A Person Talking to Herself,' 1995). Chen's stories are intensely introverted and subjective, often featuring a first-person narrator. She focuses on sexual and gender matters in contemporary and urban China and is well-known for her psychological explorations of female characters. Her stories pursue a wide range of themes in women's private lives, including growing up, heterosexual love, lesbianism, and friendship between women.

JZ

Chen Ruoxi (Ch'en Jo-hsi; Chen Lucy) (*b.* 1938), Chinese/Taiwan fiction writer. Chen Ruoxi is the pen name of Chen Xiumei. Born into a working-class family in rural Taipei, Taiwan, Chen entered National Taiwan University in 1957. That year she published her first short story in the prestigious *Literary Review*. During her junior year Chen and her classmates, including Bai Xianyong (Pai Hsien-yung), Li Oufan (Leo Ou-fan Lee), and Liu Shaoming (Joseph S. M. Lau), founded the influential *Xiandai wenxue* ('Modern Literature'). Her first collection of short stories in English translation, *Spirit Calling*, was published in 1961. That same year she entered Mount Holyoke College, transferring a year later to Johns Hopkins University, from which she received an MA in English in 1965. There she met her husband Duan Shiyao (Tuann Shih-yao), who was also from Taiwan. The couple moved to the People's Republic of China in 1966, in the hope of working toward the reconstruction of their long-lost motherland. This dream was shattered by the Cultural Revolution. After seven traumatic years they were allowed to leave China for Hong Kong. In 1979 Chen became a researcher at the Center for Chinese Studies at the University of California, Berkeley, and since then, has lived primarily in Berkeley and Taipei. Her stories written between 1974 and 1978 are mostly based on her personal experience of the Cultural Revolution and powerfully capture its unprecedented repression and distortion of humanity. These stories were an instant success and represent a watershed in the history of modern Chinese fiction.

MY

Chikwe, Kema (*b.* 1947), Nigerian children's writer, nonfiction writer, publisher. Chikwe was born in Egbu, Owerri, Imo State, Nigeria to Igbo parents, Nathan Okeoma Ejiogu and Amelia Ejiogu. She received her early education in Nigeria, and was granted both a BA in French (1976) and an MA in French education (1977) from Queens College, City University of New York. She also earned a PhD in curriculum education from the University of Nigeria, Nsukka, in 1995. She is married to Chief Herbert O. N. Chikwe and is the mother of four children. In 1999, she was sworn in as Minister of Transport in the Obasanjo government, Abuja, in Nigeria. She is the publisher of *Asha*, a children's magazine, and the owner of a publishing company, Primetime Ltd. She has written several children's books: *Kame Chameleon Tours the Garden* (1991), *Dobia's Secrets* (1992), *First School Day for Adaeze* (1992), and *My Precious Book* (1992). She is also the author of *Women and New Orientation: A Profile of Igbo Women in History* (1994). She highlights the contributions made by Nigerian women and the importance of depicting the youth, culture, and history of Nigeria in juvenile material.

MBr

Chiranan Pitpreecha (Chiranan Prasertkul) (*b.* 1955), Thai poet. Chiranan Pitpreecha, an advocate of women's rights, was born in Trang, a southern province of Thailand. Encouraged by her mother, the owner of a bookstore, and her language teacher, she started writing short poems when she was 13. She came to Bangkok to enroll as a science student at Chulalongkorn University and became very involved in the student movement of the time. She was one of the student activists who played a vital role in the October 14, 1973 uprising. She left for the 'jungles' after the political turmoil of October 6, 1976, and returned to Bangkok in 1981. She went with her husband Seksan Prasertkul, a former student leader, to the US to study for an advanced degree in history at Cornell University. She is now back in Thailand, writing poetry and working on her PhD dissertation. Her collection of poems *Bai Mai Thi Hai Pai* ('The Lost Leaf'), which recounts her experience in the 'jungles,' won the Southeast Asia (S.E.A.) Write Award in 1989.

NM

Ch'oe Chŏnghŭi (1906–1990), South Korean fiction writer. Born in a northern part of Korea, Ch'oe graduated from a special school for childcare in Seoul; she worked in a kindergarten in Tokyo and as a reporter in Seoul. She made her literary debut in 1931. Her writings tend to be confessional in style, audacious in subject matter, and emotionally engaging yet tightly controlled by objective distance. Her early works represent the difficulties 'New Women' faced in the wake of their attempts at self-determination in sexual matters. 'The Haunted House' (1937), 'Chimaek' ('Vein of Earth,' 1939), and 'Ch'ŏnmaek' ('Vein of Heaven,' 1941), among others, reveal women's struggles for psychological survival while dealing with issues of single motherhood, divorce, or illegitimate children. Her later works – most representatively, In'gansa ('Human History,' 1960) – interweave her earlier concerns into Korea's larger political and historical events in the post-liberation period. Several works of short fiction are available in English translation, including 'Hospital Room 205' (1970) and 'Round and Round the Pagoda' (1975).

K-HC

Ch'oe Yun (Choi Hyunmoo) (b. 1953), Korean fiction writer, literary critic. A precocious, avid reader of fiction, Ch'oe had a childhood dream of becoming a cartoonist. She got her BA and MA in Korean literature at Sŏgang University, Seoul, 1972–8. With a PhD in modern French literature from the University of Provence, France (1983), she has been a professor of French at Sŏgang since 1984. One of the most thought-provoking writers today, her major works address crucial sociopolitical and cultural issues of contemporary Korea. Her debut novella, 'Chŏgi sori ŏpsi hanjŏm kkonnip i chigo' ('There, a Petal Silently Falls,' 1988), depicts the brutal

victimization of innocent citizens during the Korean government's 1980 massacre in Kwangju City. 'The Gray Snowman' (1992), the winner of the Tong'in Literary Award, retraces student underground, antigovernment resistance of the 1970s. In 'Bŏngŏri ch'ang' ('A Song of a Mute,' 1989), 'His Father's Keeper' (1990), and 'Soksagim, soksagim' ('Whisper, Whisper,' 1993), she examines the ideological ambiguity and complexity of Korean War experiences. 'The Last of Hanak'o' (1994), the winner of the Yi Sang Literary Prize, critiques the fatuity of contemporary Korean male college-student culture, which devalues their female colleagues. Ch'oe, together with her husband, Patrick Maurus, has published a number of translations of contemporary Korean fiction into French.

Y-HK

Christensen, Inger (b. 1935), Danish poet, novelist. Born in Vejle, and married for seventeen years to the Danish writer Poul Borum, Christensen is likely the most important and widely read woman poet in Denmark since "Tove Ditlevsen. She received a teaching certificate from Århus Seminary, and taught for several years before becoming a full-time writer in 1964. Her first collection of poetry Lys ('Light') appeared in 1962 and was followed by Græs ('Grass') in 1963, but it was the complex, best selling, systemic poem Det ('It,' 1969) which established her reputation as a major late modernist poet. Her main concerns in her poetry are the relationships between language, nature, and biology. Her 1981 work Alfabet ('Alphabet') contains poems for each letter of the alphabet through 'n', each poem progressively longer based on the mathematical progression of the Fibonacci series. In addition to the poetry collections Brev i april ('Letters in April,' 1979) and Sommerfugledalen ('Valley of the Butterflies,' 1991), Christensen has written several experimental novels, plays, and children's books. The winner of many prestigious

European literary awards, including the Swedish Academy Stora Nordisk Pris, her work has been included in numerous anthologies and translated into several languages.

MHH

Chuah Guat Eng (*b.* 1943), Malaysian novelist, short story writer. Chuah was born in Rembau, Negeri Sembilan, and comes from a Chinese Peranakan family. She studied English at the University of Malaya, where she later taught before going to the Ludwig-Maximillan University in Munich to study modern German literature. She worked in advertising for over twenty-two years. She has three children and now writes full-time. Her first and much celebrated novel *Echoes of Silence* (1994) was one of the first two post-Independence Anglophone novels by a woman (the other is by *Marie Gerrina Louis, published the same year). The novel deals with various 'silences' encountered by colonial and postcolonial subjects in Malaysia. It examines poverty, deception, and betrayal within the female protagonist's family. By incorporating romance with the mystery genre, Chuah deals with issues of contemporary concerns as well as subverting the norms of the mystery novel. Her short stories explore diverse life situations, from the male-dominated world of business ('The Power of Advertising,' 1992) to domestic issues of extramarital affairs and guilt ('Forbidden Fruit,' 1992); her subjects range from good parenting ('The Old House,' 1992) to a woman's fear of aging and spinsterhood ('The Day Andy Warhol Died,' 1992). Often, Chuah's stories illuminate the tension between a woman's sense of empowerment and her need to depend on a man.

NFAM

Chudamani, R. (*b.* 1931), Indian short story writer, novelist. R. Chudamani became a writer with the publication of her first story, 'Kaveri,' in 1957. Her first novel, *Manathukku Iniyaval* ('Woman Close to the Heart'), was published in 1960. Born and brought up in Chennai, where she still lives, she is the daughter of Kanakavalli, her artistic mother who encouraged her to write. Although basically a Tamil writer, she also writes short stories in English as Chudamani Raghavan. Her prize-winning play *Iruvar Kandanar* ('Two Persons Witnessed') has been frequently performed. She has received many literary awards. She is a low-profile writer who has quietly made a place for herself in the Tamil literary field, resisting any bandwagon climbing, both politically and linguistically. Her stories are not loud and proclamatory. The core concern of her stories is human life as it is lived in the present day. Women in her stories emerge as characters braving the strong winds of life, fighting and resisting and sometimes succumbing. Her language is poetic and lyrical, catching the subtlest of emotions with ease and dexterity. One of her novellas, *Iravuchchudar* ('Night Spark'), was translated into English as *Yamini* in 1996.

CSL

Chudori, Leila (*b.* 1962), Indonesian short story writer. Born in Jakarta, Chudori began writing short stories during her high school years. After graduating from Trent University, Canada, in 1988, she worked as a journalist for the magazines *Jakarta Jakarta* and *Tempo*. Her short stories are frequently marked by intertextuality, with links to other works of literature both in Indonesian and English. 'Adila' (1989), for example, is the disturbing story of a teenage girl, addicted to sniffing insecticide, whose dreams of emancipation are fueled by her hallucinations of encounters with literary characters, among them Ursula Brangwen from *The Rainbow* and Stephen Dedalus from *A Portrait of the Artist as a Young Man*. 'The Purification of Sita' (1987) is a feminist 'take' on the *Mahabharata* story of Rama and Sita. In the original story, Sita is required to prove that she has been faithful to her husband during thirteen years of separation; in Chudori's version, Sita dares to ask her husband whether he was tempted to sleep with other women during their separation. 'Letter for Wai Tsz' (1998) invokes lines from Shakespeare's *As You Like It* in its exposition of the economic collapse and consequent social upheaval in Asia. The protagonists of Chudori's stories are often strong and eccentric, like the compulsive-obsessive newspaper editor in 'A Red Book and Carbolic Acid' (1985) who goes to jail rather than compromise his principles.

PA

Chughtai, Ismat (1915–1991), Indian fiction writer. Born in Badayun, India, Chughtai took her BA in Lucknow and was the first woman to earn a teaching degree from Aligarh University. A risk-taker and a feminist when the word was not yet fashionable, she created a furor in 1942 when her story 'Lihaf' ('The Quilt') was charged with obscenity by a Lahore court. Undaunted, she continued to write frankly about women's inner lives and their roles in Indian society. Her work, paving the way for those writing about women's lives who wished to scrutinize previously taboo social themes, was a turning point in Urdu fiction. She wrote novels, stories, plays, and essays, and produced scripts and stories for five films in which she collaborated with her husband, Shahid Latif. Her novels include *The Crooked Line* (1944), *The Heart Breaks Free* and *The Wild One* (published together in English translation, 1993), *Eik Qatra-e Khun* ('A Drop of Blood'), and *Masooma* (1962). She published numerous short story collections. Fifteen of her stories are available in English translation in *The Quilt and Other Stories* (1990). She received the Ghalib Award, the Maqdoom Literary Award, the President's Award for the best film story, *Garm Hawa* ('Hot Air'), and the prestigious Iqbal Award for Urdu Literature in 1989.

TN

Chukovskaia, Lidiia Korneevna (*b.* 1907), Russian critic, editor, memoirist, novelist, poet. Daughter of the famous children's writer Kornei Chukovsky, Chukovskaia dedicated most of her life to the preservation of others' achievements and writings, especially her father's, as recorded in her autobiographical *To the Memory of a Childhood* (1983), and the poet Anna Akhmatova's, preserved in her *Notes on Anna Akhmatova* (1938–41). Taught by her father to appreciate cultural values and their manifestation in political action, Chukovskaia championed the causes of Sinyavsky, Brodsky, and Solzhenitsyn, and was expelled from the Soviet Writers' Union in 1974 as a dissident critic. In addition to essays and poetry, Chukovskaia wrote two novels: *Sofia Petrovna* (1989; first translated as *The Deserted House*, 1967) and *Going Under* (1989; translated in the 1970s). Both narrate personal losses under Stalinism and the price of survival under inhuman daily conditions, while implicitly affirming the values of integrity and dedication to moral causes.

HG

Chung Ling (*see* Zhong Ling)

Churchill, Caryl (*b.* 1938), British playwright. Born in London, daughter of a political cartoonist and an actress, Churchill attended school in Montreal before returning to England to study at Lady Margaret Hall, Oxford, where her plays *Downstairs* (1958) and *Having a Wonderful Time* (1960) were produced. After graduating in 1960, she wrote radio plays, including *The Ants* (1962) and *Identical Twins* (1968), and the stage plays *Owners* (1972), written on commission for the Royal Court Theatre, *Objections to Sex and Violence* (1975), and *Light Shining in Buckinghamshire* (1976), written for the Joint Stock Theatre Company. Her acclaimed play *Cloud Nine* (1979), half of which takes place in colonial Africa in the late nineteenth century, the other half in

London in 1979, boldly counterpoints sexism and colonialism, personal and political oppression. Churchill, a socialist and feminist whose style was influenced by Brecht, experiments with cross-gender and cross-race casting with startling and powerful results. The Obie Award-winning *Top Girls* (1982) depicts the choices that women make to succeed in a capitalist, male-dominated world; the opening scene assembles famous women from history at a dinner party. Churchill has also written *Vinegar Tom* (1976), *Fen* (1983), *Softcops* (1984), which satirizes the criminal system, and *Serious Money* (1987; Obie Award), about thrills and corruption in the stock market. Recent plays include *Lives of the Great Poisoners* (1992) and *The Striker* (1994).

DVT

Cialente, Fausta (1898–1994), Italian novelist. Born in Cagliari, Sardinia, Cialente traveled widely, her family following the father, an officer in the army. In 1921 she married the music composer Enrico Terni; they had one daughter. They moved to Alexandria, Egypt, where Cialente participated intensely in literary and political life. In 1940 she began working for the Allies writing antifascist pamphlets and making daily broadcasts from Radio Cairo. In 1947 she returned to Italy where she lived until moving permanently into England in 1984. Her first book *Natalia* ('Natalie,' 1929) won the prestigious Dieci Savi Prize, but the story of a woman's lesbian relationship and her unhappy and childless marriage could hardly please the Fascist censorship and the book was suppressed. In *Cortile a Cleopatra* ('Courtyard to Cleopatra,' 1936) and *The Levantines* (1961) Cialente portrayed the lives of émigrés in Egypt in a style that fuses personal memory and fiction. Her last novel, *Le quattro ragazze Wieselberger* ('The Four Wieselberger Girls,' 1976), which won the important Strega Prize, interweaved the history of Italy with the dissolution of her family and its rebirth

through the act of writing her own and her mother's stories.

GMi

Cisneros, Sandra (*b.* 1954), US fiction writer, poet. Born in Chicago, Cisneros was educated at Loyola University and the University of Iowa. She has been a writer-in-residence at several universities in the US. Her first book, the poetry chapbook *Bad Boys*, was published in 1980. She is best known for the prose work *The House on Mango Street* (1984; American Book Award). Comprised of forty-four brief vignettes, written in simple yet beautifully lyrical language, it depicts Mexican-American life in a Chicago barrio. The young narrator, Esperanza Cordero, tells of racism and poverty but also of love and humor and community. In *Woman Hollering Creek and Other Stories* (1991), Cisneros moves out of the barrio and into the wider world, where cultures clash and her Chicana characters struggle to shape their own lives or create their own art. Her interests in gender, ethnicity, language, and place are also central to her collections of poetry. Her poetic voice in *My Wicked, Wicked Ways* (1987) and *Loose Woman* (1994) is bold, energetic, erotic, and transgressive.

JEM

Cixous, Hélène (*b.* 1937), French writer, dramatist. Born in Oran and brought up in Algeria, Cixous is of mixed heritage (French, German, Spanish, and Jewish). A professor of English literature, she founded – and is the director of – the Centre de Recherches en Etudes Féminines at the Université Paris VIII. Since her first work of fiction, *Le prénom de Dieu* ('God's First Name,' 1967), she has published a voluminous oeuvre, blending autobiography, fiction, and theory. *Inside* (1969), for which Cixous won the Prix Medicis, is about her father's death, a recurrent theme. In *The Newly Born Woman* (1975), she presents her controversial concept of 'feminine writing,' while the bilingual *Vivre l'orange/To Live the Orange* (1979) demonstrates its inventive language play to the full as well as Cixous's admiration for the Brazilian writer *Clarice Lispector. Cixous's fictions are all characterized by richly connotative poetical language and intertextuality, although she has recently moved from women-centered concerns to more universal themes such as loving and losing, as in *Déluge* ('Deluge,' 1992). In collaboration with Ariane Mnouchkine's Théâtre du Soleil, she has written a series of epic, historical, and political plays, winning the Prix des critiques for a play about AIDS, *La ville parjure ou le réveil des Erinyes* ('The Traitor Town or the Awakening of Furies,' 1994).

GR

Clampitt, Amy (1920–1994), US poet. Born in New Providence, Iowa, Clampitt was educated at Grinnell College, in Iowa, where she earned a BA in English, Columbia University, and the New School for Social Research. She worked as a secretary, librarian, editor, and freelance writer. She began writing poetry in the 1960s, and in 1974, at her own expense, published a poetry chapbook, *Multitudes, Multitudes*. Her first full-length volume of poetry *The Kingfisher* was published to great acclaim in 1983, when she was 63. It was followed by four more volumes – *What the Light Was Like* (1985), *Archaic Figure* (1987), *Westward* (1990), and *A Silence Opens* (1994) – each of which added to her reputation as an important poet. She died of ovarian cancer in 1994. Her ornate, dense, and challenging poetry has been compared by critics to that of Gerard Manley Hopkins, Marianne Moore, and Elizabeth Bishop. She focuses intensely on the natural world in her descriptions, but then shifts into surprising revelations of moral or metaphysical import. Her characteristic themes are time, change, memory, and death. Some of her most moving poems recall her parents and her Midwestern childhood. Her syntax is intricate, her vocabulary endlessly rich, her allusions plentiful though sometimes obscure. Clampitt also published *Predecessors, et Cetera* (1991), a collection of essays on poetry. She was awarded a MacArthur Fellowship in 1992 . Her *Collected Poems* was published in 1997.

JEM

Clarke, Gillian (*b*. 1937), Welsh poet. Born in Cardiff, Wales, Clarke received a BA from University College, Cardiff, in 1958. After graduation, she worked for the BBC for several years; she has also taught art history and creative writing, and served as the editor of the *Anglo-Welsh Review* from 1976 to 1984. Her first book of poetry, *Snow on the Mountain*, was published in 1971. Her poetry is concerned with the natural world and rural life in her native Wales. She writes of Celtic traditions and myths, and incorporates into the rhythms and syntax of her poetry the metrical devices of traditional Welsh poetry. She privileges the usually unrecorded domestic experiences of women, but also voices political concerns in the larger world, often feminist or environmental. Her poetry is vivid and lyrical, and its visual and sensual imagery celebrates the physical world and the evocative power of material objects. Her volumes of poetry include *The Sundial* (1978), *Letters from a Far Country* (1982), *The King of Britain's Daughter* (1993), and *Five Fields* (1998). Her *Collected Poems* was published in 1997. She translated Menna Elfyn's Welsh poems in *Cell Angel* (1996).

JEM

Clément, Catherine (*b*. 1939), French essayist, novelist. Clément studied philosophy in Paris as well as psychoanalysis with Jacques Lacan; she wrote his biography in 1981. She has worked as a professor, a journalist for the French daily *Le Matin* and a diplomat for the French government's Ministry of Foreign Relations. A postmodernist and Marxist feminist, she is a prolific author of essays and novels. She is best known for co-authoring *The Newly Born Woman* (1975) with *Hélène Cixous. She also wrote a brilliant analysis of women represented in operas as well as women who sing operas and the demands placed upon them in *Opera: the Undoing of Women* (1979). Her irony and sense of humor creep inevitably into her essays and fiction, the subjects of which include the French intellectual scene since World War II in *La putain du diable* ('The Devil's Whore,' 1996), French writer Philippe Sollers, and the Austrian Empress Sissi. Clément has written a fictional biography of Martin Heidegger, his wife, and Hannah Arendt. Her most recent works include *Le féminin et le sacré* ('The Feminine and the Sacred,' 1998), a travelogue written with *Julia Kristeva which presents their thoughts about culture and religion from a Western feminist perspective.

             JV

Cliff, Michelle (*b.* 1946), Jamaican-US novelist. Born in Kingston, Jamaica, a light-skinned daughter of the middle class, Cliff was educated at Wagner College in New York City (BA, 1969) and London's Warburg Institute (MPhil, 1974). Her work combines a scholarly reexamination of the past with a lyrical creation of histories. She describes her project in *The Land of Look Behind* (1985) to be one of writing 'as a complete Caribbean woman' and 'retracing the African part ... reclaiming as our own ... history sunk under the canefields, or gone to bush.' All three of her novels – *Abeng* (1984), *No Telephone to Heaven* (1987), and *Free Enterprise* (1993) – deal with the African diaspora in the Americas, and with women's experience of enslavement and colonization. Notable for her feminist work, she edited the journal *Sinister Wisdom* with *Adrienne Rich from 1981 to 1983. She also edited a collection of Lillian Smith's work, *The Winner Names the Age* (1978). Other writings include a prose-poem, *Claiming an Identity They Taught Me to Despise* (1980), and a collection of short stories,

Bodies of Water (1990). Cliff is currently Allan K. Smith Professor of English at Trinity College in Hartford, Connecticut.

             JES

Clifton, (Thelma) Lucille (*b.* 1936), US poet, children's writer. Born in Depew, New York, Clifton was educated at Howard University and Fredonia State Teachers' College. She married Fred J. Clifton in 1958 (who died in 1984); they had six children. She worked for government agencies in New York State and Washington, D.C. and has taught creative writing at several colleges and universities in the US. Her first volume of poetry *Good Times* was published in 1969. Her identity as an African-American woman is central to her poetry. She writes of female experience, the history of her race, and the history of her family. The inherent optimism of her work is informed by her religion. Her voice is direct, clear, full of passion and humor; her style is concentrated, unadorned, often unpunctuated. The two genres in *Good Woman: Poems and a Memoir, 1969–80* (1987) emphasize the relation of her poetry to her life. *Next* (1987) confronts death and loss, *Quilting* (1991) celebrates the history of women, and *The Terrible Stories* (1996) deals unflinchingly with cancer. Her other volumes of poetry include *Good News about the Earth* (1972), *Two-Headed Woman* (1980), and *The Book of Light* (1993). Clifton has also written numerous works for children.

             JEM

Colasanti, Marina (*b.* 1937), Brazilian short story writer, journalist. A prolific writer, born in Asmara, Ethiopia, Colasanti lived in Italy during her early childhood years and in 1948 immigrated with her family to Brazil. She received a degree in fine arts from the Federal University in Rio de Janeiro. She has worked for Brazilian television, was the editor of *Nova*, and wrote for several other magazines as well as the prestigious newspaper *Jornal do Brasil*. In addition to being a fiction writer (chronicles, short stories, and children's literature) and a journalist, she is also a translator, publicist, and artist. Her works include elements of the fantastic as she rewrites and parodies fairy tales, as in *Uma idéia toda azul* ('An All Blue Idea,' 1979), *Doze reis e a moça no labirinto do vento* ('Twelve Kings and the Girl in the Wind's Labyrinth,' 1982), and *A menina arco-íris* ('The Rainbow Girl,' 1984). Colasanti often analyzes issues related to women's sexuality and sensuality, and examines the experience of loving and being loved in *A nova mulher* ('The New Woman,' 1980), *Os contos do amor rasgado* ('Torn-up Love Stories,' 1986), and *E por falar em amor* ('Speaking about Love,' 1987).

MJB

Collen, Lindsey (*b.* 1948), Mauritian novelist. Collen was born in Umtata, Transkei, South Africa to Scottish immigrant parents. She attended the University of Witwatersrand, where she became involved in the anti-apartheid movement, and the London School of Economics. She has held a wide variety of jobs, including teacher, nurse's assistant, secretary, and potato harvester. A political activist, she has lived in Mauritius since 1974 and is married to Ram Seegobin, a doctor and trade union activist. Her first novel *There is a Trade* was published in 1990. Her second novel *The Rape of Sita* (1993; Commonwealth Writers Prize) prompted an international uproar when, shortly after its publication, Collen was faced with death threats and the book was banned in Mauritius because religious fundamentalists objected to the use of the name of a sacred Hindu deity in the title. The novel was also controversial for its powerful use of rape as a metaphor through which Collen explores questions of colonial and masculine power. Her third novel is titled *Getting Rid of It* (1997).

NW-T, JEM

Collins, Merle (*b.* 1950), Grenadian poet, novelist. Collins grew up under the

post-independence rule of E. M. Gairy and joined Maurice Bishop's revolutionary government in 1979, becoming popular as a performer of her poetry at rallies and meetings of the Workers' Parish Councils. After the US invasion of 1983, she went to England and worked as a teacher/researcher at the Polytechnic of North London. As a member of 'African Dawn,' she performed her poetry and a mix of Afro-Caribbean music and drama. Her first volume of poetry *Because the Dawn Breaks, Poems Dedicated to the Grenadian People* (1985) alludes to the inevitability of revolution. With Rhonda Cobham, she edited *Watchers and Seekers* (1987), a collection of writings by black British women. *Angel* (1987), her first novel, is a coming-of-age narrative paralleling Grenada's independence to the story of three generations of women. A short story collection *Rain Darling* appeared in 1990, and a second volume of poetry, *Rotten Pomerack*, in 1992. *The Colour of Forgetting* (1995), her third novel, is a lyrical tribute to the Caribbean, past and present. She now teaches in the Department of English and Comparative Literature at the University of Maryland (College Park)

MHL

Condé, Maryse (*b.* 1937), Guadeloupean novelist. Born to a bourgeois family in Pointe-à-Pitre, Condé later based *Tree of Life* (1987) on the racial and class dichotomies perpetuated by their obsession with social mobility. Always ready to challenge authority, she believes writing to be a revelation of painful truths and dangerous illusions. Her first novel *Heremakhonon* (1976), written after moving to Guinea with her first husband and becoming involved in African independence, was intended to denounce Sékou Touré and African socialism, and to warn against constructions of Africa as a 'paradise' for descendants distanced by geography and time. However, it was misread as a rejection of the Continent. *A Season in Rihata* (1981) relates the story of an already-decayed, contemporary African society while *Segu* (1984), which was a bestseller in France, details an African kingdom's decline through the slave trade and French colonialism. *I, Tituba, Black Witch of Salem* (1986) gives voice to a marginalized figure from the Salem 'witch trials.' The mosaic of voices in *Crossing the Mangrove* (1989) emphasizes the creation of Caribbean oral traditions through the creolized, fluid nature of Caribbean identity. The author of numerous critical essays also, Condé has garnered the prestigious Le Grand Prix Litteraire de la Femme.

GAn

Constant, Paule (*b.* 1944), French novelist. Born in Gan (Pyrénées-Atlantiques), Constant spent many years in French Guyana and in Africa, where her father served as a military doctor. She married Auguste Bourgeade, a doctor. She received her doctorate from the Sorbonne and is a Professor of French literature at the Université d'Aix-Marseille III. The three continents where she lived provide the geographic locations of her seven novels, with the most recent, *Confidence pour confidence* ('Confidence for Confidence,' 1998) taking place in the midwestern US. *Ouregano* (1980; prix Valéry Larbaud) and *Balta* (1983) present the lives of two children in a postcolonial Africa. *White Spirit* (1989; Grand Prix du Roman de l'Académie française) explores the sense of alienation felt by men and women confronting the dehumanization of 'progress.' *The Governor's Daughter* (1994) portrays a young girl taken by her parents to French Guyana, where she suffers from the repulsive life imposed on her by their neglect. Two novels set in France, *Propriété privée* ('Private Estate,' 1981) and *Le grand Ghâpal* ('The Large Ghapal,' 1991; Prix Gabrielle d'Estrées), and an essay, *Un monde à l'usage des Demoiselles* ('A World Made for Young Aristocratic Girls,' 1987), deal with the subject of the education of young women from the Middle Ages to the eight-

eenth century. The essay won the Grand Prix de l'Académie française, the first ever awarded to a woman.

GAd

Constante, Lena (*b.* 1909), Romanian writer. An artist and creator of puppets, Constante was born in Bucharest. In her youth, she traveled from Odessa to Paris and London, studied fine arts and – back home – took part in the ethno-sociological researches conducted by D. Gusti; this gave her an opportunity to discover and study Romanian folk art, which was to become her main source of inspiration. Victim of the first communist purges in postwar Romania, she was arrested and sentenced to life imprisonment in 1950, together with the musicologist Harry Brauner (whom she would marry after being released from prison in 1962). Her prison memoirs *Evadarea tăcută* ('The Silent Escape: 3000 Days of Loneliness in the Romanian Prisons,' 1990; ADELF prize, Paris, 1992; Romanian Academy prize, 1994) and *Evadarea imposibilă* ('The Impossible Escape,' 1993) are among the most important testimonies on the horrors, crimes and ways of survival in the Romanian communist prisons of the 1950s; they also offer an intellectual and moral model of 'resistance.' The literary success of Constante the writer outshone her previously established fame as an artist. A film, *Nebunia capetelor* ('The Madness of the Heads,' 1997), was made of both works by the young German director Thomas Ciulei.

IB

Cooper, Afua (*b.* 1958), Jamaican-Canadian poet. Cooper was born in Westmoreland, Jamaica and later moved to Kingston with her family. Since 1980, she has made her home in Toronto. She holds an MA from the Ontario Institute for Studies in Education and is currently pursuing a doctorate in African-Canadian women's history at the University of Toronto. Her main collection of poetry, *Memories Have Tongue* (1992), was preceded by a poetry collection for children, *The Red Caterpillar on College Street* (1989) and that by *Breaking Chains* (1984). First runner-up for the 1992 Casa de las Américas prize for poetry, the poems comprising *Memories Have Tongue* bring to life the often overlooked historical, cultural, mythological, and spiritual presences of black and indigenous women in the Caribbean, the US, and Canada. Cooper's poetry pays attention to the oral and the historical, and often employs poetic forms which are influenced by patois, Reggae music, Rastafarianism, and public traditions of informative protest.

LB

Cope, Wendy (*b*. 1945), British poet. Born in Erith, Kent, Cope attended St Hilda's College, Oxford, where she earned a BA in 1966 and an MA in 1970, and Westminster College of Education, Oxford. She taught at primary and junior schools from 1967 to 1986; she has since worked as a writer full-time. Her first full-length collection *Making Cocoa for Kingsley Amis* (1986) was a critical and popular success. Full of biting humor and satire, the volume features brilliant parodies, many of them written by 'Jason Strugnell,' an unpleasant and inferior poet invented by Cope. *Serious Concerns* (1992) also contains carefully crafted parodies and humorous poems, but includes several touching love poems as well, challenging readers, as the title indicates, to look beyond the jokes. Cope has also published two small-press volumes, *Does She Like Word-Games?* (1988) and *Men and Their Boring Arguments* (1988); *The River Girl* (1991), a long narrative poem commissioned as a play for a marionette company; and works for children.

JEM

Cordero-Fernando, Gilda (*b*. 1930), Philippine fiction writer, essayist. Noted for managing a home industry – 'the manufacturing of nursery bags for children' – in the biographical notes of her first collec-

tion of short fiction, *The Butcher, the Baker, the Candle Stick Maker* (1964), Cordero-Fernando has since moved on to the business of book production, in which she has made a name as a publisher of Filipiniana. Married to lawyer Marcelo Fernando, with whom she has four children, she obtained her AB and BSE degrees at St Theresa's College and her MA in English literature at the Ateneo de Manila University. A native of Manila, her stories often deal with the experiences of the upper middle class she was born into, although in works such as the anthologized 'The Visitation of the Gods,' she exhibits a concern for social issues such as the corruption of the public school system. A second volume of stories *A Wilderness of Sweets* was published in 1973, and a retrospective, *Story Collection*, appeared in 1998. Three books she has published and edited – *Being Filipino* (1981), *Household Antiques and Heirlooms* (1983), and *The History of the Burgis* (1987) – received the Manila Critics Circle's National Book Awards.

CJM

Cornwell, Patricia D. (*b*. 1956), US novelist. Born in Miami, Cornwell received a BA from Davidson College in North Carolina in 1979. She worked as a police reporter for the *Charlotte Observer* and in the office of the Chief Medical Examiner in Richmond, Virginia. Both jobs provided excellent preparation for her subsequent career as detective fiction writer. Her detailed and graphic novels, which feature Dr. Kay Scarpetta, a forensic pathologist, are feminist revisions of the genre. Scarpetta, a highly intelligent divorcee in her forties, investigates murders with a cool independence and formidable technical skills, which are described with fascinating specificity. The first novel in the series *Postmortem* was published in 1990, and won numerous awards. The Scarpetta series includes *Body of Evidence* (1991), *All that Remains* (1992), *Cruel & Unusual* (1993), *From Potter's Field* (1995), and

Black Notice (1999). Cornwell's first non-Scarpetta novel is *Hornet's Nest* (1997); its sequel is *Southern Cross* (1999).

JEM

Correia, Clara Pinto (*b.* 1960), Portuguese novelist, journalist. Born in Lisbon, the daughter of a medical doctor, Correia received a doctorate in cellular biology (University of Oporto, 1992) and currently is an adjunct professor in the Department of Veterinary and Animal Sciences at the University of Massachusetts–Amherst. She has had a multifaceted literary career, writing weekly columns for the Portuguese newspaper *Diário de Notícias*, and publishing over twenty-five works in a variety of genres: novels, fiction for adolescents, poetry, dramas, and essays. Her first novel, *Agrião* ('Watercress,' 1984), already delineates the themes that reappear in her later novels: the influence of mass communication in everyday life, the connection between all forms of media, alienation, sexism, and the playful relationship between writing and the social-cultural context. Her second novel *Adeus Princesa* ('Goodbye Princess,' 1985) established Correia's reputation as one of the leading contemporary voices in Portuguese fiction. The novel deals with the aftermath of the Portuguese revolution (1974) and reveals that in spite of the many changes brought about by the new sociopolitical order, patriarchy and tradition still dominate the sociocultural landscape. *Domingo de Ramos* ('Palm Sunday,' 1994) revisits the period of the Portuguese revolution and is a blending of autobiography, biography, and fiction.

JNO

Correia, Hélia (*b.* 1949), Portuguese novelist, dramatist, poet. Born in Lisbon, Correia is one of the most innovative and acclaimed narrative voices of her generation. She began as a poet, but was not recognized by the literary establishment until the publication of her first novel *O Separar das Águas* ('The Parting of the Waters,'

1981). Her fiction is informed by a rich and varied social texture and has a strong religious dimension as popular beliefs and superstitions interact with the biblical discourse. Gabriel García Márquez has been a great influence in her incorporation of the fantastic in her fiction, which she uses to question the conventionality and the banality of the bourgeois world. Her characters are moved by irrational, instinctual, mythical, unreal and extraordinary forces. Other works include *Villa Celeste* ('Celestial Village,' 1985), *Soma* ('The Sum,' 1987), and *A Casa Eterna* ('Eternal Home,' 1991). An excerpt from *Montedemo* ('The Devil's Mountain'), a long short story dealing with a mountain and a woman both impregnated with demonic forces, has been translated into English in *Sweet Marmalade, Sour Oranges* (1994). Her passion for the theatre and especially for the dramas of classical Greece has led her to write two plays, *Perdição* ('Calamity,' 1991) and *Florbela* (1991), and to become involved in acting and the development of experimental forms of theater.

JNO

Correia, Natália (1923–1993), Portuguese fiction writer, poet, dramatist. One of the most prolific and visible of all contemporary Portuguese women writers, Correia became famous for the reputedly 'libertarian' tenor of her creative and critical works and for her public oppositional voice throughout more than four decades of intense cultural and political activity. Born in the Azores, she was educated in Lisbon, where she remained for the rest of her life, regularly contributing to literary magazines and newspapers and serving as literary consultant. Although she began publishing in 1949 with a neo-realist novel with no critical repercussion, she found her decisive creative impulse in surrealist poetry, particularly concerning the irrational, magic or archetypal elements of nature and the psyche. Several of her works were banned

under Salazar's oppressive, fascistic regime due to their 'scandalous' sexual
content. Nonetheless, she boldly enacted
the right to free expression, going on to
edit the *New Portuguese Letters* in 1972
and to publicly defend the 'Three Marias'
(see entry for *Maria Velho da Costa).
One of the arguments reappearing in
Correia's more than fifty volumes of published work in virtually all genres is the
feminist notion that the nurturing force
of the feminine, potentially present in
women and men alike, must replace all
forms of chauvinism, xenophobia and
violence.

APF

Corti, Maria (1915–2002), Italian literary
critic, novelist. Born in Milan, Corti
worked as historian of the Italian language at the University of Pavia, where
she was actively involved in the important
Foundation of Manuscripts of Twentieth-
Century Italian Writers, which she created. One of Italy's most distinguished
literary critics, her work centered on
medieval and contemporary texts, as well
as on critical methodologies and theoretical issues. She was active on several
editorial boards and wrote regularly for
the newspaper *La Repubblica*. Among
her numerous scholarly works are *An
Introduction to Literary Semiotics* (1976)
and *Il viaggio testuale* ('The Textual Voyage,' 1978). Corti published her first
novel, *Otranto* (1962), at the age of 47;
after that she published several works of
prose fiction, including *Il ballo dei sapi-
enti* ('The Dance of the Wise,' 1966),
Voci dal Nord Est ('Voices from the
Northeast,' 1986), and *Il canto delle sirene*
('The Sirens' Song,' 1989). The 1986 book
is a fictionalized travel diary that grew
out of her experiences as a visiting
professor at Brown University, while the
1989 novel is a moving intellectual
autobiography in the form of a meditation on humankind's eternal search for
knowledge.

RW

Costa, Maria Velho da (*b*. 1938), Portuguese novelist, poet. Born in Lisbon, Costa
was educated in a religious school and
went on to complete an undergraduate degree in Germanic philology at the University of Lisbon with a thesis on Virginia
Woolf. Besides working in social research,
she taught in several schools, including
King's College, University of London. She
served as cultural attaché in Cape Verde
and as president of the Portuguese Writers
Association. With more than fourteen
titles published to date, she has enjoyed
critical recognition since the publication
of her first novel *Maina Mendes* (1969),
featuring the revolutionary potential of
feminine silence as a strategy against the
patriarchal, colonialist order. The condition of women, but also of those dispossessed by pervasive ideologies of gender,
class, race, nation, and empire, is explored
in the intertextually dense, hybrid feminist
text *New Portuguese Letters* (1972), co-
authored with *Maria Isabel Barreno and
*Maria Teresa Horta. The 'Three Marias'
became the center of international attention when government authorities banned
the book and legally charged them with
'immorality.' As in such prize-winning
novels as *Casas Pardas* ('Sullen Houses,'
1977), Costa's works typically align experimentalism with an ideological commitment to reflect upon the historical
fate of those who endured nearly half a
century of dictatorship.

APF

Cour, Ajeet (*b*. 1934), Indian fiction writer.
Cour was born into a middle-class Sikh
family in Lahore, where she had her early
schooling. After India's partition, her
family moved to Delhi, where she completed her education. Her father was a
devout Sikh and wanted his daughter to
follow the Sikh way, but she had an unconventional and questioning mind. She
took her BA in education and her MA in
economics, and has had a successful career
as an economic journalist. Her unhappy
marriage to a medical doctor ended in

divorce. Recipient of the Sahitya Academy Award among other honors, Cour has earned a reputation in contemporary Punjabi literature for her bold, realistic portrayal of middle-class women's lives. In her stories she deals with the complexity of the man–woman relationship with incisivenes and rare frankness. Free of traditional morality or tawdry romantic love, her fiction displays her contempt for conventional notions of marriage and openly explores female sexuality. Her major works include the collections *Gul Bano te hor Kahanian* ('Gulbano and Other Stories,' 1963), *Ehak di Maut* ('The Death of Fragrance,' 1966), *Butt Shikkan* ('The Iconoclast,' 1966), and *Dead End and Other Stories* (1997), and the novels *Faltu Aurat* ('The Dispensable Woman,' 1977) and *Gauri* (1996). She has written an autobiography, *Pebbles on a Tin Drum* (1997), and translations of her stories are included in several anthologies.

AS

Coutinho, Sonia (*b*. 1939), Brazilian novelist, short story writer. Born in the city of Itabuna, the state of Bahia, in northeast Brazil, Coutinho moved to Rio de Janeiro in 1968, where she has lived since then. *Do herói inútil* ('On the Useless Hero,' 1966), her first book, is a collection of short stories. *O jogo de Ifá* ('The Ifá Divination,' 1980), a novella, shows a protagonist, alternately male and female, leaving the city of Rio de Janeiro and going back to his/her hometown, in an attempt to recapture the past and understand who he/she is. Here Coutinho utilizes the concept of androgyny, as well as intertextuality, metafiction, and Afro-Brazilian mythology to problematize the situation of women. Her paradigmatic character, well represented in the stories of *O último verão de Copacabana* ('Last Summer in Copacabana,' 1985), is the independent woman who leaves life in a provincial town for the relative freedom – and the loneliness – of the urban center. *Atire em Sofia* ('Shoot Sofia,' 1989) and *O caso Alice*

('The Alice File,' 1991) are women-centered detective novels in which both intertextuality and metafictional discourse have an important function. They also display a fantastic dimension already seen in *Os venenos de Lucrécia* ('Lucrecia's Poisons,' 1978) and other works.

CF-P

Craig, Christine (*b*. 1943), Jamaican poet, short story and children's writer. Although she was born in Kingston, Craig's childhood in the Jamaican countryside apparently exercised a strong hold on her creative imagination, for its resonances can be found in her prose and poetry. An Honours graduate of the University of West Indies in English and mass communications, she has written fiction for children, notably *Emmanuel Goes to Market* (1970), *Emmanuel and his Parrot* (1971), and *The Bird Gang* (1990), as well as poems and short stories for adults. Craig's collection of poetry *Quadrille for Tigers* (1984) and her first collection of short stories *Mint Tea* (1993) show a sophisticated use of both standard English and a jaunty Jamaican dialect. Her men and women are sharply drawn by a sensitive authorial consciousness, and her best work explores the fragile psyches of sometimes impotent and alienated individuals who are burdened by the sense of an unfulfilled life, or who seek stability and relief from ennui. Craig currently lives in south Florida and is the Miami editor for Jamaica's *Gleaner*.

HB

Cunha, Helena Parente (*b*. 1929), Brazilian novelist, poet, short story writer. Cunha graduated in letters in 1951, received a PhD in Italian literature and literary theory in 1976, and currently teaches literary theory at the Federal University of Rio de Janeiro where she formerly held the position of Dean of Humanities. Her long-standing interest in literary theory has resulted in four books, of which *Mulheres Inventadas* ('Invented Women,'

1994) constitutes a fine example. Even though a fiction writer, her first love was poetry, collected in two volumes: *Corpo no cerco* ('Surrounded Body,' 1978) and *Maramar* ('Sea Love,' 1980). The impacts and influences that the Afro-Brazilian city of Salvador (Bahia) had on her upbringing are most apparent in her novel *Woman Between Mirrors* (1983). Her highly poetic prose combines a concern about the distribution of wealth and inequities between different social strata in Brazil, addressing these issues in the context of race, gender, and age, as in *Os provisórios contos* ('The Tentative Short Stories,' 1980) and *A casa e as casas* ('The House and the Houses,' 1990). Her writing often critically evaluates roles assigned to women in Brazilian society, especially her novels *Woman Between Mirrors* and *As doze cores do vermelho* ('The Twelve Colors of Red,' 1988).

MIB

Cusk, Rachel (*b.* 1967), British novelist. Born in Canada, Cusk was educated at New College, Oxford. She married Josh Hillman in 1995 and lives in London. Her first novel *Saving Agnes* was published in 1992 and won the Whitbread First Novel Award. With humor and sensitivity, Cusk tells the story of a self-absorbed and self-dramatizing young woman who embarks on her adult life in London and finds herself completely unprepared for the challenges of modern urban life. Cusk's second novel *The Temporary* (1995) depicts another disaffected young woman. It is a satire on the culture of fashion magazines and female vanity, in which an office temp fantasizes about her big break but is slapped with a great many unpleasant realities instead. *The Country Life* (1997) is a social comedy about Stella, who leaves London in search of a simpler life working as a nanny in Sussex. Cusk's novels have been praised for their humor, dazzling dialogue, careful observations, and precise capturing of manners and mores, particularly those of her own alienated generation.

JEM

D

Dai Houying (1938–1995), Chinese novelist, essayist. Born in Nanzhao, an historic yet impoverished town in China's Anhui Province, Dai graduated from Shanghai's East Normal University in 1960 and was assigned to work at the Literature Research Institute of the Shanghai Writers' Association. After gaining a faculty position at Fudan University, Dai wrote her first novel *Stones of the Wall* (1981). With its unabashed humanism and modernist literary techniques, the novel shook the Chinese literary establishment and garnered Dai international acclaim. By depicting the anguish of an intellectual denounced as a 'rightist' during the Maoist era, *Stones* boldly ushered in a new literary era which more candidly expressed the tragic suffering of political victims. The tragic suicide of her beloved friend Wen Jie in 1978 inspired her second novel *Shiren zhi si* ('Death of a Poet,' 1982). Dai continued to depict the fate of intellectuals in her subsequent novels, including *Xuankong de shizi lukou* ('The Suspended Intersection,' 1992), in which she explores the psychological predicament of intellectuals after the 1989 Tiananmen Square demonstrations. Prior to her heinous murder on August 25, 1995, Dai published her fifth novel *Naolie* ('Brain Fissure,' 1994), in addition to two collections of stories, two collections of essays, and the first part of her autobiography.

JN

Dai Qing (*b.* 1941), Chinese journalist and writer. Born Fu Xiaoqing in Chongqing, Sichuan Province, Dai grew up as the adopted daughter of Ye Jianying, one of China's ten military marshals. She graduated from Harbin Institute of Military Engineering in 1966 and started writing in 1979. She is known for her achievements in journalism, calling for freedom of the press, and revealing well-kept secrets of party history. An outspoken exposé of Mao's persecution of intellectuals in the 1940s, *Liang Shuming, Wang Shiwei, Chu Anping* (1989) demonstrates courage rarely found in Chinese journalism. Also written in a characteristically eloquent and forthright style, *Yangtze, Yangtze* (1989) and *The River Dragon Has Come!* (1997) are two book-length criticisms of the Three Gorges Project for its potential environmental consequences. *Wo de ru yu* ('My Imprisonment,' 1990) and *Zai Qincheng zuo lao* ('Imprisoned in Qincheng,' 1993), in which she depicts her experience in prison after the 1989 democratic movement, are a unique blending of autobiography, history, and contemporary politics. Characterized by personal sentiments and lyrical charisma, *Wo de si ge fuqin* ('My Four Fathers,' 1995) contains vivid accounts of Dai's childhood, adulthood, and career. She is married to Wang Dejia and mother of Wang Xiaojia.

JW

Dallas, Ruth (Ruth Mumford) (*b.* 1919), New Zealand poet, children's writer. Born in Invercargill, New Zealand, Dallas began writing stories and poems for the *Southland Daily News* at the age of 12. After her poems appeared in various newspapers and magazines, she published *Country Road and Other Poems* (1953), the first of numerous poetry collections. She won the New Zealand Book Award for Poetry for *Walking in the Snow* (1976). Her poems often emulate the style of nineteenth-century British romantic poetry, but have been influenced by Chinese poetry and philosophy as well as the New Zealand landscape. In her poetry and particularly in her children's books she seeks to capture impressions of her country. New Zealand historic and geographic concerns permeate much of her juvenile literature. *The Children in the Bush* (1969) is the first in a series of books about nineteenth-century children. She has won the New Zealand Literary Fund Achievement Award (1963), the Robert Burns Fellowship (1968), and the Buckland Literary Award (1977). She received an HonDLitt from Otago University in 1978 and was made a CBE in 1989. Her *Collected Poems* appeared in 1987 and her autobiography *Curved Horizon* was published in 1991.

M-RA

Dangarembga, Tsitsi (*b.* 1959), Zimbabwean novelist, playwright, filmmaker. Born in colonial Rhodesia, Dangarembga went to England when she was 2 years old and returned to Rhodesia in 1965, where she attended an American convent school. In 1977, she went to Cambridge to study medicine, but felt so alienated in England that she returned to Zimbabwe in 1980 and pursued psychology instead. Her play *She No Longer Weeps* (1987) dramatizes the experiences of a strong-willed 20-year-old, unwed, pregnant university student who rebels against familial, patriarchal, and institutionalized restrictions imposed on her gender by the post-colonial (legal) system. Dangarembga gained international success with her novel *Nervous Conditions* (1988; Commonwealth Writers' Prize), a coming-of-age story about two female teenage cousins seeking to define themselves against the forces of sexism, patriarchy, and colonialism. She has since turned her attention to film. She wrote the story on which the film *Neria* (1992) is based, and directed the acclaimed *Everyone's Child* (1996). The latter film challenges communities to take responsibility for their children, by putting the spotlight on four siblings shunned by the village after their parents die of AIDS. Dangarembga thus reclaims the African saying that an orphan is everyone's child.

JMN-A

Daniels, Sarah (*b.* 1956), British playwright. Born in London, Daniels has been a resident writer at the Royal Court Theatre and has written scripts for the television series *Grange Hill* and *Eastenders*. Her plays are powerful, innovative, often brash, sometimes darkly comic explorations of controversial social issues which affect women's lives. Her female characters are strong and complicated. *Ripen Our Darkness* (1981) is a critique of archetypal images of women. *The Devil's Gateway* (1983) concerns a working-class woman who becomes a peace activist. *Neaptide* (1986) features a lesbian schoolteacher and mother who must fight to keep custody of her child. The appropriation of women's bodies during the birthing process is examined in *Byrthrite* (1986). *The Gut Girls* (1988) is about nineteenth-century women slaughterhouse workers. *Beside Herself* (1990), Daniels' most formally experimental work, weaves together fiction and reality and different time frames in its exploration of childhood sexual abuse. Daniels is best known for *Masterpieces* (1983), a disturbing play about a woman who, made fearful by a snuff film, is driven to violence herself. The play argues that pornography not only affects everyday attitudes and behavior, but that it is also directly connected to violence against women.

JEM

Danishvar, Simin (*b*. 1921), Iranian novelist, short story writer. Born in the provincial capital city of Shiraz, daughter of a physician and a painter, Danishvar grew up enjoying an intellectual family environment and a good education. She earned a doctorate in literature in 1949 from Tehran University. She married Jala Al-i Ahmad, an author and intellectual activist in the 1950s and 1960s. She held an academic position at Tehran University until the authorities expelled her after the 1979 Islamic Revolution. She has published several novels and collections of short stories. In the pre-revolutionary period, she was preoccupied, chiefly, with political and social problems, as in *Atash-i Khamush* ('The Quenched Fire,' 1961) and *The Playhouse* (1989), and with the relations between East and West, as in *A City Like Paradise* (1962). In the post-revolutionary period she specifically confronts women's issues and writes about her experience with men (specifically her late husband) and assigns more active roles to female characters. *A Persian Requiem* (1969), her best-selling novel, is about the life of a woman who had a happy childhood and experienced personal freedom while growing up and during her school years at a British missionary school, but experiences internal conflict in her married life with a political activist.

KTa

Danticat, Edwidge (*b*. 1969), Haitian-US novelist, short story writer. Danticat emigrated from Haiti to the US at the age of 12. A similar migration appears in her first novel *Breath, Eyes, Memory* (1994), which describes a young girl's journeys between Haiti and the US, and her often-troubled relationship with her mother. This theme of complicated relationships between mothers and daughters is prevalent in Danticat's writings. She probes the ways in which separations caused by death, flight from brutal dictatorships, or economic hardship and migration in search of work can all be integral parts of the mother–child dynamic. Her short stories have appeared in over twenty-five periodicals, and she has received fiction awards from *The Caribbean Writer*, *Seventeen*, and *Essence* magazines, as well as the 1995 Pushcart Short Story Prize; she was named one of *Granta*'s Best Young American Novelists in 1996. In the same year, her second book *Krik? Krak!* was a National Book Award finalist. In Haiti, when storytellers say 'Krik?,' listeners respond 'Krak!' to signal their readiness for the tale. The title of this short story collection thus reveals another one of the central motifs of Danticat's work: the weaving of Haitian cultural forms and oral traditions through written text.

GAn

Das, Kamala (Madhavikutty) (*b*. 1934), Indian poet, short story writer. Born in Kerala to a prominent literary family, Das grew up in Calcutta, was married at the age of 15, and lived with her husband in Bombay. In 1965 she published her first volume of poetry in English, the prizewinning *Summer in Calcutta*, followed by *The Old Playhouse and Other Poems* (1973). Her 1976 autobiography *My Story* caused a controversy by portraying sexual relationships that break the bounds of marriage and heterosexuality. Her unflinching look at patriarchal oppression and open portrayal of female desire broke new ground for women's writing. Her later English works include *The Anamalai Poems* (1985) and *Padmavati the Harlot and Other Stories* (1992). In the Malayalam language, under the pseudonym Madhavikutty, she is a short story writer whose confessional mode and disturbing treatment of love, sexuality, oppression, and death have powerfully influenced the genre. The first of her fifteen collections *Mathilukal* ('Walls') was published in 1955. *The Sandal Tree and other Stories*

(1995) and a short novel *Alphabet of Lust* (1978) are English translations. In the 1984 general elections, Das ran (unsuccessfully) as an independent candidate from Trivandrum, speaking out against government corruption. She has since turned to political commentary and in 1986 won the Chimanlal Award for fearless journalism. She lives in Ernaculum.

MAg

Das, Mahadai (*b*. 1954), Indo-Guyanese poet. A descendant of East Indian indentured labourers, Das was born and grew up in Guyana where she was politically and culturally active in the 1970s. She studied economics at the University of Guyana and left for Chicago in the early 1980s to attend a doctoral program in philosophy, but severe illness forced her to return to her native country where she currently lives and writes. A militant nationalism characterizes her first collection of poetry *I Want to be a Poetess of my People* (1977), which retraces the history of thousands of Indians who 'came in ships like cattle' to the Caribbean, to replace the freed slaves on colonial plantations. Whereas *My Finer Steel Will Grow* (1982) is a sharp attack on the corrupt politics that fatally affected Guyana in the 1970s, *Bones* (1988) celebrates the transformational power of migration. This third collection, which is her most metaphorical one, explores the preoccupations of the immigrant Indo-Caribbean woman who writes from within the belly of an oppressive capitalistic society. Das's work points to the restrictions gender forces onto women but also to the instability and constant need for rebirth of identities.

VBr

De, Shobha (*b*. 1948), Indian novelist, columnist. Living in Mumbai, India, De is married with six children. Before becoming a novelist, De had a diverse set of careers as model, copywriter, and founding editor of *Stardust* and *Society*, very successful magazines reporting on the Bollywood film industry. *Socialite Evenings* (1989), *Starry Nights* (1991), and *Small Betrayals* (1995) are among her seven popular novels. She has always sparked controversy with the erotic content of her novels and their exploration of women's sexuality. Their titles suggest the ways in which her novels chronicle Indian elite society. Most of them are *Bildungsromans* narrating a young woman's development out of a sheltered, middle-class upbringing to become a model, glossy magazine editor, or popular fiction writer. Her novels sometimes venture outside the realm of elite Mumbai society to raise critical awareness about other worlds: *Socialite Evenings* tracks a young woman's journey to New York, her disillusionment with racism there, and her return 'home.' De's autobiography *Shooting from the Hip: Selected Writings* (1994) resonates with the columns and novels she has written over the years about Mumbai society. The book chronicles her relationship to the city of Mumbai and its role in producing her as a successful writer.

KA

de Cèspedes, Alba (1911–1997), Italian novelist, journalist, poet. Born in Rome, the daughter of a diplomatic family from Cuba, de Cèspedes married Franco Buonos, diplomat, and had one son. Early exposure to politics paved the way for her participation in the Italian Resistance, as radio broadcaster, during World War II and politics inform her prose fiction as well as the print journalism that followed. The collection of short stories *Anima degli altri* ('The Soul of Others,' 1935), her first publication, was followed by her bestseller *There's No Turning Back* (1938), which disavowed fascist creeds believed present in her first novel. In *There's No Turning Back* and later novels, the author carefully delineates women's lives in Italian society; her work is considered the literary antecedent to political issues Italian feminism addressed in the 1970s and 1980s. In *The Best of Husbands* (1948),

Alessandra recounts the story of her life and the events in her marriage leading up to her murder of her husband. In *The Secret* (1952), Valeria keeps a hidden diary in which she struggles with the expectations of her husband, work, and family. In her 1962 epistolary novel *Remorse*, the author examined Rome and 1950s gender and national politics.

EN

De Groen, Alma (*b*. 1941), Australian dramatist. De Groen emigrated to Australia from New Zealand in 1964. She writes for television and radio, and received a 1985 Awgie Award for her television adaptation of Glen Tomasetti's novel *Man of Letters*. However, she is best known for her stage plays. They include *The Joss Adams Show* (1970), which uses a television show format to discuss the battered-baby syndrome; *The Sweatproof Boy* (1972); *Perfectly All Right* (1973), about a woman trapped by convention; *The After-Life of Arthur Cravan* (1973), about the nephew of Oscar Wilde; *Going Home* (1976), which reveals the problems of marital relations among a group of Australian expatriates living in Canada; *Chidley* (1977), about the eccentric Sydney dress and sex reformer; *Vocations* (1982), which challenges traditional gender roles; *The Rivers of China* (1987; NSW and Victorian Premier's Awards for Best Play), which intertwines the final months of Katherine Mansfield's life and a contemporary feminist dystopia; *The Girl Who Saw Everything* (1993; Awgie Award), which affirms that individuals' perspectives can change in response to traumatic events; and *The Woman in the Window* (1998), which juxtaposes the banned poet Anna Akhmatova in Stalinist Russia with a world in which nature and the arts have been crushed by economics.

M-RA

de Jesus, Carolina Maria (1915–1977) Brazilian fiction writer. Born in a rural area of Minas Gerais, de Jesus migrated to the city of São Paulo and lived in a shantytown. Although she had only two years of schooling, she frequently read the newspapers that she collected on the streets. *Child of the Dark* (1960), her diary and first publication, became a best-seller in Brazil and was translated into twelve languages. It features a scavenger protagonist, the great-grandchild of slaves, who lives in a slum. De Jesus published two other autobiographical memoirs/diaries: *I'm Going to Have a Little House* (1961) and *Bitita's Diary: the Childhood Memoirs of Carolina Maria de Jesus* (1988). Her repetitive, documentary style, and the misspellings and grammatical mistakes that appear in her books, have often been criticized by elitist readers. While it is true that her works do not match the aesthetic standards of the best Brazilian literature, her realistic and simple style echoes her plain, unsophisticated, parched life. Her texts are powerful testimonies of the hardships encountered by those living in extremes of poverty in the richest city in Brazil; they make compelling arguments about human dignity and rights, the sorrows of poverty and hunger, and the Brazilian authorities' lack of concern for the underprivileged, while addressing questions of race, class, and gender.

MJB

del Río, Ana María (*b*. 1948), Chilean novelist, short story writer. Born in Santiago de Chile, del Río studied literature at the Universidad Católica de Chile and did graduate work at Rice University and the University of Pittsburgh. Her first collection of stories *Entreparéntesis* ('In Parenthesis,' 1985) won prizes in Chile and Argentina. It was followed by several award-winning narratives: *Oxido de Carmen* ('Carmen Oxide,' 1986; María Luisa Bombal Prize), a remarkable novella that tells of the constraints endured by a lively young woman in an upper-class family; *De golpe, Amalia en el umbral* ('Suddenly, Amalia on the Threshold'), which won the Andrés Bello Prize in 1991; and *Tiempo* *que ladra* ('Barking Time'), the 1991 'Letras de Oro' Prize from the University of Miami and the Premio Municipal de Literatura in Santiago. *Tiempo que ladra* focuses on the conflicts of daily life as seen from the perspective of a young girl whose family is deeply divided as a result of the changes introduced by the policies of the socialist government of President Salvador Allende (1970–3). Other publications include the novels *Siete días de la señora K.* ('The Seven Days of Mrs K.,' 1993) and *A tango abierto* ('Open Tango,' 1996), and a collection of stories, *Gato por liebre* ('The Swindler,' 1994).

MIL

Denser, Márcia (*b*. 1949), Brazilian fiction writer. Born and raised in the fifth largest city in the world, São Paulo, Denser places the female characters in her fiction against the impersonal backdrop of the lonely urban environment. The eroticism of her protagonists is more often than not 'anti-erotic' or intentionally pornographic. In an effort to explain that the reversal of power is not a solution to the situation of oppressed women, she places her female characters in male situations of sexual dominance. This technique of intentional reversal is similar to that used by US women writers like *Erica Jong or *Marilyn French. Denser has edited two important collections of Brazilian women writers' erotic fiction: *Muito Prazer* ('Much Pleasure,' 1980) and *O prazer é todo meu* ('The Pleasure is All Mine,' 1984). She is the author of five volumes of short stories including *Tango fantasma* ('Phantom Tango,' 1976) and *O animal dos motéis* ('Motel Bitch,' 1981). Two characteristic short stories 'The Vampire of Whitehouse Lane' (in *One Hundred Years after Tomorrow*, 1992) and 'Last Tango in Jacobina' (in *Urban Voices*, 1999) are available in English translation.

SCQ

Desai, Anita (*b*. 1937), Indian novelist. Raised in Old Delhi, Desai earned her BA in English from Miranda House. Her first story was published in 1946, and she began writing novels while raising a family of four children. Her early works articulate a woman's inner subjectivity with passionate intensity. Her first novel *Cry, the Peacock* was published in 1963, and her fourth novel *Fire on the Mountain* (1977) won the Sahitya Akademi Award and the Winifred Holtby Prize. *Clear Light of Day* (1980), a novel about family, memory, and Partition, and *In Custody* (1984), about the fate of Urdu in post-independence India, were both short-listed for the Booker Prize. *Baumgartner's Bombay* (1988) allowed her to explore her German mother's heritage through the story of an exiled German Jew in India. Finely crafted language, poetic imagery, a strong sense of place, and complex, interwoven characters distinguish her mature work. Fellow of the Royal Society of Literature and Honorary Member of the American Academy of Arts and Letters, she was awarded India's Padma Shri in 1990. Desai has been Visiting Fellow at Girton College, Cambridge, and since 1987 has taught writing in the US, first at Smith and Mt. Holyoke Colleges and now at Massachusetts Institute of Technology. Her most recent novels are *Journey to Ithaca* (1995) and *Fasting, Feasting* (1999).

JR

Desai, Kamal (*b*. 1928), Indian novelist and short fiction writer. Born in Yamkanmardi in Belgaum district, a Bombay University MA and gold medallist in Marathi, Desai has taught in small-town colleges all over Maharashtra. Her liberal reformist yet deeply religious father strongly influenced her work. Recognized as having few peers among fiction writers in Marathi, she brings an unusually forthright woman's perspective and a trenchant irony (often expressed as satire) to bear on traditionally male-defined themes such as religion and sexuality. She began writing in 1955 and has published two short story collections, *Colors* (1962) and *Ranga-2*

(1998), and three novels. Though the body of her work is not large, it is valued for its sophistication and complexity. Through a densely detailed rendering of the Maharashtrian social fabric, it presents the conditions of living as a woman in very particular regional terms. Two of her novellas, translated as *The Dark Sun and The Woman Who Wore a Hat* (1975), are renowned. They discuss the aspirations and dilemmas of lower-middle-class women who find their way through crisis to new values. Society is shown to embrace false or hypocritical morality, whereas the marginalized protagonists come to know 'real' values.

VBh

Desanti, Dominique (*b.* 1921), French novelist, biographer. Desanti was born and lived most of her life in Paris, traveling extensively as correspondent for *L'Humanité* after World War II, and as a university professor in the US. Cutting short her studies of history and sociology in 1939, she (with her husband, eminent mathematician and philosopher Jean-Toussaint Desanti) joined the Resistance in 1940, and the French Communist Party, which they left in 1956. She championed feminism in a dozen biographies, notably of Marie d'Agoult (1980), Elsa Triolet (1983), Sonia Delaunay (1988), Marina Tsvetaieva (1994), and *Flora Tristan, A Woman in Revolt* (1972). Informed by their author's intense curiosity of life, and her unflagging social and political concern, Desanti's dozen novels document the entire second half of the century, notably *La Colombe vole sans visa* ('Doves Travel Without Visas,' 1951), *Un Métier de chien* ('Drudgery,' 1972), *Les Années passion* ('The Passion Years,' 1992). She chronicled the nineteenth-century utopian movement in *Les Socialistes de l'Utopie* ('Socialist Utopians,' 1971), and examined the sway of the Communist Party over a generation of intellectuals in *Les Staliniens* ('The Stalinists,' 1975) and in her 1997 autobiography.

MBR, MLT

Deshpande, Gauri (*b.* 1942), Indian fiction writer, poet, translator. Born in Pune into an illustrious family of social reformers, educators, and social scientists, Deshpande (PhD, English, University of Pune) published her first collection of poetry in English (*Between Births*, 1968), but writes most of her fiction in Marathi. She created a stir with her first novella *Karavasatun Patre* ('Letters from Prison,' 1971), portraying the struggle of a woman to break the emotional and psychological bonds of patriarchy. It quickly became a 'standard text' for middle-class feminists. In spare, elegant prose and tightly constructed forms, she explores changing perceptions of family and self in educated urban women's lives, as her women characters take charge of their lives. Her first book of stories in English *The Lackadaisical Sweeper* (1997) is typical of her work, as are her earlier novellas *Nirgath* ('Double Knots,' 1987) and *Mukkam* ('Stopover,' 1992). She has won a wide readership and critical acclaim. Three novellas and a collection each of stories and of essays received State of Maharashtra awards. She is a prolific translator, having translated the sixteen volumes of Burton's *The Arabian Nights* into Marathi, as well as poetry, fiction, and autobiographies from Marathi into English. She herself has been translated into many Indian and foreign languages.

VBh

Deshpande, Shashi (*b.* 1938), Indian novelist, short story writer. Daughter of the dramatist and Sanskrit scholar Sriranga, Deshpande was born in Dharwad, Karnataka. After studying economics, law and journalism, she worked as a journalist. She now lives in Bangalore. Her five short story collections and seven novels examine the inner turmoil of Indian women. Kunti and Amba, the silent female characters of Indian mythology, find new voices in her stories 'The Inner Room' and 'Hear Me, Sanjaya.' Childhood trauma and marital problems torment Saru in Deshpande's first novel *The Dark holds No Terrors*

(1980), until she starts analyzing her problems. Even in her two crime novels Deshpande focuses on the feelings of the female characters. The conflicts faced by an emancipated urban woman during a return to her ancestral home are explored in *Roots and Shadows* (1983). The Sahitya Akademi Award-winning novel *That Long Silence* (1989) narrates a woman's journey of self-discovery after years of silent acquiescence in her role of wife and mother. Her recent novels include *The Binding Vine* (1993) and *A Matter of Time* (1996) whose central motif is the deep loneliness of human beings. Her stories have been widely anthologized and her novels translated into many Indian and European languages.

CHo

De Sousa, Noémia (*b.* 1927), Mozambican poet, journalist, activist. Born in Maputo (formerly Lourenço Marquez), Mozambique, De Sousa was educated in Mozambique, Brazil, and Portugal. A politically active journalist and poet who has worked for Angolan and Mozambican scholarly journals, she is recognized as the first African woman to gain an international reputation as a poet in the Francophone world. Her activism against colonial rule forced her into exile in France in the 1960s, where she still resides with her Portuguese husband. Her poetry – which appears in many anthologies including *When Bullets Began to Flower: Poems of Resistance from Angola, Mozambique and Guine* (1972), *Sunflower of Hope: Poems from the Mozambican Revolution* (1982), and *When My Brothers Come Home: Poems From Central and Southern Africa* (1985) – engages in the celebration of traditional African cultural mores, the diasporic connection, and commitment to the liberation struggle.

MU

de Souza, Eunice (*b.* 1940), Indian poet, literary critic. A daughter of Roman Catholic parents, de Souza grew up in Poona, India, graduating with a BA in English from the University of Bombay, an MA from Marquette University in the US, and a PhD from the University of Bombay. Head of the English department at St Xavier's College, Bombay, de Souza integrates pedagogy with professional activities by creating new journals, directing theater productions, and encouraging new poets. De Souza is the author of four poetry collections: *Fix* (1979); *Women in Dutch Painting* (1988); *Ways of Belonging: Selected Poems* (1990), awarded the Poetry Book Society Recommendation; and *Selected and New Poems* (1994). Her poems are characterized by innovative uses of the English language, colloquial idiom, and sharp but poignant satire of her own Goan Christian community and the gender roles confronting women in patriarchal society. In the best tradition of the personal as political, her poems radiate outward to include the social predicaments of women in India and beyond. An active literary critic and newspaper columnist, she has edited *Nine Indian Women Poets: An Anthology* (1997), with a wide ranging critical introduction. She has also written four books of children's folktales, and co-edited an anthology of Indian English prose.

KHK

Devakul, Subha (1928–1993), Thai fiction writer, TV scriptwriter. Born in Bangkok, Devakul began writing when she was in high school. She married young and became a widow before she was 30. With five children under her care, she made her living by being a full-time writer. Within ten years after her husband's death, she had written 300 short stories and countless numbers of television scripts and screenplays. Of her forty novels, the most controversial one is *Yue Arrom* ('The Victim of Lust') in which she depicts the plight of a young girl who has been raped by her stepfather. Her humorous short story 'When She Was a Major Wife' is included in the anthology *The Lioness in Bloom: Modern Thai Fiction about Women*

(1996). Devakul was president of the Writer's Association of Thailand from 1978 to 1982 and was instrumental in the establishment of the prestigious South East Asian (S.E.A.)Write Award. She died in 1993 of lung disease.

NM

Devi, Ashapurna (*see* Ashapurna Devi)

Devi, Mahasweta (*see* Mahasweta Devi)

Dhruv, Saroop (*b*. 1948), Indian poet, social activist. Dhruv grew up in Ahmedabad, Gujarat, where she acquired her MA and PhD in Gujarati literature; her doctoral thesis was titled *Covert Meanings in Folktales*. As a poet and social activist, Saroop grapples with all forms of oppression – gender, caste, and class. Her poetry bears the mark of her experiences with the disadvantaged. Over the years, her poetry registers a drastic shift; the aesthetic formalism visible in her early poems included in *Mara Hath ni Vat* ('What is Within my Reach,' 1982) has given way to a more indignant, challenging tone in *Salagti Havao* ('Burning Flames,' 1995). She has received the Sahitya Parishad award and the Mahendra Bhagat Award (1996). Her essays and articles questioning the mainstream trends of literature have appeared in leading journals. She also writes and directs plays and reinvents traditional expressive genres as a part of her developmental work for non-governmental bodies in Gujarat. English translations of her poems have appeared in *Women Writing in India* (1995), *In their Own Voice* (1990), and the forthcoming *Modern Gujarati Poetry*. Presently, she runs Darshan, an institution committed to a refashioning of folk genres in the light of issues of gender and poverty.

RK

Diallo, Nafissatou Niang (1941–1982), Senegalese novelist. Diallo was born and raised in Dakar, Senegal, where she attended Koranic school and finished her primary and secondary school education. Between 1954 and 1962 she attended a school for becoming a midwife before enrolling at the Institut de Puériculture in France. As midwife, director of a pediatrics center, mother of six, and writer, she played an active role in her community. Central to all of her writing is the Senegalese woman's role and condition in society. In her autobiography *A Dakar Childhood* (1975), she documents a vanishing way of life so as to educate future generations. Her second work *Le fort maudit* ('The Cursed Fortress,' 1980) is set in precolonial Senegal and features a heroine who seeks to avenge the many injustices done to her family. Her third book *Awa, la petite marchande* ('Awa, the Young Merchant,' 1981), written for adolescent readers, recounts the hardships of a young girl trying to find her place in society. Diallo's final work *Fary, Princess of Tiali* (1987) is the story of one woman's struggles against social inequities linked to Senegalese society.

DBH

Didion, Joan (*b*. 1934), US novelist, essayist. Born in Sacramento, California, Didion graduated from the University of California, Berkeley, in 1956, and began her writing career at *Vogue*, where she was a writer and feature editor. She married writer John Gregory Dunne in 1964; they have collaborated on several screenplays. She published her first novel *Run River* in 1963. Her next novel *Play It As It Lays* (1970) is a scathing portrait of Hollywood as a moral wasteland. Broken up into extremely brief chapters, it is narrated by a woman in the midst of a nervous breakdown. Other novels include *A Book of Common Prayer* (1977), *Democracy* (1984), and *The Last Thing He Wanted* (1996). She is perhaps best known for her two collections of essays *Slouching Towards Bethlehem* (1968) and *The White Album* (1979). Written in prose that is precise, witty, and shrewdly intelligent, these essays combine journalistic observation with personal interpretation as Didion looks at life in America (most often, in California) in the 1960s and early 1970s. Her topics range from Haight-Ashbury to Hollywood to feminism to Charles Manson to Ronald Reagan. The essays are linked by her attention to the fragmentations, disconnections, and dislocations of modern life. Although she has always been interested in politics, it has increasingly become the focus of her recent writing, as in *Salvador* (1983), which concerns the violence and political unrest witnessed during a two-week trip to El Salvador, her essays in *After Henry* (1992), and her occasional articles in the *New York Review of Books*.

DVT

Dillard, Annie (*b*. 1945), US nonfiction writer, poet. Born in Pittsburgh, Pennsylvania, Dillard recounts her middle-class upbringing in her memoir *An American Childhood* (1987). She studied English at Hollins College in Virginia. Although she has published the poetry collections *Tickets for a Prayer Wheel* (1974) and *Mornings like This* (1995), she is known primarily as an essayist and nonfiction writer. She won the Pulitzer Prize for *Pilgrim at Tinker Creek* (1974), a collection of poetic, spiritual essays on the natural world. Following in the tradition of Emerson and Thoreau, Dillard strives to understand, through her careful observations of nature, larger truths of an often mystical nature. In *Holy the Firm* (1977) and *Teaching a Stone to Talk* (1982), she continues her meditations on nature and theology. She has also written a novel *The Living* (1992), and published two books on reading and writing: *Living by Fiction* (1982) and *Writing Life* (1989).

DVT

Dimalanta, Ophelia O. (*b*. 1934), Philippine poet. The third of six children of a well-to-do family, Dimalanta enrolled for a degree in journalism at the University of Santo Tomas in 1950, and has since become an important part of the university. In 1978 she completed her PhD in literature there and became its Dean of the Faculty of Arts and Letters in 1991. Dimalanta's poems celebrate the varied roles women assume and explore how these roles inherently dictate the directions women take in their lives. Describing herself as somebody who grew up in the protective and demanding environs of home and academe, Dimalanta finds freedom for herself in the fluidity of her poetry, where sound and sense blend to create scenarios of flight, exploration, wonderment, and liberation. Critics have acknowledged that her distinct poetic style has reached its height in her collections *Flowing On* (1988), *Lady Polyester: Poems Past and Present* (1996), and *Love Woman* (1998). They are testimonies to the poet's uncompromising search for a new self as woman and artist.

DTR

Dimitrova, Blaga Nikolova (*b*. 1922), Bulgarian poet, novelist, playwright. Born in Byala Slatina, Dimitrova earned a BA in Slavic philology from the University of Sofia in 1945 and a PhD in Russian literature from the 'Maxim Gorky' Institute in Moscow in 1951. She married the literary historian Yordan Vasilev in 1967 and adopted a Vietnamese girl. Between 1950 and 1996, she published twenty-six books of poetry, six novels, two plays, and several collections of essays, travelogs, and memoirs. She also has translated extensively from classical Greek, Russian, Swedish and Polish. She has worked as editor in several literary magazines and publishing houses. A political dissident during the 1970s and 1980s and one of the leaders of the democratic forces (vice-president of Bulgaria, 1992–3) after the fall of the totalitarian government (1989), she is an equally nonconformist writer. Her first novel *Journey to Oneself* (1965) exhibits the main characteristics of her later fiction and plays: oblique parallels with her poetry, female agency, and a fusion of psychological insights and political and ethical issues. Dimitrova's poems, especially those written after her battle with cancer in the 1970s, focus on the issues of life and death, love, motherhood, nature, and the power of the word. English translations of her poems have been collected in *Because the Sea is Black* (1989) and *The Last Rock Eagle* (1992). According to *Julia Kristeva, seldom has a woman's writing been at once more cerebral and more sensual.

LPG

Dimoula, Kiki (*b*. 1931), Greek poet. Born in Athens, she earned her living working for twenty-five years in the Bank of Greece. She belongs to the so-called second generation of postwar Greek poets, yet even in her early poems, she was not carried away by the trend of postwar years toward a poetry of political commitment or social criticism. Her mature poetry is characterized by an introspectiveness, existential musing, and meditation on life's inevitable decay. Her first collection *Poiimata* ('Poems') appeared in 1952. Since then, she has published seven more collections, including *Epi Ta Ichni* ('On the Trail,' 1963), *To Ligo Tou Kosmou* ('The Little of the World,' 1971; Second State Prize for Poetry), *To Teleftaio Soma Mou* ('My Last Body,' 1981), *Haire Pote* ('Farewell Never,' 1988; First State Prize for Poetry), and *I Efiveia ti Lithis* ('Lethe's Adolescence,' 1994). The last two collections, which are available in English as *Lethe's Adolescence*, are dedicated to her late husband Athos Dimoulas, by whom she admits to having been 'discretely, invaluably, and indelibly influenced.' With each new collection, she has significantly renewed her mode of expression and her work displays a remarkable poetic development. She has developed a highly personal style and poetic idiolect that because of its originality, power, and richness, has firmly established her reputation.

DCo

Ding Ling (1904–1986), Chinese fiction writer. One of twentieth-century China's most famous writers, Ding Ling grew up in Hunan province under the influence of her progressive mother. In the 1920s she moved to Shanghai, where she pursued a brief career in film acting before making her literary debut in 1927 with her story 'Mengke.' Two months later the publication of 'Miss Sophie's Diary' created an immediate sensation in literary circles for its candid depiction of female desire. The psychological turmoil of young modern women would remain the central theme of her early fiction, which appeared in leading journals and in volumes such as *Zai heianzhong* ('In Darkness,' 1928) and *Zisha riji* ('Suicide Diary,' 1929). In 1931, her interest in socialism was sharpened by the execution of her husband Hu Yepin by the Guomingdang (Nationalist Party). She assumed the editorship of the left-wing journal *Big Dipper* and, in 1932, joined the Communist Party. At Yan'an, she actively participated in debates about the nature of revolutionary culture, and experimented with agit-prop theater, reportage, and new forms of politically engaged fiction. Her socialist realist novel *The Sun Shines over the Sanggan River* (1948) explores the effects of land reform on the peasantry; it won the Stalin Prize for Literature in 1951. Branded a rightist in 1958, Ding was exiled to Heilongjiang, and did not resume writing until her official rehabilitation in 1979.

ADD

Dini, Nurhayati Srihardini (NH) (*b*. 1936), Indonesian novelist, short story writer. Although born in Indonesia, Dini's work reflects influences from her many years living abroad, particularly in France and Japan, as the wife of a French diplomat. Since returning to Indonesia in 1980, she has become involved in the conservation movement in Indonesia and she has also developed an extensive lending library in her own home in Semarang, West Java. Her novels, almost always written in the first-person, generally revolve around a female protagonist who, by her own admission, is often a mouthpiece for Dini's own views. Although she has written a number of novels, most recently *Tanah baru, tanah air kedua* ('A New Land, a Second Mother Country,' 1997), it is her short stories which have won her the most awards. In 1987, she won a short story competition sponsored by Radio France International, Le Monde, and the French ambassador. Her stories are marked by poignant insight into the conflicting loyalties of their protagonists. 'Mortal Remains' (1982) portrays the oppression of poverty and the nature of familial obligations. The mentally handicapped girl in 'Broken Wings' (1956), the young widow in 'Warsiah' (1983), and the lazy shallow 'keeper of the temples' in the story of the same name (1973) are drawn perceptively and sensitively by a writer who has great skill in depicting emotional and psychological frailty as a feature of the human condition.

PA

Di Prima, Diane (b. 1934), US poet, dramatist. Born in New York City, Di Prima attended Swarthmore College but never graduated. She opted instead to move to Greenwich Village and write. She has been married twice and has five children. She first began publishing poetry as one of the Beat poets, and her poetry has retained the Beat spirit of rebellious unconventionality. Her work has consistently mirrored the cultural and political movements in which she has participated. She is primarily preoccupied with the magical and transformative qualities of poetry, exemplified by *The New Handbook of Heaven* (1963), but her large oeuvre is too varied to summarize. *This Kind of Bird Flies Backward* (1958) is her first volume of poetry and is representative of her Beat style. The prose work *Memoirs of a Beatnik* (1969) also effectively captures that era. *Revolutionary Letters* (1971) concerns the Vietnam War and the multipart *Loba* delves into female myths and symbols

throughout history. Recent volumes reflect her abiding interest in Buddhism and the healing arts. The revised edition of her *Selected Poems: 1956–1975* was published in 1977.

JEM

Diski, Jenny (b. 1947), British novelist. Born in London, Diski had a traumatic childhood and spent some time in a psychiatric hospital. She attended University College, London from 1982 to 1984. She married Roger Diski in 1977, and separated from him in 1980; they have one daughter. Her first novel *Nothing Natural* (1986) is a shockingly explicit first-person narrative of a divorced woman's involvement in a sadomasochistic relationship. In this and subsequent novels, Diski explores the nature of identity, often through characters in extreme psychological states who struggle to maintain their sense of themselves. Diski is also know for her innovative narrative structures, as in *Rainforest* (1987), which weaves together dreams, flashbacks, and different points of view. The narrator of the disturbing *Like Mother* (1988) is Nony, a handicapped baby. With *Happily Ever After* (1991) and *Monkey's Uncle* (1994), Diski shifts into the mode of black comedy. *The Dream Mistress* (1996) is a dark and complex narrative about identity and madness. In all of her work, she challenges the dichotomies of fact and fiction, sanity and madness, order and chaos. Diski has also published *Then Again* (1990), a novel; *The Vanishing Princess* (1995), a collection of short stories; *Skating to Antarctica* (1997), a travel memoir; and *Don't* (1998), a collection of essays originally written for the *London Review of Books*.

JEM

Ditlevsen, Tove (1918–1976), Danish poet, novelist. Born in Copenhagen, Ditlevsen was for many years one of Denmark's best-loved and most widely read writers. Her suicide in 1976 occasioned an outpouring of national grief. She published some early poems in the magazine *Vild Hvede* ('Wild Wheat'), edited by her first husband Viggo F. Møller, but her actual debut was with *Pigesind* ('A Girl's Mind,' 1939). From her first published works at the age of 18 until her death, Ditlevsen was a prolific writer, whose highly personal work reflected her poor working-class background as well as her experiences in several marriages and struggles with drug addiction. She depicted with psychological realism the world of children and women in early works such as *Man gjorde et Barn Fortræd* ('A Child was Hurt,' 1941) and *Barndommens Gade* ('The Street of Childhood,' 1943). *Faces* (1968) relates the attempted suicide and hospitalization of a young mentally ill wife and mother. In the memoir *Early Spring* (1971), originally published as two volumes in 1967, the youth of a young girl from a poor neighborhood who wants to become a published writer is portrayed with great sensitivity. *Gift* ('Married,' 1971) is a chilling autobiographical account of a young wife who leaves her husband for another man who can supply her with narcotics. Although highly personal, Ditlevsen's work reflects the existential 'angst' of the women writers of her generation.

MHH

Divakaruni, Chitra Banerjee (*b.* 1956), Indian-US poet, fiction writer. Born in Calcutta, Divakaruni lived in different parts of India before coming to America in 1976. Her BA is from Calcutta University, her MA in English from Wright State University, Ohio, and her PhD in English from the University of California, Berkeley. She is married and has two sons. She teaches creative writing at the University of Houston. She made her debut as a poet with the collection *Dark Like the River* (1987). Her writing is shaped by the folklore and rural beauty of Bengal and by her experiences in America, especially as founder of a battered women's organization. Her award-winning story collection *Arranged*

Marriage (1995) depicts the challenges confronting Indian women as contemporary life and immigration widen the gap between traditional values and individual needs. Her magical-realist novel *The Mistress of Spices* (1997) describes her Indian female protagonist's negotiations between past vows and her new life in America. The poems in *Leaving Yuba City* (1997), which won Pushcart and Allen Ginsberg Prizes, are inspired by an eclectic range of paintings, photographs, and films. The lyrical, visual poems tell haunting stories of struggle and self-discovery in immigrants' lives. Her novel *Sister of My Heart* (1999) is a coming-of-age tale about two cousins from a once wealthy family being raised together in Calcutta.

SA

Djebar, Assia (Fatima-Zohra Imalhayene) (*b.* 1936), Algerian novelist, filmmaker. Born in Cherchel, Algeria, the daughter of a schoolteacher, Djebar published her first novel, *The Mischief*, in 1957. From 1958 to 1962 she studied history in Tunis; she later taught history at the University of Rabat, Morocco and at the University of Algiers. She has directed two films: *The Nouba of the Mount Chenoua Women* (1978; Prix de la Critique Internationale at the Venice Film Festival) and *The Zerda and the Songs of Forgetting* (1982), about the colonial period in the Maghreb (1912–42). In the novel *Women of Algiers in their Apartment* (1980) she explores the fate of women of different generations from the beginning of the French colonization to the postwar years. The first volume of her autobiography *Fantasia: An Algerian Cavalcade* (1985) blends personal narratives with oral histories of women resisters in the war of liberation from France (1954–62). *Far from Medina: Daughters of Ismael* (1991) is a response to political events in Algeria and to the revision of the status of women. The novel *So Vast the Prison* (1994) combines history and family narratives with the story of the breakdown of a modern marriage. *Algerian White*

(1996; forthcoming in English) considers the lives of nineteen Algerian writers. *Oran, langue morte* ('Oran, Dead Language,' 1997) and *The Strasbourg Nights* (1997; forthcoming in English) respectively explore the current violence in Algeria and transnational and transcultural relationships. The recipient of the Neusstadt International Prize for Literature in 1996, she teaches at Louisiana State University.

JV

Djura (*b.* 1949), Algerian-Kabyle writer. Born in Ifigha, a Kabyle village in the Djurdjura mountains, Djura spent the first years of her life in the care of her paternal grandfather's second wife, Setsi Fatima, who transmitted much of her cultural heritage to her. Djura emigrated to France in 1954, where she lived in various housing projects with her family. In her autobiography *The Veil of Silence* (1990), she details her family life and the violence she endured from her older brother and father, while she was helping raise her seven younger siblings and caring for her mother. In 1968 she briefly went back to Algeria and to Ifigha where she re-acquainted herself with her culture. She co-directed two films about Algerian architecture, as well as a feature film about immigrants *Ali au pays des merveilles* ('Ali in Wonderland,' 1976). With the help of her Breton husband, Hervé Lacroix, she turned to singing traditional and modern Berber songs and recorded two albums (1993, 1998) in Tamazigh and in French, with her group Djur Djura, about women's freedom and immigration. Her second book *La saison des Narcisses* ('Narcissus's Season,' 1993) mixes autobiography and reflections about Algerian women.

JV

Dormann, Geneviève (*b.* 1933), French novelist. Dormann, who published her first novel, *The Seasons of Love*, in 1959, had since written many best-selling works which have garnered important literary prizes, including *Je t'apporterai des orages* ('I'll Bring You Storms,' 1971; Prix des Quatre Jurys) and *Le bateau du courrier* ('The Mail Boat,' 1974; Prix des Deux Magots). In general, her novels focus on strong female characters who defy social conventions in a quest for self-realization. One of her better-known works, *Le bal du dodo* ('The Ball of the Dodo Bird,' 1989), a blend of fictional and nonfictional elements of past and present, recounts the disintegration of a tightly-knit group of Franco-Mauritian families descended from eighteenth-century French settlers. Besides writing novels, Dormann is the author of several biographical works including *Colette: A Passion for Life* (1984) and *La Gourmandise de Guillaume Apollinaire* ('The Gourmandise of Guillaume Apollinaire,' 1994).

PJP, SIr

Dorrestein, Renate (*b.* 1954), Dutch novelist. Dorrestein began her writing career as a journalist. She wrote for several magazines, one of which was the feminist monthly *Opzij* ('Her Side'); she became renowned for the polemical columns she wrote for it. Her debut *Buitenstaanders* ('Outsiders') was published in 1983. In 1987 she devoted herself to writing fiction full-time. Especially her early novels contain many Gothic elements, leaving ample scope for surrealistic situations. They are often wryly comic and explicitly feminist. The more autobiographical *Het perpetuum mobile van de liefde* ('The Perpetuum Mobile of Love,' 1988), about her sister's suicide, marked a new development in her work. Her later novels are more realistic, although she has never lost her sense of absurdity. *Unnatural Mothers* (1992) is about a family secret that affects three generations of women and *Heart of Stone* (1998) gives an excellent atmospheric depiction of the 1970s. She always sides with women, children, outsiders, and others who, in general, have less power in society. Together with *Elly de Waard and others, Dorrestein was one of the founders, in 1986, of the Anna Bijns Prize, a literary prize for 'the female voice in Dutch literature.'

AAn, MMe

Douka, Maro (*b*. 1947), Greek novelist. Born in Hania, Crete, Douka began studying archaeology at the University of Athens a year before the Colonels' dictatorship was imposed on Greece in 1967. She became an active member of the student resistance movement, suffering arrest and imprisonment. During and after the dictatorship she published three collections of short stories. Her first novel *Fool's Gold* (1979; Kazantzakis Prize) drawing on her experience of those years, is a sharply observed account of a young girl's growth to maturity against the combined onslaughts of ideological friend and foe alike. In her next three novels, Douka adopts a more experimental style, juxtaposing voices and points of view, male as well as female. These are *I Ploti Poli* ('The Floating City,' 1983), *I Lefkes Asaleftes* ('The Poplars Unmoving,' 1987), and *Is ton Pato tis Ikonas* ('In the Background of the Picture,' 1990). A significant departure came with *Enas Skoufos apo Porfyra* ('A Cap of Purple,' 1995), a substantial historical novel of Byzantium at the time of the First Crusade. Her most recent work is *I Efivia tis Lithis* ('The Adolescence of Oblivion,' 1996), which was shortlisted for the European 'Aristeion' prize.

RB

Dove, Rita (*b*. 1952), US poet. Born in Akron, Ohio, Dove attended Miami University, Ohio (BA, 1973), the University of Tubingen, West Germany, and the University of Iowa (MFA, 1977). She married Fred Viebahn in 1979; she has one daughter. She has taught English and creative writing at Arizona State University and, since 1989, at the University of Virginia. The first African-American to serve as US Poet Laureate (1993–5) and the winner of numerous literary prizes and awards, Dove published her first volume of poetry *Ten*

Poems in 1977. Her work ranges widely through history, often with regard to African-American experience, but it doesn't neglect individual experience. She writes about travel, the natural world, family life, and motherhood, but does so with a distinctive objectivity. *Thomas and Beulah* (1986), a verse cycle based on her grandparents' lives, won the Pulitzer Prize. *Mother Love* (1995) explores the mother–daughter relationship through the myth of Demeter and Persephone. *On the Bus with Rosa Parks* (1999) contains meditations on public and private history. Dove's other volumes include *The Yellow House on the Corner* (1980), *Grace Notes* (1989), and *Selected Poems* (1993). She has also published *Fifth Sunday* (1985), a collection of short stories, and *Through the Ivory Gate* (1992), a novel. Her verse drama *The Darker Face of the Earth* (1994) rewrites the Oedipus myth in the antebellum South.

JEM

Drabble, Margaret (*b*. 1939), English novelist, critic. Born in Sheffield, England, Drabble followed her older sister *A. S. Byatt to study at Newnham College, Cambridge, where she graduated with first class honors in English literature in 1960. Drabble worked initially at the Royal Shakespeare Company, where she was an understudy to Vanessa Redgrave and where she met her first husband, actor Clive Walter Swift; she had three children with him. In 1982, she married biographer Michael Holroyd. She published her first novel *A Summer Bird Cage*, which explores the relationship of a woman with her successful older sister, in 1963. Her early novels, such as *The Garrick Year* (1964), *The Millstone* (1965), *Jerusalem the Golden* (1967), and *The Waterfall* (1969), focus on intelligent young women who wrestle with conflicting roles and expectations, particularly those related to sexuality, maternity, and class. In her later novels *The Needle's Eye* (1972), *The Ice Age* (1977), and the trilogy *The Radiant*

Way (1987), *A Natural Curiosity* (1989), and *The Gates of Ivory* (1991), she shifts her attention from personal relationships to larger social issues confronting modern England. Drabble's novels, written in a traditionally realistic style, are concerned with moral responsibility and social history, and show the strong influence of George Eliot and Arnold Bennett, whose biography she wrote in 1975. The editor of the fifth edition of the *Oxford Companion to English Literature* (1985), she has written several works of literary criticism.

DVT

Drakulić, Slavenka (*b*. 1949), Croatian novelist, essayist. Born in Rijeka, Drakulić graduated from the Comparative Literature and Sociology departments at the University of Zagreb. A freelance journalist contributing to Croatian, American, Italian, Swedish, and German publications, in the late 1980s she began writing novels thematically focused on taboos related to the body: illness, incest, cannibalism. Utilizing the author's own experience of prolonged sickness, *Holograms of Fear* (1987) articulates a situation in which a woman reconstructs her shattered self through writing and language when her body starts behaving as a foreign entity. *Marble Skin* (1989) revolves around a daughter's sexual obsession with her mother, and *The Taste of a Man* (1995) explores the connection between sexuality and cannibalism. Her popular nonfiction works *How We Survived Communism and Even Laughed* (1992), *Balkan Express: Fragments from the Other Side of War* (1994), and *Café Europa: Life After Communism* (1997) combine journalism with the genres of autobiography and essay. Drakulić lives in Sweden, Austria, and Croatia.

GC

Dros, Imme (*b*. 1936), Dutch children's writer. Dros has had a passion for reading and writing ever since she was a little child. She read Dutch at university and

together with Harrie Geelen, her partner, she wrote a successful Dutch television series in the early 1970s. Geelen later illustrated many of her own books. Dros has written over thirty books since 1980, for early readers as well as for older children, in addition to several plays. Her style is vivid and imaginative; a recurring theme is the (painful) contrast between dreams and reality. In the books for older children, she uses a more realistic style, as in *De trimbaan* ('The Training Circuit,' 1987), in which she explores the dilemmas of a boy who discovers he is gay. She has won many literary prizes for her work. *Annelie in the Depths of the Night* (1987), for children 7 years and older, and *The Journeys of the Clever Man* (1988), for children over 13, are available in English. Her work for adults includes translations of the visions of the medieval poet and mystic Hadewijch and Homer's *Odyssey*. She also adapted this Greek classic for children in *Odysseus, man van verhalen* ('Ulysses, Teller of Tales,' 1994).

AAu, MMe

Duckworth, Marilyn (*b*. 1935), New Zealand novelist. Duckworth was born in New Zealand, but along with her sister *Fleur Adcock, attended a dozen schools in England during World War II. She returned to New Zealand in her teens. She has held a broad array of jobs, has been married four times, and has several children and stepchildren. Her first novel *A Gap in the Spectrum* (1959) is science fiction and introduces her continuing interest in the oppression of women. Duckworth won the New Zealand Book Award for Fiction for *Disorderly Conduct* (1984) and *Leather Wings* (1995). With a background of the 1981 Springbok Rugby Tour, *Disorderly Conduct* is about a woman who is struggling to balance children, ex-husbands, and lovers, while *Leather Wings* involves the complicated relationships among a door-to-door salesman, a child, and a grandmother. Along with her dozen novels, Duckworth has published a short story collection, a book of poems, and *Cherries on a Plate: New Zealand Writers Talk about their Sisters* (1998). She has held the Scholarship in Letters (twice), literary fellowships at Victoria University and the University of Auckland, the Katherine Mansfield Memorial Fellowship, the Buddle Findlay Sargeson Fellowship, and a Fulbright Visiting Writers' Fellowship. In 1987 she was awarded the Order of the British Empire.

M-RA

Duffy, Carol Ann (*b.* 1955), British poet, playwright. Born in Glasgow, raised in Staffordshire, Duffy graduated with honors from the University of Liverpool in 1977. While still in high school, she published her first volume of poetry *Fleshweathercock and Other Poems* (1973). She has written two full-length plays *Take My Husband* and *Cavern of Dreams*, as well as the one-act plays *Loss* and *Little Women, Big Boys*. This theatrical background is evident in her first major collection of poetry *Standing Female Nude* (1985), which displays her deftness at the dramatic monologue, the form for which she is best known. Her poetry collection *Selling Manhattan* (1987) demonstrates her fine ear for patterns of speech, and her interest in giving voice to the alienated and the disenfranchised. Duffy, a prize-winning poet who has been a writer in residence at several London schools, has edited three anthologies of poetry including *I Wouldn't Thank You for a Valentine: Poems for Young Feminists* (1997). Her other collections of poetry include *The Other Country* (1990), *Mean Time* (1993), *Selected Poems* (1994), and *The World's Wife* (2000).

DVT

Duffy, Maureen (*b.* 1933), British poet, novelist, playwright. Born in Worthing, Sussex, Duffy earned a BA from King's College, London in 1956. She worked for a time as a teacher and has been an active campaigner for many social causes, including animal rights. A prolific author in many genres, her first book was a novel, *That's How It Was* (1962), a poignant story of a mother–daughter relationship. Her realistic novels offer detailed portraits of working-class life. Her best-known novel *The Microcosm* (1966) depicts both the realities and fantasies of lesbian society. In *The Paradox Players* (1967), a novelist retreats to a houseboat on the Thames, and discovers a new world of deprivation and strength. Other novels include *Love Child* (1971), *Capital* (1975), *Change* (1987), *Illuminations* (1991), and *Restitution* (1998). The central concern of Duffy's poetry, as in *Lyrics for the Dog Hour* (1968), *The Venus Touch* (1971), and *Evesong* (1975), is love, both physical and spiritual, and primarily that between women. In *Memorials of the Quick and the Dead* (1979), she turns her attention to social and environmental problems. Her *Collected Poems* was published in 1985. Duffy has also written many plays and several works of nonfiction, including *The Passionate Shepherdess* (1977), a biography of Aphra Behn.

JEM

Dunmore, Helen (*b.* 1952), British poet, novelist. Born in Yorkshire, Dunmore received a BA from York University in 1973. She is married and has two children. She is a prolific and prize-winning author of both verse and fiction. She published her first book of poetry *The Apple Fall* in 1983. Her poetry is impressively varied in its structures, concerns, and perspectives. The poems in *The Raw Garden* (1988) are all connected in their consideration of the natural and the unnatural. The richly sensual descriptions that are characteristic of both her poetry and her prose are highlighted in *Recovering a Body* (1994). Other poetry collections include *The Sea Skater* (1986), *Short Days, Long Nights* (1991), and *Bestiary* (1997). Her novels focus on the psychological and the domestic, and the imagery and rhythms of her verse are evident in her prose. Her first novel *Going* *to Egypt* was published in 1992. Her second novel, *Zennor in Darkness* (1993), won the McKitterick Prize. An unusually intense sibling relationship and destructive family secrets are at the heart of *A Spell of Winter* (1995; Orange Prize) and recur in *Talking to the Dead* (1996) and *With Your Crooked Heart* (1999), a psychological thriller with shifting narrative perspectives. She has also published the novels *Burning Bright* (1994) and *Your Blue-Eyed Boy* (1998), a collection of stories *Love of Fat Men* (1997), and several works for children.

JEM

Dunn, Nell (*b.* 1936), British novelist, playwright, nonfiction writer. Born into a wealthy upper-middle-class family, Dunn moved when she was in her twenties to Battersea, London to write about working-class urban life. Her distinctive style takes the form of vignettes or sketches, based on interviews and careful observations. Her accurate representation of dialect and mundane details, as well as her authorial distance, give her work a documentary feel. Her first group of vignettes was published initially in the *New Statesman* and then in book form as *Up the Junction* (1963). Her best-selling novel *Poor Cow* (1967) pulls together similar narrative fragments to tell the story of Joy, a 22-year-old single mother and factory worker whose life is going nowhere; it was made into a popular film by Ken Loach. In 1996, Dunn published *My Silver Shoes*, a sequel which catches up with the indomitable Joy thirty years later. Dunn has also published two books of interviews: *Talking to Women* (1965), about women in the 1960s, and *Living Like I Do* (1976), about people pursuing alternative lifestyles. She has also written several plays, of which her first, *Steaming* (1981), about a community of women in a Turkish bathhouse, is the best known.

JEM

Duong Thu Huong (*b.* 1947), Vietnamese novelist, fiction writer. Perhaps the best-known Vietnamese dissident writer, Duong Thu Huong was born in the north of Vietnam and grew up with strong beliefs in communist ideology. At 20, she led a Communist Youth brigade sent to the front during the Vietnam War. After the war, in 1975, she returned to Hanoi to study creative writing. She became disenchanted with the communist ideology and started writing about the sorrows and disillusionment of her countrymen, as depicted in her trilogy of novels *Ben Kia Bo Ao Vong* ('Beyond Illusions,'1987), *Quang Doi Danh Mat* ('Fragments of Lost Life,' 1989) and *Paradise of the Blind* (1988), the first Vietnamese novel ever translated and published in North America. It was nominated for the 1991 Prix Femina Etranger. Her fourth novel *Novel Without a Name* (1995) questions the notion of heroism in war. Postwar despair is the subject of her latest novel, *Memories of a Pure Spring* (2000). An outspoken advocate of human rights and democracy reforms, she was expelled from the Vietnamese Communist Party in 1989 and was arrested and imprisoned without trial for seven months in 1991. All of her novels have been banned in Vietnam. Her other works include more than forty short stories. Of these, the selected collection *Chuyen Tinh Ke Truoc Rang Dong* ('A Love Story Told Before Dawn,' 1988) has been translated into French and German. Duong Thu Huong lives in Hanoi with her two children.

TT

Duranti, Francesca (*b.* 1938), Italian writer, journalist. Born in Genoa, Duranti grew up in Tuscany. She studied law at the University of Pisa and worked as a journalist and translator before publishing her first novel at the age of 38. Her first two novels draw largely on autobiographical material. *La bambina* ('The Young Girl,' 1976) relates the young Duranti's perceptions of family relationships and the experience of having German soldiers billeted at their home. *Piazza mia bella piazza* ('My Beautiful Piazza,' 1977) is the story of the break-up of her marriage due to the opposition of her husband to her writing. Beginning with *The House on Moon Lake* (1984), Duranti moves away from autobiography and begins to experiment with different fictional genres, techniques and myths to express with humor and irony her main theme – the difficulty of and obsession with self-definition in the West's atmosphere of decadence, consumerism, image-making and self-promotion. Like Fabrizio in *The House on Moon Lake* and the newly divorced Valentina in *Personal Effects* (1988), Duranti's protagonists strive to create individual reputations as critics, scholars, writers, or feminists only to find that each new definition carries new limitations. In *Sogni mancini* ('False Dreams,' 1996), a young Italian woman comes to New York University to teach European culture and redefine herself with humorous, tragic, and positive results.

CL-W

Duras, Marguerite (1914–1996), French novelist, screenwriter. Born Marguerite Donnadieu to teachers in the French colony in South Vietnam, she came to Paris in 1935. She wrote more than seventy books, starting with *Les Impudents* ('The Insolents') in 1943. Memory, pain, absence, madness, violence, and erotic desire are recurrent themes in her varied oeuvre. Like Proust's, Duras's life was inextricably bound up in her writing. Obsessively returning to the story of her childhood and adolescence, she demonstrated how one's life can never fully be captured in words. Giving voice to a female desire deemed socially unacceptable, she created her own 'écriture féminine' with liberal doses of silence, inviting us to read between the lines. Best known for *The Lover* (1984; Prix Goncourt), an autobiographical novel about an adolescent girl in Indochina, she also authored the screenplay for Alain Resnais's film *Hiroshima Mon Amour* (1959). In *The War: A Memoir* (1985), she reworked her war-time journals that recount the return of her husband, Robert Antelme, from the Nazi concentration camps. She later divorced him for another intellectual, Dionys Mascolo. Placing herself along the margins of French life, Duras repeatedly brought to light stories of women's experience and inner turmoil.

JHS

E

Edgell, Zee (*b.* 1940), Belizean novelist. Born Zelma Inez Tucker, Edgell's desire to write grew out of her childhood in her native Belize (then British Honduras), among a supportive Creole family and a strong sense of community. She has traveled extensively with her North American husband, Al Edgell, who worked with CARE, Save the Children USA, and the Peace Corps in Afghanistan, Bangladesh, Nigeria, and Somalia. Having lived mostly away from Belize, she says her novels retrieve its numerous and scattered memories. Her first job, in the early 1960s, was as a reporter for the *Daily Gleaner* in Kingston, Jamaica. Her first novel *Beka Lamb* (1982) chronicles the birth of the nationalist movement in the British Honduras (1951) simultaneous with the young female protagonist's coming of age. She was the Director of the Women's Bureau in Belize, which she fictionalizes in her second book *In Times Like These* (1991), a novel that again weaves together stories of women and nation struggling toward independence. Her third novel *The Festival of San Joaquin* (1997) is from the perspective of a 'mestiza' and deals with domestic violence. Edgell has two adult children and teaches in the Department of English at Kent State University.

MHL

Edmond, Lauris (1924–2000), New Zealand poet, autobiographer. Edmond was born at Hawkes Bay, New Zealand and received a BA from Waikato University and an MA (Honours) from Victoria University. Her *In Middle Air* (1975) won the PEN New Zealand Best First Book Award, and her *Selected Poems* (1984) won the Commonwealth Prize for Poetry. Her poems tend to be direct in tone, warm, and intimate; her vivid, traditional lyrics celebrate love, family relationships, and nature. Older women are often her subject, as are the themes of aging and loss, as in her collection *A Matter of Timing* (1996; published in England as *In Position*). In addition to her ten collections of poetry, Edmond wrote and edited nonfiction and published several short stories, plays, and a novel, *High Country Weather* (1984). Her three-volume autobiography *Hot October* (1989), *Bonfires in the Rain* (1991), and *The Quick World* (1994) describes her transition from being a conventional wife and mother to a dedicated writer. She received numerous awards and honors; in 1986 she was awarded the Order of the British Empire for services to poetry and literature.

M-RA

Ega, Françoise (1920–1976), Antillean autobiographer, novelist. Born in a Martinican village, Ega completed her schooling in Fort-de-France and became a teletypist in the French Air Force. With her husband, a medic, she worked in Africa before settling in Marseilles. In France, she strove to assist others, especially Antillean immigrants, to combat racism, and to encourage intercommunity exchange. This social commitment extends to her writing. In *Le temps des madras* ('The Time of Madras Scarves,' 1967), she tells of the 'enchanted world' of a rural Martinican childhood. *Lettres à une Noire* ('Letters to a Black Woman,' 1978), a more politically engaged work, reiterates female solidarity and illustrates Ega's dream for the black diaspora through fictional letters addressed to a writer from the Brazilian slums.

AMR

Ekman, Kerstin (*b*. 1933), Swedish novelist. Born in Risinge, a small town southwest of Stockholm, Ekman in 1957 received an MA from the University of Uppsala. Before becoming a full-time writer, she wrote film scripts, worked as a literary critic, and taught literature from 1965 to 1970. Today she lives in Valsjöbyn, a small village in northern Sweden. A member of the Swedish Academy since 1978, she resigned in 1989 when the Academy did not make a statement in the Salman Rushdie case. Her first crime fiction *30 meter mord* ('30 Meters of Murder,' 1959) was followed by seven more crime novels. Her breakthrough came with *Magic Circles* (1974), the first book of her tetralogy, which depicts the history of Sweden from 1870 to 1970 from a distinct female perspective. The price for industrialization and urbanization is here seen as fragmentation and alienation, resulting in a loss of a communal 'we.' The role of community is emphasized in *Blackwater* (1993), with which she returned to crime fiction and received the Swedish Crime Academy's Award, the August Prize, and the Nordic Council's Literary Prize. In 1995 Ekman was awarded the Pilot Prize for her oeuvre. Her novels point to the importance of remembrance and stories for survival, as in *Gör mig levande igen* ('Make Me Come

Alive Again,' 1996), where seven women's lives are intertwined.

GE-C

Ekström, Margareta (*b*. 1930), Swedish novelist, short story writer, poet. Born in Stockholm, Ekström has been extremely productive. Besides writing fiction, she has worked as a critic and essayist for the Swedish media, and been the chair of Sweden PEN. Ekström has made renderings of Wole Soyinka and Virginia Woolf, among others. She lives in Stockholm with her husband, the writer Per Wästberg. In 1960 she published her first collection of short stories *Aftnar in S:t Petersburg* ('Evenings in St Petersburg'), and she has since published a book almost every year. Primarily recognized for her subtle and precise short stories, Ekström has also written several collections of poems such as *Ord till Johanna* ('Words to Johanna,' 1973), *Under bar himmel* ('Under Open Sky,' 1984), and *Skärmar* ('Screens,' 1990). In the latter collection, symbolic 'screens' hide human sufferings; yet people have learned to prevail, to doubt but not despair. The meaning of life and people's needs and longing for communication are unerringly described in *Death's Midwives: Stories* (1976) through sharp humor and psychology – narrative devices also developed in *The Day I Began My Studies in Philosophy and Other Stories* (1989). She is the recipient of many literary awards.

GE-C

Ellis, Alice Thomas (Anna Haycraft) (*b*. 1932), British novelist, nonfiction writer. Born in Liverpool, Ellis grew up in Wales, where many of her novels are set; she attended the Liverpool School of Art. She married Colin Haycraft in 1956; they have five children. She converted to Roman Catholicism at age 19, and Catholicism is an important element in her fiction. She worked as a fiction editor at Duckworth for many years. Ellis's witty and elegantly written satirical novels usually center on women, and their domestic and marital problems, and target middle-class complacency. Her first novel *The Sin Eater* (1977) depicts the clash between a daughter and daughter-in-law as the family patriarch is dying. In *Unexplained Laughter* (1985), a woman goes to Wales to recover from a love affair, but is disturbed rather than consoled by what she encounters there. Other novels include *The Birds of the Air* (1980), *The 27th Kingdom* (1982), *The Other Side of Fire* (1983), the *Summer House* trilogy (*The Clothes in the Wardrobe* [1987], *The Skeleton in the Cupboard* [1988], and *The Fly in the Ointment* [1989]; published in one volume, 1994), which tells the same story from three different perspectives, *Pillars of Gold* (1992), and *Fairy Tale* (1996). Ellis has also published several collections of essays on her home life, and *Serpent on the Rock* (1994), a personal exploration of Christianity.

JEM

Eltit, Diamela (*b.* 1949), Chilean novelist. Born in Santiago de Chile, Eltit studied Spanish literature at the Universidad Católica de Chile and film and theater at the Universidad de Chile. She worked as a full-time teacher until 1985. She was one of the founders of CADA, an art collective active in the late 1970s and early 1980s practicing alternative modes of artistic expression to counter the vacuum created by repression during the military dictatorship of Augusto Pinochet (1973–90). Her first novel *E. Luminata* (1983) was followed by *Por la patria* ('For the Fatherland,' 1986), *The Fourth World* (1988), and *Sacred Cow* (1991). Nonfiction works include *El padre mío* ('My Father,' 1989) and *El infarto del alma* ('Stroke in the Soul,' 1994; co-authored with Paz Errázuriz). In her acclaimed and highly literary work, Eltit explores the effects of social restrictions on the individual, especially those inhabiting the margins. She received a Guggenheim fellowship (1986), and the 1995 José Nuez Foundation Prize for best novel for *Los vigilantes* ('The

Guardians,' 1994). *Los trabajadores de la muerte* ('The Workers of Death,' 1998) is her latest novel. A university professor, she has lectured and taught at Berkeley, Columbia, Johns Hopkins, Stanford, Washington University, and other institutions.

MIL

Emecheta, Buchi (Onyebuchi Florence) (*b.* 1944), Nigerian novelist, autobiographer, children's writer. Born in Yaba, Lagos, Nigeria, Emecheta uses this area as well as Ibusa, her parents' hometown, as a setting in her early works. She married Francis Onwordi; they had five children before separating in 1966. She received a BS in sociology in 1974, a master's degree in philosophy in 1976 from the University of London, and a PhD in literature from Fairleigh Dickinson University in 1992. Her first books *In the Ditch* (1972) and *Second Class Citizen* (1974) are autobiographical fiction set in London, and depict the efforts of a young African mother to overcome racism, marital discord, poverty, and welfare. In *The Bride Price* (1976), a young woman is doomed for ignoring custom and eloping with the descendant of a slave. *The Slave Girl* (1977; New Statesman/Jock Campbell Award) deals with the impact of male ownership, whether father, husband, brother or master, upon the female's personal life and choices. *The Joys of Motherhood* (1979; Best British Writer's Award) explores the life of a woman who adheres to the traditional norms of having many children and enduring a polygamous marriage. In *The Family* (1990), a young, loveless girl searches for control over her life after she is raped and impregnated by her father. Emecheta's most recent novel is *Kehinde* (1994) and she is currently working on a novel titled *The New Breed*. She is the author of twelve other works, four performed plays, and numerous essays.

MBr

Enchi Fumiko (1905–1986), Japanese novelist. Born in Asakusa, Tokyo, the youngest child of renowned linguist Kazutoshi Ueda, Enchi grew up learning the importance of the Japanese classics. Her formal education ended when she abandoned Nihon Women's High School's courses on 'womanly' skills to independently study more academic subjects. In 1930 she married newspaper reporter Yoshimatsu Enchi; she had one daughter. In 1954 Enchi received the Joryū Bungaku Prize for *Himojii Tsukihi* ('Miserable Times,' 1953), which portrays the victim of an unhappy marriage like her own and incorporates the theme of spiritual liberation rooted in *The Tale of Genji*. The novel *Masks* (1958) provides a commentary on this theme. Her literature focuses on women's hardships and includes numerous award-winning works: a story of a nineteenth-century woman, *The Waiting Years* (1957); a tale of eleventh-century court life, *Namamiko monogatari* ('The Tale of Namamiko,' 1965), the semi-autobiographical trilogy *Ake o ubau mono* ('Stripped of Crimson,' 1968), and a collage of elderly women's fantasies, *Yukon* ('Wandering Spirits,' 1971). Her modern translation of *The Tale of Genji* is as well-known as her original creations. In 1985 she received Japan's highest honor in the arts, the Cultural Award.

EBM-A

Enquist, Anna (Christa Widlund-Broer) (*b.* 1945), Dutch novelist, poet. Writing is Enquist's third career. For many years, she was a professional classical pianist, and since receiving a degree in psychology in 1969, she has worked as a psychologist. During the final years of her musical career she wrote her first poems, which were published in 1988 in a Dutch literary magazine. Her first volume *Soldatenliederen* ('Soldier's Songs,' 1991) was widely praised, as well as following volumes. Translations of her poems can be found in several anthologies of Dutch literature, including *Turning Tides* (1994) and *The Defiant Muse* (1998). Her psychological and musical

backgrounds have influenced her literary work, most clearly in her novels. Enquist's prose debut, *The Masterpiece* (1994), is a family novel that can be read as a fictional exploration of classical psychoanalytical themes, such as narcissism and Oedipal rivalry. In *The Secret* (1997), the main character is a successful female pianist. The absence of a father figure is characteristic of both novels. In 1999 Enquist published a volume of short stories, *De Kwetsuur* ('The Wound'). She has received several literary prizes, for both her poetry and her prose.

AAn, MMe

Eray, Nazlı (*b.* 1945), Turkish novelist, short story writer. Born in Istanbul, Eray studied law at Istanbul University, but did not finish the program. She worked as a translator between 1965 and 1968. All her writings venture into the fantastic, which she uses to explore unchartered territories, both of the unconscious and of narration. She deals with an international cast of characters that include Dilip, an Indian fakir, Che Guevara, Marie Antoinette and a robot, among others. She appears as a character in most of her writings. Her novels are *Pasifik Günleri* ('Pacific Days,' 1980), *Orphee* ('Orpheus,' 1982), *Deniz Kenarında Pazartesi* ('Monday By the Sea,' 1984), *Arzu Sapağında İnecek Var* ('Somebody Will Get Off at the Cul-de-sac of Desire,' 1991), *Ay Falcısı* ('Fortune-teller of the Moon,' 1992), and *Yıldızlar Mektup Yazar* ('Stars Write Letters,' 1993). Of her many story collections, *Yoldan Geçen Öyküler* ('Stories that Pass by the Road,' 1987) won the Haldun Taner Story Prize in 1988. Two of her stories, 'Monte Cristo' (about a woman who escapes from her marriage by digging a tunnel out of her house) and 'The Underdevelopment Pharmacy' (about a pharmacy which sells pills that make people forget the better lives they have seen), are available in English translation. Eray is divorced and has twin daughters.

SE

Erb, Elke (*b.* 1938), German poet, essayist, editor. Erb's family moved from West Germany to the German Democratic Republic in 1949. She studied German and Slavic literatures, history, and pedagogy at the University of Halle. She moved to East Berlin in 1966. Her collections of poetry and short prose *Gutachten* ('Opinions,' 1975) and *Der Faden der Geduld* ('The Thread of Patience,' 1978) reflect her search for ways to fracture the prescriptive aesthetic of socialist realism. Writing initially about everyday reality and female experiences in a linear manner, she changed to a non-linear writing style in *Vexierbild* ('Picture-Puzzle,' 1983) and *Kastanienallee* ('Chestnut Street,' 1987). Among East Berlin's 'counter-culture' in Prenzlauer Berg, she functioned as a mediator and mentor, publishing younger writers' texts in the anthology *Berührung ist nur eine Randerscheinung* ('Touching Is only a Marginal Experience,' 1985). *Winkelzüge* ('Tricks,' 1991) challenges traditional concepts of autobiography by blurring fiction and reality, as well as the boundaries between author, narrator, protagonist, and reader. *Unschuld, du Licht meiner Augen* ('Innocence, Light of My Eyes,' 1994) contains 'text-echoes' of the works of the experimental Austrian writer *Friederike Mayröcker, and Der wilde Forst, der tiefe Wald* ('The Wild and Deep Forest,' 1995), a collection of essays and interviews, reflects on the changes brought by German unification. Erb has received several major literary prizes. Three volumes of her poetry have been translated into English as *Mountains in Berlin* (1995).

BMab

Erdrich, (Karen) Louise (*b.* 1954), US novelist. Raised in Wahpeton, North Dakota, Erdrich received a BA from Dartmouth College in 1976 and an MA from Johns Hopkins University in 1981. She married and raised six children with the late novelist Michael Dorris, whom she met at Dartmouth. Her lyrical storytelling is strongly influenced by her midwestern Ojibwa (Chippewa) heritage. Though her first publication was a collection of poems titled *Jacklight* (1984), she is best known for her novels, which depict the history and traditions as well as the adversities of Native American life. Her first novel *Love Medicine* (1984; National Book Critics Circle Award) forms a tetralogy with *The Beet Queen* (1986), *Tracks* (1988), and *The Bingo Palace* (1994). These cyclically structured works, in which short stories are woven into the narratives of the novels, follow several North Dakota families, both Native American and European immigrant, through three generations. Her creation of a community full of rich characters and history has led many critics to compare her fictional world to Faulkner's Yoknapatawpha County. Erdrich's other works include *Tales of Burning Love* (1996), the novel *The Antelope Wife* (1998), *The Blue Jay's Dance: A Birth Year* (1996), a nonfiction work which describes the challenges and joys of motherhood, and *The Birchbark House* (1999), a book for young readers.

LWT

Ernaux, Annie (*b.* 1940), French novelist. Ernaux grew up in Normandy in a blue-collar neighborhood where her parents managed a small bar–grocery store. She teaches French in high school. The ever-widening chasm between her working-class childhood and her new social status as a middle class intellectual has greatly influenced her writing, which wavers between fiction and autobiography. With her first and most fictionalized novel *Cleaned Out* (1974), she explored a young girl's physical, emotional, and sexual awakening, the effects of which are compounded by her growing awareness of her social position as an underprivileged female. After *A Frozen Woman* (1981), which chronicled Ernaux's failed marriage, *A Man's Place* (1984) and *A Woman's Story* (1988) announced an uneasy reconciliation of social spheres and linguistic levels while still focusing on class differences. Her consciousness of her social mutation surfaces even in the narration of the most intimate love affair, *Passion Perfect* (1991), as well as in her note-taking on grocery shopping, *Exteriors* (1993). In her most recent novels *Shame* (1997) and *Je ne suis pas sortie de ma nuit* ('I Have not Left my Night,' 1997) she continues her exploration of her spiraling connections to a past she cannot forget.

CLa

Espina-Moore, Lina (*b.* 1919), Philippine fiction writer. Espina-Moore was born and raised in Cebu. She obtained a BA at the Southern College (now the University of Southern Philippines) and studied law at the Far Eastern University. During World War II, she was involved in guerilla activities and was eventually arrested by the Japanese military because, she says, she was turned in by a rejected suitor. When the war ended, she returned to FEU to study foreign service, simultaneously working for the Malacanang Press Office. She married a former US army captain, Climpson 'Kip' Moore, with whom she had one son. They lived at the foot of Mount Data, the country's highest peak, which served to provide her with the details she has used in her narratives. She has written eleven novels in her native Cebuano, and two in English: *Heart of the Lotus* (1970), set in Cebu from 1920 to 1930, and *A Lion in the House* (1980), which focuses on the issue of *queridas* (mistresses). A volume of short stories *Cuentos* was published in 1985. Espina-Moore received the Southeast Asia (S.E.A.) Write Award in 1989, and has been an active member of the board of International PEN's Philippine Center.

CJM

Espinet, Ramabai (*b.* 1948), Trinidadian poet. Of East Indian heritage, Espinet is professor of literature at Seneca College (Toronto) and is active in the women's movements of Trinidad and Canada. Her poetry and critical essays have been published in such journals as *Fireweed*, *Ariel*, the *Trinidad and Tobago Review*, and many others. She edited *Creation Fire*, a significant anthology of Caribbean women's poetry (1990), and a special issue of *Race, Gender and Knowledge Production* (1995), and has been a regular speaker and poetic performer in the Caribbean women writers' conference series. Her first collection of poetry *Nuclear Seasons* (1991) examines the rural folklore and landscape of Trinidad and inscribes the complex experiences of Caribbean women's settlement in North America's urban centers. Like her Caribbean-Canadian counterparts *Dionne Brand and *Marlene Nourbese Philip, Espinet questions the restrictive ethnic contours of Canadian nationalisms which deny the (literary) contributions of Caribbean immigrants. She focuses on the multiple ethnic and national constructions of womanhood, and has written extensively on Euro-, Afro-, and Indo-Caribbean women writers. Her poetic registers move from Trinidadian Hindi to standard English, reflecting a complex Creole continuum.

ED

Esquivel, Laura (*b.* 1950), Mexican novelist, screenwriter. Born in Mexico City, Esquivel began her writing career with scripts for children's theatre, television programs, and films. In 1989, her first novel *Like Water for Chocolate* became an extraordinary best-seller in Mexico as well as in the US and other countries in its numerous translations. The story, set on a Mexican ranch during the Revolution, appeals to the intellect and the senses when telling the tale of Tita, the youngest daughter in a family, who is not permitted to marry the man she loves because of her obligation to care for her mother. The plot is interwoven with elaborate recipes whose ingredients produce magical and comical effects. *The Law of Love* (1995), her second novel, is a 'multimedia' work which, in addition to the text, is composed of comic strip panels, a compact disk with musical selections, and pre-Columbian poetry. The novel is a cosmic love story that stretches from the fall of Moctezuma to the twenty-third century. Its protagonist, Azucena, weaves a futuristic tale with space ships, regressions to previous lives, guardian angels, implanted computer chips, and divine lights. This novel has been translated into many languages.

GdB

Etcherelli, Claire (b. 1934), French novelist. Etcherelli was born in Bordeaux in a family of modest origins. A politically committed individual, she started working for unions after high school. Her genuine interest in the working class makes her one of the rare contemporary writers to portray life in factories and in modest settings. In her first novel *Elise, or the Real Life* (1967), which was awarded the Prix Fémina, she depicts a young woman from northern France, of humble origins, who falls in love with an Algerian car factory worker in Paris during the French–Algerian war, in a realistic and sensitive manner, expressed through a sober style. In her second novel *A propos de Clémence* ('About Clemence,' 1971), she examines the complexities of relationships, art, and failure as well as the plight of refugees. Her third novel *Un arbre voyageur* ('A Traveling Tree,' 1978) continues her exploration of the lives of ordinary women through the intense friendship of two working women and their attempts to survive in a capitalistic and patriarchal world, sharing revenues and family life in a revolutionary fashion.

JV

Evasco, Marjorie (b. 1953), Philippine poet. Evasco traces her family roots to her birthplace in Maribojoc, Bohol, in the southern part of the Philippines, and her literary roots to Dumaguete City where she earned her master's degree at Silliman University (1982) under the guidance of poet *Edith L. Tiempo. The inflections of the female voice engaged in the fierce struggle against oppressive modes of silence are heard in Evasco's poetic reconstructions of the female experience in Philippine society. The motifs found in Philippine indigenous weaving inspired her first collection of poetry called *Dreamweavers: Selected Poems 1976–1986* (1986; Philippine National Book Award). In 1997 she earned her PhD in literature from De La Salle University in Manila with her translation into Cebuano of poetry in English by contemporary writers from the Central Visayas region of the country. This journey back to her mother tongue brought to completion her second collection of poetry in two tongues, English and Cebuano, called *Ochre Tones and Other Poems* (1999). Evasco was given writing residencies at Hawthornden Castle International Retreat for Writers in Scotland (1991) and at Villa Serbelloni of the Rockefeller Foundation in Bellagio (1992). Every year in May, she serves as the National Writers Summer Workshop in Dumaguete City to help young Philippine writers hone their craft in poetry.

ME

Eytan, Rachel (1932–1987), Israeli novelist. Daughter of a leader of the Israeli Communist Party and a Communist herself in her youth, she had a complicated relationship with her father, who left home and sent her and her sister to a religious boarding school for underprivileged children. Her experience there is at the center of her first novel *In the Fifth Heaven* (1962), which presents her father in a negative light. She married the architect Dan Eytan, lived on kibbutz Eiyn Shemer, and had two children; her husband left her for the Israeli poet Rina Shany. Eytan's second book *Pleasures of Man* (1974) describes Israeli decadence during the end of the 1960s and the beginning of the 1970s, and includes details about her family's broken life. Both books deal with Israeli immigrant life and the creation of a new multiform society, and were written in a language combining ancient Jewish sources and modern Hebrew. She left Israel in 1967 and lived in New York for twenty years after marrying an American Jew and having a child. Eytan, a graduate of the Hebrew University in Jerusalem, taught Hebrew literature, Yiddish, and Talmud using feminist and secular points of view at Hofstra University. During the last five years of her life, she began publishing chapters from *Tzva Malachay Ha-Chabala* ('The Army of Sabotage Angels) – a novel she never finished.

IA

Ezeigbo, Akachi Adimora (*b*. 1947), Nigerian novelist, short story writer, essayist. Born Akachi Theodora Adimora in Uga, Anambra State, Nigeria, Ezeigbo attended Lagos University where she earned a BA in English in 1974, an MA in English in 1981, and a Diploma in Education in 1982. In 1986, she was awarded a PhD in English from the University of Ibadan, Nigeria. Not only is Ezeigbo a seasoned teacher and administrator, but she is also a prolific and award-winning author of many academic books, including *Fact and Fiction in the Literature of the Nigerian Civil War* (1991), *Gender Issues in Nigeria – A Feminine Perspective* (1996), and *A Companion to the Novel* (1998). Her collections of short stories are *Rituals and Departures* (1996), *Echoes in the Mind* (1994), and *Rhythms of Life* (1992). She has also written a novel *The Last of the Strong Ones* (1996), which depicts an Igbo society that falls apart because of colonial intrusion. Her children's books are *The Buried Treasure* (1992) and *The Prize* (1994). She is married with three children. At present, she chairs the department of English at Lagos University in Yaba, Lagos State.

MU

F

Fagerholm, Monika (*b*. 1961), Finland-Swedish novelist, editor. Born in Helsinki, Fagerholm has worked as a translator, critic, and editor of several literary magazines. She earned a BA in psychology and literature from the University of Helsinki in 1987, the same year she published her first collection of short stories *Sham* ('Sham'). Her breakthrough came with her first novel *Wonderful Women by the Water* (1994), for which she won the Runeberg Prize. The novel, which is set at a seaside resort in the early 1960s, depicts childhood and womanhood. The special but disconcerting friendship between Isabella and the Americanized Rosa has its consequences as seen through the eyes of Thomas, Isabella's son. The narration employs cinematic techniques. In 1998, Fagerholm edited *Leva skrivande* ('Living Writing') – an anthology of Finland-Swedish writers talking to and interviewing each other – while writing her latest novel *Diva* ('Diva,' 1998) about a woman who loves food, men and women, and words.

GE-C

Faillace, Tania Jamardo (*b*. 1939), Brazilian fiction writer. Born in Porto Alegre, Rio Grande do Sul, Faillace started her professional life as a painter and reporter, but soon began producing short stories, dramas, and novels. She has published six books: the novels *Fuga* ('Running Away,'

1964) and *Adão e Eva* ('Adam and Eve,' 1965); the story collections *Vinde a mim os Pequeninos* ('Let the Little Children Come to Me,' 1977), *O 35 Ano de Inês* ('Inez's 35th year'), and *Tradição, Família e Outras Estórias* ('Tradition, Family and Other Stories,' 1978); and *Mario/Vera – Brasil 1962/1964* (1983), a semi-autobiographical novel. Having initially dealt with subjective themes, she has developed a marked interest in life's social and political aspects and this is clearly present in her fiction, mainly in the unconventional and yet unpublished 7,748-page *roman-fleuve* titled *Beco da Velha* ('The Old Lady's Alley'). Its 200 characters tell the story of life in the mid-1970s, and though it is not a historical novel, it is based heavily on the writer's fourteen-year research on and interaction with people living in underprivileged areas in Brazil. English translations of her stories are available in several anthologies.

VLSdBF

Fakinou, Eugenia (*b*. 1945), Greek novelist. Born in Alexandria, Egypt, Fakinou grew up and went to school in Athens where she still lives with her family. She studied puppet theater in Belgrade, and in 1976 opened her own puppet theater in Athens. She wrote many children's books before attempting her first novel *Astradeni* (1982), a story of migration and loss of innocence told from the point of view of a bright and observant fifth-grade girl. This was followed by *The Seventh Garment* (1983), in which she employs the distinctive voices of a tree, representing nature, and of three women, representing three different generations, to tell the story of modern Greece from a female point of view. *I megali prasini* ('The Big Green [Sea],' 1988) deals with women's yearnings, which are shown to be in conflict with traditional gender-specific categorizations and bourgeois emphases on career, marriage, and security. Myth and ritual play a significant role in these works, all of which were best-sellers. She published four more novels between 1990 and 1997. In the last one, *Ekato dromi ke mia nihta* ('A Hundred Roads and One Night'), Fakinou delves into the world of myth, legend, and folklore as the first-person narrator wanders through the Peloponnesian countryside in search of stories about spirits and ghosts.

HDK

Fallaci, Oriana (*b.* 1930), Italian journalist, novelist. Raised in Florence, at the age of 13 Fallaci joined the Resistance movement, working against the Fascists and the Nazi occupying troops. She began work as a reporter in 1946. The first woman war correspondent, Fallaci covered hot spots around the world and, in 1968, was wounded in Mexico City when the military opened fire on demonstrators. She received an Honorary Doctorate from Columbia College in 1977. Fallaci's first book *I sette peccati di Hollywood* ('Hollywood's Seven Sins,' 1958) features interviews with the stars, and displays her hallmark blending of journalistic and literary techniques. Following *The Useless Sex* (1961), travel essays on women's conditions in foreign countries, she published her first novel *Penelope at War* (1962), the story of a young Italian woman's struggles to forge her own way in New York. Scrutinizing contemporary public figures and events, Fallaci wrote landmark works of reportage. Among them, *If the Sun Dies* (1965) focuses on the US space program,

Nothing and So Be It (1969) trains a critical eye on the Vietnam War, and *Interview with History* (1974) holds revelations about world politicians. Her best-selling novels include *Letter to a Child Never Born* (1975), a provocative reflection on motherhood and abortion, and *A Man* (1979), a literary reconstruction of the events surrounding the apparent murder of Alekos Panagoulis. The novel *InshAllah* (1990) creates an epic vision of the war in Beirut.

RP-I

Fanthorpe, U(rsula) A(skham) (*b.* 1929), British poet. Born in London, Fanthorpe was educated at St Anne's College, Oxford, where she received a BA in 1953 and an MA in 1958, University of London Institute of Education, and University College, Swansea. She taught English at Cheltenham Ladies' College for several years, but left to work, eventually, as a hospital clerk. That background is central to her poetry, and in particular to her first book *Side Effects*, which was published in 1978. Its subject matter is hospital life and physical and mental illness, its language straightforward, its tone sympathetic but cool. Often, she allows the patients to speak for themselves in moving dramatic monologues. In subsequent volumes, such as *Standing To* (1982), *Voices Off* (1984), and *Neck Verse* (1992), she moves from particular cases to broader explorations of suffering and death in verse that is disturbing, darkly humorous, and quietly erudite in its frequent allusions to the classics. The critically praised *Safe as Houses* (1996) is a thematically linked collection concerned with human vulnerability to the threats of time, war, and nature. Fanthorpe's *Selected Poems* was published in 1986.

JEM

Farmer, Beverley (*b.* 1941), Australian fiction writer, poet, critic. Born in Melbourne and educated at MacRobertson Girls High School and Melbourne University (BA, French and English), Farmer worked as a teacher before marrying a Greek immigrant in 1965 and living for some years with his family north of Thessaloniki. A novella/*recit* written at this time (*Alone*) was not published until ten years later. In 1972 the couple returned to Australia to open a restaurant in Victoria, and had a son. After six years, a separation, and the deaths of both parents, Farmer returned to teaching and writing. The short stories in *Milk* (1980), which won a NSW Premier's Award, include sensitively and sensuously rendered portraits of family and place. The collection *Home Time* (1985) more starkly and inventively interrogates origin and inheritance. In 1990, *A Body of Water*, a collage-like compilation of writer's notes, short stories, poetry, and intertextual reference, was short-listed for the National Book Council Non-fiction Banjo Award and the NSW Douglass Stewart Prize for Non-fiction. The novel *The Seal Woman* (1996) features a Danish widow confronting personal, historical, and environmental issues, and *The House in the Light* (1997) is a delicately orchestrated quartet of women's lives

LJ

Fatima, Altaf (*b.* 1929), Pakistani fiction writer. Born in Lucknow, Fatima completed her education in Lahore, Pakistan, after Partition, taking her MA and BEd from Punjab University. She taught Urdu literature at Islamia College for Women and at APWA Girls' College, Lahore. The men in her family were scholars and the women natural storytellers. In her childhood she 'turned somersaults and ran amok' with her brothers and also read Persian classics, encouraged by her mother. Her early work traces the destinies of middle-class families and cultural dislocations. She is interested in contemporary upheavals that have affected the lives of Muslim men and women all over the world, but refuses to be pigeonholed, saying that she writes about life as it 'pinches' her. A work-in-progress examines the interface between paganism and Islam in

the northern areas of Pakistan. She has published three novels, *Nishan-e-Mehfil* ('The Lost Company'), *The One Who Did Not Ask* (1993), and *Chalta Musaffir* ('The Moving Traveller'). She has published three volumes of short stories, *Woh Jisay Chaha Giya* ('One Who Was Loved'), *Jab Deewarain Girya Karti Hain* ('When Walls Weep'), and *Tar-e-Unkaboot* ('Spider's Web,' 1990). She has translated a range of fiction into Urdu.

SRah

Feinstein, Elaine (*b.* 1930), British poet, novelist, translator. Born in Bootle, Lancashire, Feinstein attended Newnham College, Cambridge (BA, 1952; MA, 1955). She married Arnold Feinstein in 1956; they have three sons. Her early books of poetry, such as *In a Green Eye* (1966) and *The Magic Apple Tree* (1971), were influenced by American poets Dickinson, Williams, and Stevens. Translating the works of Russian poet Marina Tsvetayeva (*Selected Poems* 1971, 1981, 1993) was instrumental in the expansion of her poetic range beyond her own experience; her poetry became more mythic, more passionate, but also bleaker in its subject matter, as in *The Celebrants* (1973) and *Badlands* (1986). Feinstein's characteristic themes are death and loss, suffering, and exile. Her identity as a Jewish woman has become increasingly important in her writing, and many of her novels, such as *Children of the Rose* (1975), *The Survivors* (1982), and *The Border* (1984), focus on themes related to Judaism and the Holocaust. Much of her fiction is marked by violence, fear, and pain. Other novels include *Mother's Girl* (1988), *Dreamers* (1994), and *Lady Chatterly's Confession* (1995), a sequel to Lawrence's novel. Other volumes of poetry include *City Music* (1990), *Selected Poems* (1994), and *Daylight* (1997). She has also written many radio and television plays, *A Captive Lion* (1987), a biography of Tsvetayeva, and the biography *Pushkin* (1998).

JEM

Felinto, Marilene (*b*. 1957), Brazilian novelist, short story writer, journalist. Felinto was born in Recife (Pernambuco) into a poor and racially mixed family. At the age of 12, she moved with her family to São Paulo, a city that appears in many of her works as cold and impersonal. She graduated from the University of São Paulo with a degree in literary theory, and has written for prominent newspapers in Brazil. She is also a translator and literary critic. In 1982, she received the prestigious UBE-Jabuti prize for her autobiographical novel of formation *The Women of Tijucopapo*. It is a fragmented, insightful work told from several narrative angles, describing the travel tales of an imaginary journey that the protagonist has not yet taken. Felinto's other publications include a collection of short stories, *Postcards* (1991), and a volume of literary criticism of the works of her favorite Brazilian writer, *Graciliano Ramos* (1983). Her witty, sharp, concise, and innovative prose has won her the admiration of critics and translators.

MJB

Fell, Alison (*b*. 1944), Scottish poet, novelist. Born in Dumfries, Scotland, Fell was educated at the Edinburgh College of Art and the Institute of Education, University of London. She was married for a brief time and has one son. She started out as a sculptor and painter, and then, as a co-founder of the Women's Street Theatre Group in London in 1971, turned to writing and performing. An activist for feminist causes, she contributed poems to feminist anthologies before publishing her first book *Kisses for Mayakovsky* in 1984. The emphasis on female experience in her poems is motivated by her feminism. Her political beliefs inspire her engagement with current events, especially those connected with human rights, in her poetry. Often angry and polemical, her work is driven by passion and a strong moral sense. Her other volumes of poetry are *The Crystal Owl* (1988) and *Dreams, like Heretics* (1997). Her early novels *Every*

Move You Make (1984) and *The Bad Box* (1987) are autobiographical. The narratives of the novels *Mer de Glace* (1991) and *The Pillow Boy of the Lady Onogoro* (1994) are fragmented and experimental. *The Mistress of Lilliput, or, The Pursuit* (1999), the story of the voyages of Mrs. Gulliver, is a feminist reimagining, written in the style of the eighteenth century, of Swift's classic tale.

JEM

Ferré, Rosario (*b*. 1942), Puerto Rican short story writer, novelist, poet. Ferré was born in the southern city of Ponce. Her father Luis Ferré was governor of Puerto Rico from 1968 to 1972. She graduated from Manhattanville College with a BA in English (1960) and earned an MA in Hispanic studies from the University of Puerto Rico (1985) and a PhD from the University of Maryland (1987). She began writing in 1970 when she co-founded and edited the literary review *Zona de Carga y Descarga*. Her first book *Papeles de Pandora* (1976), which won the Casa de las Américas Prize and contains some of her best-known stories, is a scalding indictment of the Puerto Rican elite and their treatment of women. Her story collection *The Youngest Doll* (1979) describes the submissive and dependent role of 'doll-women.' The poetry in *Fábulas de la garza desangrada* ('Fables of a Bleeding Crane,' 1982) rewrites women's myths of love and eroticism. In her first novel *Sweet Diamond Dust* (1986), she mixes history, fiction and myth in the saga of a family in decline as Puerto Rico changes from being a Spanish colony to an American protectorate in the early 1900s. She was nominated for the National Book Award for *The House on the Lagoon* (1995), her first novel in English. Her latest novel *Eccentric Neighborhoods* (1998) tells the history of twentieth-century Puerto Rico through the fortunes of two families.

GP, CV

Figes, Eva (*b*. 1932), British novelist, critic.

Born Eva Unger in Berlin to German Jewish parents, she moved to England in 1939. She received a BA (honors) from Queen Mary College, University of London, in 1953. Her first novel *Equinox* was published in 1966. She writes in opposition to the realistic tradition of the British novel, identifying instead with European modernist and experimental writers. Her primary influences are Kafka, Woolf, and Beckett. Her focus in her novels is on the inner self, on moments of being, rather than on traditional narrative. As in *Winter Journey* (1967; *Guardian* Fiction Prize), she eschews plot in favor of a lyrical presentation of states of consciousness. Her novels include *Konek Landing* (1969), *Days* (1974), *Nelly's Version* (1977), *Ghosts* (1988), *The Tenancy* (1993), and *The Knot* (1996). *Light* (1983) is based on the life of Claude Monet. *The Tree of Knowledge* (1990) calls up 1,000 years of women's history to explore the cycle of a woman's life. Figes is perhaps best known for her classic work of feminist analysis *Patriarchal Attitudes* (1970), in which she examines the historical and ideological bases of women's place in society. She has also written the study *Sex and Subterfuge: Women Writers to 1850* (1982). *Little Eden* (1978) is a memoir of her childhood experiences in World War II. The Holocaust figures in several of her novels.

JEM

Filkova, Fedya Raykova (*b.* 1950), Bulgarian poet, translator. Born in Yablanitsa, Filkova graduated in 1972 with a BA in German from the University of Sofia and married the poet Nikolay Kunchev. She held a series of appointments: translator for Sofia-Press, editor for the newspaper *ABV* and the publishing house Narodna kultura, lecturer in the German department of the University of Sofia, and cultural attaché in Vienna. Currently she is on the foreign relations team of President Peter Stoyanov. Her first book *Tsvetya s ochite na zheni* ('Flowers with Women's Eyes,' 1982) is characterized by an existentialist treatment of the themes of love and death. *Nezhen vuzdukh* ('Gentle Air,' 1988) and *Risunki v mraka* ('Drawings in the Darkness,' 1990) reaffirm her reputation as master of brief and subtle lyrical pieces. Many of her poems are dedicated to Austrian, Bulgarian, German, and Russian women writers. She has translated works by *Ingeborg Bachmann, *Christa Wolf, Else Aichinger and other German and Austrian authors (Austrian State Prize for Literary Translation, 1995). For English translations of Filkova's works, see the anthologies *Young Poets of a New Bulgaria* (1990), *Windows on the Black Sea* (1992), *Clay and Star* (1992), and *An Anthology of Contemporary Poetry* (1994).

LPG

Fischerová, Daniela (*b.* 1948), Czech dramatist, prose writer. Prague-born daughter of a composer and a translator, Fischerová studied scriptwriting at the Film Academy, graduating in 1971. After a short job at the Barrandov Film Studio, she worked as an editor at Orbis publishers (1973–4). Since then she has been a freelance writer. Active in public affairs, she has been on the board of the Czech branch of the International PEN Club. She is married and has one daughter. Her first play *Hodina mezi psem i vlkem* ('The Hour between the Dog and the Wolf'), depicting the trial of François Villon, was officially banned the day before its scheduled premiere in 1979. Further drawing on European tradition, her next two plays *Princezna T.* ('Princess T.,' premiere in 1986) and *Báj* ('Legend,' premiere in 1987) both focus on power and collaboration with evil. Central to her work are award-winning radio and television plays, as well as film scripts. Recently she published a collection of stories *Prst, který se nikdy nedotkne* ('A Finger that Will Never Touch,' 1995), of which one has appeared in English as 'Letter for President Eisenhower.' Fischerová's latest work *Přísudek je v této větě podmět* ('In this Sentence the

Predicate is the Subject,' 1996) is a small volume of aphoristic notebook entries.

ES

Fischerová, Sylva (*b.* 1963), Czech poet. Daughter of the philosopher and sociologist Josef Ludvík Fischer, and younger half-sister of the poet Viola Fischerová, Prague-born Fischerová returned to the city of her birth only after spending her childhood in Olomouc and a year in Brno studying French. In 1985 she began her studies at Charles University in philosophy and physics, but soon changed to classics. Since graduation in 1991, she has taught in the classics department. With her partner Martin Pokorný, a journalist, she has one daughter. Already writing as a child, Fischerová made her debut in two anthologies of young Czech poets in 1985. Her first book *The Tremor of Racehorses* (1986), awarded a prize by the Czech Literary Fund, contains remarkable self-reflective poems, depicting the conflict between freedom and love. In *Velká zdrcadla* ('Large Mirrors,' 1990) she breaks with the relatively idyllic world of youthful love, turning more to the theme of emptiness. Her latest volume *V podsvětním městě* ('In the Underworld City,' 1994) reveals a voice grown even more meditative and skeptical about life, contemplating the interconnections between the world of the living and the dead.

ES

Fitzgerald, Penelope (1916–2000), British novelist, biographer. Born in Lincoln, England, Fitzgerald studied literature at Somerville College, Oxford, graduating with first class honors in 1939. She worked for many years as an assistant at the BBC. She began her writing career with biographies, including *The Knox Brothers* (1977), which is about her father, Edmund Knox, who was the editor of *Punch*, and his three brothers. At the age of 60, Fitzgerald turned to fiction, writing *The Golden Child* (1977), a tale of murder and counterfeit art, to entertain her husband

Desmond Fitzgerald, who was dying of cancer. Her early novels drew on her personal experiences of working in a bookstore, living with her family on a houseboat on the Thames, and working for the BBC; see *The Bookshop* (1978), *Offshore* (1979; Booker Prize), and *Human Voices* (1980) respectively. Her spare and ironic prose sensitively examines human behavior, often studying the dynamic of individuals within a limited community. *Innocence* (1984) concerns two families in Florence and *The Beginning of Spring* (1988) chronicles an English community in Moscow. Other novels include *At Freddie's* (1982), *The Gate of Angels* (1990), and *The Blue Flower* (1995; National Book Critics' Circle Award), a fictionalized account of the love of Novalis, a German Romantic poet, for a 12-year-old girl.

DVT

Fleutiaux, Pierrette (*b.* 1941), French novelist. Born in Guéret in western France to a family of teachers and school administrators, Fleutiaux graduated with a BA in English from the University of Poitiers. An avid reader, she nurtured the dream of fleeing the limited horizon of her strict upbringing. Her writings eloquently mirror this desire through the fantasies of her characters and her stories. After passing the national teaching exam (the agrégation) she moved to New York where she wrote her first book *Histoire de la chauvesouris* ('The Story of the Bat,' 1975). She has published three other novels, as well as numerous short stories and children's stories. Winner of the Prix Fémina for *We Are Eternal* (1990) and the Prix Goncourt de la nouvelle for her short story 'Les métamorphoses de la reine' ('The Metamorphoses of the Queen,' 1984), Fleutiaux currently teaches at the Lycée Capital in Paris.

PP-W

Forché, Carolyn (*b.* 1950), US poet. A member of Amnesty International and an outspoken advocate for human rights,

Forché is known for her sensitive depictions of human suffering and human survival. Born in Detroit, Michigan, she received a BA from Michigan State University in 1972 and an MFA from Bowling Green State University in 1975. She is married and has one son. Her first book *Gathering the Tribes* (1976), a collection of poems with themes of kinship, growth, and sexual awakening, was published as part of the Yale Series of Younger Poets. After an extended stay in El Salvador as a human rights activist and journalist, she published *The Country Between Us* (1981), in which she gives witness to the atrocities of the civil war that occurred there in the late 1970s. Her poetry is by no means exclusively political – she has written many poems of a personal nature as well. But her interest in poetry as historical record is evident in *Against Forgetting: Twentieth-Century Poetry of Witness* (1993), an anthology she edited, and in her third collection of poetry *The Angel of History* (1994). She has translated poetry by Robert Desnos and *Claribel Alegría and has taught at many universities and colleges in the US.

DVT

Ford-Smith, Honor (*b*. 1951), Jamaican dramatist, writer. Ford-Smith was born in Montreal and raised in Jamaica. Her Jamaican mother and English father divorced when she was an infant. She was the founding artistic director of the internationally acclaimed SISTREN Theatre Collective (1977). Initially comprised primarily of black Jamaican working-class women, SISTREN promoted the expression of women's experiences and struggles, and used participatory theater as a means of education and social change. She was also the director and scriptwriter for several SISTREN productions, including *Bellywoman Bangarang*, *Bandoolu Version*, and *Domesticks* (unpublished scripts). She has conducted collaborative research on women's work, organization, and living arrangements in Jamaica and,

with the collective, co-authored *Lion Heart Gal* (1986), a book documenting the life histories of SISTREN women. *My Mother's Last Dance* (1997), a collection of prose-poems, uses Caribbean oral storytelling and mythic scenarios to examine island history. She currently studies in the doctoral program at the Ontario Institute for Studies in Education in Toronto and is married to a Cuban historian, Bernardo Garcia Dominguez.

LC

Forrest, Katherine V. (*b*. 1939), Canadian novelist. Born in Windsor, Ontario, Forrest was educated at Wayne State University and the University of California in Los Angeles, where she still lives. She is best known for her popular detective fiction series which features Kate Delafield, a lesbian homicide detective with the Los Angeles police department. The first novel in the series, *Amateur City*, was published in 1984. The novels provide the usual pleasures of suspenseful plotting and detailed depictions of police procedures and investigations, but also depict the unique tensions and complications that arise due to Kate's sexual orientation, which she tries to keep private, and her often difficult position in a working environment that is both macho and homophobic. Other books in the series include *Murder at the Nightwood Bar* (1987), *The Beverley Malibu* (1990), *Murder by Tradition* (1991), *Liberty Square* (1996), and *Apparition Alley* (1997). Forrest has also written several other novels that deal with lesbian themes in different genres. *Curious Wine* (1983) is a romantic fantasy about two women in love, told with openness and sexual frankness. *Daughters of a Coral Dawn* (1984) is a science fiction novel about a group of women who leave Earth to found a lesbian utopia.

JEM

Forsström, Tua (*b*. 1947), Finland-Swedish poet, editor. Born in Borgå in southern Finland, Forsström's childhood was filled with books – her mother was a teacher – and stories told by her father. After twenty years in Helsinki, she now lives and writes in an old schoolhouse in the area where she grew up. Besides poetry, she has written drama, lyrics, and, together with *Marta Tikkanen, anthologized Finnish women's poetry. Her first book of poetry *En dikt om kärlek och annat* ('A Book About Love and Other Things,' 1972) was followed by *Där anteckningarna slutar* ('Where the Notes End,' 1974). In the latter collection, excerpts from existing laws and regulations are challenged by the poems' depiction of freedom and longing. Her themes – memory and longing, loss and grief – are clearly developed in *Snow Leopard* (1987). Her concern for both visual and audible rhythms is displayed in *Marianerergraven* ('The Mariana Trench,' 1990), subtitled 'Oratorio.' Her latest collection, *Efter att ha tillbringat en natt med hästar* ('After Having Spent a Night with Horses,' 1997) is a dialogue with the Russian film director Andrej Tarkovskij about the concept of time. Forsström is the recipient of the Nordic Council's Literary Prize for 1998.

GE-C

Forster, Margaret (*b.* 1938), British novelist, biographer. Born in Carlisle, Cumberland, Forster attended Somerville College, Oxford and graduated with a BA in modern history in 1960. That same year, she married writer Hunter Davies; they have three children. Her first novel *Dames' Delight* was published in 1964. Based on her experiences at Oxford, it features a rebellious heroine who challenges convention – a type of woman who recurs in Forster's fiction. Her second novel *Georgy Girl* (1965) is her best-known; very funny and sexually frank, it was made into a popular film, for which Forster wrote the screenplay. The persistent subject of her fiction is family relationships, especially the mother–daughter relationship. Her style is straightforward, and the analyses of gender and class that are central to her work

are unsentimental and perceptive. Her other novels include *The Seduction of Mrs. Pendlebury* (1974), *Mother Can You Hear Me?* (1979), *Private Papers* (1986), *Have the Men Had Enough?* (1989), *Lady's Maid* (1990), *Mothers' Boys* (1994), and *Shadow Baby* (1996). She is the author of biographies of William Thackeray, Elizabeth Barrett Browning, and Daphne DuMaurier. She has also written two acclaimed works of biography/memoir about her working-class family, *Hidden Lives* (1995) and *Precious Lives* (1998).

JEM

Frabotta, Biancamaria (*b.* 1946), Italian poet, dramatist, novelist, literary critic. Frabotta was born in Rome, where she teaches contemporary Italian literature at Rome University. She is best known for her lyric poetry, which is marked by a variety of styles, from the aphorism to the long poem. She experimented with a distinctly feminine poetic voice in *Affeminata* ('Effeminate,' 1976) and *Il rumore bianco* ('White Noise,' 1982), early works which contain the nuclei of her, to date, thirty years of intense poetic and critical activity. Her often autobiographical poems address both feminist thematics and the politics of experimental poetic forms in a dense and elegant style veined with irony. She is an accomplished literary critic, with several volumes to her credit. The theme of woman's growth into creative maturity through alternating metaphors of stasis and travel appears in many poems and informs the title of her major collection *La viandanza* ('Wayfaring,' 1995), which extends the gaze of the poetic wayfarer abroad to Africa, Australia, and South America. The novel *Velocità di fuga* ('Speed of Escape,' 1989) and the collection of plays *Trittico dell'obbedienza* ('Tryptich of Obedience,' 1996) maintain earlier interests and add to them more Roman, urban, and political ones. English translations of some of her poems appear in *Italian Women Poets of the Twentieth Century*.

KJJ

Frame, Janet (*b*. 1924), New Zealand novelist. Although Frame trained at the University of Otago's Teachers College in Dunedin, the city in which she was born, she quickly decided that she did not want to be a teacher. Mistakenly believing herself to be schizophrenic, she voluntarily spent several years in New Zealand psychiatric hospitals. Subsequently, Frame spent considerable time traveling and writing in Europe and America, before returning to live in New Zealand. Her three-part autobiography *To the Is-land* (1982), *An Angel at My Table* (1984), and *The Envoy from Mirror City* (1985) won Wattie and New Zealand Book Awards. Frame's dozen novels have strong autobiographical elements. In *Owls Do Cry* (1957), Daphne struggles with a childhood of mental confusion, while in *Faces in the Water* (1961) Istina faces similar concerns in psychiatric hospitals. These and her powerful later novels often focus on key concerns such as chaos, identity, and the question of what is 'normal.' Many of her novels including *Living in the Maniototo* (1979) and *The Carpathians* (1988) are postmodernist. Frame has also published a volume of poetry and several collections of short stories. She has won numerous prestigious awards and fellowships including Commander of the Order of the British Empire (1983) and the Commonwealth Writers Prize (1989).

PW

Fraser, Sylvia (*b*. 1935), Canadian novelist, essayist. Born and raised in Hamilton, Ontario, Fraser earned a BA in English and philosophy from the University of Western Ontario in 1957. She was a successful journalist for many years. Her first novel, the autobiographical *Pandora*, was published in 1972. Other early novels include *The Candy Factory* (1975), a mystery novel that explores male female relationships; *A Casual Affair: A Modern Fairy Tale* (1978), about a failed love affair; *The Emperor's Virgin* (1980), an historical novel concerning chastity and religion set in ancient Rome; and *Berlin Solstice* (1984), which takes place during the Third Reich. The preoccupation with destructive sexual relationships evident in several of these novels was seen in a new light after the publication of Fraser's memoir, *My Father's House: A Memoir of Incest and Healing* (1987). She bravely recovers and records her memories of sexual abuse by her father, in a text that uses italics for the abuse and boldface for her recovered memories. This was followed by *The Book of Strange: A Journey* (1992; published in the UK as *The Quest for the Fourth Monkey*), in which she examines mystical experiences in her later life. Fraser's interests in premonitions, telepathy, and reincarnation are turned into fiction in *The Ancestral Suitcase* (1996), in which the heroine travels back in time to Victorian England to uncover family secrets.

JEM

French, Marilyn (*b*. 1929), US novelist, critic, nonfiction writer. Born in New York to poor Polish immigrants, French interrupted her undergraduate work at Hofstra University to marry, but after raising her family, completed her education, receiving a PhD from Harvard University in 1972. Her best-selling first novel *The Women's Room* (1977), an exploration of the restricted and frustrated lives of middle-class women, caused considerable controversy and debate due to its feminist polemics, particularly its angry criticism of male-dominated society. Her next two novels *The Bleeding Heart* (1980) and *Her Mother's Daughter* (1987) continue French's focus on feminism and the damage done by patriarchal power. In her non-fiction works *Beyond Power: On Men, Women, and Morals* (1985) and *The War Against Women* (1992), as well as in her work of literary criticism *Shakespeare's Division of Experience* (1981), French goes back to the beginnings of civilization and surveys history in order to understand the origins of patriarchy, critique its values and its hierarchies, and posit a new feminist world order. Her other works include *The Book as World: James Joyce's Ulysses* (1985), the novels *My Summer with George* (1997) and *Our Father* (1995), and *A Season in Hell* (1998), an account of her battle with cancer.

DVT

Friedman, Carl (*b.* 1952), Dutch novelist. Friedman grew up in a Jewish family that was deeply influenced by their father's traumatic experiences in a concentration camp. She started to read about World War II when she was a child. She visited former concentration camps in 1980 and wrote some sonnets about her experiences, which were published in Dutch literary magazines. Her prose debut *Nightfather* (1991) also has a clear autobiographical inspiration. Her work, however, is more than just anecdotal. Her style is sober, and the main theme of her work is her search for insight, which makes her prose less personal. All her books are driven by the same questions: How can one understand what happened during the war, and how should one tell it to others, especially to the next generation? Her novel *The Shovel and the Loom* (1993) was made into the film *Left Luggage* by Jeroen Krabbé in 1998; it won the Golden Bear at the Film Festival of Berlin. *The Gray Lover: Three stories* (1996) is her most recent work. Like her earlier books, it has been widely acclaimed by literary critics as well as by the reading public.

AAn, MMe

Frischmuth, Barbara (*b.* 1941), Austrian novelist. Born in the resort of Altaussee, Frischmuth divides her time between Styria and Vienna. She studied Turkish and Hungarian in Graz and Islamic culture at the University of Vienna. The contrast between country and city is reflected in her novels, which feature women balancing their profession and their family life in an increasingly cosmopolitan Austria. One of her major themes is the interaction between Austrians and Turks in *The Shadow*

Disappears in the Sun (1973), *Über die Verhältnisse* ('Relationships,' 1987), and *Die Schrift des Freundes* ('The Friend's Writing,' 1998), focusing on cross-cultural relationships, Islamic mysticism, and secret societies in today's Turkey. *Amoralische Kinderklapper* ('The Amoral Rattle,' 1969) and *Ida- und Ob* ('Ida and Or,' 1972) are indebted to the avant-garde program of the Grazer Forum Stadtpark, while *The Convent School* (1968) and *Chasing After the Wind* (1974) highlight gender issues. *Die Mystifikationen der Sophie Silber* ('The Mystifications of Sophie Silber,' 1976), *Amy: oder Die Metamorphose* ('Amy, or the Metamorphosis,' 1978), *Kai und die Liebe zu den Modellen* ('Kai and the Love of Models,' 1979), and *Die Frau im Mond* ('The Woman in the Moon,' 1982) construct a view of reality that intertwines the mundane with myth and folklore. Frischmuth has also written television plays and children's books.

DCGL

Frostenson, Katarina (*b.* 1953), Swedish poet, playwright. A member of the Swedish Academy since 1992, Frostenson, who grew up and lives in Stockholm, has a background in literature, film, and theater. Naming *Birgitta Trotzig as a source of inspiration, Frostenson's oeuvre is a continuing investigation of language, the spoken as well as the unspoken, its use and limitations. After her breakthrough with *Rena Land* ('Clean Land,' 1980), her following two collections of poetry *Den andra* ('The Other,' 1982) and *I det gula* ('In the Yellow,' 1985), as well as the stories in *Berättelser från dem* ('Tales from Them,' 1992) explore, expand, and question the usage of language. In her stories, the rituals of non-verbal communication are contrasted with the introduction of language by a man. In the play *Traum* ('Trauma,' 1993), furniture is rearranged while a couple quarrel; words, like furniture, change meaning depending on position and perspective. Her interests in aesthetic form, and linkage between text and music, come together in *Jan Håfström: A Suite of Poems to Jan Håfström and to Works by Him* (1994), a bilingual text with CD. In *Vägen till öarna* ('The Road to the Islands,' 1996), Frostenson's poems and prose poems accompany pictures by Jean-Claude Arnault, taken during their journey through Bergslagen, Sweden.

GE-C

Füruzan (*b.* 1935), Turkish novelist, short story and travel writer. Born in Istanbul, Füruzan left school after finishing junior high school, and joined a theater group. Her early writings depict the struggles of lonely and poor women and children with exact and penetrating detail. Her first book of stories *Parasız Yatılı* ('Free Boarding School,' 1972) won the Sait Faik Story Prize for 1972. Since then, she has published four more volumes of stories. Of these, she turned *Benim Sinemalarım* ('My Movies,' 1973) into the script of a movie in 1989, which won prizes at Cannes, Tehran, and Tokyo film festivals. Her first novel *47'liler* ('Born in 1947,' 1974), which deals with the period of the 1971 coup in Turkey from the perspective of the generation born in 1947, won the Türk Dil Kurumu (Turkish Language Association's) Novel Prize in 1975. She was invited to Germany in 1975. Her interviews with the Turkish workers there were published as *Yeni Konuklar* ('New Guests,' 1977). She writes of her travels in Germany in *Ev Sahipleri* ('The Landlords,' 1981). In *Bizim Rumeli* ('Our Rumelia,' 1994), she recounts her travels in Bosnia, Greece, and Bulgaria. The short stories 'How to Play the Piano' and 'In the Park by the Pier' appear in anthologies in English. She is divorced, and has a daughter.

SE

G

Gagnon, Madeleine (*b.* 1938), French-Canadian poet, fiction writer. Born in Amqui in the Matapédia Valley, of Huron ancestry, Gagnon studied piano in her childhood and adolescence. She pursued her musical studies at the Music Conservatory and later, in parallel, her literary studies. Having completed her MA in philosophy at the Université de Montréal and her doctorate in Aix-en-Provence in 1968, she became a professor of literature at the Université du Québec à Montréal (1969–82). She also taught at the Université de Montréal and the Université de Sherbrooke. She published her first book, a collection of short stories *Les morts-vivants* ('The Living Dead'), in 1969. She has since published in numerous feminist journals such as *La nouvelle barre du jour*. One of her best-known texts is 'Body in Writing' published in *Coming to Writing* (1977) in collaboration with *Annie Leclerc and *Hélène Cixous, in which she attempts to retrieve the maternal body as well as her female filiation through the bodies of her grandmothers. She has written more than thirty volumes of poetry that explore the relationship between the female body and language, including *Lair* (1989) and *Just an Instant* (1998). Several of her poetry volumes were awarded prestigious Canadian and Quebecer prizes.

JV

Gajadin, Chitra (*b.* 1954), Surinamese poet, children's writer. Born into an East Indian community in Suriname, Gajadin went to the Netherlands in 1972 to work as a writer and teacher. She writes in Dutch as well as in Sarnami. She has also translated from Sranantongo. Her first three collections of poetry – *Van erf tot skai: Een bundel gedichten* ('From Yard to 'skai': A Band of Poems,' 1977), *Padi voor Batavieren* ('"Padi" for Bataves,' 1979), and *De zon vloeit weg uit mijn ogen* ('The Sun Runs Away from My Eyes,' 1983) – provide the images of memories for the selections in *Kab ke yaad/Van wanneer een herinnering: 1977–1983* ('"Kab ke yaad"/ A Memory from Back When: 1977–83,' 1984). Gajadin has also written stories for children, most notably an adaptation of Rabindranath Tagore's play *Amal and the Letter from the King*.

DH

Galanaki, Rhea (*b.* 1947), Greek novelist, poet. Born in Iraklion, Crete, Galanaki earned her BA in history and archeology at the University of Athens. In the past decade she has emerged as one of Greece's most acclaimed novelists. Her novels include *The Life of Ismail Ferik Pasha* (1989), *Tha Ipografo Loui* ('I Shall Sign My Name as Louis,' 1993) and *Eleni, i Kanenas* ('Helen, or Nobody,' 1998). Poetry, however, has played a critical role in her development as a writer. Her collection of prose poems *The Cake* (1980), her most explicitly feminist text to date, provides a bridge between her early epigrammatic poems *Plin Efharis* ('Albeit Pleasing,' 1975) and *Orihta* ('*Minerals*,' 1979) her longer prose works, *Pu zi o likos?* ('Where Does the Wolf Live?', 1980) and *Omokentra Diigimata* ('Concentric Stories,' 1986). She has also published critical essays on literature, in particular on the question of women's writing. In 1987 she received the Nikos Kazantzakis Literary Award. *The Life of Ismail Ferik Pasha* was the first Greek novel to be included in the UNESCO collection of representative works. Since 1979 she has lived in Patras where her husband Ilias Kouvelas teaches in the Medical School. They have one daughter.

KVD

Gallagher, Tess (*b.* 1943), US poet. Born in Port Angeles, Washington, Gallagher attended the University of Washington, Seattle (BA, 1963; MA, 1970) and the University of Iowa (MFA, 1974). She has been married three times, the last time to the writer Raymond Carver, who died in 1988. She has taught English and writing at several universities and colleges, including University of Arizona, Tucson and Syracuse University; she is currently a professor of English at Whitman College in Walla Walla, Washington. She published her first volume of poetry *Stepping Outside* in 1974. Her voice is strong, clear, and passionate, her imagery dense, her characteristic themes love and loss. *Instructions to the Double* (1976) concerns family history, memories, and illusions. *Willingly* (1984), which is dedicated to Carver, is a portrait of their relationship. *Moon Crossing Bridge* (1992) is a work of grief and mourning. Other volumes include *Amplitude* (1987), *Portable Kisses: Love Poems* (1992), and *My Black Horse* (1995). Gallagher has published two volumes of short stories, *The Lover of Horses* (1986) and *At the Owl Woman Saloon* (1997). Her essays on poetry are collected in *A Concert of Tenses* (1986).

JEM

Gallaire, Fatima (*b.* 1944), French-Algerian dramatist. Born in Algeria, the eldest of eight children, Gallaire lives in Paris with her husband and twin children. Educated at the University of Algiers and the University of Paris VIII in film studies, she has won the Prix Arletty (1990) and the Prix de l'Académie française (1994) for her plays, in many of which she explores contemporary life in traditional Muslim settings. Performed amid controversy in New York, Paris, and Tashkent, her play *You Have Come Back* (1988) chronicles the return visit of an estranged, liberated woman to her homeland after her father's death. Leaving her non-Muslim husband and children in France, Princess tragically encounters a land transformed by intolerance and fanaticism. Gallaire's female characters find strength through collective action as in *Les Co-Epouses* ('The Co-Wives,' 1990), *Rimm, la gazelle* ('Rimm, the Gazelle,' 1993), and *Le Secret des Vieilles* ('The Secret of the Old Women,' 1996). Depicting the anguish of sexual desire, *Molly des sables* ('Molly of the Sands,' 1994) presents an isolated, immigrant wife living in Paris, while in *Madame Bertin's Testimony* (1987), an elderly couple reflect on the physical nature of their relationship.

JBG

Gallant, Mavis (*b.* 1922), Canadian short story writer. A Protestant born in Montreal, Mavis de Trafford Young shunted from school to school as a child. Married briefly, she acquired the name Gallant. She wrote for the Montreal *Standard* before moving to Europe permanently in 1950. Two novels display abiding motifs in Gallant's fiction: in *Green Water, Green Sky* (1959), a mother ruinously influences her daughter; in *A Fairly Good Time* (1970), a French–English marriage falls apart. Bilingual, and keenly aware of the accepted and the excluded in various places, Gallant writes knowledgeably about conflict between French and English cultures in many of her eleven story collections. Immigrants from Paris haunt her first book *The Other Paris* (1956) and *From the Fifteenth District* (1979). *Home Truths* (1981) concentrates on Canadian settings. In *The Pegnitz Junction* (1973), traumatized Germans reconstruct their lives after 1945. World War II forms a horizon for identity in collections such as *Overhead in a Balloon* (1985) and *In Transit* (1988). Gallant published fifty-two stories in *Selected Stories* (1996). A long-meditated account of the Dreyfus affair has not come to fruition, but a superb collection of journalism, *Paris Notebooks* (1986), shows her incisive sense of history.

AH

Galloway, Janice (*b*. 1956), Scottish novelist, short story writer. Born in Kilwinning, Scotland, Galloway earned an MA from Glasgow University in 1978. She worked as a teacher for several years in Ayrshire, before moving to Glasgow to write full-time. She has one son. She is best known for her first novel, the critically acclaimed *The Trick is to Keep Breathing* (1989). It is a disturbing yet bleakly funny account of a woman's breakdown following the death of her lover. Galloway shatters narrative conventions in her depiction of the woman's depression and self-destructiveness by tampering with typography and font size, breaking sentences into fragments, intentionally misspelling words, and including texts such as lists, lyrics, postcards, and newspaper columns. The success of the novel marked the beginning of a breakthrough for Scottish women writers, who had previously been accorded little attention. The short stories collected in *Blood* (1991; Scottish Arts Council Award) and *Where You Find It* (1996) are written in a compressed, minimalist style, sometimes macabre or bleak in tone, and continue Galloway's focus on various kinds of oppression – social, psychological, physical – that women confront in everyday life. Her second novel *Foreign Parts* (1994) is a witty exploration of how the weaknesses and strengths of a friendship between two

women are revealed during their trips to Europe.

JEM

Gambaro, Griselda (*b*. 1928), Argentine dramatist. Gambaro is one of the most respected dramatists in Argentina and author of numerous narrative works. Most of her plays focus on oppression, political or interpersonal, and on the human being's capacity to victimize and be victimized. Her early works *El desatino* ('The Blunder,' 1965), *The Walls* (1966), and *Los siameses* ('The Siamese Twins,' 1967) were labeled theater of the absurd, of the grotesque, or of cruelty. The protagonist of *El desatino* absurdly languishes and dies after his foot becomes trapped in an unidentified artifact while family and friends are too self-absorbed to offer the most basic assistance. Her best-known play *The Camp* (1968), whose title evokes both a recreation area and a concentration camp, is a nightmarish glimpse into the far-reaching effects of oppression. Although her early plays were criticized for their apparent lack of concern with issues related to women, her later works often foreground women. In *Strip* (1981), a would-be actress is stripped of her dignity and clothes while compliantly performing the roles society has assigned her. *Bitter Blood* (1982) and *Real envido* ('Royal Wager,' 1983) stage the interrelation of familial and political oppression, and *Information for Foreigners* (1987) and *Antigona Furiosa* (1986) metaphorically depict the political situation in Argentina during the late 1970s and early 1980s.

SMag

Garcia, Cristina (*b*. 1958), US novelist. Born in Havana, Cuba, Garcia grew up in New York City. She was educated at Barnard College, where she earned a BA in 1979, and Johns Hopkins University, where she earned an MA in 1981. She worked as a reporter for *Time* magazine during the 1980s. She is the author of two highly praised novels, which with poetic prose, fully imagined characters, and vivid and evocative settings, explore life in Cuba and the lives of Cuban immigrants in the US. Her first novel *Dreaming in Cuban* (1992), the story of three generations of a Cuban family, showcases Garcia's talent for storytelling. Funny, original, realistic but also lyrical, the novel moves back and forth between the past and the present, and Havana and Brooklyn, and mingles first- and third-person narration with the love letters that the family matriarch has been sending to a married Spanish man for the past twenty-five years. Garcia's second novel *The Aguero Sisters* (1997) traces the lives of two Cuban sisters. One has settled in the US, and has become a successful businesswoman with her own line of cosmetics, while the other is a skilled electrician in Cuba, reveling in a life of sexual freedom. The novel uses magic realism to explore mystical connections between the sisters and offers an optimistic and feminist perspective on the possibilities in women's lives.

JEM

Garro, Elena (1920–1998), Mexican novelist, short story writer. Garro began her career as a journalist, but soon turned to writing novels, short stories and plays. The novel *Remembrance of Things to Come* (1963), her first published and most important work, and her collection of stories *La semana de colores* ('The Week of Colors,' 1964), explore the magical and the fantastic as coexisting with objective dimensions of reality. She uses a pre-Columbian conception of cyclical time that questions Western linear time, contributing to the creation of worlds which integrate magic, myth, and history. In *Testimonios sobre Mariana* ('Testimonies about Mariana,' 1981) and *La casa junto al río* ('The House Next to the River,' 1983), the fantastic replaces myth, and surreal events, presented as if they were part of daily experience, contribute to the multivalence and ambiguity of the fictive worlds. *Felipe Angeles* (1979) and *Y*

Matarazo no llamó ('And Matarazo Did not Call,' 1991), like *Remembrance*, denounce the arbitrariness and opportunism of political power. The plight of women is also a recurrent theme in her work: most of her protagonists struggle to construct their lives in a patriarchal society while facing and enduring cruelty and persecution, misogyny and violence. As the estranged first wife of Octavio Paz, Garro lived most of her life in Spain.

PR

Gauthier, Xavière (Mireille Boulaire) (*b.* 1942), French feminist writer. From a working-class family, Gauthier graduated in liberal arts and pursued a doctorate in aesthetics with a pioneering essay on *Surrealism and Sexuality* (1971). She has a son and is a professor of bibliology or 'book-science.' She was a founding editor of the feminist creative journal *Sorcières* (1979 onwards). Her foremost creative text remains *Rose saignée* ('Bled Rose,' 1974), a 'feminine writing' piece lavishly typeset with black and red longhand streams of poetic writing to (re)present menstrual cycles as well as female discourse. The text revolves around classical European mythological and contemporary psychoanalytical references. Along with interviews with "Marguerite Duras in *Woman to Woman* (1974), Gauthier has published short stories in *Le lit clos* ('The Enclosed Bed,' 1988). Most recently she has written a novel about the nineteenth-century French socialist Louise Michel. She has also researched the history of Kanakiland, a French territory in New Caledonia, for *L'herbe de guerre, insurrection canaque* ('War Grass: The Kanaki Revolt,' 1992). Her comprehensive edition of Michel's correspondence, *Je vous écris de ma nuit* ('I Write Out of My Night') is forthcoming.

CPM

Gee, Maggie (*b.* 1948), British novelist. Born in Poole, Dorset, Gee was educated at Somerville College, Oxford, where she earned a BA in 1969, a MLitt in 1972, and a PhD in English in1980. She married Nicholas Rankin in 1983; they have one child. A scholar of surrealism, Gee cites Woolf, Beckett, and Nabokov as influences. In her formally innovative fiction, she reworks popular genres for her own unique and bleakly humorous purposes. Her first book *Dying, In Other Words* (1981) is her take on the thriller, in which the cause of a woman's death is sought through layers of stories. She turns to the family saga in her second novel *The Burning Book* (1983), which traces the lives of two families through the two world wars and the threat of a third. In this novel and in *Grace* (1988), Gee, an activist for nuclear disarmament, places her characters within the larger context of the threat of nuclear disaster. *Light Years* (1985) turns the romance around, and begins her examination of a love affair at its end. *The Ice People* (1998) is a science fiction novel about the coming of a second Ice Age. Her other novels include *Where Are the Snows* (1991) and *Lost Children* (1994).

JEM

Geetanjali Shree (*b*. 1957), Indian fiction writer. Born into a North Indian Brahmin family and trained to write in English, Geetanjali Shree (pen-name of Geetanjali Pandey) abandoned a promising career as a historian (PhD, MS, University of Baroda), and turned deliberately to Hindi for her creative writing, to become one of the most significant voices to emerge from the intensive activism and debates of the feminist movement of the 1970s and 1980s. She has worked with the experimental theater group Vivadi (Disputants), scripting feminist reinterpretations of modern Indian classics, such as the novels of Tagore. Her first short-story collection *Anugunj* ('Echoes,' 1991) explores how middle-class urban women negotiate the tensions between indigenous traditions and the modernizing impulses first generated by colonialism. Her novel *Mai* ('Mother,' 1993; forthcoming in English translation) depicts how, in recalling the painful history of her own escape into a wider world, the young narrator rediscovers her mother's inner strength. Her latest novel *Hamara Shahar us Baras* ('Our Town that Year,' 1998) deals with Hindu–Muslim relations in contemporary India in the wake of the meteoric rise of Hindu fundamentalism.

VD

Gems, Pam (*b*. 1925), British playwright. Born in Bransgore, Hampshire, Gems graduated from the University of Manchester in 1949 with first class honors. She married Keith Gems in 1949; they have four children. She did not start writing plays until after her children were grown; her first play *Becky's Wonderful Christmas* was produced in 1971, when she was 46. Her early plays were produced by the Almost Free Theatre, a feminist collective. The success of *Dead Fish*, a play about the friendship between four women, at the Edinburgh Festival in 1976 led to a long run in London, with the play retitled *Dusa, Fish, Stas and Vi*. A prolific playwright, Gems has achieved both critical and popular success with her feminist plays. As in *Queen Christina* (1977), a play about the seventeenth-century Swedish queen, she is interested in rereading the past from a feminist perspective. One of Gems's most successful plays is *Piaf* (1978), in which she undercuts the idealized myth of Piaf with the harsh truth of her life. The critically acclaimed *Stanley* (1996) looks at the life and work of the English painter Stanley Spencer. Gems has written adaptations of numerous novels and plays. Her other plays include *The Treat* (1982) and *Loving Women* (1984).

JEM

Gerhardt, Ida (1905–1997), Dutch poet. Gerhardt was taught the classics at grammar school by the Dutch poet J. H. Leopold, who was to be of great influence on her work. She read classical languages and literature at university and worked as a teacher of Latin and Greek. Her lifelong companion was the medievalist Marie van der Zeyde. Gerhardt's first book of poems appeared at the start of World War II and therefore went practically unnoticed. But she went on to become an important poet and translator of the Psalms, Lucretius, and Virgil. She produced an extensive poetic oeuvre of classical, sometimes archaic, beauty. Echoes of biblical language fill her poems, and although the tone is often lofty and prophetic, it can also be highly personal. The cycle 'In Memoriam Matris' (1954), for example, is about an adult daughter's unforgettable struggle with the ghosts of her difficult mother and a lonely and cold childhood. Gerhardt has always kept aloof from the male modernists in Dutch poetry, working more in the tradition of older poets like Leopold, Henriette Roland Holst, and even Sappho. She received the P. C. Hooft Prize in 1979. Despite her deteriorating eyesight, she continued to write brilliant poems until just a few years before her death. Five of her poems are published in The Defiant Muse (1998) and a translation of the cycle 'In Memoriam Matris' appeared in the Dutch magazine Lover in 1992.

AAn, MMe

Gerlach, Eva (Margaret Dijkstra) (b. 1948), Dutch poet. Since her debut in 1979, literary critics have been impressed by Gerlach's poetry. She combines great technical skill with an original poetic language. Her work revolves around the themes of memory and perception. Photography is an important source of inspiration for her: fixing a specific moment is what she attempts to do in her poems. In her view, poetry is a place to store essential impressions, a domicile – as one of her volumes is called (Domicilie, 1987). Dochter ('Daughter,' 1984) is the moving account of the first hours and days of a baby's life. Although this volume was biographically inspired by the birth of her own daughter, she rejects a biographical interpretation of her work. She avoids publicity in general: it was only

after six years that she agreed to an interview. Her work has been widely praised and Gerlach is now seen as one of the major Dutch poets. She has published seven volumes of poetry and numerous poems in literary magazines. English translations of her work can be found in anthologies such as Women Writing in Dutch (1994) and Turning Tides (1994).

AAn, MMe

Germain, Sylvie (b. 1954), French novelist. Born in Châteauroux, France, Germain graduated from the Sorbonne with a Doctorate in Philosophy. She then moved to Prague in 1986 where she teaches philosophy at the French School. Her first novel The Book of Nights (1985), which won the Lion's Club International Prize, depicts the story of Victor-Flandrin Péniel, a man whose destiny is marked by the violence of wars, from 1870 to World War II. In the sequel Night of Amber (1986), Péniel's grandson has to confront the forces of evil arising from the battlefields of the Algerian war. Characteristic of all her works is a style which blends fable, parable, and fantastic tale. With Medusa Child (1981), which won the Prix Fémina, she again explores the depths of the human psyche drawn by violence and madness: an adolescent girl abused by her half-brother uses her gaze as a weapon to kill her tormentor. Germain sets subsequent works, Weeping Woman on the Streets of Prague (1992) and Eclats de sel ('Salt Shards,' 1996), in Prague, showing characters bearing the mark of history's recent past and torn between God's silence and the hope for redemption.

SBo

Gersão, Teolinda (b. 1940), Portuguese novelist. Gersão is one of a select group of Portuguese women writers who has received the most prestigious literary award for fiction, the Portuguese Writers Association Grand Prize, for her novel A Casa da Cabeça de Cavalo ('The Horse's Head House,' 1995). She was born under the fascist dictatorship in Coimbra, and her works of fiction and a diary, *Os Guarda-chuvas Cintilantes* ('Shimmering Umbrellas,' 1984), focus on the suffering and the repression imposed on the individual by autocratic forces. *Paisagem com Mulher e Mar ao Fundo* ('Landscape with Woman and Sea in the Background,' 1984) paints a society suffocated by censorship, exhausted by an unjust and traumatizing colonial war, and led by a threatening and despotic figure. *Silêncio* ('Silence,' 1981) and *O Cavalo de Sol* ('The Sun Horse,' 1989), as well as other fictional works, question traditional discourses through the creation of a reality that seeks openings, expansion, and movement in order to disrupt and rupture the limitations imposed by culture. These same qualities can be found in her diary, which reflects upon and explores alternative forms of writing and of being. As in the novels, the diary writer is motivated by a desire to subvert the real and to constantly reinvent the world anew. An excerpt from an English translation of the diary appears in *Sweet Marmalade, Sour Oranges* (1994).

JNO

Gibbons, Kaye (*b.* 1960), US novelist. Born in North Carolina, Gibbons graduated from the University of North Carolina, Chapel Hill. Her first novel *Ellen Foster* (1987), which won the Sue Kaufman Prize from the American Academy and Institute of Arts and Letters, is narrated by the title character – an 11-year-old girl who seeks shelter from an abusive father with a welcoming black family. Gibbons writes in deceptively simple, direct prose, often from the first-person perspective, about strong, independent women living in the American South. In *A Virtuous Woman* (1989), a woman must prepare her husband for her impending death from cancer. In *A Cure for Dreams* (1991), Gibbons tells the stories of several generations of women, which she also does in the best-selling *Charms for the Easy Life* (1993), in which a granddaughter is in-

spired by the will of her grandmother, a local midwife. *Sights Unseen* (1995), another best-seller, is about a family headed by a manic-depressive mother. Gibbons moved in a new direction with *On the Occasion of My Last Afternoon* (1998), which is set during the Civil War. Winner of France's Knighthood of the Order of Arts and Letters, she lives in North Carolina with her husband and five children.

DVT

Gilbert, Sandra M. (*b.* 1936), US feminist literary critic, poet. Gilbert has co-authored (with Susan Gubar) several pioneering works of feminist scholarship. Refuting the patriarchal myth of pen as penis, *The Madwoman in the Attic* (1979) constructs a powerful nineteenth-century Anglo-American feminist literary canon. Its sequel, the three volumes of *No Man's Land*, asserts the artistic achievements of twentieth-century women writers by redefining masculinist modernism. *The War of the Words* (1988), *Sexchanges* (1989), and *Letters from the Front* (1994) contest the textual and sexual boundaries of modernity and celebrate an increasingly heterogeneous feminist tradition. Gilbert has also co-edited *Shakespeare's Sisters* (1979), a collection of essays, and *The Norton Anthology of Literature by Women* (1985), which masterfully produces a comprehensive history of women's world literature in English. A poet of five collections, Gilbert meditates on dreams, motherhood, and female creativity in *Emily's Bread* (1984), *In the Fourth World* (1979), and *The Summer Kitchen* (1983), and voices intense feelings of love, loss, and mourning in *The Blood Pressure* (1988), *Ghost Volcano* (1995), and the prose of *Wrongful Death* (1995).

LY

Gilchrist, Ellen (*b.* 1935), US short story writer, novelist, poet. A native of Vicksburg, Mississippi, Gilchrist earned a BA from Millsaps College in Mississippi in 1967. After marrying the first of four husbands (all of whom she divorced) and having three children, she went back to school in her forties, studying creative writing at the University of Arkansas in Fayetteville, and publishing her first book *The Land Surveyor's Daughter*, a collection of poetry, in 1979. She established her reputation with her next book *In the Land of Dreamy Dreams* (1981), a collection of short stories, which was followed by other story collections including *Victory Over Japan* (1984; American Book Award), *Drunk with Love* (1986), *Light Can be Both Wave and Particle* (1989), *Rhoda: A Life in Stories* (1995), and *Courts of Love* (1996). She is known for her compelling storytelling, her humor, and her striking and original characterizations, particularly of rebellious adolescents and discontented upper-class women. Many of her stories are interrelated and many of her characters turn up again in later stories or in her novels, which also explore the struggles of women frustrated by their lack of freedom. Gilchrist's novels include *The Annunciation* (1983), *The Anna Papers* (1988), *Net of Jewels* (1992), *Starcarbon: A Meditation of Love* (1994), and *Sarah Conley* (1997).

DVT

Gilroy, Beryl (*b.* 1924), Guyanese-British novelist. After obtaining her teacher's diploma (Government Technical Institute, 1945), Gilroy left British Guyana for England where, despite her professional qualifications, she could only find menial work. In 1953, however, she became England's first black female teacher, an experience chronicled in her autobiography *Black Teacher* (1976). Her education continued at the University of London (BSc, 1956), Sussex University (MA, 1980) and Century University (PhD, 1987). Her classroom experiences, especially her dissatisfaction with racist and xenophobic textbooks, inspired her early publications – children's books for culturally diverse

classrooms. After her first novel *Frangipani House* (1986), she wrote *Boy Sandwich* (1989), which examines intergenerational conflict as experienced by a teenager 'sandwiched' between his Guyanese grandparents' heritage and his own decidedly British identity. Black British identity, cultural conflict, and the experience of migration also figure in the novels *Gather the Faces* (1996) and *In Praise of Love and Children* (1996), the latter written over thirty years ago but only recently published. She has written two historical novels *Steadman and Joanna* (1992) and *Inkle and Yarico* (1996), and a memoir *Sunlight on Sweet Water* (1992). She lives in London where she practices psychotherapy.

JSp

Ginzburg, Evgeniia Semenovna (1904–1977), Russian prose writer, memoirist. Ginzburg is remembered as the mother of the popular writer Vasily Aksyonov and the author of women's prison camp memoirs. A Jewish Muscovite, Ginzburg worked as a teacher and a party activist before her arrest in 1937. At the labor camp of Kolyma, she performed duties as a nurse, fell in love with a doctor who was a Crimean German, and upon release in 1947 stayed in Magadan until his prison sentence expired. Upon her return to Moscow in 1955, she contributed to various papers and magazines, but died before her memoirs, published abroad in 1967, could appear in Russia. Translated into English in two separate volumes, *Journey into the Whirlwind* (1967) and *Within the Whirlwind* (1981), Ginzburg's account of the prison system under Stalin traces her personal experience in Siberia, but also offers a lively if selective portrait of the camp personnel, prisoners' habits, inmates' loyalties and lapses, and her own state of mind. Her work testifies to her stoic courage in matters of moral conscience and her profound traditionalism in gender politics.

HG

Ginzburg, Lidiia Iakovlevna (1902–1990), Russian scholar, essayist, prose writer. Born in Odessa into an intelligentsia family, in 1922 Ginzburg began studies in the Petersburg State Institute of Art History under the distinguished group of (exclusively male) literary critics known as the Formalists. Upon graduation in 1930, she maintained close relations with them, while teaching, working at a radio station, and authoring a detective novel. Her most characteristic writings, usually published after protracted delays, engage cultural history and occupy a space at the intersection of genres: essay, memoir, criticism, historical sketch, documentary fiction. Although she served as a mentor to younger generations of writers in St Petersburg, her status as a powerful cultural presence was not officially acknowledged until the last years of her life. Her best-known criticism analyzes the creativity of Lermontov (1940), the lyric (1964), psychological prose (*On Psychological Prose*, 1971), the literary hero (1979), and the relation of literature to reality (1987). One of her most successful works is *Blockade Diary* (1984), which ruminates on the human sufferings during the siege of Leningrad that it records in close-up. It condenses the historical and literary modes that for Ginzburg constitute cultural 'evidence.'

HG

Ginzburg, Natalia (1916–1991), Italian novelist, dramatist, essayist. Born in Palermo, the youngest child of an academic family of mixed religious composition (Jewish and Catholic), Natalia Levi married Jewish intellectual Leone Ginzburg in 1938; they had three children. Her mixed heritage informs the bedrock of her work, an oeuvre at once funny and sad, and profoundly shrewd in the psychological portrayal of characters in varied genres. Simplicity is integral to Ginzburg's poetics and the clarity of her language is unmistakable, especially in the plays. Unadorned language exemplifies her desire to represent life unsentimentally, a moral debt she felt authors owe their readers. Like works of the neorealist tendency, lack of emotionality is a Ginzburg staple, from *The Road to the City* (1942), her first publication and a novel about a young woman's thwarted quest for autonomy, to her award-winning memoir *Family Sayings* (1962; titled *The Things We Used to Say* in the US), and beyond. Domestic themes appear throughout; though standard fare, matrimony, as in the short novel *The Dry Heart* (1947) and the play *Ti ho sposato per allegria* ('I Married You Out of Happiness,' 1965), is not standardly reproduced any more than gender roles are normativized, something the late epistolary novel *The City and the House* (1986) makes especially clear.

EN

Giovanni, Nikki (*b.* 1943), US poet. Born Yolande Cornelia Giovanni in Knoxville, Tennessee, Giovanni attended Fisk University, where she earned a BA in 1967, the University of Pennsylvania School of Social Work, and Columbia University. She has taught English and creative writing at several universities, and is currently professor of creative writing at Virginia Polytechnic Institute and State University. Her first books of poetry *Black Feeling, Black Talk* (1967) and *Black Judgement* (1968) brought her immediate fame. Their direct, colloquial language, their expression of African-American identity, experience, and anger, and their ability to tap into the cultural moment of rebellion and revolution made them immensely popular, with critics, readers, and the black power movement. Her celebrity increased through the popularity of her album *Truth Is On Its Way*, on which she reads her poetry to the background of gospel music. But the revolutionary fervor of *Re-Creation* (1970) gave way to the personal in *My House* (1972), and Giovanni's subsequent career has been more low-key. Her poetry is characterized by plain diction, immediacy, and energy, and it remains vitally connected to the events and moods of the times. Other volumes include *Cotton Candy on a Rainy Day* (1978), *Those Who Read the Night Winds* (1983), *Selected Poems* (1996), and *Love Poems* (1997).

JEM

Glancy, Diane (*b*. 1941), US poet, fiction writer, playwright. A writer of Cherokee, British, and German ancestry, Glancy's Native American heritage was instrumental in her decision to become a writer and is central to the works she writes. Born in Kansas City, Missouri, she received a BA in 1968 from the University of Missouri and an MFA from the University of Iowa in 1988. Her books of poetry, including *One Age in a Dream* (1986), *Offering* (1988), *Iron Woman* (1990), and *Lone Dog's Winter Count* (1991), examine personal relationships, the clash of beliefs, the strong influence of culture, and problems of physical and spiritual isolation. Glancy has turned her attention to fiction in recent years. Her novels include *The Only Piece of Furniture in the House* (1996), *Flutie* (1998), and *Pushing the Bear: A Novel of the Trail of Tears* (1998). She has collected her short fiction in *Trigger Dance* (1990). The recipient of many literary awards, Glancy won the American Book Award for *Claiming Breath* (1992), a journal-like collection of notes, poems, and reactions to a year in her life. She currently teaches at Macalester College in St Paul, Minnesota.

DVT

Glück, Louise (*b*. 1943), US poet. Born in New York, Glück began her studies at Sarah Lawrence College and completed her degree at Columbia University in 1965. She has been married twice and has one son. She has taught at numerous universities and writing programs, and since 1984 has been on the faculty at Williams College. Her first book of poetry *First born* (1968) shows the influence of several American poets, including *Anne Sexton and *Sylvia Plath. In her second collection *The House on Marshland*, (1975), she de-

cisively comes into her own. Her poetic style is terse and direct, yet her lyrics, which focus on themes of loss, death, isolation, and rejection, are deeply emotional. Her third volume *The Garden*, published in 1976, consists of five interrelated poems. Biblical allusions become important in *Descending Figure* (1980) and *The Wild Iris* (1992), for which she won the Pulitzer Prize. The latter collection features a tripartite narration by God, the poet, and flowers from the poet's garden. Greek myths figure strongly in *The Triumph of Achilles* (1985; National Book Critics Circle Prize), in which she mourns the death of her father, and in *Meadowlands* (1996), which employs characters and events from the *Odyssey* to narrate the disintegration of a marriage. Other volumes include *Ararat* (1990) and *Vita Nova* (1999). In 1999, Glück received the Lannan Literary Award for Poetry.

DVT

Godwin, Gail (*b*. 1937), US novelist, short story writer. Born in Birmingham, Alabama, Godwin was raised by her mother and grandmother. Her mother worked as a journalist and writer of romance fiction to support the family, and through her, Godwin learned about the rewards and challenges of blending creativity and art with a domestic life, a theme often expressed in her novels. She received her BA in journalism from the University of North Carolina in 1968 and a PhD from the University of Iowa in 1971. Her novels, sometimes compared to works by Eliot and Wharton, portray women on the cusp of some transformation in their lives. She focuses on the pivotal as her characters are prompted, often by a death in the family, to search for their true identities and achieve previously unreachable possibilities. *The Perfectionists* (1970) was inspired by her second marriage to a psychotherapist. *The Odd Woman* (1974) is about an academic who chooses her career over her lover. *The Finishing School* (1985) is about a young woman's relationship with a droll middle-aged aristocrat. Other novels include *Glass People* (1972), *Violet Clay* (1978), *A Mother and Two Daughters* (1982), *A Southern Family* (1987), *Father Melancholy's Daughter* (1991), *The Good Husband* (1994), and *Evensong* (1999).

DVT

Golopenţia, Sanda (*b*. 1940), Romanian linguist, essayist. Born in a family of well-respected Romanian scientists (her father Anton Golopenţia was a sociologist, and her mother Stefania Cristescu was an ethnologist), Golopenţia's choice of a career in this field may seem natural. But this 'naturalness' hides a dramatic struggle against the communist authorities (her father was killed during Stalin's purges of the 1950s, and the whole family had to suffer from the authoritarian regime), which eventually made her flee the country and settle in the US in 1980. She is now a professor of French at Brown University. When she lived in Bucharest, she worked as a researcher at the Institute of Folklore and the Institute for Ethnological and Dialectological Research and published mainly studies in linguistics (*The Transformational Syntax of Romanian* with E. Vasiliu, 1972), semiotics, and anthropology. She continued this work in the US with *Les voies de la pragmatique* ('The Ways of Pragmatics,' 1988) and *Desire Machines* (1998). But, once far from home, she also started writing literary essays on American civilization, on exile, and on her way of living the confrontation between the two cultures: *Lossgainer* (1986), *Cartea plecării* ('The Book of Departing,' 1995), and *America, America* (1996).

IB

Goodison, Lorna Gaye (*b*. 1947), Jamaican poet, short story writer. Born into a lower-middle-class family in Kingston, Goodison studied at the Jamaica School of Art and at the School of the Arts Students League in New York, before returning to Jamaica in 1969 to pursue careers in art and creative writing instruction. In 1978, her six-year marriage to Jamaican radio broadcaster Don Topping ended in divorce; in 1980, she had a son. Her first major poetry collection *Tamarind Season* (1980), written in a visionary and optimistic language, a fusion of standard English and patois, focuses on the lives of Caribbean women and families grappling with race, class, and gender issues. *I am Becoming My Mother* (1986) won the Americas Region Commonwealth Poetry Prize; this work and the poems in *Heartease* (1988) personalize black womanhood in history, and resistance in rural and urban Jamaica and the US. The collection of short fiction *Baby Mother and the King of Swords* (1990) compassionately narrates the toils, loves, and losses of Caribbean women. *Poems: Selected* (1992) and *To Us All Flowers are Roses* (1995) navigate the dual African and European inheritances of Caribbean history, spirituality, and art. Her paintings illustrate her book covers and have been internationally exhibited. She has taught creative writing at various US and Canadian universities since 1991.

LB

Goodyear, Sara Suleri (*see* Suleri Goodyear, Sara)

Gooneratne, Yasmine (*b*. 1935), Sri Lankan-Australian poet, novelist, literary critic. Born in Sri Lanka, Gooneratne was educated at the University of Ceylon, Cambridge University, and Macquarie University, New South Wales, where she now holds a personal chair in English and is the Foundation Director of the Post-Colonial Literatures and Language Research Centre. She has lived in Australia since 1972. In 1990 she was awarded the Order of Australia (AO) for distinguished service to literature and education. She is married to Dr. Brendon Gooneratne and has two children. In her first book of verse *Word, Bird, Motif* (1971), she captures tones varying from the trenchant to the tender. *The Lizard's Cry* (1972) employs the Sanskrit and Sinhala message poem convention and reveals a keen and anguished perception of the socio-economic factors behind the 1971 insurgency in Sri Lanka. Her published works include two other volumes of poetry, critical studies of Jane Austen, Alexander Pope, and *Ruth Prawer Jhabvala, and *Relative Merits: A Personal Memoir of the Bandaranaike Family of Sri Lanka* (1986). Her first novel *A Change of Skies* (1991) received the 1992 Marjorie Barnard Literary Award for Fiction, and was short-listed for the 1991 Commonwealth Writers' Prize. Her second novel is *The Pleasures of Conquest* (1995).

NS

Gorbanevskaia, Natalia Evgenievna (*b.* 1936), Russian poet, journalist. Best known for her political activism of three decades ago, in August 1968 Gorbanevskaia joined the protest on Moscow's Red Square against the Soviet invasion of Czechoslovakia – an event documented in her *Red Square at Noon* (1970). A co-founder of the samizdat *Chronicle of Current Events* (1968), she was arrested in December 1969, committed to a psychiatric asylum, and released in 1972. Apart from a handful of poems published in the Soviet press in the 1960s, her verse circulated in samizdat. *Poberezhe* ('Seacoast,' 1973), the first book of her poetry issued with her permission, appeared in the US. She emigrated to Paris with her two children in 1975. A prolific poet, she authored eight volumes during the years 1973–93, all published in the West. *Angel dereviannyi* ('The Wooden Angel,' 1982) shows Gorbanevskaia at her best. Favorite themes include isolation, the balancing of political and personal impulses, religion, faith and hope. Gorbanevskaia has occupied a prominent position in the Russian emigration as editor for the influential journal *Kontinent* and the newspaper *Russkaia mysl* ('Russian

Thought'). Her *Selected Poems* appeared in English in 1972.

RMey

Gordimer, Nadine (*b.* 1923), South African novelist, short story writer, essayist. Gordimer is the daughter of Jewish immigrants – her father from Latvia and her mother from England. After growing up in a mining town, she went to Johannesburg where she met black intellectuals and artists; she responded by rejecting racism and the apartheid policies of those in power (1948–94). The impact of political events on personal lives is a prominent theme in her writings. These include ten volumes of short stories, ranging from *Face to Face* (1949) to *Jump* (1991), and twelve novels. Those new to Gordimer should read her autobiographical novel *The Lying Days* (1953). *Occasion for Loving* (1963) is about an interracial love affair, a theme developed further in two of her best novels, *A Sport of Nature* (1987) and *My Son's Story* (1990). The complex novels of the 1970s and 1980s are Gordimer's most powerful and ambitious. *A Guest of Honour* (1970) is about an educator who is killed only because he is white. *The Conservationist* (1974) features a conservative Afrikaner, while *Burger's Daughter* (1979) focuses on the daughter of white activists. *July's People* (1981) imagines the shift from white to black power through violent revolution. Two outstanding post-apartheid novels are *None to Accompany Me* (1994) and *The House Gun* (1998). Important, too, are her essays in Clingman's *The Essential Gesture*, interviews in Bazin and Seymour's *Conversations with Nadine Gordimer*, and speeches and miscellaneous writings in Gordimer's *Living in Hope and History: Notes from Our Century* (1999). Her numerous literary awards include the Nobel Prize for Literature (1991).

NTB

Gordon, Mary (*b.* 1949), US novelist, non-fiction writer. Gordon was born on Long

Island to devout Catholic parents; her father died when Gordon was 7 years old. She attended Barnard College, studying with author *Elizabeth Hardwick and receiving her BA in 1971; she later attended Syracuse University. Although Gordon broke with the Catholic Church in her teenage years, she returned to the faith in adulthood both spiritually and through her writing. Her first novel *Final Payments* (1978) tells a story of a 30-year-old woman who has sacrificed her youth to care for her strict Catholic father. The novel portrays the challenges of the new life she makes for herself after he dies, and the subsequent guilt prompted by her sexual experiences. In Gordon's second novel *The Company of Women* (1980), she returns to her exploration of Catholicism and patriarchy, and emphasizes the necessity for women to have strong female friendships for support and fulfillment. The theme of self-sacrifice recurs in *Men and Angels* (1985), in which an art historian tries to balance work and motherhood. Other novels include *The Other Side* (1989), which depicts several generations of an Irish immigrant family, and *Spending: A Utopian Divertimento* (1998). Gordon has written two very different memoirs: *The Shadow Man* (1996), in which she searches for the truth about her father's past, and *Seeing Through Places: Reflections on Geography and Identity* (2000).

DVT

Goswami, Indira (*b.* 1942), Indian novelist, short story writer. Born Mamoni Raisom in Guwahati, Assam, Goswami was influenced by her father in many ways and his death in her childhood shattered her. She studied at Hendique Girls and Cotton College in Guwahati. With her MA from Guwahati University, she went on to complete her PhD from the Institute of Oriental Philosophy, Brindavan. She has 700 short stories and fifteen novels to her credit. Her first novel *Chenabar Srota* ('The Stream of Chenab,' 1972), depicts

the exploitation faced by labourers at a construction site. *Nilakanthi Braja* ('Blue-naked Braja,' 1976) is about the confinement and ultimate rebellion of a young widow within the restrictive religious atmosphere of Brindavan. Her *Dontal Hatir Une Khowa Howdah* ('The Worm-eaten Howdah of a Tusker,' 1988) is about the power of a Vaisnavite monastic institute in Assam. Her latest novel is *Tezaru Dhulire Dhusarita Pristha* ('Pages Soiled with Blood and Dust,' 1995). Besides several anthologized stories, works published in English translation include her novel *The Saga of South Kamarupa*, her *Unfinished Autobiography*, and *The Selected Writings of Indira Goswami*. She is currently Professor and Head of the Department of Modern Indian Languages, Delhi University.

CD

Govier, Katherine (*b.* 1948), Canadian short story writer, novelist. Born in Edmonton, Alberta, Govier earned a BA from the University of Alberta in 1970 and an MA from York University, Toronto, in 1972. She has taught at York University and Leeds University in England. Her critically acclaimed collection of short stories *Fables of Brunswick Avenue* (1985) captures the lives of urban young women in the 1980s. Her fiction focuses on women and, in particular, their struggles to form relationships and find a place in the world. *Angel Walk* (1996), set in Britain in the years before and during World War II, is a richly detailed, psychologically complex portrait of a young Canadian woman who becomes a renowned photographer and has a relationship with an older man. Govier's other novels include *Random Descent* (1979), *Going Through the Motions* (1982), *Between Men* (1987), and *Hearts of Flame* (1991). *Before and After* (1989) and *The Immaculate Conception Photography Gallery* (1994) are short story collections. *Without a Guide* (1994) is a collection of her travel writings.

JEM

Govrin, Michal (*b.* 1950), Israeli writer, poet, theater director. Govrin has published six books of fiction and poetry, among them the extensively anthologized *Hold on the Sun: Short Stories and Legends* (1984), *Otah Sha'a* ('That Very Hour,' 1981), and *Gufei Milim* ('Words' Body'). Her novel *The Name* received the 1997 Kugel Literary Prize. *Ma'ase Ha-Ym: Chronikat Peirush* ('The Making of the Sea: A Chronicle of Exegesis,' 1998) combines Govrin's text and original etchings by Lilian Klapisch. In 1998 Govrin received the Prime Minister Prize for Creativity. Among her stage productions are the award-winning S. Mrojek's *The Emigrants*, and the world premiere of a stage adaptation of Samuel Beckett's novel *Mercier and Camier*. Her production *Gog and Magog*, based on Buber's novel, was performed at the 1994 Israel Festival. Since the early 1970s she has been a leading director of the Experimental Jewish Theater. She has distinguished herself in Israeli art and literature through her avant-garde poetics, which draw upon Talmudic, Kabbalistic, and liturgical sources. The daughter of a prominent Zionist and a Holocaust survivor, she presents an unconventional perception of post-Holocaust consciousness. Govrin received her PhD from the University of Paris, specializing in Jewish ritual and theater. She teaches at the School of Visual Theater in Jerusalem.

RFB

Gowdy, Barbara (*b.* 1950), Canadian novelist. Born and raised in Windsor, Ontario, Gowdy studied theater at York University. She is known for her black humor, and her fascination with the grotesque, the bizarre, and the extreme. Her works, which have been compared to those of Diane Arbus and Flannery O'Connor, are innovative, disturbing, and funny. Her first book *The Rabbit and the Hare* (1982) is a collection of poems and stories. *Through the Green Valley* (1988) is a historical novel set in Ireland in the eighteenth century. Her distinctive style and her central concerns are established in the novel *Falling Angels* (1989), which depicts three adolescent sisters in a dysfunctional family in suburban Toronto in the 1960s. The strange and shocking stories in the collection *We So Seldom Look on Love* (1992) concern physical and mental deformities of all kinds, and feature, among others, a necrophiliac and people with extra body parts. But Gowdy's perspective is honest and sympathetic, as it is in her third novel *Mister Sandman* (1995). The story of the Canary family, comprised of a pathological liar mother, a closeted homosexual father, a nymphomaniac sister, and a mute savant child, it reveals the genuine love that is expressed through their tolerance of one another's oddities. *The White Bone* (1999) asks for tolerance in an entirely different way – by showing the reader the world through the eyes of a female elephant.

JEM

Grace, Patricia (*b.* 1937), New Zealand novelist, short story writer. Wellington born Grace published the first story collection, *Waiariki* (1975), and the first novel, *Mutuwhenua: The Moon Sleeps* (1978), by a Maori woman. Born Patricia Gunson, she studied at Wellington Teacher's College, and married her fellow student Karehi Waiariki Grace, before teaching English as a second language in several rural school districts for nearly twenty years. During that time, she had seven children, and began her career as a writer. In addition to her novels and short stories, she has also published several English books and Maori readers for children. In her early work, Grace seems predisposed to an optimistic search for accommodations between European and Maori cultures and peoples. *Mutuwhenua*, for example, offers a positive treatment of the marriage of the novel's narrator, a Maori woman, to a white man, who eventually accepts some of her traditions. However, Grace's later fictions, especially the novels

Potiki (1986; New Zealand Book Award for Fiction) and *Cousins* (1992), and the collection *Electric Cities and Other Stories* (1987), suggest her growing sensitivity to the injustices suffered by Maori and to the difficulties of preserving their culture in modern New Zealand, despite her syncretic use of Christian and Maori myths.

DM

Graham, Jorie (*b*. 1951), US poet. Born in New York City, Graham grew up in Italy and was educated at the Sorbonne, New York University (BA, 1973), and the University of Iowa, Iowa City (MFA, 1978). She married her third husband James Galvin in 1983; they have one daughter. She currently teaches at the University of Iowa and Harvard University. Her first volume of poetry *Hybrids of Plants and Ghosts* was published in 1980. She has won numerous literary awards and honors, including a MacArthur Foundation Fellowship. Her selected poems *The Dream of the Unified Field* (1995) won the Pulitzer Prize. Her poetry is ambitious, difficult, dense, sober, and unique. Graham's concerns are ontological and metaphysical. The usual terrain of poetry – personal experience, the natural world – is passed through quickly on the way to an abstract realm of ideas. The syntax and rhythms of her poems are demanding, but their very difficulty fascinates, and can yield impressive insights. Her volumes include *Erosion* (1983), *The End of Beauty* (1987), *Region of Unlikeness* (1991), *Materialism* (1993), *The Errancy* (1997), and *Swarm* (2000).

JEM

Greer, Germaine (*b*. 1939), Australian feminist critic. Born in Melbourne, Australia, Greer received a BA from Melbourne University in 1959, an MA from the University of Sydney in 1963, and a PhD from Newnham College, Cambridge in 1968. She came to prominence as a major feminist critic with the publication of the best-selling *The Female Eunuch* in

1970. With humor and energy, the book critiques representations of women in literature and society and calls for women's rejection of limiting stereotypes. Greer became famous as a provocative and outspoken feminist, and in the 1970s she worked as a journalist and appeared frequently on television. She has written several other polemical works on women's issues. *The Obstacle Race* (1979) examines the conditions that have prevented women from achievement in the art world. *Sex and Destiny: The Politics of Human Fertility* (1984) celebrates motherhood and attacks the West's emphasis on family planning in third world countries. *The Change* (1991) takes issue with society's attitudes about menopause. In *The Whole Woman* (1999), she charts the achievements and failures of feminism, and offers an assessment of the current status of women. Other works include *The Madwoman's Underclothes: Essays and Occasional Writings 1968–1985* (1986), which collects her journalism; *Daddy, We Hardly Knew You* (1989), a memoir about her search for her father's identity; and *Slip-Shod Sibyls: Recognition, Rejection, and the Woman Poet* (1995). Greer has taught at Warwick University and the University of Tulsa, Oklahoma, where she was a Founding Director of the Center for the Study of Women's Literature.

JEM

Grekova, I. (*b*. 1907), Russian prose writer, mathematician. Born Elena Dolgintseva, upon marriage Grekova adopted her husband's surname of Ventsel, and later the pseudonym I. Grekova for her fiction. Like her father, she became a mathematician, graduating from Leningrad State University, earning a doctorate, and specializing in probability theory, on which she authored widely used textbooks. A resident of Moscow since the 1930s, after her husband's death in 1955 Grekova continued to teach at the Zhukovsky Military Aviation Academy until the publication of her first significant novella *Na ispytaniiakh*

('On Maneuvers,' 1967). Its unorthodox depiction of army research led to her forced resignation and transfer to the Moscow Institute of Railway Engineers, where she taught until her retirement. Grekova's fiction typically focuses on the technical intelligentsia from the perspective of a middle-aged heroine, exploring moral conflicts in tandem with 'women's' issues: the 'double burden' of professional advancement and domestic duties ('Ladies' Hairdresser,' 1963), marriage ('Hotel Manager,' 1976), abortion ('Summer in the City,' 1965), maternity (*Ship of Widows*, 1981), and orphanhood ('Malen'kii Garusov' ['Little Garusov,' 1970]). Ethical dilemmas comprise the core of such works as 'Masters of Their Own Lives' (1960), *The Department* (1978), 'No Smiles' (1975), *Porogi* ('Rapids/Thresholds,' 1984), and *Svezho predanie* (1962). The last treats Russian anti-Semitism and the trumped-up exposé of the 'Doctors' Plot' under Stalinism. Grekova favors an occasionally flaccid, zero-style realism to chronicle contemporary daily Soviet life. Vouchsafing few stylistic surprises or delights, her near-journalistic prose allows periodic strong effects to emerge with immense force

HG

Grenville, Kate (*b.* 1950), Australian short story writer, novelist. Grenville, feminist and teacher of creative writing, was born and educated in Sydney, where she earned a BA in 1972. She then lived in London and traveled in Europe and America. After an MA (University of Colorado), she worked as an editor, teacher, and journalist in Australia and the US. Grenville is married to Bruce Petty (writer and cartoonist) and has two children. Her fiction investigates gender, language, and power and the refusal of women to conform to roles ascribed to them, and includes *Lilian's Story* (Vogel Award winner 1985), in which an abused daughter eventually finds a voice and a degree of independence. *Joan Makes History* (1988) encompasses a panoramic survey of Australian women's experience: its double narrative interleaves the life of a single 'Joan' with narratives of sequential 'Joans' depicted as feminine 'others' in Australian society. *Dark Places* (1994; Victorian Premier's Award) further exposes the biases of historical discourse, as Grenville investigates misogyny, women's diminished self-worth, and the formative conditions that give rise to injustice. These are seductive fictions which effectively balance humor and bleak social truths. She also published a best-selling writing manual *The Writing Book* (1990).

LJ

Gripe, Maria (*b.* 1923), Swedish children's writer. Born in Vaxholm, Sweden, Gripe spent her childhood years steeped in the fairy tales of Hans Christian Andersen, the only author her father considered worthy of the title. Andersen left traces in Gripe's writing, which is highly poetic, somewhat dark and sentimental, and at times difficult to comprehend, especially for child readers. In her early stories, trilogy *Josephine* (1961), *Hugo and Josephine* (1962), and *Hugo* (1966), and in *The Glassblower's Children* (1964), fairy tale and fantastic elements predominate. In her later stories *Elvis and His Secret* (1972) and its sequels, Gripe moves toward a more realistic style, exploring the psychological complexities of the young protagonists. Most of the child characters that populate her books are in search of their own identity, and many live in an atmosphere of loneliness and isolation. Despite the density of her narrative and the difficulty of the subject matter, Gripe is considered one of Sweden's most prominent children's authors because of the poetry and perceptiveness of her writing. In 1974, fittingly enough, she received the Hans Christian Andersen Medal.

E-MM

Groult, Benoîte (*b.* 1920), French novelist. Born in Paris to an interior designer father and a fashion designer mother, Groult grew up in an intellectual and artistic milieu. Married three times, she has three children; her third husband is fellow journalist and novelist Paul Guimard. She wrote her first novel *Le journal à quatre mains* ('The Four Hands Diary,' 1962) with her sister Flora as well as her second book *Feminine Plural* (1965), which explores friendship between women and love triangles. In several of her subsequent novels, husbands betray their wives, yet the women become strong and the couples eventually survive. In her latest novel *Salt on Our Skin* (1988), the story of an intellectual married woman who has a lifelong affair with a sailor, also married, Groult experiments with how to speak about women's sexual pleasures. A declared feminist, she has written a manifesto *Ainsi soit-elle* ('So Be She,' 1975) and explored men's feminism. She co-founded a woman's magazine *F Magazine* in 1978 and participated in a national commission charged with creating feminine versions of position titles.

JV

Guimarães, Geni (*b*. 1947), Brazilian poet. Guimarães, a native of São Manoel, São Paulo, has published poems that reveal Brazilian blacks in their essence by speaking about the everyday life of the place she lives in – a village located in the interior of the country. *A Cor da Ternura* ('The Color of Tenderness') is a prize-winning autobiographical book for children which presents a positive role model for young black children. She has also published two volumes of poetry: *Terceiro Filho* ('Third Son,' 1970) and *Da Flor ao Afeto* ('From the Flower to the Affection,' 1981). Her poems have been included in anthologies such as *Antologia Contemporânea da Poesia Negra* ('Contemporary Anthology of Black Poetry'), *A Razão da Chama* ('Reason of Flame'), *O Negro Escrito* ('The Written Black Man') and, in English translation, in *Finally Us: Contemporary Black Brazilian Women Writers* (1995).

SVR

Gupta, Sunetra (*b*. 1965), Indian-British novelist. Born in Calcutta, India, Gupta spent her childhood in a number of African countries, where her father taught history at various universities. She graduated from Princeton University with a degree in biology in 1987 and completed her PhD in mathematical biology at Imperial College, London in 1992. She works at Oxford University researching infectious diseases. Her novels, written in a fluid, musical, and highly metaphorical language, reflect her transnational background as well as her original Bengali culture, both in characters and settings. *Memories of Rain* (1992), which won the 1996 Sahitya Akademi Award, tells the story of a failed relationship between an Englishman and his Indian wife. In subsequent works, Gupta's plot structure becomes more intricate and her language rich in both literary allusions and fairytale elements. *The Glassblower's Breath* (1993), set in London and narrated in the second-person by multiple voices, follows the wanderings of an Indian woman and recalls her past in Calcutta and New York. Here and in *Moonlight into Marzipan* (1995), the story of an accidental scientific discovery, she explores recurrent issues such as creation – human and scientific – power relations, love, death, and betrayal. Women, although not in an overtly political way, are always central characters in her novels.

PM

Gur, Batya (*b*. 1947), Israeli novelist, literary critic. A book reviewer for the highbrow daily *HaAretz*, Gur is best known for her entertaining and popular murder mysteries. She studied Hebrew literature and history at the Hebrew University in Jerusalem and taught high school. Her works blur the distinctions between genres (mystery versus novel, journalism versus fiction), question social categories, and challenge national myths. *Saturday Morning Murder* (1988) introduced the university-educated, Moroccan-born Michael Ohayon who solves murder cases through empathy. *Literary Murder* (1989), an academic *roman à clef*, both satirizes the literary establishment in Israel and offers a thoughtful discussion of aesthetics and interpretation. Changes in the ideology and practice of the kibbutz are the core of *Murder on a Kibbutz* (1991) and the key to solving the murder. *Murder Duet* (1996) is her fourth mystery. The novel *Lo Kakh Tearti Li* ('Afterbirth,' 1994) questions the essentialist nature of gender through the pairing of the protagonist with her male parallel, a patient lacking in sex characteristics, and scenes of childbirth. Her latest novel *Even Tahat Even* ('Stone for Stone,' 1998) is based on the true story of a bereaved mother's struggle against the Israeli army.

NEB

Guy, Rosa (*b*. 1928), Trinidadian-US novelist. Born Rosa Cuthbert in Trinidad, Guy grew up in Harlem after arriving in New York with her family in 1932. She left school at the age of 14, participated in the American Negro Theatre and later studied at New York University, where she began writing fiction and drama. She co-founded the Harlem Writers' Guild and has served as its president. Her writing career lagged despite the production of a one-act play *Venetian Blinds* (1954), and the publication of her first novel *Bird at my Window* (1966), until she combined her Caribbean roots with her interest in young adult literature. After editing *Children of Longing* (1971), an anthology surveying the personal experiences and hopes of young African-Americans, Guy traveled in the Caribbean, stopping in Haiti and Trinidad. She returned to the US to write a successful trilogy reflecting those Caribbean cultures: *The Friends* (1973), *Ruby* (1976), and *Edith Jackson* (1978). Most of Guy's subsequent fiction has been directed to a young adult audience, including *My Love, My Love: or, The Peasant Girl* (1985), the basis for a successful 1990 Broadway musical titled *Once on This Island*.

DM

H

Haasse, Hella (*b.* 1918), Dutch novelist. Considered to be one of the greatest authors of her generation, Haasse was born in the East Indies to Dutch parents living in Batavia (now Jakarta). She moved to the Netherlands to study Scandinavian languages at the University of Amsterdam, but soon became a professional novelist. Her novella *Forever a Stranger* (1948) put her on the Dutch literary map. The story of a friendship between an Indian and a Dutch boy in the Dutch Indies, it is an early and interesting exploration of the postcolonial condition as well as a tribute and a farewell to the country of her youth. *The Scarlet City* (1952) is the fictionalized life of Giovanni Borgia in fifteenth-century Rome. In *Threshold of Fire* (1966), set in fifth-century Rome, she develops a critique of the Oedipal structure of Christianity, which holds that the son (the human being) should blindly follow the father (Christ). After *Threshold of Fire*, she turned to female protagonists, devoting two epic novels to the life of Charlotte Sophie Bentinck, in which she explores the (im)possibilities of female emancipation in the eighteenth century. A recent, much acclaimed historical novel in letters, that once again deals with the life of the Dutch in the East Indies, is *Heren van de Thee* ('Gentlemen of Tea,' 1992). Haasse has received a number of awards, including the Constantijn Huygens Prize in 1981 and the prestigious P. C. Hooft Prize in 1983.

AAn, MMe

Hacker, Marilyn (*b.* 1942), US poet. Born in New York City, Hacker received a BA from New York University in 1964. She married the writer Samuel R. Delany in 1961; they divorced in 1980. Since 1986, her companion has been Karyn J. London. She has one daughter. Her first full-length volume of poetry *Presentation Piece* was published in 1974; it won the National Book Award for poetry. Her poetry is distinguished by her skillful use of traditional stanzaic forms and meters and by the ways she uses, modifies, or undercuts those forms to write about modern urban life. Her characteristic concerns are female, and specifically lesbian, experience, the mother–daughter relationship, love, and sexual passion. *Love, Death, and the Changing of the Seasons* (1986) is a sonnet sequence which traces the course of a lesbian love affair. Other volumes include *Separations* (1976), *Going Back to the River* (1990), *The Hang-Glider's Daughter* (1990), and *Selected Poems: 1965– 1990* (1994). Both *Winter Numbers* (1994) and *Squares and Courtyards* (2000) deal with mid-life, her dual residency in New York and Paris, and the personal losses she has suffered through cancer and AIDS.

JEM

Hagedorn, Jessica (*b. c.* 1949), Philippine-American playwright, fiction writer, poet. Born and raised in the Philippines, Hagedorn emigrated to the US in 1963. She studied theater arts at the American Conservatory Theater in San Francisco, and for ten years was the leader and lyricist for the art rock band The Gangster Choir. She has received numerous grants and awards, including two National Endowment for the Arts Inter-Arts fellowships (1984, 1987), and three MacDowell Colony fellowships (1985, 1986, 1988). Her play *Mango Tango* was originally produced by Joseph Papp at the Public Theater in New York in 1978. *Teenytown*, written in collaboration with performance artists Laurie Carlos and Robbie McCauley in the early 1990s, has been produced in New York, Los Angeles, San Francisco, and Atlanta. Her first novel *Dogeaters* (1991) was nominated for the National Book Award; her second *The Gangster of Love* was published in 1996. Her other books include *Danger and Beauty* (1993), a reissue of previously published works plus new performance texts, and *Charlie Chan is Dead* (1993), an anthology of contemporary Asian-American fiction, for which she was editor and wrote the introduction. She lives in New York City with her husband and two daughters.

                                                                CJM

Hahn Moo-Sook (1918–1993), Korean novelist. Of a highly cultured, upper-class family in Seoul, artistically gifted Hahn aspired to become a painter when young. Illnesses during her teenage years cut short her dream as well as her high school education. Home-bound, she benefited from reading Western literary masterpieces in her father's well-stocked study. She made her debut with her first novel *Tŭngpul tŭn yŏin* ('The Woman with a Lamp,' 1942), written in Japanese, the first prize winner in a magazine contest. Her post-liberation fame was established by her second novel *Yŏksa nŭn hŭrŭnda* ('History Flows,' 1948), a saga of traditional Korean families set against the turbulent political and social changes at the turn of the century. While Hahn's major works pay homage to the disappearing Korean cultural heritage, demonstrating her unsurpassed expertise in traditional Korean culture, she is noted for promoting harmony and balance between the presumably opposing cultural entities, Korean and non-Korean. Her *Sŏngnyu namujip iyagi* ('Tale of the House with Pomegranate Trees,' 1964) illustrates the necessity of accommodating modernity within the framework of Korean tradition, while *Encounter* (1986), her last novel, demonstrates the possibility of coalescence between Confucianism and Christianity.

                                                                Y-HK

Hamilton, Jane (*b.* 1957), US novelist. Born in Oak Park, Illinois, Hamilton was the youngest of five children; her mother wrote poetry, her grandmother wrote fiction. She received a BA from Carleton College in Minnesota in 1979 before settling in rural Rochester, Wisconsin with her husband Robert Willard, where she lives, works, and writes in an orchard farmhouse; she has two children. In 1988 she published her first novel *The Book of Ruth*, for which she was awarded the PEN/Hemingway Foundation Award for best first novel. Set in a rural Illinois town, its first-person narration by Ruth Grey, an insecure and inarticulate young woman, abused by her husband and numbed by alcohol and drugs, is a tour de force. Hamilton's next novel, *A Map of the World* (1994), which became an international best-seller and has been made into a major film (1999), is a painfully compelling story, narrated alternately by Alice and her husband, of how Alice's quiet rural life is completely changed when a friend's child dies in her care, and a boy accuses Alice of sexual abuse. *The Short History of a Prince* (1998) features the gay protagonist Walter McCloud, both as a teenager and an adult. Hamilton contrasts Walter's youthful aspirations, including his dreams of dancing in the ballet, to his middle-aged reality. All three novels have been praised for the believability and psychological depth of their characters.

DVT

Hanrahan, Barbara Janice (1939–1991), Australian fiction writer, artist. Hanrahan was born and died in Adelaide, South Australia. After her father's death in 1940 she was raised by her mother, her grandmother, and her great-aunt. The circumstances of her growing up form the core of her writing, from her first book, the barely fictionalized memoir *The Scent of the Eucalyptus* (1973), through her final memoir *Michael and Me and the Sun* (1992). In Adelaide, Hanrahan trained as an art teacher; in 1963 she left for London to study printmaking. For many years she and her partner, Adelaide sculptor Jo Steele, divided their time between England and Australia. Hanrahan maintained her dual careers as artist and writer. She published fifteen books, of which five can be designated as 'autobiographical fictions,' five as 'Gothic fictions' and the remainder as 'biographical fictions.' The autobiographical fictions focus on the years before she was recognized as a writer. The Gothic fictions, starting with *The Albatross Muff* (1977), are meditations upon the nature of evil. The biographical fictions, which, like *Annie Magdalene* (1985), are based on characters known to Hanrahan, are celebrations of otherwise unsung working-class people. *The Diaries of Barbara Hanrahan* (1998) reveal the spiritual underpinning of her work.

ELi

Hardwick, Elizabeth (*b.* 1916), US critic, novelist. Born in Lexington, Kentucky, Hardwick was educated at the University of Kentucky, Lexington (AB, 1938; MA, 1939) and Columbia University. She married the poet Robert Lowell in 1949 (they divorced in 1972); they had one daughter. She has taught at Barnard College. She began her career as a novelist with *The*

Ghostly Lover (1945), but discovered her true calling as a literary and social critic while working at the left-wing journal the *Partisan Review* in the 1940s. She was a founding editor of the *New York Review of Books* in 1963, for which she still writes. She is best known for her five volumes of essays: *A View of My Own* (1962), *Bartelby in Manhattan* (1983), the classic *Seduction and Betrayal: Women and Literature* (1974), *Sight-Readings* (1998), and *American Fictions* (1999), which collects her critical portraits of great American writers from Hawthorne to Mailer. Her distinctive voice, by turns wry, lyrical, and tough, and her wide-ranging interests in cultural, social, and political issues, place her critical essays closer to literature than journalism. Her other novels are *The Simple Truth* (1955) and *Sleepless Nights* (1979), a formally innovative and frankly autobiographical work about the memories of an insomniac.

JEM

Hareven, Shulamith (*b.* 1930), Israeli fiction writer, essayist. Making her debut with a book of poems *Yerushalayim Dorsanit* ('Predatory Jerusalem,' 1962), Hareven has never tired of exploring new artistic avenues, publishing in a variety of genres, including children's literature. Though she advocates a separation between 'biography and bibliography,' *The Vocabulary of Peace*, a selection of her (mostly political) essays (1981–91), includes a rare autobiographic essay 'On Being a Levantine,' in which she contrasts her adopted homeland with the gloom of her European birthplace. Having escaped the Holocaust as a child, she rarely evokes its memory, except in surrealist symbolism (*Twilight and Other Stories*, 1980), preferring to begin her life story with her participation in the Israeli War of Independence (1948). Furthermore, her first novel *City of Many Days* (1972) nostalgically imagines a multicultural and cosmopolitan Jerusalem *before* World War II. Questioning the category '*women* writers' and labeling herself 'a selective feminist,' her early novel nevertheless sports one of the most autonomous ('androgynous') heroines in Israeli fiction. In her short stories she often portrays the socially marginal. In 'Loneliness' from *Twilight*, and earlier stories, she was also the first to evoke lesbianism in Hebrew literature, although with a typical Jewish twist. The lyrical novellas of *Thirst: The Desert Trilogy* (1983–93) weave together her two major themes – the outsider (of both sexes) and the androgynous woman – framing both in a distant time (ancient Israel) that is nevertheless wholly ours.

YSF

Hariharan, Githa (*b*. 1954), Indian novelist, short story writer. Born into a Tamil household from south India, Hariharan received the finest of liberal educations in Bombay, Manila, and the US, where she took her MA in communication and worked briefly as a scriptwriter in television. She later worked as an editor in a publishing house before becoming a full-time writer. Her works display an urban sensibility engaged in the constant re-interpretation of myth, tradition, fantasy, and fable. Her first novel *The Thousand Faces of Night* (1992), which won the Commonwealth Writers Prize for the Best First Book in 1993, is a valiant, honest examination of the dilemma of identity that confronts contemporary Indian women, weighted by inherited notions of tradition, religion, and caste. The liberating recognition that a woman has to 'meet her fate alone' finally enables her heroine to locate the paradoxically emancipating impulse of these structures. Hariharan's second novel is *The Ghosts of Vasu Master* (1994). *The Art of Dying* (1993) is a collection of stories about death and its place in life. Her latest novel *When Dreams Travel* (1999) is a multi-voiced narrative with mythic qualities.

MBh

Harjo, Joy (*b*. 1951), US poet. Born in Tulsa, Oklahoma, Harjo attended the University of New Mexico, Albuquerque (BA, 1976) and the University of Iowa, Iowa City (MFA, 1978). She has two children. She has taught at several universities including University of Colorado, Boulder and University of New Mexico, Albuquerque. She has also been a writer-in-residence at numerous colleges and schools in New Mexico, Oklahoma, and Alaska. Her first volume of poetry *The Last Song* was published in 1975. She is a member of the Muscogee (Creek) Nation, and her identity as a Native American woman is central to her work. Incorporating Native American oral traditions, she writes about the landscapes of her native Oklahoma and the desert Southwest, and about Native American experience and culture. Her concerns are sometimes political, but more often spiritual, as she seeks and celebrates sources of spirituality that have not been tainted by the modern world. Her collections of poetry include *She Had Some Horses* (1985), *Secrets from the Center of the World* (1989), *In Mad Love and War* (1990, American Book Award), *The Woman Who Fell from the Sky* (1994), and *A Map of the Next World* (2000). She is a co-editor of the collection *Reinventing the Enemy's Language: Contemporary Native Women's Writing of North America* (1997).

JEM

Harmsen van Beek, Fritzi (*b*. 1927), Dutch poet, illustrator. Both of Harmsen van Beek's parents wrote and illustrated children's books. Harmsen van Beek was already a cult poet before the publication of her first book *Geachte Muizenpoot en andere gedichten* ('Venerable Mouse-foot and Other Poems,' 1965). At that time, she lived in a country house which was frequented by the Dutch literary avant-garde, of which she was the radiant center. Her poems are absurdist, desperate, yet of great technical intricacy. Her capacity to play with language is extraordinary. In this respect, she has clearly influenced Gerard

Reve, one of the major Dutch postwar writers. Besides some remarkable prose in 1968–9, she published another volume of poetry *Kus of ik schrijf* ('Kiss or Else I'll Write,' 1975). This volume deals with loss and decay, but in an extremely humorous way. Although publishers begged for more work, she has not published anything since. English translations of her work can be found in several anthologies, including *With Other Words* (1985) and *The Defiant Muse* (1998). Harmsen van Beek has received several literary prizes for her poetry.

AAn, MMe

Hartwig, Julia (*b.* 1921), Polish poet, translator. Born and raised in Lublin, Hartwig published her first poem at the age of 17. During World War II, she studied Polish and French literature at the illegally operating Warsaw University, and later at the Catholic University in Lublin. She lived in France from 1947 to 1950. Widowed in 1996, after a forty-two-year marriage to the prominent Polish poet Artur Miedrzyrzecki, Hartwig now resides in Warsaw. The author of eight volumes of verse and two volumes of what she calls poetic prose, she has also published nonfiction: *Dziennik amerykanski* ('American Diary,' 1980), an account of her sojourn in the US from 1970 to 1974. Influenced by French literature and culture, her poetry is considered predominantly aesthetic and classical. The hallmark of her poetics is a symbolic dream-vision, her favorite form that of a short poem in prose. Hartwig has published monographs on Nerval (1961) and Apollinaire (1972), as well as highly acclaimed translations of French and American poetry. The many translations of her verse may be found in the anthologies *Postwar Polish Poetry* (1983), *Spoiling Cannibals' Fun: Polish Poetry of the Last Two Decades of Communist Rule* (1991), and *Ambers Aglow* (1997).

JB

Harwood, Gwen (1920–1995), Australian poet. Born in Brisbane, Harwood published seven highly influential books of poetry, her early work often appearing under playful pseudonyms: Francis Geyer, Walter Lehmann, T. F. Kline, and Miriam Stone. Harwood is also the author of librettos and a prize-winning collection of letters *Blessed City: Letters to Thomas Riddell 1943* (1990). In 1945 Harwood married linguist Thomas Harwood and moved to Hobart, Tasmania, where she began publishing poetry in her late thirties. Her first volume *Poems* (1963) introduces two eccentric characters, Professors Eisenbart and Kröte. Often read as ironic self-projections, these figures appeared in various guises over the next twenty years, as Harwood developed her central concerns: pain and morality, the joys and struggles of art and music, spirituality, love and friendship. Her verse forms are traditional, and acclaimed for their craft, restraint, and playful rhyme, stanza, and meter. Later volumes of poetry include *Poems: Volume Two* (1968), *The Lion's Bride* (1981), *Bone Scan* (1988), and *Living in the Present Tense* (1995). Harwood's poetry received numerous prizes including the Grace Leven Poetry Prize (1975) for her *Selected Poems*, the Robert Frost Award (1977), and the Patrick White Literary Award (1978). Harwood died of cancer in 1995.

LMcC

Haslund, Ebba (*b.* 1917), Norwegian novelist, playwright, essayist. Born in Seattle to Scandinavian immigrants who returned with her to Norway in 1919, Haslund developed into a popular, mildly satirical, and insightful critic of the Norwegian middle class. Starting in 1945 and spanning half a century, her works include fourteen novels, three collections of short stories, essays, memoirs, children's books, stage and radio plays, and a biography. She has received numerous literary awards and holds distinguished member status in the Norwegian Writers' Guild, which she headed from 1971 to 1975. The novel *Nothing Happened* (1948), initially unappreciated, has won recent acclaim for its sensitive portrait of lesbian friendship, while *Bare et lite sammenbrudd* ('Just a Little Nervous Breakdown,' 1975) is more representative in its themes of marital alienation and mid-life crisis. Depicting the family as a microcosm of attitudes and problems in the surrounding society, Haslund excels in capturing the self-awareness of the conflicted housewife with her multiple allegiances and longings. Experiences during the German occupation, when her husband was a resistance worker, inspired her in *Syndebukkens krets* ('The Tropic of the Scapegoat,' 1968), which confronts readers with complex ethical dilemmas.

FS

Haushofer, Marlen (Marie Helene Haushofer) (1920–1970), Austrian prose writer. Born in rural Frauenstein in Styria, Haushofer lived as a housewife and writer in Steyr after a short episode as an aspiring young author in postwar Vienna. Her premature death was due to cancer. Simone de Beauvoir's assessment of the European woman's condition, *The Second Sex* (1949), influenced Haushofer profoundly. Alienated by the oppressive gender roles in Catholic Austria, she nostalgically records her childhood memories, associated with nature, life in the country, and freedom from social constraints in *Die Vergissmeinnichtquelle* ('The Spring of Forget-me-nots,' 1956) and *Himmel, der nirgendwo endet* ('Heaven That Knows No End,' 1969). *Wir töten Stella* ('We Kill Stella,' 1958) and *Die Mansarde* ('The Attic,' 1969) show women's adolescence and adult lives to be overshadowed by bondage, humiliation, and exploitation. *Eine Handvoll Leben* ('A Handful of Life,' 1955), *Die Tapetentür* ('The Hidden Door,' 1957), and the utopian novel *The Wall* (1963), whose protagonist kills her male assailant, explore paths to liberation. Haushofer also published numerous children's books, including *Brav sein ist schwer* ('It's Hard to be Good,' 1965) and *Schlimm sein ist auch kein Vergnügen*

('Being Bad Is Not Fun Either,' 1970). Her awards include the Theodor-Körner Prize (1963), the Arthur-Schnitzler Prize (1963), and the Austrian State Prize (1970).

DCGL

Hayashi Kyōko (*b.* 1930), Japanese novelist, fiction writer. Hayashi was born in Nagasaki, the daughter of a trading company employee. In 1931, her family moved to Shanghai. She returned to Nagasaki in 1945; she was working in a munitions plant when the atomic bomb exploded in Nagasaki on 9 August. Although she received no external wounds, she suffered severe radiation sickness for several months. She began writing in 1962. Major recognition, however, did not come until 1975, when 'Ritual of Death' won both the Gunzō Shinjin and Akutagawa Prizes. In this autobiographical account of the Nagasaki bombing, a 16-year-old schoolgirl describes in concrete, brutal detail the bombing and its aftermath. Hayashi's thirty-year high school reunion with classmates from Nagasaki (many of whom, like herself, have feared complications in childbirth resulting from radiation sickness) is the subject of several stories in *Giyaman Biidoro* ('Cut Glass and Blown Glass,' 1978). Memories of Shanghai, and the social tensions underscoring its privileged Japanese community, form another recurring theme in the author's work. 'Yellow Sand' (1977) gives a sympathetic portrait of a Japanese prostitute; 'Michelle Lipstick' (1980) depicts growing tension in the Japanese population as anti-Japanese activities escalated during the final days of World War II.

AAI

Hazzard, Shirley (*b.* 1931), US novelist. Born and raised in Sydney, Australia, Hazzard left Australia in 1947 and is now an American citizen. She married the writer Francis Steegmuller in 1963. She worked as a clerk at the United Nations in New York, and her disillusionment with the organization informs her satirical novel *People in*

Glass Houses (1967) and a nonfiction work *Defeat of an Ideal* (1973). Her first book *Cliffs of Fall*, a collection of short stories, was published in 1963. It establishes her characteristic theme of love and its complications and failures. The stories, usually told from the perspective of a female protagonist, are elegantly written, subtle, and witty. She has written two short novels, *The Evening of the Holiday* (1966) and *The Bay of Noon* (1970), both set in Italy, but is best known for her acclaimed novel *The Transit of Venus* (1980; National Book Critics' Circle Award). Intricately constructed, covering several decades and set in cities around the world, it tells the absorbing story of two expatriate Australian sisters and their experiences with love and loss. Hazzard has also written *Greene on Capri* (2000), an evocative portrait of her literary friendship with the novelist Graham Greene.

JEM

Head, Bessie (1937–1986), South African novelist, short story writer, essayist. Head, one of Africa's most acclaimed women writers, was born of mixed parentage in Pietermaritzberg in 1937 and educated mainly in Durban, South Africa. She worked as a primary school teacher and as a journalist for *Drum* magazine. She was married to the journalist Harold Head, and had one son. She left South Africa for Botswana on a one-way exit permit in 1963 and died in exile in 1986. Her untimely death was a tragic loss for African literature and for women writers in general. Notwithstanding her prominence as a writer, she lived in relative poverty all her life. She excelled as novelist, storyteller, and commentator, and wrote with extraordinary simplicity and complexity at the same time. Her first novel *When Rain Clouds Gather* (1968) is based on her time as a refugee living at the Bamangwato Development farm. Her second novel *Maru* (1971) also depicts a Botswanan community. Her third novel *A Question of*

Power (1974) concerns the complexities of the female psyche. Head also wrote many short stories which have been anthologized in various collections. Her own short story collection is titled *The Collector of Treasures* (1977). Her other works are *Serowe: Village of the Rain Wind* (1981) and *A Bewitched Crossroad* (1984). Works published posthumously are *Tales of Tenderness and Power* (1989), *A Woman Alone: Autobiographical Writing* (1990), *A Gesture of Belonging: Letters from Bessie Head, 1965–1970* (1991), and *The Cardinals* (1993).

TMR-P

Hébert, Anne (1916–2000), Quebec poet, novelist. Born in a village near Quebec City, Hébert studied at home and in Catholic girls schools in the capital. More important than formal schooling were her father's love of literature and admiration for the French language, her mother's passion for the theater, and the companionship of her cousin, the rebel poet Saint-Denys Garneau. During most of her long writing career, she lived very privately in Paris. She returned to Quebec in 1997. She self-published her first prose work *The Torrent* (1950), rejected by editors because of its violent matricide. The 'terrible and magnificent' tale condemns the repression of instincts in pre-Quiet Revolution Quebec. A published poet since 1939, Hébert finally won acclaim as a poet with another once-rejected volume, *The Tomb of Kings* (1953). Despite early struggles, she received numerous honors in North America and Europe. Two prize-winning novels, *Kamouraska* (1970) and *In the Shadow of the Wind* (1982), with their innovative narrations and explorations of the psychological motivation and social context for crimes, have become films. Hébert continually plumbed her 'deepest truth,' to rewrite history, myth, and legend, in a densely poetic style where biblical and literary allusions abound, and nature is omnipresent.

AMR

Hemmerechts, Kristien (*b*. 1955), Flemish novelist, short story writer. Hemmerechts studied Dutch, English, and comparative literature at the Universities of Brussels, Louvain, and Amsterdam. She is a literary critic, a professor of English, and a fervent feminist. She made her debut with a number of stories, written in English, published in the *Literary Review*, the *Review of Contemporary Fiction* and in Faber and Faber's *First Fictions* series (1986). But she has become most popular for her novels and short story collections written in her native Dutch. Her most recent publications are the novels *Margot en de engelen* ('Margot and the Angels,' 1997) and *Taal zonder mij* ('Language Without Me,' 1998). She is an expert at dissecting seemingly satisfactory relationships. Intimate detail is her most important weapon in her much-lauded short story collection *Kerst en andere liefdesverhalen* ('Christmas and Other Love Stories,' 1992). Her female characters casually reveal details of their erotic lives, the extreme intimacy of which is as provocative as it is evocative. Her latest book *Taal zonder mij* ('Language Without Me') is a heartrending *in momo riam* to her late husband, the Flemish poet Herman De Coninck, who died in 1997. Shying away from verbosity or emotional recollections, and with De Coninck's poetry as her guide, she has produced a moving piece of writing – a combination of both essay and biography – in which she examines his poems in order to understand and come to terms with her late husband.

AAn, MMe

Hendel, Yehudit (*b*. 1926), Israeli fiction writer. Born into a Rabbinic family in Warsaw, Hendel emigrated to Haifa, Israel in 1930. Her mother died when she was a teenager and her father remarried shortly thereafter. This tragic death is described in her collection of stories *Kesef Katan* ('Small Change,' 1988). Tragedy and conflict figure frequently in her prose. In her first collection of stories *Anashim Shonim*

Hem ('They Are Different,' 1950) as well as in her first novel, *Street of Steps* (1955), she describes the suffering of new immigrants in Israel. Hendel married an Israeli painter, Zvi Mairoitch, and lived with him and their children in Haifa. She describes this city in her second novel *Ha-Hatzer Shel Momo Ha-Gedolah* ('The Yard of Momo the Great,' 1969). She dedicated her novel *Ha-Ko'ach Ha-Aher* ('The Other Power,' 1984) to the memory of her beloved husband. She has written only one nonfiction book, *Leyad Kefarim Shketim* ('Near Quiet Places,' 1987), which describes her return to Poland. In the novel *Har HaTo'im* ('Mountain of Losses,' 1991) the characters are mourners at one of Tel Aviv's military cemeteries whose lives have been absolutely changed by tragedy. Hendel favors first-person women narrators. Her latest book is *Aruhat Boker Temima* ('An Innocent Breakfast,' 1996). She is the recipient of many Israeli literary prizes.

LR

Henley, Beth (*b*. 1952), US playwright. A native of Jackson, Mississippi, Henley wanted to follow in her mother's footsteps and become an actress. But unsatisfied with roles for contemporary women, she turned to creating them, in plays that reflect the joys and difficulties of growing up in the rural South. She attended Southern Methodist University, where her one-act play *Am I Blue* was produced in 1973, and the University of Illinois. In 1979 she wrote her most acclaimed play *Crimes of the Heart*, the story of the three McGrath sisters of Hazelhurst, Mississippi. Winner of the Pulitzer Prize, *Crimes of the Heart*, with its dark humor and regional flavor, explores the sisters' frustration with their limited options in life and celebrates the strength to be found in female relationships. Henley was nominated for an Academy Award for her screenplay for the film *Crimes of the Heart* (1986). She also wrote the screenplay for the film *Nobody's Fool* (1986). Other stage plays include *The Miss Firecracker Contest* (1980), *The*

Wake of Jamey Foster (1982), *The Debutante Ball* (1985), *The Lucky Spot* (1986), and *Abundance* (1989).

DVT

Hernández, Luisa Josefina (*b.* 1928), Mexican dramatist. Born in Mexico City and author of some fifty dramatic works, Hernández studied under the well-known Mexican dramatist Rodolfo Usigli at the Universidad Nacional Autónoma de México, where she received her MA in 1955 and later assumed his chair of dramatic theory and composition. Many of her plays have won prizes, including what is considered her earliest, *Aguardiente de caña* ('Sugar-cane Liquor,' 1951). Sometimes naturalistic, sometimes experimental, her works embrace social criticism, Mexican history, and interpersonal relationships, with particular focus on the problems of women within them. *Los frutos caídos* ('The Fallen Fruits,' 1957), her master's thesis, centers on Celia's inability to escape the limited role society has assigned her. Both *Historia de un anillo* ('The Story of a Ring,' 1961) and *The Mulatto's Orgy* (1971) expose how Church and State can work together to oppress the poor. *Los huéspedes reales* ('The Royal Guests,' 1958) ends with the young female protagonist's rejection of the patriarchal system that controls relationships both inside and outside the home. Hernández has also written several novels.

SMag

Herzberg, Judith (*b.* 1934), Dutch poet, dramatist. Herzberg was the daughter of the Jewish writer and lawyer Abel Herzberg. Both parents survived the horror of Nazi concentration camps – something which Judith had escaped by going into hiding. She made her debut as a poet in the early 1960s, and continues, with some regularity, to turn out small volumes of poetry – ten so far. With other poets of her generation, she helped to introduce colloquial speech and daily life into

Dutch poetry while shunning rhetorical ornament, verbosity, and lofty subject matter. In her subtle and accessible poems, the seemingly small things in everyday existence turn out to be mirrors of life's complexity. A representative selection of her lyrical work is *But What: Selected Poems* (1988). The author of several film scripts, she is also the most important Dutch dramatist of the present day. The aftermath of the war as seen from a Jewish perspective is often a theme of her plays, as well as the trials and tribulations of male – female relationships and family life. The play *Scratch* (1989) relates in five acts the mysterious successive burglaries in the townhouse of Ina, a 76-year-old divorcee. Although nothing is stolen, it eventually becomes apparent that, in a figurative sense, everything in her life is 'gone.' Herzberg was awarded the prestigious P. C. Hooft prize in 1997.

AAn, MMe

Hewett, Dorothy (*b.* 1923), Australian poet, dramatist. Raised on a farm in Western Australia, Hewett's nine volumes of poetry and six published drama scripts reflect her rural childhood, although the scene of her later poetry is decidedly urban. She also wrote two novels *Bobbin Up* (1959) and *The Toucher* (1993), and the prize-winning *Wild Card: An Autobiography* (1990). She is well-known for her communist commitment in the 1950s and 1960s, and for her poetic treatment of sexuality and the status of the female. Her poetry combines free verse and playful use of more conventional rhyme and meter. Her poetry publications include *Windmill Country* (1968), *Rapunzel in Suburbia* (1975), *Greenhouse* (1979), *Alice in Wormland* (1987), and *Peninsula* (1994). In all her writing, Hewett employs strong, nonconformist female voices, often criticized for self-indulgence and romantic excess. Yet other readers appreciate the honest and unblushing explorations of life as a worker, a woman, a writer, and a lover. Her plays include *This Old Man Comes*

Rolling Home (1976), *The Chapel Perilous* (1972), *Bon Bons and Roses for Dolly* and *The Tatty Hollow Story* (1976), and *The Man from Mukinupin* (1979). Hewett's later works deal openly, and for some, shockingly, with aging, sexuality, and death.

LMcC

Highsmith, Patricia (1921–1995), US novelist. Born in Fort Worth, Texas, Highsmith attended Barnard College, where she earned a BA in 1942. She lived in Europe from 1963 until the end of her life. Her first novel, *Strangers on a Train* (1950), is a suspense classic, and was made into a film by Alfred Hitchcock. It established her abiding preoccupation with the psychology of criminal behavior. In her highly entertaining but disturbing crime novels, she focuses not on detection, but on the workings of the minds of murderers and psychopaths. Highsmith's amoral characters thus become understandable, even likeable, to the reader, whose moral values are challenged. This is accomplished most effectively and chillingly in her popular and award-winning Ripley series, which features Tom Ripley, a charming American psychopath who murders without guilt those who thwart his ambitions. In the first of the series *The Talented Mr. Ripley* (1955), he murders another American in Europe and steals his identity. Other novels in the series include *Ripley Underground* (1971), *Ripley's Game* (1974), and *The Boy Who Followed Ripley* (1980). A prolific author, Highsmith also wrote, under the pseudonym of Claire Morgan, novels about lesbian identity and sexuality.

JEM

Hill, Selima (*b.* 1945), British poet. Born in London, Hill was educated at New Hall College, Cambridge. She married Roderic Hill in 1968; they have three children. Her first volume of poetry *Saying Hello at the Station* was published in 1984. Although there is a confessional element to her poetry, it is often camouflaged by her distinctive, subversive, and startling imagery. Similarly, her relaxed tone conceals a disturbing intensity. She explores the constrictions of the roles of daughter, wife, and mother with anger and frustration, which has led to comparisons with *Sylvia Plath. As in *My Darling Camel* (1988), she frequently repeats and reworks private symbols – camels, hens, blood. *The Accumulation of Small Acts of Kindness* (1989) is a journal in verse of a recovering mental patient. *A Little Book of Meat* (1993) is also a sequence, written in the voice of a farm woman. *Violet* (1997), in which the poet's late mother is a strong presence, is concerned with family relationships. *Trembling Hearts in the Bodies of Dogs* (1994) is a collection of selected poems.

JEM

Hill, Susan (*b.* 1942), British novelist, essayist, editor. Born in Scarborough, Yorkshire, Hill was educated at King's College, University of London, and received her BA (honors) in English in 1963. She published her first novel *The Enclosure* (1961) when she was only 16 years old and her second *Do Me a Favour* (1963) while still in college. Her style is straightforward and naturalistic, her tone sympathetic, her characteristic themes those of loneliness, fear, and grief. In *I'm the King of the Castle* (1970; Somerset Maugham Award), she examines a cruel conflict between two young boys. *Strange Meeting* (1971) is the story of a friendship set in the trenches of Flanders during World War I. *The Bird of Night* (1972; Whitbread Award) depicts the intense devotion of a scholar to a poet succumbing to insanity. *In the Springtime of the Year* (1974) chronicles a young widow coming to terms with her husband's death. Other novels include *Air and Angels* (1991), *The Mist in the Mirror* (1992), *Mrs. De Winter* (1993), a sequel to Daphne du Maurier's *Rebecca*, and *The Service of Clouds* (1998). A prolific writer, Hill is the author of numerous plays, radio plays, children's books, and collections of autobiographical essays about rural life, including *The Magic Apple Tree* (1982). Her short stories have been collected in several volumes, including *Listening to the Orchestra* (1996). She has also edited several fiction anthologies.

JEM

Hillar, Malgorzata (1926–1995), Polish poet. Hillar's childhood was disrupted by World War II, when her father died in a concentration camp and she moved with her mother from Piesienica in western Poland to the Warsaw area. Educated at underground high schools, Hillar studied law at Warsaw University (1946–50). In 1960 she married the Polish poet and essayist Zbigniew Bienkowski, whom she later divorced. Her first collection of poems *Gliniany dzbanek* ('A Clay Pitcher,' 1959) was followed by five more volumes of love lyrics and erotic poetry. She ceased publishing new poems in 1967, although several volumes of her selected verse have appeared since then. During her relatively short career as a poet, Hillar succeeded in speaking about love and the body from a female perspective at a time when few Polish poets broached such themes. English versions of her poems appear in the collections *The New Polish Poetry* (1978) and *Ambers Aglow: An Anthology of Polish Women's Poetry* (1996).

JB

Hilst, Hilda (*b.* 1930), Brazilian fiction writer, playwright, poet. Educated as a lawyer in the state of São Paulo where she was born, Hilst has been writing since 1950. Her career can be divided into three sections: from 1950 to 1967 she published eight volumes of poetry; from 1967 to 1969 she published eight plays; and since 1970, she has published seven works of fiction, both novels and volumes of short stories. Classified as a difficult, existential, or surreal writer by many Brazilian critics, her fiction deals with eroticism, mortality, and aging. Her works are characterized by her lyrical and innovative use of language, including neologisms, exotic names, and a kind of Joycean free association. In 1990 she published an intentionally pornographic book designed to subvert the market and attract a larger public. *Cartas de um sedutor* ('Letters from a Seducer') did just that and prompted a public debate regarding authorial intent and mass-marketing. An English translation of an early story 'Agda,' from the volume *Quadós* (1973), is included in the short story anthology *One Hundred Years After Tomorrow* (1992) and 'Glittering Nothing' from *Rútilo nada* ('Rutile Nothing,' 1993) appears in *Urban Voices: Contemporary Short Stories from Brazil* (1999).

SCQ

Hina, Zahida (*b.* 1946), Pakistani short story writer, journalist. Born in Bihar, India and now living and working in Karachi, Pakistan, Hina has been involved in both literature and journalism since the age of 16. Fiercely passionate in the causes she espouses, she locates herself to the left of the political spectrum. Her writing is scholarly and diverse, drawing on a range of philosophical and intellectual sources. Much of her work challenges the cultural and ideological underpinnings of the Pakistani State, attacking patriarchal attitudes to women and delving into the historical legacies of contemporary social configurations. She has published two books of short stories, *Qaidi Sans Layta Hai* ('Prisoner's Sigh') and *Rah main Ajal* ('Meeting Death'), and a novella, *Na Junoon Raha, na Pari Rahi* ('The Passion and the Beauty Have Fled'), which sensitively portrays the partition of the subcontinent. English translations of her work are available in many anthologies, including *Contemporary Urdu Short Stories* (1991) and *Mapping Memories: Urdu Stories from India and Pakistan* (1998). She is an acclaimed journalist who writes regularly for both the mainstream and minority press. She has also written plays and serials for television.

SRah

Hippolyte, Jane King (*b.* 1952), St Lucian poet. Born in Castries, Hippolyte earned three degrees from the University of Edinburgh, co-founded the Lighthouse Theatre Company (Castries, 1984), and attended the Lee Strasberg Theatre Institute (1986) on a scholarship. She won two Minvielle and Chastanet Literary Awards, for journalism (1984), and poetry (1990) for the manuscript of *In To the Centre* (1993). In this first collection, which also won a Witter Bynner fellowship, she explores her dream visions, relationships between women and men, and poetry's role in providing hope to a people damaged by racism and violence. *Fellow Traveller* (1994), winner of the James Rodway Memorial Award, continues these themes, and extends her feminist concerns as well as her explorations of the isolation of mixed-race individuals. Her style ranges from precise language and ironic humor, to a more lyrical line. Her work has appeared in anthologies such as *The Heinemann Book of Caribbean Poetry* (1992), *Caribbean New Voices I* (1995), and *Sisters of Caliban* (1996) and in the journals the *Literary Review* and *Massachusetts Review*. She won a James Michener Fellowship in 1993, and is currently Senior Lecturer in English at Sir Arthur Lewis Community College, St Lucia.

HS

Ho, Minfong (*b.* 1951), Singaporean novelist, children's writer. Born in Burma of Chinese parents, Ho was raised in Thailand and educated in Taiwan and the US, where she earned a BA and an MFA from Cornell University. Although fluent in Chinese and Thai, Ho writes only in English, drawing heavily on her childhood experiences to depict rural life in Southeast Asia in a way which is compelling and accessible to young readers in the West. *Rice Without Rain* (1990), based on the student movement in northern Thailand, where she taught in the 1970s, won the American Library Association's Best Book for Young Adults award and the Parents Choice award. In *The Clay Marble* (1991), her protagonist is a young Cambodian refugee who struggles to shape her own destiny against the turmoil of the Thai–Cambodian border in the early 1980s. Ho has also written several short stories and picture books set in Asia, many of which have won awards and Notable Book designations, and been widely anthologized and included in school curriculums in Singapore and the US. Her picture book *Hush! A Thai Lullaby* won a Caldecott Honor Award in 1996. Ho is also the recipient of the Southeast Asia (S.E.A.) Write Award and Singapore's Cultural Medallion.

MHo

Hobæk Haff, Bergljot (*b.* 1925), Norwegian novelist. In Hobæk Haff's first novel *Raset* ('The Landslide,' 1956), the conflict between good and evil is portrayed in a psychologically realistic fashion. But by the time she published her fourth novel *Bålet* ('The Bonfire,' 1962), she had turned from realism to an allegorical, mythical form of expression. The relationship between the human and the divine, especially the Madonna/whore figure, is a central theme in her work, appearing in several of her novels. Her protagonists are often outsiders in society, and neither characters nor plot are necessarily grounded in reality. She often combines historical settings with direct commentary to the reader, or contemporary events with myth, as in *Den guddomelige tragedie* ('The Divine Tragedy,' 1989), a modern South African tale interwoven with a biblical fable involving God's fumbling attempt at reincarnation. She combines old literary forms, like allegory and fable, with modern narrative techniques in a way that opens up new perspectives on her texts. With the publication of her latest novel *Skammen* ('The Shame,' 1996), Hobæk Haff added the Bragepris to a long list of literary honors. Twice, in 1989 and 1992, she has been nominated for the Nordisk råds litteraturpris.

TH

Hodge, Merle (*b.* 1944), Trinidadian novelist. Hodge studied French at University College, London, obtaining BA (1965) and MA (1967) degrees; the latter was on the French-Guyanese Negritude poet Leon Damas, whom she also translated. She worked and studied in France and Denmark, and traveled in Senegal and Gambia. She returned to the Caribbean in 1970, to teach at a high school in Port of Spain, and lecture in French-Caribbean and African literatures at the University of West Indies, Kingston. In 1980, she went to Grenada to work for Maurice Bishop's revolutionary government as Director of Curriculum Development, creating the *Marryshow Readers*. Having published extensively on the historical oppression of West Indian women, she sees herself primarily as an activist. Her coming-of-age novel *Crick, Crack Monkey* (1970) explores the ambivalence of the girl-narrator growing up between the world of Patois-speaking, independent Tantie and bourgeois, completely colonized Aunt Beatrice. Her second novel *For the Life of Laetitia* (1993) exposes the educational system as the primary site of subjection. Hodge lives in Trinidad, where she lectures at the University of West Indies, St Augustine.

MHL

Hodrová, Daniela (*b.* 1946), Czech prose writer. Born in Prague, the daughter of an actor, Hodrová worked briefly in a theater after completing high school in 1963. At Charles University she received a first degree in Russian and Czech literature in 1969, with postgraduate work in French and comparative literature. In 1973 her original dissertation on the novel of initiation was rejected; when published in an expanded version in 1992, it earned her the highest degree – Doctor of Sciences. After an editorship at Odeon publishers (1972–5), she began work at the Institute for Czech Literature (Academy of Sciences), where she is now a senior researcher, specializing in novel theory. She is married to writer Karel Milota. Her first

published book *Hledání románu* ('Quest for the Novel,' 1989) treats the typological opposition between the novel as reality and as fiction, anticipating her own experiments in the genre. Although she began writing earlier, Hodrová published her first novel only after 1989. In the trilogy *The Suffering City*, comprised of *The Kingdom of Olšany* (1991), *Kukly* ('Chrysalises,' 1991), and *Théta* (1992), she conveys a sense of Prague as a living time–space continuum through highly stylized and self-reflective texts. *Perun's Day* (1994) mystically and realistically links the lives of four young women connected through the image of Prague. Her latest novel *Ztracené děti* ('Lost Children,' 1997) follows a multi-layered search – for a lost daughter on a realistic level, for the meaning of existence on an abstract one.

ES

Hoffman, Alice (*b.* 1952), US novelist. Born in New York City, Hoffman received a BA from Adelphi University and an MA from Stanford University. She is married and has two children. Her first novel *Property Of* was published in 1977. Her purview is the familiar world of suburban America, but she reveals its strangeness and its possibilities by combining realism with the supernatural in her popular novels. They feature women characters, and focus on themes of family relationships, love and sex, isolation, and friendship. Yet these everyday concerns are heightened through Hoffman's use of mysticism, folklore, mythology, and symbolism in her narratives. The best-selling *At Risk* (1988) explores how a family copes when a daughter contracts AIDS through a tranfusion. In *Seventh Heaven* (1991), a mysterious woman changes the lives of the residents of a Long Island suburb in the 1950s. *Turtle Moon* (1992) is set in Florida and combines a love story with a murder mystery. In *Practical Magic* (1995), two sisters in search of love experiment with witchcraft. Other novels include *Fortune's Daughter* (1985), *Second*

Nature (1994), and *Here On Earth* (1997). *Local Girls* (1999) is a collection of short stories.

JEM

Hogan, Linda (*b.* 1947), US poet, fiction writer, essayist. Born in Denver, Colorado, Hogan received an MA from the University of Colorado in 1978. She is divorced and has two daughters. She is currently a professor of English at the University of Colorado, Boulder. Through her writing, she explores her Chickasaw heritage and the part it plays in her identity and her work. In her free verse poetry, she emphasizes the natural world, which she sees as a link to the past, the source of spiritual life in the present, and essential to the future of Native American culture. Her first volume of poetry *Calling Myself Home* was published in 1978. Other volumes include *Daughters, I Love You* (1981), *Eclipse* (1983), *Seeing Through the Sun* (1985), *Savings* (1988), and *The Book of Medicines* (1993). *Mean Spirit* (1990) is an historical novel about the exploitation of native Americans for the oil on their lands. *Solar Storms* (1995) depicts a community of Native American women who give solace to a damaged young girl. *Power* (1998) is a coming of age story about a Native American girl. Hogan is also the author of *Dwellings: A Spiritual History of the World* (1995) and *From Women's Experience to Feminist Theology* (1996).

JEM

Hong Ying (*b.* 1962), Chinese poet, fiction writer. Born Hongying Chen in Chongqing of Sichuan Province, Hong Ying studied at the Lu Xun Literature Academy, Beijing, and Fudan University, Shanghai. She started writing poetry in 1981 and writing fiction in 1988. In 1991 she left China for England, and she has lived in London since. She is married to Yiheng Zhao, a literary academician in London. Though her poetry and short stories have repeatedly won prizes in Taiwan and England, it is her novels that have

received wide critical recognition. Her novel *Summer of Betrayal* (1992) depicts the desperate and self-destructive lifestyle that permeated Beijing young artists' circles in the year of 1989. Her latest novel *Daughter of Hunger* (1997) gives an autobiographical account of her teenage years. A rebellious young woman, she discovered the secret of her birth, her sexuality, and bittersweet love. 'Hunger' in the title of the novel has several connotations. Historically, it refers to the famine in the late 1950s and early 1960s which resulted from the state policy of 'The Great Leap Forward,' which may have led to some twenty to thirty million deaths. Literally, 'hunger' refers to the dire material conditions in which the author lived throughout her childhood and adolescence. 'Hunger' also refers to the emotional and spiritual deprivations imposed on all members of a cruel, repressive society. Both of her novels have been translated into more than ten languages.

MY

hooks, bell (*b.* 1952), African-American feminist cultural critic. Writing broadly and profoundly about social, racial, and intellectual lives in black and white America, hooks is the most influential African-American feminist cultural critic and activist working today. Her first book *Ain't I a Woman* (1981), along with *Feminist Theory* (1984), *Talking Back* (1989), and *Sisters of the Yam* (1993), asserts and celebrates the black feminist subjectivity she feels is excluded by white society and the academy. Intersecting forcefully between theories of race, gender, class, and sexuality, between academic institutions and black communities, she maps critical theory as the site of cultural resistance in *Yearning* (1990), *Black Looks* (1992), *Outlaw Culture* (1994), and *Killing Rage* (1995). She explores the role, constituency, and mission of the African-American feminist intellectual in *Breaking Bread* (1991) and examines progressive multicultural pedagogy in *Teaching to Transgress* (1994). She critiques the visual politics and stereotypes of race in popular culture in *Art in My Mind* (1995) and *Reel to Real* (1996). Her autobiography *Bone Black* (1996) traces the journey of her critical awakening in girlhood, and she recollects her growth as a writer and the challenges and rewards of her career in *Wounds of Passion* (1997) and *Remembered Rapture* (1999).

LY

Horta, Maria Teresa (*b.* 1937), Portuguese poet, novelist. Born in Lisbon and educated in a religious school, Horta studied romance languages and literatures at the University of Lisbon, working subsequently as a journalist, as editor of literary supplements for the daily press, and as freelance writer for several periodicals. She became the first woman president of the ABC Film Club, an early outlet for film studies in Portugal; and, in the mid-1970s, was co-founder of the now extinct Movement for the Liberation of Women. She worked for many years as editor-in-chief of the feminist magazine *Mulheres* ('Women'). A member of the experimental movement 'Poetry 61,' she became famous for her formally challenging erotic poetry. The more than twenty-one volumes spanning from *Espelho Inicial* ('Beginning Mirror,' 1960) to *Destino* ('Destiny,' 1994) trace a poetic itinerary (also encompassing works of prose) that privileges the body as mediator of desire and of ontological knowledge. A unique voice in contemporary Portuguese literature, Horta's treatment of feminine eroticism is manifested in the *New Portuguese Letters* (1972), co-authored with *Maria Isabel Barreno and *Maria Velho da Costa. The 'Three Marias' became the center of international attention when government authorities banned the book and legally charged them with 'immorality.'

APF

Hosain, Attia (1913–1998), Indian novelist, short story writer. Born into an elite Muslim family that was part of the feudal

'Taluqdari' society in Lucknow, India, Hosain received a traditional Islamic education as well as a Western liberal education, graduating from La Martiniere and Isabella Thoburn College in Lucknow. During the 1930s, she was influenced by the growing nationalist movement and worked as a journalist and broadcaster until independence in 1947. She published several feature articles in the Indian newspapers the *Pioneer* and the *Statesman*. In 1947, she moved with her husband to England, where she later presented a women's program on the BBC Eastern Services. In 1953 she published a collection of short stories *Phoenix Fled*. Her stories give a vivid picture of pre-independence, pre-partition Muslim society in northern India. With insight and empathy, she portrays the workings of duty and honor that held the society in place at all levels. She focuses on the position of women in her best-known work, the 1961 novel *Sunlight on a Broken Column*. Considered a forerunner for later Indian feminist novels, it portrays a young woman's struggle to break free from her traditional Muslim upbringing during a period of nationalist struggle within India at large.

MAg

Hospital, Janette Turner (*b.* 1942), Australian-Canadian novelist, short story writer. Born Janette Turner in Melbourne, Australia to fundamentalist Christian parents, Hospital's life and work are characterized by the anxieties and pleasures of dislocation, from her early experience teaching in tropical Queensland to moving to Boston in 1967 and Kingston, Ontario in 1971. Her first book *The Ivory Swing* (1982), which won Canada's prestigious Seal award, shows a Canadian woman struggling with her ethnocentricity in India. *Tiger in the Tiger Pit* (1983) interweaves family relations and patriarchal self-delusion. *Borderline* (1985) handles personal and public responsibility in a multi-focused narrative straddling the Canadian–US border. *Charades* (1988) mixes a young woman's hunt for her father, a physicist's search for explanation, and the interpretive challenge of the Holocaust. *The Last Magician* (1992) is a complex mystery of power and oppression in Australia. *Oxyster* (1996) crosses the remote and suspicious independence of Australian outback with a secretive millenarian sect. Hospital's short stories *Dislocations* (1986) and *Isobars* (1990), collected and augmented in *Collected Stories 1970–1995* (1995), focus on mysteries of time, memory, and cracks in everyday reality. As Alex Juniper, Hospital has published *A Very Proper Death* (1990), a tale of conspiracy and paranoia in Boston.

DCa

Howe, Susan (*b.* 1937), US poet, literary scholar. Howe began as a visual artist, earning a BFA in painting from the Museum of Fine Arts, Boston in 1961. Her first book of poetry *Hinge Picture* was published in 1974. Her experimental poetry, sometimes classified as Language Poetry, is disjunctive, distinctive, and challenging. She works against rules of grammar and syntax, and is concerned with the history of language, the interrelations of language and history and gender, and the connections between gender and poetic voice. She explores the etymology of words, their physical placement on the page, and the dynamics of the act of reading. Her investigation of how power and authority are manifested in language is a radically political one. Her volumes of poetry include *The Liberties* (1980), *Pythagorean Silence* (1982), *Defenestration of Prague* (1983), *The Europe of Trusts* (1990), *Singularities* (1990), and *Pierce-Arrow* (1999). *Frame Structures* (1996) collects her early poetry. Howe is also known for *My Emily Dickinson* (1985), a groundbreaking feminist critical study written in an experimental prose style.

JEM

Howe, Tina (*b.* 1937), US playwright. Born in New York to Quincy Howe, a journalist and historian, and painter Mary Post Howe, Howe attended Bucknell University for two years before transferring to Sarah Lawrence, where her one-act play *Closing Time* was produced. She earned an education degree from Teacher's College, Columbia University, and taught English and drama at secondary schools in Maine and Wisconsin. She has also taught at New York University, UCLA, and Johns Hopkins University. Known for their satire and their comic dialogue, Howe's plays are typically set in unusual, seemingly banal settings where her characters encounter the absurd and the unpredictable. She has been influenced by the theater of the absurd, particularly the works of Beckett and Ionesco. Her play *Museum* (1979) takes place in the contemporary art wing of a museum, and chronicles the reactions and conversations among wandering art critics. *The Art of Dining* (1980), which takes place in a restaurant; *Painting Churches* (1983; Obie Award); *Coastal Disturbances* (1986), which takes place on the beach; and *Approaching Zanzibar* (1995), all emphasize the role of art and creativity in women's lives. *Painting Churches* was televised in 1983, and made into a film in 1993.

DVT

Huang Biyun (Bikwan Flora Wong) (*b.* 1961), Chinese/Hong Kong fiction writer. Born in Hong Kong, Huang Biyun (Bikwan Flora Wong) received a BA in journalism and communication in 1984. In 1987 and 1988, she spent time in Paris and New York. Between 1989 and 1995, she worked as a journalist in Chinese and English broadcast and print media in Hong Kong. In addition to two collections of essays and travel writings, she has published three volumes of short stories, namely *Qihou* ('Hereafter,' 1991), *Wenruan yu baolie* ('The Meek and the Violent,' 1994), and *Qizhong jingmo* ('Seven Kinds of Silence,' 1997). Lyrically evocative in style, *Qihou* focuses on the acute sense of personal and cultural alienation felt among young Chinese, a sense often exacerbated by living abroad. Adopting dialogic techniques from scriptwriting, *Wenruan yu baolie* charters the disenchantment with progressive political and personal ideals since the 1960s among Chinese men and women living in China, Taiwan, Hong Kong, Southeast Asia and the West. Philosophically oriented and psychologically descriptive in nature, *Qizhong jingmo* explores the ethical dilemmas that different segments of the population in Hong Kong face in pursuit of money, of pleasure, and of an increasingly elusive sense of cultural belonging.

PS

Hulme, Keri (*b.* 1947), New Zealand novelist, poet. Hulme began the work that was to make her reputation, *The Bone People* (1984), while working in the tobacco fields of the South Island, some twelve years before the novel was published by Spiral, a New Zealand feminist collective. Like Kerewin Holmes, the protagonist of that book, Christchurch-born Hulme is one-eighth Maori, and her writings all give thematic expression to the cultural, sexual, and environmental challenges of modern New Zealand. She attended the University of Canterbury, in Christchurch, for two years before adopting a lifestyle as unconventional as her fiction, and continues to support herself by fishing and writing. Hulme began publishing short stories in local magazines in the 1970s, winning several New Zealand Literary Fund grants. Her first book was a collection of poetry *The Silence Between: Moeraki Conversations* (1982). Her next, *The Bone People*, won the New Zealand Book Award for Fiction and the Pegasus Award for Maori literature, both in 1984, and the Booker Prize in 1985; it is probably the best-selling book by any living New Zealand writer. Her short fiction was collected in *Te Kaihau/The Windeater* (1986).

DM

Huston, Nancy (*b.* 1953), Canadian novelist, critic. Born in Calgary, Alberta, Huston was educated at Sarah Lawrence College and the École des hautes études en sciences sociales. She has taught at many universities and institutions in the US, Canada, and Europe. She is married to the writer Tzvetan Todorov and has two children; they live in Paris. Huston is fluent in and writes in both English and French. Her central concerns are, not surprisingly, language and writing, as well as the female body, sexuality, and the relation of time and space. Her first novel *The Goldberg Variations* (1981) was originally written in French and self-translated, as is the case with several of her other novels. The action of the novel lasts as long as it takes one of the characters to play Bach's *Goldberg Variations* (an hour and a half) and the narrative is comprised of thirty-two interior monologues of the pianist and her guests. Her second novel *Histoire d'Omaya* ('The Story of Omaya,' 1985) is also a formally innovative novel, in which fragments are used to represent the breakdown of a young rape victim who finds herself on trial. *Plainsong* (1993), her first novel written originally in English, is a fictional retelling of her grandfather's life in Canada. Other novels include *Slow Emergencies* (1994), *Instruments of Darkness* (1996), and *The Mark of the Angel* (1998). Huston has also written several works of literary and cultural theory and criticism.

JEM

Hyder, Qurratulain (*b.* 1927), Indian fiction writer. Recipient of India's highest literary award, the Jnanpith, Hyder, a prolific Urdu novelist, made her debut while still an undergraduate at Isabella Thoburn College, Lucknow, with stories published in major journals. Her first collection *Sitaron Se Aage* ('Beyond the Stars,' 1947) was followed by the novel *Mere Bhi Sanam-Khane* ('My Idol Houses Too,' 1949). Hyder has translated some of her own works into English, including *Fireflies in the Night* (1979) and, more recently, the widely acclaimed *River of Fire* (1959). Her fiction consistently bears witness to the partition of British India in 1947 as the founding trauma of subcontinental nationalism, and laments the passing away of a more syncretic and shared culture of the subcontinent. An underlying concern in all her work has been the sense that partition created a lost generation with no moorings; thus, questions of home, belonging, and dislocation become central to her writing. Hyder's life itself embodies the dilemmas of exile and return to a divided country: in the immediate aftermath of partition, she moved to Pakistan with her family, followed by another move to England, until her eventual return to India in 1961.

PK

Hyvrard, Jeanne (b. 1945), French novelist, poet, essayist. Born in Paris, Hyvrard is an economics teacher in a Parisian high school. She is married to a fellow economist and has one daughter. From her first work *Les Prunes de Cythère* ('Cytherea's Plums,' 1975), an economic appreciation of Martinique where she lived briefly, to her most recent, *Resserres à louer* ('Storage Space for Rent,' 1997), her writing has been multidimensional, poetical, and deeply rooted in the political and economic issues of contemporary society. She questions Western culture, deplores the inadequacy of a dehumanized language, and aims at recreating a world of inclusion rather than separation. To this effect she uses neologisms, rewrites mythology, reenacts the ancient world of alchemy and the tarot in order to voice a third or hybrid culture in which the feminine, insanity, illness, and excluded cultures have a say, as is exemplified in *Waterweed in the Wash-Houses* (1977). Her message is utopian, apocalyptic, but also pragmatic inasmuch as it prepares for the twenty-first century. Books such as *Le corps défunt de la comédie, traité d'économie politique* ('The Corpse of Comedy, Treatise of Political Economy,' 1982), *Canal de la Toussaint* ('Day of the Deads' Canal,' 1986), and *La pensée corps* ('The Body Thought,' 1989) are considered major contributions to the development of contemporary feminist thought.

JC

I

Ibrahim, Ratna Indraswari (*b*. 1949) Indonesian fiction writer. Born in Malang in East Java, Ibrahim's first passion was science; she obtained a degree in Administration of Science from Brawijaya University, Malang. She has published almost two hundred stories and ten novellas, as well as poetry, in newspapers and magazines in Indonesia, and has won several major literary competitions for her work. 'Juminten's Hair' (1993) is the poignant tale of conflict of loyalties in an Indonesian community where the old ties are still very important. The young protagonist is torn between acceding to the wishes and demands of her husband and wanting to take control of her own life.

PA

Idilbī, Ulfa al- (*b*. 1912) Syrian novelist, short story writer, essayist. Born in Damascus, Syria, Idilbī was educated in public schools. In 1929, she had to quit her studies at the Teachers' College to get married. With three children to attend to, she was not able to continue her formal education, let alone hold a public job. She did, however, continue her education on her own and founded a literary salon which met monthly at her house. She was elected to the Council of Syrian Writers' Union. She read widely and was influenced by Russian literature. She started writing short stories in 1947; they were published in Syrian and other Arab periodicals. Some of them were included in her first collection of short stories *Oiṣaṣ Shāmiyya* ('Damascene Stories,' 1954) which included an enthusiastic introduction by the prominent fiction writer Mahmūd Taymūr. In her first novel *Sabriya: Damascus Bitter and Sweet* (1980), Idilbī portrays life for women in Syria in the 1920s during the national struggle against the French mandate. She has also written scholarly studies on Arabic literature and popular culture, such as *Nazra fi Adabinā al-Sha-'bī* ('An Examination of our Popular Literature,' 1974). Her short stories have been translated into English and many other languages.

JTZ

Idström, Annikka (*b*. 1947) Finnish novelist. Idström studied TV and film in the photographic art section of Ateneum, the Institute of Applied Arts in Finland. Originally a director, dramatist, and editor at the Radio Theatre of the Finnish Broadcast Company, she became a full-time writer after her first novel *Sinitaivas* ('The Blue Heavens') appeared in 1980. *Isäni Rakkaani* ('My Father, My Love,' 1981) and *My Brother Sebastian* (1985) established her as a writer of psychological studies of the intimate, often unspoken aspects of human relations: mother-hatred, father-fixation, incest fantasies, child abuse, maltreatment of women, cannibalism. She speaks of her writing as a kind of psychoanalysis, but in the philosophical sense rather than thera-peutic sense. Thus, *Luonnollinen Ravinto* ('A Natural Diet,' 1994) studies the sub-conscious cannibalism within relation-ships between men and women and within civilization. She has said, 'For me, it's im-portant to find the violent tearing-apart. Only behind it can I find the piety and the calm.' She searches for female identity and female language to write about such things because she believes women should not write like men. Idström won the prize for best first work in 1980 and has been nominated for both the Nordic Literary Prize and the Finlandia Prize.

KMW

Ignatova, Elena Alekseevna (*b.* 1947) Rus-sian poet, documentary screenwriter. Born in Leningrad, Ignatova received her degree in language and literature in 1970 from Leningrad University, where she later held the position of lecturer in Russian phil-ology. From 1979 until 1990, when her ef-forts succeeded, she tried to emigrate to Israel when her family because it was im-possible to breathe in Russia. During this interval she worked in television and film, producing several film scripts that drew on Leningrad history and culture, above all literary history (e.g. Akhmatova, Bely, Blok). She began writing poetry at an early age, publishing her first poem, 'The Hermitage' in a Leningrad newspaper in 1963. Her poems have appeared regularly in the Russian émigré press since 1975. As her work on Petersburg's cultural figures evidences, she clearly identifies with Pe-tersburg literary and cultural traditions, exploring traditional forms and metrical patterns in her development of the Peters-burg myth. Her most recent significant publication *Zapiski o Peterburge* ('Notes on Petersburg,' 1997) offers a cultural history of the city. Important collections of Ignatova's poetry include *Stikhi o pri-chastnosti* ('Poems about Belonging,' 1976) and *Teplaia zemlia* ('The Warm Earth,' 1989).

RMey

Irigaray, Luce (*b.* 1930) Belgian franco-phone philosopher, psychoanalyst. Born in Belgium, Irigaray studied philosophy and literature at the Université de Louvain. After teaching in high school, she moved to Paris where she studied psychology, psychopathology, linguistics (Doctorate at Paris-X, Nanterre, 1968), and philosophy (State Doctorate, 1974). She also trained as a psychoanalyst at the Ecole Freudienne de Paris under Jacques Lacan's direction. She taught at the Université Paris VIII, Vincennes (1970–4). The publication of her dissertation *Speculum of the Other Woman* (1974), a feminist critique of Freudian and Lacanian psychoanalysis, caused her exclusion from the French university system and from the Ecole Freudienne de Paris. In spite of her mar-ginalization by French institutions, she is an influential feminist thinker of inter-national renown. In a style which is witty, ironic, and complex, she addresses issues such as the oppression of language for women and the necessity to create a wom-en's culture to remedy the exclusion of women by patriarchal institutions grounded in the economic and political spheres. Her most influential essays are published in *The Irigaray Reader* (1991). Her latest book is *I Love to You* (1996). She has been for many years Director of Research in Philosophy at the French Centre National de Researche Scientifique.

JV

Ishimure Michiko (*b.* 1927) Japanese novelist, non-fiction writer, activist. An awe-inspiring fusion of prayers, social activism, and literary expression is what characterizes Ishimure's career. Born a mason's daughter in Amakusa, Ku-mamoto (in Kyushu), Ishimure grew up in Minamata, Kumamoto. After her gradu-ation from a business high school, she married and became a housewife. In 1958 she joined a creative group called Circle Mura (Circle Village), founded by Gan Tanikawa and others. During her 1959 hospitalization with tuberculosis, she met some victims of the Minamata illness (mercury poisoning) and began interviewing Minamata patients. Her 1968 book *Paradise in the Sea of Sorrow* is an account that grew out of her ten-year struggle with the Minamata problem and combines documentaries and trance-like narratives with the narrator speaking as each patient. Author also of *Tenno sakana* ('Fish of Heaven,' 1974) and *Story of the Camellias* (1976), which resemble *Paradise* in style, she is highly regarded both domestically and internationally as a writer who can freely traverse the genres of reportage, novel, and biography. She has entered the Buddhist priesthood under the religious name of Ishimure Mugo.

KKa

Iskrenko, Nina Iurevna (1951–1995) Russian poet. Despite a very short publishing career, at the time of her death Iskrenko enjoyed a well-deserved reputation as one of the brightest and most promising stars of the Moscow postmodern avant-garde.

Born in Petrovsk (Saratov district), Iskrenko graduated from Moscow State University, and worked as a technical translator. Known to a small circle from her *samizdat* publications in the 1980s, she published both her first book, *Ili: Stikhi i teksty* ('Or: Poems and Texts'), and *Referendum* in Moscow in 1991. Critics have described her work as the literary equivalent of *sotsart*, represented by painters Komar and Melamid, who use socialist realism as their springboard. A more fruitful comparison might be with the prose writer *Valeriia Narbikova, who engages with similar strategies to stretch the accepted boundaries of literary language and genre. What distinguishes Iskrenko from her flashier peers with a postmodern stance is the genuine lyricism of so many poems. This lyric strain is developed even more poignantly in the posthumous collection *Interpretatsiia momenta: stikhi i teksty* ('Interpretation of the Moment: Poems and Texts,' 1996).

RMey

J

Jabavu, Noni (Nontando) (*b.* 1919) South African novelist. Born in Cape Province, South Africa, Jabavu was raised in an intellectual Xhosa family. Her grandfather was the first black African to own and edit a Xhosa-English newspaper and her father was a linguist, educated in London, who published one of the first grammars of the Xhosa language. Jabavu traveled to England at the age of 14 and attended London's Royal Academy of Music until 1939. World War II brought a halt to her studies, but she remained in London after the war, working as a feature writer and television personality. She would regularly travel to South Africa, until her marriage to Michael Cadbury Crosfield, an English film director, broke the miscegenation laws of South Africa and made visits impossible. She has lived in Mozambique, Uganda, and Zimbabwe. Her life explains her bicultural perspective and her ethnographic approach to autobiography. Her autobiographical novel *Drawn in Color: African Contrasts* (1960) is a personal account of her experiences with East Africans in Uganda and her Xhosa people in South Africa and the different ways they respond to contact with Western society. Her next novel *The Ochre People: Scenes from South African Life* (1963) is an autobiographical account of her return home to her Xhosa people and her visits to Middledrift and Johannesburg.

SDR

Jacquemard, Simonne (*b.* 1924) French novelist, poet. Although Parisian by birth, after studying at the Sorbonne, Jacquemard chose to live and work in the country outside Paris, where she and her husband, psychologist and writer Jacques Brosse, have established three nature preserves. Her work with foxes and raptors inspired *Compagnons insolites* ('Odd Companions,' 1961), among six other books on animals and birds. Highly poetic, her fifteen novels defy classification They document a vast range of knowledge and experience (real-life and imagined) derived from the sciences, psychoanalysis, mythology, folklore, mysticism, and Zen. All premise the possibility of transcending time and space, of reaching a place where duality ends and self and the universe coincide. *Les Fascinés* ('The Fascinated,' 1951), *Judith Albares* (1957) and *L'Orangerie* (1963) explore love, sexuality, and obsession. *The Night Watchman* (1962; Prix Renaudot) chronicles parallel descents to the core of the narrator's subconscious and the earth. In *L'Eruption du Krakatoa* (The Eruption of Krakatoa, 1969), her recurrent, hypothetically autobiographical heroine Anne surmounts the cataclysm, to pursue metamorphosis in Morocco in *Le Mariage berbere* ('The Berber Wedding,' 1995; Grand Prix Littéraire de Marrakesh). The quest for transcendence continues in Jacquemard's recent works.

MBR, MLT

Jaeggy, Fleur (*b*. 1945) Swiss fiction writer. Born in Zurich, Jaeggy grew up in Switzerland but now lives in Italy and writes in Italian about German-speaking Switzerland. She has written five novels, but only one of them, the autobiographical *Sweet Days of Discipline* (1989), is available in English. Winner of the Bagutta and Boccaccio Europa Prizes, it is a disturbing novel set in a girls' boarding school in Switzerland after World War II. The narrator, a 14-year-old girl, becomes obsessed with Frederique, a new student, and strives but never succeeds in breaking through her aloofness and self-discipline. Years later, when the narrator meets Frederique again, she realizes how far her discipline has gone. This brief novel, written in spare and elegant prose, masterfully evokes the oppressiveness of the boarding school and is haunting in the connections it draws between discipline, madness, and death. Also available in English is *Last Vanities* (1994), a collection of seven short stories. Written in Jaeggy's characteristic style of cool precision, the stories are set in mundane, middle-class environments, but they are filled with an eerie atmosphere of subversion and dread. The events in these compelling stories are shocking, aberrant, sometimes inexplicable, and usually violent.

SL

Jakobsdóttir, Svava (*b*. 1930) Icelandic short story writer, novelist, playwright. Svava was born in Neskaupstaður in eastern Iceland. In 1935, her family emigrated to Canada, where they lived until 1940 when they returned to Iceland. After graduating from high school, she pursued her education abroad, receiving her BA in English literature from Smith College and doing postgraduate work at Oxford and at Uppsala in Sweden. Besides being an author, she has been active in journalism and in politics, both in the Foreign Office in Iceland and as a Member of Parliament from 1971 to 1979. Svava's debut book was a collection of short stories titled *Tólf*

konur ('Twelve Women,' 1965). She has since published two novels, four collections of short stories, and a number of plays for stage, radio, and television. Her novel *Gunnlaðar saga* ('The Saga of Gunnlod,' 1987) was nominated for the 1990 Nordic Council Literary Prize. In English, her short stories have been published in various journals and collections of Icelandic short stories, such as *Icelandic Short Stories*, *Icelandic Writing Today*, and *Scandinavian Women Writers*. Considered a pioneer in the revitalization of Icelandic prose writing in the 1960s, Svava has focused on the plight of modern woman, which she often treats with a mixture of realism, irony, and satire in order to highlight the emotional crises caused by meaningless traditional role-playing in a modern society.

KG

James, P(hyllis) D(orothy) (*b*. 1920) English detective fiction writer. Born in Oxford and educated at the Cambridge High School for Girls, James married Dr. Ernest White in 1941, and worked for years in various positions as a hospital administrator. After her husband's death, she supported her two daughters by working at the National Health Service and at the Home Office Criminal Policy Department. These experiences with medical and police procedures proved valuable to her when she began writing crime novels. She published her first novel *Cover Her Face* in 1962. It introduces the character of Scotland Yard detective Adam Dalgliesh, who returns in the novels *A Mind to Murder* (1963), *Unnatural Causes* (1967), *Shroud for a Nightingale* (1971), *The Black Tower* (1975), *Death of an Expert Witness* (1977), *Original Sin* (1994), and *A Certain Justice* (1997). James's detective novels, usually set in a closed society, exhibit careful, psychological characterizations, a highly literary and sophisticated prose style, and a dedication to realism; she is credited for enriching the genre of crime fiction. Her books *An Unsuitable Job for a*

Woman (1972) and *The Skull Beneath the Skin* (1982) feature female detective Cordelia Gray, while *A Taste for Death* (1986) introduces detective Kate Miskin. Many of James's novels have been adapted for television and film.

DVT

Jamie, Kathleen (*b*. 1962) Scottish poet. Born in Johnston, Renfrewshire, Jamie received an MA (honors) in philosophy from the University of Edinburgh. She published her first volume of poetry *Black Spiders* (1982) when she was only 20 years old. Her identity as a Scottish woman is central to her work. Her characteristic subject matter is ordinary people and everyday experience. Her voice is strong and lively and direct, with the influence of Scots in its rhythms and tones. Her second book *A Flame in Your Heart* (1986) was written in collaboration with Andrew Grieg, a Scots poet. The collection *The Way We Live* (1987) highlights the difficult negotiation between just experiencing the world and the urge to interpret it. An enthusiastic traveler, Jamie has written a prose work on Pakistan, *The Golden Peak* (1992), and *The Autonomous Region* (1993), a collection of poems inspired by Tibet, with photographs by Sean Mayne Smith. *The Queen of Sheba* (1994) and *Jizzen* (1999) reveal an expansion in confidence, in themes, and in forms. In the latter, all kinds of journeys and voyages are considered, the central ones being those of birth and parenthood.

JEM

Jansson, Tove (*b*. 1914) Finland-Swedish author, illustrator. Born in Helsinki, Jansson grew up speaking Swedish, since her family belonged to the Swedish minority in Finland. Her father was a sculptor and her mother an illustrator, and she herself seemed predestined for an artistic career. In her autobiographical novel *The Sculptor's Daughter* (1968) she describes her home's bohemian and nurturing atmosphere. She studied art and design in

Helsinki, Stockholm, and Paris, and eventually became a well-known painter, but she also turned to writing at an early age. In the 1930s, the multi-talented Jansson wrote short stories and drew cartoons for the political humor magazine *Garm*, in which the Moomin trolls were already featured. They reappeared in her first picture book *Småtrollen och den stora översvämningen* ('The Small Trolls and the Great Flood,' 1945), and the lives and adventures of the extended Moomin family remained the focus of her popular children's books from *Comet in Moominland* (1946) to *Moominvalley in November* (1970), all illustrated by the author. Her children's books are characterized by warm humor and deep psychological understanding. Since 1970, Jansson has written several novels for adults. She has received many awards for her writing, among them the Hans Christian Andersen Medal in 1966 and an honorary doctorate from Åbo Academy.

E-MM

Jarunková, Klára (*b*. 1922) Slovak novelist, editor. Born in Červená Skala, district Bánska Bystrica, Jarunková started her career as a teacher, but soon became an editor at Slovak Radio in Bratislava. She subsequently joined the widely popular satirical weekly magazine *Roháč*, which risked criticism of aspects of everyday life under communism more than did other media, sometimes without dire repercussions. After retiring, she remained in Bratislava. The humor, irony, and children's slang of her first book *A Heroic Diary* (1960) offered refreshing change after a decade of stilted socialist realism. Although her fiction continued to focus on children and adolescents, after her next successful novel *The Only Girl* (1963), she avoided characters that might have typed her as a girls' author. Favoring boy protagonists in such works as *Silent Wolf's Brother* (1967) and *Tramp* (1973), she traced their transition from late childhood to early adolescence, contrasting their young ideals with the adult world of compromise. In a rare departure from her typical concerns, her novel *Black Solstice* (1979) describes a major uprising against Slovakia's government during World War II.

MV

Jayawardena, Kumari (*b.* 1931) Sri Lankan feminist, labor historian, teacher, activist. Long in the forefront of the women's movement in her native Sri Lanka, Jayawardena entered the London School of Economics in 1952, reading political science, and then qualifying as a barrister from Lincoln's Inn, London in 1958. Part of the radical left as a student, she studied industrial relations for her PhD. This resulted in her first publication *The Rise of the Labor Movement in Ceylon* (1972). Back in Colombo in 1969, she became involved in worker education, while also teaching political science at the University of Colombo till her retirement in 1985. She is best known for *Feminism and Nationalism in the Third World* (1986), cited by *Ms.* magazine as one of the twenty most important books of the feminist decades 1970–90. Targeted by the orthodox left for having deserted the fold for feminism, she has held her own, continuing to rewrite women's history and their contribution to politics and society in South Asia. Author of seven books and scores of essays on politics and history, her recent book *The White Woman's Other Burden* (1995) examines the impact of independent British women on political and social life in colonial South Asia. Her new book is *From Nobodies to Somebodies: the Rise of the Colonial Bourgeoisie in Sri Lanka*.

RMen

Jayyūsī, Salmā al-Khaḍrāʾ al- (*b.* 1926) Palestinian poet, critic, translator, editor. Born in the town of al-Salt in Jordan to a Palestinian father and a Lebanese mother, Jayyūsī received her primary education in Acre, Israel and Jerusalem. She studied Arabic and English literature at the American University of Beirut, and earned her PhD in Arabic literature from the University of London in 1970. Her husband's career in the diplomatic corps took her to many foreign lands. Before her departure for the US in 1975, she had taught at universities in the Sudan, Kuwait, Algeria, and the US. She is the mother of three. In 1980, she founded PROTA (Project of Translation from Arabic Literature) and was able to edit and publish more than thirty volumes. Jayyūsī started her literary career as a poet when she published her collection *Al-ʿAwda ilā al-Nabʿ al-Ḥālim* ('Return from the Dreamy Fountain,' 1960) which was warmly received by the critics. She suspended the publication of her second volume of poetry due to the eruption of the June 1967 war. Since then she has stopped writing poetry and concentrated on other literary activities. In 1977, her study *Trends and Movements in Modern Arabic Poetry* was published. Her edited anthologies include *Literature of Modern Arabia* (1987), *Modern Arabic Poetry* (1988), and *Modern Arabic Drama* (1995).

JTZ

Jelinek, Elfriede (*b.* 1946) Austrian novelist, dramatist. Born in Mürzzuschlag in Styria, Jelinek spent her childhood in Vienna, taking lessons in organ and piano. She enrolled in drama studies and art history and became certified as an organist. Since 1966, she has lived as a writer alternately in Vienna, Munich, and Paris. Her works are considered daring in their content and their word experiments. While applying stylistic elements used in pornography, comics, and horror literature, she constructs patterns of language connecting to patterns of conscience in *Wonderful, Wonderful Times* (1970). *The Piano Player* (1983) centers upon a masochistic mother–daughter relationship governed by the disciplined study of the piano. All of her texts investigate the relationship between societal power and the position of women in patriarchal society. Her critique of male omnipotence is expressed in *Krankheit oder Moderne Frauen* ('Illness, or Modern Women,' 1987) where vampires avenge the violence acted out by men on women. *Lust* ('Desire,' 1989) depicts a woman who is oppressed in her marriage and who perpetuates her experienced violence by murdering her son. Other recent works are *Die Kinder der Toten* ('The Children of the Dead,' 1995) and *Ein Sportstück* ('Sports,' 1998). She has received several Austrian and German awards.

MMu

Jen, Gish (Lillian Jen) (*b. c.* 1956) US novelist. The daughter of Chinese immigrants, Jen grew up in Yonkers and Scarsdale, New York and was educated at Harvard University (BA, 1977), Stanford University, and the University of Iowa, where she earned an MFA. Her first novel *Typical American* was published in 1991. It concerns Ralph and Helen Chang, Chinese immigrants in New York in the 1950s. A spare and quietly humorous portrait of assimilation and capitulation, it explores the strong pull of American values and American greed. Her second novel *Mona in the Promised Land* (1996) is a sequel set in suburban New York in the 1960s that centers on the Changs' teenaged daughter, Mona, her search for an identity, and her conversion to Judaism. A fast-paced, funny, and ultimately moving satire, the novel playfully dissects racial and ethnic stereotypes while revealing the surreal in ordinary suburban life. *Who's Irish* (1999) is a collection of short stories that return to Jen's themes of culture clash and assimilation with humor, pathos, and refreshing optimism. In 1999, Jen won the Lannan Literary Award for fiction.

JEM

Jhabvala, Ruth Prawer (*b.* 1927) Polish-Indian-British novelist, short story writer, scriptwriter. Winner of the 1975 Booker Prize for her novel *Heat and Dust*, Jhabvala has been a prolific writer for over four

decades. Born in Germany to German and Polish Jewish parents, she moved to England during World War II. In 1951 she married the Indian architect C. S. H. Jhabvala and moved to Delhi, where she lived until 1975. Her novels are snapshots of middle-class India in the post-independence years; *Amrita, or To Whom She Will* (1955), *Esmond in India* (1958), *The Householder* (1960), and *A Backward Place* (1965) portray a country caught in the disjuncture between a stagnant tradition and an uncertain future. Her short story collections, such as *How I Became a Holy Mother and Other Stories* (1976) and *Out of India* (1986), center on the viewpoints of the European woman traveler, reflecting her own position as an 'insider/outsider' in India. Her latest novel is *Shards of Memory* (1995). Together with James Ivory and Ismail Merchant, Jhabvala has also been an integral part of the Merchant Ivory film production team, winning Oscars for her screenplays for *A Room With A View* (1987) and *Howard's End* (1992). She and her husband currently reside in New York.

BMan

Jiles, Paulette (*b.* 1943) Canadian poet, novelist. Born in Salem, Missouri, Jiles was educated at the University of Missouri, where she earned a BA in Spanish literature. She moved to Canada in 1969 to work as a journalist and broadcaster for the Canadian Broadcasting Corporation. She also worked for several years as a consultant for the Cree and Ojibwa in northern Ontario, an experience she recounts in *North Spirit* (1995). Her first volume of poetry *Waterloo Express* was published in 1973. Her next volume *Celestial Navigation* (1984) won numerous literary prizes. Her poetry has the tone and rhythms of speech; it is straightforward and fast-moving, with few poetic devices. *The Jesse James Poems* (1988) began as a radio script, and contains poems written in the voices of the James gang and their women. *Song to the Rising Sun* (1989) develops her interest in the spoken word, mixing poetry with radio scripts. *Flying Lessons* (1995) is a selection of her previously published poems. Jiles also writes innovative and playful fiction. *Sitting in the Club Car Drinking Rum and Karma-Kola: A Manual of Etiquette for Ladies Crossing Canada by Train* (1986) is a feminist reworking of both the picaresque novel and detective fiction. *The Late Great Human Road Show* (1986) is science fiction. *Cousins* (1991) is a family saga in which Jiles returns to the Ozarks of her childhood.

JEM

Joenpelto, Eeva (*b.* 1921) Finnish novelist. Born in Sammatti, Joenpelto lives on land her family has occupied since the fifteenth century. Her people and these surroundings became both muse and subject matter. Graduating from secondary school in nearby Lohja in 1940, during the Winter War, she matriculated in history and literature. In 1945, she married Jarl Hellemann. She and her husband, separated in 1975, had two sons. *Kaakerholman Kaupunki* ('The Town of Kaakerholma,' 1950), became the first of twenty-two novels written within Finland's literary tradition of monumental historical novels. Richly layered with accurate historical and ethnographic details, her novels earned high regard from both the public and fellow writers. Critical acclaim, particularly for her rhythmic style and multifaceted characters, began with *The Maiden Walks Upon the Water* (1955). Like many Finnish authors, Joenpelto produced a tetralogy. Beginning with *Vetää Kaikista Ovista* ('A Draft Comes In from All the Doors,' 1974), she explored Finland from its Civil War to the 1930s. A six-time winner of the Government Prize for Literature, she received an Honorary Doctorate from Helsinki University in 1982. The Finlandia Prize, which eluded her earlier, was awarded for *Tuomari Müller, Hieno Mies* ('Judge Müller, Elegant Man,' 1994).

KMW

Johnson, Amryl (*b.* 1960) Trinidadian-British novelist, poet. Born in Tunapuna, Trinidad, Johnson emigrated to England at the age of 11. She majored in African and Caribbean Studies at the University of Kent. The experience of being a transplant in British society consistently informs her work – in her first book of poetry *Long Road to Nowhere* (1982) and in later works, *Tread Carefully in Paradise* (1991) and *Gorgons* (1992). Her first novel *Sequins for a Ragged Hem* (1988) chronicles her return to the Caribbean as native but also stranger/outsider. Immersed in her birth culture, national and cultural identities become confusing; the question of identity is embodied in her question, 'Where do you stand in all this?' She is torn by both the 'quest for memory' and the desire to escape. She explains the resilience necessary to fight the uprootedness and displacement captured in the title: 'The "ragged hem" refers to the rape of slavery and all this had done to my people. "Sequins" are the colour and sparkle they have woven into the state of being in exile.' Johnson currently lives in Oxford.

TJP

Johnson, Diane (*b.* 1934) US novelist, biographer, critic. Born in Moline, Illinois, Johnson married and had two of her four children before completing her BA at the University of Utah in 1957; she went on to earn a PhD at UCLA in 1968. Much of her satirical realist fiction is set in California and most of her protagonists are intelligent, often sophisticated, women who are displaced and dissatisfied, and take risks to find fulfillment, as in her first novel *Fair Game* (1965) and *Loving Hands at Home* (1968). Other novels include *Burning* (1971), *The Shadow Knows* (1974), a disturbing tale about a single mother plagued by oblique and actual threats of violence, *Lying Low* (1978), *Health and Happiness* (1990), and *Le Mariage* (2000). *Persian Nights* (1987), which was nominated for a Pulitzer Prize, takes place in Iran before the 1979 revolution, and *Le Divorce* (1997), which was a National Book Award finalist, is set in Paris, and explores the relationship of a young American woman and a much older Frenchman. Johnson collaborated with Stanley Kubrick on the screenplay of *The Shining* (1980) and has collected her book reviews in *Terrorists and Novelists* (1982). She is also the author of two biographies: the award-winning *Lesser Lives: The True History of the First Mrs. Meredith* (1973) and *Dashiell Hammett: A Life* (1983). Johnson currently lives in Paris.

DVT

Johnston, Jennifer (*b.* 1930) Irish novelist. Born in Ireland, the daughter of actress Shelagh Richards and playwright Denis Johnston, Johnston was educated at Trinity College, Dublin. She has been married twice, and has four children. Her first novel *The Captains and the Kings* was published in 1972. She writes about Anglo-Irish Protestants and the conflicts they face concerning class, religion, politics, and national identity. She is often associated with 'Big House' novelists, which refers to the mansions of the Anglo-Irish aristocracy that were originally serviced by the native Irish. Once the symbols of power in Johnston's novels they are symbols of decline, redundancy, and the inevitability of change. Her characters are burdened by the past, be it personal or historical. Her novels include *How Many Miles to Babylon?* (1974), *The Old Jest* (1979; Whitbread Award), and *Fool's Sanctuary* (1987). *Shadows on Our Skin* (1977) is about a working-class family in Northern Ireland. *The Invisible Worm* (1991) critiques modern Ireland through its story of the sexual abuse of a girl by her politician father. *The Illusionist* (1995) and *Two Moons* (1998) concern women and their struggles against restrictions in their lives. Johnston is also the author of several plays.

JEM

Jolley, Elizabeth (*b.* 1923) Australian novelist, short story writer. Born in England to an English Quaker and an Austrian noblewoman, Jolley worked as a nurse during World War II. She married in 1950, and emigrated to Perth, Western Australia, in 1959. Since 1978 she has taught creative writing at Curtin University. After years of rejections, her breakthrough came with *Five Acre Virgin and Other Stories* (1976). Since then, she has published two more volumes of stories, twelve novels, a three-part imaginative autobiography, a volume of essays, and one collection of radio plays. She has been awarded the Miles Franklin Award, the ASAL Gold Medal, the Canada-Australia Prize for Fiction, the France-Australia Literary Translation Prize, and an honorary doctorate by Curtin. Her first novel *Palomino* (1980) introduces her major themes: exile, particularly a woman's double exile in phallocratic Australia; cultural tensions between Australia and Europe; immigrants' quests for belonging and transfiguration; and lesbian love, which is usually doomed. *Miss Peabody's Inheritance* (1983) is a disarmingly picaresque account of the annual trip of two elderly lesbians to Vienna and London. The comical mode also predominates in *Mr. Scobie's Riddle* (1983), one of several novels and short stories dealing with the diminished lives of elderly patients. *Milk and Honey* (1984) with its incest, Jewish exiles, and Gothic atmosphere is starkly different. *The Well* (1986; made into a major Australian film in 1997) is a complex tragic lesbian tale. Her most recent novel is *Lovesong* (1997).

AWi

Jones, Gayl (*b.* 1949) US novelist, poet. Born in Lexington, Kentucky, Jones was educated at Connecticut College, where she earned a BA in 1971, and Brown University, where she earned an MA in 1973 and a DA in 1975. She taught English at the University of Michigan, Ann Arbor from 1975 to 1983. An African-American, she is particularly concerned with how the legacy of slavery continues to shape racial and sexual dynamics. In her first novel, *Corregidora* (1975), she analyzes the psychology of a black woman's double oppression by racism and sexism. In her second novel *Eva's Man* (1976), a woman who has been sexually abused uses her own sexual power to violently retaliate. These popular and critically praised novels were followed by *White Rat* (1977), a collection of short stories, and three volumes of poetry – *Song for Anninho* (1981), *The Hermit-Woman* (1983), and *Xarque* (1985). But Jones did not publish another novel until *The Healing* in 1998. She spent the intervening years in seclusion in Paris and Lexington with her husband, a troubled man who killed himself shortly after *The Healing* was published. Ironically, *The Healing* concerns a faith healer and the power of love, and, unlike her first two novels, ends on an affirmative, rather than tragic, note. *Mosquito* (1999), a massive and digressive novel about an African-American woman who operates an underground railroad for Mexican immigrants, showcases Jones's ability to represent a black vernacular voice.

JEM

Jong, Erica (*b*. 1942) US poet, novelist. Born Erica Mann to a family of Jewish artists and intellectuals on New York's Upper West Side, Jong received a BA from Barnard College and an MA from Columbia University. Married four times, her second husband was Allan Jong, a Chinese-American psychiatrist, with whom she lived in Europe for several years. She has one daughter, from her third marriage. Her first book was a volume of poetry *Fruits and Vegetables* published in 1971. It was followed by several other collections, including *At the Edge of the Body* (1979) and *Becoming Light* (1992). But Jong is best known for her first work of fiction *Fear of Flying* (1973), which is a milestone in feminist and erotic literature. The heroine of this candid, exuberant, and funny book is Isadora Wing, a feminist

who wants to enjoy sexual freedom without guilt – what she terms 'the zipless fuck.' Isadora reappears in the later novels *How to Save Your Own Life* (1977), *Parachutes and Kisses* (1984), and *Any Woman's Blues* (1990). In *Fanny: Being The True History of Fanny Hackabout-Jones* (1980) and *Serenissima, A Novel of Venice* (1987), Jong tries out different fictional genres, but her feminist perspective and her focus on female sexuality remain. Recent works include the novel *Of Blessed Memory* (1997), *Fear of Fifty: A Midlife Memoir* (1994), and *What Women Want: Bread, Roses, Sex, Power* (1998).

DVT

Jordan, June (*b*. 1936) US poet, dramatist, children's writer. Born in New York City, Jordan attended Barnard College and the University of Chicago. She married Michael Meyer in 1955 (they divorced in 1966); she has one son. She has taught at several universities and colleges in the US; currently, she is a professor of African-American studies and women's studies at the University of California, Berkeley. Her first volume of poetry *Some Changes* was published in 1971. Her identity as an African-American and a feminist informs her work. Her poetic voice is direct and powerful, her forms inventive and varied. Her sometimes angry denunciations of racism, violence, and exploitation are tempered by an abiding and optimistic vision of human unity and spiritual wholeness. She also writes lyrically about personal experience, as in *The Haruko / Love Poetry of June Jordan* (1994). Her other volumes of poetry include *New Days: Poems of Exile and Return* (1974), *Things That I Do in the Dark* (1977), *Passion* (1980), *Naming Our Destiny* (1989), and *Kissing God Goodbye* (1996). She is a prolific writer who has also published numerous plays, children's books, and collections of political essays.

JEM

Jorge, Lídia (*b*. 1946) Portuguese novelist.

Born in a rural town of the Algarve region in southern Portugal, Jorge was raised in a family of immigrant men and began reading and writing when very young. She pursued an undergraduate degree in romance philology at the University of Lisbon, and taught secondary school in Angola and Mozambique. The Revolution of April 25, 1974, ending the long history of Portuguese colonialism and nearly half a century of dictatorship, not only brought her to Lisbon; it also brought her to a career in writing. Since the publication in 1980 of her first, prize-winning, novel *O Dia dos Prodigios* ('The Day of Prodigies'), a magic-realist allegory of the revolutionary 'miracle,' she has explored in a markedly postmodern vein the artistic and political implications of representation in a society in transition toward democracy, high capitalism, and loss of referents. This comes to the fore in, for example, *O Cais das Merendas* ('Snack Pier,' 1982) and *A Última Dona* ('The Last Starlet,' 1991). The lasting agony of Portuguese colonialism is captured in *The Murmuring Coast* (1988), featuring a deconstructive female I/eye, who questions the truth value of all male-centered narratives and masternarratives of history.

APF

Joris, Lieve (*b.* 1953) Flemish travel story writer. As a child, Joris's ambition was to be a Catholic mission worker. She was indeed to travel, but not as a missionary. She went to the US as an *au pair* and for some time afterwards lived in various communes. Back in Belgium, she got a degree in journalism and wrote for several magazines, focusing on personal and literary travel stories. These stories were collected in *De golf* ('The wave,' 1986). She frequently visits countries in Africa and the Middle East. Her main concerns are the dilemmas of everyday life in countries where there is a strong tension between tradition and modernity and between colonialism and postcolonialism. An example is *Back to the Congo* (1987), in

which she travels back to the former Belgian colony, Congo, in the footsteps of her uncle, who was a missionary. In *The Gates of Damascus* (1993) and *Mali Blues: Traveling to an African Beat* (1996), she portrays local cultural figures. She explores the impossibility of escaping one's own cultural identity and, in that sense, her stories sometimes acquire an autobiographical perspective. Her own presence and experiences, however, are always less important than the people she meets. Joris travels to let other people speak.

AAn, MMe

Joseph, Sarah (*b.* 1946) Indian short story writer, novelist. Born in Kuriachira, Kerala, Joseph holds a postgraduate degree in Malayalam literature. She lives in Thrissur with her husband and her three children. Currently she is a professor of government at Sanskrit College, Pattambi. She is acknowledged as one of Kerala's outstanding contemporary feminist writers. Her publications include five volumes of short stories, two novellas, and numerous articles on women's issues. The collection *Papathara* ('Soil of Sin,' 1990) is critically acclaimed for its sensitive and powerful portrayal of the plight of the Indian woman in a male-dominated culture. One of the distinctive features of her narrative strategy is her skillful and subtle use of symbols and motifs drawn from myths religious, social, political, and ecological. Though written in simple, colloquial language, her stories are complex, metaphoric, and lyrical. As an activist she has formed the first feminist theater group in Kerala. She has served as an executive of the Kerala Sahitya Akademi. Her story *Nilave Ariyunnu* ('Moonlight Knows') won the 1994 TV Award of the Kerala State Government. She has won the Katha Award thrice for her stories *Prakasini's Children* (1991), *Asoka* (1996), and *Vanadurga* (1998), which were subsequently translated into English.

SRao

Ju (*b*. 1958) Burmese writer. Like many Burmese authors, Ju (the pen name of Dr. Tin Tin Win) qualified as a doctor in 1983 and worked in a clinic in her home town of Yenangyaung in central Burma until she was able to support herself through writing. Her first published work was a short story 'Yazawin-hteh-hma Maung-ko Hta-yiq-hkeh' ('I've Left Him Behind in the Past,' 1979). It was 'Ahmaq-taya' ('Remembrance,' 1987) which brought her to the public's attention. This is a semi-autobiographical account of a girl who falls in love and cohabits with a fellow student while at Mandalay Medical School, only to be abandoned when he marries his docile hometown sweetheart. This, and other stories such as 'Kyar-daw Thi-leh Maunt-sagar' ('Your Words Long Left Unsaid'), which explicitly refers to premarital sex, raised eyebrows at the time, but the style and the subject matter have since been copied by other writers. With some ten novels and sixty short stories, Ju is now Burma's most successful and influential female writer, although her recent more experimental writing is less popular than her love stories. In 1997, she spent a year in the US. She owns a publishing house which has published several of her short story collections. Her novels include *Pin-leh-hnin-tu-thaw meinma-mya* ('Women Like the Sea,' 1996) and *Meinma tayauq-yeh hpwin-ha-wun-hkan-jeq* ('Confessions of a Woman,' 1992).

VBo

K

Kael, Pauline (1919–2001) US film critic. Born in California, Kael received a BA from the University of California, Berkeley. She was in her mid-thirties when she published her first film review in the San Francisco quarterly *City Lights* in 1953. She wrote reviews for a local radio station and later for the *New Republic*, *Life*, *McCall's*, and other magazines; these were collected in her first two books *I Lost it at the Movies* (1965) and *Kiss Kiss Bang Bang* (1968). She joined the *New Yorker* in 1968, where she wrote a regular movie column for the next twenty-five years and became one of the most influential (and imitated) film critics in the US. Her reviews, written in a direct, spoken tone, are unabashedly, enthusiastically subjective, bitingly funny, and full of vivid imagery. Whether she loved a movie or hated it, Kael wrote with excitement and urgency; in her desire to explain her responses and judgements, she often wrote reviews that were unusually long for the genre. She published fourteen books on film, most of them collections of her reviews such as *Deeper Into Movies* (1974), which won a National Book Award, *Reeling* (1976), *When the Lights Go Down* (1980), and *For Keeps* (1994). Fascinated and repelled by the Hollywood movie industry, she examines its workings in detail in *The Citizen Kane Book: Raising Kane* (1971).

DVT, JEM

Kahana-Carmon, Amalia (*b.* 1926) Israeli fiction writer, essayist. Winner of many prestigious literary prizes (including the Israel Prize for 2000), the 'darling' of the Academe and the subject of several scholarly monographs, Kahana-Carmon, one of the foremost writers in Israel, is known as a superb (and idiosyncratic) Hebrew stylist. Born in a kibbutz, her studies at the Hebrew University were interrupted by the War of Independence (1948), in which she actively participated. However, this experience is less prominent in her work than her sojourn in England shortly after her marriage. Beginning with her first volume of lyrical stories *Bikhfifa 'ahat* ('Under One Roof,' 1966), her early work – *Veyareah be'emek ayalon* ('And Moon in the Valley of Ayalon,' 1971), *Sadot magnetiim* ('Magnetic Fields,' 1977; three novellas); *Himurim gevohim* ('High Stakes,' 1980) – mostly foregrounded the plight of women. Yet their search for an epiphanic 'vision,' for a moment of a (sometimes mutual) enchantment, 'lifts' their narratives above and beyond a narrow feminist angle. Since the mid-1980s, however, she has become *the* outspoken feminist critic of Israeli literature and Jewish culture, adding programmatic essays to her fiction. In the novellas *Lema'lah bemontifer* ('Up in Montifer,' 1984) and *Liviti 'otah baderekh leveitah* ('With Her on Her Way Home,' 1991) she probes gender difference by embedding it in other categories of otherness – race and class. Conducting a dialogue with both Simone de Beauvoir and contemporary sensitivities, Kahana-Carmon has opened in Israel a space for a postmodern, multicultural feminism.

YSF

Kahanoff, Jaqueline (1917–1979) Israeli essayist, fiction writer. Born Jacqueline Shohet in Cairo to parents who hailed from Iraq and Tunis, Kahanoff received a cosmopolitan education in Egypt and, later, in the US. In the mid-1940s she began to write essays and stories for Egyptian and foreign periodicals. In 1954 she emigrated to Israel and lived in Tel Aviv until her death. Her first notable short story 'Such is Rachel' won the *Atlantic Monthly* award for the best short story and appeared in that journal in 1946. In 1951 her only novel *Jacob's Ladder* was published in London. (Both of these works were originally written in English under the author's maiden name.) In Israel she became a major essayist, publishing her works in two central Hebrew literary reviews, *Ammot* and *Keshet*. Aharon Amir, the editor of the latter journal, who translated most of these writings from English into Hebrew, also edited a collection of her essays under the title *Mi-Mizrah Shemesh* ('From the East of the Sun,' 1978). A small number of these essays appeared, posthumously, in their original English version. The essays were well-received in Israel both for their unique literary form (a blend of autobiography and sociohistorical reflections) and their provocative ideas (an appeal to Israeli society to adopt a 'Levantine' culture).

SS

Kamienska, Anna (1920–1986) Polish poet, translator. Best known for her religious poetry rooted in the Catholic tradition, Kamienska was born in Krasnystaw, Poland and later lived in Lublin and Warsaw. When World War II interrupted her college education, she studied Polish literature on her own and took exams at the illegally operating Warsaw University. She graduated from Lodz University with a degree in classics after the war, and in 1948 married Jan Spiewak, the well-known Polish poet and translator. She made her literary debut in 1943 with a play written for an underground children's theater and she wrote for children throughout her life. A prolific reviewer, literary critic, and translator of primarily Russian literature in the postwar period, she published her first volume of poetry *Wychowanie* ('Upbringing') in 1949. Close to twenty volumes followed. Polish folklore and the Christian tradition fuel her poetry, in both theme and form: folk and religious imagery are complemented by poetic genres approximating a prayer or a litany. Her early didacticism evolved into a sense of social responsibility, expressed in her poetry of the 1970s and 1980s. Toward the end of her life, Kamienska wrote intense, meditative lyrics, translated religious verse ranging from Old Ethiopian to medieval Bulgarian, and published biblical commentaries. Translations of her poems appear in the volume *Two Darknesses* (1994) and in the anthologies *Ariadne's Thread: Polish Women Poets* (1988) and *Spoiling Cannibals' Fun: Polish Poetry of the Last Two Decades of Communist Rule* (1991).

JB

Kandre, Mare (*b.* 1962) Swedish novelist. As a child, Kandre spent some years in Canada before her family of Estonian origin settled in Gothenburg, Sweden. Wanting to become a writer, she left school at the age of 16. She made her debut with *I ett annat land* ('In Another Land,' 1984), followed by *Bübins unge* ('Bübin's Kid,' 1987) and *Aliide, Aliide* (1991). These books investigate, using landscape and imagery, young girls' experience of the world as they try to come to grips with their identity and existence. *Deliria* (1992) and *Djävulen och Gud* ('The Devil and God,' 1993), both written in poetic prose, examine how the world is being destroyed spiritually and physically. In *Quinnan och*

Dr Dreuf ('The Woman and Dr. Dreuf,' 1994), Dr. Dreuf sits by his desk ready with pen and paper, while the Woman provides him with material that will make him famous. Playing with the idea of psychoanalysis and the positions of analyst and analysand, the novel, besides being funny, questions how those roles are created. English translations of excerpts of Kandre's work can be found in several anthologies.

GE-C

Kang Sŏkkyŏng (Kang Sŏngae) (*b.* 1951) Korean fiction writer, essayist. Kang graduated from the College of Fine Arts, Ewha Women's University, in 1974. She often portrays painfully self-conscious characters on the verge of a psychological breakdown, as in 'Kun' ('Roots,' 1974) and 'Op'ŭn kaeim' ('Open Game,' 1974), her first short stories. The collection of short stories *Pam kwa yoram* ('Night and Cradle,' 1983), the story 'Mulsok ŭi pang' ('A Room in the Water,' 1984), and the novella *A Room in the Woods* (1986) explore the quest for the ideal in a chaotic world. Her prominent themes include the problems of the middle class, family tension, alienation, sexuality, gender roles, idealism versus realism, and interrogating the self. She also uses colors and space as thematic symbols. In *A Room in the Woods*, college students, the modern-day Korean youthful intellectuals, experience hypocrisy, alienation, and despair, as they feel trapped between the traditional conventions and modern demands. Those able to capture a space for themselves find hope, while others, hopeless, opt for death. Kang won the Newcomers' Prize awarded by the journal *Munhak Sasang* ('Literature and Thought') in 1974, the Nogwŏn literary award (1986), and *Writers of Today Award* (1986).

CS

Kantůrková, Eva (*b.* 1930) Czech novelist, essayist. Her father a communist journalist and mother a writer, Prague-born Kantůrková, after working for the newspaper *Mladá fronta* (Young Front), received her degree in philosophy and history from Charles University in 1956. She has one son from a first marriage; her second husband is journalist Jiří Kantůrek. Her first novel *Smuteční slavnost* ('Funeral Ceremony,' 1967) depicts the tragic fate of a farmer in the early 1950s. With the banning of her next two novels *Po potopě* ('After the Flood,' 1969) and *Pozůstalost pana Ábela* ('Mr. Abel's Legacy,' 1971), because of their political subtexts, she turned to *samizdat* and later signed Charter 77. Open dissidence – a book of interviews with the wives of political prisoners, *Sešly jsme se v této knize* ('We Met in This Book,' 1980) – led to her arrest in 1981. Ten months in prison inspired her documentary novel *My Companions in the Bleak House* (1984), for which she won the Tom Stoppard Prize. Before 1989, in addition to finely crafted essays *Valivý čas proměn* ('A Time of Upheavals,' 1995) and psychological stories *Krabička se šperky* ('A Box of Jewels,' 1992), Kantůrková wrote three novels, each an attempt to come to terms with the political situation of post-invasion 'normalization' – *Černa hvězda* ('Black Star,' 1982), *Pán věže* ('Master of the Tower,' 1992), and *Jan Hus* (1991). A founder of Civic Forum in 1989, she was elected to parliament (1990–2) and subsequently chaired the Writers' Council (1994–6). Her latest books are cultural memoirs: *Památník* ('Memorial,' 1994) and *Záznamy paměti* ('Memory Records,' 1997).

ES

Kapadia, Kundanika (*b.* 1927) Indian novelist, short story writer. Born in Limbadi, Gujarat, Kundanika graduated with a degree in politics and history. From 1962 to 1980 she lived in Bombay, where she began her career as a writer and an editor on the journals *Yatrik* (1955–7) and *Navneet*. Currently she lives in Nandigram and is married to the Gujarati poet Makarand Dave. Her first short story 'Prem na Ansu'

('Tears of Love,' 1954), and later on a collection by the same title, established her as an important writer in the Gujarati language. The conflict between an individual and society forms the overarching concern of her writings. It manifests itself in the collection *Vadhu ne Vadhu Sundar* ('More and More Beautiful,' 1967) as a quest for a meaningful and emotionally fulfilling life rather than an arid intellectual existence. Her most famous novel and the first feminist novel in Gujarati *Seven Steps in the Sky* (1984) focuses on the struggle of Vasudha, a representative of the upper-middle-class, urban, educated woman of modern India. The novel won the Sahitya Akademi Award in 1985. Her other works include the novels *Agan Pipasa* ('Burning Thirst,' 1972) and *Kagal ni Hodi* ('Paper Boat,' 1978) and essays in *Dvar ane Dival* ('A Door and a Wall,' 1964).

RK

Karapanou, Margarita (*b.* 1946) Greek novelist. One of the most widely read contemporary Greek women novelists, Karapanou was born in Athens. The daughter of writer Margarita Liberaki, she was raised in Greece and France; currently she lives in Athens. She pursued film and philosophy studies in Paris, and worked for a while as a nursery and kindergarten teacher. Written during the final period of the 1967–74 military dictatorship, her first novel *Kassandra and the Wolf* (1976) raises critical questions of class, sexuality, gender, language and censorship, and authority and politics, through its first-person narrator, the young girl Kassandra. Her second novel *O Ipnovates* ('The Sleepwalker,' 1985) also deals with authority, gender, and language within the framework of a murder committed in a cosmopolitan Aegean island. *Rien ne va plus* ('No More Bets,' 1991), written in both first- and third-person, picks up these issues yet a third time while also demonstrating how a story is written with every (re)telling. In 1988, *O Ipnovates* earned Karapanou the prestigious French award

Prix du meilleur livre étranger for best foreign fiction and confirmed her position in contemporary Greek literature.

APD

Karodia, Farida (*b.* 1942) South African novelist, short story writer. Karodia was born a 'coloured' in Aliwl North, a rural community in South Africa. She graduated from the Coronationville Teacher Training College in 1961 and taught at the Coronationville High School in Johannesburg for three years. In 1967, after a short marriage, she left South Africa with her daughter Anesia for Zambia to teach at a high school. In Zambia, her South African passport was revoked and she had to join her mother in Swaziland as a stateless person until 1969, when she was given permission to emigrate to Canada. In Canada she worked at various jobs and wrote plays for CBC while studying at the University of Calgary. She graduated in 1974 and later did graduate work. Her first novel *Daughters of the Twilight* (1986) describes a South African community not unlike the one in which Karodia grew up. In her collection of short stories *Coming Home and Other Stories* (1988), she describes various aspects of her visit home in 1981. Her second novel *A Shattering of Silence* (1993), set in Mozambique, deals with war, exile, identity, and displacement. Her second collection of short stories *Against An African Sky and Other Stories* was published in 1995.

TMR-P

Katerli, Nina Semyonovna (*b.* 1934) Russian prose writer. A Leningrader who trained as an engineer, Katerli made her literary debut in 1973. Since the 1980s she has actively combated anti-Semitism at meetings, through publications, and in court (a struggle documented in her unpublished novel *Isk* ('The Lawsuit'). Most of Katerli's fiction, contained in her collections *Okno* ('Window,' 1981), *Tsvetnye otkrytki* ('Color Postcards,' 1986), *Kurzal* (1990), and *Sennaia ploshchad'*

('Haymarket Square,' 1992), follows one of two basic modes: it freely embraces fantasy, radical temporal jumps, unexpected juxtapositions, shifts in viewpoint, and modified stream of consciousness, or it recreates in concrete detail modern urban settings as palpable contexts for romantic and familial problems, communal living, irrational, destructive daily behavior, and failure to communicate, relying on parallel plotlines and a male center of consciousness. 'The Barsukov Triangle' (1981) blends the two modes to emphasize the radical illogicality of Soviet life and the violence and frustrations of its citizens. From a feminist standpoint, *Polina* (1984) is a particularly rewarding novella in its vision of an unorthodox alternative to the paradigmatic Soviet ideal of domesticated womanhood. 'Slowly the Old Woman . . .' (1989) offers a vivid, disconcerting portrait of the stereotypical Jewish mother. Stories translated into English include 'The Farewell Light' (1981) and 'Between Spring and Summer' (1983).

HG

Katoppo, Marianne (*b.* 1947) Indonesian fiction writer. The daughter of the Minister for Education and Religion during the Indonesian revolution (1945–9), Katoppo's tertiary education and her writing have focused on the place of women in the Christian Church and the impact of Christianity on Indonesian society. The Indonesian coordinator of the Ecumenical Association of Third World Theologians, she has represented her country at conventions in Asia, Europe, and Latin America. She is also in demand as a guest lecturer on human rights issues. A keen writer since the age of 8, her first novel *Dunia tak bermusim* ('A World without Seasons,' 1974) concerns political intrigue at the time of the opening of diplomatic ties between Indonesia and South Korea. In 1982, she became the first woman to win the prestigious Southeast Asia (S.E.A.) Write Award for her second novel *Raumanen* (1975). Fluent in English, Dutch, German,

Swedish, French, and Japanese, she has published a number of translations, and her English language theological work *Compassionate and Free: An Asian Woman's Theology* has become a core textbook in theological institutions throughout the world.

PA

Katzir, Yehudit (*b.* 1963) Israeli fiction writer. Katzir was born in Haifa, Israel. She studied film and literature for her BA at Tel Aviv University. She works as a reader for a publishing house, and lives with her husband and daughter in Tel Aviv. Her first collection of stories *Closing the Sea* (1990) became a best-seller on the strength of its love story 'Schlaffstunde.' This story has been adapted for stage. Her first novel, also a best-seller, was *Le-Matisse Yesh Et Ha-Shemesh Ba-Beten* ('Matisse Has the Sun In His Belly,' 1995). Its narrator, as many of the women in her work, tends to fall in love with older men. Her latest book is *Migdalorim Shel Yabasha* ('Inland Lighthouses,' 1999) – a collection of novellas. A central theme of her writing is the disappointment of love and trust, but the death of romance or loss of faith leaves her protagonists not destroyed but renewed.

LR

Kaufman, Shirley (*b.* 1923) US-Israeli poet. Born in Seattle, the granddaughter of Eastern European Jewish immigrants, Kaufman received her BA from the University of California, Los Angeles in 1944 and her MA from San Francisco State College in 1967. Married in 1946, she raised three daughters in San Francisco; in 1974, she divorced Bernard Kaufman, Jr., and married Hillel Matthew Daleski. Her first book *The Floor Keeps Turning* appeared in 1970. In 1973, the year she published *Gold Country,* she took up permanent residence in Jerusalem, and the experience of being tied to two countries without roots in either has informed her writing since then. The titles of subsequent volumes – *Looking at Henry Moore's Elephant Skull Etchings in Jerusalem During the War* (1977), *Claims* (1984), *From One Life to Another* (1989), *Rivers of Salt* (1993), and *Roots in the Air: New and Selected Poems* (1996) – suggest her themes of duality and transition. *Mehayim Lehayim Acherim* (1995) is a selection of her poems translated into Hebrew. Though Kaufman writes only in English, she has translated the work of Abba Kovner and other Israeli poets. Her co-edited, co-translated volume *The Defiant Muse: Hebrew Feminist Poems from Antiquity to the Present* (1999) encapsulates Kaufman's lifelong Jewish and feminist commitments.

NR

Kay, Jackie (*b*. 1961) Scottish poet. Born in Edinburgh, Kay was educated at the University of Stirling, where she received a BA (honors) in English. Her first volume of poetry *The Adoption Papers* (1991) won several awards, including the Scottish Arts Council Book Award. It is a poem sequence that charts the adoption of a black child by white parents and the search of the grown-up child for her birth-mother. Significantly, three voices – those of the child, the birth-mother, and the adoptive mother – share the telling of the story. Kay's identity as a black lesbian is central to her work, as are the difficulties she has faced in Scotland as a result of that identity. The language and rhythms of her poems are simple and direct, her images vivid. Her dominant themes are identity, gender, sexuality, racial identity, and racism, and her treatment of them mixes humor with anger, the political with the personal. Her other volumes of poetry include a chapbook *That Distance Apart* (1991), *Other Lovers* (1993), *Bessie Smith* (1997), and *Off Colour* (1999). *Two's Company* (1992) and *Three Has Gone* (1994) are poetry collections for children. Kay's first novel *Trumpet* (1998; *Guardian* fiction prize) uses multiple narrative voices in its exploration of the life and death of a

female jazz trumpeter who lived her life as a man.

JEM

Kennedy, Adrienne (*b*. 1931) US playwright. Born in Pittsburgh, Kennedy grew up in Cleveland and was educated at Ohio State University and Columbia University. She has taught at many universities in the US. She is best known for her avant-garde play *Funnyhouse of a Negro* (1964; Obie Award). It is a profoundly strange and disturbing work about an African-American woman's struggle with identity, particularly her racial identity. There is no plot in a conventional sense, but rather a progression of surreal scenes which feature historical and symbolic figures which arise out of the central character's subconscious. In this and in her other plays, Kennedy explores the psychological damage of racism and sexism and the resultant fear and anger, through violent and nightmarish images. She places the real, in the figures of Jesus, Queen Victoria, Anne Boleyn, Marlon Brando, and Bette Davis, among others, amidst the distinctly unreal to powerful effect. Her plays include *The Owl Answers* (1965), *A Lesson in a Dead Language* (1966), *A Rat's Mass* (1966), *A Movie Star Has to Star in Black and White* (1976), and *The Alexander Plays* (1992). Her autobiography *People Who Led to My Plays*, was published in 1987.

JEM

Kennedy, A(lison) L(ouise) (*b*. 1963) Scottish novelist, short story writer. Born in Dundee, Scotland, Kennedy read English at Warwick University. Her first book *Night Geometry and the Garscadden Trains* (1990; Granta Award) is a collection of short stories set in Scotland, which focuses on those whose lives usually go unnoticed; the poverty, illness, and abuse they suffer are presented in a direct, realistic style. Her first novel *Looking for the Possible Dance* (1993) is about Margaret, beaten down by urban life, disaffected and directionless, but longing for escape. The story collection *Now That You're Back* (1994) expands Kennedy's previous range with its variety of settings, surreal situations, and eccentric characters. The novel *So I Am Glad* (1995) is another departure from realism. Social satire is mingled with the fantastic as Jennifer, a disillusioned radio announcer, falls in love with the reincarnation of Cyrano de Bergerac. Kennedy is also the author of *Original Bliss* (1997) and *Everything You Need* (1999), a novel set in a writers' community on an island off Wales. Intelligent, witty, and original, she was named one of Granta's Twenty Best Young British Novelists in 1993.

JEM

Kenyon, Jane (1947–1995) US poet. Born in Ann Arbor, Michigan, Kenyon attended the University of Michigan, where she received a BA in 1970 and an MA in 1972. She married the poet Donald Hall in 1972; they lived on Hall's family farm in New Hampshire. She died of leukemia at age 48. Her first volume of poetry *From Room to Room* was published in 1978. Her subjects are domestic and rural life, the cycles of nature, and the changes of seasons. She reveals unexpected beauty in her detailed descriptions of animals and human objects, but she never sentimentalizes them. Her tone is even and direct, her language and syntax simple. But as in *Constance* (1993), she also attends to the inner life, particularly as it relates to her periods of depression; she examines the power of feelings to transform the world. Her other volumes of poetry, all critically acclaimed, are *The Boat of Quiet Hours* (1986), *Let Evening Come* (1990), and *Otherwise: New and Selected Poems* (1996), a posthumous volume containing twenty poems written just before her death. *A Hundred White Daffodils* (1999) is a collection of translations, essays, interviews, and newspaper columns. She also translated *Twenty Poems of Anna Akhmatova* (1985).

JEM

Khalīfa, Saḥar (*b.* 1941) Palestinian novelist. Born in Nablus, Khalīfa received her education in Jerusalem and Amman, Jordan in addition to her hometown. She married at the age of 18, but described her marriage as a nightmare. After having two daughters and working in Libya with her husband, she left him to return to Palestine. She returned to school and earned her BA from the English department at Bir Zeit University, and her PhD in women's studies from the University of Iowa. Her first novel *Lam Naʿud Jawrārī Lakum* ('We Are No Longer Your Slaves,' 1974), reflects the problem of her failed marriage and the rigid patriarchal social values of the West Bank. Khalīfa, however, is best known for her novels that tell the saga of al-Karmī family, *Wild Thorns* (1976) and *ʿAbbād al-Shams* ('The Sunflower,' 1980). In these works, she describes life in detail for a Palestinian family under Israeli occupation without portraying the Israelis as faceless monsters. Her most recent work is *Al-Mīrāth* ('The Legacy,' 1997), a novel in which she examines life under the Palestinian Authority on the West Bank, not only criticizing the political reality, but also highlighting the social plight of women. In addition to English, her works have been translated into Hebrew, French, and German.

JTZ

Khin Myo Chit (1915–1999) Burmese journalist, historian, essayist. In the 1930s, Khin Myo Chit lived in Rangoon and associated with the Thakins ('Masters'), a group of left-wing pro-independence activists who included Aung San, father of *Aung San Suu Kyi. She later worked in the Women's Section of the pro-independence Burma Defense Army. She was an editor of the English-language *Guardian* (1958–62) and *Working People's Daily* (1964–8), but was fired from the latter for her increasingly anti-government editorials. She wrote most effectively in English, in a mischievous and ironic style. A short story 'Her Infinite Variety' won first prize in 1970 in a Southeast Asia competition run by *Horizon* magazine, and 'Thirteen Carat Diamond' was included in the collection *Fifty Great Oriental Stories* (1965). Her books which cover Burmese culture and history include *Colourful Burma* (1988), *A Wonderland of Burmese Legends* (1984), and *Anawrahta of Burma* (1968). Crippling arthritis prevented her from writing in the last ten years of her life.

VBo

Khūrī, Colette al- (*b.* 1935) Syrian novelist, short story writer, poet. Khūrī was born in Damascus, Syria into a Catholic family of some prominence. Her grandfather had served as the Syrian prime minister. She was educated in both French and Arabic. Her education included elementary schooling with the Besançon nuns, and middle and high school at the Ladaik Institute. She also studied law in Beirut at St Joseph's Jesuit University until 1955. She earned her MA in French literature at the School of French Belles Lettres in Beirut in 1972. She married a Spanish count and has one daughter. Today she is serving a second term as an elected member in the Syrian Parliament. Her literary career began with the publication of *Vingt Ans* ('Twenty Years,' 1958), a collection of poems in French that expresses her discontent with the social constraints of society. *Ayyām Ma'ahu* ('Days with Him,' 1959) describes the life of a Syrian girl who attempts to find the meaning of life in an affair with a man of the world. Over the course of the novel, the reader witnesses the girl's transition from being a submissive lover to a more independent woman. *Layla Wāḥida* ('One Night,' 1961) is the story of a woman in a loveless marriage who finds solace in a one-night affair with a stranger in Europe. Khūrī has also written about political issues in her fiction.

JTZ

Kidman, Fiona (*b.* 1940) New Zealand novelist, poet, dramatist. Kidman attended various country schools in Northland, New Zealand; trained as a librarian; and married a schoolteacher in 1960. She then began freelance writing. A decade later, after several radio and television plays, she published the poetry collection *Honey and Bitters* (1975). *A Breed of Women* (1979), her first novel, shows one woman's struggles against conventional New Zealand rural and urban society. In *Mandarin Summer* (1981) when Emily's father returns from World War II, his misguided aspirations force his family into a summer of drudgery serving the mysterious and dysfunctional Barnsley household. *Paddy's Puzzle* (1983; reprinted in the US as *In the Clear Light*) depicts Clara, whose black American Marine lover and black-marketeer friends care for her as she is dying of tuberculosis during World War II. In *The Book of Secrets* (1987; New Zealand Book Award for Fiction) fictional characters join Norman McLeod's historic migration to New Zealand. Most recently Kidman has published *Ricochet Baby* (1996) and *The House Within* (1997). She has also published several short story and poetry collections, held the New Zealand Scholarship in Letters twice, and held the Victoria University Writer's Fellowship. Kidman was awarded the Order of the British Empire.

M-RA

Kim Chiwŏn (*b.* 1943) Korean fiction writer. Kim comes from a family of prominent women writers. Her mother was *Ch'oe Chŏnghŭi, one of the most popular Korean women writers, and her younger sister is the writer Kim Ch'aewŏn (*b.* 1946). A graduate in English literature from Ewha Women's University in 1965, Kim portrays the uncertainties women face when they question social norms, as in her debut works 'Sarang ŭi kippŭm' ('Joys of Love,' 1974) and 'A Certain Beginning' (1974). In the latter, questions about traditional gender roles are intermingled with immigrant issues in the negotiations between a husband and wife united through a contract marriage. Since the 1970s, Kim has been living off and on in the New York City area, a reality reflected in 'Saebyŏk ŭi mokssori' ('Voice at Dawn,' 1979) and 'Almaden' (1979). Her favorite themes include gender roles, the hypocrisy of the middle class, and women's identity; she uses motifs that symbolize problematic aspects of Korea's patriarchal history and culture. A transformation of the space belonging only to women, such as a room or a place in nature, dominates her fictional images. In 'Lullaby' (1979) and 'P'yŏnggang kongju wa Pabo Ondal' ('Princess P'yŏnggang and Idiot Ondal,' 1985), Kim taps into Korea's common cultural memory by using myths and cultural icons.

CS

Kim Hyangsuk (*b.* 1951) South Korean fiction writer. Graduate of Ewha Women's University with a degree in chemistry, Kim started her literary career by winning a literary competition in 1977. From her first collection of stories, *Kyŏul ŭi bit* ('Light of Winter,' 1986), the depiction of the daily dystopia besetting her female protagonists as well as the combination of psychological realism and social criticism have been hallmarks of her work. In 'The Sound of Calling' (1984), she traces the genealogy of her heroine's predicament back to her husband's ideological choice during the Korean War. 'Yuri p'asukkun' ('Glass Watcher') discloses the ways in which housewives' informal sphere and their inner world are inexorably manipulated by the collusion of capitalism and patriarchy. Her subsequent collections, such as *Surye pakwi sogyesŏ* ('Within the Wheels,' 1988) and *Chong'i ro mandŭn jip* ('A House Made of Paper,' 1989), tend to be multi-focal in viewpoint and structure, effectively accommodating diverse voices and diversified social contradictions, which have gained more importance for Korean writers since the 1980s. Kim creates complex and complicated relationships in which various social factors such

as class, education, and generation are called into play, even while sustaining her key concern with gender, which is apparent in *Ttŏnanŭn norae* ('Song of Farewell,' 1991) and *Mul ŭi yŏja* ('Women of Water,' 1995).

K-HC

Kim Hyŏng-gyŏng (Kim Chŏng-suk) (*b.* 1960) Korean fiction writer, poet. Born in Kangnŭng, a northeastern seaport, Kim's early literary mentor was her schoolteacher mother. Studying Korean literature at Kyŏng-Hee University, Seoul, under renowned Korean novelists on the faculty, Kim regularly participated in student anti-government demonstrations. She debuted as a poet in 1983, but her award-winning novella 'Chugŭm chanch'i' ('Banquet of Death,' 1985) officially launched her fiction-writing career. Her first collection of short stories, *Tanjong ŭi ka chakta* ('Tanjong is Short in Height,' 1991) exposes the duplicity of charismatic leaders, the absurdity of hero worship, and the insanity of mass demonstrations. Her first full-length novel *Saedŭl ŭn che irŭm ŭl purŭmyŏ unda* ('Birds Cry Calling Their Own Names,' 1993), on the agonies and spiritual wanderings of women students of the 1980s, caused a sensation when it got the largest cash award in Korean literary history. In 'A Woman Who Smokes' (1996), Kim highlights the dangers of women's search for the meaning of life beyond their domestic comfort. Her most recent novel *Sewŏl* ('The Passage of Time,' 1995) is autobiographical, dealing with her family misfortune and her failed love – a new venture by Kim, who has consistently been reticent about personal matters.

Y-HK

Kincaid, Jamaica (*b.* 1949) Antiguan-US novelist, essayist. Born Elaine Potter Richardson in St John's, Antigua, Kincaid emigrated to New York at the age of 16 to work as an *au pair*, an experience captured in her novel *Lucy* (1990). In 1976, after several years of freelance writing, she was hired at the *New Yorker*; she attributes her maturing as a writer to the tutelage of its editor William Shawn. The stories of *At the Bottom of the River* (1983), which includes the frequently anthologized 'Girl,' appeared first in this magazine. Her first novel *Annie John* (1985) lyrically recounts the troubled adolescence of a headstrong Antiguan girl and the force of a mother's love, or its lack; the latter is a recurrent theme in Kincaid's work. The novel *The Autobiography of My Mother* (1996) is a bleak account of the life endured by a Dominican woman determined to bear no children of her own. Like her nonfiction essay *A Small Place* (1988), *My Brother* (1997), which chronicles her half-brother's death from AIDS in Antigua, is a bitter meditation on Antigua and on the devastation colonialism wrought on the land and its inhabitants. *My Garden (Book)* (1999) is a collection of essays on gardening. Kincaid, winner of the Lannan Literary Award for fiction in 1999, lives in Bennington, Vermont with her husband, composer Allen Shawn, and their two children.

JSp

Kingsolver, Barbara (*b*. 1955) US novelist. Born in Annapolis, Maryland, writer and human rights advocate Kingsolver is known for her sensitive and dignified depictions of the ordinary working American. After she graduated magna cum laude from DePauw University in 1977, she earned an MS at the University of Arizona, studying physiology, ecology, and evolutionary biology. Her novels, many of which take place in the Southwest, have been praised for their lyrical prose and Kingsolver's humorous and tender narrative voice; they are concerned with family, relationships, and cultural identity. Her first novel, the critically acclaimed *The Bean Trees* (1988; *Los Angeles Times* Book Award), introduces the character of Taylor Greer, a woman who illegally adopts a young Cherokee girl named Turtle, an abandoned child and victim of sexual abuse. *Pigs in Heaven* (1993) follows this

story into a conflict between family bonds and cultural heritage as the Cherokee Tribe demands Turtle's return. *Animal Dreams* (1990) explores the reasoning behind people's political beliefs. *The Poisonwood Bible* (1998) shifts locale to the Congo in the late 1950s and early l960s, and follows Baptist preacher Nathan Price on his troubling journey of spiritual colonialism with his wife and daughters. Kingsolver has also published a work of nonfiction, *Holding the Line: Women in the Great Arizona Mine Strike of 1983* (1989).

DVT

Kingston, Maxine Hong (*b*. 1940) US novelist, memoirist, essayist. Born in Stockton, California, the daughter of Chinese immigrants, Kingston graduated with an AB in English from the University of California, Berkeley in 1962, earning a teaching certificate in 1965. She married Earl Kingston, an actor, in 1962; they have one son. After teaching in Hawaii for many years, Kingston is now a professor of creative writing at University of California, Berkeley. Her first book *The Woman Warrior: Memoirs of a Girlhood Among Ghosts* (1976), which won the National Book Critics Circle Award for nonfiction, is a unique blending of autobiography, biography, myth, and fiction. By retelling her mother's ghost stories and legends while telling her own story of growing up amid racism and sexism, Kingston seeks to understand her identity as a Chinese-American woman. In *China Men* (1980; National Book Award), she again juxtaposes fiction and fact while rewriting North American history from the perspective of her father and other Chinese men. With *Tripmaster Monkey: His Fake Book* (1989), an allusive and complex novel about an angry young Chinese-American playwright named Wittman Ah Sing, Kingston moved in a new direction, creating an Asian-American version of James Joyce's *Ulysses*.

JEM

Kirsch, Sarah (*b.* 1935) East German poet. Born in the Harz mountains, Kirsch studied biology in Halle and literature in Leipzig. While maintaining a strong attachment to the German Democratic Republic, she sought in her early works to reveal the contradictions and problems in existing East German society. In her first lyric anthology *Gespräch mit dem Saurier* ('Conversation with the Dinosaur,' 1965), she criticizes complacency and self-aggrandizement in GDR society. In *The Panther Woman* (1973), she expresses her dissatisfaction with the socialist government's paternalistic approach toward women's emancipation. After her public protest at Wolf Biermann's expatriation in 1977, Kirsch emigrated from the GDR to West Berlin. History, particularly of the Nazi period, memory, and time have remained recurring themes in her poems. In *Irrstern* ('Wandering Star,' 1986), bucolic scenes are suddenly interrupted by associations with the Holocaust, and the title poem of *Schneewärme* ('The Warmth of Snow,' 1989) characteristically examines the intrusion of history into nature. She typically supercedes established conventions of language, using ambiguous imagery, and treating serious themes in a playful, laconic, and enigmatic manner. Kirsch has published over twenty collections of poetry and has received a number of literary awards, including the Georg Büchner Prize in 1996.

CG

Kizer, Carolyn (*b.* 1925) US poet. Born in Spokane, Washington and raised in Los Angeles, Kizer graduated from Sarah Lawrence College in 1945, and continued her studies at Columbia University and the University of Washington, Seattle. Married twice, she has three children from her first marriage. In the mid-1950s, she studied poetry under Theodore Roethke. She founded the literary journal *Poetry Northwest*, and from 1966 to 1970 was the first director of the literature program for the newly founded National Endowment for the Arts. She has also taught at many universities in the US. Kizer lived in China from 1945 to 1946, and her verse shows the strong influence of Chinese poetry and philosophy. Her controlled and elegant poems often focus on the dualities and tensions in life, particularly those which women must confront. She won a Pulitzer Prize for *Yin* (1984); the subject of the volume is indicated by the title, which is Chinese for the 'feminine principle.' She focuses on women again in *Mermaids in the Basement: Poems for Women* (1984), which she paired with *The Nearness of You: Poems for Men* (1986). Other collections of poetry include *The Ungrateful Garden* (1961), *Knock Upon Silence* (1965), *Midnight Was My Cry* (1971), and *Harping On* (1996). *Carrying Over* (1988) is a collection of her translations of Chinese, Macedonian, Yiddish, and Urdu poetry.

DVI

Klüger, Ruth (*b.* 1931) Austrian-American autobiographer, poet. In 1992, the Vienna-born Ruth K. Angress, a professor of German literature at University of California, Irvine, published her autobiography *Still Alive* under her maiden name Klüger. In *Still Alive*, Klüger takes German-language discourse on the Holocaust to a new level by combining personal narrative and feminist cultural criticism. She writes about growing up Jewish in Vienna on the eve of the Nazi takeover, her imprisonment in Theresienstadt and Auschwitz, her difficult relationship with her mother, her experiences as a teenage immigrant in the US, and, finally, her confrontation with Germany in the 1980s. *Still Alive* caused a sensation in Germany. It received several literary prizes and made Klüger a celebrity. A Berkeley PhD, Klüger has also written several critical studies, including *Frauen lesen anders* ('Women Read Differently,' 1996) and *Von hoher und niedriger Literatur* ('On High-Culture and Low-Culture Literature,' 1996).

DCGL

Kogawa, Joy (*b.* 1935) Canadian poet, novelist. Daughter of Japanese-Canadians, Kogawa and her family were moved by the Canadian government from Vancouver to the interior of British Columbia during World War II. Her first book of poems *The Splintered Moon* (1967) demonstrates a taut, imagistic style, as does her second volume of poems *A Choice of Dreams* (1974). She documents a trip to Japan in the latter collection. While working as a writer in the Prime Minister's office in Ottawa from 1974 to 1976, Kogawa produced poems for *Jericho Road* (1977) and, later, *Woman in the Woods* (1985). The experience of bureaucracy resonates in her landmark novel *Obasan* (1981), a narrative that combines legislative documents with reminiscence in an account of Japanese internment during the war. Silences and evasions weave through this novel, which won the Books in Canada First Novel Award and the Canadian Authors' Association Book of the Year Award. *Itsuku* (1992) forms a sequel to *Obasan*; one of the minor characters from *Obasan*, Naomi, records her life on the Prairies and in Toronto. Secrecy combines with religious beliefs in *The Rain Ascends* (1995), where the plot centers on child abuse in a Christian minister's family. Kogawa lives in Vancouver.

AH

Kong Chi-yŏng (*b.* 1963) Korean fiction writer. An English major at Yŏnsei University, Seoul, Kong took part in student anti-government activism, feeling guilty about her upper-middle-class family background. Upon graduation, she worked for a while as a laborer in electronics factories. Beginning with her debut work 'Tongt'unŭn saebyŏk' ('The Dawn Breaking,' 1988), the recurring theme of her works is the experience of politically radicalized young Koreans of the 1980s. Her stories 'Human Decency' (1993) and 'Dream' (1993) pay tribute to political dissenters engaged in the anti-government resistance of the 1980s. Her controversial novel *Kodŭngŏ* ('Mackerel,' 1994) describes the purity, idealism, and pains of the 1980s college students, who prioritized communal/political over private/personal, while contrasting the ethos of the 1990s as self-centered, shallow, and empty. Her novel *Muso ŭi ppul ch'ŏrŏm honjasŏ kara* ('Go Alone Like the Horns of a Rhinoceros,' 1993), about unconventional young Korean women of today who make light of gender relationships, marriage, and divorce, spotlighted Kong as a leading feminist writer despite her disclaimer. The novel became an immediate commercial success and was made into a popular movie.

Y-HK

Königsdorf, Helga (*b.* 1938) German fiction writer, essayist. Daughter of a farmer, Königsdorf studied physics and mathematics at the universities of Jena and Berlin. From 1974 to 1990, she was a professor of mathematics at the Academy of Sciences in East Berlin. Her short story collections *Meine ungehörigen Träume* ('My Impertinent Dreams,' 1978) and *Der Lauf der Dinge* ('The Way of the World,' 1982) deal with the role of women in society, including topics of love, marriage, the education of children, work, and self-realization. The novel *Respektloser Umgang* ('Irreverent Dealings,' 1986) depicts the life and work of the German scientist Lise Meitner. Since 1989, Königsdorf has repeatedly turned to problems associated with German unification. In her essay collections *1989 oder Ein Moment der Schönheit* ('1989 or a Moment of Beauty,' 1990) and *Unterwegs nach Deutschland. Über die Schwierigkeit, ein Volk zu sein* ('En route to Germany: The Problem of Being a Nation,' 1995), she views both East Germany and the united Germany critically but not without sympathy. Her recent novels *Im Schatten des Regenbogens* ('In the Shadow of the Rainbow,' 1993) and *Die Entsorgung der Großmutter* ('The Disposal of the Grandmother,' 1997) reflect satirically on the mechanisms of political systems and their influence on individuals.

PM-K

Kōno Taeko (*b.* 1926) Japanese novelist, fiction writer, literary critic. Born in Osaka, Kōno studied economics at Osaka Women's University until compulsory wartime factory work ended her formal education. Her award-winning first story 'Toddler Hunting' (1961) examines female sexuality and sadomasochism, integral themes in Kōno's fiction. In 1963, she won the Akutagawa Prize for her story 'Crabs,' which depicts a woman grappling with her feelings for her husband and her young nephew. The title story in her collection *Saigo no toki* ('The Last Time,' 1966), which won the Joryū Bungaku Prize, depicts the final day in the life of a woman preparing for death. Sadomasochism reappears in her stories 'Ants Swarm' (1964) and 'Bone Meat' (1971), as well as in her novel *Miiratori ryōkitan* ('Mummy-Hunting for the Bizarre,' 1991), which won the Noma Hiroshi Prize. Continuing her explorations into alternative sexual practices, she depicts the emotional effects of spouse-swapping in her novel *Kaiten tobira* ('Revolving Door,' 1970). 'Iron Fish' (1978) serves as a vivid depiction of the grief and loss that Japanese women experienced during the war from a postwar perspective. She has also written literary criticism on the works of Tanizaki Jun'ichirō.

KKo

Kostenko, Lina Vasylivna (*b.* 1930) Ukrainian poet. Born in Rzhyshchiv near Kiev, Kostenko is one of Ukraine's most accomplished poets, the leading representative of the 'Thaw' generation of the late 1950s and early 1960s. A Kiev resident for most of her life, she works as an editor. Her daughter Oksana Pakhl'ovs'ka (*b.* 1956) is also a poet and a literary critic. Kostenko's first collection, *Prominnia zemli* ('Earthly Rays,' 1957) was followed by *Vitryla* ('Sails,' 1958) and *Mandrivky*

sertsia ('Journeys of the Heart,' 1961). Enthusiastically received by readers, Kostenko's poetry was attacked in the official Soviet press for 'formalist tricks,' 'mannerism,' and 'sickly philosophising.' Unable to publish in her homeland until 1977, she finally overcame censorship to release a new collection of poetry, *Nad berehamy vichnoi riky* ('Above the Shores of the Eternal River'). Her historical novel in verse, *Marusia Churai* (1979), about the legendary seventeenth-century Ukrainian female folksinger-songwriter, won the Ukrainian State prize eight years later. In 1989, a major edition of her collected poetry finally saw the light, and the following year, a volume of her selected poetry in English translation, *Wanderings of the Heart*, was published. Kostenko's preoccupation with higher truths revealed in mundane events, her introspective focus, her constant search for spiritual freedom, and her transparent formal precision – as well as her hard fate – have elicited comparisons to the twentieth-century Russian poet Anna Akhmatova.

VC

Kozioł, Urszula (*b.* 1931) Polish poet, playwright, fiction writer. Born in Rakowka, Kozioł spent her childhood and adolescence in southeast Poland. Moving to Wroclaw in 1950 to study Polish literature, three years later she published her first poem, and shortly thereafter, her first collection of verse, *Gumowe klocki* ('Rubber Building Blocks,' 1957). Six additional volumes of original poetry, two novels, almost twenty theater and radio plays, a volume of short stories, and a collection of *feuilletons* followed. Having worked as a schoolteacher and freelance writer, in 1970 Kozioł joined the student theater Kalambur as a playwright and became the editor of the Polish literary journal *Odra*. A self-described outsider, she uses her poetry as a vehicle for discussing current sociopolitical issues in the context of larger conceptions of time, ethics, and traditions. Mythology, the culture of ancient Greece, and the native folklore of southeastern Poland constitute the powerful sources of imagery in her verse. Translations into English include *Poems* (1989) and entries in the anthologies *The New Polish Poetry* (1978), *Postwar Polish Poetry* (1983), *Ariadne's Thread: Polish Women Poets* (1988), and *Ambers Aglow: An Anthology of Polish Women's Poetry* (1996).

JB

Krall, Hanna (*b.* 1937) Polish journalist, prose writer. Lifelong resident of Warsaw, Krall is best known for exploring her Jewish ancestry and the tragedy of the Holocaust. A journalist by profession, since 1957 she has been publishing reportage in all the major Polish magazines and newspapers based on the life stories of ordinary people, as well as public figures. These pieces have been collected in six volumes (1972–90). During the past twenty years, her chief project has been documenting the lives of Polish Jews before, during, and after World War II and the Holocaust. Her most famous work is her book-length interview with Dr. Marek Edelman *The Last Surviving Leader of the Warsaw Ghetto Uprising* (1977), republished as *To Outwit God* (1992) in a collection with the same title. A Holocaust survivor herself, Krall has also written two semi-autobiographical novels, *The Subtenant* (1985) and *Okna* ('Windows,' 1987), based on her personal experience of having been saved by a Polish family. Her most recent books *Taniec na cudzym weselu* ('Dancing at Someone Else's Wedding,' 1993) and *Dowody na istnienie* ('Proofs of Existence,' 1995) are collections of reportage, in which the author traces the fates of Polish Jews.

JB

Kriseová, Eda (*b.* 1940) Czech prose writer. Born in Prague, daughter of an architect and a sculptor, Kriseová, after studying journalism at Charles University, worked as a reporter for the weekly *Mladý*

svět (Young World) until 1969. Losing her job in the political aftermath of the 1968 Soviet invasion, she became an active dissident and began writing fiction. During 1990–2, she was an adviser to President Vaclav Havel and wrote his biography (1991). Married to Josef Platz, a film and television director, she has two daughters. Inspired by her work in a village mental hospital, Kriseová's first novel, *Křížova cesta kočárového kočího* ('The Carriage Coachman's Calvary,' 1979; Egon Hostovsky Prize), as well as stories in the collections *Klíční kůstka netopýra* ('The Bat's Collar Bone,' 1982), *Sluneční hodiny* ('The Sundial,' 1990), and *Co se stalo . . .* ('What Happened,' 1991) combine the everyday with the grotesque, contrasting the 'freedom' of the inmates with the limitations of 'normal' totalitarian society. Her novel *Pompejanka* ('A Woman from Pompeii,' 1991), stories *Arboretum* (1987), and novella *Rybky raky* ('Fish and Crawfish,' 1991) focus on women's lives – to varying degrees lonely, unfulfilled, even despairing. Her latest novel *Kočíčí životy* ('Cat's Lives,' 1997), has a broad historical scope, depicting three generations of Volynian Czech women against the background of war and revolution.

ES

Krishnan, Rajam (*b.* 1925) Indian novelist, short story writer. Born in Tiruchi, Tamilnadu, Krishnan began her writing career in 1948 with the novel *Swarna Jyoti* ('Golden Light'). In the *New York Tribune*'s international short story competition held in 1950, her story 'Oosium Unarvum' ('Pins and Feelings') was chosen as the best short story in Tamil. Her most productive years began in 1960. She is an extremely prolific writer who has more than forty-five novels, several short story collections, essays, and biographies to her credit. Her writings, based on painstaking research, reflect the turbulent times. Her fiction, which takes the reader into hitherto unvisited spaces of body and mind, has broken new ground in Tamil fiction, in terms of both subject and style. Her subjects are often marginalized people like tribals, bandits, and children, and her novels are documents of social history as well as literature. The innermost feelings of people, especially women, are expressed in her fiction with rare perception and sensitivity. She has won several prestigious awards, including the Soviet Land Nehru Award in 1975. Her novel *Lamps in the Whirlpool* (1995) is available in English, and English translations of her stories are included in several anthologies. Krishnan lives far from the main city of Chennai in the quiet suburb of Tambaram.

                                                    CSL

Krisna Asokesin (Sukanya Cholasuek) (*b.* 1931) Thai novelist. One of Thailand's most prolific writers, Krisna Asokesin began writing at the age of 15 and has, to date, 117 novels and a countless number of short stories to her credit. After finishing high school, she spent two years studying at the Faculty of Commerce and Accountancy, Thammasat University. After seventeen years of working as a librarian at a government agency, she decided to retire and became a full-time writer. Though most of her earlier novels deal with domestic and family problems, her more recent ones touch on social and political themes. Krisna Asokesin is known for her sensitivity to human flaws and feelings and her vivid portrayal of characters. Two of her novels, *Rua Manut* ('This Human Vessel') and *Tawan Tok Din* ('Sunset'), which deal with human greed and lust, won the SEATO Literary Award in 1968 and 1972 respectively. In 1982, another novel *Poon Pid Thong* ('Disguised by Gold'), won the prestigious Southeast Asia (S.E.A.) Write Award. Krisna Asokesin was named National Artist in literature in 1988 and recently received the Gabriela Mistral medal from the Chilean government. In 1996, she was appointed senator, the first time such an honor has been given to a woman writer in Thai history.

                                                    NM

Kristeva, Julia (*b.* 1941) French-Bulgarian linguist, critic, novelist. Born in Bulgaria, Kristeva trained as a linguist before obtaining a scholarship to pursue her studies in Paris in 1966. She quickly established herself as a leading intellectual and published in the avant-garde journal *Tel Quel.* She married and later divorced the novelist Philippe Sollers. She teaches at the Université Paris VII and is Associate Professor at Columbia University. Her early publications were dense linguistic and semiological works such as *Revolution in Poetic Language* (1970), where she introduced the concept of 'the Semiotic,' and *Desire in Language* (1977). Among her best-known texts on gender are 'Women's Time' about the various generations of feminists, and 'Stabat mater' (in *Tales of Love*, 1983), where she combines a critique of dogmas about the Virgin Mary with her own experience of her son's birth. She has written on the psychoanalytical theories of abjection in *Powers of Horror* (1980) and depression in *Black Sun* (1987), and more recently, on the issues of racism, immigration, nationalism, and exile, and on Marcel Proust. She has also published three novels, *Samourais* (1990), which attempts to mirror Simone de Beauvoir's *The Mandarins,* and two police novels, *The Old Man and the Wolves* (1991) and *Possessions* (1996). Her latest publication is a correspondence with *Catherine Clément (1998).

                                                    JV

Kristof, Agota (*b.* 1935) Hungarian-Swiss novelist. Born and raised in Hungary, Kristof fled in 1956 to Switzerland, leaving behind her closest brother, Attila Kristof, also a writer. After her first poetic writing in Hungarian, she decided upon French as her literary medium. *The Notebook* (1986) begins the 'trilogy of the twins': two young brothers fend for themselves in an unnamed country ravaged by war and foreign occupation. They dutifully transcribe their fates in a common notebook. One of the twins will eventually cross the border westward. In *The Proof* (1988),

Lucas struggles alone in a repressed country, writing notes for his estranged brother, then disappears. In *The Book of Lies* (1991), Claus returns home forty years after his departure. His narration completely overthrows the preceding versions of the twins' lives. The trilogy is an allegory of Europe behind the Iron Curtain and dramatizes the twin-like alienation of the self in apparently different ideological settings. In *Yesterday* (1995), Kristof coldly portrays the impossibility of contemporary life in exile. Her world is dark, and her tone is one of resignation. For her characters, writing is not redemption but the only way to cope.

FC

Krohn, Leena Elisabeth (*b.* 1947) Finnish novelist, essayist, children's writer. Born in Helsinki, Krohn attended Helsinki University, where she studied philosophy, psychology, and literature. Her son Elias was born 1977. Her first published work, a book for children, *Vihreä Vallankumous* ('Green Revolution,' 1970) was co-authored with her sister Inari Krohn. She continued her fantasies for children with *Ihmisen Vaatteissa* ('In Human Clothing,' 1977), but her probing questions about truth and human existence gradually became poetic prose for adults. *Donna Quixote and Other City-Dwellers* (1983), a series of haunting vignettes, illuminates modern urban existence. Her critical breakthrough came with *Tainaron* (1985) which, written as letters from a world where all the citizens are insects, transforms scientifically accurate details into sensual metaphors that reexamine civilization. *Matemaattisia olioita tai Jaettuja Unia* ('Mathematical Creatures or Shared Dreams,' 1992), which won the 1993 Finlandia Prize, continues her enigmatic, though simple, allegories. *Salaisuuksia* ('Secrets,' 1992), a book for children and adults, won the 1993 Topelius Prize. As a political protest, she returned the 1997 Pro Finlandia award in 1998. Increasingly interested in how cyberspace redefines reality, she published *Sphinx or Robot*, a digital illustrated book, on the World Wide Web in 1996.

KMW

Kumin, Maxine (*b.* 1925) US poet, novelist, children's writer. Born in Philadelphia, Kumin was educated at Radcliffe College, where she received both a BA and MA. She married Victor Kumin, an engineering consultant, in 1946; they had three children. Her poems, frequently set in New England and grounded in the natural world, are often compared to those of Robert Frost. But her poetry is also rooted in the domestic world and she frequently writes about relationships, particularly those of parent and child, as well as about aging and mortality. Among her numerous collections of poetry are *Halfway* (1961), *The Privilege* (1965), *The Nightmare Factory* (1970), *House, Bridge, Fountain, Gate* (1975), *The Retrieval System* (1978), *Our Ground Time Here Will be Brief* (1982), *The Long Approach* (1985), *Nurture* (1989), *Looking for Luck* (1992), and *Connecting the Dots* (1996). In 1973, Kumin won the Pulitzer Prize for her collection *Up Country: Poems of New England, New and Selected* (1972). She has applied the wit and charm that characterizes her poetry to numerous books for children, four of which she wrote with her close friend, the poet *Anne Sexton. Kumin, who has taught or lectured at many universities in the US, is also the author of several novels, including *Through Dooms of Love* (1965), *The Designated Heir* (1974), and the mystery *Quit Monks or Die!* (1999).

DVT

Kurahashi, Yumiko (*b.* 1935) Japanese novelist, fiction writer, translator. Born in Kōchi prefecture, Kurahashi began writing while studying French literature at Meiji University. In 1966, she studied creative writing in Iowa as a Fulbright fellow. Her short story 'Partei' (1960; Joryū Bungaku Prize) satirizes the student activism of the

1960s. With her stories 'The End of Summer' (1960) and 'The Monastery' (1961), she intertwines passion and death with two love triangles. In 1963, she won the Tamura Toshiko Prize for her experimental writing style and social commentary. Her 1969 novel *The Adventures of Sumiyakist Q* satirizes political revolution and ideology. Kurahashi often plays with the notion of originality through references to other literary works. Her short story 'To Die at the Estuary' (1970) investigates the themes of aging and fate through allusions to Sophocles' *Oedipus at Colonus* and a Japanese essay on ephemerality, *Hojōki*. Her novel *Yume no ukihashi* ('The Bridge of Dreams,' 1971) presents a multi-layered depiction of spouse-swapping by alluding to *The Tale of Genji*. She won the Izumi Kyoka Prize with her fantastic novel *Amanonkoku Ōkanki* ('Journey to Amanon,' 1986), which depicts a man's experiences in the matriarchal society of Amanon.

KKo

Kuzwayo, Ellen (*b.* 1914) South African novelist, short story writer, activist. A mother and grandmother, divorced from her first husband, Kuzwayo was born in South Africa and obtained a first degree in social work at the University of Witwatersand, Johannesburg. She worked as a teacher and a social worker before beginning to write in her sixties, following the break-up of her marriage. She spent over three years writing her autobiographical novel *Call Me Woman* (1985), which pays tribute to the many South African women who are heroic but unacknowledged. She is active in Soweto community and political life and has won many awards among her people. She has helped in the making of two films: *Awake from Mourning* and *Tsiameto: A Place of Goodness*. Her collection of short stories *Sit Down and Listen: Stories from South Africa* (1990) reflects the lives of contemporary South Africans.

AUA

L

Laberge, Marie (*b*. 1950) Quebec dramatist, novelist. Born and raised in Quebec City, Laberge is the daughter of a professor. She spent two years studying journalism at Laval University before completing her studies at the Conservatory of Dramatic Arts (1972–5). Working as an actor and director in Quebec City, she soon started writing plays, teaching at various Quebec universities and drama schools, and serving as theatrical administrator. She moved to Montreal in the early 1980s. Having published the first of four novels in 1989, she has turned exclusively to fiction since 1994. Her plays, written in Québécois rather than international French, are characterized by a constant questioning of the human condition in a world that fails to fulfill basic emotional needs. She often portrays women as victims of conservative Catholic Quebec, which conditions women to subordinate personal needs to familial duties. The strong female protagonist of *C'était avant la guerre à l'Anse-à-Gilles* ('It Was before the War in Anse-à-Gilles,' 1981; Governor General's Award) rejects the traditional ideology of rural Quebec and moves to the city in search of future liberation, and the sisters of *Aurélie, ma soeur* ('Aurelia, My Sister,' 1988) triumph over family trauma and romantic disappointments by facing them together.

JM

Lacambra-Ayala, Tita (*b*. 1931) Philippine poet, short fiction writer. Lacambra-Ayala was born in Sarrat, Ilocos Norte and grew up in the mining village of Antamok, Mountain Province under the care of her maternal grandmother, who sang her lullabies and love songs. Her experiences in these places are distilled in her first poetry collection *Sunflower Poems* (1960). Her second collection *Ordinary Poems* (1969) is composed of imagist poems written in her characteristically spare style which heightens the ironic flavor in the quotidian. Married in 1955 to painter Jose V. Ayala, she moved to Mindanao with the family to settle permanently in Davao City. From this base she began editing and publishing in 1981 the art and poetry poster folio called Road Map Series, which was responsible for introducing Mindanao-based writers and visual artists to Philippine readers. The stories in her first collection of short fiction *Pieces of String and Other Stories* (1984) use minimalist narrative techniques, imbued with cutting wit and humor. *Camels and Shapes of Darkness in a Time of Olives* (1998) is a collection of poems which move through spaces and seasons of a mind that resists the dicta of the so-called 'Literature of Bitterness,' but always with humor and a tinge of tenderness. Lacambra-Ayala graduated from the University of the Philippines in 1953 with a bachelor's degree in education.

ME

Laina, Maria (b. 1947) Greek poet, drama-tist. Born in Patras, Laina is widely re-garded as one of the best writers of her generation. She studied law at the Uni-versity of Athens. She has published six collections of poetry to date: *Enilikiosi* ('Coming of Age,' 1968), *Epekina* ('Be yond,' 1970), *Allagi topiu* ('Change of Scene,' 1972), *Simia stikseos* ('Punctuation Marks,' 1979), *Hers* (1985), and *Rodinos fovos* ('Rose Colored Fear,' 1992), for which she received the National Literature Prize for Poetry (1994) and the City of Munich Literary Prize (1995). Her collec-tions involve a search for 'a place of her own,' a place that is 'hers.' The central problem is how to find a way to talk about a kind of love that others neither recognize nor approve of, a love that is 'strange.' As the introductory poem of *Hers* explains: 'The ground of love is missing.' She has also gained recognition for her theatrical pieces: *O kloun* ('The Clown,' 1985), *I pragmatikotita ine panta edo* ('Reality is Always Here,' 1990) and *Ena klefto fili* ('A Stolen Kiss,' 1966). Her translations include the short stories of Katherine Mansfield and critical writings by Ezra Pound and T. S. Eliot.

KVD

C.S. Lakshmi (*see* Ambai)

Lander, Leena (b. 1955) Finnish novelist, playwright. Born in Turku, Lander (a pseudonym for Leena Silander) earned a BA before she published her first novel *Syyspastoraali* ('Autumn Pastoral,' 1982). Her first six novels were historical ro-mances. In 1986, she began also to write radio and television plays. Her writing shifted in *Tummien Perhosten Koti* ('Home of the Dark Butterflies,' 1991), and she won critical acclaim for the som-ber, dark story centered on young boys liv-ing in a reformatory. Translated into nine languages, the novel, nominated for the 1991 Finlandia Prize, was rewritten for the theatre in 1993. *Tulkoon Myrsky* ('Tulko's Storm,' 1994) part thriller, part romance

novel, part geology textbook, part myth-ology reader, further revealed her skill at creating novels that have wide appeal and earn critical acclaim, including a second nomination for the Finlandia Prize and first nomination for the Nordic Council's literature prize. *Cast a Long Shadow* (1995) continued her signature style of large traditional novels with postmodern subjects. *Iloisen Kotiinpalun Asuinsijat* ('The Tabernacles of the Joyous Home-coming,' 1997), also nominated for the Nordic Council prize, tells a story about mining in Olkikumpu and a family's fate in the shadow of the mountain.

KMW

Lapid, Shulamit (b. 1934) Israeli novelist, dramatist. Lapid's popular novel *Gei Oni* ('Valley of My Strength/Grief,' 1982), was the first Israeli book to be labeled 'feminist.' Its feminism is displaced, however, by its setting in Palestine of the 1890s, thereby establishing a precedent in Israeli fiction for masking feminist protest by historical distancing. A gradu-ate of the Hebrew University, she con-tinued her probe into history in *Kaheres hanishbar* ('As a broken Vessel,' 1984). She finally turned to the contemporary scene, featuring a 'new Israeli woman' in a series of four thrillers (1989–96). Detective Lizzi Badihi, a single young woman whose priorities are work and love (with no strings attached and in this order), is a popular heroine. Similar male-modeled feminism also underlies some of Lapid's translated work, such as 'The Bed,' a story about a 'counter-rape' in which expected gender roles are reversed (in '*Akavishim smehim* ['Happy Spiders,' 1990]). While her earlier stories – *Mazal Dagim* ('Pisces,' 1969) and 5 other col-lections – were much more traditional, her recent work – the plays *Rekhush natush* ('Abandoned Property,' 1991) and *Rehem pundaki* ('Surrogate Mother,' 1991), and the novel '*Etzel Babu* ('Chez Babu,' 1998) – is marked by both social and feminist consciousness. 'A happily married (grand)mother,' in her own words, and former Chair of the Hebrew Writers' Association, Lapid has also published poems and children's books.

YSF

Larsen, Marianne (*b.* 1951) Danish poet, novelist. Born in Kalundborg, Larsen studied Chinese at the University of Copenhagen and translated a collection of Lu Xun's poems into Danish. Her first work *Koncentrationer* ('Concentrations,' 1971) is a collection which blends poems rich in imagery with surrealistic prose works. Larsen, a writer with Marxist convictions, speaks for the oppressed and downtrodden and believes that language functions as an integral part of societal oppression. Her conception of human isolation is often reflected in a fractured word order and lack of connection in her early work. *Ravage* ('Disorder,' 1973) and *Sætninger* ('Sentences,' 1974) are systemic collections, with insistence on language as the source for experiencing the world. In collections such as *Fælluvssprog* ('Common Language,' 1975), *Handlinger* ('Actions,' 1976), and others, she uses a variety of lyric forms for different purposes. Her latest work is a collection of prose poems *I en venten hvid som sne* ('In a Waiting White as Snow,' 1996). She has also written several novels, including the trilogy *Gæt hvem der elsker dig* ('Guess Who Loves You,' 1989), *Fremmed lykke* ('Foreign Joy,' 1990) and *Galleri Virkeligheden* ('Gallery of Reality,' 1992), about a provincial girl's education and encounters with the women's movement, first love, and the Copenhagen of the 1970s and 1980s. Larsen has won numerous Danish literary awards. *Selected Poems* (1982) is available in English.

MHH

Lê, Linda (*b.* 1963) Vietnamese francophone novelist. Lê was born in Dalat, the French-founded 'mountain-station' in South Vietnam. She began her study of French in Franco-Vietnamese schools in Saigon. In 1977, she emigrated to France, where she later pursued graduate work in French literature at the Sorbonne. She stopped writing her doctoral dissertation to devote more time to her creative writing. She now rejects her first two novels, *Un si tendre vampire* ('So Tender a Vampire,' 1987) and *Fuir* ('Escape,' 1988), which were followed by *Solo* (1989), a collection of abstract and enigmatic short narratives. A period of silence ended in 1992 with the publication of *Les évangiles du crime* ('The Books of Crime'), a stunning departure from her earlier work but foreshadowed by *Solo*. *Slander* (1993), *Les dits d'un idiot* ('The Words of an Idiot,' 1995), and *Les trois Parques* ('The Three Fates,' 1997) continue her narrative experiments. A refugee, interloper, and writer, Lê is present in her work, yet she struggles against the easy and expected autobiographical impulse. In *Voix* ('Voice,' 1998), she captures her psychological breakdown. She is currently working on the third part of a trilogy started with *Les trois Parques*.

JY

Leclerc, Annie (*b.* 1940) French novelist, essayist. Leclerc grew up in a bourgeois suburb of Paris. She studied and taught philosophy. In the early 1970s, she became active in the French women's liberation movement. Her first novel *Le pont du Nord* ('The North Bridge,' 1967) is about the sentimental education of a young woman. *Parole de femme* ('Woman's Word,' 1974) is a powerful poetical manifesto which anticipates the birth of a new woman, especially regarding female sexuality and the female body. *Epousailles* (1976) pursues the same reflection, broadened to include recognizing pleasure in simple occasions. She collaborated with *Madeleine Gagnon and *Hélène Cixous for the publication of *Coming to Writing* (1977) with her essay 'The Love Letter', inspired by a painting by Vermeer. In *Hommes et femmes* ('Men and Women,' 1985), she envisions new relationships founded in love between the sexes. *Le mal de mère* ('Mother Sickness,' 1986) is a collection of original short stories. Her masterful use of the language through puns and polysemy allows her to throw a caustic light on several aspects of society, among them the mother–daughter relationship and the idealization of the role of grandmothers. She is also known for interviewing "Marie Cardinal for *In Other Words* (1977).

JV

Leduc, Violette (1907–1972) French novelist, autobiographer. Born to a bourgeois father who refused to recognize her and a working-class mother who never forgave her for being born, Leduc's writings stage a quest for love and validation. She held various jobs before publishing *In the Prison of Her Skin* (1946). This brutal series of childhood vignettes earned her the lifelong mentorship of Simone de Beauvoir and respect of Sartre, Camus, and Genet. *L'Affamée* (1948) chronicles Leduc's unrequited passion for de Beauvoir. *Ravages* (1955) follows Thérèse and her lovers Isabelle, Cécile and Marc. Sexually explicit, the 'Isabelle' part of the book was censored. It was published later (1966) and made into a film, *Thérèse and Isabelle* (1968). Leduc achieved fame with her international best-seller *La Bâtarde: an Autobiography* (1964), telling her life from being an illegitimate child to being born as a writer. *Mad in Pursuit* (1970), about writing and life in literary Paris, and *La chasse à l'amour* ('The Hunt for Love,' 1973), relate her life through 1963. Her last work was *The Taxi* (1971).

ELo

Lee Geok Lan (*b*. 1939) Malaysian poet. Lee is often cited as one of the first Anglophone Malaysian women poets. She was born in Malacca and completed her BA (Honors) in English at the University of Malaya in Kuala Lumpur in the early 1960s. She taught English for twenty years. She was first published in 1958 in a student magazine, and later, in various literary magazines and journals like *Tenggara* and *Westerly*. However, Lee achieved international recognition when she was included in *Bunga Emas: An Anthology of Contemporary Malaysian Literature (1930–1963)* (1964); she was the only woman poet in the anthology. Her early poems are preoccupied with questions of identity, loss of innocence, and matters of relationships and human ties. These can be seen in poems like 'Credo,' 'Crossroads,' 'Cartoon,' and 'Song of Lily' (all published in the 1960s). In recent years, Lee has addressed contemporary issues like globalization, the impact of Westernization on local cultures, and the problems of immigrants becoming detached from their root-culture. This is evident in 'Violin Recital,' 'The Barbecue,' and 'Gone Overseas' (published in the 1970s), in which Lee questions the hypocrisy and pretense of Malaysian bourgeoisie who adopt Western aesthetics without fully understanding Western cultures and traditions or the richness of local traditions. Her acute understanding of people in their surroundings enables her to record effectively and convincingly Malaysian characters and foibles, making her work relevant and contemporary.

NFAM

Lee Tzu Pheng (*b*. 1946) Singaporean poet. Born and educated in Singapore, Lee is a Senior Lecturer in the English department of the National University of Singapore. Three of her poetry collections, *Prospect of Drowning* (1980), *Against the Next Wave* (1988), and *The Brink of an Amen* (1991), won National Book Development Council awards, and are widely anthologized and taught in college-level courses. Characterized by a quiet intensity, Lee's poems often reflect a feminist sensibility which is more controlled than it is controlling. She is also a strong advocate for the promotion of children's literature, and has been featured as a storyteller on television. In *Growing Readers* (1987), she recommends various ways to nurture a love of reading among the young. Her fourth collection of poems *Lambada by Galilee and Other Surprises* was published in 1997. For her contribution to poetry and children's reading, Lee was presented with the Gabriela Mistral Award by the Government of Chile in 1996. She also received the Singapore Cultural Medallion in 1985 and the Southeast Asia (S.E.A.) Write Award in 1987.

MHo

van Leeuwen, Joke (*b.* 1952) Dutch children's writer, novelist, poet. Van Leeuwen has developed her idiosyncratic talents in many different ways: as a novelist, an artist, and as an author of children's books. In her work, she fully exploits the use of children's language and logic. She has been praised for her witty and unusual plots and unsurpassed wordplay, as well as for the brilliant interweaving of her drawings and texts. Her book *Iep!* (1997), a highpoint in her oeuvre, is a philosophical and witty story about the wonders of creation, the need for selfless love and the freedom to go your own way. Her books have been translated into many languages. *Look, Listen and Play* (1984) is a highly entertaining book full of games, jokes and songs. *The Story of Bobble Who Wanted to be Rich* (1987) relates the adventures of Bo-belle (Bobble for short) who is the child of unorthodox, nomadic, poor, but happy parents.

AAn, MMe

Le Guin, Ursula K. (*b.* 1929) US science fiction writer, fantasy writer. Raised in Berkeley, California by her writer mother and her anthropologist father, Le Guin has combined her own interests in science and literature through her prolific career as a science fiction writer. She studied medieval romance literature at Radcliffe College and received an MA from Columbia University. Her books demonstrate her fascination with a range of scientific disciplines, from physics to anthropology. Her acclaimed 'Earthsea Cycle,' popular with

adolescent as well as adult audiences, contains four novels: *A Wizard of Earthsea* (1968), *The Tombs of Atuan* (1971), *The Farthest Shore* (1973), and *Tehanu* (1990). In the award-winning *The Left Hand of Darkness* (1969), which features a species of nongendered humanoids who can periodically develop the characteristics of either sex, Le Guin challenges conventional ideas about sex and gender. Her interests in feminism and environmentalism have shaped many of her novels, such as *Always Coming Home* (1985). Through the invented worlds in her novels, she creates new social orders with new ethics, taboos, myths, and histories and in so doing, she critiques contemporary social and political issues. Other works include *Rocannon's World* (1966), *Planet of Exile* (1966), *City of Illusions* (1967), *The Lathe of Heaven* (1971), *The Dispossessed* (1974), *Orsinian Tales* (1976), and *Malfrena* (1979). Le Guin has also published *Dancing at the Edge of the World* (1989), a collection of essays, speeches and book reviews.

DVT

Le Minh Khue (*b.* 1949) Vietnamese short story writer, editor. Born in Thanh Hoa, south of Hanoi, Le Minh Khue spent most of her youth on the Ho Chi Minh trail. She lost her parents at a very young age and was raised by an aunt and uncle. At fifteen, she joined the Vietnamese People's Army. From 1969 to the last day of the Vietnam War in 1975 she was a correspondent for *Tien Phong* ('The Vanguard') magazine. She has written several novellas and many volumes of short stories. She draws on the themes of love and war, the complexities of human nature, and the moral and emotional impact of postwar life. Her first story 'Distant Stars '(1971), written when she was 19, depicts the friendship of three young teenagers living in a cave. 'A Blue Sky' (1986) is set during the war. Themes of love and nostalgia are present in 'A Very Late Afternoon' (1990) and 'Fragile as a Sunray' (1992), whereas 'An Evening Away from the City' (1982) examines friendship and the change in human nature as society changes. Recurring themes including human greed, corruption, and materialism as in 'The Coolie's Tale' (1989) and 'The Almighty Dollar' (1990). She won the Writers'Association National Award for the best stories in 1987. She co-edited the anthology *The Other Side of Heaven* (1995). Le Minh Khue lives in Hanoi, where she is an editor of the Writers' Association Publishing House.

TT

Lemsine, Aïcha (*b.* 1942) Algerian novelist. Married in 1976 and mother of three, Lemsine writes using a pseudonym composed of the Arabic letters 'L' (Lem) and 'S' (Sin) which stand for her and her husband's surnames. Her first novel *The Chrysalis* (1976), which depicts the daily lives of several generations of Algerian women during the period of the War of Independence, speaks out against the traditions that stifle women in a male-dominated society: arranged marriages, polygamy, the practice of repudiation, and the pressure to bear children, especially sons. The themes of suffering and solidarity recur in *Beneath a Sky of Porphyry* (1978). Set in an Algerian village between the 1950s and the 1970s, this second novel focuses more specifically on the war, the role played by the National Liberation Front, and the mixture of violence and idealism that characterized the struggle. Lemsine is also the author of an essay titled *Ordalie des voix* ('Voices of Testimony,' 1983). Based on a series of interviews, this work examines the position of Muslim women in eleven Muslim countries, with particular emphasis on issues of education, polygamy, female circumcision, and the veil.

SIr

L'Engle, Madeline (*b.* 1918) US children's writer, novelist, poet, essayist. An imaginative only child who loved reading and writing stories, L'Engle was born in New York City, and grew up in a musical and literary household. She graduated with honors from Smith College in 1941. She married and raised three children while establishing herself as a writer. Her first novel *The Small Rain* (1945) depicts a young woman torn between love and her career; in the sequel *A Severed Wasp* (1982), L'Engle revisits the woman at the end of her career. L'Engle is best known for her several series of books for young readers. *Meet the Austins* (1960), the first book of the first series, was named the American Library Association's Book of the Year. Her most famous series, the science fiction 'Time Trilogy,' is comprised of *A Wrinkle in Time* (1962; Newbery Award), *A Wind in the Door* (1973), and *A Swiftly Tilting Planet* (1978), and depicts the travels through time and space of the Murry children. Many of her books are infused with theology, but in oblique or unconventional ways: her characters struggle to discern right from wrong, and learn to see divinity in individuality and creativity. A prolific writer, L'Engle has also published many volumes of poetry, essays, and memoirs, most notably *The Crosswicks Journal* series.

DVT

Lessing, Doris (*b.* 1919) British novelist, short story writer, playwright. Lessing was born in Kermanshah, Persia (Iran) and grew up in the British colony of Rhodesia (Zimbabwe). She dropped out of school at the age of 14 and later became active in the Communist Party and the racial politics of South Africa. After her divorce from her second husband in 1949, she moved to London. She has written over twenty works of fiction, including five science fiction novels in the 'Canopus in Argos' series; eight works of nonfiction; three plays; a libretto based on *The Making of the Representative of Planet 8*, for an opera by Philip Glass; several collections of short stories; and two volumes of autobiography – *Under My Skin* (1994) and *Walking in the Shade* (1997). Her first novel *The Grass is Singing* (1950) is a powerful examination of the sexual and racial conflicts experienced by a colonial woman living in rural Rhodesia. Lessing shifted from social realism to a style that was more experimental, mystical, and feminist in her 'Children of Violence' series, which began with the feminist *Bildungsroman Martha Quest* (1952) and continued with four more novels. Her best-known novel *The Golden Notebook* (1962) was a landmark of the new wave of feminism; it also signaled her disillusion with politics and break with conventional narrative structure. Stylistic experimentation continued in her fiction of the 1970s and 1980s, in which she explores psychology and prophecy in a range of genres and styles, from science fiction such as *Memoirs of a Survivor* (1979), to fantasy, as in *The Fifth Child* (1986), to the political realism of *The Good Terrorist* (1985).

AUA, JEM

Levertov, Denise (1923–1998) US poet, essayist, translator. Born and raised in England, daughter of a Russian Jew who converted to become an Anglican minister, Levertov never received any formal education. Her Welsh mother educated her at home and introduced her to poetry. During World War II, Levertov worked as a nurse before marrying American novelist Mitchell Goodman and returning with him to the US. Her poetry, written in free verse and emphasizing simple language and the immediacy of perception, was influenced by William Carlos Williams, H. D., and the Black Mountain poets. Her poetic works can be divided roughly into two modes – spiritual, exemplified by *Evening Train* (1992), and political, exemplified by *To Stay Alive* (1971) – although in actuality, the two modes often overlap. Her many books of poetry include *The Double Image* (1946), *Here and Now* (1956), *With Eyes at the Back of Our Heads* (1960), *The Jacob's Ladder* (1961), *O Taste and See* (1964), *The Freeing of the Dust* (1975), *Life in the Forest* (1978), and

Breathing the Water (1987). The volumes *The Sorrow Dance* (1967), *Relearning the Alphabet* (1970), and *Candles in Babylon* (1982) all have anti-war themes. Levertov also translated poetry, served as the poetry editor of the *Nation*, and published several collections of essays.

DVT

Li Ang (*b.* 1952) Chinese-Taiwan fiction writer. Born Shi Shuduan in Lugang, an old immigrant town in Taiwan, Li Ang is the youngest of three well-known sisters in Taiwan's literary circle, the other two being literary critic Shi Shunü and novelist *Shi Shuqing. Li Ang earned a BA in philosophy at the University of Chinese Culture in Taipei, and an MA in theater at the University of Oregon. She currently teaches in the Department of Theater at the University of Chinese Culture in Taipei. One of the most controversial and popular women writers in Taiwan, she is well-known for her highly charged fiction. Starting from the age of 17, she has published a series of stories, including the erotic and provocative 'Flower Season'(1968) and 'Love Letters Never Sent'(1986). Her internationally acclaimed novellas *The Butcher's Wife* (1983), *Yanye* ('The Dark Night,' 1985), and *Miyuan* ('The Labyrinth Garden,' 1991) evoked shock and outrage in her native Taiwan for their audacity in portraying sex and erotic pleasures. A firm believer in the importance of social changes, Li Ang takes an active part in the Taiwan women's movement and dissident political activities. *The Butcher's Wife* has been translated into several languages. Her latest book *Shi Mingde qing zhuan* ('A Biography of Shi Mingde'), is a biography of the Taiwan political dissident.

F-yM

Li Li (*b.* 1948) Chinese-Taiwan fiction writer. Also writing under the pen name Xue Li, Li Li was born in Nanjing, China, but moved to Taiwan with her parents in 1949. She received a BA in history from

National Taiwan University in 1969 and then studied political science at Purdue University. Like many overseas Chinese students from Taiwan, she was driven by patriotism and idealism to participate in the student movement, known as 'Protecting the Diaoyutai Movement,' protesting Japan's territorial claim to certain islands in the East China Sea in 1970–1. Because of the leftist orientation of the movement, Li was blacklisted by the Guomintang (Nationalist Party) and was not allowed to enter Taiwan until 1985. She now lives in California. Her work provides probing insights into the cultural identity crises that torment many diasporic Chinese intellectuals and the inner struggle and disillusionment that they often experience as a result of the conflict between ideals and reality. In addition to fiction she writes essays and translates Western literary works into Chinese. One of her novels, *Daishu nanren* ('The Kangaroo Man,' 1992), has been made into a movie in Taiwan. English translations of her work are available in several anthologies.

MY

Li Lienfung (*b.* 1923) Singaporean playwright, essayist. Born and educated in Shanghai, Li has remained firmly anchored to China through her cultural roots, despite a lifetime spent first in the US and later in Thailand and Singapore. As a schoolgirl, one of her essays was published as part of the influential anthology *A Day in China* (1937) edited by Guo Mo-Ro. Armed with a BA in chemistry from Mills College and an MA from Cornell University, Li went to Thailand with her husband in 1948 and worked there as a chemist for over two decades, while continuing to write poems and short stories in Chinese. After settling in Singapore in the early 1970s, Li wrote a bilingual (English/Chinese) newspaper column, 'Bamboo Green,' sharing with a whole generation of Singaporeans her own appreciation of Chinese literature. Her first play in English, *The Sword Has Two Edges* (1979),

revolves around a historically based fifth-century Chinese heroine caught in the palace intrigue of her time. Li has also written several plays in Chinese for the stage and the TV screen.

MHo

Lidman, Sara (*b.* 1923) Swedish novelist, documentary writer. The youngest of five children, Lidman grew up in Missenträsk in northern Sweden, listening to her father's and paternal grandmother's stories. In 1949, after graduating from the University of Uppsala, she worked as a teacher. Through her encounter with South Africa, Kenya, and Vietnam in the 1960s and 1970s, she became politically involved. In 1977, she returned to her native village. Her first book *Tjärdalen* ('The Tar Pit,' 1953) depicts survival and solidarity in a small northern village, while questioning issues of guilt and atonement, morality and responsibility – questions characteristic of Lidman's entire oeuvre. *The Rain Bird* (1958) and the sequel *Bära mistel* ('Carrying Mistletoe,' 1960) follow the life of Linda, whose magic power destroys those around her and finally herself. Colonialism is the subject of *Jag och min son* ('I and My Son,' 1961) and *Med fem diamanter* ('With Five Diamonds,' 1964), both set in Africa. The documentary writings *Samtal in Hanoi* ('Conversations in Hanoi,' 1966) were followed by *Gruva* ('Mine,' 1968), in which the voices of Swedish iron miners are heard and which, supposedly, brought about a strike two years later. In the five-volume Norrland railway suite (1977–85), Lidman combines her early regionalism with international concerns. The second volume, *Naboth's Stone* (1981), won her the Nordic Council's Literary Prize.

GE-C

Lie, Sissel (*b.* 1942) Norwegian novelist, children's writer. Born in Kristiansand and trained in literary studies at the University of Oslo, Lie began writing with friends in an informal café group. Her first literary work *Tigersmil* ('Tiger Smiles,' 1986), a collection of short stories, won the prestigious *Tarjei Vesaas debutantpris*. Her academic work as professor of Romance languages and literature in Trondheim enriches her complex fictions in which fantasy, folklore, and history are interwoven, such as the novels *Granateple* ('Pomegranate,' 1990), *Reise gjennom brent sukker* ('Journey through Scorched Sugar,' 1992) and *Lion's Heart* (1988), a surrealistic dialogue between a frustrated female writer in the 1980s and the exotic poetess Louise Labé in sixteenth-century France. Likewise *Rød svane* ('Red Swan,' 1994), set in America's frontier days, juxtaposes a European mother and daughter's differing views of their abduction and erotic experiences with Native American men. *Svart due* ('Black Dove,' 1997) explores the chasm between a menopausal woman's fascination with celestial movements and creation myths and her estranged husband's preoccupation with mundane events and tabloid tragedies. Lie has also published scholarly books and articles, anthologies, and several children's books featuring 'Pusegutt,' a fat, intrepid cat.

FS

Lieblich, Amia Israeli writer. Professor of psychology at the Hebrew University in Jerusalem, Lieblich is a novelist and creator of metafictional biographies. She was born in Israel, the daughter of a religious family. Her first work of psychotherapy *Hayalei bedil al hof yerushalayim* ('Tin Soldiers on the Jerusalem Shore,' 1979) was dramatized. She is best known for her investigations into the lives of two women poets, Devora Baron and Leah Goldberg. *Rikmot, sihotay im Devora Baron* ('Conversations with Devora Baron,' 1991) and *El Leah* ('To Leah,' 1995) have strong foundations in fact but include fictional elements. Her technique of 'biography' written from the point of view of a psychologist rather than a literary scholar or critic, is new to Israeli literature. In the case of Leah Goldberg, she built the poet's

character piece by piece based, among other sources, on Goldberg's diaries. Throughout, Lieblich charts her own process of discovery and writing. Her method combines research into the poet's life, mapping her own growing knowledge of her subject, and some fictional material including, in the case of Baron, fictional interviews.

GAb

Liebrecht, Savyon (*b.* 1948) Israeli short story and scriptwriter. Born in Munich to Holocaust survivors, Liebrecht grew up in Israel. She studied philosophy and English literature at Tel Aviv University. Her participation in *Amalia Kahana-Carmon's writing workshop led to the publication of her first work *Tapuhim min hamidbar* ('Apples from the Desert,' 1986), winner of the 1987 Alterman Prize for Literature. Several of her stories explore the aftermath of the Holocaust, issues of survival, memory, and family conflict. Often it is the grandchild who allows the survivor to break the silence. Many of her stories probe relationships within the family: the parents' bewilderment with their children, complications between husband and wife, revelation and the possibilities of reconciliation. Short story collections *Susim 'al kevish gehah* ('Horses on the Highway,' 1988), *Sinit ani medaberet elekha* ('It's Greek to Me, She Said to Him,' 1992), *Tsarikh sof lesipur ahavah* ('On Love Stories and Other Endings,' 1995), and the novel *Ish ve-ishah ve-ish* ('A Man, A Woman and A Man,' 1998) have followed her first book. Selections from her first three collections have been translated into English and published by the Feminist Press as *Apples from the Desert* (1998).

NEB

Likimani, Muthoni (*b.* 1926) Kenyan novelist, verse writer. Likimani grew up in a religious household in Kenya. She was educated to the secondary school level in Kenya and later studied in England, where she became interested in educational broadcasting and advertising. Before becoming a writer, she was a teacher and a popular broadcaster and producer in Kenya. Although now a full-time writer, she also maintains an advertising and promotion business in Kenya. She writes fiction primarily, although her book *What Does A Man Want* (1974), which focuses on the traditional struggles between men and women, is a collection of free-verse monologues. Her other publications include *They Shall Be Chastised* (1974), a semi-autobiographical novel of a child growing up in a church environment; *Shangazi na Watoto* ('Aunt and Children'), a work in Swahili; and *Passbook Number F47927: Women and Mau Mau in Kenya* (1985), largely considered her most ambitious work. Written from the feminine perspective, *Passbook* explores the role of women during the Mau Mau Revolution. Likimani is a natural storyteller and a keen observer of events – qualities which have led to her success as a broadcaster and a writer.

KEJ

Liking, Werewere (*b.* 1950) Cameroonian dramatist, poet, novelist. An autodidact, Liking was born in Bondè and raised by her paternal grandparents. She lives and directs her theater troupe Ki-Yi in Abidjan, Ivory Coast. In her drama *The Power of Um* (1979) and in *A New Earth: African Ritual Theater* (1980), she presents Um as the complex cosmic force, of which all individuals are a part, that gives order to the universe. She again explores the quest for Um in the novels *Elle sera de jaspe et de corail* ('She Will Be of Jasper and Coral,' 1983) and *L'amour cent-vies* ('Love-One Hundred-Lives,' 1988). She blends oral traditions and Western stylistic devices to probe the mores of modern African society in *A la rencontre de: Contes d'initiation feminine du pays Bassa* ('Encountering: Female Initiation Tales of the Bassa,' 1980) and the novel/theater piece *Orphée-dafric* ('African Orpheus,' 1981). *Spectacles rituels* ('Ritual Dramas,'

1987) recreates the ritual content of Bassa initiation rites for performance on stage. She further examines the future of Africa(ns) within the postcolonial world in *Un Touareg s'est marié à une pigmée* ('A Tuareg has married a Pigmy,' 1992). She recently released a film, *Regard de fous* ('Madmen's Gaze,' 1998).

JMN-A

Liksom, Rosa (*b.* 1958) Finnish fiction writer, performance artist, painter. Rosa Liksom (the pseudonym of Annu Ylävaara), born and raised in Lapland in northern Finland, moved to Helsinki as an adult. Her first book, a collection of short stories *Yhden Yön Pysäkki* ('A Stop for One Night,' 1985) describes nameless people existing in dead end, often morbid, situations. *Station Gagarin* (1987) juxtaposes fantasy and folk tales with jarring, contemporary Soviet life. In *Go Moskova Go* (1988), a travel book, Liksom collaborated with photographer Jukka Uotila to depict, without judgement, young Russians' empty world. *One Night Stands* (1990), an expanded version of her first book, consciously strips away coherence and meaning, and, like her naïve, brightly colored paintings, purposefully hides any seriousness. Life at the end of the millennium is ironic. Although her writing, translated into the major European languages, has made her popular, she has maintained strict anonymity, posing only for photos which hide her identity. Artifice is all. Her first novel *Kreisland* (1997), written as eight monologues in the author's own Northern Finnish dialect, tells the story of a woman who moves in a world dominated by the brutal and the banal, the past and the present, the rural and the urban.

KMW

Lim, Catherine (*b.* 1942) Singaporean novelist, short story writer. Among Singapore's earliest and most popular prose writers, Lim has published eight collections of short stories, two novels, and a book of poems. In *Little Ironies* (1978), she depicts contemporary Singaporeans with light humor and deft strokes, endearing her to a postcolonial readership newly literate in English and eager to find empathetic portrayals of themselves reflected in fiction. In her later work, however, Lim has tended to explore the more tradition-bound milieu of the 1950s. Her novel *The Bondmaid* (1977) revolves around the doomed love between a master and his servant girl in an ossified Chinese household in the Singapore of the 1950s. The novel has been translated and published in ten countries, including the US. Her newest novel *The Teardrop Woman* (1998) is also a love story set in the 1950s; it centers on the forbidden passion between a Chinese woman and a French priest in an exoticized Malaya. Lim was the 1999 recipient of the prestigious Southeast Asia (S.E.A.) Write Award. She holds a PhD in applied linguistics and lectures at the Regional Language Centre in Singapore, as well as at seminars and conferences abroad. She also contributes articles on contemporary issues to local and international newspapers.

MHo

Lim, Shirley Geok-lin (*b*. 1944) Asian-American poet, short story writer, critic. Lim was born in Malacca, Malaysia (then Malaya). She studied English at the University of Malaya and taught at Brandeis University, Queens College, and Westchester College before completing her PhD at Brandeis in 1973. She is now a professor of English and women's studies at the University of California, Santa Barbara. She has been the recipient of several prestigious fellowships and has won numerous literary awards, including the 1980 Commonwealth Poetry Prize, making her the first woman and the first Asian to win the prize. In *Crossing the Peninsula and Other Poems* (1980), Lim writes of the conflict, felt by women, between submitting to male desire, male needs, and male ascendancy, and their own awareness that they

have separate needs, desires, and goals. In *No Man's Grove* (1985) and *Modern Secrets* (1989), Lim moves away from particularism and celebrates universalism, as she writes of nature, the mutability of time, and emotions ranging from love to hate, as well as themes related to the plight of women. She has been likened to *Maxine Hong Kingston and *Amy Tan for breaking the long silence of an ethnic group, as in her memoir *Among the White Moon Faces* (1996), in which she speaks courageously and frankly of the 'clash of cultures' between Asia (Malaysian Chinese Peranakan) and the US. She argues for the necessity of women to grow out of their cocoons through active participation in the outside world, even if it means letting go of the secure world women are often associated with – that of love, romance, or marriage. In 1997, Lim published the collection *Two Dreams: New and Selected Stories*.

NFAM

Lim, Suchen Christine (*b*. 1948) Singaporean novelist. A third-generation descendant of illiterate Chinese immigrants, Lim was born in Malaysia and moved to Singapore when she was 15. Convent-educated, she graduated from the University of Singapore in 1972. Her first novel *Ricebowl* (1984) questions the regulated and pragmatic politics of Singapore in the 1960s. *Gift From the Gods* (1990) explores women's status and sense of self within an immigrant Chinese community. In *Fistful of Colours* (1993), which won the Singapore Literature Prize, Lim explores the malleability of memory, specifically as it shapes the course of history and politics in a multicultural Singapore. Her latest novel *Bit of Earth* (1999) subverts colonial stereotypes in showing a Malay chief and a Chinese refugee cynically questioning British colonial policies. Lim was awarded a Fulbright scholarship in 1997 to attend the University of Iowa International Writers Program.

MHo

Lim-Wilson, (Ma.) Fatima V. (*b.* 1961)
Philippine poet, fiction writer, essayist.
Born in Manila, Lim-Wilson received a BA
(cum laude) in English in 1982 from Ateneo de Manila University, an MA in English from the State University of New York
in Buffalo, and a PhD in English from the
University of Denver in 1992. Identifying
herself with the struggles of Filipino
women writers who write in English, she
has been very vocal in challenging the uneven definition of 'nationalism' that seeks
to invalidate women's works. Her poetry
offers lyrical renditions of insights into
sociopolitical issues, particularly those
which victimize women, and nostalgic utterances of stories – real and mythical,
witnessed and told – gathered from her
undiluted native memory. She traces her
literary lineage to such writers as *Edith
Tiempo, *Virginia Moreno, *Ophelia Dimalanta, Marra Lanot and *Marjorie
Evasco – women who create the variety
which is Philippine literature. Lim-Wilson's works include *From the Hothouse and Wandering Roots* (1991; Philippine National Book Award) and *Crossing
the Snow Bridge* (1991; Journal Award in
Poetry, Ohio State University).

DTR

Lindgren, Astrid (1907–2002) Swedish
children's writer. Born in Vimmerby, a
small town in the Swedish province of
Småland, Lindgren grew up on a farm, the
second child of four. The happy childhood
she remembers is fictionalized in her children's books about Noisy Village, but her
best-known books internationally are
undoubtedly *Pippi Longstocking* (1945),
Pippi Goes on Board (1946), and *Pippi
in the South Seas* (1948). The collected
episodes about the girl with red pigtails
and ill-fitting clothes who is strong
enough to lift a horse, tells outrageous
fibs, and defies all authorities and conventions have been translated into more
than fifty languages. Lindgren tried her
hand at a great variety of genres, from
fairy tales to detective stories, and she

renewed and enriched each genre. Her
most mature works are her epic novels
The Brothers Lionheart (1973) and *Ronia,
the Robber's Daughter* (1981). Her stories
are told from the child's point of view
and in a style that replicates the voice of
a storyteller. Lindgren received many
prestigious awards and recognitions,
among them the Hans Christian Andersen
Medal in 1958, the German Booksellers'
Peace Award (1978), the Leo Tolstoy
International Gold Medal (1987), and
UNESCO's International Book Award
(1993).

E-MM

Lipska, Ewa (*b.* 1945) Polish poet. Among
the best of the Polish poets whose debut
roughly coincided with the political upheaval in Poland in 1968, Lipska is one of
the most incisive critics of totalitarianism.
Born and raised in Cracow, where she still
lives, she enrolled in the Academy of Fine
Arts in 1963 before landing a job as editor
for the prestigious publishing house
Wydawnictwo Literackie (Literary Publishing House). She travelled widely, spending six months in the US in 1976. After the
collapse of communism in 1989, she
served as a diplomat at the Polish Cultural
Center in Vienna. Although Lipska began
to write in her teens, she published her
first volume of poetry *Wiersze* ('Poems') in
1967, followed by eight additional volumes
and several selected editions. Her verses
reflect her preoccupation with the first
postwar generation, which had to define
its place in relation to history and political
reality.

JB

Lisnianskaia, Inna Lvovna (*b.* 1928) Russian poet. A major lyric poet of her generation, Lisnianskaia published her verses
abroad in the 1980s, after her contributions to the literary almanac *Metropol*
(1979) resulted in her resignation from the
Writers' Union and a ban on publication
until 1988. Born in Baku, Azerbaijan,
where she began to publish in 1948, she

moved to Moscow in 1961, where she resides to this day with the poet Semyon Lipkin, whom she acknowledges as a major influence on her verse. Five volumes of her poetry appeared between 1957 and 1978. Even these early collections are distinctly un-Soviet, emphasizing private and not social concerns. But it was the work published abroad in the 1980s that revealed the full range of her talent. In the lyrical diary titled *Poems: On the Edge of Sleep* (1984), the 'I' persona records her hopes and disappointments as woman, mother, wife, citizen, and poet; addresses the ethical problems of conscience and responsibility; and ponders the dilemma of reconciling domestic and professional life. The religious note omnipresent in her verse becomes more pronounced in *Posle vsego* ('After Everything,' 1994) and *Odinokii dar* ('A Solitary Gift,' 1995), as does her experimentation with the formal elements of composition. The prose writer *Elena Makarova is Lisnianskaia's daughter and the addressee of some of her best work.

RMey

Lispector, Clarice (1925–1977) Brazilian fiction writer. Born in Tchetchelnik, Ukraine, Lispector moved to Brazil with her parents soon after her birth. She married a Brazilian diplomat; they had two sons before separating in 1959. For many years, she wrote chronicles for Brazilian newspapers. Her first novel *Near to the Wild Heart* (1943) surprised literary critics with its fragmented form and stream-of-consciousness narrative. Her subsequent books *O Lustre* ('The Luster,' 1946), *A Cidade Sitiada* ('The Besieged City,' 1949), *The Apple in the Dark* (1956), *The Passion According to G. H.* (1964), *The Apprenticeship or the Book of Delights* (1969), *The Stream of Life* (1973), *The Via Crucis of the Body* (1974), *The Hour of the Star* (1977) and a posthumous publication *Um Sopro de Vida* ('A Blow of Life,' 1978) all confirm her status as one of the most original and important writers of modern Brazilian fiction. Her first collection of short stories *Family Ties* (1960) was praised for its careful analyses of the female psyche and domestic intimacy. Her other short story collections – *The Foreign Legion* (1964), *Felicidade Clandestina* ('Hidden Joy,' 1971) and *Soulstorm* (1974) – explore the fragility of human nature. Her stylistic innovations, her careful consideration of language, and her emphasis on the moment, link Lispector with the great modernist writers such as Joyce, Woolf, and Faulkner. Her works have been translated into many languages.

TFC

Liu Sola (*b.* 1955) Chinese fiction writer, singer, composer. Liu Sola was born in Beijing; her parents were influential figures in the Communist Party. During the Cultural Revolution, unlike many of her contemporaries who were sent to work in the countryside, Liu stayed in Beijing and whiled away her time by extensive reading of Western books and listening to Debussy, the Beatles, and other Western music. Liu obtained her degree in composition from the Central Conservatory of Music in 1983. She began writing short stories in the early 1980s. Her first published work 'You Have No Other Choices' (1985), a novella about a group of defiantly rebellious students in a music academy, created a sensation among the reading public, particularly among young people. Other novellas include *Blue Sky Green Sea* (1986), *In Search of the King of Singers* (1986), and *Chaos and All That* (1991). In addition to writing fiction, Liu also sings and composes. In 1988 Liu went to England, and she now resides in New York City. There she continues stage performing, composing, and writing with the same kind of rebellious spirit shown in her first novella. At present, her interest has shifted from rock and pop music to 'world music.' Her music compositions blend together rock, reggae, and traditional Chinese music.

JZ

Lively, Penelope (*b.* 1933) British novelist, children's writer, short story writer. Born in Cairo, Egypt, Lively moved to England in 1945. She attended St Anne's College, Oxford, where she earned a BA (honors) in modern history in 1956. She married Jack Lively in 1957; they have two children. She wrote many critically acclaimed books for children before turning to adult fiction. Her first novel for adults *The Road to Litchfield* was published in 1977. The time travel that occurs in her children's fiction appears thematically in her adult fiction as the past, history, and memories intrude upon and affect the present. Her social novels are witty, intelligent, and elegantly written explorations of middle-class life. *Perfect Happiness* (1983) is about the adjustments a middle-aged widow must make after her husband's death. In *Moon Tiger* (1987; Booker Prize) an historian reconstructs her life as she is dying. In *City of the Mind* (1991), the story of an architect is set against multiple stories that make up a history of London. Other novels include *Treasures of Time* (1979), *According to Mark* (1984), *Passing On* (1989), *Cleopatra's Sister* (1993), *Heat Wave* (1996), and *Spiderweb* (1998). Lively has also published several collections of short stories including *Pack of Cards* (1986).

JEM

Llansol, Maria Gabriela (*b.* 1931) Portuguese fiction writer. Llansol – of Catalan origin – studied law and pedagogy, and in 1965 left Portugal for Belgium, where she resided for many years. There, she opened an experimental school for immigrant children, which confirmed her interest in questions of identity and difference and influenced her fiction. Among critics, Llansol's literary production is unanimously considered groundbreaking in that she completely redefines literature. Her work has been deemed 'unclassifiable': a hybrid genre of free-floating diaries, fiction, essays, and poetry, with no particular sequential logic and with numerous purposeful gaps. She establishes a transhistorical dialogue between fictional characters as well as major Portuguese and Western literary, philosophical, artistic, and musical figures. Beneath the dense self-referential nature of her work, there is an ongoing ethical reflection on the human condition, the power of literature, the place of Portugal within Western culture, the relations between the sexes, the material world, and spirituality. Some of her best-known works include *O Livro das Comunidades* ('The Book of the Communities,' 1977), *Um Falcão no Punho* ('A Falcon in the Fist,' 1985), *Um Beijo Dado Mais Tarde* ('A Kiss Given Later,' 1990), and *Lisboaleipzig I: o encontro inesperado do diverso* ('Lisbonleipzig I: The Unexpected Encounter with Difference,' 1995).

FA

Llewellyn, Kate (*b.* 1936) Australian poet, diarist. Born in Tumby Bay, South Australia, Llewellyn's early career was as a nurse and then as owner/director of two art galleries in Adelaide. Divorced in 1972, she has two children, her daughter Caro is the author of three books. Llewellyn won the Bundy Prize for poetry (1975) and graduated with a BA in history and classics from the University of Adelaide (1978). Her first book of poetry *Trader Kate and the Elephants* (1979) won the Ann Elder Award. Subsequent collections include *Luxury* (1985), *Honey* (1988), *Figs* (1990), and *Crosshatched* (1994). She has written 'I try for a dense, sensuous text. A voluptuous, heart-breaking art is my aim.' With Susan Hampton, Llewellyn edited the groundbreaking anthology *The Penguin Book of Australian Women Poets* (1986). After moving to the Blue Mountains, NSW, in 1985, Llewellyn produced her trilogy *The Waterlily* (1987), *Dear You* (1988), and *The Mountain* (1989). In 1997, a fourth volume, *Burning*, was published. Based on journals, these volumes include intimate reflections, recipes, and letters. She has also published a book of essays,

The Floral Mother (1995), and a series of international travel diaries: *Angels and the Dark Madonnas* (1991) on India and Italy; *Lilies, Feathers, and Frangipani* (1993) on New Zealand and the Cook Islands; *Gorillas, Tea and Coffee* (1996) on Africa.

DGi

Lochhead, Liz (*b.* 1947) Scottish poet, playwright. Born in Lanarkshire, Lochhead attended the Glasgow School of Art and worked as a teacher for several years. Her first book of poetry *Memo for Spring* (1972) was praised for its energy and its direct engagement with ordinary experience. *Dreaming Frankenstein and Collected Poems* (1984) confirms her talent for storytelling and her sensitivity to women's experiences. Lochhead cites the 'oral tradition' as an inspiration, and the dramatic nature of her poems has led naturally to the creation (and performance) of dramatic monologues, songs, and other performance pieces; many of these are collected in *True Confessions and New Clichés* (1985). She is also the author of the plays *Mary Queen of Scots Got Her Head Chopped Off* (1989), a feminist reinterpretation of Scottish history, and *Perfect Days* (1998), a social satire of contemporary Scotland featuring a Glasgow hairdresser. Lochhead has also published *The Grimm Sisters* (1981), in which she offers new versions of ballads and fairy tales, and the poetry collection *Bagpipe Muzak* (1991).

JEM

Lohrey, Amanda (*b.* 1947) Australian novelist, editor. Born in Hobart, Tasmania, Lohrey graduated with a BA (Honours) at the University of Tasmania. She studied at Cambridge in the 1970s and lived in the US before returning to Australia to edit and write. From 1987 to 1994 Lohrey worked as Lecturer in Writing and Textual Studies at the University of Technology, Sydney. She now lives in Tasmania with her husband and daughter and writes full-time. Her first novel *The Morality of Gentlemen*

(1984) is experimental in form, adapting some of Brecht's theories to a political novel. She reconstructs a crucial industrial dispute on the Australian waterfront in the 1950s, to draw out Cold War tensions and class struggle in Australian history and society. *The Reading Group* (1988; shortlisted for the NSW Premier's Fiction Awards and the Christina Stead Prize) continues her interest in political history, fiction, and form. Lohrey uses a number of narrators to give shifting and multiple perspectives to write this dystopian fantasy of the Australian political system in crisis. *Camille's Bread* (1995; Victorian Premier's Literary Award and Australian Literature Society's Gold Medal) marks a change of scene and form, to a domestic realism that portrays the subtle aspects of sexual politics, family, and relationships in urban Australia.

MAH

de Loo, Tessa (Tineke Duyvené de Wit) (*b.* 1946) Dutch novelist, short story writer. De Loo's debut did not pass unnoticed. In particular, the title story in *De meisjes van de suikerwerkfabriek* ('The Girls from the Sweets Factory,' 1983), in which a group of women assault a man, attracted a lot of publicity. It took years for her to step out of the shade of this debut, during which she wrote many more stories and two novels (*Isabelle* and *Meander*). It was only after the publication of her novel *The Twins* in 1993 that she seemed to have lost the label of 'successful débutante'. In this bestseller, which was received by critics with some scepticism, she relates the lives of two girls, during and after World War II. One of them is raised in Germany, the other in the Netherlands. They meet again when they are old, and confront each other with their prejudices. In *Een varken in het paleis* ('A Pig in the Palace,' 1998), de Loo tells of her experiences during her travels through Eastern Europe and Greece in the footsteps of the poet Lord Byron.

AAn, MMe

Lorde, Audre (1934–1992) US-born poet, essayist. Born in New York City to Barbadian and Grenadian immigrant parents, Lorde believed 'home' was the Caribbean. She detailed the complications of her relationship to homelands in *Zami: A New Spelling of My Name* (1982), a 'biomythography' which fuses autobiography, biography, cartography, and myth. She was educated at Columbia University and Hunter College, and in 1980 became professor of English at the latter. *From a Land Where Other People Live* (1973), one of her many books of poetry, was nominated for the National Book Award in 1974. *Chosen Poems: Old and New* was published in 1982. She was named New York State's poet laureate in 1991. As a black lesbian activist, her writings aimed at the destruction of white patriarchal power, and the eradication of the invisibility and denigration suffered by women, gays, and lesbians within the African-American community. She considered 'Eye to Eye: Black Women, Hatred, and Anger' and 'Poetry is not a Luxury' from *Sister Outsider: Essays and Speeches* (1984) to be the core of her prose. *The Cancer Journals* (1980) won the 1981 Book Award from the American Library Association Gay Caucus. Lorde co-founded Kitchen Table: Women of Color Press. After battling cancer, she died in 1992.

GAn

Louis, Marie Gerrina (*b.* 1964) Malaysian novelist, short story writer. Louis was born in Kuala Lumpur but was educated in Johor Bahru. She worked for a legal firm in Singapore for some years before quitting to be a full-time homemaker. She has published four children's books, two novels – *The Road to Chandibole* (1994) and *Junos* (1995) – and several short stories which have won prizes in the NST-SHELL short story writing competitions. She started writing for popular magazines like *New Thrill* and *Indian Movie News* but later turned to radio plays and children's literature. Like *Chuah Guat Eng, Louis also experiments with the detective genre in much of her writing. She addresses many of Malaysian women's issues by looking at the injustice caused by class and gender discriminations. In *The Road to Chandibole*, she explores issues of identity based on class and sexuality. Her protagonist (an Indian woman called Saras) is a tough character who struggles against class boundaries; she becomes a revolutionary figure not only in the novel but also in the Malaysian Anglophone women's writing tradition. In *Junos*, Louis explores the origin and development of the Indian descendants living in Malaysia and Singapore. She focuses on the theme of 'rags to riches' experienced by this group of immigrants.

NFAM

Løveid, Cecilie (*b.* 1951) Norwegian playwright. Born in Mysen, Norway, Løveid was raised by her grandparents in Bergen. Although her first published book *Most* (1972) was a novel, and much of her writing crosses the boundaries between poetry and prose, she considers herself primarily a playwright. She studied at the Bergen College of Art and Design and her writing retains a strong visual sense. She has worked in radio and television, and with major theaters in Bergen and Oslo. Fragmentation, lack of chronological narrative, sexual imagery, abandonment by or absence of a man, and the presence of the sea are characteristic features in her work. After *Sea Swell* (1979), she turned primarily to drama. *Seagull Eaters* won the Prix Italia for best radio play in 1983. It tells of the dreams and destruction of a poor girl in the 1940s, quoting from a popular Norwegian cookbook to comment on the protagonist's life. Løveid's work is rich in historical, literary, and highly personal allusions, as well as elaborate word play, and recent plays have varied in subject matter from *Maria Q.* (1994) about the Russian wife of Vidkun Quisling, to *Rhindøtrene* ('Daughters of the Rhine,' 1996) about Hildegarde von Bingen. One of Norway's most important contemporary playwrights, her experimental work has received more critical attention and acclaim abroad than in Norway.

TH

Loy, Rosetta (*b.* 1931) Italian novelist. Born in Rome in an upper-class family of a Piedmontese father and a Roman mother, Loy, author of seven novels and one short story collection, resides in semi-recluse fashion outside of Rome. Set in either Rome or Piedmont, her works, such as *La porta dell'acqua* ('The Door of Water,' 1974) and *Sogni d'inverno* ('Winter Dreams,' 1992), center on difficult family relationships as well as on the destructive effect of progress on the family and tradition, and the moral and political hypocrisy in upper-middle-class families especially toward the Jewish question. Her first novel *La bicicletta* ('The Bicycle,' 1974; Viareggio Prize) relates the tribulations of an upper-class family and their nonchalance toward the fascist racial laws and deportation of Jews. Winner of five prestigious literary prizes, Loy's fifth novel *The Dust Roads of Monferrato* (1987) is the saga of the progressive demise of four generations of a nineteenth-century family in rural Piedmont. Loy's most recent publications focus again on the Jewish question. *Cioccolata da Hanselmann* ('Chocolate at Hanselmann's House,' 1995) is the story of the many internal and external conflicts in an upper-class Jewish family during the war. In *First Words: A Childhood in Fascist Italy* (1997), Loy juxtaposes her personal experiences of Italian anti-Semitism as a child with a history and critique of the sentiment in Italy.

CL-W

Ludu Daw Ama (*b.* 1915) Burmese journalist, translator, publisher. Ludu Daw Ama studied science at Mandalay Degree College from 1933 to 1935 and then at Rangoon University, where she began writing articles and short stories for various Burmese language magazines and

where she met her husband, journalist Ludu U Hla. In 1937, she failed her BA Final Exams and returned to Mandalay. She and her husband established the Progress Publishing House and *Ludu* ('The People') newspaper in 1946; she wrote political articles for the latter for twenty years until it was closed down by the military regime. She has translated European, African, and Asian short stories, and books by Western pro-communist writers. Although she was a member of the Communist Party, it was her husband who spent three periods in jail before his death in 1982. Of their five children, two went underground to join the communists and the youngest son Nyi Pu Lay also a writer, was a political prisoner from 1990 to 1999. In recent years, Daw Ama has written magazine articles about Burma and Mandalay aimed at young people, which try to encourage national pride and dissuade them from embracing Western habits. Her original works include the prize-winning *Pyithu chiq-thaw a-nu-pyinnya-thi-mya* ('Favorite Artists,' 1964), a travelogue *Chindwin-hma Pin-leh-tho* ('From the Chindwin to the Sea,' 1985), and *Mandalay-thu Mandalay-tha-mya* ('Men and Women of Mandalay,' 1991). Her writing has been translated into Japanese but only two short works, on Mandalay pagodas, exist in English. She still runs the Ludu Press but censorship means that most work taken on is commercial.

VBo

Luft, Lya (*b.* 1938) Brazilian novelist, poet. Born in the southeastern state of Rio Grande do Sul, Luft published her first novel *As parceiras* ('The Partners') in 1980 at the age of 40. She subsequently published *A asa esquerda do anjo* ('The Angel's Left Wing,' 1981), *The Island of the Dead* (1984), *The Red House* (1987), and *A sentinela* ('The Sentinel,' 1994). A consistent theme in each of her five novels is the sexual and social identity of Brazilian women of German descent interacting with a Brazilian society that they view as strange or other. Taken in progression, they form a series of Brazilian women's *Bildungsromans* or coming-of-age novels. The works possess an eerily Gothic quality, reminiscent of Mary Shelley or Anne Radcliffe, as all the narratives unfold in claustrophobic atmospheres of the patriarchal home. *The Island of the Dead* takes Hieronymus Bosch's famous painting of the crossing of the River Styx as its inspiration as it recounts how the possibly accidental death of a young boy affects the members of his family, including his twin sister. Never content with easy or mundane themes, Luft is a master at dissecting contemporary problems common to many people, not just Brazilians.

SCQ

Lugn, Kristina (*b*. 1948) Swedish poet, playwright. Born in Skövde, Lugn graduated from the University of Stockholm and worked as a critic, translator, and contributor to Swedish Radio and TV. Since 1986, she has been a writer-in-residence at the Royal Dramatic Theater in Stockholm. She is the recipient of several distinguished awards. Her first collection of poems *Om jag inte* ('If I Not,' 1972) was followed by *Till min man, om han kunde läsa* ('To My Husband If He Could Read,' 1974) in which her rhythmical poems, mixed with irony and humor, contrast the familiar world with one of despair and loneliness. Her techniques are reminiscent of those of *Sonja Åkesson. *Hundstunden – kvinnlig bekännelse lyrik* ('The Dog Hour – Female Confession Poetry,' 1989) continues her investigation of alienation and the problem of communication in the midst of a seemingly secure life. In the 1990s, Lugn made a breakthrough as a playwright of short, often two-person plays, mixing her lyricism with triteness, as in *Tant Blomma* ('Mrs. Flower,' 1993) where a baby in Mrs. Flower's care is waiting to be picked up. Through associations and well-known texts – nursery rhymes, songs, romance, plays, the Bible – the play discloses our

conventional lives and expectations. In 1997, she staged and wrote the lyrics for *Astrid Lindgren's *Mio, min Mio* and won the Moa Award. Excerpts from her works in English translation can be found in several anthologies.

GE-C

Lukkari, Rauni Magga (*b*. 1943) Sami poet. Born in Utsjok, Finland, Lukkari is now a Norwegian citizen. She studied Sami and Finnish at the University in Tromsø, Norway, has taught in a Sami school, and written for radio and for the Sami theater. She debuted in 1980 with *Jienat vulget* ('The Ice Goes Out'), followed by *Báze dearvan, Biehtár* ('Farewell, Biehtar') the next year. She was the Sami candidate for the Nordisk råds litteraturpris in 1987 for *Losses beaivegirji* ('Dark Journal,' 1986). She has written two bilingual collections of poetry, one in Sami and Norwegian, *Mu gonagasa gollebiktasat* ('My King's Golden Clothes,' 1991) and another in Sami and Finnish, *Čalbmemihttu* ('Visual Estimate,' 1995). Lukkari's style is characterized by its everyday language and imagery, and the influence of the *joik*, the Sami song tradition. Her work reflects the struggle to maintain one's cultural identity while living in the modern world, and she is particularly interested in the position of women in both traditional and contemporary society. Selections from her poetry collections appear in an anthology of contemporary Sami prose and poetry, *In the Shadow of the Midnight Sun*.

TH

Lundberg, Ulla-Lena (*b*. 1947) Finland-Swedish documentary writer, novelist. Born in Kökar in the Åland Islands, Lundberg has spent several years abroad and lived in England, Japan, the US, and Siberia. She earned a masters and a doctoral degree from the University of Åbo Akademi in 1985 and 1993, respectively. Today, she lives in Borgå in southern Finland. After an early debut with a collection

of poems *Utgångspunkt* ('Point of Departure,' 1962), she spent a year in the US.
She documented her impressions in two
books: *Strövtåg* ('Wanderings,' 1966) and
En berättelse om gränser ('A Story about
Borders,' 1968). These were followed by
several documentary books based upon
various experiences abroad and one about
the place of her birth, *Kökar* (1976). Since
1982, her entire oeuvre has been translated
into Finnish. *Kungens Anna* ('The King's
Anna,' 1982) and its sequel *Ingens Anna*
('Nobody's Anna,' 1984) examine Anna's
sense of belongings as she moves from
Kökar to Stockholm and back. With *Leo*
(1989), she embarked on a seafarer trilogy
about an Åland sailing family. Her travelogue *Sibirien – ett självporträtt med vin-
gar* ('Siberia – A Self-Portrait with Wings,'
1994) depicts five ornithological trips to
Siberia between 1989 and 1993, while remembering a love-affair at a time when she
had 'wings.' Lundberg has been awarded
several prizes in Finland and Sweden. Excerpts from her work, in English translation, can be found in several anthologies.

GE-C

Lunden, Eldrid (*b.* 1940) Norwegian poet,
essayist. Lunden's poems first appeared in
1966 in *Profil*, a literary journal which embraced modernism and questioned the
traditional role of literature. Her debut
collection *f.eks. juli* ('e.g. july,' 1968) was
well received. Three collections from the
mid-1970s – one of them is the popular
hard, mjuk ('hard, soft,' 1976) – are short
and experimental in form, and explore the
relationships between identity and gender,
men and women, and among women.
Often feminist in her topics, she nevertheless skillfully and intelligently probes into
our common identities, fluid and yet separated by a variety of boundaries which
influence communication. *Gjenkjennelsen*
('Recognition,' 1982) focuses on the tension between the universality and unique-
ness of language, and on stereotypical
myths and images of women which hinder
communication. In her 1990 collection

Noen må ha vore her for ('Somebody
Must Have Been Here'), she creates a
female lineage of creative foremothers.
Lunden is now recognized as one of the
major poets of her generation. She writes
in New Norwegian, one of the two official
languages in Norway. As a creative writing
teacher and an essayist commenting on
current cultural issues, from language and
gender to canon and individual authors,
she is deservedly a major presence at home
and increasingly so abroad.

M

Lurie, Alison (*b.* 1926) US novelist. Born in
Chicago and raised in New York, Lurie
graduated from Radcliffe College in 1947.
She teaches folklore, creative writing, and
children's literature at Cornell University.
Her satirical novels focus on the American
middle class, and in particular, sophisticated, often isolated, members of academia. Her ironic, lucid prose exposes the
pretenses of American society and dissects
the institution of marriage. Adultery is a
recurring theme in her novels, its consequences being unpredictable and not always negative. Her early novels include
Love and Friendship (1962), *The Nowhere
City* (1965), *Imaginary Friends* (1967), and
Real People (1970). *The War Between the
Tates* (1974) draws parallels between the
breakup of a marriage and the generational conflicts and political unrest on a
college campus in the early 1970s. *Foreign
Affairs* (1984), which won the Pulitzer
Prize, tells the story of a professor on sabbatical and an engineer who cross paths in
London and find romance. *The Truth
about Lorin Jones* (1988), about an art historian researching the life of a dead artist,
questions the enterprise of biography. In
The Last Resort (1999), a wife tries to save
her marriage by moving to Key West with
her husband. Lurie has also written several
works of nonfiction, including *The Language of Clothes* (1982) and *Don't Tell the
Grown-Ups: Subversive Children's Literature* (1990).

DVT

M

Ma Sanda (b. 1947) Burmese writer. Born Cho Cho Tin, Ma Sanda is the daughter of the famous Burmese writer Man Tin. Her first published work was the short story 'Cama Sayama' ('My Teacher,' 1965). Since then she has published over ten novels and about a hundred short stories, which are popular for their upbeat but critical descriptions of the daily struggle with the cost of living, bureaucracy, and corruption. Her characters are the middle- and working-class residents of Rangoon's suburbs. She achieved notoriety in literary circles with her short story 'Eh-thi' ('The Uninvited Guest,' 1989), in which a rich woman 'from the western side of town' turns up and tells a simple Burmese family how she will help them rebuild their house, providing she gets to take over half of it. Some saw this – mistakenly – as an attack on *Aung San Suu Kyi. It was rather an attack on foreign aid and investment, and some of Ma Sanda's other stories have been in a similar vein, for example those which criticize Burmese girls for marrying foreigners. She obtained an architecture degree from Rangoon Institute of Technology in 1971 and has a substantial architectural practice with her husband.

VBo

MacDonald, Ann-Marie (b. 1959) Canadian dramatist, novelist. Born on a Canadian Air Force base in West Germany, MacDonald moved frequently as a child. After graduating from the National Theatre School in Ottawa in 1980, she settled in Toronto. She acted in the films *Island Love Song* (1987) and *I've Heard the Mermaids Singing* (1987); on stage she appeared in *Boom, Baby, Boom!* (1993) and *Abingdon Square* (1989). As part of Toronto's feminist theater community, she collaborated as writer-creator on *Smoke Damage* (1985) and as writer-actor on *This Is For You, Anna* (1985). *Clue in the Fast Lane* (1984), co-written with Beverley Cooper, spoofs Nancy Drew mysteries. *The Road Shows* (1986), also co-written with Cooper, satirizes road movies. MacDonald's play *Goodnight Desdemona (Good Morning Juliet)* (1990), written in blank verse, tackles Shakespeare and academia; the play won a Chalmers Canadian Play Award and a Governor-General's Award. *The Arab's Mouth* (1995) is a strange amalgam of Victorian melodrama and Gothic effects. MacDonald wrote the libretto for *Nigredo Hotel* (1992), with music by Nic Gotham. She co-wrote *The Attic, the Pearls, and Three Fine Girls* (1995). Her first novel *Fall On Your Knees* (1996), about a Scottish-Lebanese family in Cape Breton, involves piano players, maternal conflict, and opera divas.

AH

MacDonald, Sharman (b. 1951) Scottish playwright. Born in Glasgow, MacDonald was educated at Edinburgh University. She made her debut with *When I Was a Girl I Used to Scream and Shout* (1984), which was a critical and popular success. Set in Scotland, it traces the relationship between a mother and daughter by moving back and forth in time, from 1955 and the girl's early adolescence to 1960, when she was a pregnant teenager, to 1983, when mother and daughter review the past together. Emotional and humorous, with lively dialogue and convincing depictions of adolescence, the play established Mac-Donald's characteristic themes. *When We Were Women* (1988) also features a young woman in Scotland, but is set during World War II, and concerns the heroine's involvement with a bigamous serviceman. *All Things Nice* (1991) is MacDonald's most formally experimental play, in which the narrative of the adolescent Moira and her best friend is woven with a second narrative created by letters written by Moira's mother, who is living in the Middle East. *Shades* (1992) is about the relationship between a single mother in her forties and her young son. Other plays include *The Brave* (1988) and *The Winter Guest* (1993). MacDonald has also written two novels, *The Beast* (1986) and *Night, Night* (1988).

JEM

Mackay, Shena (*b.* 1944) Scottish novelist. Born in Edinburgh, Mackay is married and has three daughters. She started writing at the age of 15, and by 27 had published five novels. She established her reputation with the two novellas *Dust Falls on Eugene Schlumberger* and *Toddler on the Run* (1964; published together). Her two early novels *Music Upstairs* (1965) and *Old Crow* (1967) were notable for both their detailed realism and their black humor. After taking a break from writing to raise her children, Mackay returned with a series of striking and unusual satirical novels in which the real world is transformed into the fantastic in ways that are grimly funny and sometimes surreal. These novels include *Babies in Rhinestones* (1983), *A Bowl of Cherries*

(1984), *Redhill Rococo* (1986), and *Dreams of Bad Women's Handbags* (1987). Both *Dunedin* (1992) and *The Artist's Widow* (1998) offer richly comprehensive and scathingly ironic portraits of modern London. *The Orchard on Fire* (1996), set in the 1950s, is an elegaic portrait of a sustaining friendship between two young girls.

JEM

Madhavikutty (*see* Das, Kamala)

Magona, Sindiwe (*b.* 1943) South African novelist, memoirist, short story writer. The second of eight children and the eldest of five daughters, Magona was born in the village of Gungululu, near Umtata, South Africa. By the time she started school, her family had relocated to Cape Town, where she grew up in Blouvlei, an impoverished, sprawling tin-shack place with no running water, no electricity, and no tarred roads, but blessed with a strong sense of community. Her first book *To My Children's Children* (1990) is the story of her growing up in South Africa. With a tenth grade education and a two-year teacher training course, Magona started teaching grade school in 1962, but four years later, separated from her husband, and the mother of three children, she resorted to domestic work. She was denied her basic human rights and barred from access to good jobs by the apartheid government. In 1991, she published a collection of short stories, *Living, Loving, and Lying Awake at Night*. Her first novel *Mother to Mother* (1998) is a fictionalized account of the 1993 murder of an American Fulbright Scholar, Amy Biehl, in South Africa.

TA

Mahasweta Devi (*b.* 1926) Indian novelist, short story writer, journalist. Mahasweta, the Bengali writer and activist, was born in Dhaka into a family of artists and intellectuals. Earning her BA from Santiniketan's Visvabharati University and her MA from Calcutta University, she published her first novel *Jhansir Rani* ('The Queen of Jhansi') in 1956. This novel, a chronicle of the famous queen who battled the British in 1857, was followed by other important historical novels, including *Aranyer Adhikar* ('Rights over the Forest,' 1977), which depicts the tribal freedom fighter Birsa Munda, and *Mother of 1084* (1973), which is set amidst the political insurgencies of the 1960s and is the only one of her novels in English translation. Also available in English are two short story collections translated and introduced by *Gayatri Spivak, *Imaginary Maps* (1995) and *Breast Stories* (1997), both of which explore the interrelated effects of gender, caste, and class hierarchies upon women; the novella *Bashai Tudu* (1990); and the short story 'Rudali' (1979), which has now been adapted for stage and screen. Known for her experimental style which combines different dialects of Bengali, Mahasweta has received the Jnanpith, India's highest literary prize, as well as the prestigious Magsaysay for her campaign on behalf of India's tribal peoples.

PT

Mahbub, Maryam (*b.* 1953) Afghan short story writer. Born in Faryab, Afghanistan, Mahbub attended high school in Kabul and went to work in the Ministry of Information and Culture after graduation. She was later sent to Iran to continue her education, where she attended Teheran University. Returning to Kabul, she worked in various positions in cultural institutes while developing a writing career as a short story writer. It is believed that after the collapse of the communist government in Afghanistan, she left her country. She has a few publications, mainly in periodicals and newspapers during the time of her residence in Kabul.

FRB

Mahy, Margaret (*b.* 1936) New Zealand children's writer. Born in Whakatane, New Zealand, Mahy attended the University of Canterbury, earned her BA (1957) at the University of Auckland, and received her Diploma of Librarianship (1958) from Wellington Library School. She married and had two daughters. In 1969 an American publisher published her first stories *The Dragon of an Ordinary Family*. In 1980 she resigned from being a librarian and dedicated herself to writing full-time. Her approximately one hundred books for children, young adults, and emergent readers have won numerous prizes in New Zealand and throughout Europe. She won the UK Carnegie Medal for *The Haunting* (1982) and *The Changeover: A Supernatural Romance* (1984). She has won the New Zealand Library Association Esther Glen Award several times, the 1993 New Zealand Children's Book Award for Junior Fiction for *Underrunners*, the Order of New Zealand, and the New Zealand Literary Fund Award for Achievement. Mahy's children's books are designed to be read aloud. They have strong rhythm and vivid descriptions. Humor, astronomy, science fiction, and philosophy often permeate her texts, which tend to merge the ordinary with imaginary experiences.

M-RA

Maiden, Jennifer (*b.* 1939) Australian poet, prose writer. Maiden lives in Penrith, NSW, where she was born. She left school when she was 13 and held various jobs before she resumed formal education and earned her BA (1974) from Macquarie University. She is now a professional writer and has received fellowships from the Australia Council, the English Association Prize, the Harri Jones Memorial Prize, the Henry Lawson Festival of Arts Award, the Victorian Premier's Award, and the NSW State Literature Award. She has a dozen poetry collections, beginning with *Tactics* (1974). One of her volumes of poetry, *Mortal Details* (1977), also includes prose. Her *Selected Poems* (1990) and *Acoustic Shadow* (1993) show the range of her powerful, intimate, subtle, crisp, and controlled poetry. Some of her poems vividly record slivers of everyday life, but she writes equally about global events, for example in her Gulf War poetry. In addition, she has published two novels – *The Terms* (1982) and *Play with Knives* (1991) – and many essays.

M-RA

Maillet, Antonine (*b.* 1929) Canadian novelist, dramatist. Born and raised in New Brunswick, Maillet published her first novel *Pointe-aux-Coques* ('Clam Point,' 1958) while a schoolteacher in a religious order in Moncton. After leaving the convent, she earned a doctorate from the Université Laval in Quebec with her dissertation *Rabelais and Popular Traditions in Acadia* (1971). The affirmation of Acadian identity is central to Maillet's works, which are characterized by her colorful use of Acadian French and her resilient protagonists, drawn from the popular classes. She received the Governor General's award for *The Tale of Don l'Orignal* (1972), a mock heroic account of the origins of Flea Island. Her play *La Sagouine* (1971; revised 1974) consists of gritty, witty monologues by a charwoman, while *Evangéline the Second* (1975) debunks Longfellow's romantic image of long-suffering Acadian women. She won the Prix Goncourt for *Pélagie: The Return to a Homeland* (1979), an epic novel of the struggle by Acadians to return from deportation by the British in 1755. The author of over thirty works, including adaptations of Shakespeare and Ben Jonson, Maillet is the recipient of numerous awards and Chancellor of the Université de Moncton.

MAG

Mairs, Nancy (*b.* 1943) US essayist, poet. Born in Long Beach, California, Mairs grew up in New England. She graduated from Wheaton College in 1964 and received both an MFA and PhD from the University of Arizona. She married George Mairs, a teacher, with whom she has three children. Stricken by multiple sclerosis in the 1970s, she has been confined to a wheelchair since 1992. Her first book of poetry *Instead It is Winter* was published in 1977. Her second poetry collection *In All the Rooms of the Yellow House* (1984) won the Western States Arts Foundation Book Award. Her acclaimed work *Plaintext* (1986) collects autobiographical essays that powerfully confront her disability, her periods of depression, her fears of being crippled, and familial and romantic relationships. Her prose is typically witty, acerbic, and insightful. The memoir *Remembering the Bone House: An Erotics of Place and Space* (1989) chronicles her personal development and her physical and emotional difficulties. Mairs has also published *Carnal Acts* (1990), another collection of essays; *Ordinary Time: Cycles in Marriage, Faith, and Renewal* (1993), a spiritual autobiography; *Voice Lessons: On Becoming a (Woman) Writer* (1994), a collection of literary essays; and *Waist High in the World: A Life Among the Nondisabled* (1998).

DVT

Maitland, Sara (*b.* 1950) British novelist, short story writer, nonfiction writer. Born in London, raised in Scotland, Maitland was educated at St Anne's College, Oxford, earning a BA with honors in 1971. She married Donald Hugh Thomson Lee in 1972; they have two children. She was a co-founder of the Feminist Writers Group with *Michèle Roberts, Zoë Fairbairns, and Michelene Wandor, and collaborated with them on *Tales I Tell My Mother* (1978) and other works. Her first novel *Daughter of Jerusalem* (1978; Somerset Maugham Award, published as *Languages of Love* in the US) weaves Old Testament stories into its depiction of a woman struggling with infertility who joins a group of pro-choice radical feminists. Maitland is both a feminist and a Roman Catholic, and much of her fiction is preoccupied with negotiating the conflicts between these two identities. In *Virgin Territory* (1984), a nun tries to reconcile her religious beliefs with her lesbian sexuality. *Three Times Table* (1990) adds magic realism to Maitland's blend of feminism and religion as she compares the lives of three generations of women. Other novels include *Home Truths* (1993), *Hagiographies* (1998), and *Brittle Joys* (1999). Her short stories are collected in *A Book of Spells* (1987), *Women Fly When Men Aren't Watching* (1993), and *Angel Maker* (1996). *Very Heaven: Looking Back at the 60s* (1988) is a memoir. She has also published two works on women and Christianity, *A Map of the New Country* (1983) and *A Big-Enough God* (1995).

JEM

Makarova, Elena Grigoryevna (*b.* 1951) Russian prose writer, essayist. Born in Baku to the lyric poet *Inna Lisnianskaia, Makarova briefly studied at the Moscow Surikov Art Institute (an experience recreated in her story 'Uncle Pasha') before joining the Gorky Literary Institute. A professional teacher who worked on art and sculpture with psychologically disturbed children (reflected in her volume of essays *Osvobodite slona* ['Free the Elephant,' 1985]), she became fascinated with the work of Friedl Dicker-Brandeis, an art teacher who helped the doomed children at the Terezin concentration camp during World War II. Despite the successful exhibit Makarova mounted in Moscow of Dicker-Brandeis's work, subsequent official harassment spurred her to emigrate in 1990 to Israel with her husband and two children. Drawing on her biography, her fiction in the volumes *Katushka* ('Spool,' 1978) and *Perepolnennye dni* ('Overfull Days,' 1982) depicts marital relations in somber hues and presupposes that melancholy, frustration, and restlessness are humanity's common lot. The stories favor youthful protagonists often in search of the elusive or non-existent (see 'Fish-Needle' [1978] and 'Herbs from Odessa' [1982]), proceed elliptically at an irregular

pace, and are enriched by linguistic diversity and numerous cultural allusions. An anthology of five novellas, titled *Otkrytyi final* ('Open Final,' 1989), illuminates Russian Jewish life, exploring isolation and lost opportunities.

HG

Malā'ika, Nāzik al- (*b.* 1923) Iraqi poet, literary critic. Born in Baghdad, Iraq to an educated family, al-Malā'ika's parents and uncle were all poets. She graduated from the Higher Teachers' Training College in 1944. During this period, she was exposed to English literature and completed courses in music, acting, and Latin. After graduation, she took a teaching position and taught herself French. In 1950, she was granted a one-year scholarship to study literary criticism at Princeton University. She returned to the US in 1954 to earn her MA in comparative literature at the University of Wisconsin. Although al-Malā'ika began publishing her poetry in local journals at an early age, her first collection, *'Āshiqat al-Layl* ('Lover of Night') appeared in 1947. The poems of this collection reveal the innermost world of a young, alienated woman written within the romantic tradition. Together with Badr Shākir al-Sayyāb, she broke away from the traditional form of Arabic poetry and initiated the Free Verse movement in the mid-1940s. Her *Qaḍāyā al-Shi'r al-Mu'āṣir* ('Issues in Contemporary Poetry,' 1962) is a comprehensive study of this new form. Her poetry in the 1970s took a new turn; it became charged with religious themes. After teaching at several Iraqi universities, she moved to Kuwait to teach at Kuwait University.

JTZ

Mălăncioiu, Ileana (*b.* 1940) Romanian poet. Mălăncioiu received a BA in philosophy from Bucharest University in 1968 and completed her PhD in the same discipline seven years later. One of the most prolific and talented contemporary Romanian poets, she published her first volume

Pasarea tăiată ('The Slaughtered Fowl') in 1967. It was followed by more than ten others, among which the most important are *Inima reginei* ('The Queen's Heart,' 1971), *Crini pentru Domnişoaramireasă* ('Lilies for Her Ladyship the Bride,' 1973; Romanian Academy prize), *Ardere de tot* ('Burnt Offering,' 1976), *Across the Forbidden Zone* (1979; Romanian Writers Union prize), and *Sora mea de dincolo* ('My Sister Beyond,' 1980). As a poet, she obviously adheres to one of the most ancient and beautiful utopias of man: that of immortality, achieved through ways of love. This quest is often a battle against violence, cruelty, brainwashing, and all sorts of evils, in the metaphors of which one could easily read allegories of the Romanian communist dictatorship of the postwar period. Mălăncioiu has also worked with the Romanian National Television, has published several essays on literature and – after the fall of communism – has become a respected political columnist; her political commentaries have been published as *Cronica melancoliei* ('Chronic Melancholy,' 1998).

IB

Mallet-Joris, Françoise (*b.* 1930) Francophone Belgian novelist. Born in Anvers, Mallet-Joris grew up with her parents, Justice Minister André Lilar and novelist Suzanne Lilar. She left her family when she was 15 and studied in the US, where she was briefly married before going back alone to Paris. She wrote her first novel *The Illusionist* (1951) at the age of 21. It is about rebellion against upper-class hypocrisy and portrays a lesbian relationship. Her second novel *The Red Room* (1956) pursues this theme of rebellion, this time through a heterosexual affair. Inspired by her childhood years in Anvers, her first books take place in Belgium. Her conversion to Catholicism is chronicled in her autobiography *A Letter to Myself* (1963). She has four children and her third husband is an artist. She has written more than twenty-five books, among them

novels, autobiographies, and biographies of Marie Mancini and Jeanne Guyon. Her most recent works include *Mensonges* ('Lies,' 1998) and *Sept démons dans la ville* ('Seven Devils in the City,' 1999), in which she portrays contemporary society at the end of the millennium.

JV

Ma Ma Lay (1917–1982) Burmese writer. Born Ma Tin Hlaing in Bogale in Burma's Delta, she was active in the nationalist organization 'Do-bama Asi-ayone' in the mid-1930s. Her first published works were educational articles for women in the *Myanmar Alin* newspaper, whose editor-in-chief, U Chit Maung, she married in 1937. She helped him start *Gyaneh-gyaw* ('Thunderer') newspaper in 1939 and took it over following his death in 1946. She wrote many short stories and novels for this and other publications. She held offices in various writers' organizations and represented Burmese writers at conferences in India and Japan. Her most famous short story – and the only one translated into English (as well as French and Russian) – is 'Not Out of Hate' (1955). Set in the colonial era, an ordinary Burmese girl is gradually suffocated by an unhappy marriage to a Westernized Burmese civil servant who is keen to turn her into a 'lady.' In the end, his love and the alien culture eventually kill her. After the military coup in 1962, Ma Ma Lay was jailed for three years for communist associations, but was able to write while inside. Her last novel *Thwe* ('Blood,' 1973) was translated into Japanese.

VBo

Mamdūh, ʿĀliya (*b.* 1944) Iraqi novelist, short story writer, journalist. Born in Baghdad, Iraq, to a conservative family, Mamdūh graduated in 1971 from al-Mustanṣīriya University. She rebelled against her family, especially her father who was a police officer, by marrying the man of her choice. She edited two periodicals: *Al-Rāṣid* and *Al-Fikr al-Muʿāṣir*.

Today, she lives in Paris and contributes to several journals in the Arab world. Her first short story collection *Iftitāḥiyya li-Ḍaḥl-oaḥk* ('Introduction to Laughter'), was published in 1973. Her first novel *Laylā wa-al-Dhiʿb* ('Laylā and the Wolf,' 1981) revolves around a man and a woman who are Palestinian guerillas. They cross the desert to carry out a military mission against Israel. Her second novel *Mothballs* (1986), in which some autobiographical elements appear, narrates the story of a little girl growing up in a broken home in Baghdad during the 1940s and 1950s. In her most recent novel *Al-Walaʿ* ('The Passion,' 1995), she employs multiple points of view to examine the world of a middle-aged woman.

JTZ

Māniʿ, Samīra al- (*b.* 1935) Iraqi novelist, playwright, short story writer. Born in Basra, Iraq, al-Māniʿ obtained her BA in Arabic from the University of Baghdad in 1958. In 1976, she received a diploma in librarianship from Ealing Technical College in London, where she has lived in self-imposed exile since 1965. She has been assistant editor of *Al-Ightirāb al-Adabī*, a London-based literary magazine for Arab intellectuals in exile, since 1985. Her earliest publication was *Al-Sābiqūn wa-al-Lāḥiqūn* ('The Forerunners and the Newcomers,' 1972), a story of an Iraqi woman who follows her lover to London, defying his family's objection to their relationship. London is also the stage for two other novels: *Al-Thunāʾiyya al-Lunduniyya* ('A London Sequel,' 1979) and *Habl al-Surra* ('The Umbilical Cord,' 1990) in which she deals with the theme of exile. In the novel *Al-Qāmiʿūn* ('The Suppressive,' 1997), which was originally written in 1968, al-Māniʿ explores the private worlds of two school custodians, a man and a woman, and the custom of killing women who 'tarnish' the reputation of their families. Their relationship is presented against the politically and socially turbulent Iraq of the 1950s and 1960s. Several of her short

stories have been translated into English and Dutch. Her play *Only a Half* (1984) was staged at the International Women Playwrights' Center (IWPC) in Buffalo, New York. Some of her works have been banned in her homeland of Iraq. Al-Māniʿ is married to the poet Ṣalāḥ Niyāzī, and has two daughters.

JTZ

Manner, Eeva-Liisa (1921–1995) Finnish poet, playwright, translator. Along with Paavo Haavikko and Penti Saarikoski, Manner is Finland's greatest contribution to post-World War II modernism. Raised in Karelia by her grandparents after the death of her mother, she chose an isolated, simple adult life, dividing her time between Tampere, Finland and a small village in southern Spain (which she said closely resembled Viipuri, where she spent her childhood). Her most important work *Fahrenheit 121* (1968) reveals her introspective nature and strong moral and ethical center. She was deeply affected by World War II and her *Kirjoitettu Kivi* ('Inscribed Stone,' 1966) and *Kuollet Vedät* ('The Dead Waters,' 1977) continue her philosophically existential response to a world dominated by violence. Highly critical of her own writing, she destroyed her early work and chose which poems she wanted to be remembered by in *Runoja 1956–1977* ('Collected Poems, 1956–77'). Her influence on Finnish poetry is enormous; most writers coming after her reflect aspects of her work. She provided important Finnish translations of Chinese, English, German, Classical Greek, Spanish, and Swedish literature. Manner's plays written for the Tampere Theatre include *Snow in May*, which is available in the anthology *Modern Nordic Plays, Finland*. *Fog Horses* (1986) is a collection of English translations of her poems.

KMW

Mansour, Joyce (1928–1986) Egyptian poet. Born in Bowden, England, of Egyptian parents, Mansour was educated in

England, Switzerland, and Egypt, and resided for many years in Paris. She attracted the attention of the Surrealists with her first book of poems *Cries* (1953). She contributed to many Surrealist reviews, such as *Le Surréalisme, Front unique,* and *La Brèche.* In 1960, she participated in a BBC Broadcast, 'In Defense of Surrealism.' The Surrealist movement deeply influenced her poems, which reveal, in striking images, aggression, a dark, savage eroticism, and violent attacks on traditional bourgeois values. Freedom, cruelty, and humor inform her work, visible in *Cries and Claws* (1953), *Flash Card* (1965), *Birds of Prey* (1960), and *Shadows of Madness* (1967). As Mansour saw it, poetry, life, and thought are one and the same, and the poet's function is the 'quest for spiritual expansion.' She is currently considered to be one of the most remarkable poets published since the 1950s.

JLP

Mantel, Hilary (*b.* 1952) British novelist, critic. Born in Glossop, Derbyshire, Mantel attended the London School of Economics and the University of Sheffield, where she earned a Jur.B. in 1973. She married geologist Gerald McEwen in 1972. She worked as a social worker in a geriatric hospital and as an English teacher in Botswana from 1977 to 1980. From 1981 to 1986, she lived in Saudi Arabia. Her critically praised first novel *Every Day is Mother's Day* (1985), a darkly comic satire on British social services, examines the bizarre lives of the reclusive and fearful Evelyn and her mentally retarded daughter Muriel. *Vacant Possession* (1986) returns to Muriel ten years later, and with horror and humor, traces Muriels' destructive path. Mantel's subsequent novels display an impressive range of subject and style. Most are black comedies, many involve religious belief and the idea of redemption, but Mantel emphasizes ambiguity rather than moral judgements. *Eight Months on Ghazzah Street* (1988) is a psychological thriller set in Saudi

Arabia. *A Place of Greater Safety* (1992), about the French Revolution, and *The Giant, O'Brien* (1998), based on actual events in the eighteenth century, demonstrate her talent for historical recreation. *An Experiment in Love* (1995) is a coming-of-age story that focuses on the friendship of several young girls. Mantel's other novels include *Fludd* (1989) and *A Change of Climate* (1994).

JEM

Maraini, Dacia (*b.* 1935) Italian novelist, dramatist, poet. Maraini spent her early childhood in Japan, where her family was interned in a concentration camp from 1943 to 1946. They then moved to Bagheria, Sicily. Maraini has excelled in a variety of genres, developing a broad spectrum of topics from feminist perspectives, and co-founded the Maddalena women's theater group in Rome (1973). Since her first novel *The Holiday* (1962), the story of a young girl's sexual encounters during Fascism, she has published over thirty plays, five volumes of poetry, and numerous novels. Among them are *Memoirs of a Female Thief* (1972), based upon interviews with women in prison, and *Woman at War* (1975), which chronicles in diary form a woman's battles for autonomy. The epistolary novel *Letters to Marina* (1981) portrays lesbian love and conflict. Concerned with giving voice to historical women, *Isolina* (1985; Fregene Prize) investigates the actual murder of a working-class girl in 1900, and the legal and social trial that victimized her again. With *The Silent Duchess* (1990; Campiello Prize) Maraini crafts meanings of silence and language in a story inspired by a deaf-mute duchess from eighteenth-century Sicily. Following the autobiographical *Bagheria* (1993), *Searching for Emma: Gustave Flaubert and Madame Bovary* (1993) critiques Flaubert's utilization of Louise Colet in life and literature. The mystery novel *Voci* ('Voices,' 1994) raises the key issue of violence toward women, while the essays in *Un clandestino a bordo*

('A Stowaway Aboard,' 1996) reflect upon abortion, maternity, and images of the female body.

RP-I

Marin, Mariana (Mariana Pintilie) (*b.* 1956) Romanian poet. To Marin, 'a poem is but oblivion, extinguished in the very ashes of the fire that engendered it.' After having belonged to a group of young writers (in Bucharest) who opposed the Romanian communist regime in the 1980s, the life she has been leading after the fall of the dictatorship seems to indicate that, according to her own metaphor, Marin has chosen to be 'the ashes' of her former poems. She participated in the Romanian revolution of 1989 (and even went on hunger strike). For some time afterwards she worked as a journalist with the literary magazine *Contrapunct* ('Counterpoint'). She studied philology at the University of Bucharest. Her first volume, *Un război de o sută de ani* ('A War of One Hundred Years,' 1981) reveals a voice whose violence is barely masked by allegories. The allegorical self of the poet is Anne Frank in Marin's second book of verse *Camera secretă* ('The Secret Room,' 1986), which was widely read as a metaphorical diatribe against the dictatorship of Ceausescu. *Atelierele* ('The Workshops,' 1990), her latest collection of verse, mainly 'recovers' texts whose printing was not possible in previous times.

IB

Markandaya, Kamala (*b.* 1924) Indian novelist. Born Kamala Purnaiya, Markandaya (her pseudonym) is an upper-middle-class South Indian Brahmin whose background exposed her to both Hindu and Western traditions. Her father's job in the Indian railways enabled her to enrich her experience by traveling abroad at the age of 16. Dropping college studies during the Indian independence movement for journalism, army work, and village living, she left for England in 1948, where she married an Englishman and has lived ever since. She has one daughter. Her first novel *Nectar in a Sieve* (1954) epitomizes her major concerns – Indian social and economic ills and women's courage and stoicism. A Book-of-the-Month Club selection and translated into seventeen languages, it has been popular in US undergraduate curriculums. Like all her work, Markandaya's other novels *Some Inner Fury* (1955), *A Silence of Desire* (1955), *Possession* (1963), *A Handful of Rice* (1966), *The Coffer Dams* (1969), *The Nowhere Man* (1972), *Two Virgins* (1973), *The Golden Honeycomb* (1977), and *Pleasure City* (1982) convey her tragic and hopeful vision of the world, in their exploration of Indian–British cultural conflicts, pervaded both by cosmopolitanism and by an immigrant's sense of rootedness in her country of origin.

HA

Marlatt, Daphne (*b.* 1942) Canadian poet, novelist. Born in Melbourne, Australia, Marlatt emigrated to Vancouver, British Columbia in 1951. She earned a BA at the University of British Columbia in 1964 and an MA at the University of Indiana in 1968. An editor of the journals *TISH*, the *Capilano Review* and *Periodics*, she co-founded the feminist journal *Tessera*. Her first works appeared in 1966: a novella, 'Sea Haven' in *Modern Canadian Stories*, and fifteen poems in the anthology *New Wave Canada*. A fascination with puns, morphology, consciousness, autobiography, dislocation, and travel inflects her poetry. As adaptations of Charles Olson's theories, the long poems *Frames of a story* (1968) and *leaf/leafs* (1969) splice words and narratives into small units. *Rings* (1971), *Vancouver Poems* (1972), and *Steveston* (1974) draw on local politics, working-class history, and photographs to complement Marlatt's poetry. *Zócalo* (1977) concerns a woman traveling in Mexico; *Double Negative* (1988) documents the travels of two lesbians crossing a desert in Australia. Motherhood and family trees influence the diary-travelogue

How to Hug A Stone (1983) and the novel *Ana Historic* (1988). She examines her status as mother in *What Matters* (1980) and as daughter in *Taken* (1996). Lesbian poetics underlie much of Marlatt's work, most explicitly *Touch to My Tongue* (1984).

AH

Maron, Monika (*b.* 1941) East German novelist. After studying drama and art history, Maron worked as a reporter for the Berlin newspaper *Wochenpost*. Her first novel *Flight of Ashes* was denied publication in the GDR and was published in West Germany in 1981. The work deals with issues of environmental pollution and the impact of industrial manufacturing in the city of B. Echoes of Maron's own experience resonate in her protagonist Josefa Nadler, a journalist confronted with the discrepancy between the appalling conditions in B. and the newspaper reports about it. In her second novel *The Defector* (1986), Maron again deals with the disenfranchisement of the individual in East German society. Unlike Josefa, who retreats from her attempts to change the system, Rosalind experiences a psychological collapse. In both novels, Maron shows how individuality is destroyed in a collective society; nevertheless, she asserts the ideal of an active, multidimensional individual. In *Silent Close No. 6* (1991), published after German reunification, she openly deplores the deformation of Marxist ideals in the GDR. Her novel *Animal Triste* (1996) explores uncontrollable passion as a retreat from the past. She received the Kleist prize in 1992.

CG

Marshall, Paule (*b.* 1929) Barbadian-US novelist. Born in Brooklyn, New York to immigrant parents from Barbados, Marshall graduated Phi Beta Kappa from Brooklyn College in 1953 and attended Hunter College for postgraduate work. She married Kenneth Marshall in 1950, and had one son. Commenting that she 'grew up among poets,' a community of

Caribbean women talking and laughing in her mother's kitchen, she credits this early experience with teaching her the 'first lessons in narrative art.' In her first and best-known novel *Brown Girl Brown Stones* (1959), set in New York, the adolescent protagonist grapples with her parents' exile, her father's nostalgia, and her mother's wish for their own house. Marshall's other novels include *Praisesong for the Widow* (1983) and *Daughters* (1991). She has published several collections of short stories, *Soul Clap Hands and Sing* (1961) and *Reena and Other Stories* (1983) among them. Her other famous novel *The Chosen Place The Timeless People* (1969), set in the fictional island of Bournehills, has been described by the Caribbean critic and author Edward Brathwaite as 'a West Indies facing the metropolitan West on the one hand, and clinging to a memorial past on the other.'

JES

Martín Gaite, Carmen (1925–2000) Spanish novelist. Born into an intellectual family in Salamanca, Spain, Martín Gaite earned a doctorate in philology from the University of Madrid. Over the past five decades, she created a body of fiction that portrays the changing mores of Spain's upper middle class, a subject also depicted in her historical nonfiction. Major novels include the fantastic tale *El balneario* ('The Spa,' 1955), the coming-of-age novel *Behind the Curtains* (1958), the psychological study *Ritmo lento* ('A Slower Rhythm,' 1963), and the novel of intergenerational dialogue *Retahílas* ('Yarns,' 1974). Her best-known work is *The Back Room* (1978; winner of the Premio Nacional de Literatura), which is both a fantastic invention and a realistic memoir of growing up in Franco's Spain. Novels from the 1980s and 1990s continue to explore social themes, notably female friendship in *Variable Cloud* (1992) and familial relationships in *La reina de las nieves* ('The Snow Queen,' 1994), *Lo raro es vivir* ('Life is Strange,' 1997) and *Irse de casa*

('Leaving Home,' 1998). Recognized for her keen ear for spoken language and her astute social analysis, Martín Gaite's fiction earned Spain's major literary awards and has been widely translated.

JLB

Mason, Bobbie Ann (*b*. 1940) US short story writer, novelist. Raised on a dairy farm in Paducah, Kentucky, Mason was an introverted child whose links to the outer world were books and the radio. After she graduated from the University of Kentucky in 1962, she moved to New York and wrote for fan magazines. In 1969, she married Roger B. Rawlings, a magazine editor, and three years later earned a PhD from the University of Connecticut. Her first two books were works of criticism: *Nabokov's Garden: A Guide to Ada* (1974) and *The Girl Sleuth: A Feminist Guide to the Bobbsey Twins, Nancy Drew, and their Sisters* (1975). Her first short story collection *Shiloh and Other Stories* (1982) was critically acclaimed and won several literary awards. Written in a straightforward, minimalist prose style, her fiction, firmly located in the contemporary world by references to brand names and popular music, portrays the lives of rural Kentuckians and the tension between their Southern heritage and the forces of modernization and change. In her novel *In Country* (1985), a teenage girls confronts the Vietnam War through her veteran uncle's memories; it was made into a major film (1989). Mason has published two other novels, *Spence + Lila* (1988) and *Feather Crowns* (1993), the short story collection *Love Life* (1989), and a memoir *Clear Springs* (1999).

DVT

Masters, Olga (1919–1986) Australian fiction writer, journalist. Masters was born Olga Lawler to a poor family in a rural community in NSW. Raised in the Depression and educated at St Joseph's convent and Cobargo public school, she worked as a cadet on the *Cobargo Chronicle* and then as a clerk in Sydney. In 1940 she married a schoolteacher, Charles Masters, and lived for twenty years in NSW country towns. After the birth of the sixth of their seven children, she worked as a part-time journalist for the *Northern Star*, in Urbenville and Lismore, and then for the *Manly Daily*, *Land*, and the *Sydney Morning Herald*. Masters wrote a radio and stage play in the 1970s, but she was 58 before her fiction was published (1979). In *The Home Girls* (1982), deserted women and foster children are portrayed with relentless clarity. The themes of domestic trauma and economic domination of women recur in *Loving Daughters* (1984), *A Long Time Dying* (1985), *Amy's Children* (1987), and *The Rose Fancier* (1989). Masters's writing is notable for its wry and ironic humor, its psychological complexity, and deceptively simple style. The last novel and a collection of short stories were published posthumously after she died of cancer.

LJ

Mastoraki, Jenny (*b*. 1949) Greek poet, translator. Born in Athens, Mastoraki is regarded as one of Greece's leading poets and translators. She earned her BA in Byzantine history and literature at the University of Athens. Her first published work was a group of poems 'To Sinaksari tis Ayias Niotis' ('The Legend of Saint Youth,' 1971) about growing up in Greece in the 1950s and 1960s. The following year a more political collection of poetry *Diodia* ('Tolls,' 1972) appeared. Written under the dictatorship (1967–74), these poems were explicitly about the difficulty of writing under censorship. *Soi* ('Kin,' 1979) is also about censorship, but the more private kind associated with the family. Her last two books *Tales of the Deep* (1983) and *Me ena Stefani Fos* ('With a Crown of Light,' 1989) work out issues of censorship and literary tradition inherent in the love poem. She has published essays on literature and translation. Her own translations from American, Italian, German, and South American literature and criticism have received prizes from the Columbia University Translation Center and IBBY (International Board on Books for Young People). Mastoraki lives in Athens and has one daughter.

KVD

Mastretta, Angeles (*b.* 1949) Mexican novelist, short story writer. Born in Puebla, Mastretta came to Mexico City to study journalism and communications at the Universidad Nacional Autónoma de México. She is married to Héctor Aguilar Camín and has two children. Her first novel *Tear This Heart Out* (1985), an instant success in Mexico, has been translated into many languages. Using her storytelling skills, knowledge of history, sense of humor, and colloquial language, she weaves a two-fold tale set in Mexico of the 1940s: that of Catalina, a naïve young woman, who through a process of self-discovery comes to have ideas of her own, and that of the political career of her husband General Andrés Ascencio and his manipulation of power. *Mujeres de ojos grandes* ('Big-Eyed Women,' 1990) is a collection of short stories about extraordinary women who make unexpected decisions. Her second novel *Lovesick* (1996) moves from the pre-revolutionary years of the nineteenth century well into the twentieth century to tell the story of Emilia Sauri, who, brought up in a liberally minded family, practices non-traditional medicine and loves two men simultaneously. This work won the Premio Rómulo Gallegos in 1997 and has been widely translated.

GdB

Matalon, Ronit (*b.* 1959) Israeli fiction writer. Born to Jewish-Egyptian parents in Ganei-Tikva, Israel, Matalon's work reveals an affinity to her oriental heritage. Her writing is characterized by the need to belong, which remains an unrealized yearning, and a protest against the stereotyping of Orientalness in Israeli culture. The title of her first collection of stories

Zarim Ba-Bayit ('Strangers at Home,' 1992) emphasizes the alienation of her characters. In her novel *The One Facing Us* (1995), she defines the current world reality of uprooting, emigration and cultural rupture. The disintegration of a family in Cairo and the emigration of its members to Israel, Cameroon, and New York is the theme of this novel. The book, which was met by widespread critical acclaim, is embellished with family photographs and is a unique blending of autobiography, fiction, and discussions on image and text. Matalon's first book for young adults has been adapted to film. She took a BA at Tel Aviv University and has worked as a journalist for the Israeli daily *HaAretz*. She is a faculty member at the Camera Obscura School of the Arts in Tel Aviv, where she lives with her husband and children. Her writing is very daring, intelligent, sensitive and sensual.

LR

Matute, Ana María (*b.* 1926) Spanish fiction writer. Matute's 1996 election to the all-male Academia de la Lengua recognized her extraordinary career: ten novels, beginning with *Los Abel* ('The Abel Family,' 1948); four novellas; and ten collections of short stories, including several for children. Literary traces of her childhood – spent between city and country, poor playmates and rich classmates, a cold mother and adored father, peace and the Civil War – surface in themes of fratricidal conflict and innocence lost, and in a lifelong rejection of the Manichean vision imposed by Franco (1939–75). She has won many literary prizes: the Premio Nacional for Children's Fiction (1965, 1983), Café Gijón for *Celebration in the Northwest* (1952), Premio Nacional de Literatura for her saga *The Lost Children* (1958), and the Nadal for the affecting *Bildungsroman*, *School of the Sun* (1962), a trilogy with *Soldiers Cry By Night* (1964) and *The Trap* (1969). Matute prefers third-person narration, but her elliptical and startling prose conveys the subjective effect of circumstances, transmitting a childlike reaction to life. Nostalgia for childhood, as a time before class, gender, and age divisions are enforced, is omnipresent in her fiction, and helps explain her frequent recourse to fantasy and her admiration for Hans Christian Andersen and Peter Pan.

GCN

Matveeva, Novella Nikolaevna (*b.* 1934) Russian poet, songwriter, singer. Born in Pushkin, outside Leningrad, into a family of female lyricists, Matveeva studied at the Gorky Literary Institute and published her first poems in 1958 and her first collection *Lirika* ('Lyrics'), three years later. She released her first record of songs in 1966, soon establishing her reputation as one of Russia's 'bards.' Replete with cultural and folkloric references, her poetry and songs draw on nature, memory, childhood fantasy, art, and national traditions, projecting a romantic persona attracted to maximalism and intensity curiously at odds with the formal rigor of her lyrics. Landscape, wanderlust, artistic personalities, creative processes, and moments of self-oblivion figure largely in her poetry collections *Reka* ('River,' 1978) and *Khvala rabote* ('In Praise of Work,' 1987). Her songs, performed to the accompaniment of a guitar, create an atmosphere or capture a fleeting impression and tend toward a simplicity that occasionally seems childlike.

HG

Maxwell, Marina Ama Omowale Trinidadian novelist, dramatist. Educated in the arts and humanities at the University of the West Indies (Jamaica) and in theater in London, Maxwell has advocated a productive synthesis of Caribbean regional cultural arts as a means of promoting social change. She participated in the Caribbean Artists Movement (CAM) (1966–72) in England and Jamaica. Influenced by Beryl McBurnie's Little Carib Theatre and Derek Walcott's Basement Theatre, she experimented with 'Yard Theatre,' improvisational theatrical events that sought to join Caribbean artists across social classes. For the Jamaican Yard Theatre productions, she wrote several scripts which utilized Carnival aesthetics and costumes, Haitian Vodun ceremonies, African drumming, CAM poetry, and Rastafarian characters, including *Consciousness–I*, *One Love, Play Mas* (1976); *Hounsi Kanzo* (1976); *Jour Ouvert, Pressure*, and *Black Consciousness in Ritual*, all produced between 1969 and 1972. Her magic realist novel *Chopstix in Mauby* (1996) draws on elements of African and Indian-Caribbean spirituality and healing, Egyptian goddess imagery, Carnival, and the Black Power protests of 1970s Trinidad to chart the rebirth of Djuna, a prototypical Caribbean woman. She currently divides her time between the United States and Trinidad.

LC

Mayröcker, Friederike (*b.* 1924) Austrian poet, fiction writer. Mayröcker was born and still lives in Vienna. She started publishing poetry in 1945 and since 1954 she has collaborated with Ernst Jandl, with whom she made a US lecture tour in 1972. She is widely known for her experimental and richly metaphoric poems. *Gute Nacht, guten Morgen* ('Good Night, Good Morning,' 1982) contains poems from 1978 to 1981 which reflect key memories of childhood and religious experiences. She narrates dreams in her story collection *Je ein umwölkter Gipfel* ('A Summit, Clouded Over,' 1973) and mingles dreams and experiences of everyday life into reveries in *Das Licht in der Landschaft* ('Light in Landscape,' 1975). *Fast ein Frühling des Markus M.* ('Almost Spring for Markus M.,' 1976) deals with the problems of relationships, jealousy, and childhood experiences. *Night Train* (1984) is a story about unhappy love, and *Mein Herz mein Zimmer mein Name* ('My Heart My Room My Name,' 1988) tackles the process of aging. Other works include *Umarmungen* ('Hugs,' 1995) and

Notizen auf einem Kamel ('Notes on a Camel,' 1996). She has received several Austrian and German literary awards.

MMu

McCaffrey, Anne (*b.* 1926) US novelist. Born in Cambridge, Massachusetts, McCaffrey received a BA in Slavonic languages and literature from Radcliffe College in 1947. She is divorced, and has three children. She worked as a copywriter in New York for several years, and runs a thoroughbred horse farm in Ireland. She is a tremendously prolific and popular writer of works best described as science fantasy. Her first novel *Restoree* was published in 1967. That was followed by the award-winning *Dragonflight* (1968), the first in the Dragonrider series, for which she is best known. Set in Pern, a former colony of Earth, where the way of life has reverted to that of feudal times, the series features a group of characters who strive to protect their planet from external threats by forming symbiotic relationships with Pern's telepathic dragons. McCaffrey has been praised for breaking with the male-centered traditions of science fiction through her creation of strong female protagonists. The Dragonrider series has produced numerous sequels and prequels, most of the later ones written in collaboration with other writers.

JEM

McCauley, Sue (*b.* 1939) New Zealand novelist, scriptwriter, journalist. McCauley was born and raised in Waitahora Valley, New Zealand. She has two children from her first marriage, and none from her second. Her first radio play was *The Obituary* (1967). Since then she has written a variety of fiction and nonfiction for radio, television, film, newspapers, and magazines. Her semi-autobiographical first novel *Other Halves* (1982; New Zealand Book Award for Fiction and Goodman Fielder Wattie Book Award) depicts the involvement of a middle-class housewife and a homeless, illiterate Maori youth. She also wrote the script for the film version (1984). In *Then Again* (1986) an assortment of characters, dealing with issues including poverty, sexual orientation, mid-life and childhood memories, live and interact with one another on an off-shore island. *Bad Music* (1990) wryly examines popular culture and music from a middle-aged perspective. In *A Fancy Man* (1996) an alcoholic Australia stockman in his forties falls in love with a schoolteacher's 15-year-old daughter. McCauley transformed interview transcripts into *Aza's Story* (1997), published in New Zealand as *Escape from Bosnia*, an account of the UN observer who, breaking UN rules, smuggled out of Bosnia the local woman with whom he had fallen in love. *It Could Be You* (1997) is a collection of short stories.

M-RA

McCullough, Colleen (*b.* 1937) Australian novelist. Born in Wellington, NSW and educated at University of Sydney, McCullough hopscotched through various careers including schoolteacher, library assistant, journalist, and neurophysiologist in Sydney, England, and Yale University's School of Medicine, before making her final move to a literary career with the publication of *Tim* in 1974. This was followed by *The Thorn Birds* (1977), which was turned into a television series in 1983. This sweeping saga of several generations of the Cleary family living on Drogheda cattle station in NSW includes all the elements of a mainstream blockbuster – tragedy, forbidden love, deaths and births – set against the natural elements of the Australian landscape. Her subsequent novels *An Indecent Obsession* (1981) and *A Creed for the Third Millennium* (1985) reproduce many of the best-selling ingredients of *The Thorn Birds*. She then embarked on a prodigious research project on the Roman Empire, resulting so far in five massive novels of a planned six-book series: *The First Man in Roma* (1990), *The Grass Crown* (1991), *Fortune's Favourites* (1993), *Caesar's Women* (1996), and

Trojan Wars (1998). McCullough now lives on Norfolk Island.

LK

McDermid, Val (*b*. 1955) Scottish novelist. McDermid grew up in Scotland and read English at Oxford University. She worked at various newspapers for many years, including the *Scottish Daily Record* and Manchester *People*, but now writes fiction full-time. She made a name for herself as a detective fiction writer with *Report for Murder* (1987), which features Lindsay Gordon, are of the first lesbian private investigators in fiction. She continued the Gordon series with *Common Murder* (1989), *Final Edition* (1991), *Union Jack* (1993), and *Booked for Murder* (1996). She has begun two other detective fiction series. *Dead Beat* (1992) introduces another female private investigator, Kate Brannigan; it was followed by *Clean Break* (1995) and *Star Struck* (1998). The clinical psychologist Tony Hill is featured in *The Mermaids Singing* (1995) and *The Wire in the Blood* (1997). In her detailed, lively, and violent fiction, she critiques heterosexual prejudice and male values through her lesbian and feminist appropriation of the detective genre.

JFM

McDermott, Alice (*b*. 1953) US novelist. Born in Brooklyn, New York, McDermott was educated at the State University of New York, where she earned a BA in 1975, and the University of New Hampshire, where she earned an MA in 1978. In her first novel *A Bigamist's Daughter* (1982), a young woman who works for a vanity publisher reads a manuscript about a bigamist which leads her to reconsider her past and her memories of her father. A layered, complicated narrative, it established McDermott as an accomplished storyteller with a lyrical and detailed prose style. Her second novel *That Night* (1987) is set in suburbia of the 1960s, and narrated by a young girl who witnesses the violent and emotional events that lead to the separation of a pregnant teenager and her boyfriend. McDermott transforms a typical loss of innocence story into a complex meditation on disillusionment. *At Weddings and Wakes* (1991) begins at a family gathering where the individual stories of four very different Irish-American sisters are woven together to create a portrait of a family. *Charming Billy* (1998; National Book Award) tells the story of the late Billy Lynch and of how his life was ruined by a brief love affair and the well-intentioned lies of a friend.

JEM

McGuckian, Medbh (*b*. 1950) Irish poet. Born in Belfast, Northern Ireland, McGuckian earned a BA in 1972 and an MA in 1974 from Queen's University, Belfast. She married John McGuckian in 1977; they have three sons and a daughter. She was the first woman writer-in-residence at Queen's University, from 1986 to 1988. Her poetry is difficult, intricate, innovative, and utterly original. In a general sense, her subject-matter is everyday, especially female, experience, but her interest lies in moving beyond the surface of the real to the spiritual. Her metaphors are dense, her images evocative, and she is averse to explanation or conclusion. She sees her poetic language as the language of the subconscious or of dreams, and to fully appreciate and understand it, the reader must let go of conventional expectations. Her first book of poetry *Single Ladies* was published in 1980. Other volumes include *The Flower Master* (1982), *Venus and the Rain* (1984), *On Ballycastle Beach* (1988), *Marconi's Cottage* (1991), *Captain Lavender* (1994), and *Shelmalier* (1998). Her *Selected Poems* was published in 1998.

JEM

McMillan, Terry (*b*. 1951) US novelist. The eldest of five children, McMillan was raised in Port Huron, Michigan; her mother supported the family financially and her parents divorced when McMillan was 13 years old. She left Michigan to attend a community college in Los Angeles; she completed her BA in journalism at University of California, Berkeley and received an MFA from Columbia University in 1972. Her popular novels, known for their realistic and profanity-strewn dialogue, depict the lives of African-American women who overcome impediments to their happiness, be they socio-economic disadvantages or men who stifle their individuality. She single-handedly promoted her first novel *Mama* (1987), which has elements of auto-biography. *Disappearing Acts* (1989), for which McMillan's ex-husband sued for libel, explores the troublesome relationship between Zora Banks and Franklin Swift. She made her reputation with the best-selling novel *Waiting to Exhale* (1992), a story of friendships among four African-American women; it was made into a popular film. *How Stella Got her Groove Back* (1996), also a best-seller and also adapted to film, tells the story of a wealthy 42-year-old woman's affair with a man half her age. McMillan also has edited *Breaking Ice: An Anthology of Contemporary African-American Fiction* (1990).

DVT

McQueen, Cilla (*b.* 1949) New Zealand poet. Born in Birmingham, England, McQueen emigrated to Dunedin, New Zealand in 1953. With an MA (Honours) in French from Otago University, she was a French teacher before becoming a full-time poet. She has won the New Zealand Award for Poetry for three of her numerous collections of poetry: *Homing In* (1982), *Benzina* (1988), and *Berlin Diary* (1990). The latter volume also includes prose, and records her impressions of the months she spent in the German city a couple of years earlier. Her most recent work is *Crik'ey: New and Selected Poems 1978–1994*. Her loosely constructed, often colloquial, poems concentrate on everyday experiences, nostalgia, yearnings, the natural environment. She often focuses on the connections between disparate entities

and the roles of perception and order. Wit often permeates her verse, and she frequently presents her pieces as vibrant performance poetry. She lives at the southern extremity of the South Island of New Zealand.

M-RA

McWilliam, Candia (*b.* 1955) Scottish novelist, short story writer. Born in Edinburgh, McWilliam was educated at Girton College, Cambridge, where she earned a BA with honors in 1976. She has been married twice and has three children. Her critically acclaimed first novel *A Case of Knives* (1988), a violent and disturbing tale of homosexual love, obsession, and manipulation, establishes her distinctive, elegant style and the richness as well as the quirkiness of her language. Her second novel *A Little Stranger* (1989), depicts the tensions between a rich woman and her son's coarse but capable nanny. *Debatable Land* (1994) follows six expatriates on a voyage in the South Pacific. The short stories collected in *Wait Till I Tell You* (1997) demonstrate an expansion of McWilliam's descriptive powers and her talent for black humor.

JEM

Mehta, Gita (*b.* 1943) Indian novelist, essayist, documentary filmmaker. Daughter of prominent nationalist leader Biju Patnaik, Mehta is the wife of Knopf editor-in-chief Sonny Mehta; she has one son. Educated in India and at Cambridge, she now divides her time between the US, the UK, and India. She began her literary career in 1979 with the publication of *Karma Cola*, an ironic commentary on the West's obsession with India as its spiritual mentor. This was followed by two novels, *Raj* (1989) and *A River Sutra* (1993), and a collection of essays, *Snakes and Ladders* (1997). Her fiction, like her nonfictional work, attempts to capture the complex diversity that characterizes India, challenging stereotypical depictions of the subcontinental nation as the land of kings and gurus. In *Raj*, Mehta turns a princely romance into an insightful historical novel, tracing the negotiations between tradition and modernity, monarchy and democracy, involved in the birth of India as an independent nation. With *A River Sutra*, she moves away from political history to create a philosophically rich, episodic narrative that explores the inextricable links between material and spiritual existence in a land where ancient belief systems constantly jostle with modern systems of knowledge to define the contours of individual identity.

SMat

Merini, Alda (*b*. 1931) Italian poet. Born in Milan, when Merini was 16 her poems were published and appreciated by poets and critics. In 1951 she married Ettore Carniti; they had three children. Her first collection of poetry *La presenza di Orfeo* ('Orpheus's Presence,' 1951), presents a blend of mythical and mystical images also recurring in her later poetry. In 1965, her first prolonged stay in a mental hospital silenced her poetic voice for almost twenty years. *La terra santa* ('The Holy Land,' 1984; Cittadella Prize) is a poetic recollection of those silent years, especially of the horrors experienced in the mental facility. Since then, she has been writing extensively. Among her collections are *Il tormento delle figure* ('The Figures' Torment,' 1990), *La palude di Manganelli* ('Manganelli's Swamp,' 1993), and *Ultime poesie d'amore* ('Last Love Poems,' 1996). A widow since 1981, she married the poet Michele Pierri and moved to Taranto, in southern Italy. Her life with Pierri and her stay in the mental hospital in Taranto are recounted in the memoir *L'altra verità. Diario di una diversa* ('The Other Truth. Diary from a Misfit,' 1983) and in *Rage of Love* (1989). After Pierri's death, she moved back to Milan, where she now lives. In 1993 she was the recipient of the 'Eugenio Montale' Librex-Guggenheim Prize.

FG

Mernissi, Fatima (*b*. 1940) Moroccan sociologist, memoirist. Mernissi was born in Fez, in a harem in a traditional Muslim family, under the Spanish and French colonial administration. According to her autobiographical narrative *Dreams of Trespass – Tales of a Harem Girlhood* (1994), she learnt at an early age, from the women in her family, about the nineteenth-century Lebanese and Egyptian feminists. She was also profoundly marked by the tales of Scheherazade in the *1001 Arabian Nights*, a text that she explores in various books. She studied law in Rabat and sociology at the University Mohammad V in Casablanca before obtaining a PhD in the US in 1973. She has consistently studied the social situation of women, debunking the idea that the sacred Islamic texts justify the oppression of women rather than patriarchal conservative and political interpretations, as in *Women and Islam* (1983), *The Veil and the Male Elite: A Feminist Interpretation of Women's Rights in Islam* (1987), and *The Forgotten Queens of Islam* (1990). She has gained an international reputation, comparing different traditional societies such as Morocco and Japan, and has commented on modernity, the Gulf War, and democracy.

JV

Meulenbelt, Anja (*b*. 1945) Dutch essayist, novelist. One of the most distinguished socialist feminists of the contemporary women's movement in the Netherlands, Meulenbelt took the country by storm with her novel *The Shame is Over: a political life story* (1976). Strongly criticized by literary critics who could not see that it was part of a new international genre of feminist fictional autobiography, the novel was translated into many languages and devoured by tens of thousands of women readers. Its success in the Netherlands and abroad was comparable to that of *Erica Jong's Fear of Flying, *Verena Stefan's *Shedding*, and Kate Millet's *Flying*. In its depiction of a young woman's search for sexual and spiritual freedom, Meulenbelt's novel clearly fulfilled a need. The heroine's life becomes a mirror of everything that was new in Dutch society: active female sexuality, experimental forms of living and loving, unorthodox ways of mothering, feminism, and lesbianism. Other novels, such as *A Small Favor* (1985), the moving story about estrangement from and reconciliation with the enigmatic mother, continue in the fictional-autobiographical mode. She is also a productive scholar, working on feminist, sexual, ethnic, and political issues. An early celebratory feminist book was *For Ourselves* (1979) written with Ariane Amsberg. Meulenbelt co-edited the volume *A Creative Tension: Explorations in Socialist Feminism* (1984) which offers a map of the feminist-socialist scholarship of that time.

AAn, MMe

Míccolis, Leila (*b.* 1947) Brazilian poet, fiction writer. Míccolis has received many literary prizes since the publication of her first book of poems *Gaveta da Solidão* ('The Drawer of Solitude'), in 1965. She is a prolific writer who depicts the reality of Brazilian society with merciless sarcasm and irony. Women, whom she depicts as both oppressed and oppressive, are one of her favorite subjects. Her poems have been included in numerous anthologies but, to date, none of her books has been translated into English. Her works include *Trovas que a Vida Rimou* ('Lyrics in Rhyme with Life,' 1967); *Silêncio Relativo* ('Relative Silence,' 1977); *MPB – Muita Poesia Brasileira* ('A Lot of Brazilian Poetry,' 1982); *O Cio da Donzela* ('Maiden Heat,' 1983); *Em Perfeito Mau Estado* ('In Perfect Bad Condition,' 1987); *As Taras do Além* ('Madness of Life after Death,' 1980), a novel; and *Achadas e Perdidas* ('Women: Found and Lost,' 1997), a collection of short stories.

SVR

Michaelis, Hanny (*b.* 1922) Dutch poet. Michaelis lost both of her Jewish parents in the gas chambers of Sobibor; she was able to survive in hiding. In 1948 she married the Dutch writer Gerard Reve. The couple divorced in 1959, with Reve becoming a trail-blazing gay novelist, while Michaelis went on to become the writer of a modest but beautiful and lyrical oeuvre. Starting out as a relatively traditional poet in 1949, Michaelis's work eventually took on a more modernist lyrical form in the late 1950s, when she joined a general poetic development in Dutch literature which was geared toward more simplicity and colloquial speech. Her poems are often sober, short, and rhymeless. They frequently consist of one single sentence, as if written in one long breath. Main themes in her work are melancholy, despair, and (lost) love. In the early 1970s, she stopped publishing. A good selection of her collected poems can be found in *Against the Wind* (1987). Michaelis received the Anna Bijns Prize in 1995.

AAn, MMe

Michaels, Anne (*b.* 1958) Canadian poet, novelist. Born in Toronto, daughter of a Russian immigrant father, Michaels was educated at the University of Toronto, where she earned a BA in 1980. She has published three collections of poetry, *The Weight of Oranges* (1985), *Miner's Pond* (1991), and *Skin Divers* (1999). They feature lyrical and intimate love poems, meditative elegies, and dramatic monologues by historical figures, especially artists. These monologues highlight Michaels's interest in history, memory, and the past, all of which are central to her first novel *Fugitive Pieces* (1996). Powerfully written, wide-ranging, and intellectually ambitious, it achieved international acclaim and won several literary awards, including the Orange Prize, the *Guardian* Fiction Award, and the Chapters/*Books in Canada* First Novel Award. The novel consists of two first-person narratives: one is Jakob's, a Polish survivor of the Holocaust, and the other is Ben's, a professor in Canada whose parents survived the death camps. Both men struggle to understand the past through memories and stories, but they also long to be able to simply live in the present.

JEM

Milani, Farzaneh (*b.* 1947) Iranian poet, literary critic. Born and raised in Teheran, Milani attended French primary and secondary schools. In 1967, she emigrated to the US with her husband Faridoun; they have two children. She earned her BA in French literature in 1970 from California State University at Hayward and completed her graduate studies in comparative literature in 1979 at the University of California in Los Angeles. Her dissertation 'Forugh Farrokhzad: A Feminist Perspective' was a critical study of the poetry of a pioneering Iranian woman poet. She taught Persian language and literature at UCLA, and currently is associate professor of women's studies and Persian at the University of Virginia. She has published extensively, in Persian and English, on Iranian literature, feminism, and cultural studies. In *Veils and Words: The Emerging Voices of Iranian Women Writers* (1992) she argues that the norms and values that regulated women's physical exposure in Iran applied to their literary production as well. If the veil covered women's bodies for centuries, silence covered their public voices. *Simin Behbahani: A Fist Full of Stars* (forthcoming) is a translation (with Kaveh Safa) of the poetry of Iran's foremost contemporary woman poet. Milani's poems have been published in numerous Persian language journals and in *A Hidden Treasure: Writings and Stories of Women in Sufism, Past and Present*.

KTa

Miller, Sue (*b.* 1943) US novelist. Dissatisfied with post-feminist novels that made women's independence look easy, Miller began to write fiction that depicted realistically the struggles and difficult choices of modern women. Educated at Radcliffe College, where she earned a BA in 1964, Miller published her first novel *The Good Mother* in 1986. A best-seller that was made into a major film, it tells the story of Anna, a divorced mother whose lover is accused by her ex-husband of abusing their daughter. The novel, which follows the subsequent custody trial in which Anna is forced to judge her own behavior, is disturbing and powerful in its refusal to provide easy or expected answers. Miller's next novel *Family Pictures* (1990) was also a best-seller. The saga of an upper-middle-class family in Chicago from World War II to the 1980s, it is a wonderfully realistic and morally complex portrait of family life, rich with domestic details. *For Love* (1993) is about the mid-life crisis of a woman who has spent her life reinventing herself. *The Distinguished Guest* (1995) depicts the strained relationship between a prominent and elderly civil rights activist and her son. Miller has also published the novel *While I Was Gone* (1999) and *Inventing the Abbotts* (1987), a collection of stories.

JEM

Miłobedzka, Krystyna (*b.* 1932) Polish poet. Only recently recognized for her talent, Miłobedzka is one of the most original and complex Polish poets. Born in Margonin in western Poland, she studied Polish literature at the Adam Mickiewicz University in Pozna and at Wrocław University. The collection *Anaglify* ('Anaglyphs,' 1960) marked her debut. It consists of short, chiseled prose poems that show her linguistic virtuosity and penchant for unexpected metaphors. Author of five volumes of original verse, she has also published a collection of plays for children, and a book of theater criticism. She resides in Puszczykowko with her husband, the literary critic Andrzej Falkiewicz. A handful of her poems in English translation appeared in the anthology *Ambers Aglow: An Anthology of Polish Women's Writing* (1996).

JB

Minco, Marga (*b.* 1920) Dutch novelist, short story writer. Minco was born Sara Menco into an orthodox Jewish family. From 1938 she worked as a journalist, but was fired after the German invasion. Her parents, brother, and sister were deported to the concentration camps, but Minco miraculously escaped and went into hiding. From her family, only she, and her father's brother, survived the Shoah. After the war, she married the poet Bert Voeten and kept the name Marga, which she had used during the war. Her first and best-known novel *Bitter Herbs: A Little Chronicle* (1957) describes the deportation of a Jewish family, seen from the perspective of a 12-year-old child, in her characteristically sober and evocative style. The war is a recurring theme in her work, although she showed that she could write about other subjects in *The Other Side* (1959), a collection of stories. In her later work, the perspective shifts: she becomes more distant, and themes such as raising women's consciousness and the isolation of people in general are foregrounded, although the historical background remains the same. Minco's work has been widely acclaimed. She has written over ten novels and collections of stories, including *An Empty House* (1966), *The Fall* (1983), and most recently *Nagelaten dagen* ('Days Leftover,' 1997).

AAn, MMe

Miranda, Ana Maria (*b.* 1951) Brazilian poet, novelist. Miranda, now living in Rio de Janeiro, was born in Fortaleza, Ceará and grew up in Brasília. She is an artist as well as a writer: her poetry books *Anjos e Demônios* ('Angels and Demons,' 1978) and *Celebrações do Outro* ('Celebrations of the Other,' 1983) are illustrated with her own drawings. She writes historical fiction and her novels have been translated into Spanish, French, and English. *Bay of All Saints & every conceivable sin* (1990) takes place in seventeenth-century colonial Bahia, with the satirical poet Gregorio de Matos Guerra (1564–1636) as the main character; the novel analyzes the disorders and corruptions of colonial society. *A Última Quimera* ('The Last Chimera,' 1995) tells the story of the poet Augusto dos Anjos (1884–1914) and depicts the political disputes and literary intrigues of the first years of the Republic. Other novels include *O Retrato do Rei* ('The King's Portrait,' 1991), *Sem Pecado* ('Sinless,' 1993), and *Amrik* (1997).

VLSdeBF

Mitgutsch, Waltraud Anna (*b.* 1948) Austrian novelist. Different experiences of marginality converge in the works of the upper-Austrian scholar and freelance writer Mitgutsch: those of an Austrian woman of Jewish background, of a mother of an autistic child, and of a stranger in the US and Israel. Mitgutsch, born in Linz, her current place of residence, studied German and English at the University of Vienna and received a PhD in American literature from the University of Salzburg. She has taught in Austria and the US. Raised a Catholic, her quest for identity led her to convert to Judaism and change her first name to Anna. Her awards include the Anton Wildgans Preis (1993) and the Advancement Prize of the Austrian Ministry for the Arts (1996). Her introspective, social critical novels draw on personal experiences and insights: *Three Daughters* (1985), *Punishment* (1985), *The Other Face* (1986), *Ausgrenzung* (1989), *Jakob* (1991), *In Foreign Cities* (1992), and *Lover, Traitor* (1995). Mitgutsch has also published essays on Merwin, Strand, Simic, and D. H. Lawrence.

DCGL

Mo Mo (Inya) (1945–1990) Burmese writer. Born Ma San San, Mo Mo began writing poetry while still in high school. Her pen name derives from the Inya hostel at Rangoon University. From 1970 onwards, she published articles in various Rangoon newspapers and magazines. Her 'social realist' fiction is frequently pessimistic. Her first short story 'Ein-ni-chin'

('The Neighbor,' 1972) was broadcast on Burmese radio. She wrote over twenty novels of which her first, *Pyauq-thaw-lan-hmar san-ta-wa* ('Trying to Find a Way Out,' 1974), about a woman escaping from an unhappy marriage, won a national literary prize. It has been translated into Japanese and Russian, as have some of her many short stories, three collections of which won national awards. Her work is not available in English. At the time of her death, she was editor of *Sabeh-hpyu* ('Jasmine') magazine. At the time of its launch, it sought permission to publish as a 'women's magazine,' as this was easier to achieve. In fact, it is a literary magazine, and it is still being published, albeit at a loss. Since 1991, an annual competition for new short story writers has been established in her name by her husband's publishing house.

VBo

Moe, Karin (*b.* 1945) Norwegian sexual/textual reformer. No conventional rubric can characterize Moe's playful and often outrageous word performances. A university lecturer in French language and literature in the 1970s, she is a pioneer of *écriture féminine* in Norway. She debuted in 1980 with *Kjønnskrift* ('Sexscript' [a play on 'skjønnskrift' or 'calligraphy']) in which she made a Brechtian break with the mimetic, biographical tradition in women's writing. In *nynorsk* texts and poetry from the mid-1980s, such as *Kyka* ('Cockette' [a neologism derived from slang for male genitalia], 1984), *Motherdaughter* (1985; excerpts in *Dimension*, 1994) and *Sjanger* ('Genres,' 1986), Moe begins to blur the distinction between the teller and the told. Women's lives/bodies are treated linguistically from inside and outside simultaneously, verbally and graphically. In the 1990s, she abandoned what some feminists saw as a project of creating a composite grand feminine narrative. Instead, in the *Blove* books (1990, 1993 onward) she makes radical advances toward a literal 'body language' as an antidote

and farewell to patriarchal storytelling. A fearless stylist and political activist, Moe used her verbal art in the anti-EU campaign and established the *Snuspris* for Sunnhordaland to recognize social efforts toward gender equity.

FS

Mokeddem, Malika (*b.* 1949) Francophone Algerian novelist. Born in Kénadsa, along the Western Algerian desert, Mokeddem is of nomad ancestry. Her free-spirited grandmother was influential in securing her an education. After high school, she went to Oran to study medicine. In 1977, stifled by the Islamic fundamentalist movement, which began to infiltrate Algeria in the early 1960s, she went into exile in France. She specialized in nephrology at the Montpellier Université de Médecine and received her degree in 1985. After practicing her specialization for several years, she now devotes most of her time to writing. Her first book, auto biographical in nature, *Les hommes qui marchent* ('Men Who Walk,' 1990), retraces a childhood filled with the enchanting stories of her Bedouin grandmother and an adolescence of rebellion against the constraints of her Muslim society. In *Le siècle des sauterelles* ('The Century of Locusts,' 1992) she evokes the spiritual and ancestral quest of a poet. *The Forbidden Woman* (1993; Prix Femina) and *Of Dreams and Assassins* (1995) are diatribes against the oppression of Algerian women. Her last novel *La nuit de la lézarde* (1998) is an attempt to write about love and the search for happiness.

YH

Molina, Silvia (*b.* 1946) Mexican novelist, short story writer. Born in Mexico City, Molina is married to Claudio Molina and has two daughters. She studied anthropology, literature, and writing at the Universidad Nacional Autónoma de México. Her first novel *Gray Skies Tomorrow* (1977), in appropriating history, anthropology, and literature, characterizes much of her fiction. *La familia vino del norte* ('The Family Came from the North,' 1987) and *Imagen de Héctor* ('Image of Héctor,' 1990) deal with a woman's search to unravel her family's history and simultaneously define herself. The former tells of a woman's search to learn a family secret, whereas in the latter Molina constructs the history and puts into focus the blurred image of her father who died when she was a year old. In 1998, she published *El amor que me juraste* ('The Love You Swore to Me'), a novel about a woman who, after a brief extra-marital affair, looks into her father's past to clarify her own feelings. Several collections of short stories, among them *Dicen que me case yo* ('They're Telling Me to Get Married,' 1989) and *Un hombre cerca* ('A Man Nearby,' 1992), primarily depict women coping with contemporary problems. Molina is also a writer and publisher of children's books.

GdB

Molloy, Sylvia (*b.* 1938) Argentine novelist, literary critic. Of British and French ancestry, Molloy was born in Buenos Aires. She was educated in private schools there, attended the Universidad de Buenos Aires, and studied literature at the Sorbonne. Upon returning to Argentina she taught at the Alliance Française from 1962 to 1967, and wrote for the journal *Sur*. In 1967 she returned to Paris to finish her dissertation. After completing her degree, she came to the US. She has taught Spanish American literature at several universities, including Princeton, Yale, and now at New York University. Her novel *Certificate of Absence* (1981) tells the story of a woman who writes the story of her childhood experiences and a lesbian love affair. The text, written in the third-person, creates the impression of detachment and distance, but the narrator cannot hide her passion and obsessive fixation with the two lovers who have caused her so much pain. As literary critic, Molloy is the author of *Signs of Borges*

(1979), *At Face Value: Autobiographical Writing in Spanish America* (1991), and numerous critical essays. She has co-edited *Women's Writing in Latin America: An Anthology* (1991), *¿Entiendes? Queer Readings, Hispanic Writings* (1995), and *Hispanisms and Homosexualities* (1998).

MIL

Moníková, Libuše (1945–1998) Czech-German novelist, essayist. Born in Prague, Moníková wrote her dissertation on Shakespeare and Brecht. After the 'Prague Spring,' she worked as a lecturer in West Germany, publishing on Borges, Kafka, and Wedekind. In *Eine Schädigung* ('Damaged,' 1981), a student raped by police explores the state violence inscribed upon her body, killing her tormentor in a rhythmic beat that liberates herself from systemic oppression. The protagonist of *Pavane für eine verstorbene Infantin* ('Pavane for a Dead Infante,' 1983) rewrites Kafka's 'Castle' to have Olga leave the village. A hip injury psychosomatically converts this woman's everyday damages until she burns her wheelchair in an act of ritualistic self-liberation. Artists restoring *The Façade* (1987) of a national monument reenact a reading of textual structures that reassembles the quotes of material reality from an individual perspective. The façade is restored into a multiplicity of allusions that connect stories and history, details and contradictions on multiple levels of text. *Treibeis* ('Drift-Ice,' 1992) names a landscape of jarring edges, where a crippled Czech teacher saves a Promethean stuntwoman from the Alps while longing for love, myth, and *heimat* as places in language. Moníková received the Döblin prize in 1987.

AG

Montero, Rosa (*b.* 1951) Spanish novelist, journalist. Tuberculosis was a decisive factor in Montero's choice of career. Confined to her home, she spent the first nine years of her childhood reading and writing. She began her career as a journalist and is a columnist for *El País*. A request for a book of interviews led to her first novel *Absent Love: A Chronicle* (1979), about the daily struggles of a group of young women to find love and recognition. From this to *La hija del Caníbal* ('The Cannibal's Daughter,' 1997), a tale of a woman's search for her mysteriously disappeared husband, all her novels reflect her preoccupation with the fleetingness of life. *The Delta Function* (1981) follows the thoughts and memories of a 60-year-old dying woman. *Te trataré como a una reina* ('I Will Treat You Like a Queen,' 1983) is a detective novel with a twist, while *Amado amo* ('Beloved Boss,' 1988) and *Temblor* ('Tremor,' 1990) show the devastating effects of the lust for power, though in completely different settings. *Bella y oscura* ('Beautiful and Dark,' 1993) is about hope and betrayal, experienced by a little girl abandoned by her father. Montero's entire oeuvre displays a brilliant use of humor. She has also written a book of biographical essays on women and a children's book.

AAm

de Moor, Margriet (*b.* 1941) Dutch novelist. After a career as a classical singer, de Moor decided to pursue a career in writing – a decision which has proved a particularly happy one. Not only was she almost immediately recognized as a major talent, becoming one of the most popular writers in the Dutch language, but also as a literary presence abroad due to the international success of *First Grey, Then White, Then Blue* (1992) and her second novel *The Virtuoso* (1994). Her latest novel *Duke of Egypt* (1995) tells the story of the gypsies, the eternal wanderers, living in caravans 'through the centre of which run the coordinates of the whole of Europe.' In this novel, de Moor set herself the almost impossible task of recording the history of an oral, nomadic culture which has never kept permanent records. In shimmering, melodic prose, she sketches the story of the main character, Joseph, and

his forefathers, and with her compelling technique she makes tangible the familiar and depressing history of centuries of rejection and condemnation.

AAn, MMe

Moore, Lorrie (*b.* 1957) US short story writer, novelist. Born in Glen Falls, New York, Moore graduated summa cum laude from St Lawrence University in 1978. She continued her studies with an MFA from Cornell University in 1982. She has taught at the University of Wisconsin, Madison since 1984. Her first book *Self Help* (1985), a collection of short stories, is written in the second-person in a mock imperative style and modeled upon how-to manuals, with stories such as 'How to Talk to Your Mother (Notes)' and 'How to be the Other Woman.' Moore's subjects, in this and the story collection *Like Life* (1990), are young women, often dissatisfied with their jobs and relationships, looking for happiness. Her style is witty and ironic, her characters quick with one-liners and puns, but she can also be lyrical and moving. She has written two novels: *Anagrams* (1986), about the relationship between a college professor and a nightclub singer, and *Who Will Run the Frog Hospital?* (1994), about a woman's bittersweet memories of a childhood friendship. In the story collection *Birds of America* (1998), the women Moore writes about are now middle-aged, and the problems they try to dispel with wisecracks are much weightier, even tragic in some cases. In 1996, she was named one of *Granta*'s Best Young American Novelists.

DVT

Moorhead, Finola (*b.* 1947) Australian novelist, playwright, essayist, poet. A feminist activist, theorist, and writer, Moorhead was born in Melbourne and educated at Catholic schools. She received a BA from the University of Tasmania (1968). She has worked in a number of occupations, including teaching (for four years) before becoming a full-time writer in 1973. Moorhead was writer-in-residence at Monash University, Melbourne in 1980. She lives on the mid-north coast of New South Wales. Her first literary success came as a playwright in the mid-1970s, followed by numerous essays and short stories. Her first novel *Remember the Tarantella* (1987) chronicles the lives of feminist activists as they attempt to forge alternative forms of politics, art, and living. She weaves her story out of a non-linear narrative, a group of feminist characters rather than one central heroine, and extensive allusions to mythology, legends, literature, and contemporary politics. *Still Murder* (1991; Victoria Premier's Award) continues her experimentation in form and writing from a feminist perspective, this time subverting the genre of crime fiction. She explores the issues of violence, crime, justice, and the law.

MAH

Moraga, Cherrie (*b.* 1952) US playwright, poet, editor. Born in Whittier, California to a Chicana mother and Anglo father, Moraga was educated at San Francisco State University, where she earned an MA in 1980. She came into prominence as the co-editor of, with Gloria Anzaldúa, and contributor to, the influential anthology *This Bridge Called My Back: Writings by Radical Women of Color* (1981). Moraga's identity as a feminist Chicana lesbian is central to her work. Her poetry and prose in *This Bridge* and in her individual collections, *Loving in the War Years: Lo que nunca paso por sus labios* (1983) and *The Last Generation* (1993), deal with the cultural, racial, and personal struggles of her youth and her difficult position as a light-skinned lesbian in a Catholic, Mexican-American culture. She was also a co-editor of and contributor to *Cuentos: Stories by Latinas* (1983), which helped to establish a Latina literary tradition, and she has been instrumental in the development of Chicano theater. Her plays, which include *Giving Up the Ghost* (1986), *Shadow of a Man* (1988), and *Heroes and*

Saints (1989), continue her focus on gender, sexuality, and identity. *Waiting in the Wings: Portrait of a Queer Motherhood* (1997) is a memoir.

JEM

Morandini, Giuliana (*b.* 1944) Italian novelist, essayist. Born in the city of Udine near the border of Slovenia, Morandini revisits in her early fiction the unstable existential space of the frontier. Her first novel *Blood Stains* (1978; Prato Prize) is the story of a young woman's search for a personal and familial history lost in the rubble of the war. The clash of opposing histories and cultures is closely interwoven with a woman's pursuit of her lost identity in *The Café of Mirrors* (1983; Viareggio Prize), set in another border city, Trieste, and *Angelo a Berlino* ('An Angel in Berlin,' 1987; Campiello Prize). The commitment to telling women's stories is also central to Morandini's work as an essayist. Her first book, *E allora mi hanno rinchiusa* ('Then They Locked Me Up,' 1977; Viareggio Prize), is an anthropological study of women's experience in Italian psychiatric institutions. *La voce che è in lei* ('The Voice Within Her,' 1980) is an important critical anthology of marginalized Italian women writers of the late nineteenth and early twentieth centuries. Her last two works are historical novels: *Sogno a Herrenberg* ('Dream in Herrenberg,' 1991) and *Giocando a dama con la luna* ('Playing Checkers With the Moon,' 1996).

GMi

Morante, Elsa (1912–1985) Italian novelist, poet, short story writer. Morante grew up in Rome, and married the author Alberto Moravia in 1941 (they separated in 1962). While in her teens, Morante wrote children's stories and poems. The story 'Qualcuno bussa alla porta' ('Someone is Knocking at the Door,' serialized from 1935 to 1936) marked her literary debut, while the novel *House of Liars* (1948; Viareggio Prize) earned her critical acclaim. Set in Sicily, this fiction of family decline exposes the psychological traumas and fantasies hidden beneath the characters' deceptive masks. Destructive social ambitions and conflicted parent–child relations also figure prominently in *Arturo's Island* (1957), which contrasts the protagonist's perceptions of enchanting childhood with his passage into adulthood, brought about by the discovery of his father's homosexuality, and his own. Following two volumes of poetry, *Alibi* (1958) and the experimental *Il mondo salvato dai ragazzini* ('The World Saved by Little Children,' 1968), Morante published the controversial best-seller *History: A Novel* (1974). Set in Rome during World War II, the novel portrays the battles for survival of a widow and her two sons as emblems of history's assault on the powerless. Her final novel *Aracoeli* (1982), awarded the Médicis Prize in 1984, explores the contradictory feelings binding a disillusioned son to the memory of his mother.

RP-I

Morazzoni, Marta (*b.* 1950) Italian novelist. Morazzoni lives in Gallarate, near Milan, where she works as a high school teacher of literature. She has a degree in philosophy from the University of Milan. Her first work *The Girl with the Turban* (1986) was a tremendous success both in Italy and abroad. It is a collection of five stories, based on central themes of distance, travel, illness, cruelty, and death. Her style is notable for its attention to everyday details and subtleties, and many of the stories are fictional retellings of historical events. She won the Premio Campiello for *The Invention of the Truth* (1988), a postmodern novel which intertwines the story of the creation of the Bayeux tapestry (attributed to Queen Matilda and 300 women weavers in medieval Amiens) with the tale of Gothic art scholar John Ruskin's last trip to the cathedral in Amiens in 1879. *His Mother's House* (1992) delves into the meaning of solitude and family relations through the story of a middle-aged man's annual trip

home to his mother's house in Norway. Morazzoni's latest novels are *L'estuario* ('Estuary,' 1996) and *Il caso Courrier* ('The Courrier Case,' 1997).

DGr

Mørch, Dea Trier (*b.* 1941) Danish writer, graphic artist. Mørch, the 1977 Danish Author of the Year, was born in Copenhagen to an unwed mother. She graduated from the Royal Academy of Fine Arts, and also studied at fine arts academies in Warsaw, Crakow, Belgrade, Leningrad, and Prague. A member of the Danish Communist Party for ten years, she was also a founding member of the artists' collective Røde Mor ('The Red Mother'). Her first book *Sorgmunter socialisme. Sovjetiske raderinger* ('Bitter-sweet Socialism: Soviet Sketches,' 1968), a travel account, was an instantaneous critical success. This was followed by another travel account *Polen* ('Poland,' 1970). After becoming a mother, her writing shifted in both form and content. A version of the novel *Winter's Child* (1976) became an award-winning film. After this depiction of experiences of mothers in a prenatal unit, she explored the other end of life in *Evening Star* (1982), a novel about coming to terms with dying. *Morgengaven* ('The Morning Gift,' 1984) studies the conflicts in a marriage of two artists. Mørch's latest literary works, *Landskab i to etager* ('Landscape in Two Floors,' 1992) and *Hvide logne* ('White Lies,' 1995), written with her daughter, are epistolary novels. Mørch's woodcuts illustrate many of her books.

MHH

Mordecai, Pamela (*b.* 1942) Jamaican poet, children's writer. A prolific writer and educator, Mordecai attended the University of the West Indies and was also educated in the US. She published her early poems in such journals as *Bim*, *Savacou*, *Jamaica Journal*, and *Caribbean Quarterly*. Co-editor and contributor to the poetry anthologies *Jamaica Woman*, *From Our Yard: Jamaican Poetry Since*

Independence, and *Sunside Tide Rising* (all 1994), she has published *Story Poems* (1987), *Journey Poem* (1989), and *de man: a performance poem* (1995). She is also well-known for editing, with Betty Wilson, a collection of Caribbean women's prose entitled *Her True True Name* (1989). Mordecai has been lauded for her efforts to transform the Jamaican educational curriculum. Her collection *Ezra's Goldfish and Other Story Poems* (1995) won the Vic Reid Award for Children's Literature. She established Sandberry Press, a Kingston publishing house, and currently is editor of *Caribbean Quarterly*.

ED

Morejón, Nancy (*b.* 1944) Cuban poet, translator. Morejón was born into a working-class family in Havana. She participated in the Cuban revolution while studying French literature at Havana University. In 1966, she was the first Cuban student of African ancestry to receive a degree in the Facultad de Artes. Influenced by Angela Davis and the Cuban poet Nicolás Guillén, she focuses on explicitly political themes in her poetry, and on the linkage between race, class, gender, nationality, and revolution in the Caribbean, the United States, and Africa. Translated into many languages, her literary and critical works have received several Cuban awards, including the 1986 Premio de la Crítica. *Mutismos* ('Silences,'1962) is her earliest collection of poems. In *Elogio de la danza* ('In praise of dance,' 1982) she explores jazz and beauty; in later works, such as *Piedra Pulida* ('Polished Stone,' 1986), natural imagery and themes are used to reflect the beauty of her island. Bilingual editions include *When the Island Sleeps Like a Wing: Selected Poetry* (1985) and *Grenada Notebook/Cuaderno de Granada* (1984). Her translations of Molière and Shakespeare have been staged by Cuban theater groups, and she has translated the works of many French and English authors into Spanish.

CJG

Moreno, Virginia R. (*b.* 1925) Philippine playwright, poet. Born in Manila, Moreno graduated in 1948 with a degree in philosophy from the University of the Philippines, where she also earned her master's degree with her study of Philippine short fiction in English from 1908 to 1940. Her one-act play *Glass Altars* (1952) signaled the debut of a playwright with a formidable sense of history in a genre then dominated by male writers. In her subsequent plays, such as *Straw Patriot: A Tragedy in Five Scenes* (1967), *The Onyx Wolf* (1969; also known as *Itim Asu* in the Sao Paulo Theatre Arts Biennale), and *Indio Spoliarium* (1971), she tackled the controversial lives of colorful figures in Philippine history. Her poetry, written in the lyrical and enigmatic style of the French symbolists, is collected in one volume titled *Batik Maker and Other Poems* (1972), which won the Carlos Palance Memorial Award for Literature. Moreno went into self-imposed exile in Paris during the first year of martial law. While in Europe, she continued writing and studying drama and film. She went to Iowa on an international writing fellowship in 1973. The Don Pablo Roman award was given in 1981 for her still unpublished novel *The God Director*. For her achievements in literature, she was given the Southeast Asia (S.E.A.) Write Award in 1984 by HRH the Prince of Thailand and Queen Sirikit.

ME

Morgan, Sally (*b.* 1951) Australian autobiographer, biographer. Morgan was born Sally Milroy in Perth, Western Australia, daughter of a white father and a part-Aboriginal mother. She received a BA (1974) in psychology from the University of Western Australia, and is married with four children. Morgan's autobiographical family history *My Place* (1987) has sold more than half a million copies and won awards including the Order of Australia Book Prize. The story told by Morgan, including oral narratives from her mother, grandmother, and great-uncle, reveals a history of Aboriginal family disruption and white racism significant for its representing a general history of mistreatment affecting thousands of people over several generations. It is a moving record of how one individual found her 'place' in a society that had attempted to disguise its shameful past. She has also written a biography of Jack McPhee, her tribal grandfather, called *Wanamurraganya* (1989), which won the Human Rights Award; *The Flying Emu and Other Australia Stories* (1991), a collection of Aboriginal tales and legends; and the play *Sistergirl* (1992). She is an accomplished artist whose work is included in several important national collections.

HT

Morgner, Irmtraud (1933–1990) East German novelist. The daughter of a train conductor, Morgner attended the Leipzig literary institute and became an editor of *Neue Deutsche Literatur*. She lived as a freelance author in East Berlin, tracing a fantastic mobility through her writings on the 'entrance of woman into history.' Her erotic sense of humor subverts the gendered divisions of the world in *Leben und Abenteuer der Trobadora Beatriz* ('Life and Adventures of the Troubadour Beatrice,' 1974), a female picaresque of women's experience and irrepressible laughter. Medieval troubadour Beatrice meets GDR philologist and subway driver Laura, embracing her 'poetic of the real' beyond adventurous searches for the unicorn in Florence and Rome. In *Amanda. Ein Hexenroman* ('Amanda: A Witch Novel,' 1983), the female troubadour restores Laura's life in a 'witch novel' of imaginative frames, ranging from news and notes to speeches, tracts, essays, and other notations of novel realities. This quasialchemist literature predates a general 'revolution of the witches' devoted to undermining the boundaries of male society. A magical symbiosis of pleasure and politics moves Morgner's critique of German societies and their apocalyptic logic of history. Her catalyzing wit overcomes contemporary depression in a playful dialectic that traces unorthodox socialist positions even in the face of a postfeminist reunification of patriarchal structures.

AG

Morits, Iunna Petrovna (*b*. 1937) Russian poet, essayist, children's writer. Evacuated from her native Kiev to the Urals during World War II, in 1955 Morits moved to Moscow and enrolled in the Maxim Gorky Literary Institute, graduating and publishing the poetry collection *Mys' zhelaniia* ('Cape of Desire') in 1961. A contemporary of the more successful *Akhmadulina, she encountered difficulties publishing her poetry, and subsisted on translations (mainly from Hungarian and Latvian) and composition of children's verse. Morits's formally traditional poems celebrate nature's variety, life's vivid and intense moments, resistance and energy, and a fresh, independent perception of the world. Poems of the 1960s and 1970s refract life through history, art, and culture, alluding to the Bible and Classical Greece. 'Between Scylla and Charybdis' (1975) ironically maps the fate of women poets in Russia. Glasnost and de-Sovietization enabled the publication of numerous poems suppressed earlier, and several collections, including *Na etom berege vysokom* ('On This High Shore,' 1987) and *Muskul vody* ('Muscle of Water,' 1990). The latter teems with oblique historical references, more experimental lines and rhymes, and intense emotional convictions.

HG

Morrison, Toni (*b*. 1931) US novelist, essayist. Born Chloe Anthony Wofford in Lorain, Ohio, Morrison grew up in a working-class neighborhood that provided the setting for her early novels. She attended Howard University, where she earned a BA in English in 1953; she earned a master's degree in English from Cornell

University in 1955. She married Harold Morrison, an architect; they had two sons before separating in 1964. From 1955 onwards, Morrison has held a series of academic appointments; she is currently a professor at Princeton University. While working as an editor at Random House, she published her first novel *The Bluest Eye* (1970); its vivid language and frank depiction of the experiences of African-American women are characteristic of all of Morrison's fiction. Her second novel *Sula* (1973) intertwines the story of the friendship between two women with that of the breakdown of their community. *Song of Solomon* (1977) became a bestseller, as did *Tar Baby* (1981). The latter novel examines the tension between middle-class African-Americans and folk culture. Morrison won the Pulitzer Prize for *Beloved* (1987), a haunting novel about slavery, motherhood, and the effect of the past on the present. In 1992, Morrison published her sixth novel, *Jazz*, as well as a collection of essays, *Playing in the Dark: Whiteness and the Literary Imagination*. In 1993, she was awarded the Nobel prize in literature. Her seventh novel *Paradise* (1997) brackets the stories of a community of unconventional women with an account of their destruction by a group of men from a small black town in Oklahoma.

JEM

Mugo, Micere Githae (*b*. 1942) Kenyan poet, critic, playwright, activist. Mugo was born in Kenya and educated in Uganda at the University of Makerere. She later earned a doctorate from the University of Toronto. She is a Marxist who has always chosen to use her writings as weapons of revolution. She became involved in the revolutionary process while working as Dean of the Faculty of Arts at the University of Nairobi, where she found herself unwilling to fulfill her role of policing the thoughts and ideas of her colleagues and students. Her publications, reflecting her desire that the Kenyan

people be heard, include a collection of poetry, *Daughter of My People, Sing!* (1976); a play, *The Long Illness of Ex-Chief Kiti* (1976); and a work of criticism, *Visions of Africa* (1981). Mugo co-authored the play *The Trial of Dedan Kimathi* with author and activist Ngugi wa Thiong'o in 1976. Since 1982, Mugo has chosen to live in Zimbabwe.

KEJ

Mugot, Hazel de Silva (*b*. 1947) Kenyan novelist. Mugot was born of mixed Sri Lanka and Seychelles parentage; her father was an accountant and her mother a schoolteacher. She grew up in Kenya where she attended school until she went to the US to complete her higher education. Upon her return to Kenya, she taught social work at the University of Nairobi and worked as a professional model. Her novel *Sega of Seychelles* (1983) emphasizes the complex roles of the women of Seychelles, her mother's home island. The setting of her second novel *Makongo, the Hyena* is Kenya. *Black Night of Quiloa* (1971) evolves out of her experience from living in the US and then returning to her home island. This particular novel exhibits her unique experimental style that blends poetry and prose. The heroine of the novel, Hima, lives in London, but feels alienated, displaced, and disenchanted and longs to return to Quiloa, her homeland, and her own cultural heritage. Quiloa becomes Hima's link to her past just as Seychelles links Mugot to her past.

SDR

Muhando, Penina (*b*. 1948) Tanzanian playwright. Muhando was born in Tanzania and received a BA in theater arts, an MA in education, and a PhD in language and linguistics from the University of Dar-es-Salaam. She began her writing career by writing short scripts for Parents' Days in primary school, and has published nine plays and a collection of African tales since 1972, all in Kiswahili – due to a desire to reach her Eastern African audience (especially Tanzanians) as directly as possible. She is committed to writing plays that deal with social and developmental problems. Her plays include *Hatia* ('Guilt'), *Pambo* ('Decoration'), *Talaki si mke wangu* ('Woman, I Divorce You'), *Nguezo-mama* ('Mother Pillar,' 1982), *Harakati za Ukombozi* ('Liberation Struggles,' 1982), co-authored with Amandira Liharba and Ndyanao Balisidya, and *Lena Ubani* ('Antidote to Rot'). Her plays are on the reading lists of schools and colleges in Dar-es-Salaam and have been performed in schools and in public theaters. She is active in the Popular Theater Movement (Theater for Development). A mother and grandmother, Muhando is currently professor and head of the Department of Theater Arts at the University of Dar-es-Salaam.

AUA

Mukherjee, Bharati (*b*. 1940) US fiction writer. Born in Calcutta, India, Mukherjee came to America in 1961 after receiving her MA from the University of Baroda, and earned an MFA and a PhD from the University of Iowa. She taught at McGill University, Canada for fourteen years, and is now professor of English at the University of California, Berkeley. She is married to writer Clark Blaise; they have two sons. Her first novel *The Tiger's Daughter* (1972) describes a young, upper-class Indian woman's painfully ambiguous position between India and America. *Wife* (1975) is a story of a middle-class Bengali housewife who becomes violent when unable to adapt in America. *Days and Nights in Calcutta* (1977), co-authored with Blaise during a year's stay in India, records Mukherjee's disillusionment with the Indian middle class. Her story collections *Darkness* (1985) and *The Middleman and Other Stories*, winner of the 1988 National Book Critics' Circle Award, depict the trials and transformations of new immigrants in Canada and the United States. The latter work presents greater cultural diversity and celebrates the immigrant

experience, reflecting Mukherjee's new 'American' voice. *Jasmine* (1989), *The Holder of the World* (1993), and *Leave it to Me* (1997) constitute a loose trilogy of novels featuring a female protagonist who recreates herself in a new world.

SA

Mukherjee, Meenakshi (*b*. 1937) Indian literary critic. One of the foremost literary critics in India today, Mukherjee was born in Calcutta and educated in Patna, and at the Universities of Pennsylvania and Pune. She has taught English literature and comparative literature at the universities of Pune, New York State, Delhi, and Hyderabad, and at Jawaharlal Nehru University, Delhi, and was one of the founder-editors of *Vagartha*, a journal of Indian writing that was published from Delhi in the 1970s. Her continuing interest has been issues of nation, nationalism, and gender in Indian writing. Among her publications are *The Twice Born Fiction: Themes and Techniques of the Indian Novel in English* (1971) and *Realism and Reality: The Novel and Society in India* (1985), an important study of the factors that shaped the development of the novel form in various Indian languages. She has contributed widely to journals and books in India and abroad, and has consistently promoted literature in Indian languages that has been neglected due to contemporary conditions of literary production and circulation. She co-edited *Interrogating Post-colonialism: Theory, Text and Context* (1996), a collection that critically evaluates the institutionalization of postcolonial studies in Europe and the US. Her latest book is *The Perishable Empire and Other Essays* (1999).

UB

Müller, Herta (*b*. 1953) German-Romanian novelist. Born in Nitzkydorf in Romania, Müller belongs to the ethnic German minority of the Banat Swabians. From 1973 to 1976, she studied German and Romance literatures at the University of Temeswar and worked as a German teacher. In 1980, she lost her job after refusing to work for the Romanian secret police. These experiences are reflected in *Heute wär' ich mir lieber nicht begegnet* ('Today, I'd Have Preferred Not to Encounter Myself,' 1997). Tired of political oppression, she applied for an exit permit. Until her departure in 1987, she was not allowed to publish or to travel. Considered one of the most distinguished German-Romanian authors, Müller's writings have a high poetic quality and her language is rich in pictures and new word creations. *Niederungen* ('Lowlands,' 1982) portrays a childhood in a village in Banat governed by the cruelty of the adult world and the nationalism of the ethnic Germans in Romania. *The Passport* (1986) deals with the exit from that country. *Der Teufel sitzt im Spiegel* ('The Devil Sits in the Mirror,' 1991), *Der Fuchs war damals schon dar Jäger* ('At That Time the Fox was Already the Hunter,' 1992), and *The Land of Green Plums* (1994) reflect the specific ethnic German world from a woman's perspective. Müller has received several Romanian and German literary awards.

MMu

Munro, Alice (*b.* 1931) Canadian short story writer. Born in Wingham, Ontario, Alice Laidlaw studied at the University of Western Ontario. Without taking a degree, she left to marry James Munro in 1951 and moved to Vancouver, British Columbia. Divorced in 1976, she returned to Ontario where she lives, in Clinton, with her second husband. Her debut collection *Dance of the Happy Shades* (1968) subtly balances inner conflicts and social obligations. Munro's characters are frequently embarrassed or reserved, because they feel themselves to be different. Del in the loosely constructed novel *Lives of Girls and Women* (1971; titled *The Beggar Maid* in the US and UK), and Rose in the story collection *Who Do You Think You Are?* (1978) suffer awkwardly by virtue of their

femaleness, youth or intelligence. Munro deals with adult complexities, such as marriage, death, and parental responsibility, in *Something I've Been Meaning to Tell You* (1974), *The Moons of Jupiter* (1982), and *The Progress of Love* (1986). Munro's unparalleled craft in short fiction has resulted in sly manipulation of perspective, within a detailed, even photographic, realism, in *Friend of My Youth* (1990) and *Open Secrets* (1994). Munro included twenty-eight stories in *Selected Stories* (1996). She has won the Governor-General's Award for fiction three times (1968, 1978, 1986).

AH

Murdoch, Iris (1919–1999) British novelist, critic, essayist. One of the most important of postwar British writers, Murdoch was born an only child in Dublin and was raised in London. She studied classics and philosophy at Somerville College, Oxford, where she earned first class honors in 1942, and then pursued graduate work at Cambridge. In 1948 she became a Fellow in Philosophy at St Anne's College, Oxford. She married John Bayley, a professor of English literature at Oxford, in 1956. She published several philosophical works and is known for her brilliant and witty explorations of ethical and philosophical questions in her novels. She engages with issues such as good versus evil, the purpose of existence, the quest for freedom, and the role of art and love in human lives. In 1954 she published *Under the Net*, her first novel, about a man who tries to eradicate contingency from his existence. Her characters, normally well-educated middle-class professionals, seek spiritual, intellectual, and sexual fulfillment. Her narratives are intricately plotted and complex, yet her characters often find themselves in comically absurd or arbitrary situations. Murdoch wrote twenty-six novels. The early ones include *Flight from the Enchanter* (1956), *The Bell* (1958), *A Severed Head* (1961), *The Unofficial Rose* (1962), and *The Red and the Green* (1965).

Her prize-winning novels include *The Black Prince* (1973; James Tait Black Memorial Prize), a murder mystery exploring the power of artistic creation; *The Sacred and Profane Love Machine* (1974; Whitbread Prize); and *The Sea, The Sea* (1978; Booker Prize), about a man's obsessive fixation on a woman he loved as a boy.

Her later novels include *The Philosopher's Pupil* (1983), *The Good Apprentice* (1985), *The Message to the Planet* (1989), and *The Green Knight* (1993), an updated retelling of the Sir Gawain story.

DVT

Murthy, Janaki Sreenivas (*see* Vaidehi)

N

Naheed, Kishwar (*b*. 1940) Pakistani poet. Born in Bulund Shehr, India, Kishwar's life was shaped by her parent's involvement with the anti-colonial freedom movement and the subsequent trauma of displacement, when her family migrated to Pakistan in 1949. Witness to the rape and abduction of women that accompanied partition, her personal experience of loss and the exigencies of a new life in a new land were compounded by the patriarchal politics of the literary world. Challenging traditional poetic norms where the woman is always only the object of desire, she breached the walls of the male citadel by speaking in her own voice through poetry rather than through fiction. The most prolific poet of her generation, her work has become increasingly political, partly due to her rejection of the traditional forms of Urdu poetry which limit what can be said, and partly in response to the political climate in Pakistan, which since the 1980s has become increasingly repressive toward women. In addition to her autobiography *The Story of a Bad Woman* (1996), eight collections of her poems have been published between 1969 and 1990. *We Sinful Women* (1990) is a selection of her poems in English translation.

NH

Na'mānī, Hudā al- (*b*. 1930) Syrian poet. Born in Damascus, Syria, Na'mānī grew up in a wealthy family known for its mystical tradition and political activism. She received her early education at the Lycée-Français and the Franciscan's school where French was stressed. However, her baccalaureate was earned in 1946 from a public school where Arabic was the focus. In 1950, she graduated from the College of Law at Damascus University and went on to practice law until 1952. After her marriage in 1955, she moved to Egypt where she attended the American University in Cairo. She lived there until 1969. She later attended the American University in Beirut, pursuing her PhD degree in literature and history. She traveled extensively in Europe and the US. Today, she resides in Beirut, where she founded her own publishing house. Na'mānī has two sons. She began writing poetry in French, but never published it. Her first collection in Arabic, *Ilayka* ('To You,' 1970) is characterized by its personal tone and mystical tendency. She followed this tradition, while adding some political themes, in her seven other collections, the most recent of which is *Kitāb al-Wajd wa-al-Tawājud* ('The Book of Passion and Existence,' 1998). Her collection *I was a Point I was a Circle* (1978) was translated into English in 1993.

JTZ

Namjoshi, Suniti (*b*. 1941) Indian-Canadian-British fabulist, poet. Born in Bombay, Namjoshi took degrees from the University of Poona before entering the

Indian Administrative Service. Her first four poetry collections were published in India. Following an MS at the University of Missouri, she completed her doctorate in 1972 at McGill University in Montreal. She taught for seventeen years at the University of Toronto, and then in 1987 moved to Devon, England, where she is a full-time writer. She is currently an Honorary Fellow in Women's Studies at the University of Exeter. Her razor-sharp writing is full of wit and humor, and explores the complicated connections between feminism, lesbianism, gender, race, and writing. Her well-known *Feminist Fables* (1981) draws from both Indian and European traditions. Her fables are poetically dense, inviting readers to draw their own conclusions. Her novella *The Conversations of Cow* (1985) uses metamorphosis and talking animals to investigate the complexity of human relationships and identity. Collaborations with Gillian Hanscombe include *Flesh and Paper* (1986). Her many volumes, published in India, Canada, England, and Australia, include most importantly *Because of India: Selected Poems* (1989). *Building Babel* (1996) reflects her interest in text and technology by inviting readers to contribute to its interactive Internet web site.

MR

Na'na', Ḥamīda (b. 1946) Syrian novelist, poet, journalist. Born in the town of Idlib in Syria, to a conservative family that imposed the veil on her, Na'na' earned her BA in Arabic from Damascus University in 1971. She worked as a journalist for the Ministry of Information in Syria. She traveled to Paris where she worked for UNESCO from 1974 to 1977, and as a reporter for the Lebanese newspaper *Al-Safir*. Her first work *Anāshīd Imra'a lā Ta'rif al-Faraḥ* ('Songs of a Woman Who Does Not Know Joy,' 1970) is a collection of poems that revolves around individual and collective themes. In her novel *The Homeland* (1979), she tells the story of a leftist young woman who is dismissed from the Palestinian guerrilla movement because of her refusal to accept the military strategy of the movement and conform to the dominant patriarchal norms. *Man Yajru' 'alā al-Shawq* ('Who Dares to Yearn,' 1989) is a novel that examines the issues of emigration and alienation through the experience of a young Lebanese woman who fled the civil war in Lebanon to live in Paris. While working for *Al-Safir*, Nana published interviews with such French intellectuals as Michel Foucault and Roland Barthes. She now lives in Paris where she works as a journalist.

JTZ

Naranjo, Carmen (b. 1931) Costa Rican novelist, poet. Born and educated in Costa Rica, Naranjo has pursued successful careers in writing and in public administration. Her literary work integrates both avocations, revealing her thorough knowledge of the inner workings of bureaucracy and its alienating and frustrating effect on the individual. She has published seven books of poetry, but she is better known for her technically innovative fiction. She experiments with fragmentary structures and reduces characters to the level of a mere voice, as in *Diario de una multitud* ('Diary of a Crowd,' 1974); she drops the narrator's guidance from dialogues or selects a dialogic structure, as in *Los perros no ladraron* ('The Dogs Did Not Bark,' 1966). Her prose, especially in her short fiction, is frequently poetic, and reveals her concern with language. Her most ambitious work *Sobrepunto* ('Overpoint,' 1985) expands on a recurring theme: woman's exclusion from the spheres of political, social, and economic policy. She also highlights the imagination as a means of overcoming isolation and boredom. In 1966, she received the Aquileo Echeverría Prize for *Los perros no ladraron*, the Premio EDUCA in 1973 for *Diario de una multitud*, and again the EDUCA Prize in 1982 for *Ondina*.

PR

Naravadee (Pensri Kiengsiri) (*b.* 1931) Thai fiction writer, poet. A native of Narathiwat, a southern province in Thailand, Naravadee studied physiotherapy and graduated with a diploma from the Royal Melbourne Hospital and Melbourne University. While working as a physiotherapist, she began writing short stories and novels. Her collection of short stories *Taw and Other Thai Short Stories* has been translated into English, and an English translation of the story 'Auam Went to Bangkok' was included in the anthology *ASEAN Short Stories*. Her novel *Fa Klai, Talay Kwang* ('The Sea is Wide, The Sky is Near'), which depicts the life and culture of rural people in the South, won the National Book Award in 1995. In addition to thirty-two novels and five collections of short stories, Naravadee also has a collection of poems written in English titled *Poems From Thailand*. Currently she is president of the Writer's Association of Thailand.

NM

Narbikova, Valeriia Spartakovna (*b.* 1958) Russian prose writer, painter. A Muscovite graduate of the Gorky Literary Institute, Narbikova created a stir in 1988 with her debut publication *Day for Night*. Considered the first erotic postmodernist novel by a Russian woman, it contains the chief features of Narbikova's authorial manner: the indefatigable copulation of bodies, citations from high and low culture, paronomastic elements, and self-references. Highlighting the formidable power of language to construct reality and shape perception, she relies on the destabilizing, reconfiguring potential of triangulation in both plot and discourse. Her playful, ironic technique links her with conceptualist artists, who likewise place distancing quotation marks around the components of their art. Narbikova expands, extracts, and interpolates segments of her own narratives within her fiction, thereby intimating the contingent nature of beginnings, endings, and structure itself. English

translations include *In the Here and There* (1990) as well as *Day for Night*.

HG

Nasrallāh, Emily (*b.* 1931) Lebanese novelist, short story writer, journalist. Born in the village of Kawkaba in southern Lebanon to an illiterate Maronite father and an Orthodox Christian mother, Nasrallāh soon moved to al-Kfayr at the foot of Mount Hermon. Her father encouraged her education and in 1958 she received her BA in literature from the American University in Beirut, where she also met her husband. She has two sons and two daughters, and stresses that motherhood need not be an impediment to women's writing. Her work deals primarily with village life from the point of view of women. Her first novel *Tuyūr Aylūl* ('September Birds,' 1962), dramatized life in a Lebanese village through the use of three tragic love stories. The major theme of the work emphasized the conflict between the generations. A later novel *Shajarat al-Diflā* ('The Oleander Tree,' 1968) is a more polished work dealing with similar themes. The Lebanese civil war serves as a backdrop in the novel *Tilka al-Dhikrayāt* ('Those Memories,' 1980), against which a woman and her friend look back upon their past, recalling their own personal war against family and society. In *Flight Against Time* (1981), Nasrallāh examines the problem of emigration from Lebanon against the canvas of the civil war. Her most recent collection *Al-Layālī al-Ghajariyya* ('Gypsy Nights'), was published in 1998.

JTZ

Nasrin, Taslima (*b.* 1962) Bangladeshi poet, essayist. From 1989 to 1993, while working as an anesthesiologist in Dhaka, Nasrin wrote regularly in major national publications. Her prose and poetry – stylistically spare and bold – are marked by the open celebration of sexuality coupled with a deep ambivalence toward the female body, as well as sharp criticism of religion. The titles of her poetry collections, such as *Nirbashito Bahire Antare* ('Banished Within and Without,' 1989), *Atale Antarin* ('Captive in the Abyss,' 1991), and *Ay Koshto Jhepe, Jibon Debo Mepe* ('Pain Come Pouring Down, I'll Measure Out My Life For You,' 1994) capture the sense of isolation, entrapment, and anger that permeate her writing. They also prefigure the pain of exile she was to experience after her first novel *Shame* (1993), a critique of the persecution of Hindus in Bangladesh, was banned by the government. In 1992, she became the first Bangladeshi writer to win Calcutta's prestigious Ananda Puroskar for her *Nirbachito Column* ('Selected Columns,' 1992). A selection of her poems has been published in English as *The Game in Reverse* (1995). She remains a controversial figure in Bangladesh, her case having received worldwide media attention since the government action and religious reaction against *Shame*.

DMS

Naylor, Gloria (*b.* 1950) US novelist. Born in Tunica County, Mississippi, Naylor moved to New York City as a young child and in her twenties worked as a Jehovah's Witness missionary. She graduated from Brooklyn College in 1981 at the age of 31, and two years later she received an MA in Afro-American studies from Yale. She has taught at several colleges and universities in the US. Her bold prose, which celebrates the oral tradition and potently communicates emotion, offers kaleidoscopic depictions of African-American life. Her first novel *The Women of Brewster Place* (1982) won the National Book Award for best first fiction. It depicts, in seven 'stories,' the lives of seven strong African-American women living in a housing project; they support and nurture one another as they share their experiences of being black and female in the US. The book was adapted for television in 1989. The novel *Linden Hills* (1985), based loosely on Dante's *Inferno*, explores the possibilities for and dangers in upward socio-economic mobility. Her third novel *Mama Day* (1988) contains echoes of Shakespeare's *The Tempest*, as the protagonist, Miranda 'Mama' Day, who lives on the mythical island of Willow Springs, tries to reconcile the past with the present. Naylor has adapted her fourth novel *Bailey's Café* (1992), for the stage. *The Men of Brewster Place* (1998; American Book Award) is a sequel to her first novel.

DVT

NDiaye, Marie (*b.* 1967) French novelist. Of interracial Franco-Senegalese origin, NDiaye identifies herself as French and different rather than black and/or feminist. She declined to pursue formal higher education, having published her first novel *Quant au riche avenir* ('As Forever After') at age 18 by France's most prestigious avant-garde publishing house, Editions Minuit, in 1985. She has two children and lives outside of Paris. Considered a most gifted practitioner of the postmodern narrative mode with her ironical and uncommercial approach to fiction, she has received several literary awards. Her presence on the French literary scene was firmly established in 1990 with *Among Family*, where a female character self-destructs because she is systematically ignored because of her 'difference.' The identity quest of the female, contemporary, free-spirited 'other,' whose cultural roots remain unspecified because she naively assumes they need not be specified, defines NDiaye's protagonists. Her most recent novel about a suburban woman *La sorcière* ('The Witch,' 1996) has already been translated into several European languages.

CPM

Ngcobo, Lauretta (*b.* 1931) South African novelist, editor, fiction writer. Born Lauretta Gwina in Ixopa, Ngcobo grew up in the rural area of Natal. Her father died when she was 7 years old, and she was raised by family members who were skilled in the oral narrative tradition. She graduated from Fort Hare University with a BA degree in education. She was forced into exile in 1965 with her husband and three children because of her political activities against apartheid. Before emigrating to Britain in the 1970s, she lived in Switzerland, Tanzania, and Zambia. At present, she lives in London where she works as a day care teacher and as a tutor in the Extra-Mural Department of the University of London. Her first novel *Cross of Gold* (1981) chronicles the 1960 post-Sharpeville era and South Africans' responses to it. She edited and contributed to *Let It Be Told* (1987), a collection of writings by and about black women in Britain. *And They Didn't Die* (1991), Ngcobo's second novel, depicts the collapse of a family under the apartheid government.

MU

Niccolai, Giulia (*b.* 1934) Italian poet, prose writer. Born in Milan, of an American mother and an Italian father, Niccolai began her career as a photojournalist and her first work, the novel *Il grande angolo* ('Wide Angle,' 1966), draws on her experience in that field. For several years she edited the literary journal *Tam Tam* with her companion, the late neo-avant-garde poet Adriano Spatola. Niccolai's early poetry can be situated within the experimentalism of the Italian neo-avant-garde of the 1960s when formal issues dominated poetic creation. Her models include Lewis Carroll, Gertrude Stein (whose work she has translated into Italian), and children's verse. In *Humpty Dumpty* (1969) she uses Carroll and *Webster's Dictionary* to create visual poetry, such as the word 'cheese' written in the shape of a smile. In *Russky Salad Ballads* (1977), she plays linguistic ping-pong with Italian, English, German, and French, using many interlinguistic puns. The collection *Greenwich* (1971) contains poems made up entirely of place names. Much of her poetry is gathered in *Harry's Bar e altre poesie* ('Harry's Bar and Other Poems,'

1981). For almost two decades, Niccolai has been a dedicated follower of Buddhism, and her recent prose pieces reflect her strong spirituality as well as her keen poetic sensibility.

RW

Nichols, Grace (*b.* 1950) Guyanese-British poet, children's writer, novelist. Born in Georgetown (British Guyana, now Guyana), Nichols grew up in the coastal village of New Amsterdam. She took a diploma in communications at the University of Guyana, taught primary school, and worked as a journalist before emigrating to Britain in 1977. Blending history with African and Amerindian myths, her first collection of poetry *i is a long-memoried woman* (1983) won the Commonwealth Poetry Prize, and is a sensuous and cathartic evocation of Caribbean slavery from women's perspectives. In rewriting history, Nichols celebrates black women who resourcefully subvert and resist oppression and exploitation. *The Fat Black Woman's Poems* (1984) and *Lazy Thoughts of a Lazy Woman* (1989) cast a mischievously humorous glance at black women's lives in Britain. *Sunris* (1966) combines the themes of history and memory with contemporary experience, the long title poem using Calypso rhythms and Carnival motifs to depict a woman reclaiming herself. The semi-autobiographical *Bildungsroman Whole of a Morning Sky* (1986) takes place during the Guyanese pre-independence turbulence. Nichols has also extensively written and edited stories and poems for children. She now lives in Lewes, Sussex with poet John Agard and their two daughters.

MSt

Ní Chuilleanáin, Eiléan (*b.* 1942) Irish poet. Born in Cork, Ní Chuilleanáin received a BA in English and history in 1962 and an MA in English in 1964 from University College, Cork, and a B.Litt. in Elizabethan prose from Lady Margaret Hall, Oxford in 1969. She married

Macdara Woods in 1978; they have one son. In 1975, she was one of the founders of the literary magazine *Cyphers*. She has taught at Trinity College, Dublin since 1966, and is currently a senior lecturer there. Her first book of poetry *Acts and Monuments* (1972) won the Patrick Kavanagh Award. Her imagery is particular and visual, her descriptions often topographical, as she charts rooms and landscapes, at home and in various places around the world. She views the world through the lenses of myth, folklore, and history. Her volumes include *Site of Ambush* (1975), *The Second Voyage* (1977), *The Rose Geranium* (1981), *The Magdelene Sermon* (1989), and *The Brazen Serpent* (1994). She has been awarded the *Irish Times* prize for poetry and the O'Shaughnessy Prize.

JEM

Ní Dhomhnaill, Nuala (*b.* 1952) Irish poet. Born in St Helens, Lancashire, Ní Dhomhnaill grew up in County Tipperary in Ireland. She was educated at University College, Cork and traveled extensively, living in Holland and Turkey. She is married, and has four children. She is one of the most important modern poets writing in the Irish language. The history, traditions, and folklore of Ireland are central to her poems and to her decision not to write in English. Her sensuous and formally innovative verses depict specific places and people in Ireland, and masterfully recount the stories she has heard. She mingles the modern and the mythic, the humorous with the bleak. Her first two volumes *An Dealg Droighin* ('The Thorn of the Blackthorn,' 1982) and *Féar Suaithinseach* ('Marvellous Grass,' 1984) were highly praised. She published a bilingual edition of her poetry, *Rogha Dánta / Selected Poems* (translated by Michael Hartnett) in 1986. Her reputation grew beyond Ireland with *Pharoah's Daughter* (1990), which features translations by Seamus Heaney, *Medbh McGuckian, Paul Muldoon, and other leading Irish poets. Her other vol-

umes include *Feis* (1991), *The Astrakhan Cloak* (1992) with translations by Muldoon, *Cead Aighnis* (1998), and *The Water Horse* (1999) with translations by McGuckian and *Eiléan Ní Chuilleanáin.

JEM

Nie Hualing (*b.* 1925) Chinese fiction writer, literary critic. Born into a traditional family in Hubei Province in central China, Nie went to Chongqing as a refugee student during the Sino-Japanese War (1937–45). After she graduated from the Department of Foreign Languages and Literature at National Central University in Nanjing in 1948, she moved to Taiwan where she began her literary career. She worked as the literature editor for the liberal *Free China* until 1960 when the journal was closed down by the Guomingtang (Nationalist Party). In 1962 she taught creative writing at National Taiwan and Tung-hai universities. In 1964 she was invited to the Writer's Workshop at the University of Iowa. In 1967, she co-founded the International Writing Program (Iowa) with her husband, the poet Paul Engle. For their important contribution they were nominated for the Nobel Peace Prize. In 1991 she retired from the program in order to devote herself to writing. Nie has received many awards and honorary degrees for her multifaceted accomplishments. As a writer, she has published eighteen books of fiction, essays, translation, and literary criticism in Chinese and English. Her 1976 novel *Mulberry and Peach* stirred much controversy for its explicit description of female sexuality and for touching on political taboos. A pioneering work of Chinese diaspora literature which explores the issue of cultural identity, it has been translated into several languages.

MY

Niranjana, Anupama (1934–1991) Indian novelist, short story writer. One of the most popular writers in Kannada, Anupama Niranjana (the nom de plume of Venkatalakshmi) had an eventful life which is a source of emancipatory inspiration to numerous younger women writers. Born into a very modest, low-caste family in Tirthahalli, central Karnataka, she studied to become a physician and married outside her caste after eloping with the novelist and Marxist political activist Niranjana. Both husband and wife were active in bringing general knowledge to a broad public; she authored books on women's and children's health for lay readers. Altogether she wrote 51 books: novels such as *Snehapallavi* ('Refrain of Affection,' 1967) and *Madhavi* (1976), the short story collection *Ondu Giniya Kathe* ('Story of a Parrot,' 1983), children's stories, books on medicine, a travelogue, and two volumes of autobiography. English translations of her stories are anthologized in *Women Writing in India* (1993) and *Separate Journeys* (1998). Her great popularity is due also to her deliberately unsophisticated style of writing. She received several awards, among them the Soviet Land Nehru Award (1978) and the Kannada Rajyotsava Award (1983). The Karnataka Women Writer's Association annually bestows an all-India award for women writers, the Anupama Prasasti, in her name.

RJZ

Njau, Rebeka (*b.* 1939) Kenyan novelist, playwright, critic. Raised in a small village outside Nairobi, Njau grew up among strong women, and her critical and creative writings have focused on presenting these women, their conflicts, and the choices they make. Educated first in Nairobi and later at Makerere University in Uganda, she became a teacher, and in 1964 she founded the Nairobi Secondary School for Girls. She eventually gave up teaching, however, because she felt she needed more time for her writing. Her first work was a play *The Scar* (1965), which explores the tragedy of a family in which an unconventional woman is challenged by her brothers for the family's inheritance. This early work anticipates her later ones,

which center on women who don't fit into the prescribed traditions of a colonized society. Her most famous work is a novel *Ripples in a Pool* (1975), the first sustained portrait of a lesbian within the context of postcolonial African literature. Her interest in women's choices and the oral tradition led Njau to write a critical piece, *Kenyan Women Heroes and Their Magical Power* (1984). Njau is also a visual artist, a talent she shares with her husband Elimo Njau. At present, Njau works with the Kenyan Council of Churches in Nairobi, and has an unpublished novel, *Alone with the Fig Tree*, for which she won the East African Writing Committee Prize.

GW

Noël, Francine (*b.* 1945) Canadian novelist. Born in Montreal, Noël graduated from the University of Montreal with a BA in literature. Since 1969, she has taught drama at the University of Quebec in Montreal. She has one son. She has published three novels and a play. Her novels capture the transformations of Quebecois culture and more specifically of certain areas of Montreal. *Maryse* (1983) spans the decade 1968–78, a crucial period in the formation of Quebecois cultural and political identity. In *Myriam Première* ('Myriam the First,' 1987), she paints a host of characters inhabiting a traditional neighborhood of Montreal, the plateau Mont Royal. The narration shifts between different points of view, including that of the child Myriam. Noël introduces some fantastic elements in her novel, reminiscent of magic realism. Her most recent novel *Babel, prise deux ou Nous avons tous découvert l'Amérique* ('Babel, Take Two or All of Us Have Discovered America,' 1990, 1992) was published in two versions. It is a sophisticated novel that addresses the ethnic and cultural diversity of Montreal, especially of the old neighborhood of Outremont, which separates the francophones from the anglophones. Noël's fiction is at once an important contribution to Quebecois letters and a significant cultural comment on her times.

JV

Nolla, Olga (*b*. 1938) Puerto Rican poet, novelist. Born in San Juan, Nolla has distinguished herself as a sardonic and astute critic of social privilege and patriarchal authority, themes already present in her inaugural work *De lo familiar* ('On Things Familiar,' 1973). Her oeuvre evinces a feminist consciousness which casts a suspicious eye towards Puerto Rico's class structure and her class of origin. In *El ojo de la tormenta* ('The Eye of the Storm,' 1976), introspective and at times confessional poems about the legacy of paternal authority in her life and in language, the search for the self takes place amidst the collapse of old social conventions. The tone of her poetry is lucid and honest. She has published numerous literary essays, and was co-founder, with *Rosario Ferré, of the pathbreaking literary journal *Zona: carga y descarga* ('Zone: Loading and Unloading,' 1972–75), and, more recently, of *Cupey* (1984). With the novel *El castillo de la memoria* ('The Castle of Memory,' 1996), she delves into the island's early Spanish past. Her latest work *El Manuscrito de Miramar* ('The Miramar Manuscript,' 1998) places the mother-daughter dyad center stage, as her agile and concise prose uncovers alternate versions of reality. Nolla currently teaches literature at the Universidad Metropolitana.

MR-F

Norman, Marsha (*b*. 1947) US playwright. Born in Louisville, Kentucky to fundamentalist Christian parents, Norman graduated in 1969 from Agnes Scott College in Georgia with a degree in philosophy. She returned to Kentucky, married her former teacher Michael Norman, and completed an MA from the University of Louisville. She taught in public schools and worked with emotionally disturbed children at a state hospital. Her critically acclaimed first play *Getting Out* (1977)

won the George Oppenheimer Award, and won for Norman the Outer Critics' Award for best new playwright. Establishing two of Norman's key preoccupations – decisions and their consequences, and the problems of the mother–daughter relationship – *Getting Out* tells the story of a prostitute who decides to change her life. Norman's best-known play, *'night Mother* (1983), won the Pulitzer Prize and was nominated for a Tony award. It has only two characters – a daughter who resolutely announces that she has decided to end her bleak life by suicide, and her mother, who tries to dissuade her. Norman's other plays include *Third and Oak: The Laundromat* (1978), *Circus Valentine* (1979), *The Holdup* (1983), *Traveler in the Dark* (1984), and *Sarah and Abraham* (1988). She has published a novel, *The Fortune Teller* (1987), and has written the book and lyrics for a musical adaptation of *The Secret Garden* (1991).

DVT

Nothomb, Amélie (*b*. 1967) Francophone Belgian novelist. Nothomb was born in Japan where her father was an ambassador. She spent her childhood and adolescence in various parts of Asia. She visited Belgium for the first time at age 17 and elected to live there. She attended L'Université Libre de Bruxelles where she received a Licence in Roman philology in 1988. Her first novel *Hygiène de l'assassin* ('The Assassin's Hygiene,' 1992), a story about an odious Nobel Prize winner, instantly became a bestseller. In her second novel, *Le sabotage amoureux* ('The Love Sabotage,' 1993), she tells the tale of delirious childhood in Peking, that of an 'Alice in Horrorland!' *Les Combustibles* ('The Combustibles,' 1994), with Sartrian echoes, presents three characters trapped in an infernal situation. *The Stranger Next Door* (1995) is a frightening psychological drama. With her three most recent novels – *Péplum* (1997), *Attentat* ('Terrorist Attack,' 1997), and *Mercure* (1998) – Nothomb continues to amaze her readers with her unusual mix of wit and cynicism, innocence and perversion. Most of her novels have been adapted for the theater and some for the screen.

YH

Nu Nu Yi (Inwa) (*b.* 1957) Burmese short story writer, novelist. Nu Nu Yi's penname reflects her home town of Inwa (Ava) near Mandalay, where she took a Maths degree. Her fiction reflects first-hand research into issues such as poverty, HIV, homosexuality, and nat (spirit) worship. Her accurate portrayal of Burma's social problems has won her the praise of *Aung San Suu Kyi and close attention from the censors. Her first short story 'Htamein-lay ta-hteh' ('A Little Skirt,' 1984) gained immediate critical recognition. It describes the embarrassment suffered by a poor village girl who, while struggling in a stream to catch a fish, loses her htamein (skirt) and has to run home naked. Nu Nu Yi (Inwa) won the National Literature Prize in 1993 for *Mya-sein-pya Kamayut* ('All Change in Kamayut'), which depicts the lives of the inhabitants of a new Rangoon apartment block. Her short story 'He's Not My Father' (1992), about a boy whose father reappears after being seized for portering in Burma's war zone, is included in the anthology *Inked Over, Ripped Out: Burmese Storytellers and the Censors.*

VBo

Nwapa, Flora (1931–1993) Nigerian novelist, dramatist, short story writer, children's writer. Born in Oguta, Nwapa is regarded as Africa's first female novelist to receive international recognition. She was the first Oguta woman to gain direct entry into and graduate from University College, Ibadan (1957). She earned a Diploma in Education at the University of Edinburgh in 1958. Her first novel *Efuru* (1966) is the first African woman-centered novel in English; it tells the story of a beautiful and gifted woman's disappointments in love and marriage. Nwapa married Gogo Nwakuche in 1967 and together they raised three children. From 1970 to 1975, she was the first woman appointed as a commissioner in East Central State. In 1977, she founded Tan Press Limited, becoming the first African woman to own and manage a publishing company. Before she died in 1993, she published four additional novels, *Idu* (1970), *Never Again* (1975), *One Is Enough* (1981), and *Women Are Different* (1986); two collections of short stories, *This Is Lagos and Other Stories* (1971) and *Wives at War and Other Stories* (1975); a collection of poetry, *Cassava Song and Rice Song* (1986); two books of plays, *Conversations* (1993) and *The First Lady* (1993); many children's books, among them the acclaimed *Mammywater* (1979); and countless essays. Her novel *The Lake Goddess* (forthcoming), which is about a priestess straddling two worlds – the traditional African and the Christian – was written in 1991. For her contributions to Nigeria as an educator, author, and publisher, Nwapa garnered many accolades, including the presidential Officer of the Order of the Niger (O.O.N.) Award in 1983.

MU

O

O Chŏng-hŭi (b. 1947) Korean fiction writer. O received a BA in creative writing from Sŏrabŏl College of Art in Seoul. While a college junior, she debuted with 'The Toyshop Woman' (1968) – a study of a human psyche ridden with anxiety, frustration, and destructive impulses. O's works are permeated with a deep sense of alienation that comes from her tragic vision of human beings' fundamental inability to communicate and understand others. Most of her protagonists are women who, trapped in sterile daily routine, feel unbridgeable gaps between themselves and their family members. They usually suffer from hidden psychological wounds and slip into an abyss of loneliness without even trying to cross the interpersonal chasm, as in 'Wayfarer' (1983) and 'Param ŭi nŏk' ('Soul of the Wind,' 1986). Such relational fissures existing between married couples are exemplified in 'Pul ŭi kang' ('River of Fire,' 1970), 'Words of Farewell' (1981), and 'The Evening Party' (1981). O's works are reputed to be difficult because of her extensive use of stream of consciousness, flashback, and abstruse symbolism. Basically a short-story writer, O is a recipient of the two most prestigious Korean literary prizes: the Yi Sang Award for 'Evening Game' (1970) and the Tong'in Prize for 'The Bronze Mirror' (1982).

Y-HK

Oates, Joyce Carol (b. 1938) US novelist, short story writer, poet, playwright. One of America's most multifaceted and prolific writers, Oates publishes novels, plays, essays, collections of poetry, and short stories at a remarkable rate. Raised in Erie County, New York, the analogue to her fictional Eden County, she graduated valedictorian of her 1960 class at Syracuse University. She completed an MA at the University of Wisconsin in 1961 and has taught at Princeton University since 1978. The author of over thirty novels, twenty collections of short fiction, twenty books of plays, and ten books of poetry, she explores myriad themes and characters. Her works probe the unpleasant aspects of the human condition, straying frequently into the violent or the grotesque, depicting misfits and murderers, dealing with such issues as religion, feminism, sexual obsession, abuse, class conflicts, paranoia, and insanity. She laments modern America's failure to adhere to a coherent ethic and its intellectual and spiritual deterioration. Her novels include *With Shuddering Fall* (1964), *them* (1969; National Book Award), *Wonderland* (1971), *Do With Me What You Will* (1973) *The Assassins* (1975), *Cybele* (1979), *Bellefleur* (1980), *A Bloodsmoor Romance* (1982), *Because It Is Bitter and Because It Is My Heart* (1990), *Black Water* (1992), and *Zombie* (1995). Though her novels have met with mixed critical receptions, her short stories have been consistently acclaimed. Her story collections include *By The North Gate* (1963), *Where are You Going, Where Have You Been?* (1970), *All The Good People I've Left Behind* (1979), and *The Assignation* (1988). Oates, an active critic and frequent contributor to periodicals, has also published five detective fictions under the pseudonym Rosamond Smith.

DVT

O'Brien, Edna (*b.* 1932) Irish novelist, short story writer, playwright. Born and raised in County Clare in western Ireland in a devoutly Catholic family, O'Brien was educated in a convent as a child, and studied in Dublin at the Pharmaceutical College of Ireland. In 1952, she married Czech-Irish writer Ernest Gebler, with whom she had two sons; they were divorced in 1967. She has spent the greater part of her adult life in London. Her first and best-known novel, *The Country Girls* (1960), concerns the coming of age of two girls from western Ireland who move to Dublin. With *The Lonely Girl* (1962) and *Girls in Their Married Bliss* (1964), it forms a trilogy which is based in part on O'Brien's own life. In depicting how the girls mature, search for romance, and find disillusion instead, O'Brien is boldly frank about their sexual desires and experiences, and highly critical of the men they encounter. Her treatment of female sexuality led to several of her novels being banned in Ireland. Her other novels include *August is a Wicked Month* (1965), *Casualties of Peace* (1967), *Johnny I Hardly Knew You* (1977), *The High Road* (1988), *House of Splendid Isolation* (1994), and *Wild Decembers* (1999). She has written several stage plays and screenplays, and published several short story collections including the acclaimed *Lantern Slides* (1990). She is also the author of the biography *James Joyce* (1999).

DVT

O'Faolain, Julia (*b.* 1932) Irish novelist, short story writer. The daughter of writer

Sean O'Faolain, born in London, O'Faolain attended University College, Dublin, where she earned a BA in French and Italian in 1952, and an MA in 1953. She also studied at the University of Rome and the Sorbonne. She married an American, Lauro Martines, in 1957; they have one son. She has worked as a translator and has taught French and Italian. Her first novel *Godded and Codded* (published in the US as *Three Lovers*) was published in 1970. Her fiction is wide-ranging in subject matter, but she is consistently concerned with the lives of women and her Irish background is central to her focus on religion and politics. *Women in the Wall* (1975), set in sixth-century Gaul, blends politics with depictions of convent life. The critically praised *No Country for Young Men* (1980) follows a family involved in the troubles in Ulster from the 1920s to the present. *The Irish Signorina* (1984), the story of a young Irishwoman's encounter with her mother's past in Italy, uses multiple narratives to tell the stories of several generations. Other novels include *The Obedient Wife* (1982) and *The Judas Cloth* (1992). She has published several collections of short stories including *We Might See Sights!* (1968) and *Daughters of Passion* (1982).

JEM

Ogot, Grace (*b.* 1930) Kenyan short story writer, novelist. One of Kenya's leading writers, Ogot has contributed extensively to the literature of East Africa. She is best known for the sensitive manner in which she chronicles traditional Luo lore and history in her novels and short stories. Born Grace Emily Akinyi in Butere, Central Nyanza District of Kenya, she was trained in nursing and midwifery in Uganda and England. Her works often depict tensions between traditional folk medicine and formal medicine. Her early writing career began in 1959 as a broadcaster and scriptwriter for the British Broadcasting Company Africa Service. She was also founding chair of the Writers' Association of Kenya. She married the noted Kenyan historian Bethwell A. Ogot in 1959. Her first novel *The Promised Land* (1966), a story of Luo pioneers in Tanzania, characteristically blends the real and the fantastic. Other works, including her numerous collections of short stories, offer poignant portraits of the joys and sorrows of daily living, giving special attention to women's lives in rural traditional settings. Ogot also situates her characters in contemporary urban settings and frequently grapples with issues of post-independence Kenya, as seen in a later novella *The Graduate* (1980). Her career in public service extends from the position of Kenyan delegate to the UN to member of Kenya's parliament.

MSa

Ogundipe-Leslie, 'Molara (*b.* 1940) Nigerian poet, critic, editor, activist. Born Obiodun Omolara Ogundipe in Lagos, Nigeria, to a family of educators and clergy, Ogundipe-Leslie has two daughters. Graduating first class with honors in English from the University of London in 1963, she has been a major figure in academia and international affairs since the 1960s, holding various political and teaching appointments in Nigeria and visiting scholar positions in England, Canada, the US, Japan, India, the Netherlands, and South Africa. A leading scholar in women's, gender, and development studies, active in international women's organizations which promote research on women, she is also a well-known literary critic, editor, and poet; her work is widely anthologized. Her publications include *Sew the Old Days and Other Poems* (1985); *Recreating Ourselves: African Women and Critical Transformations* (1994), a collection of critical essays; *Moving Beyond Boundaries: Black Women's Diasporas* (1995), a two-volume co-edited anthology of writing by women in Africa and the African Diaspora; and *Women as Oral Artists* (1994), an edited special issue of *Research in African Literatures*.

NBH

Ohba Minako (*b.* 1930) Japanese novelist, fiction writer. Born in Tokyo, Ohba graduated from Tsudajuku Women's College with a degree in English, and married an engineer, Toshio Ohba, in 1955 on the condition that she would be able to continue writing. Eleven years spent in the US, mainly in Sitka, Alaska, where her husband's job took her, and courses taken in art and literature at the Universities of Wisconsin and of Washington, became important sources of material for her fiction writing. Her first story 'Koozu no nai e' ('A Picture with No Designs,' 1963) features a female Japanese art student on an American university campus. In her prize-winning story 'The Three Crabs' (1968), a middle-class Japanese housewife living with her physician husband and their daughter in Alaska feels that she has no emotional ties to her family or friends, and seeks, unsuccessfully, to fill the emptiness inside through a one-night stand with a stranger. Many of her female – and male – characters, for example those in *Funakui mushi* ('Ship Worms,' 1969), wish to escape from socially prescribed gender roles, including the institution of marriage, only to realize that they cannot yet create viable alternatives.

TK

Okoye, Ifeoma, Nigerian novelist, children's writer. Okoye is a native of Umunachi, near Onitsha. She attended St Monica's Teacher's College, Ogbunike and the University of Nigeria, Nsukka, where she received a BA in English in 1977. Her MSc in English was earned at Aston University in Birmingham, England in 1987. She married the historian and philosopher Mokwugo Okoye in 1961 and they raised five children before he died in 1998. Her first adult novel *Behind the Clouds* (1983) won the 1983 Nigerian National Festival of Arts and Culture Award. This groundbreaking work was one of the first Nigerian novels to point to male sterility as the cause of childlessness in marriage. Her second novel *Men Without Ears* (1984), which won the Association of Nigerian Authors' Best Fiction of the Year Award in 1985, attacks moral laxity and corruption during the oil-boom era in the 1980s. The novel *Chimere* (1992) looks at single-motherhood in contemporary Nigeria. She has also written many books for children, of which *Village Boy* (1978) won the Macmillan Children's Literary Prize Award in 1978 and the Nigerian National Festival of Arts and Culture Award in 1983, and *Only Bread for Eze* (1980) won the Ife Book Fair Award in 1985. She currently teaches English at Nnamdi Azikiwe University in Awka, Nigeria.

MU

Olds, Sharon (*b*. 1942) US poet. Born in San Francisco, Olds graduated with honors from Stanford University in 1964 and earned a PhD from Columbia University in 1972. She is married and has two children. In the tradition of confessional poetry, her work offers highly personal portrayals of family relationships, love, and the erotic. She is particularly concerned with complications of parent–child relationships. Her candid and compassionate poems celebrate the body with honesty, and they seek catharsis in the midst of pain, whether brought about by political injustices or personal, often sexual, violation. These themes are present in her first collection *Satan Says* (1980), which seeks to heal the emotional scars of abuse, as well as in *The Dead and The Living* (1984), for which Olds won a National Book Critics Circle Award, and *The Gold Cell* (1987), in which she looks to the past to confront her parents, and tries to capture the present through careful observations of her children. Other volumes include *The Matter of This World* (1987), which contains new and selected poems, *The Father* (1992), which express her emotions at her father's death from cancer, *The Wellspring* (1996), and *Blood, Tin, Straw* (1999).

Olds has taught at New York University since 1983.

DVT

Oliver, Mary (*b*. 1935) US poet. Born in Maple Heights, Ohio, Oliver was educated at Ohio State University and Vassar College. She has taught at several colleges and universities in the US. Her first volume of poetry *No Voyage and Other Poems* was published in 1963. Clearly influenced by Robert Frost, her poetry emphasizes rural life and landscapes. Elegant, gentle, and quiet, her poetry presents the natural world of animals and plants in beautiful detail. *American Primitive* (1983) was awarded the Pulitzer Prize. Her other volumes of poetry include *The River Styx, Ohio, and Other Poems* (1972), *The Night Traveler* (1978), *Twelve Moons* (1979), *Dream Work* (1986), *House of Light* (1990), *New and Selected Poems* (1992), which won the National Book Award, *White Pine* (1994), *Blue Pastures* (1995), and *West Wind* (1997). In 1998, she won the Lannan Literary Award for poetry.

JEM

Oliver i Cabrer, Maria-Antònia (*b*. 1946) Catalan novelist. Growing up in Mallorca, Oliver lived the dual experience of the Franco regime's repression and the island's growing pains caused by the great influx of tourists. She married writer Jaume Fuster (1945–98) and moved to Barcelona; she still maintains residences in both places. Active in anti-Franco movements, she became well-known as a defender of Catalan culture and a strong feminist and ecologist. Her novels show a variety of themes, styles and tone, and can be grouped into three categories: family, mythology, and detective. Her first novel *Cròniques d'un mig estiu* ('Chronicles of a Half Summer,' 1970) traces the coming of age of a Mallorcan youth, juxtaposed with the destruction of his town by tourists and developers. Her most compelling work, *Crineres de foc* ('Manes of Fire,' 1985; forthcoming in English), encompasses the epic, family chronicle, the founding of a town, science fiction, fantasy, and psychological and sociological studies. Her detective fiction features the female protagonist Lònia Guiu, whose sleuthing uncovers crimes against women as well as the usual adventures. *Study in Lilac* (1985) addresses the crime of rape and its aftermath, *Antipodes* (1988) uncovers a network of trafficking in women and ecological crimes; *Blue Roses for a Dead . . . Lady* (1994) exposes infantile sexual slavery. Oliver uses the conventions of the genre without falling into its clichés.

KMcN

Olsen, Tillie (*b.* 1913) US novelist, short story writer. Olsen was born into a family of Russian immigrants and grew up in Omaha, Nebraska. She is known for her humane and realistic depictions of the economically oppressed, which show the painful incompatibility of poverty and dreams. Following in the footsteps of her parents' political activism, she joined the Young Communist League after dropping out of high school and became involved in leftist politics. In the early 1930s, she started writing a novel but did not finish and publish it, as *Yonnondio: From the Thirties* (1974), until decades later. In 1936, she moved to San Francisco and married Jack Olsen, raised four daughters, and apart from some articles and poems in socialist publications, put her writing career on hold. She resumed her career in 1955, when she was awarded a creative writing fellowship at Stanford University. Her first book *Tell Me a Riddle* (1962), which collects four short stories and for which she was awarded an O. Henry Prize, chronicles survival and creativity in the face of hardship. In her classic work of nonfiction *Silences* (1978), she juxtaposes excerpts from writers' letters, diaries, and testimonies with her own experiences to examine artistic creation and the particular forces that silence women writers. Olsen has taught in numerous universities

in the US and abroad, and is a popular speaker.

DVT

Onwueme, Tess (*b.* 1955) Nigerian playwright, critic, children's writer. Born Osonye Tess Akaeke in Ogwashi-Uku, Delta State, Nigeria, Onwueme received both a BA in education/English (1979) and an MA in literature (1982) from the University Ife, and a PhD in African drama from the University of Benin (1986). She married I. C. Onwueme, an agronomist; they had five children before separating in 1994. In 1998, she married Obika Gray, a Jamaican political scientist. She has taught in academic institutions in Nigeria and the US. Currently, she is the first Distinguished Professor of Cultural Diversity and professor of English at the University of Wisconsin, Eau Claire. *A Hen Too Soon* (1983) is her first play. The Association of Nigerian Authors' Award was presented to her twice for two plays. *The Desert Encroaches* (1985), a political satire with animals representing the world powers, and *Go Tell it To Women* (1995), in which traditional rural women closely scrutinize feminism in Nigeria. *Legacies* (1989) is a play which incorporates spectacle, dance, and music to tell the story of an African-American woman's epic search for her roots. Onwueme's most recent plays are *Riot in Heaven* (1996), an allegory about the opening of 'heaven' to people of color, and *The Missing Face* (1997), in which an African-American mother and son visit Africa to find family and identity.

MBr

Oodgeroo Noonuccal (Kath Walker) (1920–1993) Australian poet. Known as Kath Walker before publicly adopting her tribal name, Oodgeroo of the Noonuccal, in 1988, she was an activist for Aboriginal rights and her *We Are Going* (1964) was the first book published by an Aboriginal writer. Born Kathleen Jean Mary Ruska, Oodgeroo was raised in the traditions of

Noonuccal culture on North Stradbroke Island, Queensland. Her growing appreciation of the heritage and plight of the Aborigines informed her work both as a writer and as an activist. The first edition of *We Are Going* sold out in three days, and it remains one of the most successful collections of poems by any Australian writer. In addition to poetry, Oodgeroo published prose works using Aboriginal traditions, including *Stradbroke Dreamtime* (1972), a popular volume of stories and recollections of her childhood and Noonuccal culture. In 1970, she was awarded an MBE for her literary and political achievements, an honor which she returned in protest to Elizabeth II in 1988, during the Queen's visit to Australia to commemorate the bicentennial of its European colonization. Oodgeroo's expression of a specifically Aboriginal inflection in her poetry has influenced subsequent Australian writers.

DM

Orozco, Olga (*b*. 1920) Argentine poet. Born in La Pampa, province of Argentina, Orozco uses her early life as a source. Her books *La oscuridad es otro sol* ('Darkness is another Sun,' 1967) and *La luz es un abismo* ('Light is an Abyss,' 1993) focus on traumatic and everyday events that reflect her Catholic indoctrination and traditions of superstition and magic. Her family moved to Buenos Aires in 1936, where she attended the university in the Faculty of Arts. She traveled extensively in South America during the late 1940s and early 1950s. In the late 1960s and early 1970s she traveled to Europe and Africa. Her first book of poetry *Desde lejos* ('From Afar') was published in 1946 and her eleventh work *Con esta boca este mundo* ('With this Mouth is this World') in 1994. She has received numerous awards for both individual books and the body of her work. She is known for long poems that plumb conventional and unconventional, supernatural and religious themes, including witchcraft, aging, death, the heroic, inter-

acting with the dead, silence, and metaphysical angst. Orozco describes her poetry as her path to knowledge and she uses fortune telling, magic, fate, astrology, and dreams to forge an unlimited and incomplete understanding of the realm of wholeness and beauty.

CJG

Orphée, Elvira (*b*. 1930) Argentine novelist, short story writer. Born in the provincial capital of Tucumán, Orphée's childhood was marked by recurrent sickness. Her mother died before she finished high school. She then left her distant father to live with an aunt in Buenos Aires. She took courses in literature and philosophy, and later moved to Paris, where she married Miguel Ocampo, a painter. After returning to Argentina and divorcing her husband, she lived in several Latin American countries and the US. She began her writing career in 1956 with the publication of *Dos veranos* ('Two Summers'), her first novel. *Aire tan dulce* ('Air So Sweet,' 1966), her third book, provides an excellent example of her elaborate lyric prose as the intimate fragmented story of the narrator unfolds. Orphée, hailed as an important writer of her generation, has continued to evolve. In *El Angel's Last Conquest* (1977), her interest in the fictional exploration of cruelty moves to political repression and torture executed by the protagonist of these stories. Other publications include *La muerte y los desencuentros* ('Death and Missteps,' 1990) and *Ciego de cielo* ('Heavenly Blind,' 1991), a collection of stories that deals with the theme of justice in the hands of common citizens.

MGP

Ortese, Anna Maria (1914–1998) Italian novelist, short story writer, journalist. Born in Rome to a family with few means, Ortese received only elementary education. She moved frequently and published her first collection of stories *Angelici dolori* ('Angelic Pains,' 1937) at a young age.

Her mentor was the 'magic realist' Massimo Bontempelli, and she maintained a surreal element in most of her fiction. Her writing combines autobiographical, realistic, and fantastic modes. Her collection of exposé stories set in Neapolitan slums *The Bay is Not Naples* (1953) brought her close to the Neorealist movement and earned her the prestigious Viareggio Prize. She moved to a more oneiric style in her novel *The Iguana* (1965), which portrays a fantastic love encounter on an ocean island between an Italian count and an iguana/woman. The latter character is a unique and haunting composite figure through which Ortese conveys two of her most important themes: the pain of exile and banishment and the sacred value of the life of all creatures. The collection of stories *Poveri e semplici* ('Poor and Simple,' 1967; Strega Prize) and many anthologies of short works followed, including wonderful travel writings in *La lente scura* ('The Dark Lens,' 1991). Ortese obtained her largest readership with a novel published only five years before her death, *Il cardillo addolorato* ('The Lament of the Linnet,' 1993). *A Music Behind the Wall* (1994) offers an excellent selection of short stories in English culled from six decades of writing.

KJJ

Ortiz, Lourdes (*b.* 1943) Spanish novelist. An acknowledged literary force of the post-Franco era, Ortiz was born in Madrid where she continues to reside. A graduate of the Complutense University of Madrid in history and an art history professor at the Royal School of Dramatic Art, she was involved in anti-Franco activism and the growing feminist movement during her university years. Her novels center on a core of themes that are conveyed by narrative structures ranging from metafiction to genre fiction. The existential theme and the fragmentation of the self appear in her first published novel *Luz de la memoria* ('Light of Memory,' 1976), as well as in *Antes de la batalla* ('Before the Battle,' 1992), a disenchanted portrayal of contemporary Spanish life. Political struggle, ideological disenchantment, and the question of violence are central to *En días como éstos* ('On Days Like These,' 1981) and *La fuente de la edad* ('The Fountain of Age,' 1995). The process of narrative/self-creation is thematically and structurally highlighted in *Urraca* ('Magpie,' 1982), a historical novel about the life of Queen Urraca, and *Arcángeles* ('Archangels,' 1986), her most metafictional novel to date. In *Picadura mortal* ('Mortal Sting,' 1979), Ortiz ventures into detective fiction and creates the first Spanish female detective.

KT-C

Ostriker, Alicia (*b.* 1937) US poet, critic. Born in Brooklyn during the Depression, Ostriker received a BA in English from Brandeis University in 1959 and earned an MA and a PhD from the University of Wisconsin. She published her dissertation as *Vision and Verse in William Blake* (1965), a study of one of her greatest influences. In the same year, Ostriker began teaching English at Rutgers University; her husband Jeremiah Ostriker, with whom she has three children, is an astrophysicist at Princeton University. An important critic as well as a poet, her critical intelligence informs her poetry, which is characterized by feminist themes, and driven by mythic, prophetic, and spiritual impulses. Her first book of poetry *Songs* (1969) has been followed by eight other collections, including *The Mother/Child Papers* (1980), a ten-year project exploring the dual role of mother and artist; *Green Age* (1989), considered one of her most powerful and original collections; and *The Crack in Everything* (1996), a National Book Award finalist. *The Little Space* (1998) contains both selected and new poems. Ostriker's critical work includes *Writing Like a Woman* (1983), *Stealing the Language: The Emergence of Women's Poetry in America* (1986), and two revisionist studies of the Bible.

DVT

Ouyang Zi (*b*. 1939) Chinese-Taiwan fiction writer, literary critic. Born Hong Zhihui in Hiroshima, Japan, Ouyang Zi returned to her parents' native place, Taiwan, after the war. In 1960, while a student at National Taiwan University, she founded with her classmates the journal *Xiandai wenxue* ('Modern Literature'). She attended the Creative Writing Workshop at the University of Iowa and earned her MFA degree in 1964. She and her husband Sian L.Yen, a linguistics professor, have resided in Austin, Texas since 1965. They have two sons and one daughter. Ouyang has published two short story collections, *Na chang toufa de nühai* ('That Girl With Long Hair,' 1967) and *Qiuye* ('Autumn Leaves,' 1971). Influenced by Freudian psychology, her fiction frequently features aberrant social behaviors and emotional crises of alienated individuals in modern society. *Wang Xietangqian de yanzi* ('Swallows in Front of the Wang and Xie Mansions,' 1976) is a highly regarded critical work on Bai Xianyong, a leading modern Chinese writer from Taiwan. She has two essay collections, *Yizhi de yinghua* ('Transplanted Cherry Tree,' 1978) and *Shengming de guiji* ('Tracks of Life,' 1988). Her latest book *Bashe shanshui lishi jian* ('Traveling Among Mountains, Rivers, and History,' 1998) consists of close-reading commentaries on the work of Yu Qiuyu, a contemporary Chinese essayist.

S-sYC

Özakın, Aysel (*b*. 1940) Turkish novelist, short story writer, poet. Özakın was born in Urfa. She studied French literature at the Ankara Gazi Educational Institute, and taught French between 1969–1980. Her teaching career came to an end for political reasons. She moved to Germany in 1981, and in 1987 moved to England. In addition to Turkish, she writes in English and German. While her childhood in Turkey is the main subject of her early prose texts, her experience as a Turkish woman living in Germany colors her later work, including two volumes of poetry. Her fiction focuses on women's lives and the struggles of the Turkish workers in Germany. Her novels are *Gurbet Yavrum* ('Exile, My Dear,' 1975), *Alnında Mavi Kuşlar* ('Blue Birds on the Forehead,' 1978; Madarali Novel Prize), *The Prizegiving* (1980), and *Mavi Maske* ('The Blue Mask,' 1988). *The Prizegiving* deals with three generations of women's lives from the period of the formation of the Turkish republic in 1920 to the student movements of the 1970s. The central character is a novelist who, while trying to decide whether or not to accept a literary prize, comes to terms with the choices of her mother, who committed suicide, and her daughter, who is involved in a political activist group. Her short story collections include *Sessiz Bir Dayanışma* ('A Silent Solidarity,' 1976) and *Kanal Boyu* ('On the Banks of the Canal,' 1982) as well as others that were published in German.

SE, SBa

Ozick, Cynthia (*b*. 1928) US short story writer, novelist, essayist. Raised during the Depression by her Russian immigrant parents in the Bronx, Ozick graduated with honors from New York University and earned an MA at Ohio State University in 1950. Fascinated by Henry James's fiction, her own prose reflects his influence, especially her first work, the six-hundred page novel *Trust* (1966). Her acclaimed short fiction has been collected in three volumes: *The Pagan Rabbi and Other Stories* (1971), which was nominated for the National Book Award, *Bloodshed and Three Novellas* (1976), and *Levitation: Five Fictions* (1982). Her identity as a Jewish woman is central to her writing, and many of her works focus on themes related to Judaism and the Holocaust, most notably *The Cannibal Galaxy* (1983), *The Messiah of Stockholm* (1987), and *The Shawl* (1989). She is interested in ethical questions, particularly concerning the perils of idolatry. Her writing is characterized by its intellectual seriousness and its imaginative, compelling storytelling; stylistically, it ranges from biting satire to the magic realism of *The Puttermesser Papers* (1997). A prolific essayist and reviewer, Ozick has published three essay collections: *Art and Ardor* (1983), *Metaphor and Memory* (1988), and *Fame and Folly* (1996).

DVT

P

Padmanabhan, Manjula (*b*. 1953) Indian short story writer, dramatist, illustrator. Born in Delhi, Padmanabhan spent her childhood travelling, and graduated from Elphinstone College, Bombay with a BA in economics. She later began, but did not complete, an MA degree in history. Instead, she turned to illustrating books for children. In 1984 she published her first short story, 'A Government of India Undertaking,' and the next year, began to write plays. These include *Lights Out* (1983), *The Mating Game Show* (1991), and *The Sextet* (1995), six short plays on sex. *The Mating Game Show* was shot as a 26-part TV serial but never aired, and another play, *The Artist's Model*, remains unproduced. Her ability to draw and her sharp, satirical wit made cartoons a natural choice and for several years she had a daily cartoon strip, *Suki*, in a national newspaper. In 1996, *Lights Out* was performed as a television play and in the same year she published her first collection of short stories *Hot Death, Cold Soup*. Written with wry humour and narrative tension, these disturbing tales paved the way for her next major piece of work, the play *Harvest* (1998), which won the prestigious first prize in the 1997 Onassis International Cultural Competition for Theatrical Plays.

UB

Pak Hwasŏng (Pak Kyŏngsun) (1904– 1988) Korean fiction writer, essayist. Pak lived through the turbulent periods of Korea's modern history, including the colonization (1910–45) and Korean War (1950–53). Although Pak enrolled in the English department of Nihon Women's College in Japan in 1926, she was unable to finish her studies. The impoverished conditions of Korean laborers and peasant farmers, often aggravated by natural disasters, appear in her socially conscious early stories such as 'Ch'usŏk chŏnya' ('Evening Before the Harvest Moon Festival,' 1925), 'Hongsu chŏnhu' ('Before and After the Flood,' 1934), and 'Kohyang ŏmnŭn saramdŭl' ('People Without Homeland,' 1936). After a series of jobs as an educator at public and private schools, Pak also worked in a variety of literary organizations including the International PEN Club. Although Pak favored women protagonists, it was only during the post-1945 period that she began to focus on women exclusively, divorced from nationalistic and political concerns. She actively promoted women's literature by forming organizations and portrayed women caught in haphazard situations. The collections *Hyuhwasan* ('Inactive Volcano,' 1977) and *Kohyang ŏmnŭn saramdŭl* ('People Without a Homeland,' 1994) contain Pak's representative short stories, dealing with multivalent themes such as socialism, ambiguity, and women's issues. Among the numerous awards Pak received are the Silver Crown literary award (1974) and the March 1st literary award (1984).

CS

Pak Kyŏngni (*b.* 1927) Korean fiction writer. Born in Ch'ungmu, an island on the southern coast and a symbol of Korea's national pride, Pak, like many other Korean women of her generation, did not attend college, and graduated only from Chinju Girls' High School. She grew up during the Colonial Period and experienced the tragedy of the Korean War as an adult, which is reflected in her first short story 'Kyesan' ('Calculation,' 1955) and in 'Pulssin sidae' ('Era of Mistrust,' 1957). Pak received the Modern Literature Newcomer's Award in 1957. Her main interest lies in how major historical events change Korean culture and people at large. In particular, the effects of the Korean War on families, the nation, and society, often seen through the eyes of a war widow, dominate Pak's work. Her *Kim Yakuk ŭi ttal tŭl* ('Daughters of the Pharmacist Kim,' 1962) and *Sijang kwa chŏnjang* ('Marketplace and Battlefield,' 1964, Korean Women Writer's Award) contain realistic depictions of ordinary people's interpretations of the Korean War. Her monumental novel *Land* (1989), originally serialized in various literary journals from 1969 to 1987, is a landmark of modern Korean literature. *Land* spans the end of the nineteenth century to Korea's liberation in 1945, with a complex web of characters drawn from several generations, exploring themes such as the disintegration of families, class antagonism, modernization of Korea, and colonization.

CS

Pak Wansŏ (*b.* 1931) South Korean fiction writer. Pak was a full-time housewife with five children when she made her literary debut in 1970 at the age of 40. Born in Kaep'ung, Kyŏngki-do, Pak was educated in Seoul and was admitted to the department of Korean at Seoul National University in 1950. Her education, however, was cut short due to the Korean War, in which her elder and sole brother tragically died. Pak's and her widowed mother's traumatic experiences give an historical dimension and a testimonial urgency to many of her autobiographical works, including *The Naked Tree* (1970), the 'Mother's Stake' trilogy (1980, 1981, 1991), and two longer memoirs (1992, 1995) which form her eleventh and twelfth novels. In many of her novels and collections, such as *Pukkŭrŏum ŭl karŭch'imnida* ('This Teaches Shame,' 1976), *Hwich'ŏnggŏrinŭn ohu* ('The Groggy Afternoon,' 1977), and *Paeban ŭi yŏrŭm* ('Summer of Betrayal,' 1978), Pak extends an unremitting critique of deteriorating morality amidst South Korea's growing capitalism. In the 1980s, Pak's concentrated treatment of women's lives took on a feminist critique, as in *Kŭdae ajiktto kkumkkugo innŭn'ga* ('Are You Still Dreaming?', 1989). Pak recently published *Nŏmuna ssŭlssŭlhan dangsin* ('All Too Lonely You,' 1998), her seventh collection of creative writings. English translations of her stories are available in anthologies.

K-HC

Palei, Marina Anatolyevna (*b.* 1955) Russian prose writer, poet. A Leningrader from a family of engineers, Palei supported herself through a series of physically and emotionally debilitating jobs (stoker, watchwoman, cleaner, medical orderly, laboratory epidemiologist) before enrolling in the Gorky Literary Institute in Moscow, from which she graduated with honors in 1990. Saturated with autobiographical elements, her fiction blends often unsettling physiological detail with dramatic situations, lyricism, irony, and verbal richness. Her stories and novellas, which consistently focus on women and their bodies, depict female 'friendship' in a communal apartment ('Evgesha and Annushka,' 1990), confront the dilemmas of birthing and abortion ('The Losers'

Division,' 1991), and deconstruct the masculine trope of Woman as Muse ('Rendezvous,' 1991). Driven by verbal zest and sweeping narrative momentum, Palei's novel *Cabiria from the Bypass* (1991) traces the adventures of the Fieldingesque heroine whose sexual insatiability personifies the indomitable life force. Works translated into English include 'The Day of the Poplar Flakes' and 'Rendezvous.'

HG

Paley, Grace (*b.* 1922) US short story writer, poet. Born into a Russian Jewish family in the Bronx, New York, Paley was educated at Hunter College and New York University. Following in the political footsteps of her socialist parents, she has been an activist for feminism and world peace all her life. She is best known for her short stories, collected in *The Little Disturbances of Man* (1959), *Enormous Changes at the Last Minute* (1974), *Later the Same Day* (1985), and *The Collected Stories* (1994; National Book Award). A masterful storyteller, she writes about ordinary people and everyday life with humor and warmth, focusing on her characters' resilience in harsh circumstances. She is particularly good at capturing the accents and inflections, as well as the attitudes and behaviors, of New York. Her depictions of relationships between men and women are astute and sexually frank. The economy, directness, and humor of her stories is also evident in her poetry, which is collected in *Leaning Forward* (1985), *New and Collected Poems* (1992), and *Begin Again: Collected Poems* (2000). The winner of numerous literary awards and honors, Paley has also published *Long Walks and Intimate Talks* (1991), a collection of poetry and prose, and *Just As I Thought* (1998), a collection of essays.

JEM

Palmen, Connie (*b.* 1955) Dutch novelist, memoirist. Palmen studied philosophy and literature, and made a spectacular debut with the best-selling novel *The Laws* (1992), which has since sold more than 300,000 copies in the Netherlands alone and has been translated into many languages. The book describes the quest of the main character, Marie Deniet, who sells her soul to seven different men in her pursuit of knowledge and wisdom. Palmen subsequently published *Friendship* (1995), a lengthy novel about two girls who are each other's opposites. The narrator grapples with such themes as the connection between mind and spirit, words and reality, family and individualism, friendship and independence. In her latest novel *I. M.* (1998), she becomes the chronicler of a tragic love. The reader is witness to a 'terrible love story, because a great love simply does to this man and woman what all great loves have always done, forcing them to deal with the other side of their love, the pain, the anxieties and the helplessness.' *I. M.* is an intimate hymn to happiness that hurts, and shows how the characters each overcome their fear of daring to know, and be known by, the other.

AAn, MMe

Paltto, Kirsti (*b.* 1947) Sami novelist, short story writer, children's writer, poet. Born in Utsjok, Finland, Paltto debuted in 1971 with the short story collection *Soagŋu* ('The Proposal Journey'). The first Sami language book written by a woman, these stories are told in the oral tradition. In Paltto's children's books, the protagonists often encounter characters from the Sami underworld, following a typical folktale motif where the small and weak outwit the large and powerful, a reflection of her views of the Sami within the majority community. She emphasizes the ties between indigenous peoples by using symbols from other folk traditions in her poetry, but she can also write realistically, as in 'Looking Back' from *Guovtteoaivvat nisu* ('Two-headed Woman,' 1989), a grim glimpse of a young Sami woman's fate. Her novel *Guhtoset dearvan min bohccat* ('Let Our Reindeer Graze in Peace') was nominated for the Finlandia Prize in 1986.

Paltto is not only one of the most prolific and versatile of Sami writers today, but also works actively on behalf of Sami artists. She was the first chairperson of the Sami Writers' Association, founded in 1979. English translations of her work appear in the anthology *In the Shadow of the Midnight Sun*.

TH

Pande, Mrinal (*b.* 1946) Indian short story writer, broadcaster. Daughter of the popular Hindi woman writer Shivani, Pande grew up in Nainital and studied English and Sanskrit at Allahabad University. Her first short story appeared in a Hindi journal in 1967. Since then she has published five volumes of short stories and two volumes of collected stories, *Yani ke Ek Bat thi* ('There was Something After All,' 1990) and *Bachuli Chaukidarin ki Karhi* ('Bachuli's Curry,' 1990). Several of her stories have appeared in her own English translation in anthologies of Indian writers. Girl-children and women surviving in the folds of society, their sensitivities scarred by the subtle and pervasive gender discrimination within the Indian family, are often the protagonists of her stories. *Daughter's Daughter* (1993) looks back at her own mother, while in *Devi, Tales of the Goddess in Our Time* (1996), Pande mixes myths of Indian goddesses with stories of ordinary women in her family. The author of two plays and two novels, she is also well-known in India as an editor and a political broadcaster – currently, on New Delhi Television. *The Subject is Woman* (1991) contains her articles on women's issues. She lives in Delhi with her husband.

FO

Pantoja-Hidalgo, Cristina (*b.* 1944) Philippine fiction writer, essayist. Currently director of the Likhaan Creative Writing Center at the University of the Philippines, Pantoja-Hidalgo obtained her bachelor of philosophy and master of arts degrees in English literature from the University of Santo Tomas, and her PhD in comparative literature from the University of the Philippines. Her marriage to former UNICEF representative Antonio Hidalgo, with whom she has three daughters, has brought her to the scenes of much of her travel writing, collected in *Sojourns* (1984), *Korean Sketchbook* (1987), *Five Years in a Forgotten Land: A Burmese Notebook* (1991), *I Remember* (1992), and *Skyscrapers, Celadon and Kimchi: A Korean Notebook* (1993). In 1996 she won the grand prize for the novel in the Carlos Palanca Memorial Awards for Literature, for her novel *Recuerdo*, an epistolary narrative of a mother recounting the family history to her daughter. Pantoja-Hidalgo's short fiction is contained in three collections: *Ballad of a Lost Season* (1987), *Tales for a Rainy Night* (1993), and *Where Only the Moon Rages* (1994).

CJM

Paretsky, Sara (*b.* 1947) US novelist. Born in Ames, Iowa, Paretsky was educated at the University of Kansas, Lawrence, where she earned a BA (summa cum laude) in 1967, and the University of Chicago, where she earned a PhD in history in 1977. She is married and has three children. She published her first novel *Indemnity Only*, which introduced her immensely popular heroine V. I. Warshawski, in 1982. An independent, tough, and funny private eye, Warshawski reinvigorates the detective fiction genre with her feminist perspective. The novels in the Warshawski series, which is set in Chicago, are intricately plotted and fast-paced, with rich characterizations and interesting depictions of the realities of the working world. Although often pessimistic in their revelations of intractable high-level corruption, they offer satisfaction through V. I.'s passionate commitment to bringing criminals to justice. Other novels in the series include *Deadlock* (1984), *Bitter Medicine* (1987), *Burn Marks* (1990), *Tunnel Vision* (1994), and *Hard Time* (1999). *Ghost*

Country (1998) is her first non-Warshawski novel.

JEM

Park, Ruth (*b*. 1918) Australian novelist, children's writer, dramatist, nonfiction writer. Born in Auckland, Park emigrated to Australia in 1942, married the author d'Arcy Niland (died 1967), and has five children. Park's early freelancing mainly consisted of children's serials for the Australian Broadcasting Commission. This work continued for twenty-five years and included the Muddle-headed Wombat series. In 1946 she won the inaugural *Sydney Morning Herald* literary competition with her first novel *The Harp in the South*. She has since won numerous awards in Australia and overseas, including the Miles Franklin Award in 1977 for *Swords and Crowns and Rings*, a novel about the Depression in which the protagonist, a dwarf, is a symbol of the young Australian nation. Park has published fifty-four books, including nine novels for adults, and several nonfiction books including a two-volume autobiography and *Home Before Dark* (1995), a biography of the boxer, Les Darcy. Several of her early works, and the first volume of her autobiography, *A Fence Around the Cuckoo* (1992), draw on her memories of New Zealand and of Maori culture, but most of her later fiction is set in Sydney where, apart from ten years on Norfolk Island, she has lived since 1942. Her adult novels, dealing mainly with the concerns of women and the underprivileged, have become best-sellers and have been translated into many languages. Several, including her multi-award-winning novel for young adults *Playing Beatie Bow* (1980), have been filmed or televised.

JGre

Parsipur, Shahrnush (*b*. 1946) Iranian novelist. Born and raised in Teheran, Parsipur received her bachelor's degree in social science from Teheran University. She began writing at the age of 13 and published her first short story at 16. Among her publications are two novels, *Sag va Zemistan-i Boland* ('Dog and the Long Wither,' 1974) and *Tuba va Mana-yi Shab* ('Tuba and the Meaning of the Night,' 1989), and four collections of short stories: *Tajrobeh'ha-yi Azad* ('Free Experiences'), *Avizeh'ha-yi Blur* ('Long Earrings') – both published in the 1970s, *Women Without Men* (1989), and *Adab-i Sarf-i Chay Dar Hozur-I Gorg* ('Tea Ceremony in the Presence of a Wolf,' 1993). She was imprisoned for several years because of her publications. Her work has been translated into English, French, and German. She has delivered numerous lectures in many Western countries including the US, where she currently resides and where she published *Prison Memoir* (1996). In works such as *Tuba* and *Women Without Men*, Parsipur is concerned with the condition of women and gender issues in Iran. Her female characters speak of women's sexual oppression throughout history, express their acceptance of their sexuality, ridicule chastity, and articulate resistance to the male-dominated culture.

KTa

Parun, Vesna (*b*. 1922) Croatian poet. An outstanding figure in Croatian letters, Perun was born on the island of Zlarin. Losses and difficulties marked her life: a childhood spent in harsh material circumstances and constant moves, a brother killed while fighting with the partisan resistance during World War II, a serious attack of typhus which forced her to abandon her postwar study of philosophy at the University of Zagreb, and the condemnation by the official representatives of socialist criticism of her first collection of poetry *Zore i vihori* ('Dawns and Gales,' 1947). Parun nonetheless established herself as a major poet and published some thirty books of poetry, the most important of which are *Crna maslina* ('Black Olive,' 1955), *Ukleti dazd* ('Cursed Rain,' 1969), *Sto soneta* ('A Hundred Sonnets,' 1972), *Stid me je* *umrijeti* ('I'm Ashamed to Die,' 1974), *Salto mortale* ('Mortal Jump,' 1981), and *Zacarana carobnica* ('Enchanted Enchantress,' 1993). Her poetry is characterized by an outstanding case of expression and richness of language, which create a unique vision of life marked by conceptual originality, emotional exuberance, and inspiring vitality. She has also written meditations, essays, fables, and almost twenty volumes of popular poems for children. Translated into numerous languages (and herself a translator from Slovene, Bulgarian, French, and German), Parun remains under-translated into English (see *Selected Poems of Vesna Parun*, 1985).

GC

Pausewang, Gudrun (*b.* 1928) German fiction writer. Born in Bohemia, Pausewang studied pedagogy and worked as a teacher in Hesse, Chile, Venezuela, and Columbia while writing books primarily for a young adult readership. The majority of her novels, such as *Bolivian Wedding* (1968), *Aufstieg und Untergang der Insel Delfina* ('The Rise and Fall of the Island of Delfina,' 1973), *Die Freiheit des Ramon Acosta* ('The Freedom of Ramon Acosta,' 1981), and *Pepe Amado* (1986), depict the social situation of thieves, beggars, prostitutes, and workers in various Latin American countries. Since the early 1980s, she has also turned to topics of peace and the environment in order to support related social movements in West Germany. The trilogy *Rosinkawiese* (1980, 1989, 1990) traces the history of an alternative, ecologically oriented lifestyle since the 1920s, while the collection of short stories *Es ist doch alles grün . . .* ('Everything is Green . . . ,' 1991), introduces young readers to an environmental perspective. Most controversial are her novels *The Last Children* (1983) and *Fall-out* (1987), in which she details the aftermath of a nuclear war as well as a nuclear meltdown in Central Europe. With the novel *The Final Journey* (1992), she turns to the problem of Germany's Nazi past and the Holocaust.

Pausewang's books have won numerous prizes in Germany and Switzerland.

PM-K

Pavlychko, Solomea (Solomiia) Dmytrivna (*b.* 1958) Ukrainian critic, memoirist, essayist, translator. Born in L'viv, Pavlychko is the daughter of Ukrainian poet and statesman Dmytro Pavlychko and has lived in Kiev since early childhood. She graduated in English and French from Kiev University, earned a PhD in English literature in 1984, and a Doctor of Sciences degree in literary theory in 1995. Since 1992, she has headed the editorial board of the Osnovy publishing house, the leading independent academic press in Ukraine. Author of three book-length studies of English literature, she has translated copiously into Ukrainian, including D. H. Lawrence's *Lady Chatterley's Lover* and William Golding's *Lord of the Flies*. More recently, she has analyzed Ukrainian literature, especially Ukrainian women writers of the modernist era. Her latest book is *Dyskurs modernizmu v ukrains'kii literaturi* ('Modernist Discourse in Ukrainian Literature,' 1997). An accomplished essayist, Pavlychko writes primarily on topics concerning contemporary Ukrainian culture and the position of women in Ukrainian society. She is best known, however, for her memoirs *Letters from Kiev*, published in English in 1992. They offer poignant eyewitness testimony of the breakdown of the old regime and the birth of democracy in Ukraine during 1990–1.

VC

Pawar, Urmila (*b.* 1945) Indian short story writer. Pawar was born in Panaswle village in Ratnagiri district. Her first short story, 'Devach Dena,' appeared in the Diwali 1975 issue of the journal *Kinara*. Her first short story collection *Sahave Boatt* ('Sixth Finger'), was published in 1988, followed by another collection *Chauthi Bhinta* (1990). In 1996, she published a book of two plays *Mukthi* ('Liberation') and a radio play *Ilas Pavnyanu Basa Basa*

('Guests, Be Seated'). Her stories are based on the lower-caste Dalit experiences of living, working, and existing. Many of her stories are derived from the pain, agony, and difficulties of living as a woman and as a Dalit. The frank and direct manner of her storytelling and the earthy language she uses in her stories have made her a controversial writer in Marathi. Two of her stories which have received critical attention have been translated into English and published by SPARROW in the booklet *Amhihi Itihas Ghadawala: Urmila Pawar and the Making of History* (1998). Another story in English translation is included in the anthology *Separate Journeys* (1998). Pawar lives in Mumbai and works in the Government Public Works Department.

CSL, MAh

Pekárková, Iva (*b.* 1963) Czech novelist. Prague-born daughter of a physicist, Pekárková spent four years studying microbiology and virology at Charles University before defecting to the West in 1985. After ten months in an Austrian refugee camp, she was offered a job in Boston with a refugee agency in 1986. A year later she moved to New York, where she supported herself as a social worker in the South Bronx. In 1988–9, she traveled to Thailand to study the refugee situation there. For the next six years she worked as a night cab driver in New York. After several short visits to post-communist Prague, in 1997 she returned with her American partner for a longer stay. Pekárková's keen interest in people and her environs, in combination with love for travel, is reflected in her prose. Written in the US, her first published novel *Truck Stop Rainbows* (1989) is a lyrical and frank portrayal of a young woman's search for freedom in the dreary world of late communist Czechoslovakia. Her second novel *The World Is Round* (1993) vividly, often brutally, depicts the experiences of East European and Asian refugees in an Austrian transit camp. In *Dej mi ty prachy*

('Gimme the Money,' 1996), she shifts the setting to New York, where her protagonist, an immigrant Czech woman cab driver, encounters multicultural America.

ES

Peri Rossi, Cristina (*b.* 1941) Uruguayan novelist, short story writer, poet. Born in Montevideo, Peri Rossi grew up in a working-class family. In 1964 she received a degree in education from the Instituto de Profesores Artigas. In 1972, the prelude of the 1973–85 military dictatorship, she was forced into exile. She went to Barcelona, becoming a Spanish citizen in 1974. Her collection of stories *Los museos abandonados* ('The Abandoned Museums,' 1968), which received the Prize Jóvenes Narradores de Arca, depicts the cultural changes in Uruguay at the end of the 1960s, with lonely and frustrated characters, presented in baroque, lyrical, and analytical prose. *El libro de mis primos* ('My Cousins' Book'), which won the newspaper *Marcha* prestigious Prize for Best Novel in 1969, raises issues of sexuality, gender, and power, characteristic of all her subsequent fiction. In 1971, she shocked Uruguayan readers with her book of erotic poetry, *Evohé*, in which she introduced lesbian love in highly metaphorical language. Her novel *The Ship of Fools* was published in 1984. In *Solitario de amor* ('Solitaire of Love,' 1988), the essay *Fantasías eróticas* ('Erotic Fantasies,' 1990), and the collection of poetry *Babel bárbara* ('Barbarian Babel,' 1990), which was awarded the Ciudad de Barcelona Prize, Peri Rossi continues her explorations into the world of human relationships.

MRO-W

Persen, Synnøve (*b.* 1950) Sami poet, visual artist. Originally from Finnmark, the northernmost district in Norway, Persen was trained as a visual artist at the National Art Academy in Oslo. She debuted as a poet in 1981 with *Alit lottit girdilit* ('Blue Birds Fly'), which she also illustrated, and which appeared in Norwegian translation in 1983. Her second book *Biekkakeahtes bálggis* ('Windless Path,' 1992), was the Sami nomination for the Nordisk råds litteraturpris in 1993. Perhaps still best known as a visual artist, Persen has been active in organizations on behalf of Sami culture, especially the founding of a Sami art museum in Karasjok. Her poetry is characterized by the concise expressiveness of the Sami *joik* tradition, nature imagery connected to the traditional Sami way of life, and the influence of her training in the visual arts. Excerpts from her two volumes of poetry appear as 'Along a Windless Path' in the anthology *In the Shadow of the Midnight Sun*.

TH

Petrescu, Ioana Emanuela (1941–90) Romanian literary critic, essayist. In contemporary Romanian academic life, Petrescu was, above all, a respected professor in the field of critical theory and poetics; at the 'Babes-Bolyai' University of Cluj-Napoca, where she taught all her life, she is looked upon as the mentor of a 'school' of literary critics and her academic achievements tend to outshine her writings. Daughter of a respected professor of literary history at the same university (D. Popovici), she first chose her career only in order to edit her father's writings (he, too, died young, in 1952). She soon became an authority in historical poetics; her first volumes, studies of the Romanian poets I. B. Deleanu and Eminescu, are constructed upon an original theoretical vision about continuity and change in modern poetry. She was also one of the first Romanian voices in the debates over postmodernism in studies such as 'M. Krieger's "Contextualism"' (1985) or *Modernism / postmodernism. O ipoteză* ('Modernism / Postmodernism: A Hypothesis,' 1988). In her opinion, criticism could profit from the suggestions of 'deconstructed' deconstruction, and thus participate in the founding of a new humanism, the opposite of the rhetorical

and individualistic humanism of the Renaissance. A charismatic personality, with a flawless moral attitude, Petrescu died at 49, after having ignored a lifelong disease in order to live fully and fulfill her projects.

IB

Petrignani, Sandra (*b*. 1952) Italian journalist, short story writer. Born in Piacenza, Petrignani now lives in Rome. She works as a journalist for *Panorama*, one of the major Italian weekly magazines. She has published interviews with famous Italian women writers in *Le signore della scrittura* ('The Ladies of Writing,' 1994) and interviews with major writers in *Fantasia e fantastico* ('Fantasy and the Fantastic,' 1985). Her first novel *Navigazione di Circe* ('Circe's Navigation,' 1987) was awarded the Premio Elsa Morante. *The Toy Catalogue* (1988) and *Poche storie* ('Few Stories,' 1993) are collections of powerful short stories. Many of her protagonists are women – often self-destructive, violent, unconventional women – and their encounters are with technology, illness, eroticism, death. Even though we find reference to historical facts, her writing is anti-realistic, transgressive, and playful. *Vecchi* ('Old People,' 1994) is a collection of intense psychological, social portrayals of old people whom she has met in a nursing home. *Ultima India* ('Last India,' 1996) is about her journey to India.

GMe

Petrushevskaia, Liudmila Stefanovna (*b*. 1938) Russian prose writer, playwright, journalist. Petrushevskaia's early childhood personally familiarized her with the bleaker aspects of life: homelessness, starvation, abject poverty, orphanages, physical brutality, and loneliness without privacy. These experiences form the psychological backbone of her prose and drama. Upon graduation from the journalism department of Moscow State University, she worked as a hospital nurse, radio reporter, and editor at a television studio. Although two of her stories were published in 1972 ('The Storyteller' and 'Clarissa's Story'), publishers rejected the bulk of her output until *perestroika*. Her stories (collected in *Immortal Love*, 1988), novel (*The Time: Night*, 1992), and plays (represented in *Cinzano: Eleven Plays*) reveal her existentialism, which conceives of life as existence 'on the edge,' devoid of palliatives, driven by appetite and self-interest. Most Petrushevskaian protagonists and narrators are women psychologically maimed through personal weakness, uncontrollable circumstances, male mistreatment, and relatives' interference or overbearing demands. Alienation, betrayal, and humiliation comprise the lot of her dysfunctional families, who eviscerate each other during confrontations in kitchens, on stairwells, and at scandalous 'intimate' gatherings ('Our Crowd' and 'Three Girls in Blue'). The seamy catastrophes in which her plots abound are conveyed in a monstrously calm narrative voice whose digressive, casual chatter is a stratagem of deflection, transference, and avoidance. Her extraordinary linguistic skills produce an 'urbanspeak' that incongruously amalgamates slang, cultural clichés, malapropisms, and solecisms, to disgorge tales of prostitution, alcoholism, suicide, child abuse, unwanted pregnancies, abortions, theft, and violence. Now the recipient of several literary prizes, during the 1990s she has been experimenting (with uneven success) in the genre of the fairy tale.

HG

Pham Thi Hoai (*b.* 1960) Vietnamese novelist, short story writer. Born in the port city of Hai Phong, Vietnam, Pham Thi Hoai graduated with a degree in archives and history from Humboldt University, Germany. She worked at the Institute of Historical Studies in Hanoi. Her two major novels are *Thien Su* ('The Heavenly Messenger,' 1989) and *Ma-ri Sen* ('The Vulgar Mary,' 1996). She has also written three collections of short stories: *Me Lo* ('The Ignorant Way,' 1990), *Tu Man*

Nuong Den AK ('From Lady Man Nuong to Teacher AK,' 1993), and *Tuyen Tap Thieu Nhi* ('Selected Stories for Children,' 1997). She has also written critical essays and translated several works of Amado, Durenmatt, Tanizaki, and Kafka into Vietnamese. Some of her works have been translated into French and German. Her style of writing is boldly unconventional. She pays little attention to structure, plot, or elements such as space and time, while she excels in exploring characters' psychological depths. Her skillful blending of the language of intellectuals and street vagabonds makes her expressions very rich and unique. Many foreign words, phrases, and symbols are also incorporated, without explanations or annotations, in her works. Pham, with her strong intellect, modern ideas, and daring style, stands out among Vietnamese woman writers and in the field of contemporary Vietnamese literature as a whole.

NTT

Phan Thi Vang-Anh (*b.* 1968) Vietnamese short story writer. Born seven years before the unification of the country, Phan Thi Vang-Anh is one of the new generation of Vietnamese writers who grew up in postwar Vietnam. Her first short story collection *Khi Nguoi Ta Tre* ('When We Are Young,' 1994) received wide attention and numerous awards. The daughter of a famous poet and high-ranking official, it has been suggested that her privileged life has shaped her work. The ordinary events of life, the desires of the individual, the loneliness and contradictions of life are depicted with poignant observations. Recurring themes include the family, as in 'Pantomime' (1994) and 'Mua Roi' ('Rain,' 1994); friendship; and love and coming of age, as in 'Truyen Tre Con' ('Children's Story,' 1988) and 'Hoa Muon' ('Late Flowers,' 1993). Known for writing very short, short stories, her style is simple and effortless. A popular writer in Vietnam, her works are widely read by young people but praised by the critics of her

parents' generation: one generation iden-
tifies with her characters, the other is nos-
talgic for a less peaceful, innocent youth.
Many of her stories have been published in
Vietnamese magazines and anthologies.
Her second short story collection,
Hoi Cho ('Market Days,' 1995), has been
translated into French.

TT

Philip, Marlene Nourbese (*b.* 1947)
Tobagan-Canadian poet, novelist. Born in
Tobago, Philip originally trained as a lawyer, taking degrees from the University of
the West Indies in Economics (BSc, 1968)
and from the University of Western Ontario in political science (MA, 1970). Living in Canada since 1968, she practiced
law from 1975 to 1982. Her first book of
poetry *Thorns* (1980) was followed by
Salmon Courage (1983). Her next work, a
novel, *Harriet's Daughter* (1988) was a finalist in the Toronto Book Awards in
1990. Philip's best-known work *She Tries
Her Tongue, Her Silence Softly Breaks*
(1989) won the Casa de las Américas prize
for a manuscript in 1988. This work represents Philip's struggle to 'decenter' English
and to find her 'mother tongue' within a
language forced on her ancestors when
they were slaves: 'English/is my mother
tongue./ A mother tongue is not/ not a foreign lan lan lang/ language/ l/ anguish/ an-
guish/ – a foreign anguish'. In 1990–1,
Philip was a Guggenheim Fellow in Poetry.
Her long prose-poem *Looking for Living-
stone* (1991) reverses the trope of the
European discovering the African, and explores the silence around the unspeakable
history of colonialism and slavery.

JES

Phillips, Jayne Anne (*b.* 1952) US novelist,
short story writer. Born in Buckhannon,
West Virginia, Phillips began writing
poetry in high school. She graduated with
honors from West Virginia University in
1974 and then traveled for several years,
working in various jobs in the western US,
before enrolling in the MFA program at
the University of Iowa, which she completed in 1976. She initially published her
stories in two small-press editions, *Sweet-
hearts* (1976) and *Counting* (1978), but
achieved national recognition with her
short story collection *Black Tickets*
(1979), which won the Sue Kaufman Prize
for first fiction. Compared to the 'dirty
realism' of writers such as *Bobbie Ann
Mason, Phillips's stories depict the lives of
the disenfranchised – working-class people
who have become alienated, disillusioned,
or numbed by the modern world. Written
with a direct and detailed realism, the
focus of these brief stories is purposely
narrow, the language spare, the observations shrewd. Her first novel *Machine
Dreams* (1984) charts the breakdown of a
West Virginian family against the backdrop of the Depression, World War II, and
the Vietnam War. Her second novel *Shelter*
(1994), set in a girls' summer camp in West
Virginia in the 1960s, contrasts the security of the friendships of two pairs of girls
with the violence and sexual dangers that
await them just outside the camp. Phillips
is also the author of the novel *How
Mickey Made It* (1981) and the short story
collection *Fast Lanes* (1987).

DVT

Piercy, Marge (*b.* 1936) US poet, novelist.
Detroit-born Piercy was the first in her
working-class Jewish family to go to college; she received a BA from the University
of Michigan in 1957 and an MA from
Northwestern University in 1958. She has
taught at numerous colleges and universities in the US. An activist in the wom-
en's movement (which is depicted in her
novels *Small Changes* [1973] and *Braided
Lives* [1982]) and a protester against the
Vietnam War, she champions the downtrodden. Her poetic work exhibits a genuine concern for the environment and for
those suffering from poverty, racism, sexism, homophobia, and violence. Political,
polemical, and direct, her works ultimately communicate hope in humanity's
ability to improve. Her poetry collections

include *Breaking Camp* (1968), *Living in the Open* (1976), *The Moon is Always Female* (1980), *Circles on the Water* (1982), *My Mother's Body* (1985), *Available Light* (1988), and *Mars and Her Children* (1992). Also a prolific novelist, her novels include *Woman on the Edge of Time* (1976) and *He, She and It* (1992), both utopian science fiction novels, and *City of Darkness, City of Light* (1996), a novel about women involved in the French Revolution.

DVT

Pinchas-Cohen, Hava (*b.* 1955) Israeli poet. The author of three books of poetry, *HaTsevah B'iqar* ('The Essence of Color,' 1990), *Masah Ayala* ('Journey of a Doe,' 1994), and *Nahar V'shikhva* ('A River and Forgetfulness,' 1998), Pinchas-Cohen writes with a passionate spiritual depth, as well as with linguistic and imaginative richness. In their symbolism, metaphors, and emotions, her poems are at once intensely and consciously womanly, while they critically and linguistically engage postmodern and post-Zionist Israel through the lenses of Jewish tradition, including the Midrash, the Bible, the Talmud, history, and religious liturgy. She often draws on English and Ladino, as well as ancient rabbinic script, to counterpoint her contemporary Hebrew. Pinchas-Cohen is also a literary critic, and editor of the journal *Dimui*, which is devoted to literature, art, and Jewish culture. She lives in Rehovot, Israel, with her family.

MGl

Pineau, Gisèle (*b.* 1956) Guadeloupean novelist. Born in Paris, Pineau moved to Guadeloupe with her family in 1961. Later, she returned to France, this time with her grandmother Man Ya, who greatly influenced Pineau and was her connection to her Guadeloupean heritage. She is portrayed in *L'exil selon Julia* ('Exile According to Julia,' 1996). Pineau abandoned her literature studies in Paris (1975–7) to study nursing. She practices as a psychiatric nurse in Guadeloupe, where she lives with her husband and two children, while also pursuing her writing career. A prolific writer, she has published eight novels (three of them for an adolescent audience), an essay about Caribbean women, and many well-crafted short stories and essays. *The Drifting of Spirits* (1993) received the Grand Prix des lectrices d'*Elle* in 1994 and the Prix Carabet de la Caraïbe. Through her unique use of language, Pineau translates Guadeloupean society, history, and culture in her stories of love, despair, and envy. She evokes the modern-day contradictions of Guadeloupean collective and intimate realities, including its natural and human violence. She focuses particularly on ordinary women's experiences.

TSp, JV

Ping Lu (*b.* 1953) Chinese-Taiwan fiction writer, journalist. Born Lu Ping, Ping Lu transposed her name to form the pen name 'peaceful road.' She graduated from Taiwan University in 1975 with a BS in psychology, earning her MA in statistics from the University of Iowa in 1979. She currently works as a senior writer for the newspaper *China Times* and teaches at Taiwan National Academy of the Arts. Her first story 'Death in a Cornfield' (1982) involves the suicide of a southern Taiwanese in a cornfield in the US, expressing the sort of diasporic angst that *Nie Hualing and other emigré writers have described before her. With 'Taiwan qiji' ('The Taiwan Miracle,' 1989), Ping Lu embarked on futuristic pieces that satirize Taiwan's society. In one strain of her recent fiction, including 'Xunide Taiwan' ('Taiwan Invented,' 1996) and 'Jinshude qishilu' ('Revelation of a Censored Book,' 1991), Ping Lu turns to a Borgesian interest in word play and structural experimentation. Ping Lu has become interested in fictional accounts of the lives of historical figures, exploring the intimate relationship between Sun Yat-sen and Song Qingling in *Xingdao tianya* ('To the Ends of the

Earth,' 1994), the affair between Jiang Jingguo (son of Chiang Kai-shek) and Zhang Yaruo in 'Shi Shui shale XXX?' ('Who Killed Mr. X,' 1994), and the inner thoughts of Song Meiling, Chiang Kai-shek's widow, in 'Bailing jian'('A Hundred Years of Letters,' 1997).

CLu

Piñón, Nélida (*b.* 1937) Brazilian fiction writer. Born in Rio de Janeiro, Piñón's family has its origins in Galicia, Spain. Although profoundly Brazilian, her work does not deny her ancestry. After graduating with a degree in journalism, she founded the first workshop of creative writing at the Federal University of Rio de Janeiro in 1970. Her first novels *Guia-mapa de Gabriel Arcanjo* ('The Guided Map of Gabriel Archangel,' 1961) and *Madeira feita Cruz* ('Wood Made into Cross,' 1963) are stylistically innovative, and are concerned with language and history. The epic narrative, already present in her first works, reaches its maturity in *O Fundador* ('The Founder,' 1969). In other novels, such as *A Casa da Paixão* ('The House of Passion,' 1972), *Tebas do meu coração* (My Agile Heart, 1974), and *Caetana's Sweet Song* (1987), linguistic invention is always balanced with that of the imagination. *A Força do Destino* ('The Power of Destiny,' 1978) is a parody of Verdi's opera. *The Republic of Dreams* (1984) is the story of a Spanish emigrant's journey to Brazil in quest of a land of hope and freedom. Piñón became a member of the Brazilian Academy of Letters in 1990 and became the first woman to preside over the institution in 1996. She was recently awarded the Juan Rulfo Prize.

TFC

Pizarnik, Alejandra (1936–1972) Argentine poet, translator. Pizarnik, a first-generation Argentine from a Jewish Eastern European family, grew up in Buenos Aries and studied philosophy, journalism, and literature at the university there. In 1960 she moved to Paris, where she wrote for literary magazines and translated French poets into Spanish. Returning to Buenos Aires in 1964, she took the city's First Prize for Poetry in 1966. Seven books of poetry were published in her lifetime. Her first book *La tierra más ajena* ('The Most Alien Land,' 1955) contains early surrealist poems that the author later rejected as her 'prehistoric poems.' Other works include *Arbol de Diana* ('The Tree of Diana,' 1962), *Extracción de la piedra de la locura* ('Extraction from the Stone of Madness,' 1968), *The Bloody Countess* (1971), and the posthumous *Textos de sombra y últimos poemas* ('Texts of Shadows and Last Poems,' 1982). Her poetry is considered a reflection of the difficult process of self-discovery through her use of many innovative techniques and visual images. She grapples with childhood, death, absence, alienation, and tragic love. Pizarnik suffered from severe and frequent bouts of depression, and after several attempts, killed herself at the age of 36. She is among the most discussed poets of the late twentieth century, and is viewed as a transitional poet bridging both traditional and modern Latin American poetry.

CJG

Plath, Sylvia (1932–1963) US poet, novelist. Born in Jamaica Plain, Massachusetts, Plath began to publish poems and fiction while in her teens. She attended Smith College on scholarships and was selected to be a guest editor for *Mademoiselle* magazine in 1953. In that same year, suffering from depression, she attempted suicide, an experience later explored in her novel *The Bell Jar* (1963). Plath returned to Smith to graduate *summa cum laude* in English and won a Fulbright fellowship to Newnham College, Cambridge in 1955. She married the British poet Ted Hughes in 1956; they had two children. The breakup of her marriage in 1962 and her recurring depression, among other troubles, led to Plath's suicide in 1963. At the time of her death, she had published only two books: *The Colossus and Other Poems* (1960) and *The Bell Jar*. But she left behind a significant body of work, most notably *Ariel*, a collection of poems written in the final months of her life, which was published posthumously in 1965. Other collections include *Crossing the Water* (1971) and *Winter Trees* (1971). Her poems – disturbing, emotional, rich in metaphor, both angry and witty – are preoccupied with female experience, male power, and death; many of them anticipate key concerns of the feminist movement of the 1960s and 1970s. Both her work and her life have been the subject of much critical and biographical analysis. Plath's *Collected Poems* was awarded the Pulitzer Prize in 1982.

JEM

Pleijel, Agneta (*b.* 1940) Swedish playwright, poet, novelist. Stockholm-born Pleijel received her MA in 1971, while working as a critic and journalist. She was the chair of Swedish PEN between 1988 and 1990, and professor of drama at the Institute of Drama, Stockholm from 1992 to 1996. Having written several plays and film scripts during the 1960s and 1970s, she regards her first book of poetry *Änglar, dvärgar* ('Angels, Dwarfs,' 1981) as her debut. The poems unleash humans' powerful potential in the midst of restriction and despair, a theme further developed in *Eyes from a Dream: Poems* (1984), which was written after a journey to Poland. With her epic novel *Vindspejaren* ('He Who Observeth the Wind,' 1987), Pleijel embarked on a career as a novelist, and received the Great Novel Prize. The novel, partially based on her family history, depicts Abel's expatriation in Indonesia and the female narrator's account of her visit to Indonesia in her grandfather's footsteps a hundred years later, while searching for identity and self-realization. *The Dog Star* (1989) depicts a troubled family and the consequences of overbearing love narrated by a teenage girl,

Ingert. Love is also the topic for *Fungi* (1993), in which the ideas of the philosopher Schopenhauer and those of the narrator, the natural scientist Junghuhn, are juxtaposed.

GE-C

Polianskaia, Irina Nikolaevna (*b.* 1952) Russian prose writer. Born in a research facility for educated prisoners under Stalinism to parents who as chemists had served sentences in the Kolyma labor camps, Polianskaia led a peripatetic childhood. She studied drama, worked as a journalist, then in 1975 enrolled at the Gorky Literary Institute in Moscow as a poet, eking out a living as a hospital orderly and watchwoman. Since her first significant publication in 1983, her most ambitious works are the novel *Predlagaemye obstoiatel'stva* ('Mitigating Circumstances,' 1989), and *Poslannik* ('The Envoy,' 1997). Psychological insight, lyric nuance, and a heightened sensitivity to nature and the surrounding world define her narratives. They unfold at a leisurely, rhythmic pace, Polianskaia's skillfully wielded language poeticizing the aura of emotional instability and bleak isolation that surrounds her personae – their existential solitude signaled by her sparse use of dialogue. Early traumas and losses, insoluble adult discord, and the compensatory potential of finely tuned perceptions are central to her fiction, in which discrete moments unexpectedly condense into epiphanies. Translations into English may be found in *Soviet Women Writing*, *Lives in Transit*, and *Present Imperfect*.

HG

Pollard, Velma (*b.* 1937) Jamaican poet, fiction writer. Pollard's family home is located in a rural parish of Jamaica. Her interest in Creole languages, and Caribbean oral and folk traditions, arises in her work as a language educator and a creative writer. She has published several critical studies of Jamaican Creole languages, including the influential *Dread Talk: The*

Language of Rastafari (1994). In addition to two collections of poetry, *Crown Point and Other Poems* (1988) and *Shame Trees Don't Grow Here ... But Poincianas Bloom* (1992), she has published two collections of short stories: *Considering Woman* (1989) and *Karl and other Short Stories* (1994), which was the recipient of the Casa de las Américas literary award in 1992. The title novella *Karl* recounts the story of a rural scholarship boy who travels abroad for an education in Canada and then descends into insanity caused by his vapid, upwardly mobile lifestyle in Kingston. *Homestretch* (1994), a novel set against the vivid rural and urban environs of Jamaica, tells the story of two generations of Jamaicans returning home after years in the 'mother country,' England. Pollard is currently a Senior Lecturer in Language Education at the University of West Indies.

LC

Pollitt, Katha (*b.* 1949) US essayist, poet. Born in New York City, Pollitt graduated from Radcliffe College in 1972 and went on to earn an MFA in poetry from Columbia University. Her first book *Antarctic Traveller* (1982), a collection of poetry, won the National Book Critics Circle Award. Her poems are characterized by their conversational tone and visual appeal; Pollitt uses direct and inventive imagery as a powerful tool to explore human emotion. But she is best known as a columnist for the *Nation*, a liberal/leftist weekly. In her biweekly column, 'Subject to Debate,' she addresses social and political issues from a distinctly feminist perspective. Her columns are perceptive, accessible, and seasoned with her biting wit. Many of those columns, along with articles from the *New Yorker* and the *New York Times*, are collected in her second book *Reasonable Creatures: Essays on Women and Feminism* (1994). The topics she covers in her characteristically provocative and passionate style include violence against women, abortion, surrogate mothers, menopause, and Hillary Clinton. Pollitt has been awarded a Guggenheim Fellowship and a grant from National Endowment for the Arts.

DVT

Poniatowska, Elena (*b.* 1933) Mexican novelist, journalist. Of Polish and Mexican ancestry, Poniatowska was born in Paris, moving to Mexico when she was 8 years old. She attended a French school in Mexico City, and completed high school in the US. She married astrophysicist Guillermo Aro, and has three children. Her first work of fiction *Lilus Kikus* (1954) tells with irony and humor the experiences and feelings of a girl who suspiciously observes the adult world trying to impose conventional values on her. Her acclaimed *Hasta no verte, Jesús mío* ('Until I See You, My Jesus,' 1969), a fictional account based on the testimonies of a witness, shows the oppressive conditions in the life of a poor uneducated woman. Other novels include *Dear Diego* (1978) and the autobiographical *La 'Flor de Lis'* ('The 'Fleur-de-Lis,'' 1988). Among her chronicles, *Fuerte es el silencio* ('Silence So Strong,' 1980); *Massacre in Mexico* (1971), about the 1968 student protests and the police's response that killed students and bystanders; and *Nothing, Nobody: The Voices of the Mexico City Earthquake* (1988), stand out. She received the Premio Mazatlán in 1970, an honorary doctorate, and the 1978 National Journalism Prize, among other honors. She has lectured extensively in the US, Canada, Latin America, and Europe. Poniatowska has distinguished herself for being a courageous voice that has not hesitated to speak up against injustice.

MIL

Porter, Dorothy Featherstone (*b.* 1954) Australian poet, novelist. Born in Sydney, Porter was educated at the University of Sydney and taught poetry and writing at the University of Technology, Sydney before moving to Melbourne. She has published seven volumes of poetry and two novels for young adults: *Rockwood* (1991) and *The Witch Number* (1993). *Little Hoodlum* (1975), Porter's first volume of poetry, published at the age of 21, was followed by *Bison* (1979), *The Night Parrot* (1984), and *Driving Too Fast* (1989). These collections developed Porter's sharp poetic style with its emphasis on witty explorations of sexual relations and lesbian and heterosexual eroticism. Her first verse novel *Akhenaten* (1992), in which she adopts the voice of the Pharaoh, considerably extended these earlier preoccupations. Porter's second verse novel *The Monkey's Mask* (1994) won both *The Age* Poetry Book of the Year and the National Book Council 'Banjo' for Poetry for its playful and parodic reworking of both poetic and detective genres and the depiction of its lesbian detective's seduction by Sydney's academic community. *Crete* (1996), Porter's latest collection, combines historical remythologizing of Cretan culture with a return to the personalized lyrics of her early volumes and was shortlisted for the 1996 National Book Council Banjo Awards.

MHe

Poświatowska, Halina (1935–1967) Polish poet, autobiographer. Born Halina Myg in Częstochowa, during World War II Poświatowska fell seriously ill, developing a heart condition that led to her untimely death at the age of 32. Educated at home by her mother, she spent most of her youth in hospitals. She met her future husband, the student Adolf Poświatowski, at a convalescent home, and he died of heart failure soon after they married. In 1958, Poświatowska traveled to the US to undergo heart surgery. With her health improved, she remained to study philosophy at Smith College, an experience described in the autobiographical *Opowieść dla przyjaciela* ('A Tale for a Friend,' 1967). Upon returning to Poland, she completed her studies at the Jagiellonian University in Cracow, where she also taught. After debuting with a volume of

verse titled *Hymn bałwochwalcy* ('Hymn to an Idol,' 1958), she published three more collections. She is most appreciated for her love poetry and those lyrics that explore the concrete expectation of death. English translations of her verses are available in a bilingual edition, *Indeed I Love/Własnie kocham* (1997) and in the anthology *Ariadne's Thread: Polish Women Poets* (1988).

JB

Prado, Adélia (*b.* 1935) Brazilian poet, fiction writer. Prado published her first book, *Bagagem* ('Baggage,' 1976) when she was 40 years old. Three other collections of poetry followed: *O coração disparado* ('The Pounding Heart,' 1977), *Terra de Santa Cruz* ('Land of the Holy Cross,' 1981), *O pelicano* ('The Pelican,' 1987), and *A faca no peito* ('The Knife in the Chest,' 1988). *The Alphabet in the Park*, a selection of her poems in English translation, was published in 1991. Although she is best known as a poet, she also writes introspective and autobiographical fiction (chronicles, short stories, and confessions) which centers upon people, places, and events in Divinópolis (Minas Gerais), her hometown. Her works combine a conversational tone with erudition and elegance as her characters discuss life, love, sex, God, the condition of women, and everyday life. She adapts her poetic techniques to her fiction, transmitting a sense of disquietude and soul searching, spiritual craving, and sensuality. Her prose works include *Solte os Cachorros* ('Let the Dogs Loose,' 1979), *Cacos para um vitral* ('Smithereens for a Stained Glass Window,' 1980), *Os componentes da Banda* ('Members of the Band,' 1984), and *O Homem da mão seca* ('The Withered-Handed Man,' 1995). Prado, who earned a degree in philosophy and religion, often compares the aesthetic experience of writing to the ecstasy felt and described by mystics. She won the prestigious Jabuti Prize in 1978.

MJB

Pritam, Amrita (*b*. 1919) Indian poet, fiction writer. Born in Gujranwala, now in Pakistan, Pritam had a lonely, restricted childhood. Losing her mother at the age of 10, she was brought up by her father, the poet Kartar Singh Hitkari. Under his guidance, she began her literary career in her early teens. She is the most prolific and popular contemporary writer in Punjabi, best known as the voice of women's suffering. Widely translated and anthologized, she has published over fifteen volumes of poetry and a dozen novels and short story collections. Her first poetry collection *Amrit Lehran* ('The Waves of Nectar,' 1932) is conventional and didactic, praising moral virtues in a simple folk style. Her early themes were India's freedom struggle, national unity, women's suffering, and social reform. Some of her major poetic works are *Lamian Vatan* ('The Long Journeys,' 1948), which describes the trauma of Partition, *Sunhere* ('Intimations,' 1953), and *Kasturi* ('Musk,' 1958). Since her divorce in the 1960s her writings have dealt largely with women who acknowledge their desires and seek independence from male domination. Her more recent Hindi fiction includes the novel *Erial* (Ariel, 1968) and the story collection, *Aksharon ki Chhaya mein* ('In the Shadow of the Alphabet,' 1977). Translator, magazine editor, and member of parliament, Pritam is the only Punjabi writer who has won the prestigious Jnanpith Award.

AS

Procházková, Lenka (*b*. 1951) Czech prose writer. Olomouc-born Procházková, daughter of writer Jan Procházka, began her studies at Charles University in journalism, but was forced to switch to literature, graduating in 1975. She has three children, the two younger ones from her more than ten-year partnership with writer Ludvik Vaculik. After signing Charter 77, she worked cleaning theaters until 1989. In addition to fiction, she has written drama, is a civic activist, and with

lawyer Aleš Pejchal has hosted a program on Radio Free Europe since 1996. Her first novel *Růžová dáma* ('The Pink Lady,' 1982; Egon Hostovský Prize) depicts the life of a rape victim in a small town. Its colloquial language and frank representation of sexual situations anticipate her later works. Subsequent novels *Oční kapky* ('Eye Drops,' 1987) and *Smolná kniha* ('Doomsday Book,' 1991) are highly autobiographical, the latter portraying a young, unmarried woman writer coping with work, partner, and children in the context of Czech dissident politics. Between novels, Procházková has published collections of stories: *Come Have a Taste* (1982), *Illídáč holubů* ('Pigeon Guard,' 1987), and *Zvrhlé dny* ('Perverse Days,' 1995), which typically have female narrators and treat problematic love relationships. In 1996 she published *Pan ministr* ('Mr. Minister'), a 'film story' interpretation of Jan Masaryk's last days.

ES

Prose, Francine (*b*. 1947) US novelist, essayist. The daughter of two New York physicians, Prose attended Radcliffe College as an undergraduate and earned an MA at Harvard University in 1969. Her first novel *Judah the Pious* was published in 1973. Her novels are cultural satires, and often use folklore elements such as prophecy, magic, and the supernatural. Her other novels include *The Glorious Ones* (1974), which focuses on seventeenth-century Italian *commedia dell'arte* actors; *Animal Magnetism* (1978); *Household Saints* (1981), which is set in Little Italy in the 1950s and examines personal faith; *Hungry Hearts* (1983); *Big Foot Dreams* (1986), which features a supermarket tabloid writer; *Primitive People* (1992), which charts the intersection of a Haitian *au pair* and an upper-class New York family; *Hunters and Gatherers* (1995), a look at the hypocrisy of the New Age movement; and *Blue Angel* (2000), a satire of academia and political correctness. *Guided Tours of Hell* (1997) contains two novellas which depict Americans in Europe. Prose has also published two short story collections, *Women and Children First* (1988) and *A Peaceable Kingdom* (1993), *Stories: Our Living Past* (1974), a collection of Jewish folktales, and several children's books, including *You Never Know: A Legend of the Lamed-Vavniks* (1998). Prose regularly writes essays and reviews for journals and newspapers.

DVT

Prou, Suzanne (1920–1995) French novelist. Born in Grimaud, France, the daughter of an army officer and a schoolteacher, Prou spent her early years in Algeria and Indochina. She studied literature in Aix-en-Provence, and then taught for a brief time before turning to writing as a profession. She published her first novel *The Patapharis Affair* in 1966. Many of her numerous literary works, set in her native Provence, evoke a confining bourgeois milieu in which repressive traditions serve as an obstacle to the self-realization of her characters. *The Bernardini Terrace* (1973; Prix Renaudot), her best-known novel, depicts the mysterious bond existing between two former rivals who eventually join forces against the man who has been exploiting them. Her keen observations of provincial life have inspired comparisons to the work of François Mauriac. Several of Prou's later works are autobiographical: *La Petite Tonkinoise* ('The Tonkinese Girl,' 1986) recounts her Indochinese experience, while *Le Dit de Marguerite* ('Margaret's Story,' 1986) narrates the life of her mother.

PJP

Proulx, E. Annie (*b.* 1935) US novelist, short story writer. Edna Annie Proulx graduated from Colby College in Maine in 1957 before earning an MA from Sir George Williams University (now the University of Concordia) in Newfoundland, Canada. She worked as a freelance writer for many years before publishing, at the age of 52, her first book *Heart Songs and Other Stories* (1988), a collection of short stories set in the isolated rural locales that have come to dominate her subsequent work. Her first novel *Postcards* (1992), which won the PEN/Faulkner Prize, is about the slow ruin of a Vermont family after the eldest son murders his wife. *The Shipping News* (1993), for which Proulx was awarded the Pulitzer Prize, the National Book Award, and the *Irish Times* International Fiction Prize, recounts the dark story of Quoyle, an awkward, directionless man who leaves New York to seek fulfillment and purpose in a small town in Newfoundland. *The Shipping News* was praised for its imaginative characters, its lyricism, and its stunning imagery. Proulx has also published the novel *Accordion Crimes* (1996; Orange Prize), about immigrants from a variety of backgrounds whose lives are linked by an accordion which is passed from one stranger to the next, and the short story collection *Close Range: Wyoming Stories* (1999). Proulx has lived in Vermont, Wyoming, and Newfoundland.

DVT

Provoost, Anne (*b.* 1964) Flemish children's writer. As one of the most innovative and important new Flemish authors of children's books, Provoost made her debut in 1991 with *My Aunt is a Pilot Whale* (1990), a book dealing with incest. The book was awarded a prestigious prize and the jury lauded Provoost's subtle, controlled style and the psychological depth of this novel in which the theme of incest is so naturally integrated. With her impressive novel *Falling* (1994), about the dangers of extremism, she garnered all the major literary prizes in 1995. *Falling* shows how ignorance and uncertainty can lead to extremist thought and fascist rhetoric. For her latest book *De roos en het zwijn* ('The Rose and the Swine,' 1997), she chose a different, less moralistic subject: the fairytale of Beauty and the Beast.

AAn, MMe

Puga, María Luisa (*b*. 1944) Mexican novelist, short story writer. Born in Mexico City, Puga is self-taught. Her fiction reflects social concerns – poverty, corruption, the conflict between generations or between men and women, and the struggle for self-realization. She possesses a rare ability to penetrate her characters and express their innermost thoughts. In 1978 she published her first work *Las posibilidades del odio* ('The Possibilities of Hatred'), composed of six novellas set in Kenya. Many of her numerous works are concerned with the act of writing, as in *Pánico o peligro* ('Panic or Danger,' 1983), the story of Susana who evolves from a bewildered young girl into an independent woman. *Antonia* (1989) deals with the life of two young Mexican women – a writer and an actress – who live together in London. Other novels are *Las razones del lago* ('The Reasons of the Lake,' 1992) and *La viuda* ('The Widow,' 1994), the former set in a small town of Michoacán and narrated by two street dogs and the latter about a widow who picks up her life where she had left it some fifty years earlier. Puga's collections of stories include *Accidentes* ('Accidents,' 1981) and *Intentos* ('Attempts,' 1987).

GdB

Q

Qalamāwī, Suhayr al- (1911–1997) Egyptian novelist, short story writer, literary critic. Born to a well-to-do family in Cairo, Egypt, al-Qalamāwī was one of the first female students in the Arab world to receive a doctorate in the humanities. After her graduation from the American College in Cairo, she joined Cairo University where she earned her MA in Arabic in 1937. She was sent to the Sorbonne University in Paris to do research for her PhD on *Arabian Nights*, a degree which she received in 1941. Upon her graduation, she was appointed as a lecturer at Cairo University. Eventually, she became the chairperson of the Arabic Department. Al-Qalamāwī served as president both of the Arab Feminist Union and the League of Arab Women University Graduates. Later, she entered the political arena to become a member of the Egyptian parliament. She also served as the director of the government-affiliated Egyptian Organization for Publishing and Distribution. In 1978, she was awarded the State Appreciation Prize for Literature – the highest literary prize in Egypt. Her literary enterprises include studies in literary criticism, classical Arabic literature, and the *Arabian Nights*. Her novel *Aḥādīth Jaddatī* ('My Grandmother's Tales,' 1935) consists of a series of tales told by a grandmother to her granddaughter. It describes the manners and customs in Cairo before the British occupation in 1882.

JTZ

Quiñones, Magaly (*b*. 1945) Puerto Rican poet. Born in Ponce, Quiñones received an MA in comparative literature and is an experienced graphic artist. Her first three collections of poems, *Entre mi voz y el tiempo* ('Between My Voice and Time,' 1969), *Era que el mundo era* ('So It Was that the World Was,' 1974), and *Zumbayllu* (1976), can be read as a journey of exploration aimed at revealing the tensions and contradictions often experienced by people living in colonized societies. To this end, the poetic voice reinterprets myths and symbols from the Puerto Rican and Latin American tradition in an effort to bring clarity and connection in the midst of chaos. *Cantándole a la noche misma* ('Singing to the Night Itself,' 1978) continues this search for balance between the world as myth and the world as history, between identity and alienation. Quiñones was awarded the Puerto Rican PEN Club poetry award for *Nombrar* ('Naming,'1985), a collection of descriptive and contemplative poems. The craft of writing is the subject of her most recent work *Sueños de papel* ('Paper Dreams,' 1996), a touching reaffirmation of the author's poetic vision. Astute political critique, compassion, and surprise are hallmarks of her writing.

MR-F

R

Radinska, Valentina Dimitrova (*b.* 1951) Bulgarian poet, essayist, translator. Born in Slivan, Radinska studied Bulgarian literature in the University of Sofia (1969–71) and earned an MA in creative writing from the 'Maxim Gorky' Institute in Moscow in 1976. Having returned to Bulgaria, she worked for the Film Company 'Boyana' and the newspaper *Kontinent*. Currently she is an editor for the magazine *Evropa 2001* and teaches creative writing at the University of Sofia. In 1986, she married Kirkor Azaryan, theater director and professor of performing arts; they have one son. In her first books, *Kum men vurvi chovek* ('A Human Walks toward Me,' 1977) and *Noshtna kniga* ('A Nocturnal Book,' 1983), she conveys intense personal feelings through studiedly simple verse. In *Ne* ('No,' 1989), *Chistilishte* (Purgatory, 1992), and *Vsichko* ('Everything,' 1995) her poetic form becomes more experimental. *Dimcho Debelyanov* (1997) contains three extensive essays about a Bulgarian Symbolist poet. She has translated works by the best twentieth-century Russian women poets – Anna Akhmatova and Marina Tsvetaeva – and other Russian writers. English translations of her poems are included in *Young Poets of a New Bulgaria* (1990), *Windows on the Black Sea* (1992), *Shifting Borders* (1993), and *An Anthology of Contemporary Poetry* (1994).

LPG

Rahimieh, Nasrin (*b.* 1958) Iranian literary critic, editor. Rahimieh was born in Bandar Anzali, Iran, a small town on the shores of the Caspian Sea. She attended school there until her last year of high school, which she spent in New London, Connecticut as an exchange student. The following year, she attended a college in Switzerland before moving to Canada, where she has lived for the past twenty years. She obtained a BA Honors degree in French and German and an MA in German literature from Dalhousie University in Nova Scotia. She pursued her doctoral studies at the University of Alberta in the field of comparative literature, where she now teaches as an associate professor. She specializes in immigrant and exile literature, cross-cultural studies, and women's studies. In 1990 she published *Oriental Responses to the West*, a collection of essays on writers of the Muslim world. Her scholarly articles have appeared in numerous academic journals such as *Iranian Studies* and *Comparative Literature Studies*. She has recently completed a book-length study of Persian transcultural writing titled *Missing Persians*.

KTa

Rambe, Hanna (*b.* 1940) Indonesian fiction writer, journalist. Born in Jakarta, Rambe is a journalist and writer whose interest in history is reflected in her fictional writings – like her short story

'Three Strands of Hair' (1991), a gentle tale of thwarted wartime love between a Japanese army major and an Indonesian princess. Rambe's writing is infused with a strong sense of irony, in particular with regard to family loyalty. 'The Love of City People' (1989) depicts the confusion of a country girl when she meets her city relatives and discovers that they care more for their pets than they do for their family. In 'The Longan Tree' (1993), an old woman is forced to sell the family home to make way for an international tourist resort; it is, however, her sophisticated, worldly son who dies of a broken heart at the end of the story.

PA

Rame, Franca (*b*. 1929) Italian dramatist. Rame, born into a famous family of strolling players, first performed at the age of eight days. In 1954 she married Dario Fo (Nobel prize winner, 1997) with whom she started a lifelong collaboration in the writing and performance of a prolific theatrical repertory. Rame became a dramatist in her own right at the end of the 1970s as a result of her involvement with the feminist movement. The collection of monologues *Female Parts: One-Woman Plays* (1977) is a hilarious and relentless exploration of the ways in which the law, state, family and church oppress women. The representation of women's submission to and subversion of patriarchy is central to the three-part farce *Open Couple* (1983). Her activity as a writer and performer is inseparable from her political commitment and personal experience as a woman. The dramatic monologues *I, Ulrike* (1975) and *A Mother* (1980), staging the relation of women to terrorism, are a direct expression of her work in the early 1970s with political prisoners. The monologue *The Rape* (1975) is the impassioned dramatization of her own kidnapping and rape in 1973 by right-wing thugs. Rame's contribution to Italian drama is closely bound to her virtuosity as a performer.

GMi

Ramondino, Fabrizia (*b*. 1936) Italian writer, essayist, screenwriter. Born in Naples, Ramondino's childhood was spent in and around Naples. Her childhood experiences during and after World War II provided the material for her first novel *Althénopis* (1981), the story of a young girl's progressive discovery of her limitations and restrictions through her experiences with different public and private spaces in and around Naples during and after the war. Major themes include the mother–daughter relationship, female sexuality, and oppressive and impotent matriarchies, all of which are found again in her 1983 short story collection *Storie di patio* ('Patio Stories'), her novel *Un giorno e mezzo* ('A Day and a Half,' 1988), the various intertwined stories of the reactions of many women of her generation to the political upheavals of 1969, and *Terremoto con madre e figlia* ('Earthquake with Mother and Daughter,' 1994). Ramondino continues her critique of confining social, familial, and political structures through innovative uses of geographical space in *Taccuino tedesco* ('A German Notebook,' 1987) and *Dadapolis. Caleidoscopio napoletano* ('Dadapolis: A Neapolitan Kaleidoscope') written with Andreas Friedrich Müller. Recent works include the script for Mario Martone's film, *Morte di un matematico napoletano* ('Death of a Neapolitan Mathematician') and a novel *L'isola riflessa* ('Reflector Island,' 1998) whose setting is the island of Ventotene, the scene of confinement for resisters of fascism.

CL-W

Randhawa, Ravinder (*b*. 1952) Indian-British short story writer, novelist. Born in India, Randhawa moved to England with her family at the age of 7. In 1973 she graduated in English from the Polytechnic of North-East London, and worked as a teacher and for the civil service. She has raised funds for Asian women's organizations and campaigned against racism in Britain. In 1984 she founded the Asian

Women Writers' Collective (AWWC) to share her experience and writing with other like-minded women. A number of her stories appeared in the AWWC's anthologies, *Right of Way* (1988) and *Flaming Spirit* (1994). Her immigrant experience, the racism suffered in Britain, and the cultural and psychological clash resulting from migration shape her fictional work profoundly, together with her commitment to exposing stereotypical images of Indian women and creating characters who defy them. The nonlinear structure of her first novel *A Wicked Old Woman* (1987) reflects the protagonist's schizophrenic identity through the conflict between her conformity to stereotypical images of Indian women and her search for a true self. Randhawa's novel *Harijan* (1992) is for teenage readers. Her manuscript *The Coral Strand* is a novel with a thriller element.

PM

Ratushinskaia, Irina Borisovna (*b.* 1954) Russian poet, memoirist, prose writer. Born in Odessa to an intelligentsia family, Ratushinskaia graduated from Odessa University in 1976 with a major in physics, and taught at Odessa Pedagogical Institute. She married an engineer, moved to Kiev, and tutored in physics and mathematics, continuing to write the poetry she had embarked on in childhood. In 1980, the couple joined the human rights movement, disseminated Ratushinskaia's poetry in *samizdat*, and in late 1981 were arrested. Rearrested in 1982, Ratushinskaia spent three years in Mordovia (Bakhtin territory), where she composed verses that comprise the collection *Beyond the Limit* (1984) and smuggled out information along with her poems. Upon release, she and her husband found asylum in England, where they currently reside. Her uneven poetry and memoirs are aureoled by her perceived role as political martyr. Spiritual values and moral commitment inform her verses in *Stikhi, Poems, Poèmes* (1986) and *Stikhi* ('Verses,'

1988), and her two translated volumes of memoirs: *Gray Is the Color of Hope* (1988) documents with a moving simplicity her three years of incarceration and *In the Beginning* (1991) moves back into her childhood as the starting point for her maturation into a poet and conscience-driven activist. Ratushinskaia has also published an unremarkable volume of stories *A Tale of Three Heads* (1986) and the novel *Fictions and Lies* (1999).

HG

Ravanipur, Muniru (*b.* 1954) Iranian novelist. Born in the coastal region of the Persian Gulf, Ravanipur grew up in Shiraz and received a BA in psychology from Shiraz University. Since the early 1980s, she has published several novels and collections of short stories including *Ahl-e Gharq* ('People of Gharq,' 1989), *Del-i Fulad* ('The Heart of Steel,' 1990), and *Satan's Stones* (1991). Her assertiveness and her literary themes have given her a prominent position among post revolutionary literary activists. Promoting the image of women who 'shout' their 'suffering,' she adheres to a feminist notion of literature which pleads that women should be portrayed not as helpless victims but as rebels. She explicitly addresses issues related to women's social conditions and gender relations by emphasizing the importance of women's literary endeavors. 'The Sad Story of Love,' from *Satan's Stones*, for example, explores these issues through the story of a woman who works in a publishing firm, where she writes fiction under the supervision of a male editor.

KTa

Ravikovitch, Dahlia (*b.* 1936) Israeli poet. Ravikovitch has been considered one of the most important voices in Israeli poetry since the publication of her first book *Ahavat Tapuah Zahav* ('The Love of an Orange') in 1959. She is also among the first to be translated into English, most recently in *The Window* (1989). Richly evocative and linguistically layered, sometimes bitter, often ironic and sharp, or filled with anguish and marked by a sense of desolation and an acknowledgement of the brutality of relationships, her eight books of poetry, including *Horef Kasheh* ('A Hard Winter,' 1965) and *Tehom Koreh* ('The Abyss Calls,' 1978), draw at once on the personal, Biblical, mythological, and historical, as well as on the Jewish liturgical and textual tradition. Poems from the newer *Ahavat Amitit* ('Real Love,' 1987) and *Eemah Eem Yeled* ('Mother with Child,' 1992) are more overtly political, incisively troubling the tragedies in the public arena. Ravikovitch's poetry has been often anthologized, including the famous 'A Dress of Fire' from the eponymous collection published in English in 1976. She has also written short stories – collected in *Mavet Bah'Mishpacha* ('A Death in the Family,' 1982) – and children's books. She lives in Tel Aviv.

MGl

Ray, Pratibha (*b.* 1944) Indian novelist. Born in the village of Alabol, Orissa, Ray was deeply influenced by her father, a freedom fighter and social activist. Graduating in botany, she discontinued her studies after her marriage to Akshaya Chandra Ray, an engineer; they have a daughter and two sons. Later she went on to complete her MA and PhD in educational psychology. Her postdoctoral research on the tribalism and criminology of one of the most primitive tribes of Orissa finds expression in some of her fictional works. She is currently a Reader in Education at Ravenshaw College, Cuttack. She has written eighteen novels, seventeen collections of short stories, one travelogue, five books for children and ten books for neoliterates, all in Oriya. Her first published novel was *Barsa Basant Baisakha* (1974). *Aranya* ('The Forest,' 1975), her second novel, anticipated the topic of artificial insemination. *Shilapadma* ('Stonelotus,' 1983), about the legends of the Sun Temple of Konark, won the Orissa Sahitya

Akademi Award in 1985 and *Yajnaseni: The Story of Draupadi* (1985), focuses on the heroine of the *Mahabharata*, making Draupadi the strong, pivotal character around whom the entire epic revolves. *Yajnaseni* won the Moorti Devi Award of the Bharatiya Jnanpith in 1991. Ray's stories have been widely translated and anthologized.

CD

Rayson, Hannie (*b.* 1957) Australian playwright, freelance writer. Rayson is a freelance writer for television, film, and newspapers. She lives in Melbourne, the city in which she was born, and received her degrees from Melbourne University, the Victoria College of the Arts, and La-Trobe University where she was awarded an Honorary Doctor of Letters. She has worked as writer-in-residence at Playbox, the Mill Theatre, and LaTrobe and Monash universities, and co-founded Theatreworks in 1981. Her plays include *Please Return to Sender* (1980); *Mary* (1985), a play about a Greek immigrant mother and her teenaged daughter; *Leave it Till Monday* (1984); *Room to Move* (1985; Awgie Award), which humorously depicts the roles and interaction of men and women in a post-feminist world; *Hotel Sorrento* (1990; Awgie Award, NSW State Literary Award, Victoria Green Room Award), which is about sisters and their judgements of each other concerning their individual decisions to remain in Australia or emigrate; *Falling from Grace* (1994), a play about female friendship and public morality; and *Competitive Tenderness* (1996), a satirical attack on bureaucracy and corruption, in which Dawn Snow is employed to reform the City of Greater Burke local government. *Hotel Sorrento* is now a feature film, starring Joan Plowright and directed by Richard Franklin.

M-RA

Redonnet, Marie (*b.* 1948) French novelist, dramatist. The only child of a seamstress and an employee of the Parisian transportation system, Redonnet taught literature in suburban high schools before devoting herself entirely to writing. Since her first book *Le Mort et Cie* ('The Dead and Co.,' 1985) – a series of haiku-like poems evoking her father's death – she has subtly blended unique narrative strategies with uncanny leitmotivs. Her collection of short stories *Doublures* ('Understudies,' 1986), revitalizes the dialectic confrontation of same and other, double and twin. In her early triptych of novels *Hôtel Splendid* (1986), *Forever Valley*, and *Rose Mélie Rose* (1987), female voices embody an unadorned and quasi-clinical prose which transforms tedious lives into hallucinatory tales of women's destinies. Fighting against a hotel's perpetually clogged plumbing, making a mission out of excavating imaginary tombs or literally dying to give birth, Redonnet's heroines acquire mythopoetic dimensions while feeling like the girl next door. *Candy Story* (1992) or *Nevermore* (1994), with its French vision of the American West Coast, and plays like *Tir et Lir* (1988) unfold disturbing yet familiar worlds of difference and repetition, absurd and violent, which linger in our memories with a Beckett-like tenacity.

F-SC

Rehmann, Ruth (*b.* 1922) German novelist, short story writer. Daughter of a Protestant minister, Rehmann grew up near Bonn. She trained as a translator and studied art history, German literature, and music, including the violin. A founding member of the Gruppe 47 and of Germany's PEN-Zentrum, she now lives in rural Bavaria. Main themes in her work are the loneliness and isolation of the individual and the restrictive possibilities for women's emancipation in German society. Her first novel *Saturday to Monday* (1959) follows four office workers who escape their meaningless and regimented existence by creating a dream world. *The Man in the Pulpit: Questions for a Father* (1979) is a

'father novel,' a largely autobiographical account of a daughter coming to terms with her father's role as a cleric during the Third Reich. Other works include *Die Leute im Tal* ('The People in the Valley,' 1968), *Abschied von der Meisterklasse* ('Graduation from the Master Class,' 1985), *Die Schwaigerin* ('The Sister-in-law,' 1987), *Der Abstieg* ('The Decline,' 1987), and *Bootsfahrt mit Damen* ('Boating with the Ladies,' 1995). Rehmann has also written numerous radio plays. She received the 'Literaturpreis des Bundesverbandes der Deutschen Industrie' in 1989.

ALC

Reinig, Christa (*b.* 1926) German novelist, poet. Born in Berlin, Reinig now lives in Munich. After working in a factory and as a florist, she studied art history and archaeology and worked as an archivist. From 1945 until 1955, while still living in East Berlin, she was a member of a writers group' and edited a journal. Since her poems and writings only appeared in West Germany and were no longer printed in the GDR, she moved to the west in 1964. *Die himmlische und die irdische Geometrie* ('Heavenly and Earthly Geometry,' 1975) is based on autobiographical materials. *Entmannung* ('Emasculation,' 1976), *Der Wolf und die Witwen* ('The Wolf and the Widows,' 1980), and *Die ewige Schule* ('Eternal School,' 1982) were written in the context of the women's movement. All three works are sarcastic portrayals of the battle of the sexes and deal with psychological and physical violence against women; they also demonstrate Reinig's mastery of dark humor, satire, and irony. *Die Frau im Brunnen* ('Woman in the Well,' 1984) is situated in an imaginary women-identified world. Other works are *Glück und Glas* ('Fortune and Glass,' 1991) and *Ein Wogenzug von wilden Schwänen* ('A Wave of Wild Swans,' 1991). She has received several literary awards.

MMu

Reinshagen, Gerlind (*b.* 1926) German playwright. Reinshagen was born in Königsberg (Kaliningrad, Russia), and originally studied to be a pharmacist. She addresses women's roles as victims or participants in nationalist, fascist, or capitalist systems and realistically depicts middle-class characters who are forced by circumstances to 'do the right thing.' Her work is underscored by Marxist social theory and is imbued with a utopian tenor through which she seeks to engage her audience. *Sonntagskinder* ('Sunday's Children,' 1976), *Frühlingsfest* ('Celebration of Spring,' 1980), and *Tanz, Marie!* ('Dance, Marie!' 1986), comprise the trilogy of a girl who grows up under fascism only to commit suicide in an affluent West Germany of the 1980s. *Sonntagskinder* and *Himmel und Erde* ('Heaven and Earth,' 1974) were made into television movies. Later dramas draw heavily on choreography and chorus recitation. Her prose includes *Die flüchtige Braut* ('The Fleeting Bride,' 1984), which depicts the city of Berlin as a mystical place where the romantic and political euphoria among a group of friends is lost to the realities of life in the 1980s. Little of her work has been translated into English. Awards include the 'Andreas Gryphius-Preis' (1982) and the 'Roswitha-Gedenkmedaille' (1988). Reinshagen lives in Braunschweig and Berlin.

ALC

Rendell, Ruth (*b.* 1930) English mystery writer, short story writer. Born in London, the daughter of two teachers, Rendell began working as a newspaper reporter and editor in Essex directly upon graduating from high school. In 1964, she published her first novel *From Doon With Death*, introducing her detective hero, Chief Inspector Reginald Wexford, a married middle-aged man with two daughters whose shrewd understanding of human behavior allows him acute insights into criminals' minds. Wexford and his assistant Mike Burden reappear in what came to be called the Kingsmarkham Series, which includes *The Best Man to Die* (1969), *No More Dying Then* (1971), *A Sleeping Life* (1978), *An Unkindness of Ravens* (1985), *Kissing the Gunner's Daughter* (1992), *Simisola* (1995), and *Harm Done* (1999). Rendell, who has also published several short story collections, is known for her construction of suspenseful, unpredictable plots and richly developed, complicated characters. Her non-series novels, including *A Demon in My View* (1976), *The Lake of Darkness* (1980), and *The Tree of Hands* (1984), are suspense thrillers which focus on child molesters, rapists, and other forms of criminal perversion. Under the pseudonym Barbara Vine, she has written a series of novels that, while still of the mystery genre, are strongly psychological and are more romantic and self-consciously literary than her work as Rendell. These novels include the award-winning *A Dark-Adapted Eye* (1986), *Gallowglass* (1990), and *The Brimstone Wedding* (1995).

DVT

Riaz, Fahmida (*b.* 1945) Pakistani poet, fiction writer. Born in Meerut, India, Riaz is known for her strong, uninhibited exploration of female sexuality. She is a controversial figure whose poetry cannot be severed from her politics. Familarized with Urdu and Persian literature by her mother and deeply influenced by left-wing politics and the Progressive Writers Movement as well as the student protests of the 1960s against martial law, she became a published poet while still in college. Later as editor of the magazine *Awaaz*, she came up against the state when she was charged with sedition. In 1991, while still on bail, she went into exile in India, where she worked as poet-in-residence at Jamia Millia University, to return in 1988 under a democratic government. Her writing challenges the female stereotype of virginal passivity and replaces her with a living, passionate, rebellious entity. Her published works include the poetry collections

Pathar ki Zaban ('The Stone Tongue'), *Badan Dareeda* ('The Injured Body'), *Dhoop* ('Sunlight'), *Apna Jurm Sabit Hai* ('My Crime is Proven') and three novels, *Karachi, Zinda Bahar,* and *Gadavri.* A selection of her poems is available in English in *We Sinful Women* (1990).

NH

Ribeiro, Esmeralda (*b.* 1958) Brazilian poet, short story writer, journalist. Born and raised in the city of São Paulo, Ribeiro is an active participant in the literary and cultural group 'Quilombhoje,' a group of black writers who edit *Cadernos negros* ('Black Notebooks'). She has published poetry and short stories in *Cadernos negros* (volumes 5, 7, 8, 9) and other anthologies such as *Criação crioula* ('Mestizo Creation,' 1987) and *Reflexões sobre a literatura afro-brasileira* ('Reflections on Afro-Brazilian Literature,' 1985). Her theoretical essays often examine the challenges involved in being a black, female writer in Brazil, and the need to theorize such a condition, as detailed in 'A escritora negra e o seu ato de escrever participando' ('The Black Woman Writer and Her Act of Writing as Participation'). She has written a short novel, *Malungos e Milongas* ('Fellow-Slave and Gossipings,' 1988), in which she traces the saga of a black family since slavery, and examines the historical process of their struggle to establish an identity.

MJB

Rice, Anne (*b.* 1941) US novelist. Born Howard Allen O'Brien in New Orleans, Rice was educated at Texas Women's University and San Francisco State College (BA, 1964; MA, 1971), and did graduate work at the University of California, Berkeley. Her first novel *Interview with the Vampire* was published in 1976; it was made into a major film in 1994. It chronicles the tortured life of a vampire, Louis, from the eighteenth century to the present. By placing him as the protagonist instead of the villain, Rice makes his feelings of isolation and frustration recognizable and sympathetic. This original twist, as well as the book's homoeroticism, made it and the subsequent books in the Vampire Chronicles, cult favorites. The Vampire Chronicles include *The Vampire Lestat* (1985), *The Queen of the Damned* (1988), and *Memnoch the Devil* (1996). Rice has begun a New Tales of the Vampires series, and has also written another series of fantasy fiction titled The Mayfair Witches, as well as several historical novels including *Cry to Heaven* (1982), the story of an Italian castrato in the eighteenth century. As with the vampire novels, her historical fiction is moodily erotic, often with overtones of sadomasochism.

JEM

Rich, Adrienne (*b.* 1929) US poet, essayist. Renowned as a feminist theorist and political activist, Rich was born into an intellectual Jewish family in Baltimore and graduated with honors from Radcliffe College in 1951. She married Harvard economist Alfred Conrad, with whom she raised three children; they divorced after seventeen years of marriage. In her nonfiction work *Of Woman Born* (1977), she uses her own experiences to examine the institution of motherhood. Her first book of poetry *A Change of World* (1951) was awarded the Yale Younger Poet series award and was lauded by W. H. Auden and other poets. Her third book of poetry *Snapshots of a Daughter-in-Law* (1963) showcases Rich's developing interest in feminism. In this and subsequent books, her goal is to write directly as a woman and to give witness to women's experiences. A stint teaching English to poor ethnic students in New York led to a sharpened sensibility about racial injustice. Her volumes of poetry include *Necessities of Life* (1966), *Leaflets* (1969), *The Fact of a Doorframe* (1984), and *Your Native Land, Your Life* (1986). *Diving into the Wreck* (1973) won the National Book Award, which she accepted on behalf of all women who have been silenced. Her acclaimed *The Dream of a Common Language* (1978) includes 'Twenty-One Love Poems,' a sequence of lesbian love sonnets. In *An Atlas of a Difficult World* (1991), Rich explores the struggles of a variety of marginalized groups in the US, though her main focus remains on women and lesbians. Her many influential essays have been collected in several volumes, including *Blood, Bread and Poetry* (1986), which contains her classic feminist essay 'Compulsory Heterosexuality and Lesbian Existence' (1980).

DVT

Richterová, Sylvie (*b.* 1945) Czech prose writer. Born in Brno, Richterová studied translation at the University of 17 November in Prague before receiving a graduate degree in French and Czech from Charles University in 1970. She moved to Italy with her husband in 1971. Studying with Slavicist Angelo Mario Repellino at the University of Rome, she earned another graduate degree and began teaching Czech literature. After working in Padua and Viterbo, she returned to Rome as a professor in 1997. Active as a literary scholar, she has published two collections of semiotic studies on Czech literature: *Slovo a ticho* ('Word and Silence,' 1986) and *Ticho a smích* ('Silence and Laughter,' 1997). Originally published in exile, her first slim books of prose, *Returns and Other Losses* (1978) and *Topography* (1983), subsequently appeared together with *Primer of the Father Tongue* (1991). This experimental prose triptych, a symbiotic memoir and dream narrative, attempts to capture lost time, as well as to comprehend life. *Roztylené podoby* ('Dispersed Images,' 1993) conveys a broken love relationship and personal crisis through an intricately fragmented narrative. In her latest novel *Second Parting* (1994), Richterová creates a challenging open text, synthesizing a fairy tale with mythological and biblical motifs.

ES

Riera, Carme (*b.* 1948) Catalan-Spanish fiction writer, literary critic. Majorcan-born Riera grew up multilingually, between Castilian (Spanish), Catalan, and the Majorcan dialect. Studying Castilian philology at the University of Barcelona, she lived the fervid Catalanism, anti-Francoism, and nascent feminism of the late 1960s. With a PhD in 1985, she is a professor of Castilian literature at the Universitat Autònoma. She writes in a distinctively evocative, Majorcan-tinged Catalan, often translating herself into Castilian. Her first short story collection became a best-seller on the strength of its stunning eponymous love story, 'I Leave You, My Love, the Sea as Token' (1975). Favorite themes include the arbitrary nature of gender, the plasticity of desire, love's transformative power, the deadening force of convention, and memory's shaping capacity. Riera favors first-person women narrators, although *Dins el darrer blau* ('In the Furthest Blue,' 1994; Premio Nacional de Literatura) is a multi-focal retelling of Majorca's last *auto de fe*. *Una Primavera per a Domenico Guarini* ('Spring for Domenico Guarini,' 1981), *Qüestió d'amor propi* ('A Question of Self Respect,' 1987), and *Mirror Images* (1989) deal with themes of psychic doubling and physical and spiritual metamorphosis, especially in women.

GCN

Rifaat, Alifa (1930–1996) Egyptian short story writer. Born Fāṭima ʿAbdallah Rifʿat in Cairo, Rifaat grew up in the countryside in a wealthy, devout Muslim family. Her formal education was minimal, but she received a substantial informal education in the teachings of Islam. After a brief arranged marriage to a mining engineer, she married a police officer cousin. Her second husband, with whom she traveled widely in many rural areas of Egypt, did not allow her to write or publish, and threatened her with divorce and the loss of custody of their young daughter. It was not until 1971, after she had suffered mental distress, that he let her publish. Her first compilation of short stories in Arabic *Ḥawwā' Ta 'ūd bi-Ādam* ('Eve Comes Back with Adam') appeared in 1975. In 1983, her collection of short stories *Distant View of a Minaret* was published in English. It reveals the intimate private world of women deprived of sexual and emotional satisfaction in their marriages. Her revolt against women's oppression, however, did not include advocating deviation from the traditionally prescribed woman's role which stresses marriage and motherhood. Rifaat published four short story collections and one novel. She embraced the veil a few years before her death.

JTZ

Rivoyre, Christine de (*b.* 1921) French novelist, journalist. Born in southwestern France to a middle-class family, de Rivoyre attended Catholic schools, then went on to complete an undergraduate degree in literature at the Sorbonne. She wrote articles on dance and on English and American literature for *Le Monde*, before becoming the literary editor of *Marie-Claire*. Her familiarity with dance is reflected in the setting of her first novel *L'Alouette au miroir* ('A Snare for the Heart,' 1955), which won the Prix des Quatre-Jurys. Since the late 1960s, de Rivoyre has devoted herself to writing fiction, producing numerous popular novels, three of which have been made into films: *The Tangerine* (1957), *The Sultans* (1964), and *Morning Twilight* (1968; Prix Interallié). The latter, set in France during the Occupation years, introduces the theme of war, which is taken up again in *Boy* (1973), a novel that evokes the Spanish Civil War. Her love of animals and of the land and ocean of southwestern France runs through much of her work; this focus on nature and attachment to a specific region has been compared to similar themes in Colette.

PJP, SIr

Roberts, Michèle (*b.* 1949) British novelist, poet. Born in Bushey, Hertfordshire,

Roberts was educated at Somerville College, Oxford, where she earned a BA with honors in 1970. Her first novel *A Piece of the Night* (1978) traces a woman's development from convent schoolgirl to a wife and mother to feminist and lesbian. She writes from a distinctly feminist perspective, employing archetypes of female power and sexuality, and mythic and biblical images of women. Her French heritage and Roman Catholicism are central to her work. *The Visitation* (1983) uses Christian myth to celebrate motherhood and female creativity. In *The Wild Girl* (1984), she retells the story of Mary Magdelene, positing a sexual relationship with Jesus. She frequently embeds interconnected stories in her novels in order to depict the fullest possible range of women's experiences through history, as in *The Book of Mrs. Noah* (1987), *In the Red Kitchen* (1990), *Flesh and Blood* (1994), and *Impossible Saints* (1997). Her critically acclaimed novel *Daughters of the House* (1992) is the story of two cousins growing up in France after the war and the secrets they uncover. Her feminist themes and her lush, sensuous style are evident in her poetry as well. Her verse collections include *Smile, Smile, Smile, Smile* (1980), *The Mirror of the Mother* (1985), and *All the Selves I Was* (1995).

JEM

Robin, Régine (*b.* 1939) French/Canadian novelist. Robin and her writing defy easy categorizations. Born in Paris to Jewish immigrants from Poland, she moved to Montreal in the 1970s, where she has taught at the University of Quebec since 1982. She holds several university degrees, including a prestigious French doctorate from the Ecole des Hautes Etudes en Sciences Sociales in Paris in 1989. Her writing is characterized by an obsession with memory and history, and a profound interest in Jewish identity. Her best-known novel *The Wanderer* (1983) wrestles with these issues while exploring three potential destinies for a recent immigrant in

Montreal, a professor of Jewish history. The same concerns are portrayed in her first novel, *Le cheval blanc de Lénine* ('Lenin's White Horse,' 1979), an imagined biography of her father. Her collection of short stories *L'immense fatigue des pierres* ('The Immense Fatigue of Stones,' 1996) further questions ideas about identity by invoking alternate, on-line identities for her characters. Robin has published several scholarly and critical works, on Kafka in particular, and most notably *Socialist Realism: An Impossible Aesthetic*, for which she received the Canadian Governor General's Award for nonfiction in 1987.

MGi

Robinson, Marilynne (*b*. 1944) US novelist, essayist. Born in Sandpoint, Idaho, Robinson grew up in Idaho and Washington State. She attended Brown University as an undergraduate and received a PhD from the University of Washington. She is married and has two sons. Her only novel *Housekeeping* (1981), the story of two teenaged girls and the different women who 'keep' them as they are passed from home to home, won an Ernest Hemingway Foundation Award for best first novel and a Pulitzer Prize nomination. This remarkable novel, lauded for its thoughtful, precise prose and elegant lyricism, addresses the tension between the civilized order that housekeeping represents and the alluring freedom of the natural world. *Housekeeping* was made into a major film in 1987. Robinson's next book *Mother Country* (1989) is a polemical and controversial nonfiction work that warns readers about the potential dangers of plutonium pollution. Having apparently renounced fiction, Robinson published her third book, the collection *The Death of Adam: Essays on Modern Thought* in 1998. In it, she criticizes the spiritual and aesthetic deficiencies of modern intellectual culture in the US.

DVT

Robles, Mireya (*b*. 1934) Cuban-US poet, novelist, short story writer. Born in

Havana, Cuba, Robles came to the US in 1957. She received a doctorate in Hispanic literatures from the University of New York at Stony Brook. She has published collections of poems, *Time, the Artisan* (1973) and *En esta aurora* ('In This Dawn,' 1974), and short stories in anthologies. Using satire, her powerful novel *Hagiography of Narcisa the Beautiful* (1985) tells the story of a girl growing up in a society that shows no respect for a female who does not adhere to the rules governing a debilitating conception of femininity. Through humor and grotesque situations, Robles offers a sharp critique of a society that relies heavily on machismo. She teaches at the University of Natal, South Africa, where she has lived since 1985.

MIL

Rochefort, Christiane (1917–1998) French novelist. Born in Paris, Rochefort started her career as a cinema reporter and journalist for *France-Soir*. She earned instant success with her first novel *Warrior's Rest* (1958). Active in the French women's liberation movements, she describes in her best-known social critiques *Josyane and the Welfare* (1961) and *Cats Don't Care for Money* (1963) how institutions such as schools, police, family, and church perpetuate inequities. To escape capitalist society, she creates neologisms and imaginary worlds, as in her anarchist utopia *Archaos ou le jardin étincelant* ('Archaos or the Glittering Garden,' 1972). She undermines the concept of order through a methodical strategy of derision and by insisting on the right to pleasure without guilt in *Une rose pur Morrisson* ('A Rose for Morrisson,' 1966). Subversive vocabulary, transposition of sexual scenes in religious settings, transformation, and interchangeability of sexes, all express her revolutionary vision. She also wrote novels and essays about the oppression of children. Among other awards, she received the Prix Médicis for *La porte du fond* ('The Back Door,' 1988), a novel about incest. She published *Conversation sans* *paroles* ('Conversation Without Words,' 1997) before her death in 1998.

IC

Rodoreda, Mercè (1908–1983) Catalan fiction writer. Rodoreda recalled her childhood with her eccentric Catalanist family as the only happy years of her life. At the age of 20, she married an uncle, bearing a son in 1929. She published five novels in the 1930s, before Franco's Civil War victory precipitated her forty-year exile. The Creixells Prize-winning *Aloma* (1938) relates a girl's seduction, impregnation, and abandonment by an older man. Its themes – men's egoism, predatory sexuality, and moral frailty versus women's psychic, physical, and economic vulnerability; paradise/childhood lost; the child as maternal parasite – recur frequently, notably in the acclaimed *Time of the Doves* (1962), with its poignant female vision of war, in the orphan Cecilia's picaresque tale, *Camellia Street* (1966; winner of Sant Jordi, 1996; Premio de la Crítica, 1967; Ramon Llull, 1969); and in *My Christina and Other Stories* (1967), Rodoreda favored indirect discourse, colloquial Caralan, and a single female narrator, but the family saga *Mirall trencat* ('Broken Mirror,' 1974), features many points of view. Her realism was increasingly complemented by fantastic elements in 'My Christina,' 'The Salamander,' *Semblava de seda* ('Like Silk,' 1978), and *Viatges i flors* ('Travels and Flowers,' 1980). Male narrators limn violent worlds in *Quanta, quanta guerra* ('War and More War,' 1980) and *La mort i la primavera* ('Death and Spring,' 1986).

GCN

Rodriguez, Judith (*b.* 1936) Australian poet, editor. Born in Brisbane, Rodriguez married a Colombian academic in 1964 and traveled and taught extensively in the US, South America, and Jamaica. Rodriguez's first volume of poetry *Four Poets* (1962), in which she appeared with David Malouf, Rodney Hall, and Don Maynard, has been followed by eight collections of verse, including *Nu-Plastik Fanfare Red* (1973), *Water Life* (1976), *Shadow on Glass* (1978), *Mudcrab at Gambaro's* (1980; 1981 PEN international prize for poetry), and *New and Selected Poems* (1988). Rodriguez's involvement in poetry editing, for the journal *Meanjin* (1979–82) and for Penguin, Australia (1989–97), and in the teaching of writing, reflects a lifetime's generous fostering of the poetic voices of younger writers. Her poetry constructs strong female voices which insist on justice, clearly perceiving the intricacies of the personal and the relational. They are not confessional, but draw deeply on experience. There is an ongoing desire, conveyed in the poetry's fluid movement between free verse and traditional verse forms, to found the self in poetic language, to give body to feisty, independent, fully-alive voices. Rodriguez is also the author of a libretto, *Lindy*, commissioned by the Australian Opera.

LMcC

Roemer, Astrid (*b.* 1947) Surinamese novelist, poet. Born in Paramaribo, Roemer left for the Netherlands in 1966 to complete her degree in elementary education. A family therapist since 1988, she joined the city council of Den Haag in 1990. In 1986, she completed an MA at the Humanist University of Utrecht. Her first novel *Neem mij terug Suriname* ('Take Me Back, Suriname,' 1974) as well as *Nergens ergens* ('Nowhere Somewhere,' 1983) show the disillusionment of Surinamese intellectuals in the Netherlands. The poems in *Noordzeeblues: Liederatuur* ('North-Sea-blues: 'Songature',' 1985) reflect her emphasis on oral-musical elements. *Over de gekte van een vrouw* ('About a Woman's Madness,' 1982) and *Levenslang gedicht* ('Lifelong Poem,' 1987) present a Surinamese woman trying to break out of cultural oppression. Lesbian relationships as well as creative activity play an important role in both novels. Her most recent novel *Lijken of liefde* ('Just Like Love,' 1997), is the second part of a trilogy which begins with *Gewaagd leven* ('To live daringly,' 1996) and envisions a tribunal for Paramaribo and a purification for Suriname, at the turn of the millennium.

DH

Romano, Lalla (*b.* 1909) Italian novelist. One of Italy's most prolific and popular writers, Romano grew up in Demonte, Cuneo. She received a degree in Italian literature in 1928 at the University of Turin. She was a schoolteacher for twenty-five years, and a painter until 1947 when she decided to dedicate herself to writing. *Fiore* ('Flower,' 1941), a book of poetry, marks the beginning of her literary career. Her writing is often autobiographical and includes such subjects as family, travel, memory, dreams, and women's issues. Among her many literary awards, she won the Librai Milanesi Prize for *La penombra che abbiamo attraversato* ('The Shade That We Crossed,' 1964), a semi-autobiographical work dealing with her mother's death. *Le parole tra noi leggere* ('Flighty Words Between Us,' 1969), which won the prestigious Premio Strega award, describes her difficult relationship with her son. Her collected works were published in two volumes, *Opere* ('Collected Works,' 1991). Although none of her works have been translated into English, a short story appears in *Italian Women Writing* (1993), an anthology of short stories including critical notes and vocabulary intended for English-speaking readers of Italian. This short story 'A Cheneil d'autunno' ('In Cheneil in the Autumn,' 1989) describes the narrator's annual retreat to the peace and simplicity of the mountain village of Cheneil.

DGr

Rong Zi (*b.* 1928) Chinese-Taiwan poet. Born into a Christian family in Jiangsu Province, Rong Zi received Christian schooling at the primary and secondary levels. She studied at an agricultural college for a year and then started working, first as a teacher and then at a radio station. The station sent her to Taipei, Taiwan in 1949, where she has been living ever since. She began writing poetry in 1950 and published her first volume of poetry in 1953; it was the first book of poetry by a woman to be published in postwar Taiwan. In 1955 she married Lo Men, a fellow poet; their well-known union has won them the accolade 'The Chinese Brownings.' Rong Zi's poetry combines traditional Chinese lyricism with a modern sensibility, as reflected in her critique of urban culture and pursuit of independence as a woman. English translations of her poetry are available in many anthologies.

MY

Rosca, Ninotchka (*b.* 1946) Philippine fiction writer, essayist. Born in the notorious Manila district of Caloocan into a political clan, Maria Antonia Rosca obtained her AB and MA degrees at the University of the Philippines, where she first became involved in the nationalist movement. She was christened 'Ninotchka' by the cinematically influenced (and now National Artist) Nick Joaquin during her fellowship at the Silliman University Summer Writers' Workshop. Her first collection of short fiction *Bitter Country and Other Stories* (1970) exhibited themes of freedom and death, in what was then described as 'committed' writing. Her second volume *Monsoon Collection* (1985), published while she was a political exile in the US, is set in Metro Manila and depicts the grotesque characters who inhabit its streets. Her first novel, *State of War* (1988) reinvents Philippine history through the metaphor of the festival and the lives of the three characters who participate in it. *Twice Blessed* (1992), her second novel, is a political satire reflecting Philippine–US relations during the Marcos era; it won for Rosca an American Book Award. She has also written for *Ms.* and the *Nation*, and has published a volume of essays *Endgame: The Fall of the House of Marcos* (1987). She lives in Manhattan.

CJM

Rose, Jacqueline (*b.* 1945) British feminist literary critic. Chair of the English Department at the University of London, Rose is one of the leading feminist psychoanalysts in the English-speaking world. In the collection *Feminine Sexuality* (1982), which she co-edited and translated, she articulates the importance of Freudian and Lacanian psychoanalysis to feminist theory. *The Case of Peter Pan* (1984) demystifies the role of childhood innocence in popular culture. In *Sexuality in the Field of Vision* (1986), Rose responds to the feminist attack on the politics of psychoanalysis, especially when psychoanalysis travels outside of its clinical domain into literary criticism. *The Haunting of Sylvia Plath* (1991) is her appraisal of the controversy over critical assessments of and approaches to *Plath's writings. *Why Wars?* (1993) makes a theoretical return to Melanie Klein, elaborating psycho-politics that mediate between psychic life and its social boundaries. In *States of Fantasy* (1996), Rose utilizes psychoanalytic terms, including fantasy, identification, guilt, and madness, to further contest the limits and assumptions of cultural politics in the public and collective categories of identity, nation, and statehood in British, Israeli, Palestinian, and South African literature and culture.

LY

Rosselli, Amelia (1930–1996) Italian poet. Daughter of an English mother and an Italian father, both activists in the struggle against fascism, Rosselli was born in exile in Paris. Her childhood was scarred by the assassination of her father Carlo in 1937 on Mussolini's order, and the family's flight to England and then the US after the invasion of France in 1940. After the war, Rosselli completed her studies of literature and music at the Saint Paul's School for Girls in England. In 1948 she settled in Italy. Since her first collection of poems *War Variations* (1964), Rosselli's poetry has blended a daring formal experimentation with language – inspired by her multilingualism and her training in musical

theory – and with the dramatic staging of her self. The experience of love and desire at the center of her first volume, and that of mourning, political disillusionment, and the pain of mental illness in the subsequent works – *Serie ospedaliera* ('Hospital Series,' 1969) and *Documento (1966–1973)* ('Document (1966–1973),' 1976) – unfold as arduous melodies that interrogate language. In her last long poem *Impromptu* (1981), she focuses on the question of history and the marginalization of poetry. In 1989 a volume of her English poems *Sleep* appeared. Silence accompanied the last years of her life leading up to her suicide in Rome in 1996.

GMi

Roy, Arundhati (*b.* 1961) Indian novelist, screenwriter. Born in Shillong, Roy grew up in Aymanam village, Kerala, the Ayemenem of her Booker Prize-winning first novel *The God of Small Things* (1997). In the novel's narrative technique, she aimed to emulate the ease with which Indian Kathakali dancers perform stories, and in its content, to challenge the social systems that placed her somewhat outside her Syrian Christian community because of her mother's marriage to a Hindu. Roy says that she was lucky to have a mother who taught her to be independent and that an education was worth more than any dowry. Her Delhi College of Architecture degree followed an education at Lawrence, a boarding school in the Ootacamund Hills. Since her novel's success, she has actively opposed India's nuclear testing and the massive Narmada Dam Project. She has also supported the cause of the Dalits (formerly known as 'Untouchables'), by donating the rights to the Malayalam translation of her novel to the Dalit literary academy. She has written two screenplays for television, *In Which Annie Gives It Those Ones* and *Electric Moon*. Roy lives in New Delhi with her husband, a film director-turned-environmentalist, and her two stepdaughters.

HA

Roy, Gabrielle (1909–1983) Canadian novelist, short story writer. Roy grew up in Saint-Boniface, Manitoba, last of ten children. Her father's work as colonizing agent exposed her to ethnic diversity, reflected in her fiction and early career as journalist. *The Fragile Lights of Earth* (1978) contains early story-articles. *Windflower* (1970) depicts an Inuit community. While recognizing diversity, Roy underlined universal elements of the human condition in all her writing in French. Her teaching experience is described in *Children of my Heart* (1977). Early years in Manitoba are depicted in first-person narratives such as *The Road Past Altamont* (1966). Her development as a writer is recounted in the autobiography *Sorrow and Enchantment* (1984), whose title echoes her characteristic use of internal emotional duality and opposition. Later years in Quebec are portrayed in *This Enchanted Summer* (1972). Her first and most celebrated novel *The Tin Flute* (1945; Prix Fémina) is a realistic description of a working-class district in Montreal during World War II. Roy's prolific writing, which has underlined common human nature while embracing individual and cultural specificity, has been widely translated.

CHa

Ru Zhijuan (*b*. 1925) Chinese fiction writer. Born in Shanghai, Ru Zhijuan lost her mother at the age of three. Raised by her grandmother, she lived in poverty and only intermittently attended school. In 1943 she joined a theatrical troupe in the New Fourth Army of the Communist Party, and carried out propaganda at the front. In 1955 she became a member of the Chinese Writers' Association in Shanghai and worked as an editor for the journal *Literary Monthly*. 'Baihe hua' ('Lilies,' 1958), a short story that won its author high praise, tells a touching story about the relationship between the Communist army and the people represented by a young soldier and a newly-wed bride. 'The Path Through the Grassland' (1979)

examines the changing social milieu after the Cultural Revolution by focusing on an abortive love relationship between a young woman and man. 'A Story Out of Sequence' (1979) critically reflects the degenerating relationship between the Party and the people in the late 1950s and contrasts it with that maintained in the 1930s and 1940s. Each of the later two stories won national awards in 1979.

LW

Rubina, Dina Il'inichna (*b*. 1953) Russian prose writer. Born into a cultured household in Tashkent, Rubina studied music, yet found early recognition as a writer of stories about adolescence and maturation, associated largely with the journal *Iunost'* ('Youth'), in which she debuted in 1970. She moved to Moscow in 1984, but four years later emigrated to Israel with her painter-husband and two children. Profoundly attuned to the shaping powers of time, until recently Rubina spotlighted the complexity of parenthood, individual maturation, and emotional realignments of children and spouses within broken marriages, as in 'The Blackthorn' and 'The Double-Barreled Name' (1990). In the 1990s she has shifted attention to Russians' life in Israel and published two collections of longer narratives, *Vot idet Messiia!* ('Here Comes the Messiah!' 1996) and *Angel konvoinyi* ('Escorting Angel,' 1997). Favoring first-person narration, the latter anthology retains her distinguishing traits of situational irony, humor, and endless fascination with the contradictions and irrationality of human behavior. An admirer of Chekhov and Salinger, Rubina ascribes to women's writing a gender-specific capacity for fine shading, an appreciation of psychological gradations.

HG

Rubinstein, Gillian (*b*. 1942) Australian novelist, children's dramatist. Born in England, Rubinstein graduated with a BA (1964) and MA (1975) from Oxford University. She worked as a journalist and film critic, and emigrated to Australia in 1973. Her first book *Space Demons* (1986) was an Honour Book in the 1987 Children's Book Council Awards, and won both the Children's Literature Peace Prize (1987) and the South Australian National Festival Award (1988). In 1989 *Beyond Labyrinth* won the CBC Book of the Year for Older Readers. She has written almost thirty books for children of all ages, many of which have won prizes and been translated. In recent years she has adapted several of her novels for the stage. *Galax Arena*, which exemplifies her interest in animals and language, won the 1996 AWGIE Award for Best Theatre for Young People. *Wake Baby*, featuring acrobatics and puppetry, was staged at the 1997 International Youth Festival in Lyons and has since toured internationally. Although her interest in exploring the issues of alienation, exploitation, fears, and insecurities have sometimes led to criticism of her 'bleak' vision of society, she is equally adept at depicting the world's positive possibilities. She lives in Goolwa, South Australia with her husband Philip. They have three children.

RS

Rubinstein, Renate (1929–1990) Dutch journalist, essayist, memoirist. Born in Berlin, the daughter of a Jewish father and a gentile mother, Rubinstein fled as a 6-year-old with her parents to the Netherlands. They settled in Amsterdam in 1939; Rubinstein's father was later killed by the Nazis. World War II, Israeli politics, and Jewishness all became important themes in Rubinstein's essays and the columns she wrote for the weekly *Vrij Nederland* from 1962 onwards. She studied political and social sciences in Amsterdam, and began her career as a journalist in the 1950s for *Propria cures*, a student's weekly magazine. Hers is an extensive oeuvre of autobiographical writings; her style is always lucid, witty, and sharp. She deliberately and consistently chose the position of the critical outsider, as in her collection of essays *Hedendaags feminisme* ('Contemporary Feminism,' 1979), in which she voices her ambivalence about feminism. But her book on the pain and anger surrounding her difficult divorce, *Niets te verliezen en toch bang* ('Nothing to Lose and Yet Afraid,' 1978), is representative of the feminist autobiographical mode made popular in the 1970s by writers such as *Anja Meulenbelt, *Verena Stefan, and Kate Millett. She contracted multiple sclerosis and wrote a moving autobiographical memoir of life as an invalid: *Take It and Leave It: Aspects of Being Ill* (1985). She died a national celebrity in 1990.

AAn, MMe

Ruebsamen, Helga (*b.* 1936) Dutch novelist, short story writer. Born in the Dutch East Indies, Ruebsamen moved to The Hague when she was 6 years old. The chaos of the war years contrasted sharply with the years that were to follow, a time when she had to conform to bourgeois life. She worked as a journalist and made her debut in 1964 with the collection *De kameleon en andere verhalen* ('The Chameleon and Other Stories'). An important theme in these stories, as in her later work, is the rejection of a 'normal,' conformist way of life. Her sympathy is always with the unexpected, the slightly crazy, and the absurd things in life. Her stories are often comical, due to her direct style and the dry tone of her prose. Physical and mental deterioration, especially of women, is another important theme, although this never becomes too oppressive. Even though the literary critics have always been enthusiastic about her stories, her early books did not sell well. Her breakthrough came with her best-selling novel *The Song and the Truth* (1997). In this book, which is clearly autobiographical, Ruebsamen relates the compelling story of a young girl who is growing up between two cultures, the Dutch East Indies and Holland.

AAn, MMe

Rule, Jane (*b.* 1931) Canadian novelist, short story writer. Born in Plainfield, New Jersey, Rule grew up in the American Midwest and in California. She earned a BA in English from Mills College in 1952, and studied at University College, London. She has lived with her partner Helen Sonthoff since 1956. Her first novel, for which she is best known, is *Desert of the Heart* (1964). Set in Reno, Nevada, it is a love story about two lesbians (narrated by both alternately) which was remarkable in its time for its honesty and positive attitude. It was made into the film *Desert Hearts. This Is Not For You* (1970) deals with the destructive effects of convention on a potential lesbian relationship. Although Rule's later novels include lesbian characters, she shifts her focus to the social dynamics of communities of different kinds of people, and does so with fictional forms that allow for a community of narrative voices to be heard. *Against the Season* (1971) looks at unconventional relationships in a small town. In *Contract with the World* (1980), events in the lives of six artists are told chronologically, but from a different perspective in each chapter. *The Young in One Another's Arms* (1977) depicts the voluntary family created by the residents of a boarding house. Both of her last two novels (she has stopped writing due to severe arthritis), *Memory Board* (1987) and *After the Fire* (1989), deal sensitively with aging and illness.

JEM

Rumens, Carol (-Ann) (*b.* 1944) British poet. Born in London, Rumens was educated at Bedford College, University of London. She married David Rumens in 1965; they have two daughters. She worked for a time as an advertising copywriter, and was the poetry editor for *Quarto* and the *Literary Review*. She is a prolific poet and her subjects and themes are wide-ranging . Her early poems are technically accomplished and quietly affecting engagements with the domestic world of marriage and parenthood. Her later volumes have been increasingly concerned with experiences beyond the personal. With emotion, imagination, and intelligence, she writes of the historical events of Europe in the twentieth century and their attendant sufferings and horrors. Her volumes of poetry include *Strange Girl in Bright Colours* (1973), *A Necklace of Mirrors* (1978), *Unplayed Music* (1981), *Star Whisper* (1983), *From Berlin to Heaven* (1989), *Thinking of Skins: New and Selected Poems* (1993), and *Best China Sky* (1995). *Holding Pattern* (1999) consists of poems written during the years Rumens lived in Belfast as an instructor at Queens' University. She has also edited *Making for the Open: The Chatto Book of Post-Feminist Poetry* (1988) and *New Women Poets* (1990).

JEM

Rushani, Layla Sarahat (*b. c.* 1952–4) Afghan poet. Rushani graduated from Kabul University and worked in various prestigious associations in Kabul. Her life has been marked by tragic personal losses. She is the daughter of the well-known Afghan journalist S. Rushani, who was executed during the communist regime of Taraki. Her beloved sister died during a journey to Australia, where she had been accepted as a refugee of war; Rushani's mother died shortly thereafter. Rushani, who refers to herself as a 'plant of the hell,' writes poems which are dominated by the pain and suffering caused by war. Her poetry collections, which have not been translated, are titled *Night Again Night*, *Constant Scream*, and *Green Sunrise*. It is believed she was not able to escape from Afghanistan and that she still lives under the tremendous pressure of the Taliban regime in Kabul. She writes modern Persian poetry predominantly, but has also written some classical-style ghazals.

FRB

Russ, Joanna (*b.* 1937) US science fiction writer, feminist critic. The daughter of two teachers, Russ was born in New York and studied with Vladimir Nabokov at Cornell University, where she received a BA in 1957. She earned an MFA from the Yale School of Drama in 1960. Although she writes in many genres, she is best known for her adult science fiction, which she uses as a medium to express her visionary feminist ideas, imagining worlds in which women exercise their power and independence as strong, self-actualized protagonists. In *The Female Man* (1975; Hugo Award), she follows a woman through three alternate realities, one of which is an ideal society in the future. Her novels include *Picnic on Paradise* (1968), *We Who Are About To* (1975), *The Two of Them* (1978), and *Extra(ordinary) People* (1984). Short story collections include *Alyx* (1976) and *The Hidden Side of the Moon* (1987). Russ has received two Nebula Awards for her fiction. The novel *On Strike Against God: A Lesbian Love Story, Out & Out* (1979) is based on Russ's experiences in coming out as a lesbian. Russ's feminist criticism includes *Magic Mommas, Trembling Sisters, Puritans and Perverts* (1985), *To Write as a Woman* (1995), and *What Are We Fighting For? Sex, Race, Class, and the Future of Feminism* (1998). Her classic *How to Suppress Women's Writing* (1983) is a humorous examination of the ways

mainstream culture marginalizes literature by women.

DVT

Ryan, Gig (Elizabeth) (*b.* 1956) Australian poet, songwriter. Born in Leicester, England, Ryan was educated at the universities of LaTrobe (1974), Sydney (1983–7), and Melbourne, where she obtained a degree in Latin and Ancient Greek in 1993. She has published four volumes of poetry to date and is also well-known as a songwriter and singer with the group 'Disband.' Ryan worked for the feminist journal *Luna* from 1975 to 1978 and was the recipient of the Australian Council Literature Board Writers grants in 1979, 1982, 1988, and 1996. Her first volume of poetry *The Division of Anger* (1980) was co-winner of the Anne Elder Poetry Award and is famous for the anger of her 'manifesto' poems 'Not Like a Wife' and 'If I Had a Gun.' Her first collection was followed by *Manners of an Astronaut* (1984), *The Last Interior* (1986), and *Evacuation* (1990). Despite this relatively small corpus, Ryan is known for her terse, bitter, and sometimes cryptic depictions of contemporary relationships which are, at the same time, poignantly evocative of the emotional detritus which often accompanies modern urban life.

MHe

S

Saalbach, Astrid (*b.* 1955), Danish play-wright. Educated at the Danish Theater Academy (1975–8), Saalbach worked as an actress for seven years before turning to writing. She married Jens Kaas, a pianist; they have two children. Her debut came in 1981 with the radio play *Spor i sandet* ('Footprints in the Sand'). In the 1980s, she published three more plays and a collection of short stories *Månens ansikt* ('The Face of the Moon,' 1985). In the 1990s, she wrote three more plays and a novel. In the play *Morning and Evening* (1993) she focuses on a single day in the life of a number of people and their superficial relations, their inability to influence or change their environment, and their fragile identities. Their lives, highly predictable and limited by expectations, yet marked by the lack of identities, are symbolized by the 'morning' and the 'evening' segments of the play, where loosely connected characters are played by the same set of actors. Marked by Saalbach's distinct poetic expression, this play exemplifies her insight into men and women in a meaningless, materially secure, contemporary environment. She is a recipient of many awards, including the Nordic Radio Play Award in 1983 and the lifelong state grant in 1997. Her latest play *Aske til aske, støv til støv* ('Ashes to Ashes, Dust to Dust,' 1997) premiered in 1998.

MŽ

Sabah, Souad al- (*b.* 1942), Kuwaiti poet, economist. Born into the Kuwaiti ruling family, Sabah earned her BA in economics from Cairo University in 1973, and her MA in Great Britain in 1976. In 1981, she received a PhD in economics from Surrey University in Britain. She is an active member of many Arab and international organizations. She founded a publishing house which carries her name in Cairo and Kuwait. As an economist, she has written about the role of Kuwaiti women in development planning in an oil economy. Her early collections *Laḥazāt min ʿUmrī* ('Moments from My Life,' 1964), *Umniya* ('A Wish,' 1971), and *Ilayka Yā Waladī* ('To You My Son,' 1982) are, to a great extent, traditional in both style and content; her second collection contains elegies to her son. With *Fragments of a Woman* (1986) and *In The Beginning Was the Female* (1988), she became more daring in her love poetry and outspoken against patriarchal values. Sabah believes that the Arab woman 'is still exiled from the world of men' and to change this reality, men must liberate themselves from the old mentality. In 1990, she enlisted her poetry and prose to protest the Iraqi invasion of Kuwait.

JTZ

Saʿdāwī, Nawāl al- (*b.* 1930), Egyptian novelist, short story writer, activist. Born in the Nile village of Kafr Tahlah, Saʿdāwī received her MD degree from Cairo University in 1955. For some time she served as Director General in the Ministry of Health, but she was fired in 1972 for her controversial views. Her first novel *Memoirs of a Woman Doctor* (serialized 1957) utilizes many autobiographical details from the author's life to emphasize the devastating impact of the Egyptian society upon the female psyche. The novel was remarkable in the Arab world for dealing with social issues from an unapologetically feminist point of view. During the 1970s, writing and political activism began to overshadow her career in medicine, as her nonfiction work *Al-Mar'ah wa-al-Jins* ('Women and Sex,' 1972) criticized the practice of female circumcision and argued that women were mentally and biologically superior to men. Later novels, such as *God Dies by the Nile* (1978), tied gender and political oppression together as related phenomena. In 1981, she was imprisoned for her criticism of Anwar Sadat's policies. She later founded the Arab Women's Solidarity Association, but it was dissolved in 1991. Her firm and sometimes militant views have led to a certain degree of popularity for her in the West, and many of her works have been translated into English. In 1997, Sa'dāwī published *Awrāqī Hayātī* ('My Papers, My Life'), the first volume of her autobiography. She currently lives in the US.

JTZ

Sadur, Nina Mikhailovna (*b.* 1950), Russian prose writer, playwright. Born into an intelligentsia family (her mother a teacher of Russian literature, her father a poet), Sadur grew up in a working-class neighborhood in Siberia. In 1978 she moved to Moscow, graduated from the Gorky Literary Institute in 1983, began writing drama, and in 1989 joined the Union of Writers. Known primarily for her plays, collected in the anthology titled *Chudnaia baba* ('Weird Woman,' 1989), Sadur has authored two cycles of stories – *Touched* (1980s) and *Bessmertniki* ('Immortals,'

1992) – in addition to several novellas and novels. Spiritual isolation and the concrete materialization of evil are her overriding, related concerns. An inimical sphere of uncontrollable powers and incessant desires, manifested in extreme and enigmatic phenomena that shade into the grotesque, her world reeks of demonism, fantasy, and folklore. This dark, mystic view of life emerges most palpably in *Pannochka*, her stage adaptation of a Gogol story, the cycle *Touched*, and her absurdist existential play *Krasnyi paradiz* ('Red Paradise,' 1988). The majority of Sadur's longer fiction, such as *Iug* ('The South,' 1992), *Chudesnye znaki spasen'ia* ('The Miraculous Signs of Salvation,' 1993), and *Sad* ('The Garden,' 1994) – a novella in which alcoholic haze and mental disintegration blur boundaries between empirical reality and irrational vision – grounds perception in female consciousness. Translations into English have appeared in *Glas* No. 3 (1992), *Half a Revolution, Lives in Transit,* and *Present Imperfect.*

HG

Saffarzadeh, Tahirih (*b.* 1936), Iranian poet. Saffarzadeh was born and raised in the small city of Sirjan. She earned a BA in English literature in 1960 from Shiraz University. In 1963, after divorcing her husband and leaving Iran for the US, she published her first collection of poetry *Rahgozar-e Mahtab* ('Moonlight Passerby'). She subsequently earned an MA in creative writing from the University of Iowa and published *Red Umbrella* (1969), a collection of poems in English. Her other publications include *Tanin Dar Delta* ('Resonance in the Bay,' 1971), *Safar-e Panjom* ('The Fifth Journey,' 1978), *Mardan-e Monhani* ('Curbed Men,' 1986), and *Selected Poems* (1987). She brings a subdued Islamic point of view to gender issues and questions of women's autonomy and emancipation. After the Islamic revolution of 1979, Saffarzadeh became one of the most famous Muslim poets in the country. During this period, she did not hesitate to use literature as an informative medium to promote her religious beliefs.

KTa

Sagan, Françoise (*b.* 1935), French novelist, dramatist. Born Françoise Quoirez in Cajarc, France, Sagan moved to Paris in 1945. After failing the Sorbonne entrance exams, she wrote her first novel *Bonjour Tristesse* (1953), whose heroine Cécile discovers her sexuality and takes control of her life, driving her stepmother-to-be to suicide. It was an overnight critical and popular success. The Sagan legend was born, emphasizing fast cars, gambling, and alcohol. In the more than twenty-five novels which followed, she became known for creating moods with strong emotional overtones. Never challenging traditional fictional conventions, she created mostly female protagonists who struggle as atheists in an amoral universe to control their destinies, facing the transience of love, the inevitability of solitude, and the reality of death. In *La Chamade* (1965) Lucile rejects the passionate Antoine to return to her former lover Charles and the security his wealth represents. *The Still Storm* (1983) parodies nineteenth-century romantic novels featuring a male/female protagonist who wrestles with meaning and the act of writing. In 1985 Sagan won the Prix de Monaco for her life's work. Her latest novel *Le Miroir Egaré* ('The Distorting Mirror,' 1996) chronicles a couple's unintentional breakup.

LMS

Sahgal, Nayantara (*b.* 1927), Indian novelist, memoirist. Born in Allahabad, Sahgal is the daughter of Vijaya Lakshmi and Ranjit Sitaram Pandit. Her family was deeply involved in the independence struggle, most notably her maternal uncle, Jawaharlal Nehru. In 1943, her parents sent her to study at Wellesley College for four years, a period she reflects on in her memoir *Prison and Chocolate Cake* (1954). Returning to an independent India in 1947,

she published her first novel *A Time to be Happy* (1958) followed by *This Time of Morning* (1965), *Storm in Chandigarh* (1969), *The Day in Shadow* (1971), *A Situation in New Delhi* (1977), and *Plans for Departure* (1985), which won the Commonwealth Writer's Prize for Eurasia. Her writing explores the nationalist movement, the meaning of freedom in postcolonial India, the erosion of Gandhian values, the rise of consumerism, political corruption, and the exploitation of religious sentiment, best captured in *Rich Like Us* (1985), which won the Sinclair Prize. Conflicts between women's desire for autonomy and patriarchal expectations for their roles as daughters, wives, and mothers preoccupy her novels. A regular commentator on Indian politics, Sahgal was outspoken against the authoritarian turn in her cousin Indira Gandhi's government during the Emergency, culminating in *Indira Gandhi: Her Road To Power* (1978).

JD

Said, Bahar (*b. c.* 1954), Afghan poet. After receiving her BA in literature from Kabul University, Said went to Iran where she earned an MA in Persian literature from Teheran University. She began writing poetry at the age of 10 and has been influenced by ghazal poetry. Although she writes love poems predominantly, she has stated that she wants to be the voice of the oppressed feelings of the women in her country. She has published in various newspapers and periodicals in Kabul, but presently lives and publishes in the US. The outspoken nature of her most recent poetry collection *Shukufa-i Bahar* ('Spring's Blossom,' 1994) prompted angry criticism from conservative members of émigré Afghan communities.

FRB

Said, Titie (*b.* 1935), Indonesian fiction writer. Born in Bojonegoro, Titie Said (the pen name of Siti Raya), completed her secondary schooling in Malang and graduated from Universitas Indonesia in Jakarta in 1959 with a degree in archaeology. She has worked for a number of Indonesian magazines and journals. 'Kelimutu' (1962), set on the Indonesian island of Flores, is an essay about the treachery of war. 'The Rambutan Season' (1961) is a poignant tale of thwarted love and emotional barrenness, which no amount of material success can overcome.

PA

St Aubin de Teran, Lisa (*b*. 1953), British novelist, poet, travel writer. Born in London, St Aubin de Teran married her first husband Jaime Teran when she was 17, and returned with him to his family farm in Venezuela. Her experiences during the seven years she lived there formed the basis for her first novel *Keepers of the House* (1982; published in the US as *The Long Way Home*), which won the Somerset Maugham Award. The novel was praised for its vivid sense of place and its use of magic realism. Her second novel *The Slow Train to Milan* (1983; John Llewelyn Rhys Memorial Prize), also autobiographical, is an episodic account of a train journey taken by a newly-married couple. *The Tiger* (1984), a disturbing tale of cruelty and domination, is also set in Venezuela. Other novels include *The Bay of Silence* (1986), *Black Idol* (1987), *Joanna* (1990), *Nocturne* (1992), and *The Palace* (1997), the last two set in Italy, where St Aubin de Teran now lives. She published her first book of poetry *The Streak* in 1980. She has also written a nonfiction account of her years in Venezuela *The Hacienda: My Venzuelan Years* (1997), several works of travel writing, including *Off the Rails* (1989), and *Southpaw* (1999), a collection of short stories.

JEM

Salivarová, Zdena (*b*. 1933), Czech prose writer. Prague-born Salivarová was not permitted to study beyond high school, after her father defected to New York and her older brother was sentenced to ten years in the mines. She sang in the State Song and Dance Ensemble until 1960, helping support her mother and younger sister. She married the writer Josef Škvorecký in 1958 and in 1965 she was admitted to the Film Academy to study scriptwriting. In 1969 she traveled with Škvorecký to Berkeley, California, and then Toronto, where they settled. With him she founded Sixty-Eight Publishers in 1971, producing over 230 Czech books in exile before closing the enterprise in 1994, the same year she was awarded an honorary doctorate from the University of Toronto. Her first book, *Pánská jízda* ('Gentlemen's Ride,' 1968) contains three stories treating adolescent sexuality, in part a feminine response to Kundera's *Laughable Loves*. Her first novel *Summer in Prague* (1972), subtitled 'Protest Song,' depicts a young woman's life in the context of totalitarianism. Her novella *Ashes, Ashes, All Fall Down* (1976; Egon Hostovský Prize) confronts innocent love with stark authoritarian reality. In her documentary novel *Hnůj země* ('Dung of the Earth,' 1994), Salivarová conveys émigré experience through letters from 1850 to the present.

ES

Salter, Mary Jo (*b*. 1954), US poet. Born in Grand Rapids, Michigan, Salter was educated at Harvard University, where she earned a BA (cum laude) in 1976, and at New Hall, Cambridge, where she earned an MA (first class honors) in 1978. She married Brad Leithauser in 1980; they have two daughters. She published her first volume of poetry *Henry Purcell in Japan* in 1985. She is considered one of the 'New Formalists,' whose poetry is strongly influenced by poetic tradition and traditional forms. In particular, the influence of Emily Dickinson on Salter's work has been noted. The formal precision and grace of her poems is balanced by a conversational tone and a playful alertness to linguistic humor. Often her poems involve the careful observation of foreign settings and different cultures, as in her first volume and *Unfinished Painting* (1989), reflecting her time living abroad, in Japan, Paris, and Iceland. Her third collection *Sunday Skaters* (1994) contains poems on domestic life, love, and motherhood, but also includes two ambitious, longer poems on the lives of Thomas Jefferson and Robert Frost. She continues this interest in poetic biography in *A Kiss in Space* (1999), in which she tells stories from the lives of Helen Keller, Alexander Graham Bell, and Arthur Conan Doyle.

JEM

Sammān, Ghāda al- (b. 1942), Syrian novelist, short story writer, journalist. Born in Damascus, Sammān was tutored in French by her father, who was a rector at Damascus University. She received her BA degree in English literature at the same university in 1961. She moved to Beirut and earned her MA from the American University there. While traveling extensively in Europe, her father died; his death forced her to become financially independent. Several of her early articles angered religious conservatives and incited controversy by calling for the emancipation of Syrian women. Her first collection of short stories *ʿAynaka Qadarī* ('Your Eyes Are My Destiny,' 1962) deals with the quest for personal identity. Later collections address the 1967 Arab defeat and the need for social and political change. She switched to writing novels with the publication of *Beirut 75* (1975), a work that predicted the looming Lebanese civil war. A subsequent novel *Beirut Nightmares* (1976) is unique in its use of dream sequences to portray most of the action, as the main characters are trapped in an apartment building. Another novel *Laylat al-Milyār* ('The Night of the Billion,' 1986) deals with the theme of alienation. Later Sammān wrote *The Square Moon* (1994), a collection of psychic stories. *Al-Riwāya al-Mustaḥīla* ('The Impossible Novel,' 1997) contains some autobiographical material.

JTZ

Sanchez, Sonia (b. 1934), US poet, dramatist. Born Wilsonia Benita Driver in Birmingham, Alabama, Sanchez received a BA in political science from Hunter College in New York in 1955 and a PhD in fine arts from Wilberforce University, Ohio in 1972. Divorced, she has three children. She has taught at many universities and colleges in the US. Her first collection of poetry *Homecoming* was published in 1969. The black power movement of the 1960s was central to her development as a writer, and her poetry is driven by her political and social concerns, particularly those related to African-Americans. Her voice is direct, intense, sometimes militant, sometimes abrasive. She speaks unabashedly as a teacher and a prophet. Her early volumes, such as *WE a BaddDDD People* (1970) and *It's A New Day: Poems for Young Brothas and Sistuhs* (1971), establish her focus on black empowerment and the distinctive chanting rhythms of her poetic voice. In her later volumes, she tempers her unflinching portraits of human pain and tragedy with visions of spiritual wholeness. Her other volumes of poetry include *Love Poems* (1973), *I've Been a Woman* (1978), *Homegirls and Handgrenades* (1984), *Wounded in the House of a Friend* (1995), *Like Singing Coming Off Drums* (1998), and *Shake My Skin Loose: New and Selected Poems* (1999).

JEM

Sander, Helke (b. 1937), German filmmaker, prose writer. Born in Berlin, Sander married, had a son, and studied psychology and German literature in Helsinki. She worked as a theater and TV director in Finland, then attended the German Film and Television Academy from 1966 to 1969. The founder of the influential journal *Frauen und Film*, she has worked as a critic as well as a director of documentaries and feminist films. Since 1980, she has been a professor at the Hamburg art academy. Her films include *The All-Round Reduced Personality – Redupers* (1977), *The*

Subjective Factor (1980), *The Trouble With Love* (1983), and *Liberators Take Liberties*: *War, Rapes, Children* (1992). Feminizing Brecht's didactic parables of 'Mr. K.,' Sander tells her own instructive stories of *The Three Women K.* (1987), feminist tales about love under the conditions of long-distance commuting, the intersections of personal relations and professional achievements, and the aspirations of women facing an art-funding bureaucracy beset by old men. Sander's literary vignettes render a complex kaleidoscope of the familiar hypocrisies and everyday realities of sexist discrimination in a post-feminist era. In *Oh Lucy* (1991), the narrator engages in an imaginary dialogue with the prehistoric ancestress of all women, reviewing the enduring constellations and experiences of femininity over the ages, such as sex, love, violence, and childbirth.

AG

Sanvitale, Francesca (*b.* 1928), Italian novelist, journalist. Originally from Milan, Sanvitale resided for twenty years in Florence where she earned a degree in Italian literature before moving to Rome in 1961. Her articles on cultural and political topics frequently appear in literary journals and newspapers. Her first novel *Il cuore borghese* ('The Bourgeois Heart,' 1972) received the Premio Viareggio award. Her semi-autobiographical novel *Madre e figlia* ('Mother and Daughter,' 1980) brought her public recognition and won her the Premio Fregene and the Premio Pozzale. The book's title refers to both the protagonist's difficult relationship with her mother, and to the various female roles she assumes throughout her life, including mother and daughter. Sanvitale has since written four additional novels, and most recently two short fiction collections which investigate themes of isolation and communication: *La realtà è un dono* ('Reality is a Gift,' 1987) and *Separazioni* ('Separations,' 1997). English translations of

several of her short stories have been anthologized.

DGr

Sarraute, Nathalie (1900–1999), French novelist, dramatist. Born into a Jewish family in Russia, Sarraute moved to Paris in 1902. After a BA in English from the Sorbonne, she studied history at Oxford, literature in Berlin, and law in Paris. In 1925, she joined a Paris law firm and married a fellow lawyer, Raymond Sarraute. They had three daughters. She started to write *Tropisms* (1939), a work that defines her style based on subtle reactive communication between characters and their private thoughts, in 1932. Her second book *Portrait of a Man Unknown* (1948) was prefaced by Jean-Paul Sartre. Her best-known novel is *The Planetarium* (1959), a challenging work in which she displays her mastery of 'sub-conversation' between bourgeois members of a Parisian family, in a new form of psychological realism. Sarraute is associated with the Nouveau Roman movement because plots, characters, and chronology are less important in her works than fragmented moments. In 1959, she published a book of essays to explain her technique, *The Age of Suspicion*. She continued to write until the end of her life, her later publications including the novels *You Don't Love Yourself* (1990) and *Here: A Novel* (1995), an autobiography, *Childhood* (1983), also written in her distinctive style, and *Ouvrez* ('Open,' 1997), a denunciation of the impoverishment of the French language. Her complete works are now published in the prestigious Pléiade Series.

JV

Sarumpaet, Ratna (*b.* 1949), Indonesian dramatist. Indonesia's most prominent female playwright, Sarumpaet is driven by her belief that 'when a woman dares to speak, there seems to be a great force or desire to silence her.' Her play *Marsinah: A Song from the Underworld* (1994), which deals with the true story of a female worker who was found murdered four days after she led a factory worker's strike, is banned in Indonesia. As well as being a writer, performer, and stage and television director, Sarumpaet runs the 'Satu Merah Panggung' theater group in Jakarta. Her theatrical adaptations include versions of *Hamlet*, *Romeo and Juliet*, and *Antigone*. She has presented her work in Avignon, France, Adelaide, Australia, and Galway, Ireland. In March 1998, Sarumpaet was arrested for her involvement in a pro-democracy meeting in Jakarta, and faced up to twelve years in prison on charges of organizing a meeting without a permit and spreading hatred against the Soeharto government. Three months later, Soeharto stepped down and Sarumpaet was released. She was given a hurried trial and convicted of a lesser charge with a sentence of time already served.

PA

Sa'ūdī, Munā al- (*b.* 1945), Jordanian poet, artist. Born in Amman, Jordan, Sa'ūdī studied art at l'Ecole Nationale des Beaux Arts in Paris (1965–9) which she combined with independent study in Carrara, Italy (in 1967 and 1972). She has contributed articles and poems to leading Arabic literary periodicals in Lebanon, and was a member of the editorial board of the quarterly *Mawāqif*. She lived in Beirut from 1969 until 1983, when she returned to Amman to reside. She is not married. In 1970, Sa'ūdī published *Shihādāt al-Atfāl fī Zaman al-Harb* ('In Times of War Children Testify'), a bilingual book which contains drawings and conversations with Palestinian children from a refugee camp in Jordan. Her first collection of poems *Ru'yā Ūlā* ('First Vision'), which appeared with drawings in 1972, reflects a great deal of anxiety and a tendency to create a dreamlike world. Her sculpture *Provisions on Stone* is exhibited in a public square in Paris.

JTZ

Schine, Cathleen (*b.* 1953), US novelist. Born in Westport, Connecticut, Schine attended Sarah Lawrence College, Barnard College, and the University of Chicago. She is married to David Denby, a journalist and the film critic for the *New Yorker*; they have two sons. Her novels are modern comedies of manners, her style witty and erudite. Her first novel *Alice in Bed* (1983) examines the eventful hospital stay of a college student who for no apparent reason loses the use of her legs. Alice reappears years later as she prepares for her marriage in Schine's second novel *To the Birdhouse* (1990), which features Alice's mother Brenda. *Rameau's Niece* (1993; Los Angeles Times Book Prize) is an academic satire in which the intellectual heroine's erotic quest is accented with French enlightenment philosophy. The bestselling novel *The Love Letter* (1995), which has been made into a film, chronicles a romantic relationship between Helen, a book shop owner, and Johnny, a much younger university student. *The Evolution of Jane* (1998) takes place on the Galapagos Islands, where Jane learns about the origin of species and the origin of friendship.

DVT

Schmidt, Annie M. G. (1911–1995), Dutch children's writer, poet. Schmidt's father was a Protestant minister, which might explain her lifelong rebellion against the Dutch petite bourgeoisie. Although she started out as a journalist in Amsterdam, Schmidt became most famous for the prose and poetry she wrote for the very young. Generations of Dutch children have grown up with her unforgettable stories, such as *The Island of Nose* (1977) and the stories from her 'Dusty and Smudge' (Floddertje) series, such as *Dusty and Smudge and the Soap Suds* (1971) and *Dusty and Smudge and the Bride* (1977). The main character in these lovely books for the very young is Dusty (Floddertje) and her inseparable little dog Smudge. *Minnie* (1970) is the story of a lady who used to be a cat. Schmidt's read-aloud books, such as *Bob and Jilly are Friends* (1963) and *Bob and Jilly in Trouble* (1963), have been bedtime reading for millions of Dutch children. Their charm comes from Schmidt's simple but humorous use of language and the nonconformism which emanates from her work. She also wrote a great number of cabaret songs, musicals, plays, television series, radio plays, and columns for grown-ups, all of which still enjoy great popularity. A selection of her poems for children can be found in *Pink Lemonade*. Schmidt has received many prizes and been widely translated.

AAn, MMe

Schoultz, Solveig von (1907–1996), Finland-Swedish poet, short story writer. Born in Borgå in southern Finland, the youngest of eight children of the theology teacher Albert Segerstråle and the painter Hanna Frosterus-Segerstråle, Schoultz became a teacher, married, and had two daughters. After divorcing her first husband, she married the composer Erik Bergman in 1961, who has set her poems to music. Awarded numerous prizes in Finland and Sweden, Schoultz in 1980 received the Pro Finlandia Medal and in 1986 an honorary doctorate from Helsinki University. Her first collection of poems *Min timme* ('My Hour,' 1940) marks her actual breakthrough, after some earlier attempts as a novelist. Whether she writes poetry or short stories, her language is subtle and stringent, catching the essence of human experiences and complex relationships through an image or everyday situation. Her daughters' first years are captured in *De sju dagarna* ('The Seven Days,' 1942), and her own mother is portrayed in *Porträtt av Hanna* ('Portrait of Hanna,' 1973). Between 1947 and 1984, she wrote seven collections of short stories, selections from which are included in *Heartwork* (1989). The cream of her poetry from thirteen collections is found in *Snow and Summers: Poems 1940–1989*. Her last collection of poems *Molnskuggan* ('Cloud Shadow,' 1996) appeared a few months before her death.

GE-C

Schwaiger, Brigitte (*b.* 1949), Austrian novelist. Born in Freistadt in Upper Austria, Schwaiger studied German and Spanish literatures, philosophy, and psychology, and lived in Spain. After her divorce in 1972, she became an actress. Since 1975 she has lived as a writer in Vienna and Linz. Her first novel *Why is there Salt in the Sea?* (1977) is a satirical report about a failing marriage which mocks societal double standards fostered by a bourgeois upbringing. *Mein spanisches Dorf* ('My Spanish Village,' 1978) deals with specific suffocating experiences during a childhood and youth in rural Austria and attacks the hypocrisy of bourgeois relations. *Lange Abwesenheit* ('Long Time Absent,' 1980) focuses on Schwaiger's troubled relationship to her father and his National Socialist past. In *Die Galizianerin* ('The Woman from Galicia,' 1982), she reworks biographical reports by the Jewish woman Eva Deutsch, who was the only member of her family to survive the Holocaust. *Der Himmel ist süß* ('The Sky is Sweet,' 1986) centers upon a young woman's conflict between her own wishes and the religious demands of a school run by nuns. *Jaro heißt Frühling* ('Jaro is Called Spring,' 1994) deals with feelings of alienation. Schwaiger has received several Austrian literary awards.

MMu

Schwarz-Bart, Simone (*b.* 1938), Guadeloupean novelist. Born in Charente-Maritime, raised in Guadeloupe from the age of 3, Schwarz-Bart returned to France to study and later attended the university in Senegal. She married the Jewish novelist André Schwarz-Bart; they moved to Switzerland in the 1970s. Later, she returned to Guadeloupe, raised her two children, and continued to write while managing her own business. Her first novel *Un plat de porc aux bananes vertes* ('A Dish of Pork with Green Bananas,' 1967) was written in collaboration with her husband. She is best known for her second novel *The Bridge of Beyond* (1972), which received the French Prix Elle. It gives a voice to an old peasant woman telling the story of the women in her family emerging out of slavery. Through courage, pride, and self-confidence, they forge the path for other Caribbean women to follow in their quest for self-reliance from male domination and French colonial customs. The use of local imageries and the integration of Creole oral structures make a unique contribution to contemporary Caribbean literature. The novel *Between Two Worlds* (1979) concerns the connection between modern inhabitants of Guadeloupe and their African ancestors. Schwarz-Bart is also the author of a six-volume celebration of black women titled *Homage à la Femme Noire* ('Homage to Black Women,' 1989).

GAd, DM

Sebbar, Leïla (*b.* 1941), French-Algerian novelist, short story writer. The daughter of an Algerian father and a French mother, Sebbar was born and raised in Algeria. At 17, she left North Africa to pursue her studies, first in Aix-en-Provence and then in Paris, where she has lived since 1963. Although she began her literary career by writing essays on the conditions of immigrant women, she eventually turned her attention to writing fiction, publishing her first novel *Fatima ou les Algériennes au square* ('Fatima, or the Algerian Women in the Park') in 1981. Her best-known work is her Shérazade trilogy – *Shérazade: Missing, Aged 17, Dark Curly Hair, Green Eyes* (1982); *Les Carnets de Shérazade* ('Shérazade's Notebooks,' 1985); *Le fou de Shérazade* ('Shérazade's Fool,' 1991) – which traces the voyage of self-discovery of a young *beure*, an Arab woman born in France of immigrant parents. Calling into question the validity of commonly accepted social, ethnic, and cultural boundaries, the novels explore the unsettling, yet ultimately productive, consequences of resisting a fixed cultural and gender identity. In a recent collection of short stories *La jeune fille au balcon* ('The Young Girl on the Balcony,' 1996), Sebbar examines the effects of political, religious, and identity conflicts on the struggle for self-definition in present-day Algeria.

DS

Sedakova, Olga Aleksandrovna (*b.* 1949), Russian poet, prose writer. A major poet of the avant-garde New Wave, Sedakova also teaches in the Department of Languages and Literatures at Moscow University, from which she received a BA in 1973 and an advanced degree in cultural anthropology within the Institute of Slavic and Balkan Studies in 1980. Until *glasnost*, she published only one verse collection, *Deti pishut stikhi* ('Children Write Verses,' 1960), in Russia, the bulk of her poems, which date from her childhood, appearing in samizdat. *Vorota, okna, arki* ('Gates, Windows, Arches'), an anthology of her poetry, came out in Paris in 1986, followed almost a decade later by a volume in Moscow titled *Stikhi* ('Verses,' 1994), which contains school verses from the 1970s and several cycles (e.g. 'Wild Rose,' 'Tristan and Isolde,' 'Old Songs'), as well as an essay 'Pokhvala poezii' ('In Praise of Poetry,' 1982). Mortality and life's meaning, spiritual self-assessment, and the order of the universe constitute Sedakova's perennial preoccupations. Metaphysical themes and the allusive, often concrete images that figure them recur from poem to poem, conveyed via a lucid, controlled tone, thickened textually through cultural references, and complicated through shifting perspectives, as in 'Stanzas in the Manner of Alexander Pope' (1979–80). For English translations of her poems, see the anthology *Contemporary Russian Poetry*.

HG

Seghers, Anna (1900–1983), German novelist, short story writer. Seghers was one of the greatest German woman writers of her century and a literary mentor of *Christa Wolf. Born Netty Reiling, she came from a Jewish family of art dealers and earned her PhD at Heidelberg. Influenced by European and East Asian art, legend and myth, Dostoyevsky and Kafka, her early prose, notably *The Revolt of the Fishermen* (1928), brought her international acclaim. Exiled in 1933, she was an active speaker and essayist within the anti-fascist movements in France, Spain, and Mexico. Her anti-fascist resistance novel *The Seventh Cross* (1942) was translated into over 40 languages. *Transit* (1944) reflects on her own fate and that of other European Jews trapped at the Mediterranean in 1940–1. *The Excursion of the Dead Girls* and *Post to the Promised Land* respond to the Holocaust and her mother's deportation. Influenced by the Mexican muralists, she returned to Europe in 1947 with the aim of reeducating a generation of Germans raised under National Socialism. Her Mexican and Caribbean novellas and stories about German life, as in the collection *The Power of the Weak* (1965), thematize the ravages and hopes of her time and anticipate the South African realism of *Nadine Gordimer. She was a nominee for a Nobel prize and President of the German Writers Union in the GDR from 1952 to 1978. The success of East German women's writing is unimaginable without the example of her person and work.

HF

Segun, Mabel (*b.* 1930), Nigerian fiction writer, essayist, poet. Born Mabel Aig-Imoukhuede in Ondo State, she graduated from the University College, Ibadan in 1949, with a BA in English, Latin, and history. She was married to Oluwajimi Jalaoso from 1952 to 1957, and to Oludotun Segun from 1960 to 1975; she and Segun had three children. Her career has included working as a teacher, an editor, Deputy Permanent Delegate of Nigeria to UNESCO (1979–81), and Senior Research Fellow, Institute of African Studies, University of Ibadan (1982–9). Her other accomplishments include being an international table-tennis champion, a singer, a

pianist, an advertising copywriter, and a broadcaster, for which she won the Nigerian Broadcasting Corporation 1977 Artiste of the Year Award. Her first book *My Father's Daughter* (1965) is about the experiences of a young girl growing up in a Christian family. This was followed by a tribute to her mother titled *My Mother's Daughter* (1987). She has written many books for young children. Her collection of essays *Friends, Nigerians, Countrymen* (1965) includes the texts of several radio broadcasts which satirize life in Nigeria. *Conflict and Other Poems* (1987) focuses on the struggles of Nigerian women and the relationships between men and women. In *The Surrender and Other Stories* (1995), she grapples with such subjects as legal polygamy, female chastity, and marital fidelity. Segun is currently Director of the Children's Literature Documentation and Research Centre in Ibadan.

SDR, MU

Semel, Nava (*b.* 1954), Israeli fiction writer, dramatist. A Tel Aviv native who completed an MA in art history from Tel Aviv University, Semel, the daughter of Holocaust survivors, has probed the legacy of the Holocaust for second-generation children and adults in many of her books and plays, which have been translated into many European languages and English. Her collection of stories *Kova Z'khukheet* ('A Hat of Glass,' 1985) was the first Israeli book to address this painful topic. She continued to explore the theme in her radio play and short story 'Hunger.' The novella *Flying Lessons* (1995), adapted for Israeli television, sensitively portrays a young girl's dawning awareness of the Holocaust legacy in her own Israeli village. The recipient of a Women Writers of the Mediterranean Award in 1994, Semel also received Israel's prestigious Prime Minister's Award for Literature (1996), and her 1990 novel *Becoming Gershona* won the National Jewish Book Award in the US. Her monodrama of a developmentally disabled child

The Child Behind the Eyes was produced in Israel, throughout Europe, and in the US. She also authored the 1996 novel *Eeshah al Hàneyar* ('Bride on Paper') and stories for children, including *Liluna* (1998) and *Shirai Laila* ('Night Poems', 1999). She lives in Tel Aviv with her husband Noam and three children.

MGl

Sen, Nabaneeta Dev (*b.* 1938), Indian fiction writer, poet, critic. Born in Calcutta to parents who were poets in the 1920s and 1930s, Sen studied English at Presidency College and comparative literature at Jadavpur. She earned her MA and PhD from Harvard and Indiana University respectively. Her first collection of poems was *Pratham Pratyay* ('First Confidence,' 1959) and her first novel was *Ami, Anupam* ('I, Anupam,' 1976), about an urban middle-class Naxalite youth. Other works include *Karuna Tomar Kon Path Diye* ('The Path of Thy Grace,' 1978), about a lone women's pilgrimage to the Kumbhamela; *Truck Bahoney Mac Mahoney* (1984), about her own journey to the military-patrolled area of northeastern India; the story collection *Monsieur Hulot's Holiday* (1980); a collection of essays, *Nati Nabaneeta* ('Actress Nabaneeta,' 1983); and her fourth novel, *Sheet Sahasheet Hemantalok* ('Autumnal Abode of Brave Winter People,' 1990), about the problems of aging in middle-class women. She has been professor and chairperson of comparative literature in Jadavpur, a visiting professor at Harvard, Columbia, and Oxford Universities, and during her marriage to the economist Amartya Sen, a post-doctoral fellow at Newnham College, Cambridge. When the marriage ended Sen moved with her two daughters to Calcutta, where she has lived and taught since.

RMa

Senior, Olive (*b.* 1941), Jamaican short story writer, poet. Born and raised in Jamaica, Senior has worked as a journalist and writer in both Canada and the Caribbean. She studied journalism in the UK and Canada, earning a Bachelor of Journalism degree from Carleton University in Ottawa. She is perhaps still best known for her first work of fiction, *Summer Lightning* (1986), which won the Commonwealth Writers Prize in 1987. The former editor of *Social and Economic Studies* and *Jamaica Journal*, she combines her poetic voice with social concern in exploring women's lives in the English-speaking Caribbean, as in her nonfictional *Working Miracles* (1991). Her works of fiction include *Arrival of the Snake Woman* (1989) and the linked short story collection *Discerner of Hearts* (1995), set in both urban and rural Jamaica and containing stories which often shift seamlessly between the past and the present. One of her defining features is her gift for recreating the music of everyday Jamaican speech. The poetry collected in *Gardening in the Tropics* (1994) rings with just such a richness of speech, particularly in the title section. Senior currently lives and writes in Toronto.

LM

Sexton, Anne (1928–1974), US poet. Born Anne Harvey in Newton, Massachusetts, Sexton had an unhappy childhood which would later figure significantly in her poetry. She eloped with Alfred (Kayo) Sexton in 1948; they had two daughters. She suffered from depression and attempted suicide several times before ending her life in 1974. At the suggestion of her therapist, she began writing poetry in the late 1950s. In 1957 she met the poet *Maxine Kumin at a poetry workshop (where she also met *Sylvia Plath). Sexton and Kumin developed a close friendship and an important working relationship, reading and critiquing each other's poetry. Sexton's first volume of poetry *To Bedlam and Part Way Back* was published in 1960. It was followed by *All My Pretty Ones* (1962), *Live or Die* (1966; Pulitzer Prize), *Love Poems* (1969), and *The Death Notebooks* (1974). Her intensely personal poems are preoccupied with death, madness, and suicide.

Often characterized as a confessional poet, Sexton boldly explored female experience, including sexuality, motherhood, and social restrictions. Other works include *Transformations* (1972), revisions of Grimm's fairy tales, *The Book of Folly* (1972), a collection of poetry and prose, and, published posthumously, a play *45 Mercy Street* (1976) and her final poetry collection *The Awful Rowing Towards God* (1975).

JEM

Shange, Ntozake (*b.* 1948), US dramatist, poet, novelist. Born Paulette Williams in Trenton, New Jersey, Shange earned a BA from Barnard College in 1970, and an MA from the University of Southern California, Los Angeles in 1973. She is best known for her play *for colored girls who have considered suicide when the rainbow is enuf*, which was first produced in 1975. Dubbed a 'choreopoem' by Shange, it combines dance, poetry, and music in a distinctive dramatic work about the lives of black women and their struggles against racism and physical and emotional abuse by men. Critically and popularly acclaimed, it is considered a classic of African-American feminist writing. In her effort to express the distinctive voices and experiences of black women, she also subverts traditional form in her fiction and poetry. The novel *Sassafras, Cypress and Indigo* (1977) examines women and their relationships, and celebrates female culture with an unusual mixture of fiction, poetry, journal entries, letters, and recipes. In her poetry, Shange experiments with language as she explores, in her vivid and lyrical voice, the imagery and rhythms of the female body, as well as the racial and social struggles of black women. Her volumes of poetry include *Nappy Edges* (1978), *A Daughter's Geography* (1983), and *Ridin' the Moon in Texas* (1988). She has also written numerous plays and the novels *Betsey Brown* (1985) and *Liliane: Resurrection of the Daughter* (1995).

JEM

Shapcott, Jo (*b.* 1953), British poet. Born in London, Shapcott was educated at Trinity College, Dublin (BA 1976), Dublin College of Music, St Hilda's College, Oxford (BA, 1978), Harvard University, and University of Bristol. Her strange, surreal poetry is intellectually challenging but playful, her language sensuous but her images disturbing. Her subject matter is too eclectic to summarize, but in each volume she returns to the themes of communication, transgression, and the power and limitations of language. War figures frequently in her poems, as do animals, but never in expected ways. Her volumes of poetry include her first *Electroplating the Baby* (1988; Commonwealth Prize), as well as *Phrase Book* (1992), *Motherland* (1996), and *My Life Asleep* (1998). She has twice been awarded the Poetry Society National Poetry prize.

JEM

Shaykh, Ḥanān al- (*b.* 1945), Lebanese novelist, short story writer, journalist. Born in Beirut, al-Shaykh was raised in a strict Muslim family environment. She attended primary and middle school in Beirut, but went to Cairo for secondary school, and later attended the American College for Girls in Cairo from 1964 to 1966. Her educational experiences abroad perhaps contributed to the theme of exile in her works. A poor student by her own admission, she nevertheless loved to read, and wrote her first novel, *Intiḥār Rajul Mayyit* ('Suicide of Dead Man,' 1970) when she was still in college. Her most famous work, however, is *The Story of Zahra* (1980), which describes the life of an abused woman both before and during the Lebanese civil war. Paradoxically, the protagonist finds greater freedom and happiness during the war than in the period preceding it. This novel was widely read in the Arab world despite it being banned in a number of countries for its sexual descriptions. It represents one of the greatest contributions to women's literature written in Arabic. An equally controversial novel is her *Women of Sand and Myrrh* (1988), in which there is a frank description of a lesbian relationship in an Arab 'desert country.' The impact of the civil war in Lebanon was, again, the focus of *Beirut Blues* (1992). Her most recent work is a collection titled *I Sweep the Sun off Rooftops* (1994). She is married and lives with her husband and two sons in London.

JTZ

Shcherbakova, Galina Nikolaevna (*b.* 1932), Russian prose writer, scriptwriter. A native of Dzerzhinsk, Shcherbakova graduated from the department of languages and literatures at Rostov University and taught school before turning to journalism. In the 1970s she started writing fiction and in the 1980s film scripts to augment her income. Married to the journalist Alexander Shcherbakov, she has two adult children. Her early novella of youthful idealism *Vam i ne snilos'* ('You Wouldn't Dream of It,' 1979), adapted into a popular film, brought her wide acclaim. Like most of her works in the collections *Sprava ostavalsia gorodok* ('The Little Town to the Right Remained,' 1979), *Otchaiannaia osen'* ('Autumn of Despair,' 1985), and *Krushenie* ('Collapse,' 1990), it examines moral choices, the psychology of love, and the effects of time's passage on the postwar generation in a modern urban setting. The dynamics of marriage, divorce, and generations play a focal role in her more recent works, including the diptych titled *Anatomiia razvoda* ('Anatomy of Divorce,' 1990), consisting of an 'ideal version,' *Mandarinovyi god* ('The Year of Tangerines') and an 'ironic version,' *God Aleny* ('Alyona's Year'). Since *perestroika*, she has favored a rather light, risqué treatment of sex and family relations, reflected in the stories 'Uncle Khlor and Koriakin' (1988) and 'Dochki, materi, ptitsy i ostrova' ('Daughters, Mothers, Birds, and Islands,' 1991). An ironic, down-to-earth individual, in such stories as 'The Three "Loves" of Masha Peredreeva' and in her narratives of the 1990s, Shcherbakova freely acknowledges female sexual appetites and the marketability of women's bodies, especially in post-Soviet Russia.

HG

Shcherbina, Tatiana Georgievna (*b.* 1954), Russian poet. Born in Moscow, Shcherbina attended Moscow University from 1971 to 1976 as a student in the Department of Languages and Literatures. She dates the beginning of her career in poetry to 1975. No official literary journal published her work until 1985, although her books circulated in *samizdat* in the 1980s. The volume *Nol'-Nol'* ('Nothing-Nothing,' 1991) collects verse written from 1979 onwards. From 1989 to 1992, she worked for Radio Liberty in Munich, continued to write poetry, and developed her international contacts, primarily in France and Germany. She has been described by one critic as 'traditionally avant-garde' for her adoption of modernism's salient devices and stances (e.g. fragmentation, nonlinear development, irreverence, irony, and paronomasia). Regarded by some as the (un)-official spokeswoman of the avant-garde, Shcherbina has succeeded in bridging the gap between nontraditional literary culture and the establishment. She is a shrewd manager of her career, as attested by the several translations of her work, invitations abroad, and her growing reputation at home.

RMey

Shen Rong (*b.* 1936), Chinese fiction writer. Originally named Shen Derong, Shen Rong was born in Hankou, Hubei Province and had a turbulent childhood. In 1954 she went to Beijing to study Russian; after graduation she worked as a translator in a radio station. In 1963 she was released from the station due to illness. In 1973 she went to live with a peasant family in Shanxi Province, which provided the setting for her first novel

Wannianqing ('Eternal Green,' 1975). Shen is currently a professional writer in Beijing and also the head of a private film and TV studio. Her story 'At Middle Age' (1980), which won its author wide recognition as well as a literary prize, vividly depicts the life experience of one generation of professionals who reached middle age toward the end of the Cultural Revolution. It tells of a female oculist's life-and-death struggles over competing responsibilities as a career woman, wife and mother, and political subject. Shen has written on a wide range of topics regarding contemporary Chinese intellectuals. Her recent short stories tend to be humorous and sarcastic in style.

I.W

Shi Shuqing (*b.* 1945), Chinese-Taiwan fiction writer, dramatist. Born in Lugang, an old immigrant town in Taiwan, Shi Shuqing is the sister of writer *Li Ang and literary critic Shi Shunü. Shi Shuqing earned a BA in English at Tamkang University, and an MA in theater at the City University of New York. She taught at the National Chengchi University in Taipei before she moved to Hong Kong in 1978. She was the director of Asian Programs at the Hong Kong Art Center and is now a consultant at the same institution. Her writings range from the experimental depiction of the psychological grotesque (using Lugang as the setting of her stories) in the 1960s, to the portrayal of the Chinese expatriates in America in the 1970s, and her later devotion to the hybridized Hong Kong society and people. Her early works, such as 'Yuebo de houyi' ('The Last Descendants of Job,' 1969) and 'Shiduo naxie rizi' ('Sorting Out Those Days,' 1971), are experimental in language and style and are marked by deliberate treatment of sexual oppression and desire. Her later works, however, are loaded with historical details that evoke the landscape, realities, and history of Hong Kong colonial life in the past hundred years. *The Barren Years and Other Short Stories and*

Plays is a collection of her works in English translation.

F-yM

Shields, Carol (*b.* 1935), Canadian novelist. Born in Oak Park, Illinois, Shields was educated at Hanover College, Indiana, where she earned a BA in 1957, and the University of Ottawa, where she earned an MA in 1975. She married Donald Shields, a Canadian, in 1957; they have five children. She became a Canadian citizen in 1971, and has taught at the Universities of Ottawa and Manitoba. Her award-winning first novel *Small Ceremonies* was published in 1976. Shields's central subjects – the domestic life of married couples, the chronicling of lives, and the tension between biography and fiction – are all launched here. She is interested in the ways we try to make sense out of our lives or the lives of others by turning them into stories, but in her sympathetic satirical novels, she emphasizes how incomplete those stories necessarily are. In *Happenstance* (1980), she narrates the events of the same few days twice, from the perspective of a husband and from that of his wife. *The Stone Diaries* (1993), which won the Pulitzer Prize, is the 'autobiography' of Daisy Flett, from her birth in 1905 to her death over ninety years later. Told in the third-person by Daisy, who describes both her birth and her death, and complete with family tree and photos, the novel raises fascinating questions about truth and fiction. Other novels include *The Box Garden* (1977), *Swann: A Mystery* (1987), *The Republic of Love* (1992), and *Larry's Party* (1997; Orange Prize). Shields has also published three volumes of poetry, two plays, and a collection of stories, *Dressing Up for the Carnival* (2000).

JEM

Shin Kyŏgsuk (*b.* 1963), South Korean novelist. Shin was born and raised in Chŏngŭp, Chŏllabuk-do, a small village in the countryside. She moved to Seoul and worked, under poor conditions, in an electronics factory while attending a special night school for workers. She later enrolled in the creative writing program at Seoul College of Arts and made her literary debut in 1985. The trajectory of her life is crucial to understanding the themes in her work: rupture from, and ardent longing for, both a long-lost primal bonding and the selves left behind in the past. These themes recur in her first two short story collections *Kyŏul uhwa* ('Winter Fable,' 1990) and *P'unggŭm i ittŏn chari* ('Where the Organ Once Stood,' 1993), as well as in her first novel, *Kip'ŭn sŭlp'ŭm* ('Deep Sadness,' 1994). Shin's revisit to the sites of memory culminates in her second novel *Woettan pang* ('An Out-of-the-Way Room,' 1995), a fine example of the literature of interiority and Shin's most representative work so far. She recently published her third novel *Kich'a nŭn ilgopssi e ttŏnane* ('The Train Leaves at Seven,' 1999). The title of her collection of essays, *Arŭmdaun kŭnŭl* ('Beautiful Shadow,' 1995), pithily captures the general milieu of her works, which are written mostly in her characteristically delicate, confessional, and poetic style.

K-HC

Shinebourne, Janice (*b.* 1947), Guyanese short story writer, novelist. Born in the Canje region of Guyana to parents of East Indian and Chinese heritage, Shinebourne attended university in both Georgetown and London, and won the Guyana Prize for a first work of fiction, for *Timepiece* (1986). Like her critically acclaimed novel *The Last English Plantation* (1988), her work is concerned with the coming of age for young Guyanese women, and their psychological and social experiences in the transition from rural to urban environments. She is equally concerned with the impact of colonial education in the multiethnic schools of Guyana, and the process of nation-building in a country with a highly complex ethnic constitution. She has also published short stories and essays

in anthologies such as *Her True True Name* and *Caribbean Women Writers*. She currently resides in London but is also a writer-in-residence at New York University; her travels have facilitated complex national and Asian ethnic constructions, which are reflected in her current lectures and scholarships on creoleness.

ED

Showalter, Elaine (*b.* 1941), US feminist literary critic. A leading feminist intellectual during the past three decades, former chair of the English Department at Princeton University and former president of the Modern Language Association (MLA), Showalter received her BA from Bryn Mawr and her PhD from the University of California, Davis. *A Literature of Their Own* (1976) asserts the diverse and evolving female literary tradition of nineteenth- and twentieth-century British women writers from Charlotte Brontë to Doris Lessing. *The Female Malady* (1987) is a feminist archeology of the discourse of madness in eighteenth- and nineteenth-century psychiatry and culture. *Sexual Anarchy* (1990) studies the historical materialism of sexuality in *fin-de-siècle* Anglo-American culture. *Hystories* (1997) is a feminist interpretation of the history and cultural narrative of the concept, syndromes, and social appropriations of hysteria. In the two collections of essays she has edited – *The New Feminist Criticism* (1985) and *Speaking of Gender* (1989) – Showalter historicizes the genesis and formation of American feminist theory and establishes gender as a central critical category. *Sister's Choice* (1991) considers the hybrid, intertextual nature of American women's writing. Challenging male-dominated canons, Showalter has edited plays, poetry, prose, short stories, and autobiographies by women in *Women's Liberation and Literature* (1971), *These Modern Women* (1978), *Alternative Alcott* (1988), and *Daughters of Decadence* (1993).

LY

Shree, Geetanjali (*see* Geetanjali Shree)

Shu Ting (*b.* 1952), Chinese poet. A native of Xiamen, Fujian Province, Shu Ting was sent to the countryside as a child because her father was accused of being a 'rightist' during the 'Anti-Rightist Campaign' of 1957–8. Her junior high school education was interrupted by the Cultural Revolution, which broke out in 1966; during the next ten years she held many odd jobs, including working on the assembly line at a light bulb factory. In the late 1970s the senior poet Cai Qijiao introduced her to the group of young poets in Beijing who had founded the first underground literary journal in the People's Republic of China, *Today*. She became a frequent contributor to *Today* and gained national prominence by 1980 as a leading practitioner of 'Misty Poetry,' which broke many lyric conventions and was informed by Western modernism. Although she was criticized by the establishment for her negative portrayals of society in some of her early poems, she became a member of the official Chinese Writers' Association and is now a vice chair at the Fujian provincial branch of the Writers' Association. Her early poetry has also won her international acclaim, and she has been invited to the West many times, most recently as a writer in residence in Berlin. *The Mist of My Heart: Selected Poems of Shu Ting* is a collection of English translations of her poetry.

MY

Shvarts, Elena Andreevna (*b.* 1948), Russian poet. Born in Leningrad, Shvarts was raised by her mother, a scriptwriter at the Leningrad Dramatic Theater. Shvarts studied philology at Leningrad State University and later graduated as a correspondent student from the Leningrad Theater Institute in 1971. From the start, her verse eloquently testified to the vitality of the religious and metaphysical traditions in Russian poetry. The religious thematics, exploration of passion both spiritual and sensual, and wide-ranging cultural references, however, for the most part rendered her verse unprintable in the Soviet Union, despite her reputation in literary circles. Her first poems appeared in 1973 in the newspaper of Tartu University, and subsequent poems were printed in émigré publications. Of her three books published abroad in the 1980s, the most important is *The Works and Days of Lavinia, A Nun of the Order of the Circumcision of the Heart* (1987). The imaginary Convent of the Circumcision of the Heart stands at the intersection of time, space, and religions, where Lavinia, who embodies both wisdom and heresy, contemplates her place in a world seemingly ruled by evil. Shvarts established her reputation in Russia with the publication of *Storony sveta* ('Compass Points,' 1989) and *Stikhi* ('Poems,' 1990).

RMey

Si Pha (M. L. Sipha Ladavalya Mahawann), (*b.* 1930), Thai fiction writer. Si Pha was born in Bangkok and was a student at the Faculty of Commerce and Accountancy at Chulalongkorn University. She left the university to become a teacher, but after eighteen years in the teaching profession, she decided to become a full-time writer. Her first published novel *Prasad Mued* ('The Dark Castle') became very popular and was made into a TV series and films. Si Pha is one of the most prolific writers in Thailand and her work reflects social and political aspects of Thai life. Many of her novels and short stories have received awards from both public and private organizations. One of her short stories 'Ai Nin' received the John A. Ekin Memorial Fund Award in 1979. Of her seventy novels, eleven have won the National Book Award. Her highly acclaimed novel *Khao Nok Na* ('Rice Outside the Rice Field'), which deals with adolescence problems caused by the presence of GIs in Thailand, has been translated into Japanese, while her collection of short stories *Grandmother the Progressive* has been translated into English. In 1996, Si

Pha was named National Artist in Literature.

NM

Sidaoruang (Wanna Sawatsi), (*b.* 1943), Thai fiction writer. Daughter of a railway worker and a market vendor, Sidaoruang was born in Phitsanulok, a northern province of Thailand. Because of family hardships, she was forced to leave school at the age of 10 and sent to work in Bangkok when she was only 12. Her experiences in working at different menial jobs proved later to be of great value to her writing. Drawing upon her personal experience as a factory worker, she began writing short stories depicting the plight of the poor and the underprivileged. These short stories, mostly written from 1973 to 1976, had great impact on the 'Literature for Life' movement of the 1970s. They were later published as a collection titled *A Drop of Glass* (1983), which was translated into several languages. In her more recent collected short stories, *Matsi* (1987) and *Mae Salue* (1993), she has moved away from the 'social injustice' theme and focuses more on the problems of motherhood, gender inequality, and female identity. She has also become increasingly experimental and innovative in her technique and style. Sidaoruang is married to Suchat Sawatsi, a well-known editor and prominent literary figure, who undeniably has exerted an influence on her development as a writer.

NM

Sidhwa, Bapsi (*b.* 1938), Pakistani novelist. Sidhwa was born in Karachi and grew up in Lahore. She received no formal education until she was 14 years old but later graduated from Kinnaird College for Women, Lahore and became a social worker. Her first published novel *The Crow Eaters* (1978), set in colonial India, parodies the eccentricities of her own Parsi community through the Junglewalla family. Though it was published second, Sidhwa began her writing career with *The Bride* (1983). Based on a story of a runaway bride caught and killed by her husband, *The Bride* explores the resonances and conflicts between urban and rural, and Eastern and Western, patriarchal interests in postcolonial Pakistan. *Cracking India* (1990; originally published as *Ice-Candy Man*) is narrated from the perspective of a young Parsi girl coming of age in Lahore during the partition of India in 1947. Like Sidhwa's other novels, *An American Brat* (1993) uses an episodic structure and self-reflexive realism to investigate the impact of conservative attitudes on women's lives in cross-cultural contexts. Currently, Sidhwa lives in the US. She has taught creative writing at Columbia, Rice and the University of Texas, Houston and received numerous awards including the Sitara-i-Imtiaz (1991), Pakistan's highest honor in the arts.

JD

Siekkinen, Raija (*b.* 1953), Finnish novelist, essayist, children's writer. Born in Kotka, Finland, Siekkinen studied Finnish literature, philosophy, and folklore at Helsinki University. She lives as a writer in Kotka. Childhood and many-sided classical symbolism are the most important building blocks in her novels. Her debut as a published writer was *Talven tulo* ('Coming of Winter,' 1978). In her fourth volume of short stories *Kuinka rakkaus syntyy* ('*How Love Begins*,' 1991), she describes solitude and alienation. Her characters live ordinary contemporary urban lives. She narrates the soul of the landscape rather than the concrete reality. In *Metallin Maku* ('The Taste of Metal,' 1992), she deals with the theme of tenderness and cruelty in relations between the sexes. This work brought her the Runeberg Prize. In her first novel *Disturbance in the Landscape* (1994), Siekkinen continues her dissection of the soul with an account of a woman who finds that many lives are being lived through her own experiences. Her latest work *Kaunis Nimi* ('A Beautiful Name') is a collection of stories about women who, for one reason or another, ponder and remember their lives more accurately than ever before. She was twice awarded Finland's State Literature Prize and also the Mika Waltari Prize. Her works have been translated into several languages.

TSi

Sigurðardóttir, Fríða Á. (*b.* 1940), Icelandic novelist, short story writer. Born in Hesteyri, a small, now-abandoned village in the western fjords of Iceland, Fríða grew up in a large family in which her older sister was also an author. When she was quite young, the family left the western fjords and moved to Keflavik. She studied at the University of Iceland in Reykjavik, earning a master's degree in Icelandic. Currently she lives in Reykjavik with her husband and two sons. In 1980 she debuted with a collection of short stories titled *þetta er ekkert alvarlegt* ('This is Nothing Serious'). Since then she has published another collection of short stories and four novels. Her novel *Nightwatch* (1990), thus far her only work translated into English, has won several awards, including the Icelandic Literary Prize (1990) and the prestigious Nordic Council's Literary Prize (1992). In 1994 Fríða also received the honorary Icelandic Order of the Falcon. *Nightwatch* captures some of the most typical features of traditional Icelandic storytelling as a woman sitting by the bedside of her dying mother reflects on the stories of her female ancestors, attempting to discover who she is and how her story fits in with those women who have gone before her. A prominent feature of Fríða's writing is a sense of history and connectedness to her native geography, especially the western fjords where she was born.

KG

Sigurðardóttir, Steinunn (*b.* 1950), Icelandic novelist, short story writer, poet, playwright. Steinunn was born and grew up in Reykjavik. After graduating from

high school, she went abroad and in 1972 received her BA (honors) in psychology and philosophy from the University of Dublin. Upon her return to Iceland, she worked as a journalist and reporter for radio and television until 1982. She and her daughter currently live in Reykjavik. In 1969 she debuted with a collection of poems enigmatically titled *Sífellur*. Since then she has published four volumes of poetry, two collections of short stories, five novels, and several television plays. For her literary production, Steinunn has received several Icelandic literary awards, among them the Icelandic Literary Prize (1995), and two nominations for the prestigious Nordic Council's Literary Prize. Although none of her novels has been translated into English, her poetry ('The Direction of Beauty,' 'To Descartes,' and 'When I'm Sixty-four') is included in a 1980 collection of Icelandic poetry *The Postwar Poetry of Iceland* and one of her short stories – 'Twenty-five Crosses' – appears in English in the publication *Icelandic Writing Today*. Her versatility in genre makes her a particularly interesting and important contemporary writer in Iceland; her prose works in particular constitute breaks with traditional novel writing, for she uses diary notations, letters, poems, and even the obituaries in the daily newspapers to tell her stories. Her novel *Tímaþjófurinn* ('The Thief of Time,' 1986) was made into a major motion picture in France in 1998.

KG

Silko, Leslie Marmon (*b.* 1948), US novelist, poet, short story writer. Born in Albuquerque, New Mexico, and raised on a Laguna Pueblo reservation, Silko is of Laguna Pueblo, Plains Indian, Anglo-American, and Mexican descent. She graduated with honors from the University of New Mexico in 1969 and has taught writing at several colleges and universities. While living for two years in Ketchikan, Alaska, she wrote her remarkable first novel *Ceremony* (1977). It is the story of Tayo, a troubled mixed-blood Native American, who struggles to adjust to life on the reservation after being a Japanese prisoner of war during World War II. The novel asserts the importance of Native American traditions and presents a powerful critique of white Americans' values and metaphysics. In 1981, Silko published *Storyteller*, a collection of stories, poems, essays, and autobiography, which stresses the importance of the oral storytelling tradition. That same year, she was awarded a five-year MacArthur Fellowship, which allowed her to begin work on the novel *Almanac of the Dead* (1991), an epic 'moral history' of North America told from a Native American viewpoint, which took her ten years to complete. Silko has also written *Laguna Woman* (1974), a collection of poems; *Sacred Water* (1993), a collection of short fiction; and *Yellow Woman and a Beauty of the Spirit: Essays on Native American Life Today* (1996). Her novel *Gardens in the Dunes* was published in 1999.

DVT

Simonsuuri, Kirsti (*b*. 1945), Finnish poet, essayist, prose writer. Simonsuuri was born in Helsinki into a family with a folklorist father who died when she was a teenager and a mother who was a Finnish literature and language teacher. Despite these firm roots in Finland, she has spent most of her life abroad. She earned an MA in Latin, Greek, and English at the University of Helsinki in 1971. Her doctoral thesis at Cambridge in 1977 was on Homer. Her first published work was a collection of poems *Murattikaide* ('Ivy Balustrade,' 1980), which brought her the J. H. Erkko award for the best first book published in Finland. This collection includes 'Mother Tongues.' In the novel *The Demon Boy* (1986), the 'demon boy' is taught the meaning of true love. In the collection of poems *Euroopan Ryöstö* ('Abduction of Europe,' 1984), people are depicted as pieces of the universe, always in motion. *Miehen Muotokuva* ('Portrait of

a Man,' 1992) presents a question of an almost mythic father and his son's survival without him, alone with his guilt. Simonsuuri ponders motherhood in her works; she believes it stifles a woman's chances of expressing herself. In 1991, she was awarded the Columbia Translation Center's award for the best translation into English for *The Enchanting Beasts*, an anthology of Finnish modern women poets.

TSi

Simpson, Mona (*b*. 1957), US novelist. Born in Green Bay, Wisconsin, Simpson earned a BA from the University of California, Berkeley in 1979 and an MFA from Columbia University in 1983. Her critically acclaimed first novel *Anywhere But Here* was published in 1986. A psychologically complex and unsentimental portrait of a mother–daughter relationship, it concerns an eccentric mother who dreams of Hollywood success for her adolescent daughter and romance for herself, but who ends up with only a dreary job and a daughter who cannot wait to live on her own. Simpson's next two novels also focus on broken families and a peculiarly American kind of restlessness. *The Lost Father* (1991) is a sequel to her first novel, in which the daughter Ann is now a medical school student. It tells the story of her quest, which takes her halfway around the world, for the Egyptian immigrant father who abandoned her. Simpson returns to the same triad in *A Regular Guy* (1996), in which an illegitimate daughter seeks out her absent father, who has become a biotechnology tycoon. Simpson gives this search for legitimacy an allegorical tone by weaving the story of Genesis into the narrative. She was named one of *Granta*'s Best Young American Novelists in 1996.

JEM

Sjöwall, Maj (*b*. 1935), Swedish crime fiction writer. Born in Malmö, Sjöwall started out as a reporter for several magazines. While working as an editor for the woman's magazine *Idun*, she met Per Wahlöö (1926–1975) in 1961. After their marriage in 1962, they collaborated on a ten-book crime fiction series which features police detective Martin Beck's work and life while critically depicting contemporary Swedish society. *Roseanna*, the first book of the series, was published in 1965. All the books, psychological and sociological in nature, pay attention to minute details while keeping the reader in suspense. The fourth book *The Laughing Policeman* (1968), in which Beck investigates the murders of nine people in Stockholm, won the Edgar Allan Poe Award in 1970 and was made into a movie with Walter Matthau as Beck. The last and longest book, *The Terrorists* (1975), further enlarged the critique of society. Besides translating books by Ed McBain, Sjöwall and Wahlöö also made a comparative study of police methods in Sweden, England, Russia, and the US.

GE-C

Skinner, Michelle Cruz (*b.* 1965), Philippine fiction writer. Born in Rizal to a Filipina from Manila and an American from Indiana, Skinner spent her formative years at the Subic Bay Naval Base and moved to Honolulu in 1983. She received her BA in English with highest honors from the University of Hawaii at Manoa, and her MFA in creative writing from Arizona State University. 'Faith Healer' (1988), which dramatizes one family's experience of the Martial Law years, was one of fifty-four stories selected for the 7th Annual PEN Syndicated Fiction Project in 1988. Her first collection of short stories *Balikbayan: A Filipino Homecoming* (1988) reflects her insights on Philippine–US military base towns. Her second collection *Mango Seasons* (1996) is a series of interconnected narratives told from different perspectives within a middle-class family. Skinner resides in Oahu where she writes and teaches English.

CJM

Smiley, Jane (*b.* 1949), US novelist, short story writer. Born in Los Angeles, Smiley was raised in St Louis. She received a BA from Vassar College in 1971 and an MFA and a PhD from the University of Iowa. She currently teaches at Iowa State University. Many of her early novels focus on the dynamics of family relations and are set in the rural Midwest. Her first novel *Barn Blind* (1980) explores the tension between a mother and her children on a family farm. *At Paradise Gate* (1981) charts how domestic life is affected by a father's cancer diagnosis. *Duplicate Keys* (1984), a mystery novel set in Manhattan, analyzes romantic and platonic love, while *The Age of Grief* (1987), a collection of short stories, examines marital relationships. Smiley conducted extensive research for *The Greenlanders* (1988), an historical novel set in fourteenth-century Greenland. Her best-known book *A Thousand Acres* (1991), lauded for its vivid language and attention to landscape, is a contemporary rewriting of *King Lear*; it was awarded the Pulitzer Prize and a National Book Award. With *Moo* (1995) and *Horse Heaven* (2000), Smiley turned to multi-plot satirical novels with large casts of characters; the former is a comic look at academia while the latter takes on the world of horse racing. Other works include the novellas *Ordinary Love and Good Will* (1989) and the novel *The All-True Travels and Adventures of Lidie Newton* (1998).

DVT

Smither, Elizabeth (*b.* 1941), New Zealand poet, fiction writer. Smither was born and has lived most of her life in New Plymouth, New Zealand. She attended Massey and Victoria universities, but did not graduate. In 1963 she qualified as a librarian, and married Michael Smither; they later divorced. She has two sons and one daughter. Her first collection of poems was *Here Come the Clouds* (1975). Smither's later collections include *You're Very Seductive William Carlos Williams* (1978), *The Legend of Marcello Mastroianni's*

Wife (1981), *Casanova's Ankle* (1981), *Shakespeare's Virgins* (1983), and *Professor Musgrove's Canary* (1986). The titles of her poems indicate her diverse interests, including literature, legend, and history. Most recently she has published *The Tudor Style* (1993). This volume includes poetry from eight earlier collections as well as thirty-three new selections. Her poems are generally intellectual and witty, and sometimes startling, their tone direct. She has won numerous prizes for her poems including the New Zealand Book Award for Poetry. Her first novel *First Blood* (1983) is historical fiction, while *Brother-love Sister-love* (1986) is an autobiographical novel about visiting Britain. Her lively short stories have been collected in *Nights at the Embassy* (1990), *Mr Fish and Other Stories* (1994) and *The Mathematics of Jane Austen* (1997).

M-RA

Sobti, Krishna (*b.* 1925), Indian fiction writer. Born in Gujrat (now in Pakistani Punjab), raised in New Delhi, and educated in Lahore, Sobti is one of Hindi's most singular, important, and prolific writers. She began writing in 1944 with the story 'Lama,' and has written ten novels and a collection each of stories and essays. Although her chosen language is Hindi, Sobti's idiom is heavily Punjabi, making her remarkable books tremendously difficult to translate. She focuses on the lives of ordinary people, principally women, and touches on the generally taboo area of women's sexuality, giving her characters the *joie de vivre* which is so much a mark of her own personality. Like many Punjabis of her generation, she comes from a family of Partition refugees and much of her writing is preoccupied with that experience of dislocation and uprooting – notably her autobiographical *Zindaginama* (1980), honoured with the Sahitya Akademi and the Sahitya Shiromani awards. She has been writer-in-residence at the Indian Institute of Advanced Study, Simla, and honoured with a fellowship from Punjab University, Patiala. Her best-known early works are *Dar se Bichudi* ('Separated from the Flock,' 1958), *Mitro Marjani* ('Damn You, Mitro,' 1968), and, more recently, *Dil-o-Danish* ('Heart and Wisdom,' 1993), a novel about Old Delhi. Her novella *Ai Ladki* ('Hey Girl,' 1991) and an excerpt from *Mitro Marjani* have been anthologized in English translation. Sobti lives in Delhi.

UB

Sofola, Zulu (1935–1995), Nigerian playwright. Sofola, one of the major innovators of contemporary drama in Nigeria, was born Nwazuluoha Okwumabua in Issele-Uku, Nigeria. Although she received her BA and MA in the US, she earned her PhD from the University of Ibadan and taught at the University of Ibadan and the University of Ilorin. She married the sociologist J. A. Sofola in 1960. She became the first Nigerian woman to publish a play in English with *The Disturbed Peace of Christmas* (1971). Her most popular plays, such as *King Emene* (1974) and *Wedlock of the Gods* (1972), raise questions about society, which reflect her initial literary research – the basis of tragedy and the implication for the individual and the community. A linking focus in her work is also the role of women in society, as illustrated in her more humorous plays *Old Wines are Tasty* (1981) and *The Sweet Trap* (1977). A major collection of her plays *Lost Dreams and Other Plays* was published in 1992. Sofola has achieved much fame for basing her contemporary plays on indigenous forms, although some critics have admonished her for allegedly preferring the traditional over the modern. Still, her plays are produced throughout Nigeria as well as the rest of West Africa, leaving her with a legacy of the living community theater she envisioned.

GW

Song, Cathy (*b.* 1955), US poet. Born in Honolulu, Song was educated at Wellesley College (BA, 1977) and Boston University

(MFA, 1981). She is married to Douglas Davenport; they have three children. She has taught creative writing at several universities. Her first collection of poems *Picture Bride* (1983) was selected for publication by the Yale Series of Younger Poets. Although she resists being classified as a Hawaiian or Asian-American poet, Song's Korean and Chinese heritage is central to poetry. In *Picture Bride*, she tells of her grandmother, who came from Korea to the US to marry a man she had never met, and considers the importance of the past as well as the lure of assimilation. Her subjects are family life, specifically her ties to children, parents, community, and tradition. Her poems are carefully crafted and visually aware. Her voice is quietly strong, her language lucid and spare. *Frameless Window, Squares of Light* (1988) contains narrative poems about family history and relationships as well as powerful poems that shift to a more intimate perspective. *School Figures* (1994) returns again to family stories, but Song dwells in particular on her parents and on the death of her father.

JFM

Sontag, Susan (*b.* 1933), US essayist, novelist, cultural critic. A precocious student who graduated from high school at age 15, New York-born and Los Angeles-raised Sontag was educated at the University of California, Berkeley and at the University of Chicago, where she earned a BA in philosophy in 1951. She continued her education with an MA in English and philosophy at Harvard University and graduate study in Oxford and Paris. She married psychologist Philip Rieff, with whom she had one son; they divorced in 1959. Her first book, the novel *The Benefactor*, was published in 1963. She came to prominence with *Against Interpretation and Other Essays* (1966), in which she argues for a reevaluation of contemporary schools of criticism. The collection includes her famous essay 'Notes on Camp,' in which Sontag defends camp as a

legitimate art form, and established her reputation as a postmodern critic and intellectual. *Illness as Metaphor* (1978), influenced by her own diagnosis of breast cancer, and *AIDS and its Metaphors* (1989) both examine the language and images through which modern society copes with illness. She has written the play *Alice in Bed* (1993), as well as several novels, including *Death Kit* (1967), *I, Etcetera* (1978), *The Volcano Lover* (1992), and *In America* (2000). Her nonfiction includes *On Photography* (1977; National Book Critics Circle Award) and *Under the Sign of Saturn* (1980), which explores the intellectual influences of Benjamin, Barthes, Artaud, and other modern thinkers. Sontag has written and directed several films.

DVT

Sow Fall, Aminata (*b.* 1941), Senegalese novelist. The most prestigious and prolific woman writer in contemporary francophone Africa, Sow Fall was born in St Louis, Senegal. She earned a degree in French language and literature in 1967 from the Sorbonne. Like *Mariama Bâ, she is bicultural and bilingual and her vision is profoundly Islamic. Her work deals with a wide range of the social, political, economic, and personal difficulties posed by the need to adapt traditional African society to the Western world originally introduced by French colonialism. Her work is never didactic, but it implicitly shows that such a coexistence is possible. Her first novel *Le Revenant* ('The Ghost,' 1976) deals with the conflict between family loyalty and the materialism of contemporary Dakar society. In *L'Appel des arènes* ('The Call of the Arenas,' 1982), a young mother has become so Westernized that she tries to separate her young son from his African heritage. *The Beggars' Strike* (1979) criticizes political cronyism, technocrats, and especially the disrespectful treatment of the poor and disabled in a Westernizing city. *L'Ex-père de la nation* ('The Ex-Father of the Nation,' 1987) examines the conflict between traditional family loyalty and the need for a representative African government. *Le Jujubier du patriarche* ('The Patriarch's Jujube Tree,' 1993) returns to this theme and ingeniously uses a traditional African epic to reconcile family conflicts. Her most recent novel is *Douceurs du Bercail* ('The Sweetness of the Home,' 1998).

SGC

Soysal, Sevgi (1936–1976), Turkish short story writer, novelist. An activist for the rights of women and children, Soysal received a BA in classical philology from Ankara University before studying archaeology and drama in Germany. She married three times, and had two children with her last husband. She died of cancer. Of her three novels, *Yürümek* ('Walking,' 1970) was initially banned because of its sexual explicitness, but it also won the 1970 Turkish Radio and Television Award for Art. Her second novel *Yenişehirde Bir Öğle Vakti* ('Noontime in Yenişehir,' 1973) won the Orhan Kemal Novel Prize in 1974. Her last novel *Şafak* ('Dawn,' 1975). All her novels have dramatically tight structures, depicting several hours in the characters' lives. Her characters are rebels, usually from provincial backgrounds, trying to find solutions to personal problems which are connected to larger social issues. Her short stories were published in three volumes. Two stories are available in English: 'Hanife,' which depicts a young girl who is punished for entering into a sexual relationship without marriage, and 'The Junk Peddler,' which is about a newly divorced woman who gives away her marriage bed. Both stories play with points of view in ingenious ways, allowing the full narrative situation to be clear only in the end.

SE

Spark, Muriel (*b.* 1918), Scottish novelist, poet, short story writer. Born in Edinburgh, of Jewish-Italian heritage, Spark attended Heriot-Watt College before moving, at age 19, to South Africa, to marry her fiancé, S. O. Spark. They had one son

and later divorced. She moved to London in 1944, where she worked for the Political Intelligence Department, writing anti-Nazi propaganda. She worked as an editor for the *Poetry Review*, started a literary magazine titled *Forum*, and published *Child of Light* (1951), a study of Mary Shelley, before publishing her first novel *The Comforters* in 1957. Spark's conversion, in 1954, to Catholicism, has had a profound influence on her fiction. Her acerbically witty and often satirical novels combine realism with the supernatural and the allegorical. Fascinated with the tension between free will and God's plan, she often calls attention to her own role as creator/author within her narratives. Her most famous novel *The Prime of Miss Jean Brodie* (1961) is about a romantic but manipulative teacher at a girl's school in Edinburgh. Other novels include *Robinson* (1958), *Memento Mori* (1959), *The Ballad of Peckham Rye* (1960), *The Bachelors* (1960), *The Girls of Slender Means* (1963), *The Mandelbaum Gate* (1965), *The Abbess of Crewe* (1974), and *Symposium* (1990). She has also published novellas, several volumes of short stories, poetry collections, and an autobiography *Curriculum Vitae* (1992). The winner of many literary awards, Spark was awarded an OBE in 1967.

DVT

Spaziani, Maria Luisa (*b.* 1924), Italian poet, critic. Born in Turin, Italy, Spaziani studied French literature in college and taught it at the University of Messina for many years. Her first collection of poetry *Le acque del Sabato* ('The Sabbath Waters,' 1954) showed her indebtedness both to Hermetic poetry and to high lyric tradition. Spaziani is often linked with the Nobel prize-winning poet, Eugenio Montale, with whom she had a close personal and professional relationship. She is currently the president of the Eugenio Montale International Center, which forwards the study and dissemination of poetry and awards the annual 'Montale Prize' for publications and translations of Italian verse. Two of her books are available in English translation: *Star of Free Will* (1986) and *Sentry Towers* (1992). Her poetry reflects her deep literary culture, her respect for traditional forms, and her love of nature. Although never an openly autobiographical poet, some recent writing speaks more to personal experience and memories. She has never espoused feminist causes, but in the past decade she has completed a narrative poem *Giovanna d'Arco* ('Joan of Arc,' 1990) and has published *Donne in poesia* ('Women in Poetry,' 1992), a collection of imagined conversations with women poets from many countries, both of which emphasize the gendered nature of art and life.

RW

Spivak, Gayatri Chakravorty (*b.* 1942), Indian-US cultural theorist. One of the world's most renowned postcolonial, deconstructionist, and Marxist feminist intellectuals, Spivak was born in Calcutta, educated at University of Calcutta and Cornell University, and is currently Avalon Professor of Humanities at Columbia University. Her 1976 translation of Jacques Derrida's *Of Grammatology*, with its masterful 'Translator's Preface,' introduced Derridian deconstruction to the English-speaking world. Her postcolonial project is an ambitious dialectic between the micropolitics of the First World academy and the violence of global capitalism in the Third World. In over 100 articles and numerous books, including *In Other Worlds* (1988), *The Post-Colonial Critic* (1990), *Outside in the Teaching Machine* (1993), and *Imaginary Maps* (1995), she performs her unique cultural politics of problematizing Eurocentrism in French feminism, translating and reading *Mahasweta Devi's stories, or examining the uses and abuses of multiculturalism. In essays such as 'Can the Subaltern Speak?' (1988), she theorizes the key concept of subalternity, articulates the theory, subject-positions and limits of Third

World feminism, and warns against the desire to speak for the muted native Other. Spivak's latest book *A Critique of Postcolonial Reason* (1999) analyzes the structure and production of postcolonial cosmopolitanism, and its complicity with various power mechanisms it strategically contests.

LY

Springer, Eintou Pearl (*b.* 1944), Trinidadian poet, dramatist. Born in Santa Cruz, in Trinidad and Tobago, Springer completed her early education at San Juan Presbyterian School, later attending St George's College, Barataria, followed by an MPhil. in information sciences from City University of London. In 1962, she joined the Trinidad Theatre Workshop and helped found the Caribbean Theatre Guild. She has written stage adaptations of C. L. R. James's *Minty Alley* (1977) and Sam Selvon's *A Brighter Sun* (1979). She conducts workshops throughout the Caribbean, using theater and poetry to teach AIDS awareness, family planning, and self-esteem. In *Out of the Shadows* (1986), a collection of poems, she connects the colonial past with images of the West Indian present, both at home and in exile, in sensual language. A second volume, *Focussed*, was published in 1991. In 1996, she was honored with a national award for her contribution to Art and Culture in Trinidad and Tobago. She is currently director of the National Heritage Library at Port of Spain in Trinidad.

JSp

Stefan, Verena (*b.* 1947), Swiss-German prose writer, poet. Born in Bern, Stefan moved in 1968 to Berlin, the center of the German students' rebellion. She joined the woman's group 'Bread + Roses' and contributed to the 'Women's Manual Nr.1.' After publishing her autobiographical feminist narrative *Shedding* (1975), she left the city and worked as a physical therapist, writer, and poet. Regarded as the 'bible' of the German women's movement and widely distributed in universities and alternative bookstores, *Shedding* gave voice to previously unwritten, overlooked forms of female experience. The text explores a woman's identity by uncovering traces of her colonization that are inscribed indelibly into the alienation from her own body. Passing through urban environs and affairs with men, Stefan's narrator begins to take note of the differences between a male gaze and her real desires, becoming aware of the lack of a German sexual vocabulary that is not hostile to women. She withdraws from these misogynies of heterosexist reality into intense observations of female bodies, 'creating [themselves] anew through touching looking talking.' This new sexuality is expressed through an innovative language of both linguistic experiments and nature metaphors. Stefan's claim to familiar tropes of women's bodies – colors, petals, pumpkins – has also provoked criticism of her regressive attempts to recreate an alternative myth of matriarchy.

AG

Steinwachs, Ginka (*b.* 1942), German novelist, dramatist, essayist. Born in Göttingen, Steinwachs studied religion, philosophy and comparative literature in Munich, Berlin, and Paris. Her PhD thesis on André Breton has developed into a seminal work and was published as *Mythologie des Surrealismus* ('Mythology of Surrealism,' 1985). She has lectured at several universities. Since 1974 she has lived as a writer and performance artist in Europe and the US. Her studies in art history and literary theory continue to influence her creativity. While most of her writings are governed by surrealism, her plays, performance scripts, and prose are centered upon concepts of feminist aesthetics emphasizing the female body, especially the mouth and lips. Her play *George Sand* (1980) concentrates on the artist's attempts to find her identity, and *Tränende Herzen* ('Crying Hearts,' 1977) emphasizes women's 'deficiencies' while

simultaneously urging women to acquire 'masculine' qualities. Her novel *Marylinparis* (1978) applies montage and polysemie, the title implying both Marylin in Paris, or the identity of Marylin and Paris. *Berliner Trichter/Berliner Bilderbogen* ('Berlin Funnel/Berlin Picture Page,' 1979) compares literary theory with practice. *Ein Mund von Welt* ('A Mouth Full of World,' 1989) and *Vollmund* ('Full Mouth,' 1991) contain performance scripts and other texts. She has received several German and Austrian literary awards.

MMu

Stenberg, Eira (*b.* 1943), Finnish poet, novelist. Stenberg was born in Tampere, Finland and received a BA in philosophy, literature, and art history from the University of Helsinki. She also studied music and film dramaturgy at the Sibelius Academy, Helsinki. Her first book of poems was *Kapina huoneessa* ('Revolt in the Room'), which won her the J. H. Erkko prize for the best first book of the year (1966). In her other poetry collections – *Rakkauden pasifismit* ('Love's Pacifisms,' 1967), *Vedenalainen Silta* ('The Submerged Bridge,' 1979), *Erokirja* ('The Book of Parting,' 1980), and *Parrakas madonna* ('The Bearded Madonna,' 1983) – she questions the place of the child, the woman, and the family in this world. Her first novel *Paratiisin Vangit* ('The Prisoners of Paradise,' 1984) is about the power struggle within the family. This work received the Government Literature Prize. The themes of family relationships, and power and submission, continue in her novels *Häikäisy* ('Dazzle,' 1987) and *Kuun Puutarhat* ('The Gardens of the Moon,' 1990). In 1997, she returned to poetry with *Halun ikoni* ('Icon of Desire'). Its theme is female sexuality, which she approaches both passionately and ironically through the myths of the Minotaur and Grimm's fairy tales. She has also written children's books and plays for radio and TV. *Wings of Hope and Daring* (1993) is a selection of Stenberg's poems in English translation.

TSi

Stevenson, Anne (*b.* 1933), British poet, biographer. Born into an American family in Cambridge, England, Stevenson attended the University of Michigan, Ann Arbor, where she received a BA in 1954 and an MA in 1962. She married her fourth husband, Peter Lucas, in 1987; she has three children. She has taught writing at various colleges and universities in Great Britain. She moved to England with her first husband, and the challenges of being a transplanted American are central to her early poetry. Her first volume of poetry *Living in America* was published in 1965. Her poems are technically accomplished, carefully crafted, reserved and wry. She writes about nature, place and displacement, and the hopes and failures of love. *Travelling Behind Glass* (1974) excoriates suburban motherhood. *Enough of Green* (1977) is preoccupied with both aesthetic and spiritual renunciation. *Minute by Glass Minute* (1982) contrasts Vermont and Wales, the old and the new world. *The Collected Poems 1955–1995* was published in 1996. *Between the Iceberg and the Ship* (1999) is a collection of essays and lectures. Stevenson has also written a critical study of Elizabeth Bishop and the controversial *Bitter Fame* (1989), a biography of *Sylvia Plath.

JEM

Strauss, Jennifer (*b.* 1933), Australian poet, essayist, critic. Born in Heywood, Victoria and educated at the universities of Melbourne and Glasgow, Strauss obtained her PhD in 1992 from Monash University (where she now is Associate Professor in English) for her critical study of *Gwen Harwood. Strauss has had a distinguished academic and poetic career, winning the *Westerly* Sesquicentenary Prize in 1979, and having been a visiting scholar at the universities of North Carolina (1974), Toronto (1982), and ANU

(1988). She has published numerous scholarly articles in collections and journals in addition to *Judith Wright* (1995), her second critical study in Australian poetry. She is the editor of the highly successful *Oxford Book of Australian Love Poems* (1993) and *Family Ties: Australian Poems of the Family* (1998), and is co-editor of *The Oxford Literary History of Australia* (1998). Strauss's own poetry is notable for its intimate and sensitive responses to both personal and political injustices and for her ability to evoke personal awareness of the emotional ambivalence which accompanies the lives of modern women. Her poetry has been published in various journals as well as in her four volumes *Children and Other Strangers* (1975), *Winter Driving* (1981), *Labour Ward* (1988), and *Tierra del Fuego: New and Selected Poems* (1997).

Mhe

Ström, Eva (*b.* 1947), Swedish poet, novelist, critic. Born on Lidingö, Stockholm, Ström became a medical doctor in 1973. Before becoming a full-time writer in 1988, she worked at the clinic for Infectious diseases in Kristianstad. She is married to a gynecologist; they have three children. Together with the stage director Suzanne Osten, Ström has also staged plays. Her first book of poetry *Den brinnande zeppelinaren* ('The Burning Zeppelin,' 1977) was followed by *Steinkind* (1979) and *Akra* (1983). In the latter collections, which both won literary awards, the yearning for freedom is thematized and developed. In the novel *Det mörka alfabetet* ('The Dark Alphabet,' 1982), the rational language of a doctor is contrasted with that of a schizophrenic woman. The dichotomy between the professional, but mother-fixated, Dr. Ulfson and his rich inner life is highlighted in *Mats Ulfson* (1991). *Berättelser* ('Stories,' 1997), a collection of poems and prose poems, discusses the unknown and the impossibility of knowing, while still searching for order and meaning. English translations of

Ström's poems are included in several anthologies.

GE-C

Su Weizhen (*b*. 1954), Chinese-Taiwan fiction writer, editor. Born in Taiwan, Su Weizhen is a second-generation immigrant from the mainland. She is one of the few women writers to have graduated from the Political Staff College, a college operated by the Ministry of National Defense in Taiwan to cultivate military and political staff officers. She served in the army and then worked at a local radio station. She is now editor of the literary supplement of the *United Daily*, one of Taiwan's leading newspapers. She has received several literary awards in Taiwan, including the 1980 *United Daily* Short Story Award, the 1981 *United Daily* Novelette Award, and the 1994 *China Times* Novel Award. In contrast to her military educational background, her early novels are known for their mesmerizing emotional details stripped of any political overtones. Her works include *Hongyan yilao* ('The Beauty Has Aged,' 1980), *Peita yiduan* ('Keep Him Company for a While,' 1983), and *Suiyue de shengyin* ('The Sound of Time,' 1984). More recently, works such as *Chenmo de daoyu* ('The Silent Island,' 1994) demonstrate a greater diversity of style and subject matter. She is married and currently lives in Taipei.

F-yM

Suleri Goodyear, Sara (*b*. 1953), Pakistani-US prose writer, critic. Pakistani-born Suleri was educated at Punjab University, Lahore and Indiana University, and now teaches English at Yale University. Her first book *Meatless Days* (1989) is a memoir reconstructing postcolonial Pakistan. Her subtle poetic style juxtaposes the violent birth of Pakistan with her father's political idealism, her Welsh–Pakistani heritage, and her own migration to the West. In *The Rhetoric of English India* (1992), she critically examines the historical documentation of British rule in India and the Anglo-Indian fictional narrative from the eighteenth to the twentieth century. She emphasizes the irreducible intimacy and complicity in colonial exchange and encounter, which defies any binarism between colonizer and colonized, imperial Center and marginalized Other. Particularly illuminating is her analysis of numerous tropes and rhetorical devices in the colonial/postcolonial representation of British India, such as the feminization of colonial discourse, rape, homoeroticism, and the geography of the female body. This postcolonial feminist trajectory continues in her essay 'Woman Skin Deep: Feminism and the Postcolonial Condition' (1992). Suleri carefully problematizes easy assumptions from within and in-between the two discourses of postcoloniality and feminism through an enabling differentiation of the concepts and categories of race, gender, ethnicity, Afro-American feminism, and Third World feminism.

LY

Sunder Rajan, Rajeswari (*b*. 1950), Indian feminist cultural critic. Born in Tiruchirapalli, Tamil Nadu, Sunder Rajan completed her BA and MA in English at Bombay University, and her English PhD at George Washington University. She is the editor of *The Lie of the Land*: *English Literary Studies in India* (1993) and *Signposts*: *Gender Issues in Post-Independence India* (1999); co-editor of *Austen in the World*: *Postcolonial Mappings* (1999); and author of *Real and Imagined Women*: *Gender, Culture and Postcolonialism* (1995) and *Women, Law, Citizenship and the Post-Colonial State* (1999). Ranging from essays on Austen, Eliot, and Dickens to South Asian cultural studies, her work powerfully integrates literary criticism with feminist analysis, interrogating culture, politics, and the written word. She examines literary works and their 'social text,' the meanings which surround the production and reception of texts, be they fiction, film, or cultural commentary. Her landmark essays on sati (widow immolation), the contest over women's legal rights in India, and narratives of violence such as rape, address critical issues in the politics of representation of women and the nation in postcolonial settings. She has taught at Delhi University and George Washington University, and was a Senior Fellow at the Nehru Memorial Museum and Library, New Delhi. She is currently a Fellow at Wolfson College, University of Oxford.

AWa

Supunpasaj Supasiri (*b.* 1948), Thai short story writer, memoirist. Supunpasaj first published in her native Thai as a schoolgirl and by the 1970s had developed a dedicated following as a biting humorist. By contrast, 'The Umbrella' (1993), her first short story in English, written as a 44 year-old Harvard summer student, is a touching memoir about the death of her grandfather when she was 9 years old. The title story of her collection *The Umbrella and Other Stories* (1998), it received second prize in the 1993 UNESCO-PEN International competition for non-native English writers. With no college degree, Supunpasaj wryly describes herself as a 'housewife and storyteller' interested in recording fast-disappearing traditional Thai customs and rituals. Critical readers, however, see in her stories powerful depictions of socially approved sexual and educational inequalities in a Thai-Asian context. While her themes are Thai with an upper-class perspective, her fresh, vivid imagery transcends cultural differences. Her spare English style exhibits poetic cadences along with a true ear for dialogue. Although her English output to date is still small, her stories are widely used in classroom teaching, giving her considerable influence on younger readers.

NM

Sutherland, Efua Theodora (1924–1996), Ghanaian playwright, activist. Born Theodora Olivia at Cape Coast to Harry Peter Morgue and Harriet Efua Maria Parker,

Sutherland was raised by her grandmother Araba Mansa. She studied at Homerton College, Cambridge University and the School of Oriental and African Studies, University of London. In 1954, she married William Sutherland, an African-American educator living in Ghana; they had three children. An inspiring educator, writer, and developer of experimental and community theater, she joined the Institute of African Studies in 1963. Among her credits are the founding of the Ghana National Theatre, the Ghana Society of Writers, the Ghana Experimental Theatre, the Ghana Drama Studio and *Okyeame*, a literary magazine. Her advocacy of children's rights and education culminated in the Children's Drama Development Project in the late 1970s and her work as founding chair of the National Commission on Children in the 1980s. Her best-known plays are *Edufa* (1962), *Foriwa* (1967), and *The Marriage of Anansewaa* (1975). She was awarded an honorary doctorate by the University of Ghana in 1991 and the Arts Critics and Reviewers Association of Ghana Flag Star Award in 1995.

NDII

Suwanni Sukhontha (Suwanni Sukhonthiang), (1932–1984), Thai fiction writer. Suwanni Sukontha was born in Phitsanulok province where her father practiced medicine. She studied and taught fine arts at Silapakorn University in Bangkok during the 1950s. In the early 1960s, following the success of her short story writing, she left her teaching career and became a full-time writer. Suwanni was noted for her profound understanding of women's psyche and her use of 'brush stroke' technique to create rich imagery. In her novel *Khao Chue Karn* ('His Name is Karn'), which won the SEATO Literary Award in 1971, she depicts the predicament of a frustrated young wife whose womanly needs are completely ignored by her husband, an idealistic doctor who chooses to work in a small village in the middle of nowhere. In some of her best-known works, two of which won the National Book Award in 1972 and 1976, she draws on personal experience to portray the turbulent romantic lives of the female protagonists. Her short stories have been translated into English and Japanese and are popular among international readers. In 1984, Suwanni was stabbed to death in the midst of a Bangkok traffic jam by two young men apparently attempting to hijack her car.

NM

Swir, Anna (1909–1984), Polish poet, playwright. Born Anna Swirszczynska – the signature appended to Polish editions of her verses – the poet had her surname shortened to Swir in the West when two volumes of her poetry (*Happy As a Dog's Tail* [1985] and *Talking to My Body* [1996]) appeared in English translations by the 1980 Nobel prize laureate Czeslaw Milosz, in collaboration with Leonard Nathan. The daughter of a painter, Swir could not afford to pursue her strong interest in art, and graduated from Warsaw University in 1932 with a degree in Polish literature. She published her first book *Wiersze i proza* ('Poems and Prose') in 1932. During World War II she held a series of menial jobs and served as a nurse in the Warsaw Uprising in 1944. She moved to Cracow in 1946. It took Swir exactly thirty years to shape her war experiences into verse form. *Building the Barricade* (1974; bilingual edition, 1979) is a chilling report of life in Nazi-occupied Warsaw, written in precise, sparse language. Her controversial lyrics about female life have garnered her considerable attention. Included in five volumes of poetry published between 1958 and 1985, they represent the woman's body, sexuality, physiology, childbirth, rape, and physical abuse in an unmediated, graphic manner. The author, also, of plays and children's literature, Swir served as director of the Children's Theater in Cracow. Additional English translations of her poems appear in the collection *Fat*

Like the Sun (1986) and in several anthologies.

JB

Syal, Meera (*b.* 1963), British-Indian screenwriter, novelist. Self-described 'British Indian,' Syal was born in the mining town of Essington, near Wolverhampton, to an accountant and a schoolteacher from the Punjab. She describes in affectionate but clear-eyed detail the experience of growing up in the only Asian family in town in *Anita and Me* (1996), her first novel, which won the Betty Trask Award for its poignant mixture of humour, nostalgia, and lost innocence. She read English and drama at Manchester University, and was a successful actress before, irked by the 'boring' roles available to Asian actresses, she began to write her own. Her screenplays 'explode' stereotypes of Asian women. *My Sister Wife* (1992) stars a Westernized, sophisticated British Pakistani woman who chooses to become a wealthy businessman's second wife. The Asian lady-cabdriver of *It's Not Unusual* (1996) adores rock star Tom Jones. A surprising crossover success, the film *Bhaji on the Beach* (1993) follows a group of Asian women on a day-trip to Blackpool. It was both criticised and acclaimed by British Indians for considering controversial issues such as racism and domestic abuse within the Asian community. Syal's hilarious skits for the radio and TV show *Goodness Gracious Me!* (1998) have proven equally popular among all British ethnicities. Her second novel is *Life Isn't All Ha Ha Hee Hee* (1999).

SIy

Szymborska, Wislawa (*b.* 1923), Polish poet. Nobel prize winner in 1996, Szymborska was born in Bnin, near Poznan, in western Poland. A Cracow resident since 1931, she studied Polish literature and sociology at the Jagiellonian University. Her marriage to poet Adam Wlodek in 1948 lasted six years, whereas her liaison with the prose writer Kornal Filipowicz ended only with his death in 1990. Szymborska was poetry editor of the Cracow literary weekly *Zycie Literackie* (Literary Life) from 1953 to 1981 and wrote tongue-in-cheek reviews subsequently published in two volumes, *Lektury nadobowiązkowe* ('Non-compulsory Reading,' 1973, 1981). Her first poem was published in 1945 and her first collection *Dlatego żyjemy* ('That's Why We Live') in 1952, but she views her true debut as the third volume *Wołanie do Yeti* ('Calling Out to Yeti,' 1957). Two of her collections are particularly significant: *People on a Bridge* (1986) and *Koniec i początek* ('The End and the Beginning,' 1993). In them Szymborska achieves unparalleled mastery at delving into philosophical and ethical dilemmas by asking deceptively simple questions, frequently sparked by a mundane, everyday situation or detail. The language of her poetry is lucid and spare, while the ironic, analytical tone often turns playful or outright comic. For English translations, see *Sounds, Feelings, Thoughts* (1981), *View with a Grain of Sand* (1995), *Nothing Twice/Nic dwa razy* (1997), a bilingual edition, and *Poems New and Collected 1957–1997* (1999), which includes her Nobel prize acceptance speech.

JB

T

Tadjo, Véronique (b. 1955), Côte d'Ivoire (Ivory Coast) poet, novelist. Born in Paris and raised in Côte d'Ivoire, Tadjo graduated with a BA in English from the Université Nationale de Côte d'Ivoire in 1978, where she now teaches. She earned a master's degree and PhD in English with a specialization in African-American literature at the Sorbonne. She is married and has two sons. She entered the literary world with *Laterite* (1984), a book that can be read as a collection of poems or as a single long poem. This book won the Prize of the ACCT (Agence de Cooperation Culturelle et Technique) in 1983. Her first novel *A vol d'oiseau* ('As the Crow Flies,'1986), is a deeply original, unclassifiable piece made of ninety-two vignettes. Her second novel *Le royaume aveugle* ('The Kingdom of the Blind,' 1990) is an allegorical work which sets a love story in the midst of political turmoil and moral decay. Tadjo is also well-known for her children's books which she illustrates herself with exquisite, colorful drawings. Among the books translated in English are *Lord of the Dance: An African Retelling* (1988), *The Lucky Grain of Corn* (1996), and *Mamy Wata and the Monster* (1997). She has two forthcoming works: a book of poetry, *A mi-chemin* ('Half-Way Through'), and a novel, *Champs de bataille et d'amour* ('Battlefields and Fields of Love').

IAD'A

Tafdrup, Pia (b. 1952), Danish poet, playwright. After receiving her BA from the University of Copenhagen in 1977, Tafdrup made her debut in 1981 with the poetry collection *Når det går en hul på engel* ('When an Angel's Been Grazed'). A prolific poet, she followed with almost an annual collection through 1988, then again in 1992 and 1994. She is married and has two sons. She has written two plays, *Døden i bjergene* ('Death in the Mountains,' 1988) and *Jorden er blå* ('The Earth is Blue,' 1991), and is also a translator and editor. Her work has appeared in over forty literary journals and nearly as many anthologies. She is a recipient of many grants and awards. In 1989 two collections appeared in English: *Ten Poems* and *Spring Tide* (1985). Taking the rhythm of the body and its desire as a point of departure, her poetry imitates, transgresses, and redefines the body's language. While body and sexuality constitute an important, indeed crucial, part of her poetry, she also explores broader social issues like war and loneliness. By referring in her poetry to other contemporary or earlier poets, and by being an active participant in the debate about art and culture, Tafdrup positions herself squarely in the contemporary poetic network rooted in tradition.

MŽ

Takahashi Takako (b. 1932), Japanese

novelist, fiction writer. Takahashi received an unusually extensive education for a Japanese woman of her time, graduating from Kyoto University in 1954, and obtaining a master's degree in French literature from the same institution four years later. She worked primarily on essays and translations until her short story 'Kodomo Sama' ('Honorable Child') appeared in 1969. She soon published other stories, including 'Byōbō' ('Boundlessness,' 1970) and 'Congruent Figures' (1971). Both works present female protagonists' disturbingly ambivalent fantasies of relations with children or other women in their family group. In 1975, she received baptism as a Catholic convert. Many of her subsequent works, including Lonely Woman (1977), which won the Joryū Bungaku Prize, and 'Kou' ('To Yearn,' 1985), which won the Kawabata Yasunari Prize, display a shift in psychological emphasis to more abstract portrayals of heroines' spiritual isolation. In other stories, a motif of spiritual quest combines with that of erotic encounter. Like 'Higi' ('Secret Rites'), such works often describe ecstatic, sado-masochistic unions between a middle-aged woman and an adolescent boy. Takahashi entered a convent in France in 1985. In 1990, however, she resumed secular life in Japan, and has voiced an interest in writing new fictional works.

AAl

Takenishi Hiroko (b. 1929), Japanese novelist, critic. Concern with warfare based on her own experience and rediscovery of classic Japanese literature form the double focus of Takenishi's literature. Born in Hiroshima, she attended Hiroshima Girls' High School and witnessed the August 6, 1945 atomic bomb explosion. After Japan's defeat, she earned a BA in Japanese literature from Waseda University and became an editor. Her writing career began with Ookan-no ki ('Literary Travels to the Past,' 1964), a collection of essays that reread Japanese literary classics, such as The Tale of Genji, as contemporary literature. As a fiction writer, she debuted with 'The Rite' (1963), a story that depicts the life of a female atomic bomb survivor in postwar Japanese society. She established herself with Kangensai ('Music Festival,' 1978), which takes place in Hiroshima during and after World War II. Another novel Heitai yado ('The War Barracks,' 1981) portrays, from a young boy's point of view, life at an inn which boards soldiers on their way to the war, and invites the reader to contemplate the nature of everyday life in wartime through its low-key description of military men.

KKa

Takvam, Marie (b. 1926), Norwegian poet. Raised on a small farm in western Norway, Takvam had 'roots in the earth' that nurtured nature imagery for poems about seasons and life cycles, joy and suffering, love and conflict. But it was her urban experiences as a psychology student in Oslo and her involvement with literary circles there that inspired her to become a poet. The cosmic context of love and longing in her debut work Dåp under sju stjerner ('Baptism under Seven Stars,' 1952) persists through the decade alongside harsher details of everyday reality and the increasingly destructive effects of technology and capitalism. 'Scars of Life,' the title poem of Merke etter liv (1962), affirms maturing, yet maturing experiences, but other poems about flawed love and motherhood reveal bitterness and indignation. Collections from the late 1960s and 1970s, including Brød og tran ('Bread and Cod Liver Oil,' 1969), decry social injustice and encouraged the growing women's movement, but contain undertones of resignation and acceptance of the formulaic nature of life and art. The final collections from 1980 to 1990 (excerpts in Contemporary Norwegian Women's Writing) revisit earlier themes, ever mindful of life's transient pleasures and the sustaining power of words.

FS

Tamaro, Susanna (*b.* 1957), Italian novelist, short story writer, children's writer. Born in Trieste, the author uses the solitude of the cityscape and of the Carso, the surrounding countryside, as foil to the essential isolation of her works' principal characters. Trieste and environs furnish the setting for her epistolary novel *Go Where Your Heart Takes You* (1994), which has sold more copies than any other book in the history of Italian literature, been translated into 34 languages, and was made into a successful film in 1995. Although the author's reputation was founded on the creation of a multi-generational chorus of women's voices, *Anima mundi* (1997) signals a shift in perspective. This best-seller, about the friendship between two men in three different phases of their lives, has been attacked by some critics as 'anti-communist' and by others as 'fascist,' charges the author vehemently denies. With a degree in teaching and a background as an animator, Tamaro's work also includes children's literature – her first published work was *La testa fra le nuvole* ('Head in the Clouds,' 1989) – and a concern for the well-being of children is evident in the 1995 collection of adult short stories *For Solo Voice*.

EN

Tan, Amy (*b.* 1952), US novelist. A first-generation American, Tan was born in Oakland, California to Chinese immigrants who had emigrated from Beijing in 1949. She received a BA in 1973 and an MA in linguistics in 1974 from San Jose State University. She married Louis de Mattei in 1974. She worked as a freelance technical writer and traveled to China with her mother in 1984 before writing her first book, the popular *The Joy Luck Club* (1989), which was nominated for both a National Book Critics Circle Award and a *Los Angeles Times* Book Award. The novel, which was made into a film in 1993 (for which Tan wrote the screenplay), weaves together the stories of four Chinese-American mothers and their first-generation daughters, exploring the cultural misunderstandings in their often difficult relationships. Her next novel *The Kitchen God's Wife* (1991), in which a mother recounts to her daughter a parable of survival in wartime China, is also concerned with relations between generations and the importance of family stories in forging one's identity. *The Hundred Secret Senses* (1995) incorporates ghost stories into the main narrative, which is set in both the US and in China, and which concerns two half-sisters, one Chinese, the other Chinese-American. Tan has also written *The Moon Lady* (1992), a book for children.

DVT

Taraqqi, Goli (*b.* 1939), Iranian novelist, short story writer. Taraqqi grew up in a period of transition and modernization in Iran. Her father was a member of parliament, and a publisher, editor, and journalist; her mother was from a cultured family. She studied in universities in the US and Iran, and earned a position at Tehran University teaching courses in philosophy, myth, and symbolism. She has published a number of short stories about the urban life before and after the 1979 Iranian Revolution. She first gained fame with a collection of short stories titled *Man Ham Che Gevara Hatam* ('I Too am Che Guevara,' 1969). Her experiences with the contradictions between modern life and religion are reflected in her *Winter Sleep* (1994), a short novel which delves into the individual psyches of eight urban middle-class 'friends' and illustrates, in an unusual and symbolic manner, the disorientation and 'anomie' resulting from Iran's rapid modernization of the 1960s under the Shah. One of her short stories 'The Great Lady of My Soul' (1982) won the Contre-Ciel Short Story Prize. *Khatereh-ha-ye Parakandeh* ('Scattered Memories,' 1994) depicts the emotional world of alienated Iranians who deal with dislocation in their society and separation from their family due to the Iran–Iraq war.

KTa

Tawfīq, Saḥar (*b.* 1951), Egyptian short story writer. Born in Cairo, Tawfīq earned her degree in Arabic from al-Azhar University in 1974. She started her literary career in the early 1970s by publishing short stories in Egyptian and other Arab periodicals. She is a teacher of Arabic at a Cairo public school and has also taught in Saudi Arabia. She lives with her artist husband and their two children in Cairo. The characters in Tawfīq's stories are predominately women who suffer from alienation and a hostile environment while trying to cope with new realities. Often she resorts to creating a dream world as a framework for her stories. Her only anthology of short stories is *An Tanḥadir al-Shams* ('That the Sun Should Set,' 1985). *Points of the Compass* (1995) is a collection of stories that have been translated into English.

JTZ

Tekin, Latife (*b.* 1957), Turkish novelist. Tekin was born in the village of Karacefenk, near Kayseri. Her family moved to Istanbul in 1966, where she finished Beşiktaş High School. She recounts the effects of this move, after which her father quickly became working-class and eventually unemployed, in her autobiographical first novel *Sevgili Arsız Ölüm* ('Dear Cheeky Death,' 1983). The element of fantasy and the depiction of the inanimate world as living imbues this novel with the atmosphere of a fairy tale. *Berji Kristin: Tales from the Garbage Hills* (1983) portrays the difficult life in a squatter settlement from an insider's perspective which emphasizes the quiet dignity and the quirky humor of the people living there. *Gece Dersleri* ('Night Lessons,' 1986), which criticizes leftist revolutionary politics for attempting to speak for the poor without knowing or understanding them, was attacked by leftist critics. Tekin's critique of any ideology that claims to speak for others has led her to experiment with language since her first book. In *Buzdan Kılıçlar* ('Swords of Ice,' 1989), there is an attempt to create a totally different language for the poor, which will narrate their story, but will not reveal their secrets. Her latest novel *Aşk İşaretleri* ('Love Signs,' 1995) suggests that silence is the last repository of personal freedom and resistance.

SE

Telles, Lygia Fagundes (*b.* 1923), Brazilian novelist, short story writer. Born in São Paulo, Telles spent her childhood in many small towns before her family settled down in that state's capital. She has a son from her first marriage; divorced in 1961, she later married Paulo Emílio Salles Gomes, a film critic and writer. Her first book *Praia viva* ('Living Beach,' 1944) was followed by another volume of short stories *O cacto vermelho* ('The Red Cactus,' 1949), which won a prize from the Brazilian Academy of Letters. Her novel *The Marble Dance* (1954), about a young woman's development of a sense of identity, displays the main characteristics of her fiction: a concern with women's social situation and self-realization; psychological introspection; the creation of a language adequate to the expression of the character's reality; and the use of elements of the fantastic. Her novel *The Girl in the Photograph* (1973) portrays the political turmoil during the Brazilian military dictatorship through the eyes of three college-age female friends. In the novel *As horas nuas* ('Bare Hours,' 1989), the stories of *A noite escur e mais eu* ('The Dark Night and Me,' 1996), and other recent works, Telles continues to discuss women's condition in Brazil, addressing issues such as sexuality, abortion, and aging.

CF-P

Tennant, Emma (*b.* 1937), British novelist. Born in London, daughter of a wealthy titled businessman of Scottish descent, Tennant was educated at St Paul's Girls' School in London and a finishing school in Oxford. She published her first novel *The Colour of Rain* (1964) under the pseudonym Catherine Aydy. Her second novel *The Time of the Crack* (1973), a black comedy set in the future, establishes her distinctive postmodern style. Tennant appropriates and fractures a variety of genres in her explorations of social decay and historical change. Her perspective is feminist and satirical, her style innovative and imaginative. *The Last of the Country House Murders* (1975) is a detective story parody set in the future. *Hotel de Dream* (1976) also uses science fiction conventions and characteristically mingles reality and fantasy. She reworks Hogg's *Confessions of a Justified Sinner* in *The Bad Sister* (1978) and changes the gender of *Lord of the Flies* in *Queen of the Stones* (1982). *The Magic Drum* (1989) is a Gothic murder mystery. Other novels range from comedies of manner of the British upper class, such as *The House of Hospitalities* (1987), to the magic realism of *Wild Nights* (1979) and *Alice Fell* (1980), to a feminist revision of *Dr. Jekyll and Mr. Hyde* and sequels to *Pride and Prejudice* and *Sense and Sensibility*. Tennant has also published two memoirs – *Strangers* (1998), about her prominent family, and *Girlitude* (1999), about her own early life.

JEM

Tham, Hilary (*b.* 1946), Asian-American poet. Tham was born in Klang, Malaya, shortly after the end of the Japanese Occupation and the return of the British to Malaya. She graduated from the University of Malaya with an Upper Class Honours in English. She married an American, Joseph Ray Goldberg, and moved to the US in 1971 upon completing her postgraduate studies in American literature. She is now a US citizen, living in Arlington, Virginia. She is the author of five books of poetry and a book of memoirs and poems. She teaches poetry in high schools and is the recipient of numerous literary awards and fellowships. Her lively poetry, which employs startling and original language, deals with the traditions of two worlds – those of the Chinese and

the Jewish. Tham has moved away from the soul and identity searches evident in her pioneering works of poetry in the 1960s such as *No Gods Today* (1969), to promoting world peace, love, and understanding in her later works such as *Lane with No Name* (1997), *Tigerbone Wine* (1992), and *Bad Names for Women* (1989). Her persona 'Mrs. Wei' in *Bad Names for Women* is a delightful invention of a wise, old, diasporic Chinese matriarch living in the US who makes intelligent comments on and interpretations of the modern world she lives in.

NFAM

Tharu, Susie (*b.* 1943), Indian feminist cultural theorist. Born in Uganda and educated at Makerere University, Uganda, and at Oxford, Tharu is currently a professor in the Department of English at the Central Institute of English and Foreign Languages, Hyderabad. A scholar and activist, her research interests are in the areas of gender and caste, the teaching of English, cultural history and critical legal theory. Her current work is on citizenship in the field of the imaginary and includes essays titled 'The Impossible Subject: Caste in the Scene of Desire' and 'Citizenship and its Discontents.' Her major works as editor include the path-breaking two-volume anthology *Women Writing in India: 600 B.C. to the present* (1993; co-edited with K. Lalitha), *We Were Making History: Women in the Telengana People's Struggle* (1998; co-edited), and *Subject to Change: Literary Studies in the Nineties* (1998). A founding member of Stree Shakti Sangatana and Anveshi Research Centre for Women's Studies, Tharu was awarded the Jawaharlal Nehru Fellowship in 1994–6, and has been a visiting professor at a number of universities in India and abroad.

JK

Thomas, Audrey (*b.* 1935), Canadian novelist. Born in Binghamton, New York, Thomas was educated at Smith College, St

Andrews University, Scotland and the University of British Columbia (MA, 1963). She emigrated with her husband Ian Thomas to Canada in 1959. She lived in Ghana for two years, an experience that frequently informs her fiction. Her first collection of stories *Ten Green Bottles* was published in 1967. Her first novel *Mrs. Blood* was published in 1970, and portrays the psychological disintegration of a woman who suffers a miscarriage. Her feminist fiction is allusive, sophisticated, and experimental in narrative form and use of language. She is particularly interested in women being pushed to the edge, either due to personal or domestic circumstances, or because of social pressures. *Songs My Mother Taught Me* (1973) is a formally complex coming-of-age story about a girl who takes a summer job at a mental hospital. *Blown Figures* (1974), her most experimental novel, is a kind of narrative collage that depicts a woman's schizophrenia. The acclaimed and popular *Intertidal Life* (1984) traces a mother–daughter relationship against the background of their study of marine life. Her other novels include *Latakia* (1979), *Graven Images* (1993), *Coming Down from Wa* (1995), and *Isobel Gunn* (1999). Her short stories are collected in *Ladies and Escorts* (1977), *Real Mothers* (1981), *Goodbye Harold, Good Luck* (1986), and *The Wild Blue Yonder* (1990).

JEM

Thomyanti (Wimol Siriphaiboon), (*b.* 1945), Thai fiction writer. A native of Bangkok, Thomyanti was enrolled as a student at the Faculty of Commerce and Accountancy, Thommasat University, but she left the university to become a teacher of Thai language at St Joseph Convent School. She began writing short stories at the age of 14. By the age of 25 when her first novel *Nai Phan* ('In the Dream') was published, she had become one of the most popular novelists in Thailand. Her novel *Khu Kum* ('Star-Crossed Lovers,' 1979), with its World War II setting, in

which an idealistic young Japanese soldier and a young Thai woman become lovers, became a best-seller overnight. The TV series and film made from this novel were also instant successes. In addition to novels with romantic themes, Thomyanti's works also include novels which explore women's potential, human psychology, and spiritual and mystical forces in human existence. By royal command, her novel *Perils of Passion* has been translated into English in order to be given to foreign dignitaries. To date, Thomyanti has a hundred short stories and eighty-five novels to her credit.

NM

Thon, Melanie Rae (*b.* 1957), US novelist, short story writer. Born in Kalispell, Montana, Thon was educated at the University of Michigan, where she earned a BA in 1980, and Boston University, where she earned an MA in 1982. She has taught creative writing at Syracuse University and Ohio State University. Her first novel *Meteors in August* was published in 1990. She followed with a critically acclaimed collection of short stories *Girls in the Grass* (1991), which established her characteristic subject matter, style, and themes. Hers are bleak, intense, interior stories of the hard and desperate lives of runaway adolescents, drug addicts, unwed mothers, and prostitutes in the American West and East Coast cities. But Thon tells these stories with psychological insight and lyrical, beautiful prose. Her second novel *Iona Moon* (1993) concerns the hard luck adventures of a teenage girl growing up in the 1960s in rural Idaho, who goes on the road after her mother dies of cancer. Thon's second collection of short stories is *First, Body* (1996). She has won the Whiting Writers' Award and was named one of *Granta*'s Best Young American Novelists in 1996.

JEM

Thorup, Kirsten (*b.* 1942), Danish novelist, poet. Thorup's debut came with a collection of poems, *Indeni-Udenfor* ('Inside-Outside,' 1967), followed by a collection of stories, followed in turn by *Love From Trieste* (1969). In her novel *Baby* (1973), she experimented with both content and form; the stark, seemingly disinterested portrayal of marginals who vegetate amidst the Danish welfare state is a critical representation of the symptoms of the modern, structured, and alienating way of living. A highly complex and original writer, she investigates the gap between our own expectations and those of others as well as the importance of utopian visions and how lamentable life is without them. In her novels *Lille Jonna* ('Little Jonna,' 1977) and *Den lange sommer* ('The Long Summer,' 1979), the focus is on the 1950s and early 1960s in the provinces. The extraordinary *Himmel og helvede* ('Heaven and Hell,' 1982), set in the urban milieu, examines the utopian project of the late 1960s. Looking backwards with *Den yterste grense* ('The Outer Limit,' 1987), Thorup both recognizes the limits of utopian vision and affirms its importance for human existence. She is also the author of radio and TV plays, and film scripts, and the recipient of many literary awards.

MŽ

Tie Ning (*b*. 1957), Chinese fiction writer. Born in Beijing, Tie Ning graduated from senior middle school in Baoding, Hebei Province in 1975. In the same year she set off for the countryside to experience rural life. In 1979 she was transferred to the Baoding branch of the Chinese Federation of Art and Literature. She is now a professional writer as well as a council member of the Chinese Writers' Association. Her first influential story 'Ah, Fragrant Snow' (1982), which won a national award as the best short story of the year, truly refreshed the literary world of the time. It tells a touching story of a young girl in a remote mountain area who is prompted to dreaming of the outside world by seeing the trains passing through

her village. Another story 'Haystacks' (1986) explores love, desire, and marriage among the villagers and young students who are sent to the countryside during the Cultural Revolution. Her semi-autobiographical novel *Meigui men* ('The Gate of Roses,' 1989) best demonstrates Tie Ning's superb and sophisticated manner of structuring stories. Set against the background of turbulent twentieth-century China, it presents the complex psychological and physical development of Si Yiwen and her granddaughter Meimei, two women of different times and social backgrounds.

LW

Tiempo, Edith L. (*b*. 1919), Philippine poet, novelist. Born in Nueva Vizcaya to a Gaddang mother and an Ilocano father who was a mining engineer, Tiempo grew up in various parts of the Philippines and later used these places in her stories. Her first novel *A Blade of Fern* (1979) is set in a Mindanao village and explores the problems of gold miners. In her subsequent novels *His Native Coast* (1979), *The Alien Corn* (1992), and *One, Tilting Leaves* (1995), she dramatizes the endurance of the spirit. Her short stories in *Abide, Joshua and Other Stories* (1964) celebrate the will to transcendence. Writing in the spirit of the Romantic tradition and using the style of modern metaphysical poetry, her poems in *Tracks of Babylon and Other Poems* (1966), *The Charmer's Box* (1992), and *Beyond, Extensions* (1993) evoke the power of art in providing the existential point of balance between despair and hope. Tiempo married Philippine novelist Edilberto K. Tiempo; they have a daughter and a son. She graduated from Silliman University, Dumaguete City in 1947 and received an international writing fellowship (1947–50) from the University of Iowa, where she also finished her master's degree. She earned her PhD from the University of Denver in 1958. As director of the thirty-eight-year-old National Writers Summer Workshop in Dumaguete City, she continues to guide Filipino writers in the craft of creative writing.

ME

Tikkanen, Märta (*b.* 1935), Finland-Swedish novelist, editor. Tikkanen grew up in Helsinki, graduated from Helsinki University in 1958, and worked as a journalist, teacher, and principal. While working at *Hufvudstadsbladet*, she met her second husband, the artist and novelist Henrik Tikkanen. In 1970 she published her first book, *Nu imorron* ('Now Tomorrow') followed by *Ingenmansland* ('No Man's Land') in 1972. These novels of marriage questioned women's roles, the possibility of liberation, and the importance of being seen. *Manrape* (1975) won international attention and was made into a film by Jörn Donner. Tikkanen's autobiographical prose poem *The Love Story of the Century* (1978) tells the story of her marriage to an alcoholic. While displaying feelings of love and guilt, hope and despair, the prose poem also questions female roles in a patriarchal world. The book, a source of inspiration for Scandinavian women, won the Nordic Women's Literary Prize in 1979. Both *Mörkret som ger glädjen djup* ('The Darkness that Gives Happiness Depth,' 1981) and *Sofias egen bok* ('Sofia's Own Book,' 1982) focus on motherhood. Using her own life, Tikkanen continues her investigation of love and desire, dependence and survival in *Rödluvan* ('Little Red Riding Hood,' 1986) and *Storfångaren* ('The Great Catcher,' 1989).

GE-C

Tjitrawasita, Totilawati (1945–1982), Indonesian fiction writer. Born in Kediri, East Java, Tjitrawasita was the second of thirteen children. An aspiring journalist, in 1967 she became assistant editor of a Javanese-language weekly magazine called *Jaya Baya*, and in 1970 she won the national Zakse Award for young journalists. Her collection of short stories *Sebuah Cinta Sekolah Rakyat* ('A School Crush,'

1977) was awarded first prize for fiction by the Book of the Year Foundation. Her contribution to the arts, specifically through her membership in the Surabaya Arts Council, was recognized in 1979 when she was made an honorary citizen of the City of Surabaya. Tjitrawasita's short story 'Jakarta' (1976), like many of her stories, was first published in Javanese in 1972. It is a poignant story about a humble village schoolteacher who makes an arduous and expensive trip to the capital to visit his brother, who has become a high-ranking government official. The breakdown in familial ties and the treachery of power are portrayed through the brother's refusal to see his country brother, due to his busy schedule.

PA

Tlali, Miriam (*b.* 1933), South African novelist, journalist, short story writer. Born in Doornfontein, Johannesburg, Tlali grew up in South Africa and attended the University of Witwatersrand until it was closed to black people. She completed her education at the University of Roma, Lesotho. She worked for a time as a clerk in a hire-purchase store, the basis for her first novel. A positive experience at the Iowa Writers' Workshop kindled her love of writing into a full time career. She wrote her first autobiographical novel *Muriel at Metropolitan* in 1968, but it was not published until 1976. Her second novel *Amandla* (1980) is based on the school children's rebellion in Soweto in 1976. Both novels were banned in South Africa until the lifting of apartheid as a system of government in South Africa. Tlali writes a regular column 'Soweto Speaking' in an arts journal, *Staffrider*. Some of her journalism is included in the collection *Mihloti* (1984), along with interviews and samples of her travel writing. In 1989, Tlali published *Footprints in the Quag* (called *Soweto Stories* in Britain), a collection of short stories based on the oral tradition.

AUA

Tokareva, Viktoriia Samoilovna (*b.* 1937), Russian prose writer, playwright, scriptwriter. Tokareva abandoned both her early training as a pianist at the Leningrad Music School and her acting classes at the Moscow State Institute of Cinematography for writing. She achieved instant acclaim with her first story in 1964, published her first collection *O tom, chego ne bylo* ('About Things that Didn't Happen') in 1969, and has released a steady stream of fiction ever since. A prolific scriptwriter for film and television, she has adapted her own and others' works for the screen, including *I. Grekova's Ship of Widows.* Discrepancy is Tokareva's major theme, whether between ways and means, expectation and realization, ideals and empirical reality, or style and essence. Relying on irony, lightness of touch, plot reversals, paired contrasting characters, naturalizing metaphors, and inconclusiveness, she portrays individuals seeking authenticity and happiness in the teeth of human fallibility and discouraging circumstances, as in *Nothing Special* (1983). With *glasnost* and *perestroika*, Tokareva's fiction has acquired a topical flavor and moralistic overtones, illustrated in 'Pasha and Pavlushka' (1987) and 'First Try' (1989). *The Talisman and Other Stories* contains English translations of her stories. Additional English versions may be found in anthologies of contemporary Russian women's fiction.

HG

Tolstaya, Tatyana (*b.* 1951), Russian short story writer. A Leningrader from an illustrious literary family, Tolstaya specialized in classics at Leningrad State University, graduated in 1974, and moved to Moscow, where she worked at the Nauka publishing house. After her literary debut with the story 'On the Golden Porch' (1983), during *glasnost* she acquired international fame when the slim collection of her stories by the same title (1987) was translated into ten languages. Since 1988 she has divided her time between Moscow and the

US, where she has taught, lectured on Russian culture, and written review essays for mainstream publications. Tolstaya's fictional oeuvre consists of twenty-one stories, all but one translated in *On the Golden Porch* and *Sleepwalker in a Fog* (1992). These inordinately condensed narratives meditate, in vivid, trope-saturated prose, on such universal concerns as time, language, imagination, and memory. With the aid of myth, folklore, and numerous intertexts, she muses on the elusive significance of a given life in 'Sonia' (1984); the isolation of the individual personality in 'Sweet Dreams, Son' (1986); the conflicting claims of spirit and matter in 'Hunting the Wooly Mammoth' (1985); the complex interplay between perception and language in 'Night' (1987); and the transforming power of imagination and memory in 'Sweet Shura' (1985). A highly colorful, kaleidoscopic style is her authorial signature, with lush, metaphor-freighted sentences marked by perpetual shifts in perspective, voice, and mood, elaborate instrumentation, alternation between poetic lyricism and irony, between elevated diction and colloquialisms. A stylist par excellence, Tolstaya spotlights the dazzling capabilities of the Russian language in a mode that reviews the aesthetics of Russia's 1920s.

HG

Tomioka Taeko (*b.* 1935), Japanese poet, novelist, fiction writer. Born in Osaka, Tomioka started writing poetry in 1954 shortly after she entered college to study English. Her first collection of poetry *Henrei* ('Returning the Gift,' 1957) received the Mr. H. Prize. After teaching high school, she relocated to Tokyo with her lover, painter Masuo Ikeda, in 1960. While continuing to write poetry, she translated Gertrude Stein's *Three Lives*, wrote a screenplay, and published an autobiography and essay collections, before turning to fiction writing in 1971. Though prolific in all these genres, she may be best known to the general reading public through her fiction, some of which is unmistakably autobiographical. For example, 'Family in Hell' (1974) and its sequels feature a female protagonist whose parents are street-smart but unsophisticated, and who leaves her native Osaka in order to follow her painter boyfriend to Tokyo. One of Tomioka's strengths as a fiction writer resides in her ability to catch people's live dialogues and to add theatrical vividness to them. In later works such as 'Namiutsu tochi' ('The Undulating Land,' 1983), she departs from autobiographical material to create contemporary narratives in which potentials of women's sexuality are candidly explored.

TK

Torrevillas, Rowena Tiempo (*b.* 1951), Philippine poet, fiction writer, essayist. Born in Dumaguete City, Torrevillas earned an AB in 1971, an MA in creative writing in 1978, and a PhD in English literature in 1983, all from Silliman University, Dumaguete City. She was also the associate program administrator of the International Writing Program, University of Iowa, until 1998. Her poetic voice spans the relaxed and beautiful university town of Dumaguete and the Midwestern US where she spent many years of her youth. Being the daughter of Edilberto and *Edith Tiempo, two famous literary figures who came from different parts of the Philippines and hence spoke different dialects, has given her insight into the versatile workings of language. Though she initially considered herself an 'other' in the US, she eventually recognized the unrelenting riches of being the recipient of two languages. Poetry has served as a creative locus for this rough negotiation which joyfully contains her native wonder in a foreign tongue. Her publications include two volumes of poetry, *Mountain Sacraments/Selected Poems* (1991) and *The Sea-Gypsies Stay* (1999); *Upon the Willows and Other Stories* (1980), a collection of short stories; and two collections of

essays, *Flying Over Kansas* (1998) and *The World Comes to Iowa* (1987), co-edited with Paul Engle.

DTR

Townsend, Sue (*b.* 1946), British novelist, playwright. Born in Leicester, England, Townsend left school at the age of 14. She married and started a family at a young age, and supported her family with menial positions before beginning to write dramas. Her plays, of which she has written over a dozen, are marked by social commentary and sensitivity to class issues. They include *Womberang* (1980), which critiques England's socialized medicine; *Bazaar and Rummage* (1982), which focuses on the mental health system; and *Groping for Words* (1983), which is about adult illiteracy. Her best-selling first novel *The Secret Diary of Adrian Mole, Aged 13¾* (1982), introduced the feisty and self-dramatizing title character who has remained central to Townsend's writing for over a decade. The popular sequels, which include *The Growing Pains of Adrian Mole* (1984), *Adrian Mole: The Wilderness Years* (1993), *Adrian Mole: The Lost Years* (1994), and *Adrian Mole: The Cappucino Years* (1999), trace the adolescence and maturation of Adrian, whose witty and astute observations offer a scathing satire of Thatcher's Britain. The Adrian Mole series has been adapted for stage, television, and radio. Townsend is also the author of the novels *Rebuilding Coventry: A Tale of Two Cities* (1988), *The Queen and I* (1992), and *Ghost Children* (1997).

DVT

Traba, Marta (1930–1983), Argentine-Colombian art critic, poet, novelist. Born in Buenos Aires to Spanish immigrants, Traba studied literature at the Universidad de Buenos Aires, graduating in 1948. Between 1949 and 1958, she lived in Paris and Rome where she pursued a career in art criticism. She married Colombian journalist Alberto Zalamea in 1950, and in 1958 she arrived in Colombia, where she became a prominent, and at times controversial, figure. She was a professor at the Universidad de América, and promoted the founding of a museum of modern art in Bogota, which was inaugurated in 1962. In 1966 she published her first novel *Las ceremonias del verano* ('Summer Ceremonies'), which won the prestigious Casa de las Américas literary award. In 1969 she married Uruguayan literary critic Angel Rama. They lived in Venezuela and the US. Moving to Paris in 1983, they both died that year in an airplane accident near the Madrid airport. In 1981 Traba published her most widely read novel *Mothers and Shadows*, an examination of life under the 1976 Argentine military regime. She explored the theme of exile and life as an outsider in two novels, *En cualquier lugar* ('Any Place,' 1984) and *Casa sin fin* ('House with no End,' 1988), published posthumously.

MGP

Tremain, Rose (*b.* 1943), British novelist, short story writer. Born in London, Tremain studied literature at the Sorbonne before obtaining a BA with honors from the University of East Anglia. She worked as a French teacher before publishing a biography of Stalin and *The Fight for Freedom for Women* (1971), a study of the suffrage movement in England. Her first novel *Sadler's Birthday* (1976) tells the story of a retired butler who inherits his master's mansion. As in many of her novels, the protagonist is lonely and alienated but feels too paralyzed to imagine a new life. Though her characters and settings are varied, Tremain consistently depicts, with sensitivity and humor, the pain of the isolated or the disenfranchised. *The Cupboard* (1981) juxtaposes the uninspired life of a reporter with the meaningful life of an elderly suffragist whom he interviews. *Letter to Sister Benedicta* (1978), in which a woman reviews her life by writing letters to a childhood teacher, and *The Swimming Pool Season* (1985) both feature adults restrained by unfulfilling marriages. *Restoration* (1989) takes place in the court of King Charles II, and in *Music and Silence* (1999) multiple plots are woven around the central figure of King Christian IV of Denmark. *Sacred Country* (1992; James Tait Black Memorial Prize) charts a transsexual's thirty-year transition from girl to man. *The Way I Found Her* (1997), a coming-of-age thriller, is narrated by a 13-year-old boy. Tremain has published several volumes of short stories, with her *Collected Short Stories* appearing in 1996.

DVT

Trollope, Joanna (*b.* 1943), British novelist. Born in Gloucestershire, Trollope was educated at St Hugh's College, Oxford and received an MA in English in 1965. She has been married twice and has two children. She is a descendent of the nineteenth-century novelist Anthony Trollope, and like him, is prolific and popular. Her best-selling novels are about middle-class people living in English villages, the plots set in motion when a crisis disrupts their ordinary lives. The appeal of her fiction lies in its strong characterizations, realistic and minutely detailed descriptions, and the author's sympathetic attitude. Her first novel *Eliza Stanhope* was published in 1978. Other novels include *The Choir* (1986), *A Village Affair* (1989), *A Passionate Man* (1990), *The Rector's Wife* (1991), and *The Men and the Girls* (1992). In her recent novels, she has turned toward a more ambitious and morally ambiguous realism; serious critical attention has followed. *The Best of Friends* (1995) chronicles the breakup of a marriage and its implications for three generations of two families. In *Next of Kin* (1996), Trollope shifts to a different milieu and a darker mood in a story about a dairy farmer coming to terms with the death of his wife. *Other People's Children* (1998) explores the dynamics of stepfamilies.

JEM

Trotzig, Birgitta (*b.* 1929), Swedish novelist, essayist. Born Birgitta Kjellén in Gothenburg, Trotzig moved to Kristianstad, a town in southern Sweden, which later provided the setting for several novels. In 1949 she returned to Gothenburg to study literature and art history, establishing herself as a critic. She married the painter Ulf Trotzig and they settled in Paris in 1955; the same year, Trotzig converted to Catholicism. The proximity of the Algerian War formed her and influenced her writing, which is marked by a religious and ethical conviction. She uses stylized and poetic language while looking deep into the human soul. She returned to Sweden in 1969. With *De utsatta* ('The Exposed,' 1957), she made her breakthrough. Using the landscape of the war-torn province Skåne in the seventeenth century, the novel depicts suffering, betrayal, greed, and the need for redemption seen through the priest Isaac Graa and his family. Continuing the investigation of human suffering and the meaning of life, *Dykungens dotter* ('The Marsh King's Daughter,' 1985), the title taken from Hans Christian Andersen's fairy tale, contrasts individual needs with societal demands. In 1985, Trotzig received the Pilot Prize for her oeuvre. She has been a member of the Swedish Academy since 1993. Excerpts from her work in English translation can be found in several anthologies.

GE C

Tsushima Yuko (*b.* 1947), Japanese novelist, fiction writer. Born in Tokyo as youngest daughter of renowned writer Osamu Dazai, Tsushima began writing fiction while in college, debuting with 'Rekuiemu – Inu to Otona no tame ni' ('Requiem – for Dogs and Adults') in 1969. She has won numerous major literary prizes for her fiction, which focuses on family relationships with unambiguously autobiographical details, such as dead or otherwise absent father figures, retarded male siblings who resemble her beloved real-life brother, and women single-handedly raising children born out of wedlock. Her strong desire to reconnect to her father, who committed suicide when she was an infant, sometimes takes the form of a fictional incestuous relationship, as in *Hi no kawa no hotori de* ('On the Bank of the River of Fire,' 1983). Much critical attention has been paid to her portrayal of women's experiences of motherhood with particular emphasis on its biological aspects of pregnancy and childbirth, as in *Child of Fortune* (1978). Mother of an illegitimate son as well as a daughter, Tsushima problematizes society's definition of motherhood, oftentimes depicting mothers relating to their children on an animal-like, instinctive level, or presenting women who put their heterosexual relationships before their maternal responsibilities.

TK

Ṭūqān, Fadwā (*b.* 1917), Palestinian poet. Born in Nablus, Palestine to a conservative landowning family, Ṭūqān was forced to quit school at the age of 11. Her brother tutored her in the art of poetry. Eventually a prisoner in her own home, she began to read widely. She deepened her knowledge of English by taking courses at Oxford University (1962–3). Her early poetry, as evident in her first collection *Waḥdī ma'a al-Ayyām* ('Alone with the Days,' 1952), is romantic in nature, reflecting an anxious and alienated soul yearning for love. Whereas traditional forms are employed in this collection, she started writing in the free verse tradition with her second collection *Wajadtuhā* ('I Found It,' 1956). After the June 1967 war, her poetry became more politicized, centering upon the Palestinian struggle for self-determination, as is evident in *Al-Layl wa-al-Fursān* ('Night and the Knights,' 1969) and *'Alā Qimmat al-Dunyā Waḥīdan* ('Alone on Top of the World,' 1973). In her autobiography *The Mountainous Journey* (1985), she recounts the story of her life from a miserable childhood to a rude awakening with the 1967 war. *Al-Riḥla al-As'ab* ('The Tougher Journey,' 1993) continues the story, but the emphasis shifts to the public sphere. Ṭūqān has traveled extensively in the Arab world, Europe, China, and Russia. She remains single and lives in Nablus.

JTZ

Turkka, Sirkka (*b*. 1939), Finnish poet. Turkka was born in Helsinki, where she received a BA in literature at the University of Helsinki and studied the care of horses at an equestrian school. Her first published work was *Huone avaruudessa* ('A Room in Space,' 1973). In her poetry, she moves from meager nature poems to political drama, from lyrics filled with emotions to crazy family chronicles. She defends all that is small, humble, and forgotten. She sees innocent animals, dogs or horses, as the poet's missionaries in the world. By defending animals, she discovers something fundamental about the place of humans in the world and universe. Turkka's pacifism is revealed by her absolute support for the protection of life. *Mies, joka rakasti vaimoaan liikaa* ('The Man Who Loved His Wife Too Much,' 1979) earned her the State Literature Prize in 1980. *Kaunis hallitsija* ('The Beautiful Sovereign,' 1981) describes how eroticism results in the birth of the new, but also in someone's death – it subordinates one's will and kills another's. *Tule takaisin, pikku Sheba* ('Come Back, Little Sheba,' 1986) won the 1987 Finlandia Prize. *Sielun veli* ('Brother of My Soul,' 1993) depicts the social realities of contemporary Finnish life.

TSi

Turnbull, Patricia (*b*. 1952), St Lucian and Virgin Islands poet. Turnbull, born in St Lucia, obtained her BA from University of West Indies (Barbados, 1974), and her MSc in English education (Syracuse University, 1986). She has been a business communication consultant, Patois/Kweyole translator and speech coach, and an English teacher and department chair. In *Rugged Vessels* (1992), her first collection of poetry, she writes of girlhood and female sexuality, mothers and children, the need for mythologies and ritual, and US–Caribbean conflicts. Her poetry emphasizes rhythmic quality, and she often uses patois to shape her character portraits. She edited the UNESCO Multi-Island Project Readers in 1982, and is currently editing *Let Me Speak of These Islands: An Anthology of Virgin Islands Writing*. Her literary work and essays have appeared in *Caribbean New Voices 1* (1995) and *Moving Beyond Boundaries* (1995), and in the journals *The Caribbean Writer*, *English Journal*, and *The New Voices*. She has won the Cedars Prize for Contemporary Poetry (1991), the James Michener Fellowship (1993), and the BVI Department of Education and Culture Local Writers Award (1990). Turnbull now resides in Tortola, British Virgin Islands, and is Director and Coordinator at H. L. Stoutt Community College.

HS

Tusquets, Esther (*b*. 1936), Spanish fiction writer. *The Same Sea as Every Summer* (1978), first of a trilogy, launched a late writing career for Tusquets, a well-known publisher. Its nameless fiftyish protagonist, suffering an identity crisis provoked by her husband's desertion, narrates her affair with Clara as she searches for the roots of her unhappiness. *Love is a Solitary Game* (1979) and *Stranded* (1980) continue the search, with similar protagonists. Tusquets's sinuous sentences, demanding syntax, and the overt eroticism of her love stories – heterosexual and lesbian – are unusual among the writers of the 'women's boom' in 1970s Spain. More common is her narrative device of having the protagonist recollect the constant diminishments of growing up female in Francoist Spain, coldly overseen by an alienated bourgeois mother. The stories of *Siete miradas en un mismo paisaje* ('Seven Glances at the Same Landscape,' 1981) present those curtailments from a girl's perspective. *Never to Return* (1985) reverts to the adult protagonist bereft of husband, now undergoing psychoanalysis in spite of distrusting its patriarchal structure. Tusquets's novels invariably end with the protagonist returning to the security of her deeply flawed marriage.

GCN

Ty-Casper, Linda (*b. c.* 1930s), Philippine fiction writer. Ty-Casper says that her long-term purpose as a writer has been to present a composite portrait of the Filipino. A graduate of the College of Law at the University of the Philippines, she went on to pursue her LLM degree at Harvard. It was the erroneous and biased statements in books at Widener Library that led her to champion the Filipino quest for self-definition, which she seeks to achieve through faithfully researched historical fiction. *The Peninsulars* (1963) is set in eighteenth-century Manila; *The Three-Cornered Sun* (1979) chronicles the 1896 revolution, and *Ten Thousand Seeds* (1987) focuses on the start of the Philippine American War. Her other novels – *Dread Empire* (1980), *Hazards of Distance* (1981), *Fortress in the Plaza* (1985), *Awaiting Trespass* (1985), *Wings of Stone* (1986), *A Small Party in a Garden* (1988), and *Dream Eden* (1996) – are set in contemporary times, which include the Martial Law years and the Edsa Revolt. *Transparent Sun* (1963), *The Secret Runner* (1974), and *Common Continent* (1991) are anthologies of her short stories. Ty-Casper is married to Leonard Casper, noted critic and professor emeritus of Boston College; they have two daughters.

CJM

Tyler, Anne (*b.* 1941), US novelist, short story writer. Born in Minneapolis, Tyler was raised in Quaker communes in the South and Midwest. She graduated Phi Beta Kappa with a degree in Russian from Duke University at the age of 19. She did graduate work at Columbia University and later returned to Duke as a Russian bibliographer at the university library. Her first novel *If Morning Ever Comes* was published in 1964. Other early novels include *A Slipping-Down Life* (1970), *Celestial Navigation* (1974), *Searching for Caleb* (1976), and *Earthly Possessions* (1977). With their straightforward, humorous prose and deft characterizations of quirky individuals, Tyler's novels have been extremely popular. She reveals the remarkable in the everyday as her characters try, usually unsuccessfully, to break free from the limitations of their lives. In *Dinner at the Homesick Restaurant* (1982; PEN/Faulkner Award), five members of a family remember the past in five different ways. *The Accidental Tourist* (1985; National Book Critics Circle Award), which was made into a major film, centers on the author of travel guides for people who want to feel like they've never left home. *Breathing Lessons* (1988), the story of a marriage, won the Pulitzer Prize. *Saint Maybe* (1991) is about the power of guilt, and *Ladder of Years* (1995) is about a woman who creates a new identity for herself. In *A Patchwork Planet* (1998), a 30-year-old underachiever earns a living by doing odd jobs for a variety of eccentrics in Baltimore – the setting of many of Tyler's novels.

DVT

U

Ugrešić, Dubravka (b. 1949), Croatian fiction writer, literary scholar. After studying Russian and comparative literature at the University of Zagreb, Ugrešić began writing fiction that humorously commented on given cultural modes of behavior and literary conventions through a juxtaposition of high and low literary genres. In the short novel *Steffie Speck in the Jaws of Life* (1981), the narrator constructs the subjectivity of her female protagonist as a mélange of various popular cultural discourses shaping femininity, including gossip, romance novels, and practical advice from women's magazines. The novel *Fording the Stream of Consciousness* (1988) revolves around a self-ironic account of the events during a literary conference. Her other works include collections of stories, *Pose for Prose* (1978) and *Life Is a Fairy Tale* (1983), a collection of essays, *Have a Nice Day: From the Balkan War to the American Dream* (1993), and three prize-winning children's books. A scholar of literary theory and Russian literature (especially of the 1920s avant-garde), Ugrešić is a co-editor of the international 'Glossary of the Russian Avant Garde.' After a stint at the University of Zagreb, she currently teaches in Europe and the US.

GC

Ulasi, Adaora Lily (b. 1931), Nigerian journalist, novelist. Ulasi is part of African literary history as the first Nigerian woman to write mystery and detective fiction in English. Born in Aba, she is the daughter of the late chief J. C. Ulasi. After receiving her early education in Nigeria, she attended Pepperdine University and the University of Southern California where she earned a BA in 1954, becoming the first West African woman to earn a degree in journalism. Upon her return to Nigeria in the 1960s, she became the editor of the woman's page for the *Lagos Sunday and Daily Times*. She left Nigeria to travel with her British-born husband to Zimbabwe and later to England, where they raised three children in Kent. Her first novel *Many Thing You No Understand* (1970) is a satire on the inefficiency of British administrators in Nigeria during the colonial era. In *Many Thing Begin for Change* (1971), Chief Obieze III commits suicide rather than admit his complicity in the mysterious death of a British expatriate in Nigeria. Ulasi's third novel *The Night Harry Died* (1974) is set in the US. Her other two novels – *The Man from Sagamu* (1973) and *Who Is Jonah?* (1978) – are also mysteries. After her divorce, Ulasi returned to Nigeria in 1972 as editor of *Woman's World* magazine. In 1976 she moved to London, where she worked for the BBC as a radio broadcaster before retiring from public life in England.

MU

Ulitskaia, Liudmila Evgen'evna (*b*. 1943), Russian prose writer, scriptwriter. Born in Bashkiria to a biochemist and agricultural engineer, Ulitskaia grew up in a communal Moscow apartment, graduated as a geneticist from Moscow State University (1967), married a physicist, and bore two sons. After a stint in a genetics laboratory, she worked in the theater, then began writing film scripts and prose. She has authored two story cycles, *Bednye rodstvenniki* ('Poor Relatives,' 1994) and *Devochki s deviati do odinnadtsati* ('Girls from Nine to Eleven,' 1994), which explore familial and romantic love, integrity, spirituality, and sensualism. Her rich casts of characters, often Jewish and on the fringe of society, tend to be poverty-stricken and vulnerable to the vagaries of history, physical impairment, or human cruelty, but learn reconciliation. Her matter-of-fact acceptance of sexuality as one of life's driving forces informs her handling of extreme or anomalous sexual acts (rape in the story 'Bron'ka,' a 'one-night stand' between a middle-aged man and a woman old enough to be his mother in 'Gulia'). Humor, strong narrative momentum, focus on character, and conciseness are Ulitskaia's stylistic trademarks. Her novella *Sonechka* (1993) and novel *Medea i ee deti* ('Medea and Her Children,' 1996) were both shortlisted for the Russian Booker Prize. The former creates a credible icon of understated female strength, while the latter recasts the Medea myth as a nurturing cultural source in her role of surrogate mother.

HG

Umpierre-Herrera, Luz María (*b*. 1947), Puerto Rican poet, critic. Umpierre-Herrera received her BA in Spanish and completed most of the law curriculum in Puerto Rico. She came to the continental US to get a PhD in Latin American literature from Bryn Mawr. Her first book of poetry *Una puertoriqueña en Penna* ('A Puerto Rican in Penna') was written during her graduate studies in 1979. She has held several academic appointments in the US, including at Rutgers University and Bates College. Her five books of poetry reveal her struggle with authority, her desire to find her personal and sexual voice, and the need to combat societal oppression. She uses Spanglish, English, and Spanish in her poetry as well as contrasting themes to invite others to find their own voice. Her use of wit, satire, frankness, and anger are also noted elements in her writing. In her *Margarita Poems* (1987) she openly explores her lesbianism and the requirement for self-love.

CJG

Uno Chiyo (1897–1996), Japanese novelist, essayist. Born in the castle town of Iwakuni, Uno was the first child of a family with high social status but lacking the corresponding wealth. After graduating from Iwakuni Girls High School in 1914, she worked as a teacher's assistant, maid and waitress, and eventually opened a kimono boutique. She was involved with several men, three of whom she married. Her first story *Shifun no kao* ('Painted Face,' 1921) depicts an impoverished waitress and represents Uno's early focus on struggling young women. Although much of her fiction is autobiographical, best-known are narratives based on stories she heard. *Confessions of Love* (1935) relates a man's affairs prior to his attempted love-suicide; *Ohan* (1958) portrays a man caught between wife and geisha. After her third divorce, Uno wrote several personal narratives: *To Stab* (1966), *Happiness* (1970), and *The Story of a Single Woman* (1972). She later concentrated on her memoirs *Ikite yuku Watashi* ('I Go on Living,' 1983). Despite numerous honors, including the Academy of Arts Award (1972) and Person of Cultural Merit (1990), Uno remained a free spirit, working, until her death, on her two loves: writing and kimonos.

EBM-A

Urquhart, Jane (*b*. 1949), Canadian poet, fiction writer. Born in Little Long Lac, Ontario, Urquhart grew up in Toronto, and was educated at the University of Guelph, where she earned a BA in English in 1971 and a BA in art history in 1976. Her first book, a volume of poetry, *I'm Walking in the Garden of His Imaginary Palace*, was published in 1982. In this, and in her subsequent volumes *False Shuffles* (1982) and *The Little Flowers of Madame de Montespan* (1984), she creates personal poetic narratives for figures ranging from the mistress of Louis XIV to her own grandmother. Her rich imagery and fascination with memory and transformation are also evident in her fiction. The novel *The Whirlpool* (1986) connects the stories of three nineteenth-century Canadians through symbols and metaphors. In *Changing Heaven* (1990), a scholar of Emily Brontë travels to England and finds herself involved in the world of *Wuthering Heights*. *Away* (1993; Trillium Award) explores Irish and Canadian history through the stories passed down by four generations of women. It won the Marian Engel Award for Outstanding Prose written by a Canadian Woman. Other works include *Storm Glass* (1978), a collection of stories, and the novel *The Underpainter* (1997).

JEM

'Usayrān, Laylā (*b.* 1934), Lebanese novelist, journalist. Born in Baghdad, Iraq to a Lebanese family, 'Usayrān received her primary and secondary education at the American College in Cairo before returning to Beirut in 1949. She earned her BA in political science from the American University there and subsequently worked as a correspondent for Egyptian periodicals. In 1958 she married a professor of economics, Dr. Amīn al-Ḥāfiz, who was a member of the Lebanese parliament and who eventually became Prime Minister of Lebanon in the late 1970s. Her first novel *Lan Namūt Ghadan* ('We Will Not Die Tomorrow,' 1962) deals with an alienated young woman from a wealthy family who searches for meaning and fulfillment in her work and life. However, the tenor of 'Usayrān's work changed after the Arab defeat in the 1967 war; she began to depict men and women caught up in the Palestinian resistance movement. Her scope widened to include novels dealing with the Lebanese civil war as well, as in the novels *Qal'at al-Usṭah* ('The Headman's Fortress,' 1979) and *Ṭā'ir min al-Qamar* ('A Bird from the Moon,' 1996). When she began her literary career, she was married and had a child. Her work often lacks the rebelliousness of her contemporaries. In 1994 she published her autobiography, *Sharā'iṭ Mulawwana min Ḥayātī* ('Colored Ribbons of My Life').

JTZ

'Uthmān, Laylā al- (*b.* 1945), Kuwaiti novelist, short story writer, journalist. 'Uthmān was born in Kuwait to a conservative family. She was denied higher education and was discouraged from publishing, although her father was a published poet. She read widely and after her marriage to a Palestinian poet who encouraged her to write, she began to publish articles in local periodicals in 1965. In 1966, she began producing cultural programs for the radio. She published her first work *Hamasāt* ('Whispers'), a compilation of light pieces on social and literary topics, in 1972. Since 1976, she has focused on writing short stories, which have appeared in periodicals in Kuwait and other Arabic-speaking countries. Her first collection *Imra'a fī Inā'* ('A Woman in a Vessel,' 1976) was followed by nine other collections of short stories. In 1987 'Uthmān published her first novel *Al-Mar'a wa-al-Qiṭṭa* ('The Woman and the Cat'), in which she portrays the life of a young man who falls victim to a merciless, sadistic aunt. In *Wasmiyya Takhruj min al-Baḥr* ('Wasmiyya Leaves the Sea,' 1986), she depicts a tragic love story between a wealthy man and a poor woman. In her collection *Al-Hawājiz al-Sawdā'* ('The Black Barriers,' 1994), she examines the impact of the Iraqi occupation of Kuwait in 1990. She is recently divorced and lives in Kuwait with her four children.

JTZ

V

V. **Vinichayakul** (Khunying Vinita Ditee-yont), (*b.* 1949), Thai fiction writer. Born in Bangkok, V. Vinichayakul received her BA degree from the Faculty of Arts, Chulalongkorn University, and her doctorate in curriculum and instruction (literature) from the University of Northern Colorado. She taught Thai literature and creative writing at Silapakorn University until her early retirement in 1995. Her first published novel *Mithila Wesalee* was written when she was a university student and was later serialized in a leading women's magazine. Many of her novels have been made into TV series and films. V. Vinichayakul is noted for her ability to write on a wide variety of subjects. Her works include realistic novels that reflect various aspects of Thai life as well as historical and fantasy novels. Of her fifty novels, nine have received the prestigious National Book Award. 'The Night Full of Light,' a short story written in English, was included in UNESCO's 1994 collection of Asian and Australian short stories.

NM

Vaidehi (*b.* 1945), Indian short story writer, novelist. Born in the small town of Kundapura, Vaidehi (the nom de plume of Janaki Sreenivas Murthy) is one of the foremost prose writers in the Kannada language today. After her debut collection of short stories in 1979, she developed a distinctive style, characterized by a refined introspection on the part of the characters, often from her high-caste background in coastal Karnataka, through which unexpected aspects of people's inner lives are brought to light. She does not identify herself with any ideological program, and her writings are marked by honest and subtle analysis. A journalist by profession, she has four story collections – the best-known being *Antarangada Putagalu* ('Pages from the Inner Self,' 1984) – a collection each of essays and of poems, and eight children's dramas. In her award-winning novel *Asprsyaru* ('Untouchables,' 1992), she analyzes two types of untouchability: that of caste, but also that of gender, which seeks to keep women away from the world outside the family. She has twice won the national Katha Award and received the prestigious Karnataka Sahitya Akademi Award and the Attimabbe Award. English translations of her stories have appeared in several anthologies, including *The Inner Courtyard* (1992), *Katha Prize Stories* (1992), and *Women Writing in India* (1993).

RJZ

Valenzuela, Luisa (*b.* 1938), Argentine novelist, short story writer. Daughter of writer Luisa Mercedes Levinson, Valenzuela grew up in Buenos Aires, surrounded by writers and other intellectuals. She lived in France for several years where she wrote her first novel *Clara* (1966). Later, she lived in New York for ten years where she wrote *The Lizard's Tail* (1983) and *Other Weapons* (1982), both of which are thinly veiled critiques of the Argentine political situation during the late 1970s and early 1980s. Her more recent *Black Novel (with Argentines)* (1990), set in New York but written after her return to Buenos Aires, uses the detective story format to explore both that political situation and our capacity for interpersonal oppression. Her three main preoccupations are consistently women, language, and politics. Both *The Heretics* (1967) and *Strange Things Happen Here* (1975) playfully yet seriously explore the ways in which we presume to know what we know and how we use language to manipulate even as we are manipulated by it. Her most recent work *Simetrías* ('Symmetries,' 1993) is a powerful collection of short stories, some of which rewrite traditional fairy tales from a feminist perspective, while others examine some of the most frightening (and censored) aspects of society such as torture and matricidal impulses. In 1995 Valenzuela was honored at the fifteenth biennial Puterbaugh Conference.

SMag

Vaneeva, Larisa L'vovna (*b.* 1953), Russian prose writer. Born into a family of teachers in Novosibirsk, Vaneeva worked as a journalist before enrolling in Moscow's Gorky Literary Institute. Rejected by journals and publishers during the Soviet era, her fiction saw print only in the 1990s. Evidencing her passion for nature and environmental issues, her prose embraces modernist devices: abrupt, unexplained temporal and spatial shifts, an elliptical style, blurred boundaries between empirical and mental phenomena, and an affinity for the relational structures of modernist painting, to which the title of her collection *Iz kuba* ('Out of the Cube,' 1990) adverts. Violence, degradation, and physical dissolution interplay with lyrical nature descriptions and philosophical ruminations in her texts. Her female

protagonists muse about cosmic issues while coping with rape, as in 'Antigrekh' ('Anti-sin') and 'Venetian Mirrors,' or alcohol and drug addiction, as in 'Parade of the Planets' (1981), while her male characters appear weak or/and brutal. Her language mixes slang, vulgarisms, poetic lexicon, and often ironic allusions to high and low culture. Silent for several years after moving to Estonia with her son so as to save him from conscription in the Russian army, Vaneeva has resumed publishing her fiction and collaborating with fellow female writers in Moscow through the journal *Raduga* ('Rainbow').

HG

van Herk, Aritha (*b.* 1954), Canadian novelist. Born in Wetaskiwin, Alberta, van Herk was educated at the University of Alberta, where she earned a BA in 1977 and an MA in 1978. In 1978, she won the Alberta Achievement Award in Literature. She teaches at the University of Calgary. Her prize-winning first novel *Judith* (1978) depicts the feminist awakening of a secretary and mistress who becomes a pig farmer. It established van Herk as a formally innovative, feminist novelist who writes boldly about female experiences through her reworkings of myths, literary conventions, and even maps. In *The Tent Peg* (1981), the presence of a young woman disguised as a man transforms a geological survey team in the Yukon. *No Fixed Address: An Amorous Journey* (1986) is a picaresque novel about Arachne Manteia, a sexually free traveling saleswoman for ladies' underwear (but who wears none herself). It is a consciously feminist appropriation of male myths, roles, and territories which ends with Arachne taking off for the unmapped North. *Places Far From Ellesmere: A Geografictione: Explorations on Site* (1990) is a combination of travel writing, fiction, and criticism which continues van Herk's preoccupations with gender roles, female rebellion, alternative mappings, and the lure of the North. Similarly, *In Visible Ink: Crypto-Fictions*

(1991), *A Frozen Tongue* (1992), and *Restlessness* (1998) blur the lines between fiction, autobiography, and criticism.

JEM

Vanita, Ruth (*b.* 1955), Indian feminist critic, literary historian, poet. Born in Delhi, Vanita received her MA and doctorate in English literature from the University of Delhi, where she also taught until 1997. She currently teaches at the University of Montana. She was one of the founders of *Manushi – a journal about women and society*, and co-edited it (with Madhu Kishwar) from 1978 to 1990, writing and publishing poems, interviews, analyses of gender in Hindi films, and a regular column on women and the law, and also translating fiction and poetry by and about women. Her articles also appeared regularly in leading Indian dailies and magazines. She published two books in 1994, *A Play of Light: Selected Poems* and *Strangers on the Roof* (a translation of Rajendra Yadav's Hindi novel *Sara Aakash*). In *Sappho and the Virgin Mary: Same-Sex Love and the English Literary Imagination* (1996), she demonstrated the centrality of an imagined lesbian literary ancestry in English literature and explored friendships between gay men and women in the late nineteenth century. Her latest book, co-edited with Saleem Kidwai, is a collection of Indian writings on same-sex love in India (1999).

SK

Van Steen, Edla (*b.* 1936), Brazilian novelist, journalist, editor. Born E. Lucy Vendhausen in Florianópolis, Santa Catarina, the daughter of a Belgian father and a German mother, Van Steen started a career in journalism, and participated in a daily radio program. She also worked as an actress on stage and in films before turning to writing full-time. Her debut as a writer was with a collection of short stories *Cio* ('Heat') in 1955. In her second work, a novel titled *Memórias do Medo* ('Memories of Fear,' 1974), she carefully multiplies characters, situations, and story lines. Her capacity for dealing concomitantly with various situations in the same narrative process is also present in *Village of the Ghost Bells* (1983) and *A Bag of Stories* (1991). She has edited several anthologies, including *Viver e Escrever* ('To Live and to Write,' 1981, 1982), a series of interviews with Brazilian writers collected in two volumes.

TFC

Varlamova, Inna Gustavovna (Klavdiia Landau), (1922–1990), Russian prose writer. After a peripatetic childhood and youth due to her father, Varlamova briefly worked in the Urals before Stalin's death, whereupon she settled in Moscow as a journalist. In 1957 she turned to fiction and translation. Her stories of the 1960s and 1970s, dealing with adjustment to change, divided loyalties, integrity, and love, appeared in the collections of stories and novellas *Tret'ego ne dano* (1969) and *Dve liubvi* ('Two Loves,' 1974). Her most memorable novel is the autobiographical *Counterfeit Life* (1978), set in a cancer hospital. The personal drama of its heroine, stricken with breast cancer and alienated from her husband, meshes with the sociopolitical background of the 1960s. Though occasionally tending toward slackness, Varlamova's writing is animated by compassion, gentle humor, and a faith in human perseverance. Additional translations in English include the stories 'Ladle for Pure Water' and 'A Threesome.'

HG

Vasilenko, Svetlana Vladimirovna (*b.* 1956), Russian prose writer, scriptwriter. Born into an officer's family, Vasilenko spent her early years within the wired fence of the security zone at Kapustin Iar, the equivalent of America's Cape Canaveral. Her 'cosmic childhood' meant distance from her perennially absent father and intimacy with her mother, whose surname she adopted. After moving to Moscow, Vasilenko worked as a fruit hauler and mailwoman, married a much older engineer, whose child she was carrying, and enrolled in the Gorky Literary Institute, graduating in 1983. By 1989, when she completed her education in film directing, she had acquired fame as the author of 'Going after Goat-Antelopes', her prize-winning first publication. During *glasnost* she wrote film and video scripts and participated in several collections of women's writing, notably *Ne pomniashchaia zla* ('She Who Doesn't Remember Evil,' 1990) and *Novye Amazonki* ('The New Amazons,' 1991), which she edited. She currently heads the Writers' Union in Moscow. Vasilenko's fiction belongs to the New Women's Writing, with its female subjectivity, unproblematic engagement with physiology, and unflinching treatment of sexuality, rape, birthing, obsession, and identity in a world contaminated by nuclear waste and postlapsarian categories of existence. Translated texts include the stories 'Shamara' and 'Piggy.'

HG

Vega, Ana Lydia (*b*. 1946), Puerto Rican short story writer. Born in Santurce, Puerto Rico, Vega grew up in a working-class neighborhood that provided the setting for her short stories. She studied at the University of Puerto Rico and the University of Aix-en-Provence, where she earned an MA and PhD in Comparative Literature in 1975. Since 1976 she has taught French and Caribbean Literature at the University of Puerto Rico. Her first book *Encancaranublado y otros cuentos de naufragio* ('Cloudy Sky and Other Shipwreck Stories,' 1982), a collection which won the Casa de las Américas prize, highlights the lack of solidarity among peoples of the Caribbean, who are left to the mercy of more powerful nations. Her second book *Pasión de historia* ('A Passion for History,' 1987) parodies the detective story genre and social satire; the collection includes a short story by the same name which won the prestigious Juan Rulfo

International Prize in 1984. *Falsas crónicas del sur* ('False Southern Chronicles,' 1991) is a short story collection inspired by historical documents and popular oral tradition that documents the history of southern Puerto Rico. The collection *True and False Romances: Stories and a Novella* (1994) includes selected stories.

GP

Velmar-Janković, Svetlana (*b*. 1949), Serbian novelist, literary critic. Born in Belgrade, where she still resides, Velmar-Janković studied French language and literature, and for many years worked as an editor in the publishing house Prosveta. Her novel *Dungeon* (1990) portrays six decades of Serbian history, refracted through the eyes of a cultured Belgrade woman. Flashbacks into the past recount the narrator's personal history, and her internal monologue is interspersed with other characters' fragmented thoughts, as well as reflections on contemporary world events. The novel constructs a mosaic of life in Belgrade from the prewar 1930s to the 1980s. Velmar-Janković's other works include an early novel *Ožiljak* ('The Scar,' 1956), collections of essays on Serbian literary figures, *Savremenici* ('Contemporaries,' 1968) and *Ukletnici* ('The Cursed,' 1993), and several radio plays.

GC

Vera, Yvonne (*b*. 1964), Zimbabwean short story writer, novelist. Vera is one of Zimbabwe's most talented and prolific young writers. Her novels focus on Zimbabwe's liberation struggle and are unique in the ways they challenge common assumptions about freedom, fictional form, and modes of reading. She attended York University for undergraduate and doctoral studies and started writing seriously in 1992. She has published four novels and a collection of short stories titled *Why Don't You Carve Other Animals* (1992) as well as edited an anthology of women's writing. Her first novel *Nehanda* (1993), centered on Zimbabwe's first war of liberation, rewrites the rebellion against white settlers as communal resistance and affirmation. *Without A Name* (1994), set in 1977 at a heightened moment of the liberation war, focuses on a peasant woman's search for personal freedom, and questions assumptions about liberation, national identity, and history. Her third novel *Under the Tongue* (1996, Commonwealth Writers Prize) explores the subject of incest in the context of national struggle and interrogates cultural taboos in the transitional moment of struggle and freedom. Her latest novel *Butterfly Burning* (1999) recreates township life of the 1940s. Her exciting and experimental writing has earned several literary awards both nationally and internationally.

NW-T

Vestly, Anne-Cath (Catharina) (*b.* 1920), Norwegian children's writer. Born in Rena, Norway, Vestly lived in several places around the country before her parents settled in Oslo. There she studied at Studioteatret and began her acting career. She also wrote scripts for cabaret performances and radio dramas for children. In 1950 she started working full-time for Norwegian radio's children's program, writing and performing her own material. In 1953 she published her first children's book *Ole Aleksander F∎libom-bom-bom*; Ole's adventures grew into a series of five books. More than forty children's books followed. Aurora and Guro are some of the beloved characters who reappeared in seven books each. Among Vestly's books that have been translated into English are *Hello, Aurora* (1966) and *Aurora and Socrates* (1969). All of her books are illustrated by her husband, the artist Johan Vestly. Vestly broke new ground in Norwegian children's literature by placing her protagonists in urban environments and challenging gender stereotypes in a nondidactic fashion. Her books are loved in Norway because of her humor and the refreshing openness with which she addresses social and psychological problems.

She has received the Peer Gynt Prize (1980), the Prize of Honor of the Norwegian Board of Culture (1994), and the Brage Prize (1995).

E-MM

Vianen, Bea (*b.* 1935), Surinamese novelist, poet. Born in Paramaribo, the daughter of an East Indian mother and an Afro-Caribbean father, Vianen was educated at a Roman Catholic boarding school and worked in Paramaribo as an elementary school teacher until 1957, when she left for Amsterdam. Her autobiographical novel *Sarnami, hai* ('Suriname, I am,' 1969) presents the coming of age of a young Surinamese who finally sacrifices everything, including her child, to study biology in the Netherlands. The problems of gender, class, and race confronted in this first novel also affect a group of idealistic Surinamese intellectuals in her second novel *Strafhok* ('Punishment Coop,' 1971). Whereas these first two novels are set in Suriname, *Het paradijs van Oranje* ('The Paradise of Orange,' 1972) shows how Sindja, a Surinamese writer, experiences discrimination, racism, and hypocrisy in the former 'mother country.' *Geen Onderdelen* ('No Parts,' 1979) finally suggests a complete loss of faith in the possibility of change.

DH

Vicuña, Cecilia (*b.* 1948), Chilean poet. Born in La Florida, Chile, Vicuña was raised among intellectuals and artists. At the age of 14, she started a diary that remains the source of her writing and work. Her writing career began in a collective (Tribu) during the late 1960s and early 1970s. In 1972 she completed her studies at the School of Fine Arts at the University of Chile in Santiago and traveled to England, where she lived for three years, followed by a move to Colombia. Her early, erotic poetry *Sabor a mí* ('My Flavor,' 1973) was first published bilingually in London. In 1980 she married Cesar Paternosto, with whom she studies the Colombian indigenous and contemporary world. Her first video-poem 'Tres Trabajos' ('Three Works') was shown at the Museum of Modern Art in New York. She has published an award-winning book *Precario/ Precarious* (1983) and *PALABRARmas- =wurdwapppinschaw* (1984). Using indigenous oral traditions, Vicuña developed a series of 'ritual readings' of poetry that include speech, song, and movement. In 1990 *La Wik'uña* ('Vicuna') was published in Chile. She lives in New York City.

CJG

Vik, Bjørg (*b.* 1935), Norwegian short story writer, novelist, playwright. A prolific writer in many genres, Vik was born in Oslo, and many of her stories reflect the mundane, everyday details of life for girls and women in a lower-middle-class milieu. She attended the College of Journalism and in 1956 began working for the *Porsgrunn Dagblad*. Her first collection of short stories, *Søndag ettermiddag* ('Sunday Afternoon') appeared in 1963 and created a stir because of the stories' frank approach to sexuality. As a co-founder of the feminist journal *Sirene* in 1973, Vik was in the forefront of the feminist movement of the 1960s. Winner of many literary awards and nominated three times for the Nordisk Råds Litteraturpris, her other works include the short story collections *Nødrop fra en myk sofa* ('Cries for Help from a Soft Sofa,' 1966), which explores the corrosive effects of materialism on relationships, *An Aquarium of Women* (1972) and *Out of Season and other stories* (1979). A recurring theme in Vik's work is how society's expectations and gender stereotypes mold personality. The play *To akter for fem kvinder* ('Two Acts for Five Women,' 1974), about the differing, but typical, fates of five old friends, was a long-running theatrical success. More recent works include a trilogy whose heroine has much in common with Vik herself, and a collection of reminiscences *Gatenes magi* ('Magic of the Streets,' 1996).

MHH

Vilalta, Maruxa (*b.* 1932), Mexican dramatist, journalist. Born in Barcelona in 1932, Vilalta has lived in Mexico City since 1939. With an MA from the Universidad Nacional Autónoma de México, she has written more than a dozen plays, several of which she has directed herself. Her career began in 1960 with *Los desorientados* ('The Lost Ones'). Her earliest works, such as *A Happy Country* (1964) and *Number 9* (1965), generally dramatize the discrepancies between discourse and praxis. Her plays of the early 1970s depict the unexpected cruelty inherent to many relationships between couples: *Together Tonight, Loving Each Other So Much* (1970), *Nothing Like the Sixteenth Floor* (1975). In the late 1970s she experimented with theater of the absurd while still focusing on interpersonal relationships: *The Story of Him* (1978), *A Woman, Two Men, and a Gunshot* (1981), and *A Little Tale of Horror (and Unbridled Love)* (1985). Most recently Vilalta has employed religious motifs to critique contemporary mores and power struggles: *A Voice in the Wilderness* (1991), *Francis of Assisi* (1992), *Jesucristo entre nosotros* ('Jesus Christ Among Us,'1994), and *En blanco y negro* ('In Black and White,'1997). She has won numerous prizes.

SMag

Vilariño, Idea (*b.* 1920), Uruguayan poet. Vilariño was born in Montevideo, Uruguay, into a family of poets and readers. Childhood illnesses made her a voracious reader and precocious poet. She received degrees from the University in Montevideo in both literature and science. In her lifelong relationship with Manual Claps, she began publishing, editing, translating, and writing essays. Today, she lives a life of deliberate solitude, facing the sea, in Montevideo. Her first book of poetry *La Suplicante* ('The Supplicant,' 1945) examines the perishability of love and life. In her second book *Cielo cielo* ('Heaven Heaven,' 1947) she eliminates most punctuation and conventional syntax, but uses repetition and ellipses to gain rhythmic effect. Her books of lyrical poetry, *Nocturnos* ('Nocturnes,' 1951) and *Poemas de amor* ('Love Poems,' 1957), have been the most widely read. Other works include *Pobre Mundo* ('Poor World,' 1966), *Poesia* ('Poetry,' 1970), and *Segunda antologia* ('Second Anthology,' 1980). Her later work expresses hope for political liberation for women, who, Vilariño believes, are morally superior to men. She finally agreed to accept the Uruguayan Municipal Grand Prize for her work in 1987.

CJG

Vilhjálmsdóttir, Linda (*b.* 1958), Icelandic poet, playwright. Linda was born and grew up in Reykjavik, where she currently lives and works part-time as a nurse. In 1990, she published her first collection of poems titled *Bláþráður* ('Hanging by a Thread'), which critics in Iceland considered an unusually fine debut book. Since then she has published two more volumes of poetry and written two plays which have been staged in Reykjavik. For her work she was awarded the DV Daily Newspaper Literary Prize in 1993. Her poetry is included in English translation in the anthology of Icelandic poetry *Brushstrokes of Blue: The Young Poets of Iceland* and in a small bilingual volume devoted solely to her poetry titled *Mona Lisa* (1993). She is considered an important young poet for the depth she achieves in her introspective poems and for her original approach to nature poetry. As with many contemporary Icelandic writers, Vilhjálmsdóttir draws on a long tradition of seeking the exotic in the mundane; for example, in her series of poems titled 'Weather,' included in *Mona Lisa*, wind, rain, and winter become the protagonist's mysterious opponents.

KG

Vine, Barbara (see Rendell, Ruth)

Viramontes, Helena Maria (*b.* 1954), US fiction writer, editor. Born in East Los Angeles, Viramontes made a critically acclaimed debut with the collection *The Moths and Other Stories*, which was published in 1985. Her feminism and her Mexican-American background inform her fiction, which features Chicana and Latina women struggling with their families, their communities, and the Catholic Church to redefine gender roles and reimagine possibilities for their lives. The stories are written in an impressionistic style that employs magic realism, flashbacks, and multiple narrative perspectives. Her second collection of stories *Paris Rats in E.L.A.* (1993) examines sexual and economic oppression in the barrio from a female point of view. Her first novel *Under the Feet of Jesus* (1995) depicts the precarious and dangerous lives of migrant farm workers in California. Her second novel *Their Dogs Came With Them* (2000), set in East Los Angeles in the 1960s, combines poetry, myth, and realism to depict a neighborhood threatened by a new free way. Viramontes also co-edited *Chicana Creativity and Criticism: New Frontiers in American Literature* (1991), an important collection of Chicana poetry, prose, and critical essays. She was awarded the John Dos Passos Prize for Literature in 1995.

JEM

Vogel, Paula (*b.* 1951), US playwright. Born in Washington, D.C., Vogel was educated at Bryn Mawr College, Catholic University (BA, 1974), and Cornell University, where her first plays were produced. These include *Apple-Brown Betty* (1979) and *Desdemona* (1979), a comic rewrite of Shakespeare's play that fleshes out the female characters and chillingly ends just before Desdemona's murder. Vogel first gained critical attention with *The Oldest Profession* (1981), a play about a group of elderly prostitutes and their madam who cannot afford to retire. A satire of Reagan era social policies, it is also a sympathetic portrayal of sisterhood and the joy of work. *And Baby Makes Seven* (1986) is a comedy about a lesbian couple, the gay man who has fatherered a child with one of them, and their three imaginary children. Fantasy and death are mingled with a powerful effect, as they are in *The Baltimore Waltz* (1992), a formally daring play made up of lectures, language lessons, a slide show, and quick two or three person scenes that wittily satirize US AIDS policy without actually naming the syndrome. Vogel approaches serious issues from a feminist perspective, such as domestic violence in *Hot 'n' Throbbing* (1992) and sexual abuse in the Pulitzer Prize-winning *How I Learned to Drive* (1997), but no matter how dark the subject, she manages to unearth humor. *The Minealoa Twins* (1998) is a satire on gender roles in the 1950s, 1960s, and 1980s.

JEM

Volach, Yona (1944–1985), Israeli poet. During her brief career in which she published seven books of poetry, Volach became a powerful literary presence in Israel and a startlingly original poetic voice, one at once psychologically and spiritually complex, flamboyant, self-aware, provocative, satiric, sophisticated, and tender. In collections such as *Dvarim* ('Things/ Words,' 1966), *Shnai Ganim* ('Two Gardens,' 1969), *Tsurot* ('Forms,' 1985) and *Mufah* ('Appearance,' 1985), she dug into and challenged the nuances of identity, religion, gender and sexuality, as well as the Hebrew language itself, inscribing within it street slang, Jungian psychology, the Bible, liturgy, rock and roll. Born in a suburb of Tel Aviv, she was active in the 'Tel Aviv poets' circle centered on the journals *Siman Kriyah* and *Achshav* in the 1960s, and wrote for and appeared with an Israeli rock group. Her own poetry was set to music and a record was released in 1982. Her 1983 collection *Ohr Parah* ('Wild Light'), for example, challenges civic, religious, familial, and theological expressions of patriarchal authority, in poems like 'When You Come Sleep With Me, Come Like God.' *Tot Hakarah Niftachat Kmo Menifa; Mivchar Hashirim 1963–*

1985 ('Selected Poems') appeared in a posthumous collection in 1992.

MGl

Voznesenskaia, Juliia Nikolaevna (*b.* 1940), Russian prose writer, poet, essayist. Expelled from the Leningrad Theater, Music, and Cinema Institute, where she studied theater, Voznesenskaia immersed herself in the city's unofficial culture during the 1960s and 1970s, circulating her poetry in *samizdat*, editing and organizing such underground publications as *Chasy* ('Clock,' 1976) and *Mariia*, the journal of the religious feminist group Mariia. After multiple arrests, imprisonment, and exile, she emigrated in 1980 to Germany, where she worked for the Society for Human Rights and Radio Liberty, while simultaneously authoring three prose works in addition to poetry and essays. Her best-known 'novel' is the Boccaccio-inspired *Women's Decameron* (1987), which orchestrates the voices of ten women at a Leningrad maternity hospital, narrating the checkered fate of womanhood as individually experienced in Soviet Russia. *The Star Chernobyl* (1987) presents reactions to the Chernobyl nuclear disaster from the perspective of three contrasting sisters, interspersed with citations from the media's consequence-laden cover-up campaign. *Letters of Love* (1991) consists of extracts from female camp inmates' letters to their 'loved ones.' Gendered multivocalism is Voznesenskaia's major narrative device, and she increasingly collapses womanhood into spirituality.

HG

Vrkljan, Irena (*b.* 1930), Serbian prose writer, poet, screenwriter. A native of Belgrade, as a child Vkrljan moved to Zagreb, Croatia, where she lived until her departure for West Berlin in the mid-1960s. While in Zagreb, she wrote poetry and screenplays for Zagreb television. She is best known, however, for her autobiographical works, to which she turned later in her career. The changing forms of her bold experiments in the genre of autobiography reflect the changing form of female identity created through them. In *Silk, Scissors* (1984), autobiography is conceived as literally *my* biography, with a succession of numerous short narratives following the chronology of the author's life from childhood to the present. *Marina, or on Biography* (1986) reacts to the closure of individualism itself – as 'separateness' between 'I' and others – through its articulation of a specific 'contact zone' on the basis of an individual. The text of *Marina* is thus a collage of countless short fragments from Vkrljan's and other people's biographies. Her latest works, *Berlinski rukopis* ('Berlin Manuscript,' 1988) and *Dora, ove jeseni* ('Dora, This Autumn,' 1990), represent an even more radical experimentation with the possibilities of autobiography. Her *Ispred crvenog zida* ('In Front of the Red Wall,' 1995) muses on the violence in the Balkans in the 1990s.

GC

W

de Waard, Elly (*b*. 1940), Dutch poet. Before she started to write poetry, de Waard worked as a critic for a newspaper. She studied Dutch literature and lived with the poet Chris van Geel for many years. After his death in 1974, she took care of his poetic legacy and in 1978, she started to publish her own poems, which were well received. She is a true lyrical poet. Her style is baroque and she does not avoid strong words. Romantic love is the most important theme in her work. The reception of her work changed when it became explicitly lesbian. Male critics in particular were negative and they even ignored an entire volume, which was actually one of her best: *Een Wildernis van verbindingen* ('Wilderness of Connections,' 1986). English translations of her work can be found in anthologies such as *With Other Words* (1985) and *The Defiant Muse* (1998). She is a prolific poet: since 1978 she has published ten volumes of poetry. Together with *Renate Dorrestein, among others, she was the founder of the Anna Bijns Prize in 1989, a literary prize for 'the female voice in Dutch literature.' In the 1980s she also organized a number of workshops and festivals for women poets.

AAn, MMe

Waciuma, Charity (*b. c*. 1930s), Kenyan autobiographer, children's writer. Waciuma's parents fled Kenya for a Western education but returned to bring public health and education to the Kenyan people. She was born and raised in Kenya during the seven years of the Mau Mau Emergency period. Her autobiographical book *Daughter of Mumbi* (1969) depicts her adolescence during this time. Her writing emphasizes the woman's role in Kenya, and the pressures and conflicts of living in a rapidly changing society. Her children's books *The Golden Feather* (1966), *Mweru, the Ostrich Girl* (1966), *Merry-Making* (1972), and *Who's Calling?* (1973) are based on Kikuyu legends and oral narrative traditions. In all of her writing, she stresses the importance of traditions as well as family values and unity.

SDR

Wahidi, Surraya (*b*. 1955), Afghan poet. Born in Kabul, Wahidi completed her education at the Kabul Teacher Training College and taught in various schools. She later became a member of the Afghan Writers Association and was given two literary awards by the Ministry of Information and Culture in Afghanistan. She has a free style of writing and writes modern short poems. She has two poetry collections in Persian, published in Kabul a few years before the Taliban regime. Until two years ago, she was living in Kabul. No accurate information is available about her present situation.

FRB

Wakoski, Diane (*b*. 1937), US poet, essayist. Raised in an impoverished family in Whittier, California, Wakoski earned a BA from the University of California, Berkeley in 1960. After graduation, she moved to New York City. She has taught at many universities and colleges, and has been writer-in-residence at Michigan State University since 1976. Her emotional, confessional poetry draws on her personal experiences, often written in the first-person, and often expressing rage at betrayal, hostility toward men, and lamentation for an unhappy childhood. Praised for its intense imagery, spontaneous form, and direct language, her poetry frequently takes on a prose-like structure. Her first volume of poetry *Coins and Coffins* was published in 1962. Other poetry collections include *Discrepancies and Apparitions* (1966), *The George Washington Poems* (1967), *The Diamond Merchant* (1968), *Inside the Blood Factory* (1968), *The Moon Has a Complicated Geography* (1969), *The Motorcycle Betrayal Poems* (1971), *Smudging* (1972), *Dancing on the Grave of a Son of a Bitch* (1973), *Looking for the King of Spain* (1974), *The Collected Greed: Parts 1–13* (1984), and *Emerald Ice: Selected Poems 1962–1987* (1988). Wakoski has also published essays on writing, including *Creating a Personal Mythology* (1975) and *Toward a New Poetry* (1979). She was awarded the Williams Carlos Williams Prize in 1989.

DVT

Walker, Alice (*b*. 1944), US novelist, poet, short story writer, essayist. A self-labeled 'womanist,' Walker was born to sharecropper parents in Eatonton, Georgia. At the age of 8, she was accidentally blinded in one eye by her brother's BB gun; her father's delay in getting medical help created a lifelong rift between them. She attended Spelman College for two years before transferring to Sarah Lawrence College, earning a BA in 1965. She was a teacher and civil rights advocate in Mississippi, where she married Melvyn

Leventhal; they were the state's first legally married interracial couple. Her novels focus on the two major forces of oppression endured by black women – racism and sexism. Her work, influenced by Zora Neale Hurston, demonstrates concern for the culture and character of African-American women in her depictions of their search for identity and meaningful relationships. Her first book *Once* (1968) is a collection of poetry. She won the Pulitzer Prize for *The Color Purple* (1982), an epistolary novel which treats rape, abuse, and interracial violence; it was made into a film by Stephen Spielberg. Her other novels include *The Third Life of Grange Copeland* (1970), the roughly autobiographical *Meridian* (1976), *The Temple of My Familiar* (1989), and *Possessing the Secret of Joy* (1992), which concerns female genital mutilation, a practice Walker has actively campaigned against. Her short story collections are *In Love and Trouble* (1973) and *You Can't Keep a Good Woman Down* (1981). She has written several collections of essays, including the influential *In Search of Our Mother's Gardens* (1983).

DVT

Wander, Maxie (1933–1977), German prose writer. Born in Vienna, Wander died in Berlin. She left school without a diploma and worked in factories, offices, and as a housekeeper. In 1958 she moved with her husband, a member of the Communist Party in Austria, to the GDR. There she worked as a secretary, a photographer, and a journalist. She became famous with a series of interviews which she rewrote in a literary style titled *Guten Morgen, du Schöne. Protokolle nach Tonband* ('Good Morning, Beautiful,' 1977). In that collection of interviews, women in the GDR talk about their work, their concepts of love, their sexuality, and their everyday life experiences. They simultaneously expose the lack of emancipation for women in the GDR and the small chances for self-realization. The book became a best-seller and was sold in both East and West Germany; it had a great influence on the perception of emancipation in the GDR. *Leben wär' eine prima Alternative* ('Going On Living Would Be Great,' 1980) contains a selection of her letters and excerpts from her diaries edited by her husband.

MMu

Wang Anyi (*b*. 1954), Chinese fiction writer. Born in Nanjing, daughter of writer *Ru Zhijuan, Wang grew up in Shanghai. Sent down to Anhui Province during the Cultural Revolution (1966–76), she returned to Shanghai in 1978 and began her career as a writer. The winner of many national literary prizes for fiction, she is one of the most versatile and prolific Chinese writers of the 1980s and 1990s. Her stories from the early 1980s are explorations of subjective perspectives, as in the collection *Yu, shashasha* ('Gentle Rain,' 1981). Later she shifted her concern to portray broad social events, as in the novella *Baotown* (1984). In the mid 1980s, Wang expanded her exploration to the 'forbidden' area of sexuality by publishing three novellas on the theme of 'love' – *Brocade Valley* (1986), *Love in a Small Town* (1986), and *Love on a Barren Mountain* (1986). In the 1990s, a tremendous change in the narrative styles and perspectives is evident in her construction of grand epics combining surrealism and myth with extended family history, as in the novels *Shangxin Taipingyang* ('Grieving over the Pacific Ocean,' 1992) and *Jishi he xugou* ('Reality and Fiction,' 1993). Other important works include *Shushu de gushi* ('A Story of an Uncle,' 1990), a satirical account of a revolutionary hero seen through the eyes of a younger generation, and *Changhen ge* ('The Song of Eternal Regret,' 1995), a saga of a Shanghai woman whose life mirrors many changing phases in modern China.

JZ

Wang, Lulu (*b*. 1960), Dutch novelist. Wang got off to a flying start in literature with her novel *The Lily Theatre* (1997), which won the Dutch prize for the best-selling literary debut and was immediately sold to foreign publishers. Wang, who was born in China and studied English at the University of Beijing, published several literary works in China. In 1989, as a teacher of Chinese for the School for Interpreters and Translators, she came to the Netherlands, where she continues to live and work. She wrote *The Lily Theatre* directly in Dutch. Her Dutch is noticeably influenced by Chinese: she uses Chinese expressions and sometimes translates literally, which makes her prose very lyrical and quite exceptional. Some critics have praised these linguistic innovations, while others have thought them rather weak. The novel tells the story of a young woman in communist China. Wang describes the cruel totalitarian regime from within. Apart from *The Lily Theatre* she has published several stories and columns in magazines, and a novella in early 1999. Her second novel is forthcoming.

AAn, MMe

Warner, Marina (*b*. 1946), English novelist, critic, children's writer. Born in London and educated at Lady Margaret Hall, Oxford, where she earned an MA in 1967, Warner began her writing career with the study *The Dragon Empress: The Life and Times of Tz'u-hsi 1835–1908* (1972). Her elegantly written feminist cultural histories focus on verbal and visual representations of and myths about women, as in *Alone of All Her Sex: The Myth and Cult of the Virgin Mary* (1976), *Joan of Arc* (1981), *Monuments and Maidens* (1985), and *From the Beast to the Blonde: On Fairy Tales and Their Tellers* (1995). Her interest in fairy tales is also expressed in her fiction; her own versions of classic tales are collected in *Mermaids in the Basement* (1993). Identity and sexuality are important themes in her novels *In a Dark Wood* (1977), *The Skating Party* (1982), and *Indigo: or, Mapping the Waters* (1992), which is a retelling of

Shakespeare's *The Tempest*. Her autobiographical novel *The Lost Father* (1988) won the Commonwealth Writers' Prize and was short-listed for the Booker Prize. A visiting professor at universities in England, Holland, and the US, Warner has also published several books for children.

DVT

Warner-Vieyra, Myriam (*b*. 1939), Guadeloupean novelist. Born in Pointe-à-Pitre, Guadeloupe, Warner-Vieyra moved to Paris at the age of 12, where she attended high school. In 1961 she married filmmaker and critic Paulin Vieyra and moved to Senegal, where she still resides and works as a librarian at the University of Dakar. She has three children. She has written two novels and a book of short stories. She considers herself to be Guadeloupean, French, and Senegalese; however, her childhood emigration from the Caribbean led to a deep nostalgia that is embodied in her first novel *As the Sorcerer Said* (1980). *Juletane* (1982) is her best-known novel. It details the psychological disintegration of a Caribbean woman who marries an African man and struggles to accept her role as his second wife. Warner-Vieyra's short stories, like her novels, often revolve around sexual violence against women, madness, and cultural issues.

GAn, JV

Wasserstein, Wendy (*b*. 1950), US playwright. Born in Brooklyn and raised in Manhattan, Wasserstein earned a BA from Mount Holyoke College in 1971 and an MFA from the Yale School of Drama. Her first play *Any Woman Can't* (1973), a farce about a woman establishing independence in a man's world, was first produced at Yale. Her plays, known for their humor, cultural satire, clever dialogue, and believable characters, focus on intelligent and affluent contemporary women. She explores choices these women make, conventions imposed upon them, and tensions between traditional and feminist viewpoints. *Uncommon Women and Others*

(1975), which began as her master's thesis, reunites five Mount Holyoke College graduates six years after graduation. *The Heidi Chronicles* (1988), for which Wasserstein won a Pulitzer Prize and a Tony Award, traces twenty-five years of a woman's growing disillusionment. Other plays include *Isn't it Romantic* (1981), which concerns marriage and motherhood, *The Sisters Rosensweig* (1992), and *An American Daughter* (1998), in which a woman nominated for Surgeon General faces up to the compromises she's made. The winner of many awards for her dramas, Wasserstein adapted *Uncommon Women* and John Cheever's 'The Sorrows of Gin' for television and has also published *Bachelor Girls*, a collection of humorous essays.

DVT

Wassmo, Herbjørg (*b*. 1942), Norwegian novelist, poet. Born in Vesterålen in northern Norway, Wassmo has quickly become one of Norway's most critically acclaimed and widely read novelists, and the foremost regional writer of northern Norway. Educated as a teacher, she began writing poetry as a child. Two early poetry collections, *Vingeslag* ('The Flapping of Wings,' 1976) and *Flotid* ('Tides,' 1977), were followed in 1981 by *The House with the Blind Glass Windows*, the first novel in the trilogy about Tora, a child of a Norwegian mother and German soldier father, who suffers emotional and physical abuse both at home and in Norwegian society right after World War II. Already part of the literary canon, Tora's story is continued in *Det stumme rommet* ('The Silent Room,' 1983) and reaches its tragic end in *Hudløs himmel* ('The Skinless Sky,' 1986). *Dina's Book* (1989), selected the best book of the 1980s by the Norwegian Bookseller's Association, features a strong and ruthless heroine, and begins a new trilogy set in the nineteenth century. Dealing with themes of guilt and atonement and spanning three generations, the trilogy continues with the story of Dina's son Benjamin in *Lykkens sønn* ('Son of Joy,' 1992) and her granddaughter Karna in *Karnas arv* ('Karna's Inheritance,' 1997). Wassmo received the Critic's Prize in 1981 and Nordisk Råds Litteraturpris in 1987. She has also written several plays and a children's book.

MHH

Webb, Phyllis (1927–1997), Canadian poet. Born in Victoria, British Columbia, Webb was educated at the University of British Columbia and McGill University. Her first individual volume of poetry *Even Your Right Eye* was published in 1956. Webb's poetic method involved slow and careful crafting, honing, and polishing of each poem, so her oeuvre is relatively small. Her early poetry, as in *Naked Poems* (1965), is formal, austere, simple yet elegant. Her later poems, as in *Wilson's Bowl* (1980), are still economical and controlled, but are no longer minimalist. While treating her characteristic subjects of personal life, loneliness, and death, the later volumes reveal more complexity in their ideas and their musicality. Other volumes of poetry include *Selected Poems* (1971), *Sunday Water* (1982), *The Vision Tree* (1982; Governor-General's Award), *Water and Light* (1984), and *Hanging Fire* (1990).

JEM

Weigel, Sigrid (*b.* 1950), German feminist literary theorist. Weigel received her PhD from the University of Hamburg in 1977 with a thesis on revolutionary pamphlet literature in 1848 in Berlin. During her years as a professor of German literature in Hamburg, she produced such influential feminist works as *Die verborgene Frau* ('The Hidden Woman,' 1983, with Inge Stephan), in which she developed criteria for a feminist critique of German literature, and *Die Stimme der Medusa* ('The Voice of Medusa,' 1987), which examined the history of contemporary German women's writing. Her often interdisciplinary approach has resulted in collaborative works on topics ranging from historical

feminist journalism to the fine arts to the relationship between Jewish culture and femininity in the modern era. She is well-known in the English-speaking world for numerous translated essays, among them '"Woman begins Relating to Herself." Contemporary German Women's Literature,' and for her book on Walter Benjamin, *Body-and Image Space. Rereading Walter Benjamin* (1992). Weigel taught German literature at the University of Zurich for three years before becoming the acting chair of the Einstein Forum in Potsdam in 1998.

JH

Weldon, Fay (*b.* 1933), English novelist, short story writer, playwright. Born in Worcestershire, England, Weldon grew up in New Zealand with her divorced writer-mother, sister, and grandmother. She graduated from the University of St Andrews in Scotland, having studied economics and psychology, and worked for a time as an advertising copywriter. Her first works were dramas for the stage, radio, and television, including the television play *The Fat Woman's Joke* (1966) which she adapted into her first novel in 1967. Weldon's bold and darkly comic feminist novels focus on the lives of modern women as they struggle with relationships, men, children, sex, their bodies, and the vicissitudes of contemporary culture. Her many novels include *Down Among the Women* (1971), *Female Friends* (1975), *Remember Me* (1976), *Puffball* (1980), *The Life and Loves of a She-Devil* (1983), which was made into a film in 1990, *The Hearts and Lives of Men* (1987), and *Big Women* (1997). *The Cloning of Joanna May* (1989) is a tale of creation and genetic manipulation. In *Darcy's Utopia* (1990), a woman's vision of the future clashes with modern realities. *Big Girls Don't Cry* (1998) takes on the feminist movement as it follows the founders of a feminist press from the 1970s to the 1990s. Weldon's nonfiction includes *Letters to Alice on First Reading Jane Austen* (1984), *Sacred*

Cows (1989), a polemic against censorship, and the essay collection *Godless in Eden* (1999). She has also published several collections of short stories, including *Wicked Women* (1995) and *A Hard Time To Be a Father* (1998).

DVT

Wertenbaker, Timberlake (*b.* 1951), English playwright, translator. Born to Anglo-American parents and raised in France, Wertenbaker is bilingual and has translated dramatic works by Anouilh, Marivaux, Lorca, Sophocles, and Euripedes. She has worked as a journalist and teacher, has been a writer-in-residence at the Royal Court Theatre in London, and has lived and worked in Greece, where some of her plays have been performed. Her award-winning plays, which include *This is No Place for Tallulah Bankhead* (1978), *Case to Answer* (1980), *Breaking Through* (1980), *The Grace of Mary Traverse* (1985), *Break of Day* (1995), and *After Darwin* (1999), are radical in their feminism and their formal experimentation. *New Anatomies* (1981), about the nineteenth-century explorer Isabelle Eberhardt; *Abel's Sister* (1984), which changes the gender in the Cain and Abel story; and the award-winning *Our Country's Good* (1988), about a band of Australian convicts performing George Farquhar's eighteenth-century play *The Recruiting Officer*, all demonstrate Wertenbaker's inventive reinterpretation of mythical and historical events.

DVT

Wicks, Susan (*b.* 1947), British poet, novelist. Born in Tunbridge Wells, Kent, Wicks was educated at the University of Hull (BA, 1971) and the University of Sussex (PhD, 1975). She married John Collins in 1974 and has two daughters. She has taught English in France and French in Ireland, and has been a tutor and instructor at the University of Kent. Her first volume of poetry *Singing Underwater* was published in 1992. It establishes her pre-

occupation with the details of domestic life and her fascination with the evocative nature of its material objects. *Open Diagnosis* (1994), which deals in part with the author's multiple sclerosis, is a more confessional volume. *Driving My Father* (1995), an autobiographical prose work about the death of her mother and the deterioration of her father, is closely observed and moving, yet unsentimental. She approaches the same subject matter, but from a greater distance, in her third volume of poetry *The Clever Daughter* (1996), in which she focuses on death, the past, and memories. Her two novels *The Key* (1997), about a woman's affair with a younger man, and *Little Thing* (1998), about an Englishwoman teaching in France, are both studies of manipulation and betrayal, elegantly written, subtle and spare.

JEM

Wicomb, Zoë (*b.* 1948), South African short story writer, essayist, activist. Born in Cape Province, South Africa, Wicomb was educated locally in rural Namaqualand. She completed her first degree in Arts at the University College for Cape Coloureds in Western Cape. In 1970 she left South Africa to study English literature at Reading University in England. Her book *You Can't Get Lost in Cape Town* (1987) is a collection of ten short stories. The stories are connected by a central character, Frieda Shenton, who leaves the veld to go to the colored locality and then to Capetown, to England, and back home again to a country she once escaped because of its racially oppressive laws. Wicomb's essays have been published in journals and anthologies such as *Snow on the Cane Fields: Women's Writing and Creole Subjectivity* (1996). She teaches English and Black literature courses in Nottingham, England, where she resides. An active member of her community's post-apartheid movement, she lectures widely on South African politics.

MU

Wiggins, Marianne (*b.* 1947), US novelist. Born in Lancaster, Pennsylvania, Wiggins began her career with two somewhat autobiographical novels, *Babe* (1975) and *Went South* (1980), which depict the struggles of a single mother with a young child. She establishes her intelligent, poetic, and quietly witty style in her third novel *Separate Checks* (1984) and in *Herself in Love* (1987), a collection of short stories. *John Dollar* (1989), her first critical and popular success, marked a significant development in her writing. Set on an island off Burma in the 1910s, it is a shocking yet lyrical account of a shipwreck and the subsequent savagery that emerges in a group of English schoolgirls. The novel was highly acclaimed but was overshadowed by events in the life of her then husband, Salman Rushdie, who went into hiding shortly after its publication. The stories in the collection *Bet They'll Miss Us When We're Gone* (1991; published in the US as *Learning Urdu*) were written while living in hiding with Rushdie. Wiggins and Rushdie have since divorced. *Eveless Eden* (1995) is a dramatic novel set across Europe about a love triangle between a war correspondent, a photographer, and an unscrupulous Romanian businessman. Some of its characters reappear in the novel *Almost Heaven* (1998).

JEM

Willumsen, Dorrit (*b.* 1940), Danish novelist, short story writer. Raised by her maternal grandparents, Willumsen has a keen sense of absence, disconnection, and the search for identity, expressed in a style that is sparse, absurd, and grotesque. These have become her trademark features, already demonstrated in her debut collection of stories *Knagen* ('The Hook,' 1965). She is married to Jess Ørnsbo, a writer, and has one son. A modernist in style and often a feminist in content, she is a detailed observer of our contemporary environment, and a fine interpreter of times and persons removed either in time or geography. In her novel *Marie* (1983), she probes into the life of the famous French wax figure artist. The novel *Bang, En roman om Herman Bang* ('Bang: A Novel about Herman Bang,' 1996) is about the Danish turn-of-the-century writer, with whom Willumsen feels a special kinship. The novel brought her the 1997 Nordic Council Prize, amidst a lively debate about fiction and history. *Manden som påskud* ('The Man as a Pretext,' 1980) presents modern living as hostile and alienating to men and women. Her highly original art of short story writing can be admired in the collection *If It Really Were a Film* (1987). Her latest work is *De kattens feriedage* ('The Damn Holidays,' 1997).

MŽ

Winterson, Jeanette (*b.* 1959), British novelist, short story writer. Adopted by a Pentecostal Evangelical family in Lancashire, England, Winterson was prepared for life as a religious missionary when, at age 15, a lesbian love affair led to her banishment from the church. She worked at odd jobs before reading English at St Catherine's College, Oxford, from 1978 to 1981. Her first book *Oranges Are Not the Only Fruit* (1985), an autobiographical *Bildungsroman*, won the Whitbread Award for a first novel and was adapted into an award-winning television series. Her second novel *Boating for Beginners* (1985), a reworking of the story of Noah's Ark, marks the beginning of her imaginative and witty narrative experiments. Her fantastical, playful, and challenging novels, linguistically and philosophically rich, mythic and prophetic, revise history, fairy tales, and the Bible. *The Passion* (1987) follows the intersecting lives of Napoleon's chef and the web-footed daughter of a Venetian boatman. *Sexing the Cherry* (1989) is another 'historical novel' of sorts, in which a young boy in seventeeth-century London travels on magical journeys through time. *Written on the Body* (1992), in which the gender of the main character is not revealed, and *Gut Symmetries* (1997), in which physics and love are intertwined, both deal with triangular relationships. *Art and Lies* (1994) features Handel, Picasso, and Sappho. Winterson has also published *Art Objects* (1995), a collection of essays, and *The World and Other Places* (1998), her first collection of short stories.

DVT

Wittig, Monique (*b*. 1935), French writer. Born in Alsace, Wittig moved to Paris to pursue her studies. She became an influential radical feminist leader in the French women's liberation movement in the late 1960s and early 1970s. She co-founded several groups such as the Petites Marguerites and the Féministes révolutionnaires. Her subversive writing has influenced Western feminists. Her first novel *The Opoponax* (1964), about lesbianism and the role of language in the social construction of sexuality and femininity, received the Prix Medicis. She pursued her exploration of language's oppression in *Les Guérillères* (1969), a classic work of feminism. This intensely poetic novel expresses the need to assert a womanist culture and to rework androcentric myths. *The Lesbian Body* (1973) is a rewriting of the Orpheus myth from a lesbian perspective; it is also a revalorizing of the female body. In her subsequent works, she continues to rewrite the great Western works in a feminist utopian fashion. In her book *The Straight Mind and Other Essays* (1992), she debates the concept of gender, the role of language in culture, the role of women in the social contract and political theory. Since 1976, she has been living in the US and she currently teaches at the University of Arizona.

JV

Witting, Amy (Joan Levick, née Fraser) (1918–2001), Australian fiction writer, poet. Witting was born in Annandale, at the time a 'tough' inner suburb of Sydney and a rich source of subject matter. Educated at the local Catholic school and Fort Street High School, she attended Sydney University in the 1930s, where she was known for her sharp intellect and acerbic wit. She then taught French and German in NSW high schools, and continued to write. Her first short story 'Goodbye Ady, Goodbye Joe' was published in the *New Yorker* in 1965, and others followed in Australian literary journals. Retiring from teaching in 1974, Witting published her first novel *The Visit* in 1977 – a perceptive study of small-town relationships. The self-published poetry collection *Travel Diary* (1985) gained critical acclaim, and the autobiographically influenced *I for Isobel* (1989) and the short stories collected in *Marriages* (1990) brought her wider recognition. Her second book of poetry *Beauty is the Straw* (1991) made plain Witting's strength as a fine poet. In 1993 she received the Patrick White Award. To coincide with her eighteenth birthday, Witting's *Collected Poetry* was published in January 1998. Her fourth novel *The Ante-room* was also published that year.

YM

Wohmann, Gabriele (*b*. 1932), German novelist. Born in Darmstadt, Wohmann studied German and Romance literatures, music, and philosophy in Frankfurt am Main and worked as a teacher. Since 1956 she has lived as a writer in Darmstadt. She 'diagnosed' herself as being obsessed with writing, and she accepted this 'mania' which results in her impressive production. *Abschied für länger* ('Farewell for Long,' 1965) centers upon a woman who finally emancipates herself from her parents. However, she has to return to them after leaving her partner. *Ernste Absicht* ('Serious Intention,' 1970) describes the thoughts of a woman who finds herself during a stay in a hospital. A conflict between public image and private person is thematized in *Schönes Gehege* ('Beautiful Preserve,' 1975). *Glücksspiel* ('Gamble,' 1981) shows the individual in conflict with expectations in family and society. *Flötentöne* ('Flute-Tones,' 1987) deals with the isolation of the individual and *Aber* *das war noch nicht das Schlimmste* ('But That Was Not Yet the Worst,' 1995) narrates how death and the fear of death are dealt with in extreme life circumstances. Other works are stories about women: *Die Schönste im ganzen Land* ('The Prettiest Woman in the Country,' 1995) and *Das Handicap* ('The Handicap,' 1996). She has received several German literary awards.

MMu

Wolf, Christa (*b.* 1929), East German fiction writer, essayist. Wolf was born in Landsberg and studied German literature at the universities of Jena and Leipzig; she received a PhD from the latter in 1953. In her writings, she has always tried to combine a historical perspective with personal experience, a style which has been called 'subjective authenticity.' Her novels *Divided Heaven* (1963) and *The Quest for Christa T.* (1968) deal critically with the social and political development of East Germany and the failure of individualist attitudes in a tightly planned society. Other topics of her novels include Germany's Nazi past, which she narrates in *Patterns of Childhood* (1976), German romanticism, exemplified in *No Place on Earth* (1979), and the growing conflict between technological progress and individual destiny, depicted in *Accident: A Day's News* (1987). Wolf is fascinated by ancient myths, which she explores in *Cassandra: A Novel and Four Essays* (1983) and in the novel *Medea: A Modern Retelling* (1996). The collections *What Remains and Other Stories* (1990) and *Parting from Phantoms: Selected Writings* (1994) combine public speeches, essays, letters and diary entries with short prose, thematizing the interaction between public and private spheres. A prolific author, Wolf has received numerous prizes in East Germany as well as honorary degrees and awards in Austria, Italy, France, and the US.

PM-K

Wong, Bikwan Flora (*see* Huang Biyun)

Wright, Judith (*b.* 1915), Australian poet, children's writer, essayist. Born in Armidale, NSW, Wright's responsive and responsible depictions of word and world have vitally influenced Australian cultural life. A social and political activist, her poetry reflects passionate concerns about Australian land-use and heritage, indigenous rights, and environmental sustainability, which partly arose from an interrogation of the privileges of her NSW inheritance. Educated locally and then at the University of Sydney (1943–7), she married the philosopher J. P. McKinney. In her poetry, Wright has striven to create a language to express Australian vision and has courageously written of love, creativity, and regenerative processes. Her collections *The Gateway* (1953) and *Two Fires* (1955) articulate a sense of a world threatened by disunity. Wright has consistently emphasized the gap between knowledge of material existence and understanding of human emotion. The sparer, occasionally satiric, poetry of *Alive* (1973) prefigures *Birds* (1982). Wright was a foundation member of the Australian Academy of Humanities and member of the Australia Council. She has been awarded seven honorary doctorates and numerous prizes: among them are the Grace Leven award (twice), the *Encyclopedia Britannica* award (1964), the Robert Frost Memorial Award (1976), the Asian World Prize for poetry (1984), and the 1992 Queen's Gold Medal for Poetry.

LJ

Wynter, Sylvia (*b.* 1928), Jamaican novelist, dramatist. Born in Cuba to Jamaican parents, Wynter attended school in Jamaica and the University of London, receiving a BA (1949) and an MA (1953). In 1958 she married Guyanese writer Jan Carew. In 1962 she established a professional theater company in Jamaica. She wrote and produced *Shh, It's a Wedding* (1961), *Miracle in Lime Lane* (1962; with Carew), an adaptation of Roger Mais's *Brother Man* (1965), and a pageant about the 1865 Jamaican Morant Bay Rebellion (1965). With the publication of *The Hills of Hebron* (1962), she became the first black woman novelist from the English-speaking Caribbean. The novel depicts the struggle for leadership of a religious sect following the death of its messianic leader, and addresses such themes as the validity of folk culture, the oppression of women, racial discrimination, and political and religious corruption. In the 1970s, Wynter moved to the US and resumed her academic career. A professor of Spanish and Portuguese at Stanford University since 1977, she has published many scholarly articles on Afro-Caribbean writing and culture.

JSp

X

Xi Xi (*b*. 1938), Chinese-Hong Kong fiction writer, essayist. Xi Xi is the pen name of Zhang Yan. Born in Shanghai, she moved to Hong Kong in 1950. In 1958, after her graduation from Grantham College of Education, she worked as a primary school teacher. Taking an early retirement in 1979, she devoted herself to writing. Her first short story 'Maliya' ('Maria,' 1965), which won critical acclaim, describes the experience of a Belgian nun encountering a captured French mercenary during the Congo war of liberation. This attempt to write on subjects beyond Hong Kong exemplifies Xi Xi's willingness to use exotic settings. The novel *Xiao lu* ('Deer Hunt,' 1982) adopts two contrasting perspectives to narrate the life of ordinary people and that of the imperial emperor Qianlong during the Qing Dynasty. But Xi Xi is best known for works which are directly related to women's experiences, such as *A Girl Like Me* (1984) and *Aidao ru fang* ('Elegy for a Breast,' 1992). The former is a monologue of a young woman beautician working in a funeral parlor in Hong Kong; the latter is based on the writer's personal experience of breast cancer. Other important works relating to the city of Hong Kong include 'My City' (1979), 'The Story of Fertile Town' (1982), 'Marvels of a Floating City' (1986), and *Fei zhan* ('Flying Carpet,' 1996). Xi Xi has also published essays, poems, and critical comments. Her fiction has won many awards in Hong Kong and Taiwan.

SC

Xia Yu (*b*. 1956), Chinese-Taiwan poet, songwriter. Xia Yu was born in Taipei, Taiwan. After graduating from the National Academy of Arts, she worked for various publishing companies and television stations. Besides writing poetry, she is a successful writer of lyrics and music for popular songs. She has lived in southern France in recent years and travels often. Xia's poetry typically describes personal experiences in an urban setting; it is imaginative, experimental, and refreshingly unpredictable. She challenges poetic conventions in every respect, from subject matter, form, and language to physical production. She designed and published her first volume of poetry *Beiwanglu* ('Memoranda,' 1984) by herself, in an unusual size and color of paper, with a handwritten title on the cover. The poetry book enjoyed phenomenal success. In a poem from her second book of poetry *Fuyushu* ('Ventriloquism,' 1991), she mixes and matches disparate elements of Chinese characters to create simulacra that look tantalizingly familiar yet are unintelligible and meaningless. Her recent book of poetry *Moca, buke mingzhuang* ('Rubbing, Indescribable,' 1995) is a recreation of the poems in *Fuyushu* through random rearrangements of words and phrases. The intent is to test the elasticity of signification. Although Xia dislikes being labeled a feminist, her poetry often parodies gender stereotypes and highlights the woman as the creator-poet.

MY

Xiao Sa (*b.* 1953), Chinese-Taiwan fiction writer. Born in Nanjing, China, Xiao Sa (pen name of Xiao Qingyu) was taken to Taiwan by her parents soon after her birth. She taught at a primary school in Taipei after earning a degree at the Girl's Teacher Institute. She was married to film director Zhang Yi until their divorce in 1986. First published at the age of 17, and prolific ever since, Xiao Sa deals mostly with the dilemmas of urban men and women caught in Taiwan's economic and political transition. She writes about the pitiable yet despicable lives of working women, the struggle of disoriented men to fulfill traditional obligations while searching for themselves, and people's reluctant choices in marriage, career, relationships with children and parents. Xiao is also known for her treatment of juvenile problems encountered in her teaching experience. While her stories deal with universal issues, they also address the specific reality of Taiwan society striving for political and economic standing under the military threat of communist China. Her major works include *Wo er Hansheng* ('My Son Hansheng,' 1981), *Shaonian Ahxin* ('The Youth Ahxin,' 1984), and *Xiafei zhi jia* ('A Family from Xiafei,' 1981), which was made into a film by her former husband titled *Wo zheyang guole yisheng* ('The Life of Guimei,' 1986).

F-yM

Y

Yamada Eimi (**Amy**) (*b.* 1959), Japanese novelist, fiction writer. Born Yamada Futaba in Tokyo, Japan, Yamada studied literature at Meiji University in Tokyo and spent several years as an illustrator for girls' comics. Her award-winning first novel *Bedtime Eyes* (1985) gained attention for its frank depiction of sexuality and its portrayal of the romantic relationship between a Japanese woman and an African-American man. This paradigm occurs throughout Yamada's fiction, including *Jeshii no sebone* ('Jesse's Backbone,' 1986) and *Trash* (1991). Her short story 'When a Man Loves a Woman' (1987) is characteristic of her collection *Sōru myujikku rabaazu onrii* ('Soul Music Lovers Only,' 1987), which received the 97th Naoki Prize. This story investigates love and sexuality in the relationships of African-Americans in the US. Her 1988 novel *Kneel Down and Lick My Feet* depicts the lives of several women working as dominatrices at an S&M club. She has also written about the difficulties of adolescence in *Fūsō no kyōshitsu* ('Classroom Burial,' 1988), which won the Hirabayashi Taiko Prize, and *Afterschool Keynotes* (1989). Her playful use of the English language, especially slang, is apparent in both her texts and their titles, *24/7* (1992), *120% COOOL* (1994), and *4U* (1997).

KKo

Yamanaka, Lois-Ann (*b.* 1961), US novelist,

poet. Born in Ho'olchua, Molokai, Hawaii, of Japanese-American heritage, Yamanaka was educated at the University of Hawaii at Manoa, where she earned a BEd in 1983 and a MEd in 1987. She lives in Honolulu. Her first book *Saturday Night at the Pahala Theatre*, a collection of four verse novellas, was published in 1993. Through powerful dramatic monologues and a combination of pidgin English and teenage slang, she explores the hard lives of working-class Japanese-American adolescents in Hawaii. Those lives are also the subject of her trilogy of coming-of-age novels set in Hilo, Hawaii. The first, *Wild Meat and Bully Burgers* (1996), set in the 1970s, explores how ethnic identity complicates the other, more typical adolescent crises of the heroine. A series of connected vignettes, the novel is funny, realistic, and utterly distinctive in its setting and use of pidgin English. *Blu's Hanging* (1997) is a darker work about an impoverished and troubled family trying to cope with their mother's death. *Heads by Harry* (1999) concerns a teenaged girl who wants to learn her father's trade of taxidermy instead of going away to college. Yamanaka has won two Pushcart Prizes for her poetry and the Lannan Literary Award for fiction.

JEM

Yang Jiang (*b.* 1911), Chinese dramatist, fiction writer. Born in Beijing, Yang earned a BA in foreign literature at Dongwu University, and attended graduate school at Qinghua University. After she married the eminent scholar Qian Zhongshu in 1935, the couple studied abroad in England and France. Since returning to China in 1938, she has held academic positions at Fudan Women's College, Qinghua University, and the Chinese Academy of Social Sciences. Yang began writing fiction and drama in her spare time in the 1930s. Her early comedies *Chenxin ruyi* ('As You Desire,' 1943) and *Nongzhen chengjia* ('The Cheat,' 1944) received favorable reviews when performed in Shanghai during the Japanese Occupation. A keen comic sensibility pervades much of Yang's writing. *Six Chapters from My Life 'Downunder'* (1981), a memoir of the Cultural Revolution (1966–76), captures the profound absurdity of life at the cadre school where she and Qian underwent 'reeducation' through agricultural labor. *Xizao* ('Shower,' 1988), Yang's first novel, satirizes intellectuals in the 1950s. In addition to her creative writing and literary criticism, Yang also translated three major European novels: *Gil Blas*, *La Vida de Lazarillo de Tormes*, and *Don Quixote*.

ADD

Yang Kwi-ja (*b.* 1955), Korean fiction writer. Yang is a native of Chŏnju, a provincial capital in southwestern Korea, where she obtained her BA in Korean literature at Wŏn'gwang University. Since her debut work, 'Tasi sijakhanŭn ach'im' ('A Morning Begun Anew,' 1978), her major focus has been on the enervated daily lives of the socially and economically displaced. Most representative is her collection of short stories *Wŏnmi-dong saramdŭl* ('People in Wŏnmi-dong,' 1987), with 'The Wŏnmi-dong Poet' (1986) illustrating the crushed life of a promising young man victimized by police. In 'Ch'ŏnmach'ong kanŭn kil' ('The Road to the Heavenly Horse Ancient Tomb,' 1988), she indicts the government's human rights violations by tracing the torture in-

flicted on a magazine reporter. In her first full-length novel *Hŭimang* ('Hope,' 1991), she offers a possibility for healing the collective wounds of the socially uprooted. Her 'Sumun kkot' ('Hidden Flowers,' 1992; Yi Sang Prize) underscores the importance of inner strength necessary for survival through the political oppression of 1980s Korea. Yang's recent novel *Mosun* ('Contradictions,' 1998) suggests a new thematic interest, exploring the ultimate meaning of love, happiness, and gender relationships – a marked departure from her trademark preoccupation with public or politically oriented issues.

Y-HK

Yang Mo (1914–1995), Chinese fiction writer. Yang Mo (originally Yang Chengye) was born into a university president's family in Beijing. She attended an all-girl high school but was forced to drop out after three years because of her family's bankruptcy. She worked as a schoolteacher, private tutor, and bookstore clerk, and audited classes at Beijing University. In the early 1930s she began to be involved in underground communist activities. She published essays, reports, and stories to expose the atrocities committed by the Japanese armies in North China. After the founding of the People's Republic of China, Yang worked in several official posts. In 1958 she published her first novel *The Song of Youth*, a portrait of the growth of a young female intellectual during the revolution. The novel carries on the autobiographical tradition of the women writers of the early twentieth century, but at the same time focuses on affirming the Communist Party's political strength and its absolute authority to speak in the name of the nation. It was an instant success and provoked heated national debates about the protagonists. Republished in 1960, with revisions based on the readers' suggestions and enlarged sections on the rural class struggle, the novel was made into an award-winning film of the same title (1960). After the Cultural Revolution,

Yang published two other novels, *Fangfei zhi ge* ('The Song of Fangfei,' 1985) and *Yinghua zhi ge* ('The Song of Yinghua,' 1989), as sequels to *The Song of Youth*.

JZ

Yared, Nazik Saba (*b*. 1928), Palestinian novelist. Born in Jerusalem to supportive parents, Yared received her BA from Cairo University. After marrying and giving birth to three children, she resumed her education, earning an MA and a PhD in Arabic literature from the American University of Beirut. She began her literary career after her children were grown. Her first novel *Nuqṭat al-Dā'ira* ('Center of the Circle,' 1983) is concerned with the financial independence of a married woman who is caught in the traditional role of being a wife and mother. In *Al-Ṣadā al-Makhnūq* ('The Strangled Echo,' 1986), she examines the impact of the civil war in destroying the family. *Improvisation on a Missing String* (1992) recounts the story of an unattractive young woman struggling to assert herself in a hostile environment. Yared's nonfiction works include *Arab Traveller and Western Civilization* (1979). She received the Chevalier de L'Ordre des Palmes Académiques from the French government. She is currently a professor of Arabic literature at the Lebanese American University in Beirut.

JTZ

Yoshimoto Banana (*b*. 1964), Japanese novelist, short story writer, essayist. In 1987 Yoshimoto Mahoko adopted the pen name 'Banana' and burst onto the Japanese literary scene with the novella *Kitchen*, which won two major prizes and quickly became a worldwide best-seller. Written while she waitressed in a golf-club café, the sweetly melancholic tale examines love, food, and death in the lives of orphaned Mikage, her friend Yuichi, and his transsexual mother/father. Born and raised in Tokyo, Yoshimoto graduated from Nihon University in 1987 with a Fine Arts degree. Her award-winning BA thesis

'Moonlight Shadow,' about teenage bereavement, was published with *Kitchen*. She has subsequently written more than a dozen novels, essay collections, and volumes of short stories. Of these, *Kitchen* (1987), *NP* (1990), *Amrita* (1994), and the short story collection *Lizard* (1993) have been translated into English. Recurring themes include gender-bending, the family, alienation, sexuality, death and mourning, and nostalgia; her latest novel *SLY* (1996) is about the impact of HIV on a group of friends. The daughter of a renowned philosopher, Yoshimoto herself has become an ambiguous voice of her generation: while some readers regard her writing as cartoon-like, others praise her wistful visions of young people haunted by the dilemmas of late-twentieth-century life.

JGra

Yosifova, Ekaterina Petrova (*b*. 1941), Bulgarian poet. Born in Kyustendil, Yosifova graduated with a BA in Russian from the University of Sofia in 1964. She is divorced and has two children. As a high school teacher in Kyustendil, she published *Kuso putuvane* ('Brief Journey,' 1969) and *Noshtem ide vyatur* ('The Wind Comes at Night,' 1972). Criticized by the establishment, her poems were enthusiastically received by open-minded readers. From 1971 onwards, she worked as a newspaper editor and repertoire consultant for the theater in Kyustendil. At present, she is editor-in-chief of the literary magazine *Struma*. In *Posveshtenie* ('Dedication,' 1979), *Kushta v poleto* ('House in the Field,' 1983), and *Imena* ('Names,' 1984), she discovers unexpected ways to infuse symbolic significance into images taken from nature or daily routine. The somber mood of *Podozreniya* ('Suspicions,' 1993) and *Nenuzhno povedenie* ('Useless Conduct,' 1994) is partly counterbalanced by the playful *Prikazka za drakoncheto Poli* ('Tale about the Little Dragon Poli,' 1995). English translations of Yosifova's works are published in the anthologies *Devil's*

Dozen (1990), *Windows on the Black Sea* (1992), *Clay and Star* (1992), *The Many-Voiced Wave* (1993), and *An Anthology of Contemporary Poetry* (1994).

LPG

Yourcenar, Marguerite (1903–1987), French-writing novelist, translator. Born Marguerite de Crayencour in Brussels, raised motherless in Belgium and France, resident of Mount Desert Island, Maine from 1937 until her death, with her companion Grace Frick, Yourcenar considered herself a wanderer by education and inclination. She adopted the anagram of her aristocratic family name with the 1921 publication of a poem financed by her father. An early novella *Alexis* (1929), the story of a man who abandons his wife to live out his true sexuality, won her critical acclaim. Blurring boundaries of gender and genre in classic, lyrical French prose, she fashioned primarily male protagonists characterized by their pursuit of knowledge, whether traditional, esoteric, or carnal. Best known for her first-person narrative *Memoirs of Hadrian* (1951), a compelling analysis of statesmanship, love, and loss, she fashioned another 'uncertain and evasive self' in Zeno, the Renaissance philosopher, physician, and alchemist of *The Abyss* (1968). This erudite 'poet historian' was the first woman elected to the prestigious Académie Française in 1980. A lover of Greek civilization, the translator of Cavafy's poetry and Virginia Woolf's *The Waves*, the chronicler of family history in *Le labyrinthe du monde* ('Labyrinthine World,' 3 vols, 1974, 1977, 1988), Yourcenar hid herself in the careful literary production that spanned her lifetime.

JHS

Yu Lihua (*b*. 1931), Chinese fiction writer. Born into a middle-class intellectual family in Shanghai, Yu Lihua moved to Taiwan in her teens and graduated from National Taiwan University with a BA in history in 1953. Subsequently she majored in journalism at the University of California at Los Angeles, from which she received an MA in 1956. Since 1968 she has taught at the State University of New York at Albany. In 1957 she received the Samuel Goldwyn Creative Writing Award for her short story 'Sorrow at the End of the Yangtze River,' written in English. Yu is a pioneer of 'overseas Chinese student literature' and of feminist literature. Her work on women examines and critiques the patriarchal institutions in which Chinese women live, though her female characters are endowed with psychological complexity, individuality and, above all, a strong will to live. English translations of her works are available in several anthologies.

MY

Yu Luojin (*b*. 1946), Chinese fiction writer. Born in Beijing, Yu Luojin graduated from the Academy of Industrial Arts in Beijing in 1965. During the Cultural Revolution (1966–76), she spent three years in a labor camp because of political statements found in her diary. Her brother Yu Luoke was executed by the government for his dissident views. After her release in 1970, Yu married a farmer; they had a son and divorced in 1974. Returning to Beijing in 1976, she married a worker in 1977. In the early 1980s, her televised lawsuit for a second divorce was a public scandal. In 1982 she married a teacher and in 1986 sought political asylum during a trip to West Germany, where she now lives. After another divorce, she married a German. Yu's works are often autobiographical and courageous in revealing her vulnerability and the need to use her sex to gain power and to improve her personal circumstances. Marriage for convenience is a central theme in her fiction. Her first autobiographical novel *A Chinese Winter's Tale* (1980) mingles the personal with political and social history by presenting a subjective account of events in a woman's life during the Cultural Revolution. Her second work of autobiographical fiction

Chuntian de tonghua ('A Spring Tale,' 1982), the story of an adulterous relationship, maintains the same deeply personal tone. Her third autobiographical writing *Qiu suo* ('Seeking,' 1983) defends a woman's personal life within the scope of the politically sanctioned discourse of the time.

LW

Yu, Ovidia (*b.* 1960), Singaporean playwright. With twenty-six of her plays performed, Yu is arguably the most versatile and prolific playwright in Singapore. Abandoning medical school despite parental misgivings, she earned a BA from the University of Singapore and in quick succession wrote several plays. *Six Lonely Oysters* (1994), *The Land of a Thousand Dreams* (1996), and *The Woman in a Tree on a Hill* (1992) are among her best-known plays, the latter winning an Edinburgh Fringe First when it was performed at the Edinburgh Arts Festival in 1992. Adopting a humorous tone and diction which often segues into sly mockery, her plays treat traditional themes such as family piety and femininity in innovative ways, which clearly resonates with her young, savvy audience. She has also written a novel *Miss Moorthy Investigates* (1989), and several prizewinning short stories. In 1996 she received the Japan Chamber of Commerce and Industry Young Artist Award as well as the Singapore National Arts Council's Young Artist Award.

MHo

Yuan Qiongqiong (*b.* 1950), Chinese-Taiwan fiction writer. Born to parents who followed Chiang Kai-shek's Nationalist army in its retreat to Taiwan from mainland China in 1949, Yuan is among a group of second-generation mainlander writers whose family histories form important backdrops to their fictional worlds. After graduating from Tainan Business Vocational School, she married Guan Guan (Guan Yunlong), a poet, in 1972; they had two children before separating. Yuan's first book *Chunshui chuan* ('Spring Boat'), a short story collection, was published in 1979. In 1980 her story about a divorced woman's journey to independence, 'A Space of One's Own,' won a prize in the *United Daily* Short Story Contest. Her story anthologies *A Space of One's Own* (1981) and *Cangsang* ('Vicissitudes of Life,' 1985) contain some of Taiwan's finest stories on middle-class young urbanites caught in personal dilemmas and trying situations. In 1988 Yuan published her best-known novel *Jinsheng yuan* ('Affinities in This Life'), which traces back to years following the Retreat when mainlander refugee families struggled to resettle in Taiwan. In the 1990s, she devotes her energy to writing scripts for prime-time television drama series, several of which have received high ratings. She is currently a regular contributor to the Book Review section of the *United Daily*.

S-sYC

Z

Zabuzhko, Oksana Stefanivna (*b.* 1960), Ukrainian poet, novelist, essayist. Born in Luts'k into an intelligentsia family (her father a prominent dissident, her mother a literary scholar), Zabuzhko soon moved with her parents to Kiev, where she later graduated from Kiev University with a PhD in philosophy. Now employed at the Institute of Philosophy of Ukraine's National Academy of Sciences, she is Vice-President of the Ukrainian PEN Center. The strongest feminist voice in contemporary Ukrainian literature, Zabuzhko has developed a highly original poetic vision. Her verse combines intimately personal overtones with explorations of the embattled position of a postcolonial woman intellectual. The latter, more public aspect increasingly dominates her writing. Her collections of poetry are *Travnevyi inii* ('May Hoarfrost,' 1985), *Dyryhent ostann'oi svichky* ('Conductor of the Last Candle,' 1990) and *Avtostop* ('Hitchhiking,' 1994). A book of her poetry and essays in English translation, *A Kingdom of Fallen Statues*, appeared in 1996. Her prose includes the philosophical novella *Inoplanetianka* ('Extraterrestrial Woman,' 1992) and the novel *Pol'ovi doslidzhennia z ukrains'koho seksu* ('Field Research in Ukrainian Sex,' 1996). This highly controversial work, partly based on the author's American experiences as a Fulbright scholar, combines a critique of the contemporary Ukrainian cultural condition with elements of a narrative 'working through' a personal trauma similar to *Sylvia Plath's *The Bell Jar*. Indeed, Zabuzhko cites Plath, whose poetry she has translated into Ukrainian, Marina Tsevetaeva, and *Ingeborg Bachmann as her major literary influences. She currently is working on a study of the position of women in Ukrainian culture.

VC

Zaman, Dina (*b.* 1969), Malaysian poet, short story writer. Zaman was born in Kuala Lumpur but spent most of her childhood abroad in Japan, Russia, and other countries. She began to write seriously when enrolled as a student of creative writing at Western Michigan University. Since then, she has won several writing awards for poems such as 'How To Go To Heaven' and 'Carpe Diem.' She is currently completing a master's degree in creative writing at Lancaster University. She is also a celebrated short story writer and upcoming playwright. Her published works include *Night and Day* (1997), a collection of short stories, the poems 'The Pickpocket' and 'Snapshot of a Family Holiday' (1999), and the stories 'The Fat Woman' (1996), 'The Kacang Puteh and Assam Lady' (1996), and 'Phillipa' (1994). Her plays include *Why Did He Sleep With Me If I'm So Fat?* (1995) and *Penganggur Terhormat* (1995). Her subjects are usually simple and personal, but provocative. In a society in which Asian moral values are so fiercely guarded, she challenges pretentious concepts of beauty, virtue, morality, and aesthetics. Her lucid prose addresses important questions for marginalized people in Malaysia and gives fresh insights into her unconventional characters (often fat, ugly, or perverted women). Sadly, however, Zamanian endings are often gloomy and pessimistic.

NFAM

Zangana, Haifa (*b*. 1950), Iraqi novelist, short story writer, artist. Born in Iraq to a Kurdish father and an Arab mother, Zangana graduated from the School of Pharmacy at the University of Baghdad in 1974. A year later, she moved to Damascus, Syria to work with the Palestinian Red Crescent. In 1976 she left for London, where she still lives and works in journalism. She has contributed collages to *Memoth*, *Freedom Surrealist* (London), *The Moment*. *Le Désir libertaire* (Paris), *Kayak*, and *Dream Helmet* (US), in addition to several Arabic periodicals. She also participated in Surrealist group exhibitions in England and the US, with one-woman shows in Reykjavik (1982) and London (1988). She has been publishing short stories in local and Arab periodicals since 1973. Her first novel *Through the Vast Halls of Memory* (serialized 1986–9) draws on her life in Iraq as a political activist who was persecuted and jailed by the regime. In addition to her novel, Zangana has published two short story collections, *Bayt al-Naml* ('The Ants' Nest,' 1996) and *Akthar mimmā Narā* ('Further Than We Can See,' 1997). The theme of alienation and nostalgia and the relationship between the sexes are prevalent in her stories.

JTZ

Zaryab, Spojmai Rauuf (*b*. 1952), Afghan short story writer. Born in Kabul, Afghanistan, Zaryab received a BA from Kabul University in French language and literature and an MA in modern French literature from a French university. She is married to an Afghan writer, Rahnaward Zaryab. It is believed that she lives in France with her family. Her short stories were published in various newspapers and magazines in Afghanistan before the Islamic government came to power, and have been published outside Afghanistan in recent years.

FRB

Zayyāt, Laṭīfa al- (1923–1996), Egyptian novelist, writer, activist. Born in Damietta, Egypt, al-Zayyāt received her PhD in English literature from ʿAyn Shams University in Cairo in 1957. Having witnessed violent demonstrations against the British in her youth, her years of study were marked by extensive political activity with the Communist Party of Egypt. This landed her in jail several times in the late 1940s. Her first novel *Al-Bāb al-Maftūḥ* ('The Open Door,' 1960), ties together the emancipation of a young woman from her conservative family with the nationalist struggle of the Egyptian people against the British. Egypt's defeat in 1967, however, led to a long hiatus in her writing, as she became disillusioned with the power of literature in the face of political and military failure. In addition, her thirteen-year unhappy marriage to another academic with opposing views also troubled her. Her opposition to normalizing relations with Israel led her to jail in 1981. It was not until the publication of the short story collection *Al-Shaykhūkha wa Oiṣaṣ Ukhra* ('Old Age and Other Stories,' 1986) that she returned to writing. She dissected her life and career with brutal honesty in her autobiography *The Search: Personal Papers* (1992). She died of cancer in 1996, shortly after receiving the State Prize for Literature, Egypt's highest literary award.

JTZ

Zei, Alki (*b*. *c*. 1926), Greek children's writer, novelist. Born in Athens, Zei is Greece's best-known children's writer and author of the novel *Achilles' Fiancée* (1987). Zei's husband, the dramatist and director Yiorgos Sevastikoglu, died in 1991; the couple had two children. Zei studied philosophy and drama in Athens and attended the Institute of Cinematography in Moscow. From 1954 to 1964 she and her husband lived in political exile in the Soviet Union. In 1964 she returned to Greece only to flee again following the military takeover in 1967, at which time she moved to Paris. Her first stories for children were published in the magazine *Neaniki Foni* ('Youthful Voice') in 1943–4. Three of her children's novels – *Wildcat Under the Glass* (1963), *Petros' War* (1971) and *The Sound of the Dragon's Feet* (1977) – won Mildred L. Batchelder Awards for outstanding books translated into English from a foreign language. Among her other books for children are *O Theios Platon* ('Uncle Plato,' 1975) and *I Mov Ombrela* ('The Mauve Umbrella,' 1995). *Achilles' Fiancée*, the only work Zei wrote for adults, is a loosely autobiographical novel. Written from the perspective of a woman disillusioned with communism, the book caused a sensation when it was published, going through twenty-two editions in three years.

GH-W

Zelda (Zelda Shneurson Mishkowsky) (1914–1984), Israeli poet. Known simply as Zelda, the poet was born in Chernigoff, the Ukraine, to the famous Chasidic family Shneurson. Her father was a rabbi. The family emigrated to Israel (Palestine) in 1926 and settled in Jerusalem where Zelda lived most of her life. She studied at a teachers' seminary and taught in a religious academy for girls. Although her first collection of poetry *Pnai* ('Leisure') did not appear until 1968, she had written poetry since her childhood but did not want to publish it. Her religious poetry is widely loved and appreciated by the predominantly secular Israeli readership. Her poetry is acclaimed for its directness, precision, and simplicity, and the poet was

awarded a number of literary prizes. The tragic death of her beloved husband is one of the themes in her collections *Ha-Carmel Ha-i Nir'a* ('The Invisible Carmel,' 1971) and *Al Tirhak* ('Let Me Not Be Forsaken,' 1974). In her collections *Ha-Lo Har Ha-Lo Esh* ('Surely a Hill, Surely a Fire,' 1977) and *Ha-Shoni Ha-Marhiv* ('The Magnificent Other,' 1981), Zelda's symbolism is steeped in biblical and Chasidic allusions. Her last book *She-Nivdelu Mi-Col Merhak* ('Beyond All Distance,' 1984) describes her illness and her prayers confronting death. Zelda felt contact with the divine to be a precondition to the creative act, and wrote about genuine mystical experiences.

LR

Zha Jianying (*b.* 1959), Chinese fiction writer, essayist. Born in Beijing, Zha has successfully pursued a bilingual writing career. She attended Beijing University, where she earned a BA in Chinese in 1982, she received an MA in English from the University of South Carolina in 1984, and an MPhil in Comparative Literature from Columbia University in 1987. She married Benjamin Lee, an anthropology professor, in 1992; they have one daughter. Zha's 'Zhijiage chongfeng' ('Reunion in Chicago') won the Best Short Story Award from *Xiaoshuojie* ('Fiction World') in 1988. Her writings of fiction, mostly novellas and short stories about Chinese students' experiences in the United States, are collected in two books, *Dao Meiguo qu, dao Meiguo qu* ('Going to America, Going to America,' 1991) and *Conglin xia de binghe* ('River Frozen under the Jungle,' 1995). While she is based in Houston, Zha's literary network extends globally; her essays and reviews appear in magazines and journals in the US, Hong Kong, China, England, and Australia. Her first English book, *China Pop* (1995), which was included in the *Village Voice*'s list of the '25 best books of 1995,' consists of in-depth reports on the drastically changing sociocultural realities in post-Tiananmen

China. The book is a popular textbook for college courses on contemporary China.

S-sYC

Zhai Yongming (*b*. 1955), Chinese poet. A native of Sichuan, Zhai was relocated to the countryside during the Cultural Revolution (1966–76). Her memory of the experience is movingly captured in a poem sequence titled *Jing'an zhuang* ('Jing'an Village') in the early 1980s. In 1984 she published another sequence called *Nüren* ('Woman') with a prose preface titled 'Heiye yishi' ('Consciousness of the Dark Night'), by which she refers to the world of female consciousness. It is characterized by a terse yet suggestive language that creates a mysterious, hallucinatory ambience in which to explore women's repressed desires and needs. *Nüren* and her subsequent work established Zhai as the leading woman poet among the new generation in the People's Republic of China, although her recent work since the early 1990s is more anchored in mundane reality and less concerned with female consciousness. Zhai now lives in Chengdu, Sichuan Province.

MY

Zhang Ailing (Eileen Chang) (1920–1995), Chinese fiction writer and essayist. One of the towering figures of modern Chinese literature, Zhang brought to her writing an exquisite sense of language and a sharp eye for the details of contemporary society. From an elite social background, she attended St Mary's Hall Girls' School and the University of Hong Kong. With the Japanese invasion in 1942, she abandoned her undergraduate studies and returned to Shanghai to pursue a literary career. Her first story 'Aloeswood Ashes' (1943) was published in the popular journal *Ziluolan*, and was followed by a steady stream of essays and fiction that quickly captured a wide audience. Many of these works subsequently appeared in the volumes *Chuanqi* ('Romances,' 1944) and *Liuyan* ('Gossip,' 1945). 'The Golden Cangue'

(1943) unfolds the psychological breakdown of its heroine, the despised daughter-in-law of an old-style family; its rich imagery and attention to the shades of human emotion are characteristic of Zhang's early fiction. Critical of the new political regime, Zhang moved to Hong Kong in 1952, where she wrote two anticommunist novels *Naked Earth* (1954) and *Rice Sprout Song* (1954), a haunting account of rural poverty after 'liberation.' After she emigrated to the US in 1955, her publications included several works of fiction, a monograph on the classical Chinese novel *Dream of The Red Chamber*, and numerous film scripts. The Hong Kong journal *Renditions* published a special issue on Zhang in 1996.

ADD

Zhang Jie (*b*. 1937), Chinese fiction writer. One of the most celebrated woman writers of her generation, Zhang has written essays, poetry, and screenplays, but is best known as a fiction writer. Her first short story 'The Child from the Forest' (1978) won the National Prize for fiction. A Beijing native, Zhang's parents separated early in her life, and she spent her youth with her mother in Liaoning Province. A 1960 graduate of People's University in economics, Zhang was sent to the countryside during the Cultural Revolution. Her famous story 'Love Must Not Be Forgotten' (1979) was the first story published in the post-Mao era to place 'love' in the center of public discourse. Zhang's *Heavy Wings* (1980) scrutinizes the frustration and optimism felt by intellectual families during the first years of China's economic reforms. Largely written from the perspective of a female journalist, this novel was awarded the Mao Dun Prize for literature in 1985. 'The Ark' (1988) gives full voice to Zhang's concern for the personal and professional struggles of independent women in the mid-1980s. Zhang continued to write and publish in the 1990s.

JML

Zhang Xinxin (*b.* 1953), Chinese fiction writer. Well-known and politically controversial during the 1980s, Zhang has written for the stage, screen, and television. Raised in Beijing, she was just out of middle school at the start of the Cultural Revolution (1966–76), when she was sent to work in China's rural northeast. She served as an army medic in Hunan Province, and was then reassigned to Beijing, where she worked for some years as a nurse. Zhang was accepted to the Directors' Program at the Central Academy of Drama in 1979 and graduated in 1984. While at the Academy, Zhang published fiction in a number of literary journals. The protagonist in 'The Dreams of Our Generation' (1982) is a married proofreader whose memories of her adolescence in the countryside during the Cultural Revolution yield a lyrical and emotional critique of urban life in the 1980s. Zhang's well-known work of reportage, *Chinese Lives* (1985), was compiled during the early 1980s with a journalist collaborator. Through edited interviews with people in Beijing, *Chinese Lives* provides a series of biographical portraits articulating the hopes and private struggles of Beijing residents from various walks of life. Zhang now lives in the United States.

JMI

Zheng Min (*b.* 1920), Chinese poet, literary critic. Born in Beijing, Zheng entered the Department of Foreign Languages and Literatures at the Southwest Associate University in 1939 and later transferred to the Philosophy Department. After she graduated in 1943, she studied English literature first at Brown University and then at Illinois State University, from which she received an MA in 1951. In 1955 she returned to China and worked in the Literature Institute of the Chinese Academy of Social Sciences. In 1960 she became a professor at Beijing Normal University, where she remains to this day. Zheng started writing poetry in 1942; her early work was heavily influenced by Goethe and Rilke and displays a strong philosophical, even metaphysical bend. Together with *Chen Jingrong, she belongs to the 'School of Nine Leaves' retroactively. Like many intellectuals in China during the Cultural Revolution (1966–76), she stopped writing. After the Cultural Revolution she resumed writing poetry and has been productive in both creative and scholarly work. English translations of her poetry are available in several anthologies.

MY

Zhong Ling (Chung Ling) (*b.* 1945), Chinese-Taiwan fiction writer, poet, translator. Born in Chongqing, China, Zhong Ling arrived in Taiwan with her family in 1950. Zhong grew up mainly in Gaoxiong where she attended a girls' school and fell in love with classical Chinese literature. She graduated from the Foreign Languages Department of Taiwan's Tunghai University in 1966 and received a PhD in comparative literature from the University of Wisconsin at Madison in 1972. Zhong taught at the State University of New York at Albany and at Hong Kong University before returning to Taiwan to teach at National Sun Yat-sen University, where she is currently the director of the Literature Program. She married film director Hu Jinquan in 1977. Zhong began publishing essays and short stories while still in college and has produced many collections of essays, short stories, and poems, including *Chizu zai caodi shang* ('Barefoot on the Grass,' 1970), *Qunshan huhuan wo* ('The Mountains Are Calling Me,' 1981), and *Fenfang de hai* ('Fragrant Sea,' 1989). Much of her creative writing explores themes of female sexuality, oppression, and liberation, and is often inspired by fantasy and Chinese folklore. She has edited and translated collections of Chinese poetry into English, most notably, with Kenneth Rexroth, *Orchid Boat: Woman Poets of China* (1972). *Running Wild: New Chinese Writers* contains English translations of her stories.

KTo

Zhong Xiaoyang (*b.* 1962), Chinese-Hong Kong fiction writer. Zhong Xiaoyang was born in Guangzhou (Canton) and grew up in Hong Kong; her father is an Indonesian Chinese and her mother is originally from the northeastern part of China. In 1981 she entered Michigan University, where she studied film. In 1986 she returned to Hong Kong and became a professional writer. Zhong's writing career began when she was still a high school student. Her first essay 'Zhu fu' ('Blessing,' 1979) and first novel *Bing* ('Sickness,' 1979) won second prize in the junior section of the Sixth Hong Kong Youth Literary Award in 1979. Her novel *Tingzhe zhan jie wen* ('Stop a While and Ask,' 1981) established her literary reputation in both Taiwan and Hong Kong. It is a historical story set in northeast China during the Japanese occupation. The political analogy between a part of China under the Japanese occupation and a Hong Kong soon to be returned to mainland China was obvious. Her later works are about the metropolitan, commercial Hong Kong, a place where young people have neither roots nor clear ethical orientation. A prolific writer of poetry, essays, and fiction, Zhong left Hong Kong before the Chinese takeover and now lives in Australia. *Nativism Overseas: Contemporary Chinese Women Writers* contains English translations of her work.

SC

Zhu Tianwen (*b.* 1956), Chinese-Taiwan fiction writer, screenwriter. The eldest daughter of a well-known literary couple (fiction writer Zhu Xining and translator Liu Musha), Zhu grew up in a military housing compound, the site of a unique subculture in Taiwan's post-1949 era, which constituted an important component of Zhu's creative work. While attending Tamkang University as an English major, Zhu founded the 'Double-Three Series Club,' a literary society of young writers that later developed into a private publishing house. Her first collection of short stories *Qiao Taishou xinji* ('New Stories of Magistrate Qiao'), was published in 1977, a year before she graduated from college. Since 1982, Zhu has been closely associated with the Taiwan New Cinema movement. She is the screenwriter for nearly all well-known movies by director Hou Xiaoxian, including *City of Sadness*, winner of the Golden Lion Award at the 1989 Venice Film Festival. Zhu's career as fiction writer reached a climax with the publication of *Shijimo de huali* ('Splendor of the Fin de siècle,' 1990), a collection of short stories on the rapidly transforming middle-class lifestyles in urban Taiwan. In 1994 her first novel *Huangren shouji* ('The Ravished Man'), narrated in a confessional mode by the homosexual protagonist, won top prize in the *China Times* Novel Contest. *Running Wild: New Chinese Writers* contains English translations of her work.

S-sYC

Zhu Tianxin (*b.* 1958), Taiwan fiction writer, essayist. Born into a family of distinguished writers and literary translators, Zhu Tianxin was a precocious writer whose short stories and essays written in her high school years were collected in two volumes, *Fangzhou shang de rizi* ('Days on the Ark') and *Jirang ge* ('Songs of Rustic Pleasures'), and published in 1977. She earned her BA degree in history from National Taiwan University in 1981; married Xie Caijun, a writer and editor, in 1984; and gave birth to a daughter in 1986. Zhu's art of literary writing matured amid radical transformations of Taiwan's cultural and political climate between the mid-1980s and mid-1990s, which provided the setting and thematic focuses for her celebrated stories in *Wo jide . . .* ('I Remember . . . ,' 1989) and *Xiang wo Juancun de xiongdi men* ('Thinking of My Brothers in Juancun,' 1992). Her 1994 book *Xiaoshuojia de zhengzhi zhouji* ('Political Diaries of a Fiction Writer') consisted principally of essays she wrote as a columnist for *China Times* weekly. In 1997 Zhu published her eleventh book

Gudu ('Ancient Capital,' 1997). Written in the hybrid genre of essay-fiction, *Gudu* mixes nostalgia, identity quest, and harsh criticisms of cultural, political, and ecological environments in contemporary Taiwan. Her work in English translation is available in the journals *Renditions* and *The Chinese Pen.*

S sYC

Zürn, Unica (1916–1970), German novelist, poet. Born in Berlin, Zürn worked as an archivist and a dramatic adviser with the German film company UFA. Married in 1942, divorced in 1949, she earned her living by writing radio plays, fairy tales, and short stories. In 1953 she met the Surrealist painter Hans Bellmer, followed him to Paris, and became friends with other Surrealists. She learned to write poems in anagrammatic style and exhibited her drawings. She was diagnosed with paranoid schizophrenia and was hospitalized several times. Written between 1962 and 1965, *The Man of Jasmine* (1977) describes a severe mental disease in a language rich with surrealistic images. Zürn expresses her suffering in visions, states of depression, and hallucinations. A recurring motif is 'love in distance,' a bodiless love as protection against the disappointment of longing. *Dunkler Frühling* ('Dark Spring,' 1969) narrates her significant psychological and sexual development. Written in similarly dense images are her other works *Im Staub dieses Lebens* ('In the Dust of this Life,' 1980), *Das Weiße mit dem roten Punkt* ('White with Red Spots,' 1959), and *The House of Illness: Stories and Pictures from a Case of Jaundice* (1958). Zürn committed suicide in Paris.

Due to an increasing interest in women's literature, her writings became more widely known after her death.

MMu

Zwicky, (Julia) Fay (*b.* 1933), Australian poet, essayist. Zwicky completed an undergraduate degree at Melbourne University before being published in a number of anthologies and periodicals in Australia and abroad. Although she is a concert pianist, has edited three anthologies, and has published a collection of essays, reviews, and articles in *The Lyre in the Pawnshop* (1986; the Western Australian Literary Award for Non-Fiction), and a collection of short stories *Hostages* (1983), it is as a poet that she is best known. Her first anthology of poetry *Isaac Babel's Fiddle* (1975) was followed by *Kaddish and Other Poems* (1982; NSW Premier's Award), *Ask Me* (1990; WA Premier's Award for Poetry), *A Touch of Ginger* (1991, with Dennis Haskell), *Fay Zwicky: Poems 1970–1992* (1993), and *The Gatekeeper's Wife* (1997). 'Kaddish,' a lament for her dead father, is among her most famous and well-received poems. With its poignant, sometimes comic overtones, it limns the experience of growing up in a Melbourne Jewish family in unexpected and provocative ways. In much of her poetry Zwicky explores similar fractures and ambivalence in relationships, the conflicts and contradictions in experience, and the relationship between the individual artist and the community. She was Senior Lecturer in English at University of Western Australia from 1972 to 1987.

LK

Further reading

Africa

Berrian, B. F. (1985) *Bibliography of African Women Writers and Journalists*, Washington, D.C.: Three Continents Press.

D'Almeida, I. A. (1994) *Francophone African Women Writers: Destroying the Emptiness of Silence*, Gainesville, Florida: University Press of Florida.

James, A. (1990) *In Their Own Voices: African Women Writers Talk*, London: James Currey.

Lindfors, B. (ed.) (1979, 1989, 1995) *Black African Literature in English*, Vol. I, II, and III, Detroit: Gale Research.

Wilentz, G. (1992) *Binding Cultures: Black Women Writers in Africa and the Diaspora*, Bloomington: Indiana University Press.

Arab Countries

Accad, E. and Ghurayyib, R. (1985) *Contemporary Arab Women Writers and Poets*, Beirut: Beirut University College.

Badran, M. and Cooke, M. (eds) (1990) *Opening the Gates: A Century of Arab Feminist Writing*, Bloomington: Indiana University Press.

Booth, M. (trans.) (1994) *My Grandmother's Cactus: Stories by Egyptian Women*, Austin: University of Texas Press.

Boullata, K. (trans.) (1978) *Women of the Fertile Crescent: Modern Poetry by Arab Women*, Washington, D.C.: Three Continents Press.

Cohen-Mor, D. (trans.) (1993) *An Arabian Mosaic: Short Stories by Arab Women Writers*, Potomac, Maryland: Sheba Press.

Fayad, M. (1987) *The Road to Feminism: Arab Women Writers*, Lansing, Michigan: Michigan State University.

Malti-Douglas, F. (1991) *Woman's Body, Woman's Word: Gender and Discourse in Arabo-Islamic Writing*, Princeton: Princeton University Press.

Shahham, A. Al- (1988) *Rebellious Voices: Selections of Poetry by Arab Women Writers*, Amman.

Zeidan, J. (1996) *Arab Women Novelists: The Formative Years and Beyond*, Albany: State University of New York Press.

Australia and New Zealand

Adelaide, D. (1988) *Australian Women Writers: A Bibliographic Guide*, London: Pandora.

Clancy, L. (1992) *A Reader's Guide to Australian Fiction*, Melbourne: Oxford University Press.

Jackson, M. P. and O'Sullivan, V. (1983) *The Oxford Book of New Zealand Writing Since 1945*, Auckland: Oxford University Press.

Page, G. (1995) *A Reader's Guide to Contemporary Australian Poetry*, St Lucia: University of Queensland Press.

Sturm, T. (ed.) (1991) *The Oxford History of New Zealand Literature in English*, Auckland: Oxford University Press.

Wilde, W., Hooton, J., and Andrews, B. (eds) (1994) *The Oxford Companion to Australian Literature*, Melbourne: Oxford University Press.

Brazil

Foster, D. W. and Reis, R. (1981) *A Dictionary of Contemporary Brazilian Authors*, Tempe: Center for Latin American Studies, Arizona State University.

Lobo, L. (1987) 'Women Writers in Brazil Today,' *World Literature Today* 61, 1: 49–54.

Quinlan, S. C. (1991) *The Female Voice in Contemporary Brazilian Narrative*, New York: Peter Lang.

Sadlier, D. J. (1992) *One Hundred Years after Tomorrow: Brazilian Women's Fiction in the Twentieth Century*, Bloomington: Indiana University Press.

Stern, I. (ed.) (1988) *Dictionary of Brazilian Literature*, New York: Greenwood Press.

Burma

Allott, A. J. (1993) *Inked Over, Ripped Out: Burmese Storytellers and the Censors*, New York: PEN American Center.

Allott, A. J. (1994) 'Burma,' in A. Dingwall (ed.) *Traveller's Literary Companion to South-east Asia*, Brighton: In Print.

The Caribbean

Berrian, B. (1989) *Bibliography of Women Writers from the Caribbean*, Washington, D.C.: Three Continents Press.

Cudjoe, S. R. (ed.) (1990) *Caribbean Women Writers: Essays from the First International Conference*, Wellesley, Massachusetts: Calaloux Publications.

Davies, C. B. and Fido, E. S. (eds)

(1990) *Out of the Kumbla: Caribbean Women's Literature*, Trenton, New Jersey: African World Press.

Fenwick, M. J. (1992) *Writers of the Caribbean and Central America: A Bibliography*, 2 vols, New York: Garland.

Meyers, E. and Adamson, G. (eds.) (1987) *Continental, Latin American, and Francophone Women Writers*, New York: University Press of America.

Niesen de Abruña, L. (1988) 'Twentieth-Century Women Writers from the English-Speaking Caribbean,' *Modern Fiction Studies* 34, 1: 85–96.

Phaf, I. (1985) 'Women and Literature in the Caribbean,' in M. Schipper (ed.) *Unheard Words: Woman and Literature in Africa, the Arab World, Asia, the Caribbean, and Latin America*, trans. B. P. Fasting, London: Allison & Busby.

China

Barnstone, T. (ed.) (1993) *Out of the Howling Storm. The New Chinese Poetry*, Middletown, Connecticut: Wesleyan University Press.

Carver, A. C. and Chang, S-s. Y. (eds) (1990) *Bamboo Shoots after the Rain: Contemporary Stories by Women Writers of Taiwan*, New York: The Feminist Press.

Cheung, D. (ed.) (1987) *The Isle Full of Noises: Modern Chinese Poetry from Taiwan*, New York: Columbia University Press.

Gunn, E. (1983) *Twentieth-Century Chinese Drama: An Anthology*, Bloomington, Indiana: Indiana University Press.

Hsu, V. L. (ed.) (1981) *Born of the Same Roots: Stories of Modern Chinese Women*, Bloomington, Indiana: Indiana University Press.

Hung, E. (ed.) (1990) *Contemporary Women Writers: Hong Kong and Taiwan*, Hong Kong: Research Center for Translation, Chinese University of Hong Kong.

Kao, H-s. (ed.) (1993) *Nativism Overseas: Contemporary Chinese Women Writers*, Albany, New York: State University of New York Press.

Liu, N. *et al.* (eds) (1988) *The Rose-Colored Dinner: New Works by Contemporary Chinese Women Writers*, Hong Kong: Joint Publishing Company.

Morin, E. (ed.) (1990) *The Red Azalea: Chinese Poetry since the Cultural Revolution*, Honolulu: Hawaii University Press.

Roberts, R. A. and Knox, A. (trans.) (1988) *One Half of the Sky: Stories from Contemporary Women Writers of China*, London: Heinemann.

Wang, D. D-w. (ed.) (1994) *Running Wild: New Chinese Writers*, New York: Columbia University Press.

Yeh, M. (ed.) (1992) *Anthology of Modern Chinese Poetry*, New Haven, Connecticut: Yale University Press.

Zhong, L. and Rexroth, K. (eds and trans.) (1972) *The Orchid Boat: Women Poets of China*, New York: McGraw-Hill.

Zhu, H. (trans.) (1991) *The Serenity of Whiteness: Stories by and about Women in Contemporary China*, New York: Ballantine Books.

Germany

Eigler, F. and Kord, S. (eds) (1997) *The Feminist Encyclopedia of German Literature*, Westport, Connecticut: Greenwood Press.

Fox, T. C. (1993) *Border Crossings: An Introduction to East German Prose*, Ann Arbor: University of Michigan Press.

Frederiksen, E. P. (ed.) (1989) *Women Writers of Germany, Austria, and Switzerland: An Annotated Bio-Bibliographical Guide*, Westport, Connecticut: Greenwood Press.

Frederiksen, E. P. and Ametsbichler, E.
G. (eds) (1998) *Women Writers in German-Speaking Countries: A Bio-Bibliographical Critical Sourcebook*, Westport, Connecticut: Greenwood Press.

Lukens, N. and Rosenberg, D. (1993) *Daughters of Eve: Women's Writing from the German Democratic Republic*, Lincoln, Nebraska: University of Nebraska Press.

Weedon, C. (ed.) (1997) *Postwar Women's Writing in German*, Providence and Oxford: Berghahn.

Greece

Alexiou, M. and Lambropoulos, V. (eds) (1985) *The Text and its Margins: Post Structuralist Approaches to Twentieth-Century Greek Literature*, New York: Pella.

Beaton, R. (1998) *An Introduction to Modern Greek Literature*, Oxford and New York: Oxford University Press.

Dalven, R. (ed. and trans.) (1994) *Daughters of Sappho: Contemporary Greek Women Poets*, Rutherford, New Jersey: Fairleigh Dickinson University Press.

Lambropoulos, V. (1988) *Literature as a National Institution: Studies in the Politics of Modern Greek Literature*, Princeton: Princeton University Press.

Van Dyck, K. (1998) *Kassandra and the Censors: Greek Poetry since 1967*, Ithaca: Cornell University Press.

Van Dyck, K. (ed. and trans.) (1998) *The Rehearsal of Misunderstanding: Three Collections by Contemporary Greek Women Poets*, Middletown, Connecticut: Wesleyan University Press.

Indonesia

McGlynn, J. (trans.) (1979) *A Taste of Betel and Lime: An Anthology of Poetry by Women*, Jakarta: Pustaka Jaya.

Iran

Green, J. and Yazdanfar, F. (eds) (1993) *A Walnut Sapling on Masih's Grave and Other Stories*, Portsmouth, New Hampshire: Heinemann.

Milani, F. (1992) *Veils and Words: The Emerging Voices of Iranian Women Writers*, Syracuse, New York: Syracuse University Press.

Sullivan, S. P. (trans.) (1991) *Stories by Iranian Women since the Revolution*, Austin, Texas: Center for Middle Eastern Studies, the University of Texas at Austin.

Talattof, K. (1997) 'Iranian Women's Literature: From Pre-Revolutionary Social Discourse to Post-Revolutionary Feminism,' *International Journal of Middle East Studies* 29: 531–58.

Israel

Diament, C. and Rattok, L. (eds) (1994) *Ribcage: Israeli Women's Fiction*, New York: Hadassah.

Domb, R. (ed.) (1996) *New Women's Writing from Israel*, London and Portland, Oregon: Vallentine Mitchell.

Feldman, Y. S. (1999) *No Room of Their Own: Gender and Nation in Israeli Women's Fiction*, New York: Columbia University Press.

Glazer, M. (ed.) (1981) *Burning Air and a Clear Mind: Contemporary Israeli Women Poets*, Athens, Ohio: Ohio University Press.

Glazer, M. (ed.) (2000) *Dreaming the Actual: Contemporary Fiction and Poetry by Israeli Women Writers*, Albany, New York: State University of New York Press.

Sokoloff, N. B., Lerner, A. L., and Norich, A. (eds) (1992) *Gender and Text in Modern Hebrew and Yiddish Literature*, New York: Jewish Theological Seminary of America.

Italy

Aricò, S. (ed.) (1990) *Contemporary Women Writers in Italy: A Modern Renaissance*, Amherst, Massachusetts: University of Massachusetts Press.

Ballerini, L. (ed.) (1992) *Shearsmen of Sorts: Italian Poetry 1975–1993*, Stony Brook, New York: Center for Italian Studies, State University of New York at Stony Brook.

Baranski, Z. and Pertile, L. (eds) (1993) *The New Italian Novel*, Edinburgh: Edinburgh University Press.

Caesar, A. and Caesar, M. (eds) (1993) *The Quality of Light: Modern Italian Short Stories*, London and New York: Serpent's Tail.

King, M. (ed.) (1989) *New Italian Women: A Collection of Short Fiction*, New York: Italica Press.

Lazzaro-Weis, C. (1993) *From Margins to Mainstream: Feminism and Fictional Modes in Italian Women's Writing, 1968–1990*, Philadelphia: University of Pennsylvania Press.

O'Brien, C. (ed.) (1996) *Italian Women Poets of the Twentieth Century*, Dublin: Irish Academy Press.

Russell, R. (ed.) (1994) *Italian Women Writers: A Bio-Bibliographical Sourcebook*, Westport, Connecticut: Greenwood Press.

Russell, R. (ed.) (1997) *The Feminist Encyclopedia of Italian Literature*, Westport, Connecticut: Greenwood Press.

Japan

Lippet, N. M. and Selden, K. I. (trans. and eds) (1991) *Japanese Women Writers: Twentieth Century Short Fiction*, Armonk, New York: Sharpe.

Schalow, P. G. and Walker, J. A. (eds) (1996) *The Woman's Hand: Gender and Theory in Japanese Women's Writing*, Stanford, California: Stanford University Press.

Schierbeck, S. (1994) *Japanese Women Novelists: 104 Biographies, 1900–1993*, Copenhagen: Museum Tusculanum Press, University of Copenhagen.

Tanaka, Y. (ed.) (1991) *Unmapped Territories: New Women's Fiction from Japan*, Seattle: Women in Translation.

Tanaka, Y. and Hanson, E. (eds) (1984) *This Kind of Woman: Ten Stories by Japanese Women Writers, 1960–76*, New York: Perigee Books.

Vernon, V. V. (1988) *Daughters of the Moon: Wish, Will, and Social Constraint in Fiction by Modern Japanese Women*, Berkeley, California: Institute of East Asian Studies, University of California.

Korea

Fulton, B. and Fulton, J.-C. (trans. and eds) (1997) *Wayfarer: New Fiction by Korean Women*, Seattle: Women in Translation.

Fulton, B. and Fulton, J.-C. (trans.) (1989) *Words of Farewell: Stories by Korean Women Writers*, Seattle: Seal Press.

Malaysia

Brewster, A. (1989) *Post-colonial and Ethnic Minority Literatures in English in Singapore and Malaysia: A Cultural Analysis*, The Flinders University of South Australia.

Chan, M. and Harris, R. (eds) (1991) *Asian Voices in English*, Hong Kong: Hong Kong University Press.

Karim, W. J. (1992) *Women and Culture: Between Malay Adat and Islam*, Boulder, Colorado: Westview Press.

Koh, T. A. (1987) 'Biographical and Literary Writings and Plays in English by Women from Malaysia and Singapore: A Checklist', *Commentary* 7, 2 and 3: 94–6.

Wignesan, T. (ed.) (1964) *Bunga Emas: An Anthology of Contemporary Malaysian Literature (1930–1963)*, Malaysia: Anthony Blond with Rayirath Publications.

The Netherlands and Flanders

Aercke, K. (1994) *Women Writing in Dutch (Women Writers of the World, Vol. 1)*, New York and London: Garland Publishing.

Bakker, M. A. and Morrison, B. H. (eds) (1994) *Studies in Netherlandic Culture and Literature* (publication of the American Association for Netherlandic Studies), Lanham, New York and London: University Press of America.

Brems, H. and Zuiderent, A. (1992) *Contemporary Poetry of the Low Countries*, Rekkem: Stichting Ons Erfdeel.

Meijer, R. P. (1978) *Literature of the Low Countries: A Short History of Dutch Literature in the Netherlands and Belgium*, Boston/The Hague: Martinus Nijhoff.

Meijer, M., Eijsker, E., Peypers, A., and Prins, Y. (eds) (1998) *The Defiant Muse: Dutch and Flemish Feminist Poems, from the Middle Ages to the Present: A Bilingual Anthology*, New York: The Feminist Press.

Robson, C. (ed.) (1997) *A Touch of the Dutch: Plays by Women*, Aurora Metro Press.

Vermij, L. Th. (1992) *Women Writers from the Netherlands and Flanders*, Amsterdam: International Feminist Book Fair Press.

Zwart, M. and Grene, E. (1998) *Kaleidoscope: Dutch Poetry in Translation, from Medieval Times to the Present* (with parallel Dutch text), Wilmette, Illinois: Fairfield Books.

The Philippines

Abad, G. H. (1993) (ed.) *A Native Clearing: Filipino Poetry and Verse from English since the 50s to the Present*,

Quezon City: University of the Philippines Press.

Abad, G. H. (1999) (ed.) *A Habit of Shores: Filipino Poetry and Verse from English, 60s to the 90s*, Quezon City: University of the Philippines Press.

Bernad, M., SJ (1961) *Bamboo and the Greenwood Tree: Essays on Filipino Literature in English*, Manila: Bookmark.

Breshnahan, R. J. (ed.) (1977) *Literature and Society: Cross-Cultural Perspectives*, Manila: USIS.

Dimalanta, O. (1976) *The Philippine Poetic*, Manila: Colegio de San Juan de Letran.

Galdon, J., SJ (ed.) (1972) *Philippine Fiction*, Quezon City: Ateneo de Manila University Press.

Galdon, J., SJ (ed.) (1979) *Essays on the Philippine Novel in English*, Quezon City: Ateneo de Manila University Press.

Manlapaz, E. Z. and Evasco, M. (1996) *Six Women Poets: Inter/Views*, Manila: Aria Edition, Inc.

Valeros, F. and Gruenberg, E. V. (1987) *Filipino Writers in English: A Biographical and Bibliographical Directory*, Quezon City: New Day Publishers.

Romania

Deletant, A. and Walker, B. (trans.) (1986) *Silent Voices: An Anthology of Romanian Women Poets*, London and Boston: Forest Books.

Deletant, A. and Walker, B. (trans.) (1998) *An Anthology of Contemporary Romanian Women Poets*, London and Boston: Forest Books.

Dutescu, D. (ed. and trans.) (1982) *Romanian Poems*, Bucharest: Eminescu Publishing House.

Walker, B. with Celea-Leach, M. (trans.) (1991) *Young Poets from a New Romania*, London and Boston: Forest Books.

Scandinavia

Carpelan, B. *et al.* (1992) *A Way to Measure Time: Contemporary Finnish Literature*, Helsinki: Finnish Literature Society.

Clareus, I. (ed.) (1989) *Scandinavian Women Writers: An Anthology from the 1880s to the 1980s*, New York and Westport, Connecticut: Greenwood Press.

Garton, J. (ed.) (1995) *Contemporary Norwegian Women's Writing*, Norwich: Norvik Press.

Gaski, H. (ed.) (1996) *In the Shadow of the Midnight Sun: Contemporary Sami Prose and Poetry*, Karasjok, Norway: Davvi Girji.

Hanson, K. (ed.) (1995) *An Everyday Story: Norwegian Women's Fiction*, Seattle: Seal Press.

Heitmann, A. (ed.) (1987) *No Man's Land: An Anthology of Modern Danish Women's Literature*, Norwich: Norvik Press.

Weinstock, J. (ed.) (1994) *Dimension: Contemporary Nordic Literature*, Special Issue of *Contemporary German Arts and Letters Magazine*, Austin, Texas.

Slavic Countries

Baranczak, S. and Cavanagh, C. (trans. and eds) (1991) *Spoiling Cannibals' Fun: Polish Poetry of the Last Two Decades of Communist Rule*, Evanston, Illinois: Northwestern University Press.

Bassnett, S. and Kuhiwczak, P. (trans. and eds) (1988) *Ariadne's Thread: Polish Women Poets*, London and Boston: Foreign Books/Unesco.

Cummins, W. (ed.) (1993) *Shifting Borders: East European Poetry*, London and Toronto: Associated University Press.

Decter, J. (ed.) (1990) *Soviet Women Writing*, New York: Abbeville Press.

Gessen, M. (ed.) (1995) *Half a*

Revolution: Contemporary Fiction by Russian Women, Pittsburgh and San Francisco: Cleis Press.

Goscilo, H. (ed.) (1991) *Balancing Acts: Contemporary Stories by Russian Women*, New York: Laurel/Dell Publishing Company.

Goscilo, H. (ed.) (1995) *Lives in Transit: Recent Russian Women's Writing*, Dana Point, California: Ardis.

Grol, R. (trans. and ed.) (1996) *Ambers Aglow: An Anthology of Polish Women's Poetry (1981–1995)*, Austsin, Texas: Host Publications.

Hogan, E. (ed.) (1996) *From Three Worlds: New Writing from Ukraine*, Somerville, Massachusetts: Zephyr Press.

Kagal, A. and Perova, N. (eds) (1996) *Present Imperfect: Stories by Russian Women*, Boulder, Colorado: Westview Press.

Leonidov, R. (ed.) (1994) *An Anthology of Contemporary Poetry*, Sofia: Free Poetry Society, Soros Center.

Meredith, W. (ed.) (1986) *Poets of Bulgaria*, Greensboro, North Carolina: Unicorn Press.

Milosz, C. (ed.) (1983) *Postwar Polish Poetry*, Berkeley and Los Angeles: University of California Press.

Tonchev, B. (ed.) (1990) *Young Poets of a New Bulgaria*, London and Boston: Forest Books.

Walker, B. *et al.* (trans. and eds) (1990) *The Devil's Dozen*, London and Boston: Forest Books.

South Asia and the South Asian Diaspora

Ahmad, R. (trans. and ed.) (1990) *We Sinful Women: Contemporary Urdu Feminist Poetry*, London: The Women's Press.

Asian Women Writers' Workshop (1988) *Right of Way: Prose and Poetry from the Asian Women Writers' Workshop*, London: The Women's Press.

Azim, F. and Zaman, N. (trans. and eds) (1998) *Different Perspectives: Women Writing in Bangladesh*, Dhaka: Rachana and UPL.

Butalia, U. and Menon, R. (eds) (1990) *The Slate of Life: An Anthology of Stories by Indian Women*, New Delhi: Kali for Women.

Dharmarajan, G. (ed.) (1998) *Separate Journeys*, New Delhi: Katha.

George, K. M. *et al.* (eds) (1993) *Inner Spaces: New Writing by Women from Kerala*, New Delhi: Kali for Women.

Gill, G. (guest ed.) (1996) *Yatra 6: Writings from the Indian Subcontinent*, Special Issue of New Writings by Women in Hindi, New Delhi: Harper Collins.

Holmstrom, L. (ed.) (1991) *The Inner Courtyard: Stories by Indian Women*, Calcutta: Rupa & Co.; London: Virago.

Kali for Women (eds) (1987) *Truth Tales: Stories by Indian Women*, London: The Women's Press.

Kothari, R. and Ramanathan, S. (trans. and eds) (1998) *Modern Gujarati Poetry: A Selection*, New Delhi: Sahitya Akademi.

Natarajan, N. (ed.) (1996) *Handbook of Twentieth-Century Literatures of India*, Westport, Connecticut: Greenwood Press.

Rajan, R. S. (1993) *Real and Imagined Women: Gender, Culture and Postcolonialism*, New York: Routledge.

Tharu, S. and Lalita, K. (eds) (1993) *Women Writing in India: Volume II – The Twentieth Century*, New York: The Feminist Press.

Spain

Brown, J. L. (ed.) (1991) *Women Writers of Contemporary Spain: Exiles in the Homeland*, Newark, Delaware: University of Delaware Press.

Galerstein, C. L. and McNerney, K. (eds) (1986) *Women Writers of Spain: An Annotated Bio-Bibliographical*

Guide, Westport, Connecticut: Greenwood Press.

Levine, L.G., Marson, E. E., and Waldman, G. F. (eds) (1993) *Spanish Women Writers: A Bio-Bibliographical Source Book*, Westport, Connecticut: Greenwood Press.

Manteiga, R. C., Galerstein, C. L., and McNerney, K. (eds) (1988) *Feminine Concerns in Contemporary Spanish Fiction by Women*, Potomac, Maryland: Scripta Humanistica.

McNerney, K. and de Salamanca, C. E. (eds) (1994) *Double Minorities of Spain: A Bio-Bibliographic Guide to Women Writers of the Catalan, Galician, and Basque Countries*, New York: MLA.

Miller, B. (ed.) (1983) *Women in Hispanic Literature: Icons and Fallen Idols*, Berkeley, California: University of California Press.

Ordóñez, E. (1991) *Voices of Their Own: Contemporary Spanish Narrative by Women*, Lewisburg, Pennsylvania: Bucknell University Press.

Pérez, J. (1988) *Contemporary Women Writers of Spain*, Boston: Twayne.

Pérez, J. (1996) *Modern and Contemporary Spanish Women Poets*, New York: Twayne.

Thailand

Kepner, S. F. (trans. and ed.) (1996) *The Lioness in Bloom: Modern Thai Fiction about Women*, Berkeley, California: University of California Press.

Turkey

Erol, S. (1992) 'Feminism in Turkey', *New Perspectives on Turkey* 8: 109–21.

Erol, S. (1995) 'Sexual Discourse in Turkish Fiction: Return of the Repressed Female Identity,' *Edebiyat* 6: 187–202.

Gün, G. (1986) 'The Woman in the Dark Room: Contemporary Women Writers in Turkey,' *World Literature Today* 60, 1–2: 275–9.

Paker, S. (1991) 'Unmuffled Voices in the Shade and Beyond. Women's Writing in Turkish,' in H. F. Scott (ed.) *Textual Liberation: European Feminist Writing in the Twentieth Century*, New York and London: Routledge.

Reddy, N. M. (trans.) (1988) *Twenty Stories by Turkish Women Writers*, Bloomington, Indiana. Indiana University Turkish Series.

Author nationalities

Authors are listed under each nationality by which they identify themselves. The listing for 'British' includes all English authors and any other British authors who prefer that designation over a more specific one, such as 'Scottish.'

Afghan

Barlas, Fevziye Rahgozar
Mahbub, Maryam
Rushani, Layla Sarahat
Said, Bahar
Wahidi, Surraya
Zaryab, Spojmai Rauuf

Algerian

Amrouche, Fadhma Aïth Mansour
Djebar, Assia
Djura
Gallaire, Fatima
Lemsine, Aïcha
Mokeddem, Malika
Sebbar, Leïla

American

Accad, Evelyne
Acker, Kathy
Adams, Alice
Adnan, Etel
Agosín, Marjorie
Alexander, Meena
Allen, Paula Gunn
Allison, Dorothy
Alther, Lisa
Alvarez, Julia
Angelou, Maya
Beattie, Ann
Blume, Judy
Bradley, Marion Zimmer
Brown, Rita Mae

Butler, Octavia E.
Castillo, Ana
Chavez, Denise
Cisneros, Sandra
Clampitt, Amy
Cliff, Michelle
Clifton, Lucille
Cornwell, Patricia D.
Danticat, Edwidge
Di Prima, Diane
Didion, Joan
Dillard, Annie
Divakaruni, Chitra Banerjee
Dove, Rita
Erdrich, Louise
Forché, Carolyn
French, Marilyn
Gallagher, Tess
Garcia, Cristina
Gibbons, Kaye
Gilbert, Sandra
Gilchrist, Ellen
Giovanni, Nikki
Glancy, Diane
Glück, Louise
Godwin, Gail
Gordon, Mary
Graham, Jorie
Guy, Rosa
Hacker, Marilyn
Hagedorn, Jessica
Hamilton, Jane
Hardwick, Elizabeth
Harjo, Joy
Hazzard, Shirley
Henley, Beth

Highsmith, Patricia
Hoffman, Alice
Hogan, Linda
hooks, bell
Howe, Susan
Howe, Tina
Jen, Gish
Johnson, Diane
Jones, Gayl
Jong, Erica
Jordan, June
Kael, Pauline
Kaufman, Shirley
Kennedy, Adrienne
Kenyon, Jane
Kincaid, Jamaica
Kingsolver, Barbara
Kingston, Maxine Hong
Kizer, Carolyn
Klüger, Ruth
Kumin, Maxine
L'Engle, Madeleine
Le Guin, Ursula K.
Levertov, Denise
Lim, Shirley Geok-lin
Lord, Audre
Lurie, Alison
Mairs, Nancy
Marshall, Paule
Mason, Bobbie Ann
McCaffrey, Anne
McDermott, Alice
McMillan, Terry
Miller, Sue
Moore, Lorrie
Moraga, Cherrie
Morrison, Toni
Mukherjee, Bharati
Naylor, Gloria
Norman, Marsha
Oates, Joyce Carol
Olds, Sharon
Oliver, Mary
Olsen, Tillie
Ostriker, Alicia
Ozick, Cynthia
Paley, Grace
Paretsky, Sara
Phillips, Jayne Anne
Piercy, Marge

Plath, Sylvia
Pollitt, Katha
Prose, Francine
Proulx, E. Annie
Rice, Anne
Rich, Adrienne
Robinson, Marilynne
Robles, Mireya
Russ, Joanna
Salter, Mary Jo
Sanchez, Sonia
Schine, Cathleen
Sexton, Anne
Shange, Ntozake
Showalter, Elaine
Silko, Leslie Marmon
Simpson, Mona
Smiley, Jane
Song, Cathy
Sontag, Susan
Spivak, Gayatri Chakravorty
Suleri Goodyear, Sara
Tan, Amy
Tham, Hilary
Thon, Melanie Rae
Tyler, Anne
Viramontes, Helena Maria
Vogel, Paula
Wakoski, Diane
Walker, Alice
Wasserstein, Wendy
Wiggins, Marianne
Yamanaka, Lois-Ann

Antiguan

Kincaid, Jamaica

Antillean

Ega, Françoise

Argentine

Gambaro, Griselda
Molloy, Sylvia
Orozco, Olga
Orphée, Elvira
Pizarnik, Alejandra
Traba, Marta

Valenzuela, Luisa

Australian

Adams, Glenda
Anderson, Jessica
Astley, Thea
Bedford, Jean
Bobis, Merlinda
Cato, Nancy
De Groen, Alma
Farmer, Beverley
Gooneratne, Yasmine
Greer, Germaine
Grenville, Kate
Hanrahan, Barbara Janice
Harwood, Gwen
Hewett, Dorothy
Hospital, Janette Turner
Jolley, Elizabeth
Llewellyn, Kate
Lohrey, Amanda
Maiden, Jennifer
Masters, Olga
McCullough, Colleen
Moorhead, Finola
Morgan, Sally
Oodgeroo Noonuccal
Park, Ruth
Porter, Dorothy Featherstone
Rayson, Hannie
Rodriguez, Judith
Rubinstein, Gillian
Ryan, Gig
Strauss, Jennifer
Witting, Amy
Wright, Judith
Zwicky, Fay

Austrian

Bachmann, Ingeborg
Frischmuth, Barbara
Haushofer, Marlen
Jelinek, Elfriede
Klüger, Ruth
Mayröcker, Friederike
Mitgutsch, Waltraud Anna
Schwaiger, Brigitte

Bahamian

Bethel, Marion

Bangladeshi

Nasrin, Taslima

Barbadian

Marshall, Paule

Belgian

Beck, Beatrix
Irigaray, Luce
Mallet-Joris, Françoise
Nothomb, Amélie

Belizean

Edgell, Zee

Belorussian

Aleksievich, Svetlana

Brazilian

Alves, Miriam
Assunção, Leilah
César, Ana Cristina
Colasanti, Marina
Coutinho, Sonia
Cunha, Helena Parente
de Jesus, Carolina Maria
Denser, Márcia
Faillace, Tania Jamardo
Felinto, Marilene
Guimarães, Geni
Hilst, Hilda
Lispector, Clarice
Luft, Lya
Míccolis, Leila
Miranda, Ana Maria
Piñón, Nélida
Prado, Adélia
Ribeiro, Esmeralda
Telles, Lygia Fagundes
Van Steen, Edla

British

Atkinson, Kate
Bainbridge, Beryl
Barker, Pat
Bawden, Nina
Beer, Patricia
Brooke-Rose, Christine
Brookner, Anita
Byatt, A. S.
Carter, Angela
Churchill, Caryl
Cope, Wendy
Cusk, Rachel
Daniels, Sarah
Diski, Jenny
Drabble, Margaret
Duffy, Carol Ann
Duffy, Maureen
Dunmore, Helen
Dunn, Nell
Ellis, Alice Thomas
Fanthorpe, U. A.
Feinstein, Elaine
Figes, Eva
Fitzgerald, Penelope
Forster, Margaret
Gee, Maggie
Gems, Pam
Gilroy, Beryl
Gupta, Sunetra
Hill, Selima
Hill, Susan
James, P. D.
Jhabvala, Ruth Prawer
Johnson, Amryl
Lessing, Doris
Lively, Penelope
Maitland, Sara
Mantel, Hilary
Murdoch, Iris
Namjoshi, Suniti
Nichols, Grace
Randhawa, Ravinder
Rendell, Ruth
Roberts, Michèle
Rose, Jacqueline
Rumens, Carol
St Aubin de Teran, Lisa
Shapcott, Jo

Stevenson, Anne
Syal, Meera
Tennant, Emma
Townsend, Sue
Tremain, Rose
Trollope, Joanna
Warner, Marina
Weldon, Fay
Wertenbaker, Timberlake
Wicks, Susan
Winterson, Jeanette

Bulgarian

Basheva, Miryana Ivanova
Dimitrova, Blaga Nikolova
Filkova, Fedya Raykova
Radinska, Valentina Dimitrova
Yosifova, Ekaterina Petrova

Burmese

Aung San Suu Kyi
Ju
Khin Myo Chit
Ludu Daw Ama
Ma Ma Lay
Ma Sanda
Mo Mo (Inya)
Nu Nu Yi (Inwa)

Cameroonian

Beyala, Calixthe
Liking, Werewere

Canadian

Anderson-Dargatz, Gail
Atwood, Margaret
Aude
Barfoot, Joan
Birdsell, Sandra
Bowering, Marilyn
Brand, Dionne
Brossard, Nicole
Butala, Sharon
Carson, Anne
Cooper, Afua

Forrest, Katherine V.
Fraser, Sylvia
Gallant, Mavis
Govier, Katherine
Gowdy, Barbara
Hospital, Janette Turner
Huston, Nancy
Jiles, Paulette
Kogawa, Joy
MacDonald, Ann-Marie
Maillet, Antonine
Marlatt, Daphne
Michaels, Anne
Munro, Alice
Namjoshi, Suniti
Philip, Marlene Nourbese
Robin, Régine
Roy, Gabrielle
Rule, Jane
Shields, Carol
Thomas, Audrey
Urquhart, Jane
van Herk, Aritha
Webb, Phyllis

Catalan

Oliver i Cabrer, Maria-Antònia
Riera, Carme
Rodoreda, Mercè

Chinese

Bai Fengxi
Bing Xin
Can Xue
Chen Jingrong
Chen Ran
Dai Houying
Dai Qing
Ding Ling
Hong Ying
Liu Suola
Nie Hualing
Ru Zhijuan
Shen Rong
Shu Ting
Tie Ning
Wang Anyi
Yang Jiang

Yang Mo
Yu Lihua
Yu Luojin
Zha Jianying
Zhai Yongming
Zhang Ailing
Zhang Jie
Zhang Xinxin
Zheng Min

Chinese-Hong Kong

Huang Biyun
Xi Xi
Zhong Xiaoyang

Chinese-Taiwan

Chen Ruoxi
Li Ang
Li Li
Ouyang Zi
Ping Lu
Rong Zi
Shi Shuqing
Su Weizhen
Xia Yu
Xiao Sa
Yuan Qiongqiong
Zhong Ling
Zhu Tianwen
Zhu Tianxin

Chilean

Agosín, Marjorie
Allende, Isabel
del Río, Ana María
Eltit, Diamela
Vicuña, Cecilia

Colombian

Angel, Albalucía
Traba, Marta

Costa Rican

Naranjo, Carmen

Côte d'Ivoire

Tadjo, Véronique

Croatian

Drakulić, Slavenka
Parun, Vesna
Ugrešić, Dubravka

Cuban

Cabrera, Lydia
Campos, Julieta
Morejón, Nancy
Robles, Mireya

Czech

Berková, Alexandra
Boučková, Tereza
Brabcová, Zuzana
Fischerová, Daniela
Fischerová, Sylva
Hodrová, Daniela
Kantůrková, Eva
Kriseová, Eda
Moníková, Libuše
Pekárková, Iva
Procházková, Lenka
Richterová, Sylvie
Salivarová, Zdena

Danish

Balle, Solvej
Bødker, Cecil
Brøgger, Suzanne
Christensen, Inger
Ditlevsen, Tove
Larsen, Marianne
Mørch, Dea Trier
Saalbach, Astrid
Tafdrup, Pia
Thorup, Kirsten
Willumsen, Dorrit

Dominican

Allfrey, Phyllis Shand

Alvarez, Julia

Dutch

Bloem, Marion
Burnier, Andreas
Dorrestein, Renate
Dros, Imme
Enquist, Anna
Friedman, Carl
Gerhardt, Ida
Gerlach, Eva
Haasse, Hella
Harmsen van Beek, Fritzi
Herzberg, Judith
van Leeuwen, Joke
de Loo, Tessa
Meulenbelt, Anja
Michaelis, Hanny
Minco, Marga
de Moor, Margriet
Palmen, Connie
Rubinstein, Renate
Ruebsamen, Helga
Schmidt, Annie M.G.
de Waard, Elly
Wang, Lulu

Egyptian

ʿĀshūr, Raḍwā
Bakr, Salwā
Bint al-Shāṭi
Mansour, Joyce
Qalamāwī, Suhayr al-
Rifaat, Alifa
Saʾdāwī, Nawal al-
Tawfīq, Saḥar
Zayyāt, Laṭīfa al-

Finland-Swedish

Fagerholm, Monika
Forsström, Tua
Jansson, Tove
Lundberg, Ulla-Lena
Schoultz, Solveig von
Tikkanen, Märta

Finnish

Idström, Annikka
Joenpelto, Eeva
Krohn, Leena Elisabeth
Lander, Leena
Liksom, Rosa
Manner, Eeva-Liisa
Siekkinen, Raija
Simonsuuri, Kirsti
Stenberg, Eira
Turkka, Sirkka

Flemish

Hemmerechts, Kristien
Joris, Lieve
Provoost, Anne

French

Arnothy, Christine
Avril, Nicole
Baroche, Christiane
Beck, Beatrix
Billetdoux, Raphaële
Bouraoui, Nina
Cardinal, Marie
Césaire, Ina
Chandernagor, Françoise
Chawaf, Chantal
Chedid, Andrée
Cixous, Hélène
Clément, Catherine
Constant, Paule
Desanti, Dominique
Dormann, Geneviève
Duras, Marguerite
Ernaux, Annie
Etcherelli, Claire
Fleutiaux, Pierrette
Gallaire, Fatima
Gauthier, Xavière
Germain, Sylvie
Groult, Benoîte
Hyvrard, Jeanne
Jacquemard, Simonne
Kristeva, Julia
Leclerc, Annie
Leduc, Violette

Ndiaye, Marie
Prou, Suzanne
Redonnet, Marie
Rivoyre, Christine de
Robin, Régine
Rochefort, Christiane
Sagan, Françoise
Sarraute, Nathalie
Sebbar, Leïla
Warner-Vieyra, Myriam
Wittig, Monique
Yourcenar, Marguerite

French-Canadian

Bersianik, Louky
Blais, Marie-Claire
Gagnon, Madeleine

German

Brückner, Christine
Erb, Elke
Kirsch, Sarah
Königsdorf, Helga
Maron, Monika
Moníková, Libuše
Morgner, Irmtraud
Müller, Herta
Pausewang, Gudrun
Rehmann, Ruth
Reinig, Christa
Reinshagen, Gerlind
Sander, Helke
Seghers, Anna
Stefan, Verena
Steinwachs, Ginka
Wander, Maxie
Weigel, Sigrid
Wohmann, Gabriele
Wolf, Christa
Zürn, Unica

Ghanaian

Aidoo, Ama Ata
Sutherland, Efua Theodora

Greek

Anagnostaki, Loula

Anghelaki-Rooke, Katerina
Dimoula, Kiki
Douka, Maro
Fakinou, Eugenia
Galanaki, Rhea
Karapanou, Margarita
Laina, Maria
Mastoraki, Jenny
Zei, Alki

Grenadian

Collins, Merle

Guadeloupean

Condé, Maryse
Pineau, Gisèle
Schwarz-Bart, Simone
Warner-Vieyra, Myriam

Guyanese

Das, Mahadai
Gilroy, Beryl
Nichols, Grace
Shinebourne, Janice

Haitian

Chauvet, Marie
Danticat, Edwidge

Hungarian

Kristof, Agota

Icelandic

Árnadóttir, Nína Björk
Jakobsdóttir, Svava
Sigurðardóttir, Fríða Á.
Sigurðardóttir, Steinunn
Vilhjálmsdóttir, Linda

Indian

Alexander, Meena
Ambai
Appachana, Anjana
Ashapurna Devi

Bhandari, Mannu
Chudamani R.
Chughtai, Ismat
Cour, Ajeet
Das, Kamala
De, Shobha
Desai, Anita
Desai, Kamal
Deshpande, Gauri
Deshpande, Shashi
de Souza, Eunice
Dhruv, Saroop
Divakaruni, Chitra Banerjee
Geentanjali Shree
Goswami, Indira
Gupta, Sunetra
Hariharan, Githa
Hosain, Attia
Hyder, Qurratulain
Jhabvala, Ruth Prawer
Joseph, Sarah
Kapadia, Kundanika
Krishnan, Rajam
Mahasweta Devi
Markandaya, Kamala
Mehta, Gita
Mukherjee, Meenakshi
Namjoshi, Suniti
Niranjana, Anupama
Padmanabhan, Manjula
Pande, Mrinal
Pawar, Urmila
Pritam, Amrita
Randhawa, Ravinder
Ray, Pratibha
Roy, Arundhati
Sahgal, Nayantara
Sen, Nabaneeta Dev
Sobti, Krishna
Spivak, Gayatri Chakravorty
Sunder Rajan, Rajeswari
Syal, Meera
Tharu, Susie
Vaidehi
Vanita, Ruth

Indonesian

Chudori, Leila
Dini, Nurhayati Srihardini (NH)

Ibrahim, Ratna Indraswari
Katoppo, Marianne
Rambe, Hanna
Said, Titie
Sarumpaet, Ratna
Tjitrawasita, Totilawati

Iranian

AmirShahi, Mahshid
Bihbahani, Simin
Danishvar, Simin
Milani, Farzaneh
Parsipur, Shahrnush
Rahimieh, Nasrin
Ravanipur, Muniru
Saffarzadeh, Tahirih
Taraqqi, Goli

Iraqi

Amīr, Daisy al-
Malā'ika, Nāzik al-
Mamdūḥ, ʿĀliya
Mānīʿ, Samīra al-
Zangana, Haifa

Irish

Binchy, Maeve
Boland, Eavan
Boylan, Clare
Johnston, Jennifer
McGuckian, Medbh
Ní Chuilleanáin, Eiléan
Ní Dhomhnaill, Nuala
O'Brien, Edna
O'Faolain, Julia

Israeli

Aini, Leah
Almog, Ruth
Bat Shahar, Hannah
Bejerano, Maya
Ben Yehuda, Netiva
Castel-Bloom, Orly
Chalfi, Rahel
Eytan, Rachel
Govrin, Michal

Gur, Batya
Hareven, Shulamith
Hendel, Yehudit
Kahana-Carmon, Amalia
Kahanoff, Jacqueline
Katzir, Yehudit
Kaufman, Shirley
Lapid, Shulamit
Lieblich, Amia
Liebrecht, Savyon
Matalon, Ronit
Pinchas-Cohen, Hava
Ravikovitch, Dahlia
Semel, Nava
Volach, Yona
Zelda

Italian

Capriolo, Paola
Cavarero, Adriana
Cialente, Fausta
Corti, Maria
de Cespedes, Alba
Duranti, Francesca
Fallaci, Oriana
Frabotta, Biancamaria
Ginzburg, Natalia
Loy, Rosetta
Maraini, Dacia
Merini, Alda
Morandini, Giuliana
Morante, Elsa
Morazzoni, Marta
Niccolai, Giulia
Ortese, Anna Maria
Petrignani, Sandra
Rame, Franca
Ramondino, Fabrizia
Romano, Lalla
Rosselli, Amelia
Sanvitale, Francesca
Spaziani, Maria Luisa
Tamaro, Susanna

Jamaican

Adisa, Opal Palmer
Bennett, Louise
Breeze, Jean 'Binta'

Brodber, Erna
Campell, Hazel
Cliff, Michelle
Cooper, Afua
Craig, Christine
Ford-Smith, Honor
Goodison, Lorna Gaye
Mordecai, Pamela
Pollard, Velma
Senior, Olive
Wynter, Sylvia

Japanese

Ariyoshi Sawako
Enchi Fumiko
Hayashi Kyōko
Ishimure Michiko
Kono Taeko
Kurahashi Yumiko
Ohba Minako
Takahashi Takako
Takenishi Hiroko
Tomioka Taeko
Tsushima Yuko
Uno Chiyo
Yamada Eimi (Amy)
Yoshimoto Banana

Jordanian

Saʿūdī, Muni al-

Kenyan

Likimani, Muthoni
Mugo, Micere Githae
Mugot, Hazel de Silva
Njau, Rebeka
Ogot, Grace
Waciuma, Charity

Korean

Ch'oe Chŏnghŭi
Ch'oe Yun
Hahn Moo-Sook
Kang Sŏkkyŏng
Kim Chiwŏn
Kim Hyangsuk

Kim Hyŏng-gyŏng
Kong Chi-yŏng
O Chŏng-hŭi
Pak Hwasŏng
Pak Kyŏngni
Pak Wansŏ
Shin Kyŏgsuk
Yang Kwi-ja

Kuwaiti

Sabah, Souad al-
ʿUthmān, Laylā al-

Lebanese

Accad, Evelyne
Adnan, Etel
Baʿlabakkī, Laylā
Barakāt, Hudā
Naṣrallāh, Emily
Shaykh, Ḥanan al-
ʿUsayrān, Laylā

Malaysian

Amin, Khalidah Adibah
Chuah Guat Eng
Lee Geok Lan
Lim, Shirley Geok-lin
Louis, Marie Gerrina
Tham, Hilary
Zaman, Dina

Martinican

Césaire, Ina

Mauritian

Collen, Lindsey

Mexican

Berman, Sabina
Boullosa, Carmen
Campos, Julieta
Castellanos, Rosario
Esquivel, Laura
Garro, Elena

Hernández, Luisa Josefina
Mastretta, Angeles
Molina, Silvia
Poniatowska, Elena
Puga, María Luisa
Vilalta, Maruxa

Moroccan

Abouzeid, Leila
Mernissi, Fatima

Mozambican

De Sousa, Noémia

New Zealander

Adcock, Fleur
Anderson, Barbara
Dallas, Ruth
Duckworth, Marilyn
Edmond, Lauris
Frame, Janet
Grace, Patricia
Hulme, Keri
Kidman, Fiona
Mahy, Margaret
McCauley, Sue
McQueen, Cilla
Smither, Elizabeth

Nicaraguan

Belli, Gioconda

Nigerian

Acholonu, Catherine
Alkali, Zaynab
Amadiume, Ifi
Chikwe, Kema
Emecheta, Buchi
Ezeigbo, Akachi Adimora
Nwapa, Flora
Ogundipe-Leslie, 'Molara
Okoye, Ifeoma
Onwueme, Tess
Segun, Mabel
Sofola, Zulu
Ulasi, Adaora Lily

Norwegian

Brantenberg, Gerd
Haslund, Ebba
Hobæk Haff, Bergljot
Lie, Sissel
Løveid, Cecilie
Lunden, Eldrid
Moe, Karin
Takvam, Marie
Vestly, Anne-Cath
Vik, Bjørg
Wassmo, Herbjørg

Pakistani

Fatima, Altaf
Hina, Zahida
Naheed, Kishwar
Riaz, Fahmida
Sidhwa, Bapsi
Suleri Goodyear, Sara

Palestinian

ʿAzzām, Samīra
Badr, Liana
Jayyūsī, Salmā al-Khaḍrāʾ al-
Khalīfa, Saḥar
Ṭūqān, Fadwā
Yared, Nazik Saba

Philippine

Aguilar, Ma. Luisa B.
Aguilar, Mila
Alfon, Estrella D.
Alunan, Merlie M.
Bobis, Merlinda
Brainard, Cecilia Manguerra
Cordero-Fernando, Gilda
Dimalanta, Ophelia O.
Espina-Moore, Lina
Evasco, Marjorie
Hagedorn, Jessica
Lacambra-Ayala, Tita
Lim-Wilson, Ma. Fatima V.
Moreno, Virginia R.
Pantoja-Hidalgo, Cristina
Rosca, Ninotchka

Skinner, Michelle Cruz
Tiempo, Edith L.
Torrevillas, Rowena Tiempo
Ty-Casper, Linda

Polish

Hartwig, Julia
Hillar, Malgorzata
Kamienska, Anna
Kozioł, Urszula
Krall, Hanna
Lipska, Ewa
Miłobedzka, Krystyna
Poświatowska, Halina
Swir, Anna
Szymborska, Wislawa

Portuguese

Barreno, Maria Isabel
Bessa-Luís, Agustina
Botelho, Fernanda
Carvalho, Maria Judite
Correia, Clara Pinto
Correia, Hélia
Correia, Natália
Costa, Maria Velho da
Gersão, Teolinda
Horta, Maria Teresa
Jorge, Lídia
Llansol, Maria Gabriela

Puerto Rican

Ferré, Rosario
Nolla, Olga
Quiñones, Magaly
Umpierre-Herrara, Luz María
Vega, Ana Lydia

Quebec

Hébert, Anne
Laberge, Marie
Noël, Francine

Romanian

Albu, Florenţa

Bantaş, Ioana
Banuş, Maria
Blandiana, Ana
Cârneci, Magda
Cassian, Nina
Cesereanu, Ruxandra
Constante, Lena
Golopenţia, Sanda
Mălăncioiu, Ileana
Marin, Mariana
Müller, Herta
Petrescu, Ioana Emanuela

Russian

Akhmadulina, Bella Akhatovna
Baranskaia, Natalia Vladimirovna
Berberova, Nina Nikolaevna
Bonner, Elena
Chukovskaia, Lidiia Korneevna
Ginzburg, Evgeniia Semenovna
Ginzburg, Lidiia Iakovlevna
Gorbanevskaia, Natalia Evgenievna
Grekova, I.
Ignatova, Elena Alekseevna
Iskrenko, Nina Iurevna
Katerli, Nina Semyonovna
Lisnianskaia, Inna Lvovna
Makarova, Elena Grigoryevna
Matveeva, Novella Nikolaevna
Morits, Iunna Petrovna
Narbikova, Valeriia Spartakovna
Palei, Marina Anatolyevna
Petrushevskaia, Liudmila Stefanovna
Polianskaia, Irina Nikolaevna
Ratushinskaia, Irina Borisovna
Rubina, Dina Il'inichna
Sadur, Nina Mikhailovna
Sedakova, Olga Aleksandrovna
Shcherbakova, Galina Nikolaevna
Shcherbina, Tatiana Georgievna
Shvarts, Elena Andreevna
Tokareva, Viktoriia Samoilovna
Tolstaya, Tatyana
Ulitskaia, Liudmila Evgen'evna
Vaneeva, Larisa L'vovna
Varlamova, Inna Gustavovna
Vasilenko, Svetlana Vladimirovna
Voznesenskaia, Juliia Nikolaevna

St Lucian

Hippolyte, Jane King
Turnbull, Patricia

Salvadoran

Alegría, Claribel

Sami

Lukkari, Rauni Magga
Paltto, Kirsti
Persen, Synnøve

Saudi Arabian

Abū Khālid, Fawziyya

Scottish

Fell, Alison
Galloway, Janice
Jamie, Kathleen
Kay, Jackie
Kennedy, A. L.
Lochhead, Liz
MacDonald, Sharman
Mackay, Shena
McDermid, Val
McWilliam, Candia
Spark, Muriel

Senegalese

Bâ, Mariama
Diallo, Nafissatou Niang
Sow Fall, Aminata

Serbian

Velmar-Janković, Svetlana
Vrkljan, Irena

Singaporean

Ho, Minfong
Lee Tzu Pheng
Li Lienfung
Lim, Catherine

Lim, Suchen Christine
Yu, Ovidia

Slovak

Blazková, Jaroslava
Jarunková, Klára

South African

Gordimer, Nadine
Head, Bessie
Jabavu, Noni
Karodia, Farida
Kuzwayo, Ellen
Magona, Sindiwe
Ngcobo, Lauretta
Tlali, Miriam
Wicomb, Zoë

Spanish

Martín Gaite, Carmen
Matute, Ana María
Montero, Rosa
Ortiz, Lourdes
Tusquets, Esther

Sri Lankan

Gooneratne, Yasmine
Jayawardena, Kumari

Surinamese

Gajadin, Chitra
Roemer, Astrid
Vianen, Bea

Swedish

Åkesson, Sonja
Ekman, Kerstin
Ekström, Margareta
Frostenson, Katarina
Gripe, Maria
Kandre, Mare
Lidman, Sara
Lindgren, Astrid
Lugn, Kristina

Pleijel, Agneta
Sjöwall, Maj
Ström, Eva
Trotzig, Birgitta

Swiss

Accad, Evelyne
Bille, Stéphanie Corinna
Jaeggy, Fleur
Kristof, Agota
Stefan, Verena

Syrian

ʿAṭṭār, Samar al-
Idilbī, Ulfa al-
Khūrī, Colette al-
Naʿmānī, Hudā al-
Naʿnaʿ, Ḥamīda
Sammān, Ghāda al-

Tanzanian

Muhando, Penina

Thai

Anchan
Boonlua
Botan
Chamnongsri Rutnin
Chiranan Pitprcccha
Devakul, Subha
Krisna Asokesin
Naravadec
Si Pha
Sidaoruang
Supunpasaj Supasiri
Suwanni Sukhontha
Thomyanti
V. Vinichayakul

Tobagan

Philip, Marlene Nourbese

Trinidadian

Brand, Dionne
Espinet, Ramabai

Guy, Rosa
Hodge, Merle
Johnson, Amryl
Maxwell, Marina Ama Omowale
Springer, Eintou Pearl

Tunisian

Béji, Hélé

Turkish

Ağaoğlu, Adalet
Eray, Nazlı
Füruzan
Özakın, Aysel
Soysal, Sevgi
Tekin, Latife

Ugandan

Akello, Grace

Ukrainian

Andiievsʼka, Emma
Bilorserkivers', Natalka
Kostenko, Lina Vasylivna
Pavlychko, Solomea Dmytrivna
Zabuzhko, Oksana Stefanivna

Uruguayan

Peri Rossi, Cristina
Vilariño, Idea

Vietnamese

Duong Thu Huong
Le Minh Khue
Lê, Linda
Pham Thi Hoai
Phan Thi Vang-Anh

Welsh

Clarke, Gillian

Zimbabwean

Dangarembga, Tsitsi
Vera, Yvonne